PHILOSOPHIC CLASSICS

THALES to ST. THOMAS

BASIC TEXTS

SELECTED AND EDITED WITH PREFACES

BY

Walter Kaufmann

PRENTICE-HALL, INC.

ENGLEWOOD CLIFFS, N.J.

PRENTICE-HALL PHILOSOPHY SERIES

Arthur E. Murphy, Ph.D., Editor

Books by Walter Kaufmann

Author

NIETZSCHE: PHILOSOPHER, PSYCHOLOGIST, ANTICHRIST (1950)
CRITIQUE OF RELIGION AND PHILOSOPHY (1958)
FROM SHAKESPEARE TO EXISTENTIALISM (1959)
THE FAITH OF A HERETIC (1961)

Editor and translator

THE PORTABLE NIETZSCHE (1954)
EXISTENTIALISM FROM DOSTOEVSKY TO SARTRE (1956)
JUDAISM AND CHRISTIANITY: ESSAYS BY LEO BAECK (1958)
GOETHE'S FAUST (1961)
PHILOSOPHIC CLASSICS: THALES TO ST. THOMAS (1961)
PHILOSOPHIC CLASSICS: BACON TO KANT (1961)
RELIGION FROM TOLSTOY TO CAMUS (1961)

Third printing . . . . June, 1963

66232–C

✿
PREFACE

I

There is no better introduction to philosophy, whether one reads for oneself or takes a course, than to read some of the great philosophers. But few books are more difficult than Aristotle's *Metaphysics* or Spinoza's *Ethics* or Kant's *Critique of Pure Reason*. And even works that are less puzzling are sometimes like snippets of a conversation that one overhears on entering a room: what is said is clear, only one can't be sure one has got the point because one does not know just what has gone before. A slight point may be crucial to refute some earlier suggestion, and a seemingly pointless remark may contain a barbed allusion. Too often nonphilosophers despair: It does not occur to them that whenever they choose to begin, they can still get in at the beginning of the conversation. They need only to commence with Thales and the other pre-Socratics. Nobody should fear that going back so far will expose him to a tedious excursion. On the contrary, in quick succession one encounters some of the most fascinating thinkers of all time and finds oneself regretting that so little of their writings has survived.

Soon one comes to Socrates and Plato and becomes involved in philosophical discussions that continue to this day. In the early dialogues of Plato, the most brilliant literary power is employed to introduce us to philosophy; but one gains ever so much more from one's reading if one knows the pre-Socratics.

The later dialogues are much more difficult, and so is much of Aristotle, but no serious student will be satisfied to remain completely innocent of all these classics, and most teachers will want to read at least some of this material with their students.

Altogether, it is not the point of either this book or its companion volume to avoid all difficulties. On the contrary, philosophy begins in perplexity, as both Plato and Aristotle noted; and those who spurn perplexity and want unquestioned answers have not begun to understand philosophy. One of the first things one discovers in the study of philosophy is that intelligent and even brilliant men are frequently in disagreement, and that some of the most interesting problems seem to have no ready-made solutions. It might be argued that anyone who has not found this out still needs an education.

It is an uncomfortable discovery, however, and many people try to dodge it. Instead of being challenged by one great philosopher after another to reconsider preconceived opinions and to become more careful, thoughtful, and conscientious, many a student would like to learn, once and for all, the "central doctrines" of the great philosophers: that way one has something definite that one can memorize, and one does not have to think, oneself.

Alas, the "central doctrines" of a great philosopher often turn out to be very problematic in the context of the whole work in which they are said to be presented; and matters become yet less reassuring as we move to compare the first edition of some classics with the second, or one book with another by the same philosopher. Often, there are passages in which the "central doctrine" seems to be presented; but the philosopher did not always oblige us by ceasing to think after formulating his position in this manner: typically, he continued to reflect on the same topic and on other problems that have some relation to it; and in the end his position turns out to be hotly disputed by scholars. The greatest Plato scholars still argue not only about Plato's meaning in specific sentences but also about "central doctrines"; and the situation is no better in the case of Aristotle. No one who loves philosophy is seriously dismayed by that: what Plato and Aristotle teach us is not a body of assured results but rather a way of thinking—the delights of thinking.

The most damning comment on a course I ever heard came from a student who, after a semester's freshman course which he had taken with one of my colleagues, said that now he knew all about modern philosophy—adding only, as he noted my surprise, "at least since Descartes."

Carving up great books to excerpt "essential doctrines" is one of the sins against the spirit of philosophy. If the reading of a whole Platonic dialogue leaves a man more doubtful and less sure of himself than the perusal of a brief epitome, that is all to the good, as Plato himself noted many times; for example, at the end of the *Theaetetus*. It is part of the point of philosophy to make men a little less sure about things. And Socrates, who converted Plato to philosophy, insisted that what distinguished him from other men was not that he knew all, or even most, answers but rather that he realized his ignorance.

Nobody can be introduced to philosophy without being exposed to wonder and perplexity, without being made aware of his ignorance, and without discovering that the great philosophers, far from settling all our doubts, present us with a host of puzzles. Not the least of these is often what precisely the philosopher's position was. Those who have never read a complete book by a philosopher are very often sure about his doctrines, while those who have studied the man thoroughly are usually much less sure—and those who do feel sure often disagree with each other.

No reader of this book or its companion volume should feel that he now knows all about Plato or Kant, Aristotle or Spinoza. He will find many complete and unabridged works, supplemented with selections, but these, far from being tailored to some one interpretation of the man, should give some impression of the range of his thought and of the problems that confront interpreters. The reader should not emerge with a spurious sense that he knows what in fact he does not know; rather he should come, if possible, to love philosophy. The *Apology* may communicate the philosophic spirit, and the *Symposium* and the *Phaedrus,* also uncut, might convince the reader that here are works of great beauty which may well require many a delightful reading before they yield up even most of their treasures. It is thus that one is won for philosophy, not by reading books that make everything easy and simple.

II

There is a good deal of continuity in these selections: those from the pre-Socratics turn out to be relevant for an understanding of Plato, Aristotle, Epicurus, and a lot of later writers, and the previously suggested metaphor of the conversation should be taken seriously. Hobbes' objections to Descartes have been included with Descartes' replies before Thomas Hobbes is introduced in his own right; but even where the dialogue is not quite so explicit it is well to ask oneself to what ideas of his predecessors a philosopher is probably responding.

Where translations had to be used, versions in the public domain that could be reprinted without permissions and fees were usually available, but a great deal of effort was devoted to attempts to obtain some of the fine translations done in recent years by the best scholars. Professionals will appreciate instantly what it means (to give but a very few examples) that Kirk and Raven's work on *The*

Presocratic Philosophers (1957) could be used along with Cornford's and Hackforth's excellent translations of some of Plato's more difficult dialogues; that Aquinas is offered in the translation edited by Pegis; that there is an entirely new, previously unpublished version by Willis Doney of material from Malebranche, not hitherto available in English; and that Philip Wiener's revised versions of his fine Leibniz translations are presented.

A single case may be discussed in just a little more detail. Old translations, in the public domain but not respected by the scholars in the field, are available of much material by and about the pre-Socratics. The versions reprinted in two of the most popular texts come from Arthur Fairbanks' *The First Philosophers of Greece* (1898), of which R. D. Hicks showed in *The Classical Review* (1899, pp. 450 ff.) that "a pupil who followed the translation . . . would be liable to serious misconceptions at almost every step"—a verdict seconded by Gregory Vlastos in *The Philosophical Review* (October 1959). The student who wants versions based on the latest scholarship can turn to Kathleen Freeman's *Ancilla to The Pre-Socratic Philosophers* (1947) and find their fragments but none of the often equally important paraphrases or reports about their doctrines—though much of their thought is known to us only indirectly in this manner. For additional material he can consult Freeman's *The Pre-Socratic Philosophers: A Companion to Diels, Fragmente der Vorsokratiker* (1946). Or he can turn to Kirk and Raven and find many of the testimonies and those fragments—often all too few—which the authors cite in the course of their scholarly discussions. But to give only two examples, those who consult Kirk and Raven will miss out on a good many of Heraclitus' most striking sayings and on almost all of the abundant sayings of Democritus on ethics. In Freeman's *Ancilla*, on the other hand, they will miss the atomistic world view of Democritus, which is known almost exclusively from testimonies. What is offered in the following pages, then, is—quite apart from some emendations of the translations presented—no mere reprint but, at least in places, material never previously presented in anything like the present form.

Zeno represents an especially dramatic case. Few, if any, pre-Socratic fragments have elicited as much interest and discussion as his famous paradoxes; but in recent years some of the foremost scholars have repudiated earlier translations of this material and proposed new readings. No English version hitherto in print is really up to date. The section on Zeno, therefore, was contributed by Gregory Vlastos and constitutes an important contribution to pre-Socrati scholarship.

III

Nothing has been offered of Chinese and Indian philosophy. The little that might have been put into these two volumes could not have done justice to India or China and would only have taken away valuable space from Western thinkers. To do justice to Oriental thought, another volume as large as one of the present volumes would be necessary. The same reasoning applies to Western philosophy since Kant. Not enough could have been included along with the men from Bacon to Kant to be satisfactory for students of nineteenth or twentieth-century philosophy. It therefore seemed best to devote as much space as possible to philosophers of the seventeenth and eighteenth centuries.

The treatment of medieval thought also requires comment. In line with the points just made, it could be argued that the Middle Ages should have been left out entirely; but for two reasons a few samples of medieval philosophy have been presented. Unlike Oriental philosophy—which stands entirely apart from the development recorded in these volumes—and unlike philosophy since Kant, which comes afterwards as the sequel, medieval philosophy must be conceded to have been either a link or an interruption, and probably both, in the story that is here presented. Our understanding of Bacon, Descartes, and Spinoza is enhanced by even a slight knowledge of Augustine, Anselm, and Aquinas. Moreover, interest in St. Thomas Aquinas is widespread, and his thought is as much discussed in the twentieth century as ever before. It is therefore customary in many colleges to bring in just a little of medieval philosophy at the end of a course on Greek philosophy, and this makes good sense. But any great expansion of this section, either by way of offering more of the writings of the three men represented here or by way of introducing others, such as Erigena, Scotus, Eckhart, and Occam, was not feasible for the same reasons that led to the exclusion of Oriental and recent philosophy: not enough could have been offered for the serious student or for a semester's course, and the value of the remaining part of the volume would have been impaired too seriously by the required cuts. Everything considered, it seemed best to concentrate chiefly on one medieval philosopher—and to select St. Thomas Aquinas for this purpose.

Those who use one of these volumes as the basis of a one-term course need hardly to be told that there is more material here than can easily fit into one semester. But the editor does not apologize for offering some choice or for giving teachers who offer the same course years after year an easy opportunity for varying their fare.

The last quotation from Xenophanes may serve as a motto for both volumes: "Not from the beginning have the gods revealed all things to mortals, but by long seeking, men find what is better."

IV

In making my selections for these two volumes, I have had the invaluable advantage of discussions with, and advice from, many of my colleagues: Dennis O'Brien, George Pitcher, and Gregory Vlastos at Princeton University; Richard Cartwright and Irving Copi at the University of Michigan; and Willis Doney at Dartmouth College. Having taught a variety of courses in the history of philosophy, they gave me the benefit of their considerable experience, and I am glad to have this opportunity to express my gratitude.

Professor Vlastos has also contributed the section on Zeno—both the translations and the editorial matter—and Professor Doney has contributed that on Malebranche. For this, too, I am deeply indebted to them.

Everybody with whom I have dealt at Prentice-Hall has been most cooperative and helpful, and special thanks are due Mrs. Maurine Lewis.

Acknowledgments to other publishers who have kindly given permission to reprint material in this volume will be found on page 630.

NOTE: In many instances, the page numbers of a standard edition have been retained—in the running heads at the top of the page in the selections from Aristotle; in brackets at the end of the line in the selections from Plato and (in the second volume) from Hobbes and Kant. This should facilitate the checking of scholarly citations as well as comparison with the original or with other editions. Moreover, where omissions are indicated, this device shows at a glance approximately how much has been omitted.

W. K.

CONTENTS

This volume is dedicated to

JOHN WILLIAM MILLER

*Mark Hopkins Professor of Intellectual and Moral Philosophy
in Williams College
emeritus*

PART ONE

BEFORE

SOCRATES

I

Almost all histories of philosophy and all philosophers agree that the so-called pre-Socratics were the first philosophers, at least in the Western world. Unlike most of the early thinkers of India and China, the pre-Socratics did not think exegetically: they did not read their ideas into, or out of, ancient scriptures or poems. On the contrary, they spoke as disrespectfully of the greatest poets as they did of each other. They made bold to speak out on their own behalf, each for himself, claiming neither the authority of divine inspiration nor the sanction of tradition. They come before us as thinking men who challenge us to think for ourselves as they did.

There are excellent reasons for beginning a study of philosophy with these men and then proceeding to Socrates and Plato. This, after all, is how Western philosophy did begin, and we can still recapture the movement from the bald statements of Thales to the all-embracing questioning of Socrates, and hence to Plato's efforts to fuse criticism with construction.

If a deep dissatisfaction with all facile answers is the starting point of philosophic thought, the fragments of the pre-Socratics are doubly appropriate for a beginning. Not one of their works has survived complete: all we have are quotations and reports in later writers.

1

As a result, pre-Socratic thought has a mysterious quality that makes flat statements highly questionable. Cryptic passages and forceful aphorisms whose original context is lost give us food for thought and stimulate our imagination. Instead of looking for "the" answer, one is fascinated by reflecting on a wealth of possibilities. And in the effort to show why some suggested interpretations are untenable, one can develop one's critical faculties, too.

Some of these fragments may remind the reader of archaic statues, heads with broken noses, torsos without heads or arms—pieces so perfect in the form in which they have survived that one has no regrets and even feels that the freshly completed work could not have been so fascinating.

For all that, most interest in the pre-Socratics is motivated by the fact that they furnish the backdrop for the thought of Socrates, Plato, and Aristotle: that is why one lumps them together as "the pre-Socratics." But the magnificent succession of thinker upon thinker was anything but luck. The Chinese *Tao-Teh-Ching* is also wonderful and enigmatic, but one understands why the book was never followed by a philosophic crescendo. Though they are often enigmatic and at times somewhat oracular, the pre-Socratics are distinguished by their appeal to reason. In this way each one makes it possible for his successors to subject his thought to criticisms, to amend it, to develop an alternative, to go beyond it.

In the pre-Socratics, wisdom ceases to soliloquize and becomes dialogue. Sage speaks to sage, often acidly, but not with the finality of monologue or revelation. In the Upanishads of ancient India we are invited to ponder infinite wisdom that claims to be derived from still more ancient poems, and any failure to assent is charged to lack of understanding. There is no room for argument and disagreement. The pre-Socratics confront us with constant disagreement. They are not mystagogues but heretics.

To picture them either as positivistic scientists, as John Burnet came close to doing in his *Early Greek Philosophy,* or as theologians, as Werner Jaeger did in *The Theology of the Early Greek Philosophers,* is to miss something of their very essence. Theology suggests the exegetic mode of thought, a loyalty to a traditional religion, and an effort to provide a systematic statement of, and rational foundation for, traditional beliefs and rites. In all three respects, the pre-Socratics stand opposed to all theology. None of them condoned traditional religion or any popular beliefs or cults. Some were scientists, but their world was not devoid of mystery—on the contrary. They neither denied mystery, nor did they try to expound it to the point where it might cease to be mysterious. They were exuberant in their reliance on reason, and they wrote poetry about it, or superbly fashioned aphorisms. They delighted in the light of sane thought but always retained a profound sense of the outer darkness, the unexpected, and the uncanny.

II

Their influence on Plato was so great that a study of their thought is essential to an understanding of many passages in his dialogues, of his intentions—many problems were suggested to him by Heraclitus, the Eleatics, and the Pythagoreans—and, of course, his originality. Aristotle studied the pre-Socratics closely and discussed them at length in the first book of his *Metaphysics*, which is reprinted in its entirety below, under Aristotle. Of the later Greek philosophers it has often been remarked that the Stoics were particularly influenced by Heraclitus, the Epicureans by Democritus. Elements of Orphism, an early Greek religious movement, also found their way into the pre-Socratics—most obviously, but by no means only, into Pythagoreanism—and hence into Plato and, later, into Christianity. In fact, a few of the fragments survived as quotations in the works of early Christian writers.

Most scholars would probably agree that the most important work on the pre-Socratics has been done by an international cast of philologists. Even so, there is still a great deal of discussion about the meaning of many fragments and the views of some of these early philosophers; and not only classical philologists have taken an interest in this literature.

Among modern philosophers, Hegel was the first to deal with pre-Socratic thought at loving length, in his posthumously published lectures on the history of philosophy. As a professor of classical philology at the University of Basel, Switzerland, Friedrich Nietzsche dealt in great detail with "The Pre-Platonic Philosophers" or, as he put it in the title of another posthumously published manuscript, with "Philosophy in the Tragic Era of the Greeks." In the books he, himself, published, too, there are occasional suggestions that in some respects these early thinkers may have been superior to their successors and that in some ways Plato may represent a decline, with his bifurcation of the world and of man and with his pre-Christian depreciation of *this* world and the senses.

In his first philosophic book, "The Psychology of World Views" (1919), Karl Jaspers based his discussion of "Types of Philosophic Thinking" on "the pre-Socratics, on account of their relative simplicity, on account of their greatness, and above all on account of Nietzsche's example" (p. 204). Jaspers' comments were admittedly based mainly on Nietzsche's essay on "Philosophy in the Tragic Era of the Greeks." The other great protagonist of German existentialism, Martin Heidegger—actually, both Jaspers and Heidegger repudiate the label of existentialism—has published a large body of interpretations of pre-Socratic fragments and has suggested again and again that the whole of Western philosophy from Plato to Nietzsche represents a tragic fall from the sensibility, the world feeling, the insights of the pre-Socratics to which our generation must somehow recover an approach. Philologists do not take Heidegger's laborious exegeses seriously, and it is worth pointing out that he quite misses their most distinctive break with the past: their refusal to think exegetically. Even so, it is interesting that the so-called existentialists, at least in Germany, have done their utmost to redirect attention to the pre-Socratics. Some feeling for at least a few of these early thinkers might be expected among a generation that has rediscovered archaic Greek art and has come to prefer the best of it to the (till recently) more celebrated classical and post-classical works.

III

The surviving quotations from the works of the pre-Socratics were collected by a nineteenth century German scholar, Hermann Diels, in *Die Fragmente der Vorsokratiker*. Diels assembled the original Greek texts and furnished German translations of all the fragments. He also collected and printed, but did not translate, reports of ancient authors about the lives, works, and ideas of the pre-Socratics. His work went through several editions and has been periodically revised and kept up to date since his death. No other work has ever replaced the latest edition of Diels.

In English there are primarily, though certainly not only, three works that offer pre-Socratic fragments in English. First, John Burnet translated and discussed many of the fragments in his *Early Greek Philosophy* (1st ed., 1892; 4th ed., 1930, reprinted as a paperback by Meridian Books; for some brief comments on his work, see section I, preceding). Then Kathleen Freeman published *An Ancilla to The Pre-Socratic Philosophers: A complete translation of the Fragments in Diels, Fragmente der Vorsokratiker* (Harvard University Press, 1947). Like Diels, she translated only the fragments, not the ancient paraphrases and reports about the philosophers' lives and works. Finally, there is *The Presocratic Philosophers: A Critical History with a Selection of Texts* by G. S. Kirk and J. E. Raven (Cambridge University Press, 1957). Here the emphasis falls on a careful critical discussion of some of the texts against the background of recent scholarly books and articles, and in the course of the discussion many, but not most, of the fragments, paraphrases, and reports are both cited in Greek and, at the bottom of the page on which the original is cited, rendered into English. For the serious student of the pre-Socratics, the book is a delight and constant help; for the less serious reader, and especially for those with no Greek, Freeman's book is likely to be more satisfactory, if only because it offers all of the fragments.

Almost all of the translations that follow are either those of Kirk or Raven (marked accordingly with a *K* or *R*, followed by the number which the passage bears in their book) or those of Freeman (marked with an *F*). An asterisk (*) indicates that the translation has been revised slightly—often, but not always, very slightly indeed, for purely stylistic reasons. In a very few cases the translation is my own and marked *WK*. After direct quotations, these symbols (*K, R, F,* and *WK*) are preceded by the number which the fragment bears in the fifth edition of Diels's standard work. Freeman's numbering is the same as Diels's. After paraphrases, the ancient works in which they occur are cited briefly, using the standard abbreviations. Those interested in an evaluation of these paraphrases, which are by no means always completely reliable, will find illuminating, if occasionally controversial, discussions in Kirk and Raven.

The reason for often using Kirk's and Raven's versions is that they embody the latest scholarship; the reason for not relying solely on them is that there is so much material which they have not translated. Moreover, their wording—and Miss Freeman's, too—is now and then excessively academic. Miss Freeman also uses capital letters very profusely—to the point of distraction—and I have departed from this practice.

The reader should not forget that some of the pre-Socratics were very great writers, but that both here and throughout these readings every effort has been made to take into account the work of the best scholars in the field. Nowhere has accuracy been knowingly sacrificed to beauty; but one need not give the impression, in the name of accuracy, that the pre-Socratics wrote like classical philologists.

What follows is a selection. There is no such thing as a complete roster of the pre-Socratics. The so-called Sophists were Socrates' contemporaries, but Protagoras and Gorgias were older than he and acquired great reputations before he came along and challenged them; and they are included here. After all, it was partly in response to their teaching that his thought was developed. Among the older writers, it is arguable who was, and who was not, a philosopher. Various poets, for example, are occasionally included among the pre-Socratics. Not counting the Sophists, the present selection concentrates on the twelve major figures. They might conveniently be arranged in four groups of three: the Milesians (Thales, Anaximander, and Anaximenes), then three men who came from different places and stood each by himself (Pythagoras, Xenophanes, and Heraclitus), then the so-called Eleatics (Parmenides, Zeno, and Melissus), and finally the pluralists (Empedocles, Anaxagoras, and Democritus). The only major name that is missing in this list is that of Leucippus, the founder of the atomistic philosophy, who is presented together with his great follower, Democritus.

Offering all the fragments of the twelve main figures, one would have to include such items as the following, each of which I now proceed to cite in its entirety: "The joint connects two things"; "as when fig juice binds white milk"; and "having kneaded together barley-meal with water" (Empedocles, fragments 32, 33, 34).

The selections that follow are generally very inclusive. They are meant to give an idea not only of each man's major teachings, as far as possible in his own words, but also of his way of thinking and feeling, his style—in short, of the man who still confronts the student across roughly 2,500 years. Where a striking sentence has given rise to widely different translations, this is noted.

THE
MILESIANS

THALES

Thales is quite generally considered the first Western philosopher
—not so much by virtue of some one thing he said as because an
unbroken line leads from him to Socrates, Plato, and Aristotle. He
lived in Miletus in Asia Minor and is said to have predicted an
eclipse of the sun that occurred in 585 B.C. He was thus a contemporary of the Hebrew prophet, Jeremiah, who predicted the fall of
Jerusalem which, to his regret, he lived to see in 586 B.C.

According to both Herodotus, the great 5th century historian who
has been called "the father of history," and Diogenes Laertius, who,
in the 3rd century A.D., composed the fascinating, anecdotal, but by
no means always reliable *Lives of Famous Philosophers,* Thales was
of Phoenician descent. But not all scholars are convinced that he
was a pure Semite. In any case, the Greek-speaking population of
Miletus was racially very mixed, and Greek philosophy originated in
a melting pot of many cultures. The ancients were agreed that Thales
had learnt a great deal from the Egyptians, Babylonians and Phoeni-
cians.

Like many of the other pre-Socratics, Thales was by no means a
philosopher only. Among other things, he was also a statesman, an
astronomer, a geometer, and renowned sage. He probably did not
write any book, but ancient literature contains many statements
about him, a few of which follow.

.   .   .

A witty and attractive Thracian servant-girl is said to have mocked Thales for falling into a well while he was observing the stars and gazing upwards; declaring that he was eager to know the things in the sky, but that what was behind him and just by his feet escaped his notice.

[Plato, *Theaetetus* 174A; K 74]

When they reproached him because of his poverty, as though philosophy were no use, it is said that, having observed through his study of the heavenly bodies that there would be a large olive-crop, he raised a little capital while it was still winter, and paid deposits on all the olive presses in Miletus and Chios, hiring them cheaply because no one bid against him. When the appropriate time came there was a sudden rush of requests for the presses; he then hired them out on his own terms and so made a large profit, thus demonstrating that it is easy for philosophers to be rich, if they wish, but that it is not in this that they are interested.

[Aristotle, *Politics* A11, 1259a; K 75]

When he came to the Halys river, Croesus then, as I say, put his army across by the existing bridges; but, according to the common account of the Greeks, Thales the Milesian transferred the army for him. For it is said that Croesus was at a loss how his army should cross the river, since these bridges did not yet exist at this period; and that Thales, who was present in the army, made the river, which flowed on the left hand of the army, flow on the right hand also. He did so in this way: beginning upstream of the army he dug a deep channel, giving it a crescent shape, so that it should flow round the back of where the army was encamped, being diverted in this way from its old course by the channel, and passing the camp should flow into its old course once more. The result was that as soon as the river was divided it became fordable in both of its parts.

[Herodotus I, 75; K 67]

. . .

Moist natural substance, since it is easily formed into each different thing, is accustomed to undergo very various changes: that part of it which is exhaled is made into air, and the finest part is kindled from air into aether, while when water is compacted and changes into slime it becomes earth. Therefore Thales declared that water, of the four elements, was the most active, as it were, as cause. [Heraclitus Homericus, *Quaest. Hom.* 22; K 89. These may not really have been Thales' reasons.]

He [Thales] said that the world is held up by water and rides like a ship, and when it is said to 'quake' it is actually rocking because of the water's movement. [Seneca, *Qu. Nat.* III, 14; K 90]

Thales, too, seems, from what they relate, to have supposed that the soul was something kinetic, if he said that the (Magnesian) stone possesses soul because it moves iron. [Aristotle, *De Anima* A2, 405a; K 91]

Some say that it [soul] is intermingled in the universe, for which reason, perhaps, Thales also thought that all things are full of gods.

[Aristotle, *De Anima* A5, 411a; K 93]

ANAXIMANDER

The second Milesian philosopher hazarded quite a number of interesting guesses about nature. He may also have been the first among the Greeks to compose a book of prose. But what has fascinated his successors, down to the present, far more than anything else about him is the one sentence, or half-sentence, from that book which has survived because Simplicius quoted it. In these few words one may detect an echo of ancient Orphic notions of original sin, though this interpretation is by no means certain. It was Anaximander at any rate who introduced the notion of the *apeiron*, the unlimited, boundless, infinite, or indefinite, which he considered the fundamental principle of the world, thus replacing Thales' conception of water.

. . .

Anaximander son of Praxiades, of Miletus, philosopher, was a kinsman, pupil and successor of Thales. He first discovered the equinox and solstices and hour-indicators, and that the earth lies in the center. He introduced the gnomon [a vertical rod whose shadow indicates the sun's direction and height] and in general made known an outline of geometry. He wrote *On Nature, Circuit of the Earth,* and *On the Fixed Stars,* and *Celestial Globe,* and some other works. [Suda s.v.; K 97. Some of this has been disputed.]

[Anaximander] was the first of the Greeks whom we know who ventured to produce a written account on nature. [Themistius *Or.* 26; K 98]

. . .

Of those who say that it is one, moving, and infinite, Anaximander son of Praxiades, a Milesian, the successor and pupil of Thales, said that the principle and element of existing things was the *apeiron* [indefinite, *or* infinite], being the first to introduce this name of the material principle. He says that it is neither water nor any other of the so-called elements, but some other *apeiron* nature, from which come into being all the heavens and the worlds in them. And the source of coming-to-be for existing things is that into which destruction, too, happens 'according to necessity; for they pay penalty and retribution to each other for their injustice according to the assessment of time,' as he describes it in these rather poetical terms. It is clear that he, seeing the changing of the four elements into each other, thought it right to make none of these the substratum, but something else besides these; and he produces coming-to-be not through the alteration of the element, but by the separation off of the opposites through the eternal motion. [Simplicius, *Phys.* 24; K 103A and 121. The phrase quoted from Anaximander's work has elicited a large literature, including a 48-page essay by Martin Heidegger. Some scholars believe that the quotation begins earlier and comprises the whole sentence.]

He says that that which is productive from the eternal of hot and cold was separated off at the coming-to-be of this world, and that a kind of sphere of flame from this was formed round the air surrounding the earth, like bark around a tree. When this was broken off and shut off in certain circles, the sun and moon and stars were formed.

[Ps.-Plutarch, *Strom.* 2; K 123]

He says that the earth is cylindrical in shape, and that its depth is a third of its width.   [*Ibid.*; K 124A]

Its shape is curved, round, similar to the drum of a column; of its flat surfaces we walk on one, and the other is on the opposite side.

[Hippolytus, *Ref.* I, 6, 3; K 124B]

Anaximander says the sun is a circle 28 times the size of the earth, like a chariot wheel, with its rim hollow and full of fire, and showing the fire at a certain point through an aperture as though through the nozzle of a bellows.   [Aetius II, 20; K 128*]

Anaximander said that the first living creatures were born in moisture, enclosed in thorny barks; and that as their age increased they came forth on to the drier part and, when the bark had broken off, they lived a different kind of life for a short time.   [Aetius V, 19; K 136]

Further he says that in the beginning man was born from creatures of a different kind; because other creatures are soon self-supporting, but man alone needs prolonged nursing. For this reason he would not have survived if this had been his original form.

[Ps.-Plutarch, *Strom.* 2; K 137]

Therefore they [the Syrians] actually revere the fish as being of similar race and nurturing. In this they philosophize more suitably than Anaximander; for he declares, not that fishes and men came into being in the same parents, but that originally men came into being inside fishes, and that, having been nurtured there—like sharks—and having become adequate to look after themselves, they then came forth and took to the land.

[Plutarch, *Symp.* VIII, 730E; K 140]

ANAXIMENES

The third and last of the Milesian philosophers proposed air as the basic principle of the world. Perhaps this suggestion can be understood as an attempted synthesis of the ideas of his predecessors: air, more than water, seems to partake of the nature of the boundless, the unlimited, the infinite, the indefinite—the *apeiron* of Anaximander.

. . .

Anaximenes son of Eurystratus, of Miletus, was a pupil of Anaximander ... He said that the material principle was air and the infinite; and that the stars move, not under the earth, but round it. He used simple and un-superfluous Ionic speech. He was active, according to what Apollodorus says, around the time of the capture of Sardis [by Cyrus in 546/5 B.C.?], and died in the 63rd Olympiad.   [Diogenes Laertius II, 3; K 141]

He [Anaximander] left Anaximenes as his disciple and successor, who attributed all the causes of things to infinite air, and did not deny that there were gods, or pass them over in silence; yet he believed not the air was made by them, but that they arose from air.
[Augustine, *City of God*, VIII, 2; K 149]

And all things are produced by a kind of condensation, and again rare-faction, of this [air]. Motion, indeed, exists from everlasting; he says that when the air felts, there first of all comes into being the earth, quite flat—therefore it accordingly rides on the air; and sun and moon and the remaining heavenly bodies have their source of generation from earth. At least, he declares the sun to be earth, but that through the rapid motion it obtains heat in great sufficiency.   [Ps.-Plutarch, *Strom.* 3; K 151]

THREE
SOLITARY
FIGURES

PYTHAGORAS

Born on the island of Samos, just off the coast of Asia Minor and very close to Miletus, Pythagoras moved to southern Italy, where the Greeks had colonies, and settled at Croton, on the bay of Tarentum. He founded a quasi-religious sect which still existed in Plato's time, 150 years later. It exerted a decisive influence on Plato's thought, second only to the impact of his revered teacher, Socrates.

Pythagoras was soon associated with so many legends that few scholars would dare to say much about his life and personality, or even about his teachings, without adding that we cannot really be sure whether our information is accurate. That there really was a man named Pythagoras who founded the sect, we need not doubt: among the witnesses to that was his younger contemporary, Heraclitus, who thought ill of him (see below under Heraclitus, section D). The big question is this: what did Pythagoras himself do and say, and what did others later ascribe to him?

Today he is best known for the so-called Pythagorean theorem in geometry (cited below). His interest in mathematics is as well attested to as his concern with religion and philosophy, and we may safely surmise that, like Plato after him, he considered the study of mathematics essential for the conversion of the soul from the world of the senses to the contemplation of the eternal.

The following ideas evidently influenced Plato especially: the

12

dualistic juxtaposition of body and soul and the conception of the body (*soma* in Greek) as the tomb (*sema* in Greek) of the soul; the belief in the immortality of the soul; the doctrine of the transmigration of souls; the idea that knowledge and a philosophic life are required for the salvation of the soul; the notion that one might design a society that would be an instrument of salvation for its members; the admission of women to this society; the suggestion that all members should hold their property in common; and, finally, the division of mankind into three basic types—tradesmen being the lowest class; those in whom the competitive spirit and ambition are highly developed, a little higher; while those who prefer contemplation are considered most excellent.

The whole development of Plato's thought from his early works to his last ones may be understood as a gradual departure from the heritage of Socrates and a sustained effort to absorb Pythagoreanism. And it was the Pythagorean Plato rather than the Socratic one who decisively influenced the subsequent development of Christian thought.

· · ·

According to my information from the Greeks who live beside the Hellespont and Pontus, this Salmoxis, a real man, was a slave in Samos to Pythagoras son of Mnesarchus ... but I believe that this Salmoxis lived many years before Pythagoras. [Herodotus IV, 95; R 255]

Aristoxenus says that at the age of forty, seeing that the tyranny of Polycrates had grown more intense, ... he eventually migrated to Italy. [Porphyry *V.P.* 9; R 256]

He emigrated to Croton in Italy and there, by legislating for the Italians, won renown together with his pupils. They numbered nearly 300, and they administered the affairs of state so well that the constitution was virtually an aristocracy. [Diogenes Laertius VIII, 3; R 257]

Pythagoras wrote nothing, nor did Socrates ...
[Plutarch, *Alex. fort.* I, 4, 328; R 267]

· · ·

Ten is the very nature of number. All Greeks and all barbarians alike count up to ten, and having reached ten revert again to the unit. And again, Pythagoras maintains, the power of the number ten lies in the number four, the tetrad. This is the reason: if one starts at the unit and adds the successive numbers up to four, one will make up the number ten; and if one exceeds the tetrad, one will exceed ten, too. If, that is, one takes the unit, adds two, then three, and then four, one will make up the number ten.... So the Pythagoreans used to invoke the tetrad as their most binding oath: 'Nay, by him that gave to our generation the tetractys, which contains the fount and root of eternal nature.'
[Aetius I, 3, 8; R 280]

The square of the hypotenuse of a right-angled triangle is equal to the sum of the squares on the sides enclosing the right angle. [The text of the next sentence is corrupt, but the sense is:] If we pay any attention to those who like to recount ancient history, we may find some of them referring this theorem to Pythagoras, and saying that he sacrificed an ox in honor of his discovery.   [Proclus, *In Eucl.*, p. 426 Friedl.; R 281]

. . .

On the subject of reincarnation, Xenophanes bears witness in an elegy which begins: 'Now I will turn to another tale and show the way.' What he says about Pythagoras runs thus: 'Once they say that he was passing by when a puppy was being whipped, and he took pity and said: Stop, do not beat it; for it is the soul of a friend that I recognized when I heard it giving tongue.' [Diogenes Laertius VIII, 36; Xenophanes, fragment 7; R 268]

Moreover, the Egyptians are the first to have maintained the doctrine that the soul of man is immortal and that, when the body perishes, it enters into another animal that is being born at the time, and when it has been the complete round of the creatures of the dry land and of the sea and of the air it enters again into the body of a man at birth; and its cycle is completed in 3000 years. There are some Greeks who have adopted this doctrine, some in former times and some in later, as if it were their own invention; their names I know but refrain from writing down.   [Herodotus II, 123; R 270]

None the less the following became universally known: first that he maintains that the soul is immortal; next, that it changes into other kinds of living things; also that events recur in certain cycles, and that nothing is ever absolutely new; and finally, that all living things should be regarded as akin. Pythagoras seems to have been the first to bring these beliefs into Greece.   [Porphyry, *Vita Pythagorae* 19; R 271]

If one were to believe the Pythagoreans that events recur in an arithmetical cycle, and that I shall be talking to you again sitting as you are now, with this pointer in my hand, and that everything else will be just as it is now, then it is plausible to suppose that the time, too, will be the same as now.   [Eudemus *ap.* Simplic. *Phys.*, 732, 30; R 272. The doctrine of the eternal recurrence of the same events at gigantic intervals was revived in modern times by Friedrich Nietzsche; cf. Walter Kaufmann's *Nietzsche*, Princeton 1950, Meridian Books 1956, Chapter 11, "Overman and Eternal Recurrence."]

. . .

Let the rules to be pondered be these:

1. When you are going out to a temple, worship first, and on your way neither say nor do anything else connected with your daily life.

2. On a journey neither enter a temple nor worship at all, not even if you are passing the very doors.

3. Sacrifice and worship without shoes on.
4. Turn aside from highways and walk by footpaths. . . .
6. Follow the gods and restrain your tongue above all else. . . .
8. Stir not the fire with iron. . . .
10. Help a man who is loading freight, but not one who is unloading.
11. Putting on your shoes, start with the right foot; washing your feet, with the left.
12. Speak not of Pythagorean matters without light.
13. Never step over a cross-bar.
14. When you are out from home, look not back, for the furies come after you. . . .
22. Do not wear a ring. . . .
23. Do not look in a mirror beside a lamp. . . .
30. Eat not the heart. . . .
32. Spit upon the trimmings of your hair and finger-nails. . . .
37. Abstain from beans. . . .
39. Abstain from living things.
[Iamblichus, *Protr.* 21; R 275. These were some of the rules of the sect founded by Pythagoras.]

Pythagoras turned geometrical philosophy into a form of liberal education by seeking its first principles in a higher realm of reality.
[Procl., *In Eucl.*, p. 65 Friedl.; R 277]

Life, he said, is like a festival; just as some come to the festival to compete, some to ply their trade, but the best people come as spectators, so in life the slavish men go hunting for fame or gain, the philosophers for the truth. [Diogenes Laertius VIII, 8; R 278]

XENOPHANES

A contemporary of Pythagoras, he came from Colophon on the mainland of Asia Minor, a few miles inland and approximately 50 miles north of Miletus and less than 15 miles north of Ephesus. He traveled a great deal and recited his poetry of which only a few fragments survive. At one time he was supposed to have been Parmenides' teacher and the founder of the Eleatic school, no doubt on account of his conception of one sole, unmoving god—a notion readily associated with Parmenides' idea of being. But this supposition is now generally rejected, and Xenophanes is seen as an essentially solitary figure. Little of his work has come down to us, but what little there is is unforgettable.

.   .   .

Xenophanes son of Dexios or, according to Apollodorus, of Orthomenes, of Colophon . . . being expelled from his native land, passed his time in

Zancle in Sicily and in Catana.... He wrote in epic metre, also elegiacs and iambics, against Hesiod and Homer, reproving them for what they said about the gods. But he himself also recited his own original poems. He is said to have held contrary opinions to Thales and Pythagoras, and to have rebuked Epimenides, too. He had an extremely long life, as he himself somewhere says: 'Already there are seven and sixty years tossing my thought up and down the land of Greece; and from my birth there were another twenty-five to add to these, if I know how to speak truly about these things.'   [Diogenes Laertius IX, 18; K 164]

.   .   .

Homer and Hesiod ascribed to the gods whatever is infamy and reproach among men: theft and adultery and deceiving each other.   [11; WK]

Mortals suppose that the gods are born and have clothes and voices and shapes like their own.   [14; WK]

But if oxen, horses, and lions had hands or could paint with their hands and fashion works as men do, horses would paint horselike images of gods and oxen oxlike ones, and each would fashion bodies like their own.
[15; WK]

The Ethiopians consider the gods flat-nosed and black; the Thracians blue-eyed and red-haired.   [16; WK]

There is one god, among gods and men the greatest, not at all like mortals in body or mind.   [23; F*]

He sees as a whole, thinks as a whole, and hears as a whole.   [24; F]

But without toil he moves everything by the thought of his mind.
[25; F*]

He always remains in the same place, not moving at all, nor is it fitting for him to change his position at different times.   [26; F]

Everything comes from earth and returns to earth in the end.   [27; F*]

No man knows or ever will know the truth about the gods and about everything I speak of: for even if one chanced to say the complete truth, yet oneself knows it not; but seeming is wrought over all things.
[34; K 189]

Not from the beginning have the gods revealed all things to mortals, but by long seeking men find what is better.   [18; WK]

HERACLITUS

Heraclitus of Ephesus flourished around 500 B.C. The ancients already called him "the dark philosopher," but there is nothing obscure about his cutting strictures of Xenophanes and Pythagoras,

Homer and Hesiod, or about his contempt for common sense and common men. He was clearly a man of very great literary genius, and his epigrams, though often paradoxical and elusive, are immensely suggestive, invite frequent rereading, and haunt the mind. In his sayings, as in those of no previous philosopher, one feels that one encounters the personality of the thinker. After almost 25 centuries, he still evokes instant antipathy in some readers and the highest admiration in others. Among those who have paid lavish tribute to him are Hegel and Nietzsche.

Because so many of his sayings have survived and are worth quoting here, it seemed advisable to arrange them under a few topical headings. Regarding the two items in the first section (A), it may be noted that the claim about the three parts of his book has been questioned; indeed, some have doubted that he wrote any book at all—but this doubt strikes me as unreasonable.

The term *Logos,* left untranslated in section B, is sometimes rendered as reason, sometimes as word (as in the first sentence of the fourth Gospel: "In the beginning was the Word"); and it may also denote a rational principle in the world. The so-called river fragments are included in section C. In the following section, the role assigned to fire is striking. Thales had considered water the basic principle; Anaximenes, air; now Heraclitus introduces fire. It would seem that fire was associated in his mind with both change, which it represents even much more strikingly than water, and with strife and war; but the last two fragments in that section also raise the question whether he may not possibly have been influenced by the religion of the Persians, who had conquered the Babylonian empire during Heraclitus' lifetime. It was the Persians who put an end to the Babylonian exile of the Jews, and it was probably from the Persians that the conception of a fiery judgment day entered first Jewish speculation and later the Christian religion. The Persians, following their great prophet Zarathustra, or Zoroaster, also believed that there were two great gods, one of the good and of light, the other of evil and darkness, and that man must assist the former, Ormuzd, against the latter, Ahriman. This idea, which the Jews emphatically rejected, was not accepted by Heraclitus either (cf., e.g., fragments 57 and 102 in section D). That Heraclitus knew something of the religion of the Persians is by no means established. It seems probable to me, but some eminent scholars doubt it. It has also been suggested that Heraclitus associated fire not only with change but also with permanence.

Plato frequently referred to Heraclitus and named one of his dialogues after Heraclitus' follower, Cratylus. In the *Cratylus* he speaks of "the opinion of Heraclitus that all things flow," and this phrase, "all things flow" (*panta rhei*) has often been cited as the quintessence of Heracliteanism. With some slight oversimplification, one might say that Plato was convinced by Heraclitus that in this world all things are in a flux; that he also believed that if everything were in a flux no rational discourse would be possible; and that he concluded that there must be another world beyond the world of sense experience—a realm utterly free from change, motion, and time. At that point he was probably influenced not only by the Pythagoreans but also by Parmenides, the next great pre-Socratic after Heraclitus.

.   .   .

A. THE MAN

Antisthenes, in his *Successions*, quotes as a sign of his [Heraclitus'] arrogance that he resigned the hereditary kingship to his brother.
[Diogenes Laertius IX, 6; K 194]

The book said to be his is called *On Nature*, from its chief content, and is divided into three discourses: On the Universe, Politics, Theology. He dedicated it and placed it in the temple of Artemis, as some say, having purposely written it rather obscurely so that only those of rank and influence should have access to it, and it should not be easily despised by the populace. . . . The work had so great a reputation that from it arose disciples, those called Heracliteans.   [*Ibid.*, IX, 5; K 195]

B. LOGOS AND SENSES

Those awake have one ordered universe in common, but in sleep every man turns away to one of his own.   [89; WK]

The thinking faculty is common to all.   [113; F]

Of the Logos, which is as I describe it, men always prove to be uncomprehending, both before they have heard it and when once they have heard it. For although all things happen according to this Logos men are like people of no experience, even when they experience such words and deeds as I explain, when I distinguish each thing according to its constitution and declare how it is; but the rest of men fail to notice what they do after they wake up just as they forget what they do when asleep.   [1; K 197]

Therefore it is necessary to follow the common; but although the Logos is common the many live as though they had a private understanding.
[2; K 198]

Listening not to me but to the Logos it is wise to agree that all things are one.   [50; K 199]

The things of which there is seeing and hearing and perception, these I prefer.   [55; K 200]

The eyes are more exact witnesses than the ears.   [101a; F]

If all existing things turned to smoke, the nose would be the discriminating organ.   [7; F]

Evil witnesses are eyes and ears for men if they have souls that do not understand their language.   [107; K 201]

C.   COSMOS

The path up and down are one and the same.   [60; K 203*]

The sun is new each day.   [6; F]

Sun will not overstep his measures; else the Erinyes, Justice's ministers, will find him out.   [94; K 299*]

In the same river we both step and do not step, we are and are not.
[49a; F*]

It is not possible to step twice into the same river.   [91; F]

Upon those that step into the same rivers different and different waters flow.   [12; K 217]

Sea is the most pure and polluted water: for fishes it is drinkable and salutary, but for men undrinkable and perilous.   [61; K 202*]

Disease makes health pleasant and good, hunger satiety, weariness rest.
[111; K 204]

What is in opposition is in concert, and from what differs comes the most beautiful harmony.   [8; F*]

War is the father of all, the king of all; and some he shows as gods, some as men; some he makes slaves, some free.   [53; K 215*]

One must know that war is common and justice is strife, and that all things happen by strife and necessity.   [80; K 214*]

For souls it is death to become water, for water death to become earth; from earth water comes-to-be, and from water, soul.   [36; K 232*]

Immortals are mortal, mortals immortal: (each) lives the death of the other and dies their life.   [62; F*]

After death things await men which they do not expect or imagine.
[27; F*]

Time is a child playing a game of draughts; the kingship is in the hands of a child.   [52; F]

D.   RELIGION AND FIRE

Being a polymath does not teach understanding: else Hesiod would have had it and Pythagoras; also Xenophanes and Hekataeus.   [40; WK]

Homer deserves to be thrown out of the contests and whipped, and Archilochus, too.   [42; WK]

The most popular teacher is Hesiod. Of him people think he knew most —he who did not even know day and night: they are one.   [57; WK]

They purify themselves by staining themselves with other blood, as if one stepped into mud to wash off mud. But a man would be thought mad if one of his fellowmen saw him do that. Also, they talk to statues as one might talk with houses, in ignorance of the nature of gods and heroes.
[5; F*]

The consecrations of the mysteries, as practised among men, are unholy.
[14; WK]

Corpses should be thrown away more than dung.   [96; WK. To appreciate the full measure of this heresy, one should recall Sophocles' *Antigone* and Homer's *Iliad*.]

To god all things are beautiful and good and just, but men have supposed some things to be unjust, some just.   [102; K 209*]

Man is called childish compared with divinity, just as a boy compared with a man.   [79; F]

Fire lives the death of earth, and air the death of fire; water lives the death of air, earth that of water.   [76; F*]

Fire, having come upon them, will judge and seize upon (condemn) all things.   [66; F]

This cosmos [the same of all] none of gods or men made, but it always was and is and shall be: an everlasting fire, kindling in measures and going out in measures.   [30; K 220*]

E.   MEN AND MORALS

Asses prefer chaff to gold.   [9; F*]

Dogs bark at those whom they do not recognize.   [97; F]

If happiness lay in bodily pleasures, we should call oxen happy when they find vetch to eat.   [4; F*]

It is not good for men to obtain all they wish.   [110; F*]

Sane thinking is the greatest virtue, and wisdom is speaking the truth and acting according to nature, paying heed.   [112; F*]

All men are granted what is needed for knowing oneself and sane thinking.   [116; WK]

A dry soul is wisest and best.   [118; K 233]

A man when he is drunk is led by an unfledged boy, stumbling and not knowing where he goes, having his soul moist.   [117; K 234]

The best choose one above all else: everlasting fame above mortals. The majority are contented like well-fed cattle.   [29; WK]

The people must fight on behalf of the law as though for the city wall.   [44; K 252]

One man to me is ten thousand if he is the best.   [49; F*]

The Ephesians would do well to hang themselves, every adult man, and leave their city to adolescents, since they expelled Hermodorus, the worthiest man among them, saying: Let us not have even one worthy man; but if we do, let him go elsewhere and live among others!   [121; F*]

F.   EPILOGUE

I sought myself.   [101; WK]

If one does not expect the unexpected one will not find it, for it is not reached by search or trail.   [18; WK]

Character is man's fate.   [119; WK]

Nature loves hiding.   [123; WK]

The Sybil, uttering her unlaughing, unadorned, unincensed words with raving mouth, reaches out over a thousand years with her voice, through the god.   [92; F*]

The lord whose oracle is in Delphi neither speaks out nor conceals, but gives a sign.   [93; K 247]

THE ELEATICS

PARMENIDES

Parmenides, a younger contemporary of Heraclitus and an older contemporary of Socrates, lived in Elea in southern Italy, on the west coast, a few miles south of the ancient Posidonia (now Paestum) where a magnificent temple of Poseidon stands to this day along with two other fine temples which also belong to the time of Parmenides. He may have been born about 510 B.C., something like 30 years after Heraclitus. Plato gave free expression to his reverence for Parmenides and introduced him into one of his dialogues, named after him (part of it is reprinted in the present volume). According to that dialogue, Parmenides visited Athens when he was about 65, accompanied by his chief pupil, Zeno, then nearly 40, and conversed with Socrates who was still "quite young." Whether the visit to Athens really took place, we do not know; that Socrates met Parmenides is not especially likely; but that they did not have the conversation reported in the dialogue is absolutely clear: for that discussion presupposes Plato's own earlier work and explores difficulties in the theory of forms expounded in the *Phaedo* and the *Republic*—difficulties which Plato evidently had not noticed when he wrote those dialogues long after the death of Socrates.

That Plato raised Parmenides to such heights, allowing him to instruct the young Socrates (generally, Socrates bests or teaches those with whom he converses in Plato's dialogues), confirms the impression one gets in any case, that there were few men to whom Plato felt a greater debt. Specifically, his dichotomy of knowledge and

22

belief and of an unchanging, eternal, timeless reality and ever changing, temporal appearance was derived from Parmenides. The Eleatic idea that reality is one, devoid of any plurality, Plato did not accept: he peopled the "real" world with a number of unchanging, eternal forms. But when he realized later that this theory was open to serious objections, he put the criticisms that occurred to him into the mouth of the great Parmenides. And in a still later dialogue, the *Sophist* (also reprinted in large part in the present volume), Plato occupied himself with another Parmenidean dichotomy: that of being and non-being.

Parmenides' distinction between the one, undifferentiated, timeless, changeless reality and the merely apparent world of sense experience invites comparison with the slightly older philosophy of the Indian Upanishads; and Pythagoras' belief in the transmigration of souls points in the same direction. No Indian influence on the pre-Socratics has ever been demonstrated, but this, of course, does not prove that there was no such influence.

Parmenides, as the philosopher of changeless being, has often been contrasted with Heraclitus, as the philosopher of change and becoming. But it should not be overlooked that both are at one in repudiating the wisdom of tradition as well as common sense. One is as radical as the other.

The fragments that follow are parts of a poem in which, after an imposing prologue, the ways of knowledge and belief, of being and non-being, are distinguished.

· · ·

The steeds that bear me took me as far as my heart's desire after they brought me to the renowned way of the goddess that leads the man who knows through every town. On that way I was borne, for there the wise chariot-steeds bore me, and the maidens led the way.   [Lines 1-5]

The axle, glowing in the socket, urged round by the whirling wheels at each end, made the naves sing, as the daughters of the sun, hastening to convey me to the light, left the abode of night and threw back the veils from their faces.   [Lines 6-10]

There are the gates of the ways of night and day, with a lintel above and a threshold of stone below. They themselves, lofty, are filled with huge doors, and avenging Justice wields the changing bolts.

[Lines 11-14]

Her the maidens entreated with gentle words, persuading her cleverly to unfasten the bolted bar quickly from the gates. Flung open, they revealed a wide, gaping space, as the brazen posts with their rivets and nails swung in turn on their hinges. There, straight through the gates, on that road the maidens guided the chariot and steeds.   [Lines 15-21]

Then the goddess greeted me kindly, took my right hand in hers, and spoke to me, addressing me thus: [Lines 22-23]

O youth, companion of immortal charioteers and steeds that brought you to our abode: welcome! No evil fate, but right and justice, sent you on this way, far from the beaten track of men. You must needs learn all: both the unshaken heart of well-rounded [1] truth and the opinions of mortals in which there is no true belief. Nevertheless, you shall learn these things also, how, passing right through all things, one should judge the things that seem to be.   [Lines 24-32; fragment 1 comprises lines 1-32. Raven's translation is based on Burnet's; the above version was arrived at after also consulting Diels's and Freeman's.]

Come, I will tell you; hear my word and carry it away. These are the only ways of inquiry that can be thought of [literally: that exist for thinking (Raven)]: one way, that it is and cannot not-be, is the path of persuasion, for it attends upon truth; the other, that it is-not and needs must not-be, that, I tell you, is a path altogether unthinkable. For you could not know that which is-not (that is impossible), nor utter it.

[2; R 344*]

For thinking and being are the same thing.   [3. This striking sentence seems to be continuous with the preceding two fragments. Interpretations differ. Burnet: for it is the same thing that can be thought and that can be. Raven: for the same thing can be thought as can be. Raven construes the literal meaning as: the same thing exists for thinking and for being. Freeman: For it is the same thing to think and to be. Diels: Denn *das Seiende* denken und sein ist dasselbe.]

Look steadfastly at things which, though far off, are yet present to your mind; for you shall not cut off what is from clinging to what is, neither scattering itself everywhere in order nor crowding together.   [4; R 349]

It is all one to me where I begin; for I shall come back there again in time.   [5; R 343]

That which can be spoken and thought needs must be; for it is possible for it, but not for nothing, to be; that is what I bid you ponder. This is the first way of inquiry from which I hold you back, and then also from that way on which mortals wander, knowing nothing, two-minded; for helplessness guides the wandering thoughts in their breasts: they are carried along, deaf and blind at once, dazed altogether, hordes without judgment, persuaded that to be and to be-not are the same, yet not the same, and that the path of all things turns back.   [6; R 345*. Freeman renders the final words: in everything there is a way of opposing stress. Either way, many interpreters believe that Parmenides here alludes to Heraclitus.]

---

[1] Cf. Fragment 5, following.

For never shall this be proved, that things that are not are. Hold back your thought from this way of inquiry, nor let custom, born of much experience, force you to let roam along this road your eye, sightless, your ear, noise-filled, or your tongue. But by means of the logos judge the much-debated proof that I utter.   [7; R 346*]

Only one way remains; that it is. To this way there are very many sign-posts: that being has no coming-into-being and no destruction, for it is whole of limb, without motion, and without end. And it never was, nor will be, because it is now, a whole all together, one, continuous; for what creation of it will you look? How, whence sprung? Nor shall I allow you to speak or think of it as springing from not-being; for it is neither expressible nor thinkable that what-is-not is. Also, what necessity impelled it, if it did spring from nothing, to be produced later or earlier? Thus it must be absolutely, or not at all. Nor will the force of credibility ever admit that anything should come into being, beside being itself, out of not-being. So far as that is concerned, justice has never released (*being*) from its fetters and set it free either to come into being or to perish, but holds it fast. The decision on these matters depends on the following: it is, or it is not. It is therefore decided, as is inevitable: ignore the one way as unthinkable and inexpressible (for it is no true way) and take the other as the way of being and reality. How could being perish? How could it come into being? If it came into being, it is not; and so too if it is about-to-be at some future time. Thus coming-into-being is quenched, and destruction also into the unseen.

Nor is being divisible, since it is all alike. Nor is there anything there which could prevent it from holding together, nor any lesser thing, but all is full of being. Therefore it is altogether continuous; for being is close to being.

But it is motionless in the limits of mighty bonds, without beginning, without cease, since becoming and destruction have been driven very far away, and true conviction has rejected them. And remaining the same in the same place, it rests by itself and thus remains there fixed; for powerful necessity holds it in the bonds of a limit, which constrains it round about, because it is decreed by divine law that being shall not be without boundary. For it is not lacking; but if it were (*spatially infinite*), it would be lacking everything.[2]

To think is the same as the thought that it is; for you will not find thinking without being to which it refers. For nothing else either is or shall be except being, since fate has tied it down to be a whole and motionless; therefore all things that mortals have established, believing in their truth, are just a name: becoming and perishing, being and not-being, and change of position, and alteration of bright colour.

But since there is a (*spatial*) limit, it is complete on every side, like the mass of a well-rounded sphere, equally balanced from its centre in every

---

[2] Reading and meaning doubtful. Diels-Kranz: 'if it lacked Limit, it would fall short of being a Whole', but without any certainty. [F]

direction; for it is not bound to be at all either greater or less in this direction or that; nor is there not-being which could check it from reaching to the same point, nor is it possible for being to be more in this direction, less in that, than being, because it is an inviolate whole. For, in all directions equal to itself, it reaches its limits uniformly.

At this point I cease my reliable theory (*Logos*) and thought, concerning Truth; from here onwards you must learn the opinions of mortals, listening to the deceptive order of my words.

They have established (*the custom of*) naming two forms, one of which ought not to be (*mentioned*): that is where they have gone astray. They have distinguished them as opposite in form, and have marked them off from another by giving them different signs: on one side the flaming fire in the heavens, mild, very light (*in weight*), the same as itself in every direction, and not the same as the other. This (*other*) also is by itself and opposite: dark night, a dense and heavy body. This world-order I describe to you throughout as it appears with all its phenomena, in order that no intellect of mortal men may outstrip you.   [8; F*]

But since all things are named light and night, and names have been given to each class of things according to the power of one or the other, everything is full equally of light and invisible night, as both are equal, because to neither of them belongs any share (of the other).   [9. Kranz takes ἐπεί with the previous line, and translates: 'For nothing is possible which does not come under either of the two' (*i.e.* everything belongs to one or other of the two categories light and night); F*.]

You shall know the nature of the heavens, and all the signs in the heavens, and the destructive works of the pure bright torch of the sun, and whence they came into being. And you shall learn of the wandering works of the round-faced moon, and its nature; and you shall know also the surrounding heaven, whence it sprang and how necessity brought and constrained it to hold the limits of the stars.   [10; F]

(*I will describe*) how earth and sun and moon, and the aether common to all, and the milky way in the heavens, and outermost Olympus, and the hot power of the stars, hastened to come into being.   [11; F]

For the narrower rings were filled with unmixed fire, and those next to them with night, but between (*these*) rushes the portion of flame. And in the centre of these is the goddess who guides everything; for throughout she rules over cruel birth and mating, sending the female to mate with the male, and conversely again the male with the female.   [12; F]

First of all the gods she devised Love.   [13; F]

(*The moon*): Shining by night with a light not her own, wandering round the earth.   [14; F]

ZENO [1]

According to Plato's *Parmenides*, Zeno was "close to forty" when Parmenides was sixty-five and Socrates (born 469 B.C.) was a very young man (127b); while still young (128d) he wrote a book (128a) [2] whose purpose was "a defence of Parmenides' argument against those who try to ridicule it by arguing that ludicrous and self-contradictory consequences follow from the hypothesis that [only] One exists. This book talks back to those who affirm the Many [i.e. that many things exist]. It pays them back in the same coin, and with something to spare. What it aims to make clear is that, if the case is properly made, their own hypothesis, that there are many, has still more ridiculous consequences than the hypothesis that there is (only) One (128cd)." In other words: the purpose of Zeno's book was not to expound his own doctrine, or that of his master, but to counter-attack Parmenides' critics. Elsewhere (*Phaedrus* 261d) Plato speaks of Zeno as "that Eleatic Palamedes [3] who by his art makes the same things appear to his listeners both like and unlike, both one and many, both at rest and in motion."

---

[1] The section on Zeno of Elea has been contributed by Gregory Vlastos, with the following comment:

I have put together this material at the request of the editor of this book in the hope that it may be of some use to students who cannot dig it out for themselves from the sources. I consented only because I know, from my own experience in teaching Zeno to undergraduates, how hard it is for the non-specialist to get from currently available textbooks an even approximately adequate idea of what the historical Zeno is likely to have thought and written. I have no illusions that the present brief account will fully meet their difficulty, but hope it may prove of some help, if only because it frees the exposition and analysis of Zeno's arguments from the dubious hypothesis that they have to be understood as wholly or mainly anti-Pythagorean polemic. (For objections to this hypothesis see G. E. L. Owen, "Zeno and the Mathematicians," *Proceedings of the Aristotelian Society*, 1958, pp. 199 ff.; my reviews in *Gnomon* 25 (1953), pp. 29 ff., and *Philosophical Review* 68 (1959), pp. 531 ff.; and N. B. Booth, "Were Zeno's Arguments Directed Against the Pythagoreans?" *Phronesis* 2 (1957), pp. 90 ff.). I should add that everything in this chapter represents purely *provisional* results of work-in-progress which will be published elsewhere in due course; that I try to avoid, so far as possible, controversial questions; and that when I find it necessary to take sides (as I do in almost every paragraph) I do not burden the text by explaining, or even naming, respectable scholarly alternatives to the views I expound, nor do I attempt to marshall *all* the evidence that can be cited for my own positions.

[2] Or books? Several titles are mentioned by Suidas, *Vorsokratiker* 29 A 2. Plato speaks of "writings" at 127c, but this is inconclusive.

[3] "(Παλαμήδης, 'the handy or contriving one'), a proverbially (cf. Aristophanes *Frogs* 1451) clever hero . . . His chief distinctions are the invention of letters and his cunning while serving with Agamemnon . . ." H. J. Rose, *s.v.*, *Oxford Classical Dictionary*, Oxford, 1941.

Zeno's puzzles have fascinated philosophers, logicians, and mathematicians ever since, and never more than in our own time: probably more has been written on his paradoxes in the last hundred years than in all the preceding two thousand.[4] Much of this work is cheerfully unconcerned with the connection, if any, between its "Zeno" and Zeno. Reading it one might form extravagant notions of the reasoning powers of this remote Greek. One might come to think of him as a logical superman who enjoyed a charmed infallibility and an uncanny insight into difficulties which baffled all others for more than two millennia after his time. Anyone who has swallowed this legend will get a shock when he comes face to face with what Zeno wrote and sees how, on the best available evidence, this man must have thought and reasoned.[5] But if one persists in seeking facts, instead of wish-fulfilments, and is not totally lacking in historical imagination, one may still come to feel in the end that, for all his crudities and blunders, this pioneer in the art of argument deserves an honored place in the history of thought.

A. ARGUMENTS AGAINST PLURALITY

Hermann Diels identified four fragments as verbatim citations from Zeno's original book (or books), and numbered them as B1, B2, B3, and B4.[6] The authenticity of the first three has never been called into question. The third of these, B3, is a beautifully self-contained logical argument that speaks for itself; it will be cited as such without much commentary as "The Second Argument Against Plurality." The first two fragments, B1 and B2, are almost certainly pieces from a much longer piece of argumentation, which preceded

---

[4] For some idea of the vast literature on Zeno see F. Cajori, "The History of Zeno's Arguments on Motion," *American Mathematical Monthly* 22 (1915), pp. 1 ff., 39 ff., 77 ff., 109 ff., 143 ff., 179 ff., 253 ff., 292 ff.; the bibliography in H. D. P. Lee, *Zeno of Elea*, Cambridge, 1936, pp. 124-5. Interesting samples of the more recent literature: The nine papers in *Analysis* 12-15 (1951-5), most of them listed in Max Black, *Problems of Analysis*, Ithaca, 1954, p. 109, n. 1; the whole of the section on Zeno's Paradoxes in this book by Max Black; the chapter on "Achilles and the Tortoise" in *Dilemmas* (Cambridge, 1954) by Gilbert Ryle; and A. Gruenbaum, "Modern Science and the Refutation of the Paradoxes of Zeno," *Scientific Monthly* 81 (1955), pp. 234 ff.; D. S. Schwayder, "Achilles Unbound," *Journal of Philosophy* 52 (1955), pp. 449 ff.

[5] The most important paper by a philologist which established the right perspective for understanding the historical Zeno is H. Fraenkel, "Zeno of Elea's Attacks on Plurality," *American Journal of Philology* 63 (1942), pp. 1 ff. and 193 ff.

[6] This number has been preserved in current editions of *Vorsokratiker,* in spite of the fact that it is now generally recognized that B2 preceded B1 in Zeno's text.

B3 in Zeno's text,[7] and may for that reason be called Zeno's "First Argument Against Plurality." [8] To figure out the structure of this whole argument and tell just where B1 and B2 fit and what part they play in it is a difficult problem of historical scholarship. But I think it is fair to say that it has been solved in principle by Hermann Fraenkel.[9] The main lines of his reconstruction, but with important modifications of my own,[10] are incorporated in the following version:

First Argument Against Plurality

This began with a section which has been lost to us, though this sentence from Simplicius (*Physics* 131, 19), gives us some idea of what it tried to prove and how: "He showed earlier [i.e. prior to the parts of the argument constituting B1 and B2] that nothing has size because each of the many is self-identical and one."

It so happens that Zeno's contemporary and fellow-disciple of the great Parmenides, Melissus, has an argument which runs as follows (in verbatim citation):

If it existed, it would have to be one; but if it were one, it could not have body; but if it had thickness, it would have parts; and then it would not be one.[11]

This gives us a fair idea of the logical bridge a disciple of Parmenides would build from 'x is one' (or, more fully, from 'x is one and self-identical') to 'x has no size.' If it is one, he would argue, it can have no parts, and hence, can have no size. The latter inference would be drawn on the assumption that anything which does have size is at least *logically* divisible and has at least logically discriminable parts; [12] the former, on the assumption that anything which has parts in any sense whatever cannot be strictly or absolutely "one".[13] Thus the whole of this argument might have gone somewhat as follows:

---

[7] Simplicius, *Physics* 140, 34.

[8] It may, or may not, have been preceded by other arguments against plurality in Zeno's original text.

[9] In the paper cited above, n. 5.

[10] Some of these are defended in my review of H. Fraenkel, *Wege und Formen fruehgriechischen Denkens* (Munich, 1955), in *Gnomon* 31 (1959), pp. 193 ff.; and in a paper entitled, "A Zenonian Argument Against Plurality," which I presented to the Society for Ancient Greek Philosophy at Harvard on December 27, 1957: this paper has not been published, but copies of it were distributed to the members of the Society and to some other scholars.

[11] *Vorsokratiker* 30 B 9.

[12] Zeno (or Mellissus) would not, of course, have used such language. Words for what *we* express by "logical" and "physical" did not exist at that time.

[13] For various versions of arguments, attributed to Zeno by later writers, which ring the changes on this theme, see items 1, 3, 5 in Lee, *op. cit.*

If anything is one and self-identical, it would not have parts, and then it would not have size. But if anything exists, it must be one and self-identical. Hence if the Many exist (or, if there are many), then each of the Many would have to be one and self-identical, and hence none of them would have size.

Zeno's next move was to turn around and argue that, on the contrary, if the many exist, they *must* have size, on the ground that something without size would not even exist. This part of the argument (B2 in Diels) survives intact in a verbatim citation by Simplicius:

For [a] if it [something having no size] were added to another, it would make it [the latter] no larger. For [b] having no size, it could not contribute anything by way of size when added. And thus [c] the thing added would be nothing. [d] If indeed when [something is] subtracted from another, the latter is not reduced, nor again increased when [someing is] added [to it], it is clear that what is added or subtracted is nothing.

This is not a smooth translation—which is all to the good, for the original is just as rough; and this is not surprising, for the use of written prose for this kind of abstract argumentation was something new under the sun: it had never been done before, so far as we know, except in geometry. What may seem a bit more disturbing than the clumsy formulation is the peculiar inverted order, which is best seen if we compare the text above with a modernized version of it (simplified by using symbols to cut out unnecessary verbiage), exhibiting the true logical order of the intended argument:

(1) If x did not increase y, when added to it, nor decrease y, when subtracted from it, then x would be nothing.
(2) If x had no size, then x would not increase y, when added to it, nor decrease y, when subtracted from it. Therefore,
(3) If x had no size, it would be nothing.

A comparison with the above text will show that the last proposition there, (d), is in fact (1) here, the first premise of the argument; and the conclusion here, (3), appears at (c) above, *before* (d). This is odd, but commits no logical fault; it is no rule of logic that the premise *has* to be written (or spoken) ahead of the conclusion (and sometimes it is not in live arguments; e.g., 'A and B are both right angles, so they must be equal—*all* right angles are equal.') What does look like a logical fault is not that the premise (1) should be stuck at the end of the argument, but that it should be used as a premise at all.

A modern reader might object: 'How can Zeno ask me to agree to (1), when he professes to have proved to me a moment ago that no existent has size; that would entail that all existents are incorporeal, and hence that (1) is false, since it could only be true if all existents

were corporeal.' But this objection would misconceive the purpose
of Zeno's argument, which is purely dialectical. Addressed to *his*
contemporaries—not ours, or even Plato's—its aim was to show them
that their thinking was criss-crossed with contradiction. And since
the notion of incorporeal existence cannot be claimed for anyone at
this time outside of Eleatic circles, Zeno's own readers would have
been assuming the truth of (1) all along. Hence Zeno, given his
purpose to convince them they had been holding inconsistent beliefs, could claim the right to use the premises he did in the first
section *and* (1) in this section, since prior to this argument they
would have agreed right off to all of them. It was clumsy of him to
do it in just this way; but it committed no fault of logic.

We are now ready for the climax of the whole argument:

So if [the many] exist, each one [of them] must have some size and
thickness and one part [of each] must extend beyond the other [part of
the same existent]. And the same reasoning holds of the projecting [part].
For this too will have size and some part of *it* will project. Now to say
this once is as good as saying it for ever. For no such [part, i.e., no part
resulting by subdivision, no matter how far this process is carried out]
will be the last or without one [part similarly] related to another [part].

Thus, if there are many, they must be both small and great: on one
hand, so small as to have no size; on the other, so large as to be infinite.

The reasoning in this lap of the argument (on the above translation) is perfectly straightforward: If there are many existents, each
of them must have some size; this is just a carry-over from the preceding section, B2. But if something has size, it must be spread out
in space, so you can distinguish in it a "here" from a "there"; having
such non-overlapping parts, Zeno might have explained, is part of
what we mean by having size. These parts are clearly not intended
to be physically separate; they don't arise by splitting an object, or
cutting it up, but a purely logical process of discriminating different
regions within it. And this process can go on *ad infinitum;* we can
distinguish parts *b* and *c* within *a*, parts *d* and *e* within *c*, and so
forth, as in the accompanying diagram:

The series—*a, c, e, g*, . . .—has no last member.

So far so good. But how could Zeno expect us to go from this point to the extraordinary conclusion he wants to reach and which he evidently thinks *can* be reached by moving along this road: that *a* (which stands for any existent) is infinitely large? He must have assumed, as too obvious for mention, some such additional intervening steps as these:

(4) *a* is the sum of an infinite number of terms, each of which has a finite size ($a = b + d + f + h \dots$) This follows correctly from the preceding.

(5) The sum of an infinite number of terms, each of which has a finite size, is infinitely large. Therefore,

(6) *a* is infinitely large. This follows from (4) and (5).[14]

That something has gone wrong here is evident, and it is not hard to see just where: (5) is clearly false. To show this it is sufficient to call attention to any convergent series, e.g. to the series, ½, ¼, ⅛, ⅟₁₆, such as the *b, d, f, h,* . . . series might well have been by the terms of the construction. It is false to say that the sum of this series is infinitely large, and Zeno himself might have satisfied himself that this is false by the arithmetic at his disposal. He could have reasoned: when there are two terms in this series, ½ + ¼, their sum is ¾; when there are three, ½ + ¼ + ⅛, the sum is ⅞; in both cases it is less than 1; and this will always be true, no matter how many terms are put into the series, since the last term added will never be the whole of the difference between 1 and the sum of the preceding terms, but always half of that difference. So the sum could never be more than 1. Or, if Zeno were averse to arithmetic, he might have seen the error of (5) by just reasoning from a diagram, like the one in the text above: since *all* the magnitudes included in the *b, d, f, h,* . . . series are non-overlapping *parts* of *a,* their sum will always fall

---

14 Many a modern reader will find it impossible to believe that such a vital part of the chain of argument was left purely tacit in the original text. Before he makes up his mind on this point, he would do well to study other arguments in Greek philosophical texts, and note how elliptical they sometimes are, even in authors like Plato and Aristotle, who have the benefit of enormous intervening progress in the art of argument. Only long and bitter experience teaches philosophers that every argument must be made as fully explicit as possible, even at the risk of saying the obvious at tedious length, for it is in just those stretches of it that look most obvious that mistakes are likely to occur. As for the present case, it is, of course, not *certain* that the gap in the reasoning was also present in Zeno's original text; it is possible that something dropped out of the text at this point. But since it would be just this portion of the argument that would have had the greatest interest for Zeno's own contemporaries and successors all the way down to the faithful Simplicius, the chance that such a portion as this was lost in the transmission is so small that no historian can reasonably bank on it.

short of *a*, so long as a finite number of terms have been put into the series; and if the whole infinite lot of them could be put in, they would *exhaust a* (no part of *a* would be left unincluded), and hence the sum of the series would be precisely equal to *a;* and since *a* is finite, how could that sum be infinite? So there is no getting around the point that here, at (5), our clever Zeno walked into a booby-trap which, one would think, he could have avoided with the materials at his disposal. What is it then that could have made him go wrong?

Consider the following proposition, (5a), and compare it carefully with (5) above:

(5a) The sum of an infinite number of terms, the *smallest* of which has a finite size, is infinitely large.

The only difference between (5a) and (5) is that "the smallest" at (5a) replaces "each" at (5). But what a difference that makes: (5a) refers only to a collection which does have a smallest term (or, smallest terms), while (5) refers to any collection whatever, *including* series which have no smallest term. The result of the difference is that (5a) is true, as one can see by noting (i), that given an infinite number of things such that the smallest of them has any size at all, their sum would be infinitely large, since if that smallest term were added to itself an infinite number of times the sum would be infinitely large, and hence *a fortiori* if added to an infinite number of terms larger than itself the sum would certainly be infinitely large; and (ii), that the convergent series which falsified (5) would not falsify (5a), for it would be irrelevant to (5a): having no last term, it would have no smallest term. But after seeing all this, note finally how easily even a very clever man *could* have confused (5a) with (5). Since at (5) he is thinking of an infinite number of parts *all of which have size,* it would be easy for him to say, 'Well, if they *all* have size, it must be the case that even the smallest of them has size,' failing to see that, in saying this, he is making the fatal assumption that "smallest" does apply to this *infinitely* decreasing series. This failure would be a symptom of the tendency to extrapolate from what remains true of the series so long as it has a finite number of terms to what would be the case if *all* its terms were present in it. Zeno's best hope of checking this tendency lay in making the assumption as explicit as possible. Had he actually *said,* 'the series *b*, *d*, *f*, *h*, . . . must have a smallest member,' his chances of noticing the contradiction with the fact that, as he himself says, it has no last, would have immeasurably improved. He threw this chance away when he treated the steps intervening between the argument that makes up the first paragraph of B1 above and the conclusion to 'a is infinitely large' as too obvious to deserve a place in his text.

We can now look back over the whole argument, and see how, on the present reconstruction of it, Zeno thought he could prove the conclusion at B1: If there are many existents, then each of them must be both (I) so small as to have no size and (II) so large as to be infinite. (I) he would infer from the first section of the argument: if no existent has *any* size, then it is indeed "so small as to have no size." (II) he would infer by the long-drawn out process which begins by propping up again, at B2, the commonsense belief knocked down in the first section, that existents have size, and deducing therefrom by the explicit reasoning at B1 and its tacit sequel—(4), (5), (6), above—that every one of them must be "so large as to be infinite." [15]

Second Argument Against Plurality

B3 (Simplicius, Physics 140, 30). "If there are many, they must be just so many as they are, neither more nor fewer. But if they are just so many as they are, they must be finite [in number]. If there are many, the existents are infinite [in number]: for there are always other [existents] between existents, and again others between these. And thus the existents are infinite [in number]."

The first horn of the dilemma is proved by arguing that if there are many things, they must be just so many, i.e., they have a number; and then inferring that this must be a *finite* number. This is a very respectable inference. It could not have been known to be false prior to the discovery of transfinite cardinal numbers by Georg Cantor, more than 2,300 years after this time.

The second horn is proved by arguing that given any two distinct existents, there must be other existents between them. The existents Zeno is thinking of here must be physically separate objects, and he must be assuming that to be separate, any two objects, a and b, must be separated by at least one separate object c; hence he infers correctly that a must be separated from c by d, so too a from d by e, and so forth.

---

[15] For a new interpretation of the last sentence of B1, which puts an entirely different face on the logical structure of the whole of this First Argument against Plurality, see now F. Solmsen, *Aristotle's Physical World,* Ithaca, 1960, p. 172 and n. 56. Though I find this an extremely interesting and attractive suggestion, I do not waver in my adherence to the interpretation I have set out here.

B. ARGUMENTS AGAINST MOTION

The Race Course

Aristotle has four references to this argument:

Topics, 160b 7 For we have many arguments contrary to (common) beliefs, whose solution is yet difficult, like Zeno's that it is impossible to move or to traverse the race course.[16]

Phys. 233a 21 For this reason Zeno's argument too assumes falsely that it is impossible to traverse or to come in contact with each one of an infinite number [of things] in a finite time.

Phys. 239b 11 The first [of Zeno's arguments against motion "which cause difficulty to those who try to solve the problems they raise"] says that there is no motion, because the moving [body] must reach the midpoint before it gets to the end.

Phys. 263a 5 In the same way one should reply to those who pose [literally, 'ask'] Zeno's argument, claiming that it is always necessary to traverse the half [i.e., to traverse any given distance we must first traverse its first half], and these [*sc.* half-distances] are infinitely numerous, while it is impossible to traverse an infinity. . . .

We get a somewhat different version of the argument in the late commentators.[17] The following, from Simplicius (*Phys.* 1013, 4ff.), is typical:

If there is motion, the moving object must traverse an infinity in a finite [time]: and this is impossible. Hence motion does not exist. He demonstrates his hypothesis thus: The moving object must move a certain stretch. And since every stretch is infinitely divisible, the moving object must first traverse half the stretch it is moving, and then the whole; but before the whole of the half, half of that and, again, the half of that. If then these halves are infinite, since, whatever may be the given [stretch] it is possible to halve it, and [if, further,] it is impossible to traverse the infinity [of these stretches] in a finite time . . . it follows that it is impossible to traverse any given length in a finite time.

If this was the original version, Zeno started his argument by saying that the runner cannot get from the starting-point, S, to the goal, G, unless he first gets to the mid-point, M, then went on to argue that neither can he get to M, unless he first gets to the mid-point of

---

16 Evidently the stage-setting of the argument is a race course. On this ground it is better to call the argument by this name, instead of "The Dichotomy," as is often done in the literature, keeping "The Stadium" as the generally accepted name of the fourth argument.

17 They are all in Lee, *op. cit.*, pp. 44 ff.

SM, N; nor to *N,* unless first to the preceding mid-point, *O;* and so forth, as in the following diagram:

(I)   S...O   N   M   G

Now none of Aristotle's accounts need to be read in this way. They permit the alternative construction, which puts the mid-points after *M* between *M* and *G:* he must first get to *M,* then to the mid-point of *MG, N;* then to the mid-point of *NG, O,* and so forth, as in this diagram:

(II) S   M   N   O...G

Which of these two versions is more likely to have been Zeno's? Pretty certainly, (I I). For had (I) been Zeno's line of argument, the most obvious conclusion to be drawn from it (and the one that would have pleased best Zeno's taste for theatrical logic) is that the runner *can't even get started.* But as Aristotle understood the argument its point was that the runner *can't finish.* For otherwise Aristotle would not have tried to break the argument (as will be explained shortly) by refuting the assumption that the runner cannot traverse an infinite number of stretches *in a finite time.* That Zeno's conclusion must hang on this assumption would never have occurred to Aristotle, had he taken Zeno to be arguing that the runner can't get started: if he can't start, there would be no journey, and the finite time-length of that journey would be totally irrelevant. So only (I I) could be the version of the argument Aristotle had in mind. Now if we had any reason to think that Simplicius wrote his own account with Zeno's original text before him, we would still have to rule in favor of (I) and put down Aristotle's commitment to (I I) as an exceptionally stupid misunderstanding. But in point of fact we can be fairly sure that Simplicius did *not* have the text of this argument or of any of the other arguments against motion. For when he does have original texts it is his habit to make one or more verbatim citations, as we have seen him do in the case of Zeno's arguments against plurality. But in all of his copious and fulsomely explicit accounts of the arguments against motion there is nothing that looks like a quotation. This is fairly good reason to think he was not working from a text, but from second- or nth-hand accounts. We have no choice then but to take (II) as the most likely original version.[18] Let us look more closely into its logic:

---

18 Another reason: two other accounts of this argument in Simplicius himself (Lee, items 20(b), 24) reason quite definitely from the impossibility of traversing a distance, rather than from the impossibility of leaving a starting-point, *and* are entirely free from any commitment to (I). Reading *these* accounts in Simplicius, (I) would not even occur to one.

Zeno points out that to get from S to G the runner must traverse the series of successive half-stretches, *SM, MN, NO,* . . . , in diagram (II) above. (Let us call this for convenience "the Z-series"; and let us speak of running through any member of this series as "making a Z-run.") But this series is infinite. Hence the runner cannot traverse it; he cannot make *all* of an infinite number of runs.

This is as far as Zeno's own statement of the puzzle is likely to have gone.[19] The modern reader may find this hard to believe. 'Surely,' he will say, 'Zeno has no business stopping at just this point. He still has to tell us *why* the runner cannot traverse the whole of the Z-series. He says it is infinite. Is that reason enough?'

(i) It is entirely possible that Zeno would have replied, 'Yes,' counting on the mere infinity of the series as quite sufficient to convince a reasonable mind that it cannot possibly be traversed. If provoked to further argument, he might have proceeded as follows: 'That all the Z-runs can be made is a self-contradictory hypothesis. For if they can, suppose that they all have been made; in that case a definite number of runs would have been made ("just so many" as have been made, in the phraseology of B3) and hence a finite number (reasoning as in B3), which is impossible since the runs in the Z-series are infinitely many.'

(ii) Alternatively, he might have been more circumspect and simply argued, as did one of his acute interpreters in our own day: 'The very notion of making an infinite series of runs or of performing an infinite series of any other tasks is self-contradictory. For an infinite series of runs is one in which there are always more (and infinitely more) to be performed no matter how many have been performed; hence it is one in which all the runs can never (in the logical sense of 'never') be performed' (See Max Black, *op. cit.*, pp. 99ff. Black subsequently revised this view; but the fact that he once expounded it with such gusto shows its continuing appeal even for minds equipped with logical and mathematical apparatus incomparably superior to Zeno's). This very appealing argument is not really convincing, as will appear when we get to (iv) below.

But now (iii) there is another line of argument that Zeno might have followed. This is the one Aristotle confidently ascribes to Zeno (though without actually saying that Zeno stated this argument in so many words; cf. the second of the Aristotelian citations given above, "For this reason Zeno's argument too assumes [*not* 'states'] . . ."). On this construction, 'Since every Z-run takes time, and there are an infinite number of them, to run through all of them would

---

[19] Leaving a gap in the reasoning comparable to the one at the end of the First Argument against Plurality; cf. note 14, above.

take infinite time.' If that is how he argued (reenacting the error at B1 above, assuming that the sum of an infinite collection *must* be infinite), Aristotle's refutation would be utterly crushing: since running half a given stretch takes half the time needed to run the whole of it, the "divisions of time and of spatial magnitude will be the same" (*Physics* 233a 16)—which is Aristotle's terse way of saying that the time required to make successive Z-runs will decrease by the same ratio as does the length of the Z-runs; as the stretches get smaller, so will the times required to run them; so with a finite time-budget for the whole run, the runner will still have plenty of time to make it. He will never run out of time.

(iv) But let us give Zeno a chance to make his case in still another way. This, I think, is the most powerful case he could have made with the materials at his disposal, and though there is no evidence whatever that he did make it,[20] it is well worth considering for its own intrinsic interest:

(1) To make all the Z-runs the runner would have to make a run that reaches G. But

(2) No Z-run reaches G. Therefore,

(3) He cannot make all the Z-runs.

What is wrong with this argument? The premises are quite all right. (2) is true since, by the terms of the construction, every Z-run terminates at a point to the left of G. (1) is no less true, since until G has been reached there are further Z-runs to be made, and our runner (who is man, not jinn, nor orbit-jumping electron) can only reach G by a run that reaches G. But what follows from (1) and (2)? Does (3)? Not at all. What does follow is

(4) To make all the Z-runs he must make a run reaching G that is not a Z-run.

Would he have any trouble doing that? Why should he? There are plenty of such runs: SG, or MG, or NG, for example. Call these "G-runs." Since all G-runs terminate at G, any of them will get him there. And if he makes any G-run, *he will have made all the Z-runs*, the whole infinite lot of them, in the perfectly good sense that he will have run through all the members of the Z-series, since he would have traversed the whole SG stretch, of which *all* the members of the Z-series are sub-stretches.[21] Now if it were the case that he can-

---

20 Though neither is there any evidence *against* it, as there would certainly be if Aristotle had told us that Zeno had said (instead of "assumed") that the runner cannot finish for lack of time. Had Aristotle said any such thing, no construction of the argument other than (iii) would have a leg to stand on.

21 This is the reason why the argument at (ii) above is unconvincing. It assumes that no good sense can be given such an expression as 'an infinite number of

not run through the whole of the Z-series, it would indeed follow that he can't make any G-run. But is there any reason to believe that this *is* the case? The ones at (i), (ii), and (iii) all turned out to be bad reasons. And what we are given here—(1) and (2) above—is quite irrelevant, since the only conclusion *this* warrants is that if (A) all the Z-runs are made, then (B) a G-run is made. Who then would believe that because of (1) and (2) all the Z-runs cannot be made? *Only one who tacitly assumed that (A) and (B) are incompatible;* i.e. someone who tacitly assumed that limiting one's physical exertions to making Z-runs prevented one from making a G-run.

This assumption is very plausible on the face of it. How in the world, one is bound to feel, can one limit one's exertions to making Z-runs and yet make a G-run—when no Z-run is a G-run? There is a trick here. But what is it?

Think of the way "runs" have been spoken of in this argument. As we ordinarily think of them, consecutive runs have to be temporally separate events which are *uniquely individuated*. Thus if a man were to run without a break from one point to another, the question, 'How many runs has he made?' would have just one true answer: 'One run.' To say, 'Two runs,' would be simply false; so too (though no more so) would be, 'An infinite number of runs.' But this restriction was quietly ignored in the concept of run we employed in our definition of "making Z-runs" (p. 37 above), where 'to make a run' is simply to traverse any arbitrarily selected interval, so that the very same physical event can be truly said to be as many runs as we please depending on the intervals or sub-intervals into which we choose to divide the trajectory. Thus the motion from S to G, be it ever so smooth and uninterrupted, could be described indifferently as one run (traversal of SG) or two runs (traversals of, for example, SM, MG) or an infinite number of runs (traversals of all the members of the Z-series). To mark the difference between these two radically different concepts, let us use "run_a" for the first kind of uniquely individuated motions, and "run_b" for the second kind of run, where the same motion could be correctly said to be *any* number of runs, small or large, finite or infinite.[22]

---

runs have been (or, can be) completed.' For this point, and much else in section (iv), I am heavily indebted to J. F. Thomson's, "Tasks and Super-Tasks," *Analysis* 15 (1954), pp. 1 ff., a paper of rare brilliance. Before reading it, (iv) had not occurred to me as a possible way of construing Zeno's argument.

[22] The relation of $runs_a$ to $runs_b$ is analogous to that between (a) physically separate and (b) logically discriminated parts. 'How many $parts_a$ does this drop of water have?' has a unique answer, once we decide on the physical parts we are talking about—say, water molecules. 'How many $parts_b$ does it have?' admits infinitely many different answers: it is two halves, four quarters. a trillion trillionths, and so forth.

Now we can see the trick: The Z-runs are obviously runs$_b$. For it is understood right along that the runner is making a continuous motion;[23] described in *run$_a$* language, this could only be correctly said to be *one* run$_a$, namely the G-run$_a$ from S to G. The impossibility of his making all the Z-runs$_a$ *and* some run$_a$ that reaches $G-$(A) *and* (B), above—would then follow by definition. But if the Z-runs are runs$_b$, they can be described just as well in any number of other ways; there is then not the slightest reason why our runner cannot make all the Z-runs$_b$ *and* the G-run$_b$ from S to G: he may do either by making the same physical motion, the G-run$_a$ from S to G.[24]

The Achilles

Aristotle, *Phys.*, 239b 14 The second [of Zeno's arguments against motion] is the so-called 'Achilles'. This is that the slowest will never be overtaken by the swiftest; for the pursuer must first reach [the point] whence the pursued started, so that the slower must always be some distance ahead.

As Aristotle goes on to say, the reasoning here is (substantially) the same as in the Race Course (which, incidentally, is an additional reason for saying that he understood the Race Course in accordance with version (II) above; for in the case of the Achilles the conclusion is so obviously that the task can't be finished, *not* that it can't be started). All four of the above reconstructions of Zeno's argument in the Race Course will apply *mutatis mutandis* here. The reader may do this for himself, if he finds it amusing; he will learn nothing new from this that he cannot learn, with greater ease, because of its sparer staging, from the Race Course.

The Arrow

Aristotle, *Phys.* 239b 5 Zeno argues fallaciously. For if, he says, everything is at rest, when it is in a place equal to itself, and the moving object is always [in a place equal to itself] in the present moment [literally, in the now], the moving arrow must be motionless.[25]

---

23 That is to say, nothing has been done to show that there are any physical interruptions of the runner's motion at $M, N, O, \ldots$, or even that there is any change of speed at, or in the vicinity of, any of these points. For all that has been said to the contrary, the runner is moving along in the usual way.

24 I am deeply indebted to my colleague, Paul Benacerraf, for a searching criticism of an earlier draft of (iv) and for many suggestions I have incorporated. Whatever mistakes I may still be making are not to be charged to him.

25 The text on which my translation is based is that of F. M. Cornford in the Loeb edition of the *Physics*, Harvard University Press, 1934, generally followed by English editors thereafter, but unfortunately still ignored in later editions of *Vorsokratiker*.

"When it is in [or, at] a place [26] equal to itself" is the best I can do to English ὅταν ᾖ κατὰ τὸ ἶσον, literally, "when it is in [or, at] the equal," which can only be understood as an ellipsis for the longer expression I have used in my translation.[27] The crux of the argument then is the contention, (1), that when the arrow is at a given place (the one here designated as the "place equal to itself") it is at rest. To see what is wrong with this, one need only consider (as Black has pointed out in a penetrating discussion of the "Arrow," *op. cit.*, pp. 127 ff.) the two entirely different senses in which time-specifying words like "when" can be used: (a) "When did you write your paper?" ["when" = "during what stretch of time" or "in what period of time"]; (b) "When did you start to write it?" ["when" = "at which point of time"]. In the case of (a) the "when" is a duration; in that of (b) it is the limit of a duration. 'When$_a$' is to 'when$_b$' as a segment of a line is to a point. 'When$_a$' has temporal length. This may be as long as a trillion years, or as short as a trillionth of a second. In either case it is totally different from 'when$_b$' to which the notion of length is logically inapplicable; it makes no sense to ask, for example, 'how long is eight o'clock?' Once this distinction is straightened out, we can see that (1) is true for 'when$_a$', false for 'when$_b$'. If the arrow is in a given place for any stretch of time, no matter how small, it *is* at rest throughout that stretch of time. This is certain, since 'to be in the same place for some stretch of time' is part of what we mean by 'rest'. But if we substitute 'when$_b$', (1) is certainly false: for now we are no longer saying, 'in the stretch of time at which A is in a given place,' but only 'at the point of time (or, at the instant) at which A is in a given place'; and from the latter it doesn't follow that A is at rest. If we were told that the arrow was just over a particular flag-pole at twelve o'clock sharp, we wouldn't be able to tell whether it was moving or at rest; it might be flying past the flag-pole, or have been stuck over the flag-pole as a surrealist decoration, and it would still be true, in either case, that it was over the flag-pole at just that instant.[28]

---

[26] Not "space" as in Lee and the Oxford translation. The word that must be understood here (see next note) is τόπος (used also at B4, in the Argument against Space below, and in Parmenides B 8, 41); and the natural translation for this is "place."

[27] That Zeno himself used just this expression would be a very dubious assumption, considering the frequency with which Aristotle has been using κατά τι εἶναι in this context (259a 25 ff.) for a thing's having a given position. But neither is there good reason to think it misrepresents the sense of the Zenonian original.

[28] For further discussion of the Arrow see especially Owen, *op. cit.*, pp. 216 ff.

We can now consider another fragment:

B4 (Diogenes Laertius, *Lives of the Philosophers*, 9, 72) Zeno refutes motion, saying: 'the moving object moves neither in the place in which it is, nor in the place in which it is not.'

This looks like a truncated version of an argument preserved in somewhat fuller form by Epiphanius (Lee, *op. cit.*, item 18): "Zeno argues thus: the moving object moves either in the place in which it is, or in the place in which it is not; and it moves neither in the place in which it is, nor in the place in which it is not, hence nothing moves." B4 may or may not be the original citation Diels thought it: there is not much evidence either way, and it matters little what decision is made, since, in any case, there would be no reason to doubt that, if not a verbatim citation, it is, at least, a reliable reproduction of Zeno's thought. The same is true for the longer version in Epiphanius.[29] The thought is clear enough: a dilemma is constructed (a favorite device of Zeno's, as we have seen in the two arguments against plurality), and one leg of the dilemma—"moves in the place in which it is not"—would be easily refuted by some such reasoning as we meet in another version of this argument in Sextus Empiricus (*Pyrrh. Hyp.* 3, 71):[30] it cannot move where it is not, for "it can neither do nor suffer anything where it is not." That leaves us with the other leg—"moves in the place in which it is." Clearly Zeno would be equally bent on destroying this one, too. How would he do it?

The supporting reason in Sextus Empiricus is, "for it must rest in that place, if it is in it." But this is lame. If something is in (or, at) a place, why must it be *resting* there? Why should position in space entail rest in space? Zeno could scarcely expect his audience to grant that inference without further argument; and if we ask what sort of argument this would be, why need we look further than the Arrow? By adding that the place in which it happens to be is "a place [just]

---

[29] There is no justification for Diels' decision to accept B4 as an original fragment, and deny the same status to Lee 18, which Diels printed in *Doxographi Graeci* (590, 21) but omitted from the section on Zeno in *Vorsokratiker*. He might have thought that the greater conciseness of B4 was more likely to represent the original. But this is not a good reason. When we can actually compare Zeno's own version with a later paraphrase (B2 with Aristotle, *Metaphysics* 1001b 8) the original is much the more longwinded, and with no appreciable gain in content.

[30] Cf. also Sextus, *Adv. Phys.*, 2, 87. Sextus speaks of this as a "current" argument against motion which Diodorus Cronus also used. Sextus does not ascribe it specifically to Zeno; but that it is his originally is evident by comparison with B4 and Lee 18.

equal to itself," Zeno would enforce the notion that this place is a strictly *limited* portion of space, a kind of immaterial crate, as it were, which becomes a fixed, immovable cage insofar as the time-reference of the occupancy (the "when" of its being there) implies temporal *stretch,* no matter how small. If this then is the complement of the thought of B4, it would be reasonable to suggest that it was *contained* along with B4 in the Zenonian original of the Arrow, from which Aristotle, with his habit of seizing the bare essential of an argument, clipped the part paraphrased in his text above. That original might have run somewhat as follows:

(a) The arrow moves either in the place in which it is, or in the place in which it is not.
(b) It cannot move in the place in which it is not: for it can do nothing whatever where it is not. Therefore,
(c) If it moves, it must move in the place in which it is. But
(d) When the arrow is in the place in which it is it is in a place equal to itself. And
(e) When something is in a place equal to itself, it is at rest. Therefore,
(f) It cannot move in the place in which it is. Therefore,
(g) The arrow can move neither in the place in which it is, nor in the place in which it is not. Hence
(h) It is always at rest.

The Stadium

Aristotle's account of this argument may be consulted at *Phys.* 239b 33. [See under Aristotle, below. WK] Modern commentators have made Zeno a present of an entirely different and vastly more ingenious argument, which may be read e.g. in T. Heath, *Mathematics in Aristotle,* Oxford, 1949, pp. 139-140, or G. E. L. Owen, *op. cit.,* pp. 148 ff.[31] The problem is too complicated for discussion here.

---

[31] But Owen does not commit himself to the historicity of the argument he expounds. For someone who sticks by Aristotle see, e.g., N. B. Booth, "Zeno's Paradoxes," *Journal of Hellenic Studies* 63 (1942) Part Two, pp. 187 ff. at pp. 193-5. I accept Booth's conclusion, but a good deal more could be made of the point to which he alludes on p. 195: to set aside Aristotle's interpretation we would have to assume not only that he misunderstood Zeno's text (Aristotle often misunderstands texts), but that he did so in the following special circumstances: at 233b 15-31, not long before citing the Stadium, he has an argument of his own which no one could reasonably claim he borrowed from Zeno or anyone else) which is similar in all essentials to the one the commentators now wish to give Zeno. It is not reasonable to think that Aristotle was capable of *constructing* this very beautiful argument, but incapable of *understanding* its logical twin when he met it in Zeno's text.

C. AGAINST SPACE

Aristotle, *Phys.* 210b 23 Zeno's puzzle—'if place exists, in what does it exist?'—is not hard to solve. *Ibid.* 209a 23 Further, if it [place] is itself an existent, where will it exist? For Zeno's puzzle demands some explanation. For if every existent is in a place, clearly there will have to be a place of a place, and so on *ad infinitum.*

'Why think that such a thing as place exists?', asks Zeno. If his contemporaries reply, as they doubtless would, 'Because whatever exists must be somewhere—in some place,' they are caught in his trap, unless they can then go on to explain what sort of "existent" place (or, space) is, how different from the things we ordinarily think of as existents which do 'exist in space.' To do this would be to launch an inquiry into the different senses of the word *to be* (there is no separate word for *to exist* in Greek), anticipating Aristotle by a century. No wonder Zeno's question went begging for a hundred years.

D. THE PARADOX OF THE MILLET SEED

Simplicius, *Physics* 1108, 18 ff. By this means he [Aristotle at *Phys.* 259a 19] solves the puzzle which Zeno the Eleatic put to Protagoras the Sophist. 'Tell me, Protagoras,' he said, 'does a single millet seed, or the ten thousandth part of a seed, make a noise when they fall?' When Protagoras said they did not, he said: 'does the bushel then make a noise when it falls or not?' When Protagoras said this did, Zeno said: 'Is there not then some ratio of the bushel to one seed and to a ten thousandth of a seed? When Protagoras said there was, Zeno said: 'But then must not the respective noises stand to one another in the same ratios? For as the sounding bodies are to one another, so must be the sounds they make. This being so, if the bushel of millet makes a noise, then the single millet seed must also make a noise, and so must the ten thousandth of a millet seed.'

The dialogue form in which this argument is is not Zeno's, and Simplicius does not pretend that it is. But neither is there any reason to doubt that the gist of the argument did go back to Zeno. (Cf. H. D. P. Lee, *Zeno of Elea*, Cambridge, 1936, p. 110.)

The argument speaks for itself. Along similar lines Leibniz argued that because we hear the roar of the sea we must have a "small perception" of "the little sounds" that come from each wave. *New Essays of Human Understanding, Introduction* (R. Latta, Leibniz, *The Monadology etc.*, Oxford, 1898, p. 371). If Leibniz were trying to show, not that we have "small perceptions," but that sense-perception as such is delusive, he would not have stopped at the sounds made by each wave but would have gone on, like Zeno, to the vastly smaller ones made by each of the minute particles that compose each wave.

MELISSUS

Melissus is said to have come from Samos, like Pythagoras, and to have flourished about 440 B.C. He wrote a book "About Nature or Reality," probably some time after the completion of Zeno's more celebrated work. Melissus, too, was concerned to defend Parmenides, and it is therefore convenient to have a single label for the philosophy of these three men. They are traditionally called Eleatics, after the small town in southern Italy where Parmenides made his home, Elea.

.   .   .

Melissus son of Ithagenes, a Samian. He was a pupil of Parmenides. . . . He was a statesman, and was held in great honor by the citizens; and later, when he was elected admiral, he won even greater fame for his personal courage. . . .   [Diogenes Laertius, IX, 24; R 379]

When Pericles had set sail, Melissus son of Ithagenes, a philosopher who was then in command of Samos, was so contemptuous of the small number of the Athenian ships or of their commander's inexperience that he persuaded the Samians to attack. A battle took place which the Samians won. They took so many prisoners and destroyed so many ships that they had command of the sea, and they devoted to the prosecution of the war certain supplies which they did not till then possess. Pericles himself, according to Aristotle, had also been defeated by Melissus in an earlier naval battle.   [Plutarch, *Pericles* 26; R 380. The great battle referred to took place in 441/40 B.C.]

.   .   .

All of his genuine fragments follow, in Freeman's translation:

1. That which was, was always and always will be. For if it had come into being, it necessarily follows that before it came into being, nothing existed. If however nothing existed, in no way could anything come into being out of nothing.
2. Since therefore it did not come into being, it is and always was and always will be, and has no beginning or end, but it is eternal. For if it had come into being, it would have a beginning (for it would have come into being at some time, and so begun), and an end (for since it had come into being, it would have ended). But since it has neither begun nor ended, it always was and always will be and has no beginning nor end. For it is impossible for anything to be, unless it is completely.

3. But as it is always, so also its size must always be infinite.

4. Nothing that has a beginning and an end is either everlasting or infinite.

5. If it were not one, it would form a boundary in relation to something else.

6. If it were infinite, it would be one; for if it were two, (*these*) could not be (*spatially*) infinite, but each would have boundaries in relation to each other.

7. (1) Thus therefore it is everlasting and unlimited and one and like throughout (*homogeneous*).

(2) And neither could it perish or become larger or change its (*inner*) arrangement, nor does it feel pain or grief. For if it suffered any of these things, it would no longer be one. For if being alters, it follows that it is not the same, but that that which previously was is destroyed, and that not-being has come into being. Hence if it were to become different by a single hair in ten thousand years, so it must be utterly destroyed in the whole of time.

(3) But it is not possible for it to be rearranged either, for the previous arrangement is not destroyed, nor does a nonexistent arrangement come into being. And since it is neither increased by any addition, nor destroyed, nor changed, how could it have undergone a rearrangement of what exists? For if it were different in any respect, then there would at once be a rearrangement.

(4) Nor does it feel pain; for it could not be completely if it were in pain; for a thing which is in pain could not always be. Nor has it equal power with what is healthy. Nor would it be the same if it were in pain; for it would feel pain through the subtraction or addition of something, and could no longer be the same.

(5) Nor could that which is healthy feel pain, for the healthy—that which is—would perish, and that which is not would come into being.

(6) And with regard to grief, the same reasoning applies as to pain.

(7) Nor is there any emptiness; for the empty is nothing; and so that which is nothing cannot be. Nor does it move; for it cannot withdraw in any direction, but (*all*) is full. For if there were any empty, it would have withdrawn into the empty; but as the empty does not exist, there is nowhere for it (*being*) to withdraw.

(8) And there can be no dense and rare. For the rare cannot possibly be as full as the dense, but the rare must at once become more empty than the dense.

(9) The following distinction must be made between the full and the not-full: if a thing has room for or admits something, it is not full; if it neither has room for nor admits anything, it is full.

(10) It (*being*) must necessarily be full, therefore, if there is no empty. If therefore it is full, it does not move.

8. (1) This argument is the greatest proof that it (*being*) is one only; but there are also the following proofs:

(2) If things were many, they would have to be of the same kind as I say the one is. For if there is earth and water and air and fire and iron

and gold, and that which is living and that which is dead, and black and white and all the rest of the things which men say are real: if these things exist, and we see and hear correctly, each thing must be of such a kind as it seemed to us to be in the first place, and it cannot change or become different, but each thing must always be what it is. But now, we say we see and hear and understand correctly,

(3) and it seems to us that the hot becomes cold and the cold hot, and the hard soft and the soft hard, and that the living thing dies and comes into being from what is not living, and that all things change, and that what was and what now is are not at all the same, but iron which is hard is worn away by contact with the finger, and gold and stone and whatever seems to be entirely strong (*is worn away*); and that from water, earth and stone come into being. So that it comes about that we neither see nor know existing things.

(4) So these statements are not consistent with one another. For although we say that there are many things, everlasting(?), having forms and strength, it seems to us that they all alter and change from what is seen on each occasion.

(5) It is clear therefore that we have not been seeing correctly, and that those things do not correctly seem to us to be many; for they would not change if they were real, but each would be as it seemed to be. For nothing is stronger than that which is real.

(6) And if it changed, being would have been destroyed, and not-being would have come into being. Thus, therefore, if things are many, they must be such as the one is.

9. If therefore being is, it must be one; and if it is one, it is bound not to have body. But if it had bulk, it would have parts, and would no longer be. [Cf. Vlastos's translation on page 29 above.]

10. If being is divided, it moves; and if it moved, it could not be.

.   .   .

❧

THE
PLURALISTS

EMPEDOCLES

The philosophers who came after the Eleatics, down to Plato and Aristotle, were concerned to show how change *was* possible. The first three philosophers to make this attempt are sometimes lumped together as "the Pluralists," for each of them tried to explain change by invoking several ultimate principles.

The first of these was Empedocles of Agrigentum, in Sicily, where an excellently preserved Greek temple of his time still stands, along with the ruins of several others. Like the more legendary Pythagoras, he fused scientific thought with religious concerns and left other people with the definite impression that he had performed miracles. He is said to have ended his life by leaping into the crater of Mount Etna. Friedrich Hölderlin, one of the greatest German poets, who was also a close friend of Hegel's, left several drafts, one almost finished, for a drama on "The Death of Empedocles," in five acts.

Empedocles wrote two poems, "On Nature" and "Purifications." The former is said to have been divided into two books, totalling 2,000 lines, of which less than 400 have survived. According to Diogenes Laertius, the two poems together came to 5,000 lines; if so, even less than one-fifth of the "Purifications" has come down to us.

As a person, Empedocles comes to life for us more than any other pre-Socratic, save only Heraclitus. Of an aristocratic family, he opposed tyranny and reputedly refused the crown of his native town. Like Pythagoras, he believed in the transmigration of souls; also like Pythagoras, he spoke of himself as a god. E. R. Dodds, in his splendidly illuminating and suggestive book on *The Greeks and the Irrational* (published as a paperback by the Beacon Press), speaks of Empedocles as a shaman.

Empedocles was the first great synthesizer of the history of philosophy. Around 450 B.C., a full century before Aristotle, he tried to find a place in his thought for all the major contributions of his predecessors. By explaining generation and destruction, if not all change, in terms of mixture and separation, Empedocles tried to reconcile Heraclitus' insistence on the reality of change with the Eleatic claim that generation and destruction are unthinkable. Going back to the Greeks' traditional belief in four elements, he found a place for Thales' water, Anaximenes' air, and Heraclitus' fire, adding to them earth. In addition to these four, which Aristotle might have called "material causes," Empedocles postulated two "efficient causes": strife (Heraclitus' great principle) and love. He envisaged four successive ages: an age of love or perfect mixture in the beginning; then gradual separation as strife enters; then complete separation as strife rules; finally, as love enters again, a gradual mixture.

The fragments are given in Freeman's translations.

. . .

Empedocles of Agrigentum was born not long after Anaxagoras, and was an admirer and associate of Parmenides, and even more of the Pythagoreans.   [Simplicius, *Phys.* 25, 19; R 411]

Anaxagoras of Clazomenae, though older than Empedocles, was later in his philosophical activity. [Aristotle, *Metaphysics* A 3, 984 a; see below under Aristotle.]

. . .

2. For limited are the means of grasping (*i.e. the organs of sense-perception*) which are scattered throughout their limbs, and many are the miseries that press in and blunt the thoughts. And having looked at (*only*) a small part of existence during their lives, doomed to perish swiftly like smoke they are carried aloft and wafted away, believing only that upon which as individuals they chance to hit as they wander in all directions; but every man preens himself on having found the Whole: so little are these things to be seen by men or to be heard, or to be comprehended by the mind! But you, since you have come here into retirement, shall learn—not more than mortal intellect can attain.

. . .

8. I shall tell you another thing: there is no creation of substance in any one of mortal existences, nor any end in execrable death, but only mixing and exchange of what has been mixed; and the name 'substance' (*Physis, 'nature'*) is applied to them by mankind.

9. But men, when these (*the Elements*) have been mixed in the form of a man and come into the light, or in the form of a species of wild animals, or plants, or birds, then say that this has 'come into being'; and when they separate, this men call sad fate (*death*). The terms that right demands they do not use; but through custom I myself also apply these names.

· · ·

12. From what in no wise exists, it is impossible for anything to come into being; and for being to perish completely is incapable of fulfilment and unthinkable; for it will always be there, wherever anyone may place it on any occasion.

13. Nor is there any part of the whole that is empty or overfull.

14. No part of the whole is empty; so whence could anything additional come?

· · ·

17. I shall tell of a double (*process*): at one time it increased so as to be a single one out of many; at another time again it grew apart so as to be many out of one. There is a double creation of mortals and a double decline: the union of all things causes the birth and destruction of the one (*race of mortals*), the other is reared as the elements grow apart, and then flies asunder. And these (*elements*) never cease their continuous exchange, sometimes uniting under the influence of love, so that all become one, at other times again each moving apart through the hostile force of hate. Thus in so far as they have the power to grow into one out of many, and again, when the one grows apart and many are formed, in this sense they come into being and have no stable life; but in so far as they never cease their continuous exchange, in this sense they remain always unmoved (*unaltered*) as they follow the cyclic process.

But come, listen to my discourse! For be assured, learning will increase your understanding. As I said before, revealing the aims of my discourse, I shall tell you of a double process. At one time it increased so as to be a single one out of many; at another time it grew apart so as to be many out of one—fire and water and earth and the boundless height of air, and also execrable hate apart from these, of equal weight in all directions, and love in their midst, their equal in length and breadth. Observe her with your mind, and do not sit with wondering eyes! She it is who is believed to be implanted in mortal limbs also; through her they think friendly thoughts and perform harmonious actions, calling her joy and Aphrodite. No mortal man has perceived her as she moves in and out among them. But *you* must listen to the undeceitful progress of my argument.

All these (*elements*) are equal and of the same age in their creation; but each presides over its own office, and each has its own character, and they prevail in turn in the course of time. And besides these, nothing else comes into being, nor does anything cease. For if they had been perishing continuously, they would be no more; and what could increase the whole? And whence could it have come? In what direction could it perish, since nothing is empty of these things? No, but these things alone exist, and running through one another they become different things at different times, and are ever continuously the same.

.   .   .

20. This process is clearly to be seen throughout the mass of mortal limbs: sometimes through love all the limbs which the body has as its lot come together into one, in the prime of flourishing life; at another time again, sundered by evil feuds, they wander severally by the breakers of the shore of life. Likewise too with shrub-plants and fish in their watery dwelling, and beasts with mountain lairs and diver-birds that travel on wings.

21. But come, observe the following witness to my previous discourse, lest in my former statements there was any substance of which the form was missing. Observe the sun, bright to see and hot everywhere, and all the immortal things (*heavenly bodies*) drenched with its heat and brilliant light; and the rain, dark and chill over everything; and from the earth issue forth things based on the soil and solid. But in (*the reign of*) wrath they are all different in form and separate, while in (*the reign of*) love they come together and long for one another. For from these (*elements*) come all things that were and are and will be; and trees spring up, and men and women, and beasts and birds and water-nurtured fish, and even the long-lived gods who are highest in honour. For these (*elements*) alone exist, but by running through one another they become different; to such a degree does mixing change them.

22. For all these things—beaming sun and earth and heaven and sea— are connected in harmony with their own parts: all those (*parts*) which have been sundered from them and exist in mortal limbs. Similarly all those things which are more suitable for mixture are made like one another and united in affection by Aphrodite. But those things which differ most from one another in origin and mixture and the forms in which they are moulded are completely unaccustomed to combine, and are very baneful because of the commands of hate, in that hate has wrought their origin.

.   .   .

24. ... Touching on summit after summit, not to follow a single path of discourse to the end.

25. For what is right can well be uttered even twice.

26. In turn they get the upper hand in the revolving cycle, and perish into one another and increase in the turn appointed by fate. For they alone exist, but running through one another they become men and the tribes of other animals, sometimes uniting under the influence of love into one ordered whole, at other times again each moving apart through the hostile force of hate, until growing together into the whole which is one, they are quelled. Thus in so far as they have the power to grow

into one out of many, and again, when the one grows apart and many are formed, in this sense they come into being and have no stable life; but in so far as they never cease their continuous exchange, in this sense they remain always unmoved (*unaltered*) as they follow the cyclic process.

27. (*The sphere under the dominion of love*): Therein are articulated neither the swift limbs of the sun, nor the shaggy might of earth, nor the sea: so firmly is it (*the whole*) fixed in a close-set secrecy, a rounded Sphere enjoying a circular solitude.

.   .   .

28. But he (*god*) is equal in all directions to himself and altogether eternal, a rounded sphere enjoying a circular solitude.

29. For there do not start two branches from his back; (*he has*) no feet, no swift knees, no organs of reproduction; but he was a sphere, and in all directions equal to himself.

.   .   .

35. But I will go back to the path of song which I formerly laid down, drawing one argument from another: that (*path which shows how*) when hate has reached the bottommost abyss of the eddy, and when love reaches the middle of the whirl, then in it (*the whirl*) all these things come together so as to be one—not all at once, but voluntarily uniting, some from one quarter, others from another. And as they mixed, there poured forth countless races of mortals. But many things stand unmixed side by side with the things mixing—all those which hate (*still*) aloft checked, since it had not yet faultlessly withdrawn from the whole to the outermost limits of the circle, but was remaining in some places, and in other places departing from the limbs (*of the sphere*). But in so far as it went on quietly streaming out, to the same extent there was entering a benevolent immortal inrush of faultless love. And swiftly those things became mortal which previously had experienced immortality, and things formerly unmixed became mixed, changing their paths. And as they mixed, there poured forth countless races of mortals, equipped with forms of every sort, a marvel to behold.

36. As they came together, hate returned to the outermost.

.   .   .

45. There whirls round the earth a circular borrowed light.

.   .   .

48. It is the earth that makes night by coming in the way of the (*sun's*) rays.

.   .   .

55. Sea, the sweat of earth.

.   .   .

58. Limbs wandered alone.

.   .   .

60. Creatures with rolling gait and innumerable hands.
61. Many creatures were created with a face and breast on both sides; offspring of cattle with the fronts of men, and again there arose offspring of men with heads of cattle; and (*creatures made of elements*) mixed in part from men, in part of female sex, furnished with hairy limbs.

.   .   .

100. The way everything breathes in and out is as follows: all have tubes of flesh, empty of blood, which extend over the surface of the body; and at the mouths of these tubes the outermost surface of the skin is perforated with frequent pores, so as to keep in the blood while a free way is cut for the passage of the air. Thus, when the thin blood flows back from here, the air, bubbling, rushes in in a mighty wave; and when the blood leaps up (*to the surface*), there is an expiration of air. As when a girl, playing with a water-catcher of shining brass—when, having placed the mouth of the pipe on her well-shaped hand she dips the vessel into the yielding substance of silvery water, still the volume of air pressing from inside on the many holes keeps out the water, until she uncovers the condensed stream (*of air*). Then at once when the air flows out, the water flows in in an equal quantity. Similarly, when water occupies the depths of the brazen vessel, and the opening or passage is stopped by the human flesh (*hand*), and the air outside, striving to get in, checks the water, by controlling the surface at the entrance of the noisy strainer until she lets go with her hand: then again, in exactly the opposite way from what happened before, as the air rushes in, the water flows out in equal volume. Similarly when the thin blood, rushing through the limbs, flows back into the interior, straightway a stream of air flows in with a rush; and when the blood flows up again, again there is a breathing-out in equal volume.

.   .   .

110. If you press them deep into your firm mind, and contemplate them with good will and a studious care that is pure, these things will all assuredly remain with you throughout your life; and you will obtain many other things from them; for these things of themselves cause each (*element*) to increase in the character, according to the way of each man's nature. But if you intend to grasp after different things such as dwell among men in countless numbers and blunt their thoughts, miserable (*trifles*), certainly these things will quickly desert you in the course of time, longing to return to their own original kind. For all things, be assured, have intelligence and a portion of thought.
111. You shall learn all the drugs that exist as a defence against illness and old age; for you alone will I accomplish all this. You shall check the force of the unwearying winds which rush upon the earth with their

blasts and lay waste the cultivated fields. And again, if you wish, you shall conduct the breezes back again. You shall create a seasonable dryness after the dark rain for mankind, and again you shall create after summer drought the streams that nourish the trees and [which will flow in the sky].[1] And you shall bring out of Hades a dead man restored to strength.

KATHARMOI (PURIFICATIONS)

112. Friends, who dwell in the great town on the city's heights, looking down on yellow Agrigentum, you who are occupied with good deeds, who are harbours treating foreigners with respect, and who are unacquainted with wickedness: greeting! I go about among you as an immortal god, no longer a mortal, held in honour by all, as I seem (*to them to deserve*), crowned with fillets and flowing garlands. When I come to them in their flourishing towns, to men and women, I am honoured; and they follow me in thousands, to inquire where is the path of advantage, some desiring oracles, while others ask to hear a word of healing for their manifold diseases, since they have long been pierced with cruel pains.

113. But why do I lay stress on these things, as if I were achieving something great in that I surpass mortal men who are liable to many forms of destruction?

114. Friends, I know that truth is present in the story that I shall tell; but it is actually very difficult for men, and the impact of conviction on their minds is unwelcome.

115. There is an oracle of necessity, an ancient decree of the gods, eternal, sealed fast with broad oaths, that when one of the divine spirits whose portion is long life sinfully stains his own limbs with bloodshed, and following hate has sworn a false oath—these must wander for thrice ten thousand seasons far from the company of the blessed, being born throughout the period into all kinds of mortal shapes, which exchange one hard way of life for another. For the mighty air chases them into the sea, and the sea spews them forth on to the dry land, and the earth (*drives them*) towards the rays of the blazing sun; and the Sun hurls them into the eddies of the Aether. One (*Element*) receives them from the other, and all loathe them. Of this number am I too now, a fugitive from heaven and a wanderer, because I trusted in raging Hate.

.   .   .

117. For by now I have been born as boy, girl, plant, bird, and dumb sea-fish.

118. I wept and wailed when I saw the unfamiliar land (*at birth*).

119. How great the honour, how deep the happiness from which (*I am exiled*)!

.   .   .

---

[1] Reading corrupt.

136. Will ye not cease from this harsh-sounding slaughter? Do you not see that you are devouring one another in the thoughtlessness of your minds?

. . .

ANAXAGORAS

He came from Clazomenae on the coast of Asia Minor, not far northwest of Colophon (Xenophanes' home) and Ephesus (Heraclitus' home). He was the first of the Greek philosophers to move to Athens, where he became a good friend of Pericles, the greatest statesman of the time, who gave his name to the whole epoch. The dates are uncertain, but he may have been born about 500 B.C. and come to Athens around 480. He lived in Athens during the time of her greatest glory, a contemporary of Aeschylus, Sophocles, and Euripides.

He taught that everything consists of an infinite number of particles or seeds, and that in all things there is a portion of everything. Hair could not come from what is not hair, nor could flesh come from what is not flesh. The names we apply to things are determined by the preponderance of certain kinds of seeds in them; e.g., hair seeds or flesh seeds. Like Empedocles, he added to such "material causes" an "efficient cause" to account for the motion and direction of things—however, he added only one "efficient cause," which was mind, *nous* in Greek. The introduction of mind led Aristotle to hail Anaxagoras as the only sober man among the pre-Socratics; but Aristotle found fault with Anaxagoras for not making more use of this new principle to explain natural events. The modern reader is more likely to commend Anaxagoras on that score, having wearied of centuries of purposive explanations.

Anaxagoras was the first philosopher to be tried formally on a charge of heresy or impiety. He went into exile at Lampsacus on the Hellespont, where he died about 428/7, a year after Pericles. His sole book was still on sale in Athens at the end of the century, for one drachma.

The fragments are given in Freeman's translations, for once with her profuse capitals.

. . .

He is said to have been twenty years old at the time of Xerxes' crossing, and to have lived to seventy-two.... He began to be a philosopher at Athens in the archonship of Callias, at the age of twenty, as Demetrius Phalereus tells us in his *Register of Archons,* and is said to have spent thirty years there.... Of his trial different accounts are given. Sotion, in his *Succession of Philosophers,* says that he was prosecuted for impiety

by Cleon, because he claimed that the sun was a red-hot mass of metal, and that after Pericles, his pupil, had made a speech in his defense, he was fined five talents and exiled. Satyrus, in his *Lives*, on the other hand, says that the charge was brought by Thucydides in his political campaign against Pericles; and he adds that the charge was not only for impiety but for Medism ["treasonable correspondence with Persia," as another translator puts it] as well; and he was condemned to death in absence. . . . Finally he withdrew to Lampsacus, and there died. It is said that when the rulers of the city asked him what privilege he wished to be granted, he replied that the children should be given a holiday every year in the month in which he died. The custom is preserved to the present day. When he died, the Lampsacenes buried him with full honors.
[Diogenes Laertius II, 7-15; R 487]

Anaxagoras, the natural philosopher, was a distinguished Clazomenion . . . and his own pupils included . . . Euripides, the poet.
[Strabo 14, p. 645 Cas.; R 490]

Those who wrote only one book include Melissus, Parmenides, and Anaxagoras.   [Diogenes Laertius I, 16; R 494]

.   .   .

1. (*Opening sentences from his book 'On Natural Science'*): All Things were together, infinite in number and in smallness. For the Small also was infinite. And since all were together, nothing was distinguishable because of its smallness. For Air and Aether dominated all things, both of them being infinite. For these are the most important (*Elements*) in the total mixture, both in number and in size.
2. Air and Aether are separated off from the surrounding multiplicity, and that which surrounds is infinite in number.
3. For in Small there is no Least, but only a Lesser: for it is impossible that Being should Not-Be, and in Great there is always a Greater. And it is equal in number to the small, but each thing is to itself both great and small.
4. Conditions being thus, one must believe that there are many things of all sorts in all composite products, and the seeds of all Things, which contain all kinds of shapes and colours and pleasant savours. And men too were fitted together, and all other creatures which have life. And the men possessed both inhabited cities and artificial works just like ourselves, and they had sun and moon and the rest, just as we have, and the earth produced for them many and diverse things, of which they collected the most useful, and now use them for their dwellings. This I say concerning Separation, that it must have taken place not only with us, but elsewhere.
Before these things were separated off, all things were together, nor was any colour distinguishable, for the mixing of all Things prevented this, (*namely*) the mixing of moist and dry and hot and cold and bright and dark, and there was a great quantity of earth in the mixture, and

seeds infinite in number, not at all like one another. For none of the other things either is like any other. And as this was so, one must believe that all Things were present in the Whole.

5. These things being thus separated off, one must understand that all things are in no wise less or more (for it is not possible for them to be more than All), but all things are forever equal (*in quantity*).

6. And since there are equal (*quantitative*) parts of Great and Small, so too similarly in everything there must be everything. It is not possible (*for them*) to exist apart, but all things contain a portion of everything. Since it is not possible for the Least to exist, it cannot be isolated, nor come into being by itself; but as it was in the beginning, so now, all things are together. In all things there are many things, and of the things separated off, there are equal numbers in (*the categories*) Great and Small.

7. So that the number of the things separated off cannot be known either in thought or in fact.

8. The things in the one Cosmos are not separated off from one another with an axe, neither the Hot from the Cold, nor the Cold from the Hot.

9. Thus these things circulate and are separated off by force and speed. The speed makes the force. Their speed is not like the speed of any of the Things now existing among mankind, but altogether many times as fast.

10. How can hair come from not-hair, and flesh from not-flesh?

11. In everything there is a portion of everything except Mind; and some things contain Mind also.

12. Other things all contain a part of everything, but Mind is infinite and self-ruling, and is mixed with no Thing, but is alone by itself. If it were not by itself, but were mixed with anything else, it would have had a share of all Things, if it were mixed with anything; for in everything there is a portion of everything, as I have said before. And the things mixed (*with Mind*) would have prevented it, so that it could not rule over any Thing in the same way as it can being alone by itself. For it is the finest of all Things, and the purest, and has complete understanding of everything, and has the greatest power. All things which have life, both the greater and the less, are ruled by Mind. Mind took command of the universal revolution, so as to make (*things*) revolve at the outset. And at first things began to revolve from some small point, but now the revolution extends over a greater area, and will spread even further. And the things which were mixed together, and separated off, and divided, were all understood by Mind. And whatever they were going to be, and whatever things were then in existence that are not now, and all things that now exist and whatever shall exist—all were arranged by Mind, as also the revolution now followed by the stars, the sun and moon, and the Air and Aether which were separated off. It was this revolution which caused the separation off. And dense separates from rare, and hot from cold, and bright from dark, and dry from wet. There are many portions of many things. And nothing is absolutely separated off or divided the one from the other except Mind. Mind is all alike, both the greater and the less. But nothing

else is like anything else, but each individual thing is and was most obviously that of which it contains the most.

13. And when Mind began the motion, there was a separating-off from all that was being moved; and all that Mind set in motion was separated (*internally*); and as things were moving and separating off (*internally*), the revolution greatly increased this (*internal*) separation.

14. Mind, which ever Is, certainly still exists also where all other things are, (*namely*) in the multiple surrounding (*mass*) and in the things which were separated off before, and in the things already separated off.

15. The dense and moist and cold and dark (*Elements*) collected here, where now is Earth, and the rare and hot and dry went outwards to the furthest part of the Aether.

16. From these, while they are separating off, Earth solidifies; for from the clouds, water is separated off, and from the water, earth, and from the earth, stones are solidified by the cold; and these rush outward rather than the water.

17. The Greeks have an incorrect belief on Coming into Being and Passing Away. No Thing comes into being or passes away, but it is mixed together or separated from existing Things. Thus they would be correct if they called coming into being 'mixing', and passing away 'separation-off'.

18. It is the sun that endows the moon with its brilliance.

19. We give the name Iris to the reflection of the sun on the clouds. It is therefore the sign of a storm, for the water which flows round the cloud produces wind or forces out rain.

.   .   .

21. Through the weakness of the sense-perceptions, we cannot judge truth.

.   .   .

DEMOCRITUS (AND LEUCIPPUS)

Democritus of Abdera, on the coast of Thrace, was probably born in 460 B.C. Together with Leucippus, his teacher, he was the prime exponent of the philosophy known as atomism. Leucippus' work has perished, but we have many reports about the atomistic philosophy, especially in its Democritean form; a few of Democritus' remarks on knowledge and reality have survived; a collection of Democritus' ethical maxims—the so-called *Gnomae*—has come down to us; and finally we also have a large number of fragments from his other writings, dealing with ethics. This material is offered in four sections here: first, the reports (in Raven's translations); then the metaphysical and epistemological fragments; next, the *Gnomae;* and eventually the fragments on ethics—all in Freeman's versions.

There are three reasons for allotting so much space to Democritus.

First, we have ever so much more material on him than on any of his predecessors. Second, although atomism represents another pluralistic answer to Parmenides, along with the philosophies of Empedocles and Anaxagoras, and although Leucippus was a pre-Socratic, Democritus was actually a slightly younger contemporary of Socrates and an older contemporary of Plato. His philosophy may be viewed as an important alternative to Platonism—as one follows the development of pre-Socratic thought, the road forks in the end, one path leading to Democritus, the other to Plato. Third, Democritus does not by any means represent a dead end; his thought was taken up first by Epicurus and then, in Roman times, by Lucretius. Epicurus is represented later in the present volume, but Lucretius is not. Because we are here dispensing with Roman copies, we are in a position to give more space to the Greek originals.

That so much of Democritus' thought on ethics has come down to us, is our good fortune: atomism has often been contrasted with Platonism as materialism versus idealism. It is worth noting, then, that Democritus' ethic was no less lofty than Plato's.

.   .   .

A. ANCIENT REPORTS ON ATOMISM

Leucippus of Elea or Miletus (both accounts are current) had associated with Parmenides in philosophy, but in his view of reality he did not follow the same path as Parmenides and Xenophanes but rather, it seems, the opposite path. For while they regarded the whole as one, motionless, uncreated, and limited, and forbade even the search for what is not, he posited innumerable elements in perpetual motion—namely the atoms—and held that the number of their shapes was infinite, on the ground that there was no reason why any atom should be of one shape rather than another; for he observed too that coming-into-being and change are incessant in the world. Further he held that not-being exists as well as being, and the two are equally the causes of things coming-into-being. The nature of atoms he supposed to be compact and full; that, he said, was being, and it moved in the void, which he called not-being and held to exist no less than being. In the same way his associate, Democritus of Abdera, posited as principles the full and the void.

[Simplicius, *Phys.* 28, 4; R 546]

Apollodorus in the *Chronicles* says that Epicurus was instructed by Nausiphanes and Praxiphanes; but Epicurus himself denies this, saying in the letter to Eurylochus that he instructed himself. He and Hemarchus both maintain that there never was a philosopher Leucippus, who, some (including Apollodorus the Epicurean) say, was the teacher of Democritus. [Diogenes Laertius X, 13; R 547]

Leucippus postulated atoms and void, and in this Democritus resembled him though in other respects he was more productive.

[Cicero, *Academica pr.* II, 37, 118; R 548]

Later he [Democritus] met Leucippus and, according to some, Anaxagoras also, whose junior he was by forty years. . . . As he himself says in the *Little World-System,* he was a young man in the old age of Anaxagoras, being forty years younger.   [Diogenes Laertius IX, 34; R 549]

Demetrius in his *Homonyms* and Antisthenes in his *Successions* say that he [Democritus] traveled to Egypt to visit the priests and learn geometry, and that he went also to Persia to visit the Chaldaeans, and to the Red Sea. Some say that he associated with the 'naked philosophers' in India; also that he went to Ethiopia.   [*Ibid.,* IX, 35; R 551]

Leucippus thought he had a theory which, being consistent with sense-perception, would not do away with coming-into-being or perishing or motion or the multiplicity of things. So much he conceded to appearances, while to those who uphold the one [the Eleatics] he granted that motion is impossible without void, that the void is not-being, and that no part of being is not-being. For being in the proper sense is an absolute *plenum.* But such a *plenum* is not one, but there is an infinite number of them, and they are invisible owing to the smallness of their bulk. They move in the void (for the void exists), and by their coming together they effect coming-into-being, by their separation perishing.

[Aristotle, *de gen. et corr.,* A 8, 325a; R 552]

They [Leucippus, Democritus, and Epicurus] said that the first principles were infinite in number, and thought they were indivisible atoms and impassible owing to their compactness, and without any void in them; divisibility comes about because of the void in compound bodies.

[Simplicius, *de caelo* 242, 18; R 556]

To this extent they differed, that one [Epicurus] supposed that all atoms were very small and on that account imperceptible; the other, Democritus, that there are some atoms that are very large.

[Dionysius *ap.* Eusebium P.E. XIV, 23, 3; R 560]

Democritus holds the same view as Leucippus about the elements, full and void . . . he spoke as if the things that are were in constant motion in the void; and there are innumerable worlds which differ in size. In some worlds there is no sun and moon, in others they are larger than in our world, and in others more numerous. The intervals between the worlds are unequal; in some parts there are more worlds, in others fewer; some are increasing, some at their height, some decreasing; in some parts they are arising, in others failing. They are destroyed by colliding with each other. There are some worlds without any living creatures, plants, or moisture.   [Hyppolytus *Ref.* I, 13, 2; R 564*]

Everything happens according to necessity; for the cause of the coming-into-being of all things is the whirl, which he calls necessity.   [Diogenes

Laertius IX, 45; R 565; cf. "the only extant saying of Leucippus himself, R 568, Fr. 2, Aetius I, 25, 4: Nothing occurs at random, but everything for a reason and by necessity."]

As they [the atoms] move, they collide and become entangled in such a way as to cling in close contact to one another, but not so as to form one substance of them in reality of any kind whatever; for it is very simple-minded to suppose that two or more could ever become one. The reason he gives for atoms staying together for a while is the intertwining and mutual hold of the primary bodies; for some of them are angular, some hooked, some concave, some convex, and indeed with countless other differences; so he thinks they cling to each other and stay together until such time as some stronger necessity comes from the surrounding and shakes and scatters them apart.

[Aristotle *On Democritus ap.* Simplicium *de caelo* 295, 11; R 581]

Democritus says that the spherical is the most mobile of shapes; and such is mind and fire. [Aristotle, *de anima*, A 2, 405a; R 583]

Democritus and the majority of natural philosophers who discuss perception are guilty of a great absurdity, for they represent all perception as being by touch. [Aristotle, *de sensu* 4, 442a; R 585]

Leucippus, Democritus, and Epicurus say that perception and thought arise when images enter from outside; neither occurs to anybody without an image impinging. [Aetius IV, 8; R 586]

Democritus explains sight by the visual image, which he describes in a peculiar way; the visual image does not arise directly in the pupil, but the air between the eye and the object of sight is contracted and stamped by the object seen and the seer; for from everything there is always a sort of effluence proceeding. So this air, which is solid and variously colored, appears in the eye, which is moist (?); the eye does not admit the dense part, but the moist passes through [Theophrastus, *de sensu* 50; R 587]

B. METAPHYSICAL AND EPISTEMOLOGICAL FRAGMENTS

7. We know nothing about anything really, but opinion is for all individuals an inflowing (? *of the atoms*). (*From 'On the Forms'*.)
8. It will be obvious that it is impossible to understand how in reality each thing is. (*From 'On the Forms'*.)
9. Sweet exists by convention, bitter by convention, colour by convention; atoms and void (*alone*) exist in reality . . . We know nothing accurately in reality, but (*only*) as it changes according to the bodily condition, and the constitution of those things that flow upon (*the body*) and impinge upon it.
10. It has often been demonstrated that we do not grasp how each thing is or is not.
11. There are two sorts of knowledge, one genuine, one bastard (*or 'obscure'*). To the latter belong all the following: sight, hearing, smell,

taste, touch. The real is separated from this. When the bastard can do no more—neither see more minutely, nor hear, nor smell, nor taste, nor perceive by touch—and a finer investigation is needed, then the genuine comes in as having a tool for distinguishing more finely. (*From 'The Canon'*).

.   .   .

156. Naught exists just as much as Aught.

C. THE SO-CALLED GNOMAE (COMPLETE)

35. If any man listens to my opinions, here recorded, with intelligence, he will achieve many things worthy of a good man, and avoid doing many unworthy things.

36. It is right that men should value the soul rather than the body; for perfection of soul corrects the inferiority of the body, but physical strength without intelligence does nothing to improve the mind.

37. He who chooses the advantages of the soul chooses things more divine, but he who chooses those of the body, chooses things human.

38. It is noble to prevent the criminal; but if one cannot, one should not join him in crime.

39. One must either be good, or imitate a good man.

40. Men find happiness neither by means of the body nor through possessions, but through uprightness and wisdom.

41. Refrain from crimes not through fear but through duty.

42. It is a great thing, when one is in adversity, to think of duty.

43. Repentance for shameful deeds is salvation in life.

44. One should tell the truth, not speak at length.

45. The wrongdoer is more unfortunate than the man wronged.

46. Magnanimity consists in enduring tactlessness with mildness.

47. Well-ordered behaviour consists in obedience to the law, the ruler, and the man wiser (*than oneself*).

48. When inferior men censure, the good man pays no heed.

49. It is hard to be governed by one's inferior.

50. The man completely enslaved to wealth can never be honest.

51. In power of persuasion, reasoning is far stronger than gold.

52. He who tries to give intelligent advice to one who thinks he has intelligence, is wasting his time.

53. Many who have not learnt reason, nevertheless live according to reason.

53a. Many whose actions are most disgraceful practise the best utterances.

54. The foolish learn sense through misfortune.

55. One should emulate the deeds and actions of virtue, not the words.

56. Noble deeds are recognised and emulated by those of natural good disposition.

57. Good breeding in cattle depends on physical health, but in men on a well-formed character.

58. The hopes of right-thinking men are attainable, but those of the unintelligent are impossible.

59. Neither skill nor wisdom is attainable unless one learns.

60. It is better to examine one's own faults than those of others.

61. Those whose character is well-ordered have also a well-ordered life.

62. Virtue consists, not in avoiding wrong-doing, but in having no wish thereto.

63. To pronounce praise on noble deeds is noble; for to do so over base deeds is the work of a false deceiver.

64. Many much-learned men have no intelligence.

65. One should practise much-sense, not much-learning.

66. It is better to deliberate before action than to repent afterwards.

67. Believe not everything, but only what is approved: the former is foolish, the latter the act of a sensible man.

68. The worthy and the unworthy man (*are to be known*) not only by their actions, but also their wishes.

69. For all men, good and true are the same; but pleasant differs for different men.

70. Immoderate desire is the mark of a child, not a man.

71. Untimely pleasures produce unpleasantnesses.

72. Violent desire for one thing blinds the soul to all others.

73. Virtuous love consists in decorous desire for the beautiful.

74. Accept no pleasure unless it is beneficial.

75. It is better for fools to be ruled than to rule.

76. For the foolish, not reason but advantage is the teacher.

77. Fame and wealth without intelligence are dangerous possessions.

78. To make money is not without use, but if it comes from wrong-doing, nothing is worse.

79. It is a bad thing to imitate the bad, and not even to wish to imitate the good.

80. It is shameful to be so busy over the affairs of others that one knows nothing of one's own.

81. Constant delay means work undone.

82. The false and the seeming-good are those who do all in word, not in fact.

83. The cause of error is ignorance of the better.

84. The man who does shameful deeds must first feel shame in his own eyes.

85. He who contradicts and chatters much is ill-fitted for learning what he ought.

86. It is greed to do all the talking and not be willing to listen.

87. One must be on one's guard against the bad man, lest he seize his opportunity.

88. The envious man torments himself like an enemy.

89. An enemy is not he who injures, but he who wishes to do so.

90. The enmity of relatives is much worse than that of strangers.

91. Be not suspicious towards all, but be cautious and firm.

92. Accept favours in the foreknowledge that you will have to give a greater return for them.

93. When you do a favour, study the recipient first, lest he prove a scoundrel and repay evil for good.

94. Small favours at the right time are greatest to the recipients.

95. Marks of honour are greatly valued by right-thinking men, who understand why they are being honoured.

96. The generous man is he who does not look for a return, but who does good from choice.

97. Many who seem friendly are not so, and those who do not seem so, are.

98. The friendship of one intelligent man is better than that of all the unintelligent.

99. Life is not worth living for the man who has not even one good friend.

100. The man whose tested friends do not stay long with him is bad-tempered.

101. Many avoid their friends when they fall from wealth to poverty.

102. In all things, equality is fair, excess and deficiency not so, in my opinion.

103. The man who loves nobody is, I think, loved by no one.

104. In old age, a man is agreeable if his manner is pleasant and his speech serious.

105. Physical beauty is (*merely*) animal unless intelligence be present.

106. In prosperity it is easy to find a friend, in adversity nothing is so difficult.

107. Not all one's relatives are friends, but only those who agree with us about what is advantageous.

107a. It is proper, since we are human beings, not to laugh at the misfortunes of others, but to mourn.

108. Good things are obtained with difficulty if one seeks; but bad things come without our even seeking.

109. The censorious are not well-fitted for friendship.

110. A woman must not practise argument: this is dreadful.

111. To be ruled by a woman is the ultimate outrage for a man.

112. It is the mark of the divine intellect to be always calculating something noble.

113. Those who praise the unintelligent do (*them*) great harm.

114. It is better to be praised by another than by oneself.

115. If you do not recognise (*i.e. understand*) praise, believe that you are being flattered.

D.   FRAGMENTS ON ETHICS

3. The man who wishes to have serenity of spirit should not engage in many activities, either private or public, nor choose activities beyond his power and natural capacity. He must guard against this, so that when good fortune strikes him and leads him on to excess by means of (*false*)

seeming, he must rate it low, and not attempt things beyond his powers. A reasonable fullness is better than overfullness.

4. Pleasure and absence of pleasure are the criteria of what is profitable and what is not.

. . .

31. Medicine heals diseases of the body, wisdom frees the soul from passions.

32. Coition is a slight attack of apoplexy. For man gushes forth from man, and is separated by being torn apart with a kind of blow.

33. Nature and instruction are similar; for instruction transforms the man, and in transforming, creates his nature.

34. Man is a universe in little (Microcosm).

. . .

118. (*I would*) rather discover one cause than gain the kingdom of Persia.

. . .

159. If the body brought a suit against the soul, for all the pains it had endured throughout life, and the illtreatment, and I were to be the judge of the suit, I would gladly condemn the soul, in that it had partly ruined the body by its neglect and dissolved it with bouts of drunkenness, and partly destroyed it and torn it in pieces with its passion for pleasure—as if, when a tool or a vessel were in a bad condition, I blamed the man who was using it carelessly.

160. (*To live badly is*) not to live badly, but to spend a long time dying.

. . .

169. Do not try to understand everything, lest you become ignorant of everything.

170. Happiness, like unhappiness, is a property of the soul.

171. Happiness does not dwell in cattle or gold. The soul is the dwelling-place of the (*good and evil*) genius.

. . .

174. The cheerful man, who is impelled towards works that are just and lawful, rejoices by day and by night, and is strong and free from care. But the man who neglects justice, and does not do what he ought, finds all such things disagreeable when he remembers any of them, and he is afraid and torments himself.

175. But the gods are the givers of all good things, both in the past and now. They are not, however, the givers of things which are bad, harmful or non-beneficial, either in the past or now, but men themselves fall into these through blindness of mind and lack of sense.

180. Education is an ornament for the prosperous, a refuge for the unfortunate.

181. The man who employs exhortation and persuasion will turn out to be a more effective guide to virtue than he who employs law and compulsion. For the man who is prevented by law from wrongdoing will probably do wrong in secret, whereas the man who is led towards duty by persuasion will probably not do anything untoward either secretly or openly. Therefore the man who acts rightly through understanding and knowledge becomes at the same time brave and upright.

182. Beautiful objects are wrought by study through effort, but ugly things are reaped automatically without toil. For even one who is unwilling is sometimes so wrought upon by learning . . . . . (*? MSS. corrupt*).

.   .   .

184. Continuous association with base men increases a disposition to crime.

.   .   .

186. Similarity of outlook creates friendship.

.   .   .

188. The criterion of the advantageous and disadvantageous is enjoyment and lack of enjoyment.

.   .   .

190. One must avoid even speaking of evil deeds.

191. Cheerfulness is created for men through moderation of enjoyment and harmoniousness of life. Things that are in excess or lacking are apt to change and cause great disturbance in the soul. Souls which are stirred by great divergences are neither stable nor cheerful. Therefore one must keep one's mind on what is attainable, and be content with what one has, paying little heed to things envied and admired, and not dwelling on them in one's mind. Rather must you consider the lives of those in distress, reflecting on their intense sufferings, in order that your own possessions and condition may seem great and enviable, and you may, by ceasing to desire more, cease to suffer in your soul. For he who admires those who have, and who are called happy by other mortals, and who dwells on them in his mind every hour, is constantly compelled to undertake something new and to run the risk, through his desire, of doing something irretrievable among those things which the laws prohibit. Hence one must not seek the latter, but must be content with the former, comparing one's own life with that of those in worse cases, and must consider oneself fortunate, reflecting on their sufferings, in being so much better off than they. If you keep to this way of thinking, you will live more serenely, and will expel those not-negligible curses in life, envy, jealousy and spite.

.   .   .

194. The great pleasures come from the contemplation of noble works.

.   .   .

198. The animal needing something knows how much it needs, the man does not.

199. People are fools who hate life and yet wish to live through fear of Hades.

200. People are fools who live without enjoyment of life.

201. People are fools who yearn for long life without pleasure in long life.

202. People are fools who yearn for what is absent, but neglect what they have even when it is more valuable than what has gone.

.   .   .

206. Fools want to live to be old because they fear death.

207. One should choose not every pleasure, but only that concerned with the beautiful.

208. The self-control of the father is the greatest example for the children.

.   .   .

210. A rich table is provided by luck, but a sufficient one by wisdom.

211. Moderation multiplies pleasures, and increases pleasure.

212. Sleep in the daytime signifies bodily trouble or aberration of mind or laziness or lack of training.

213. Courage minimises difficulties.

214. The brave man is not only he who overcomes the enemy, but he who is stronger than pleasures. Some men are masters of cities, but are enslaved to women.

215. The reward of justice is confidence of judgement and imperturbability, but the end of injustice is the fear of disaster.

216. Imperturbable wisdom is worth everything.

.   .   .

219. The passion for wealth, unless limited by satisfaction, is far more painful than extreme poverty; for greater passions create greater needs.

.   .   .

222. The excessive accumulation of wealth for one's children is an excuse for covetousness, which thus displays its peculiar nature.

223. The things needed by the body are available to all without toil and trouble. But the things which require toil and trouble and which make life disagreeable are not desired by the body but by the ill-constitution of the mind.

.   .   .

226. Freedom of speech is the sign of freedom; but the danger lies in discerning the right occasion.

227. Misers have the fate of bees: they work as if they were going to live for ever.

. . .

231. The right-minded man is he who is not grieved by what he has not, but enjoys what he has.

. . .

234. Men ask in their prayers for health from the gods, but do not know that the power to attain this lies in themselves; and by doing the opposite through lack of control, they themselves become the betrayers of their own health to their desires.

. . .

236. It is hard to fight desire; but to control it is the sign of a reasonable man.

. . .

239. Bad men, when they escape, do not keep the oaths which they make in time of stress.

. . .

242. More men become good through practice than by nature.
243. All kinds of toil are pleasanter than rest, when men attain that for which they labour, or know that they will attain it. But whenever there is failure to attain, then labour is painful and hard.
244. Do not say or do what is base, even when you are alone. Learn to feel shame in your own eyes much more than before others.

. . .

247. To a wise man, the whole earth is open; for the native land of a good soul is the whole earth.

. . .

249. Civil war is harmful to both parties; for both to the conquerors and the conquered, the destruction is the same.

. . .

251. Poverty under democracy is as much to be preferred to so-called prosperity under an autocracy as freedom to slavery.
252. One must give the highest importance to affairs of the state, that it may be well run; one must not pursue quarrels contrary to right, nor acquire a power contrary to the common good. The well-run state is the greatest protection, and contains all in itself; when this is safe, all is safe; when this is destroyed, all is destroyed.

. . .

260. Anyone killing any brigand or pirate shall be exempt from penalty, whether he do it by his own hand, or by instigation, or by vote.

261. One must punish wrong-doers to the best of one's ability, and not neglect it. Such conduct is just and good, but the neglect of it is unjust and bad.

262. Those who do what is deserving of exile or imprisonment or other punishment must be condemned and not let off. Whoever contrary to the law acquits a man, judging according to profit or pleasure, does wrong, and this is bound to be on his conscience.

. . .

264. One must not respect the opinion of other men more than one's own; nor must one be more ready to do wrong if no one will know than if all will know. One must respect one's own opinion most, and this must stand as the law of one's soul, preventing one from doing anything improper.

265. Men remember one's mistakes rather than one's successes. This is just; for as those who return a deposit do not deserve praise, whereas those who do not do so deserve blame and punishment, so with the official: he was elected not to make mistakes but to do things well.

. . .

270. Use slaves as parts of the body: each to his own function.

. . .

272. The man who is fortunate in his choice of a son-in-law gains a son; the man unfortunate in his choice loses his daughter also.

273. A woman is far sharper than a man in malign thoughts.

274. An adornment for a woman is lack of garrulity. Paucity of adornment is also beautiful.

275. The rearing of children is full of pitfalls. Success is attended by strife and care, failure means grief beyond all others.

276. I do not think that one should have children. I observe in the acquisition of children many great risks and many griefs, whereas a harvest is rare, and even when it exists, it is thin and poor.

277. Whoever wants to have children should, in my opinion, choose them from the family of one of his friends. He will thus obtain a child such as he wishes, for he can select the kind he wants. And the one that seems fittest will be most likely to follow on his natural endowment. The difference is that in the latter way one can take one child out of many who is according to one's liking; but if one begets a child of one's own, the risks are many, for one is bound to accept him as he is.

. . .

284. If your desires are not great, a little will seem much to you; for small appetite makes poverty equivalent to wealth.

285. One should realise that human life is weak and brief and mixed with

many cares and difficulties, in order that one may care only for moderate possessions, and that hardship may be measured by the standard of one's needs.

286. He is fortunate who is happy with moderate means, unfortunate who is unhappy with great possessions.

.   .   .

289. It is unreasonableness not to submit to the necessary conditions of life.

290. Cast forth uncontrollable grief from your benumbed soul by means of reason.

291. To bear poverty well is the sign of a sensible man.

292. The hopes of the unintelligent are senseless.

293. Those to whom their neighbours' misfortunes give pleasure do not understand that the blows of fate are common to all; and also they lack cause for personal joy.

294. The good things of youth are strength and beauty, but the flower of age is moderation.

.   .   .

❧
THREE
SOPHISTS

PROTAGORAS

Protagoras, like Democritus, came from Abdera, on the Thracian coast. He was the first of those traveling teachers of philosophy and rhetoric who became known as "Sophists." Plato considered it his task to oppose these men, and since his dialogues survive while their writings do not, his highly polemical pictures of the Sophists have been widely but unreasonably accepted as fair and accurate portraits, and the very name "Sophist" has become an opprobrium. Yet one should no more accept Plato's image of the Sophists at face value than one should take the picture of the Pharisees in the Gospels for the gospel truth.

The Sophists are the great representatives of the Greek enlightenment. They come after the bold speculators and metaphysicians and ask what we can really know. Their thought is critical, not constructive; and their criticisms do not stop before all kinds of prejudices and traditions. Some of them question the hallowed distinction between Greeks and barbarians and that between masters and slaves: is not the supposition that barbarians and slaves are more similar to the animals than to the Greeks based on convention rather than on evidence? They do not only question prejudices of this sort—which Plato and Aristotle sought to revive—but all knowledge and all ethics: how much can be defended rationally, and how much is merely a matter of convention?

Questioning of that sort is inseparable from honesty, at least at a certain level of maturity. But the Sophists do not seem to have boasted of their honesty; on the contrary, their manner tended to be somewhat playful and occasionally somewhat cynical. They enjoyed debating, liked to construct skilful, craftsmanlike speeches, and offered to teach young men how to do likewise. For such instruction they accepted money, insisting quite reasonably that the skills they taught were likely to spell success, especially in politics.

This combination of qualities made it easy for Plato to picture the Sophists in the darkest colors. One as hostile to Plato as Plato was to the Sophists could easily portray him as a reactionary who sought some sanction in another world for convictions threatened by the Greek enlightenment. Plato makes skilful use of Socrates, contrasting his ironic modesty with the Sophists' pomp, his acid questioning with their big speeches, his concern with the moral fiber of a man with their admitted interest in success. Even if one agrees that Socrates was inimitably greater than any of the Sophists, this does not settle any of the crucial issues. After all, he was greater than almost any other man; he would have balked at the ideas which Plato in the dialogues put into his mouth quite as much as he had ever balked at any of the Sophists' views. The question of the limits of knowledge and the role played by convention, especially in ethics, cannot be answered by making capital of the less appealing traits of one or another Sophist.

In sum, the Sophists represent a milestone in the history of human thought. But exceedingly few fragments survive. The following selections concentrate on three representative figures.

Of Protagoras, born in Abdera about 480 B.C., an ancient story relates that he was at first a porter and that Democritus of Abdera saw him, admired his poise, and decided to instruct him; but this story is very doubtful. Protagoras reflected on language and developed a system of grammar. Having settled in Athens where he taught the youths, he won the respect of Pericles who commissioned him to frame laws for the new colony of Thurii, in Italy. At the age of seventy, he was accused and convicted of atheism and is said to have left for Sicily and to have drowned at sea.

Plato introduces him in one of his dialogues, which is named after Protagoras. Some of Protagoras' ideas about truth are also considered at some length in one of Plato's later dialogues, the *Theaetetus;* and the relevant sections are reprinted below under Plato. The fragments are given in Freeman's translations.

·   ·   ·

1. (*From 'Truth' or 'Refutatory Arguments'*). Of all things the measure is Man, of the things that are, that they are, and of the things that are not, that they are not.

2. (*From 'On Being'*).
(PORPHYRY: *'Few of the writings of Plato's predecessors have survived, otherwise Plato perhaps would have been detected in further plagiarisms. At any rate, in the place where I happened to have been reading in Protagoras' book "On Being" the argument he uses against those who make Being One, I find that he uses the same refutatory terms. For I took the trouble to memorise the passage word for word'*).
3. (*From a treatise entitled 'Great Logos'*). Teaching needs endowment and practice. Learning must begin in youth.
4. (*From 'On the Gods'*). About the gods, I am not able to know whether they exist or do not exist, nor what they are like in form; for the factors preventing knowledge are many: the obscurity of the subject, and the shortness of human life.

.   .   .

6b. To make the weaker cause the stronger.

.   .   .

9. When his sons, who were fine young men, died within eight days, he (Pericles) bore it without mourning. For he held on to his serenity, from which every day he derived great benefit in happiness, freedom from suffering, and honour in the people's eyes—for all who saw him bearing his griefs valiantly thought him great-souled and brave and superior to themselves, well knowing their own helplessness in such a calamity.
10. Art without practice, and practice without art, are nothing.
11. Education does not take root in the soul unless one goes deep.

GORGIAS

Next to Protagoras, Gorgias was probably the most renowned of all the Sophists. (Regarding the Sophists, see the preface to the selections from Protagoras.) Gorgias came from Leontini, in southern Sicily, a little to the east of Agrigentum. His dates are uncertain, but he is said to have died at the age of 108, possibly as late as 375 B.C. He first came to Athens on a mission from his countrymen, who had asked him to enlist Athenian help against Syracuse; in this he succeeded.

Like Protagoras, he is introduced as one of the two main figures (the other being Socrates) in one of Plato's dialogues, which is named after him. The following selections, all translated by Freeman, comprise the one philosophic fragment that has come down to us (as a long quotation in Sextus Empiricus), a sample speech (the encomium on Helen), and three very short bits that may help to round out the picture of Gorgias.

.   .   .

3. (SEXTUS, *from 'On Being' or 'On Nature'*):

I.   Nothing exists.
(*a*) Not-Being does not exist.
(*b*) Being does not exist.
    i.   as everlasting.
    ii. as created.
    iii. as both.
    iv. as One.
    v.   as Many.
(*c*) A mixture of Being and Not-Being does not exist.

II.   If anything exists, it is incomprehensible.

III. If it is comprehensible, it is incommunicable.

I.   Nothing exists.
If anything exists, it must be either Being or Not-Being, or both Being and Not-Being.

(*a*) It cannot be Not-Being, for Not-Being does not exist; if it did, it would be at the same time Being and Not-Being, which is impossible.

(*b*) It cannot be Being, for Being does not exist. If Being exists, it must be either everlasting, or created, or both.
i. It cannot be everlasting; if it were, it would have no beginning, and therefore would be boundless; if it is boundless, then it has no position, for if it had position it would be contained in something, and so it would no longer be boundless; for that which contains is greater than that which is contained, and nothing is greater than the boundless. It cannot be contained by itself, for then the thing containing and the thing contained would be the same, and Being would become two things—both position and body—which is absurd. Hence if Being is everlasting, it is boundless; if boundless, it has no position ('is nowhere'); if without position, it does not exist.
ii. Similarly, Being cannot be created; if it were, it must come from something, either Being or Not-Being, both of which are impossible.
iii. Similarly, Being cannot be both everlasting and created, since they are opposite. Therefore Being does not exist.
iv. Being cannot be one, because if it exists it has size, and is therefore infinitely divisible; at least it is threefold, having length, breadth and depth.
v. It cannot be many, because the many is made up of an addition of ones, so that since the one does not exist, the many do not exist either.

(*c*) A mixture of Being and Not-Being is impossible. Therefore since Being does not exist, nothing exists.

II.   If anything exists, it is incomprehensible.
If the concepts of the mind are not realities, reality cannot be

thought if the thing thought is white, then white is thought about; if the thing thought is non-existent, then non-existence is thought about; this is equivalent to saying that 'existence, reality, is not thought about, cannot be thought.' Many things thought about are not realities: we can conceive of a chariot running on the sea, or a winged man. Also, since things seen are the objects of sight, and things heard are the objects of hearing, and we accept as real things seen without their being heard, and vice versa; so we would have to accept things thought without their being seen or heard; but this would mean believing in things like the chariot racing on the sea.

Therefore reality is not the object of thought, and cannot be comprehended by it. Pure mind, as opposed to sense-perception, or even as an equally valid criterion, is a myth.

III. If anything is comprehensible, it is incommunicable.

The things which exist are perceptibles; the objects of sight are apprehended by sight, the objects of hearing by hearing, and there is no interchange; so that these sense-perceptions cannot communicate with one another. Further, that with which we communicate is speech, and speech is not the same thing as the things that exist, the perceptibles; so that we communicate not the things which exist, but only speech; just as that which is seen cannot become that which is heard, so our speech cannot be equated with that which exists, since it is outside us. Further, speech is composed from the percepts which we receive from without, that is, from perceptibles; so that it is not speech which communicates perceptibles, but perceptibles which create speech. Further, speech can never exactly represent perceptibles, since it is different from them, and perceptibles are apprehended each by the one kind of organ, speech by another. Hence, since the objects of sight cannot be presented to any other organ but sight, and the different sense-organs cannot give their information to one another, similarly speech cannot give any information about perceptibles.

Therefore, if anything exists and is comprehended, it is incommunicable.

11. (*'Encomium on Helen': summary*)

(1) The glory (*cosmos*) of a city is courage, of a body, beauty, of a soul, wisdom, of action, virtue, of speech, truth; it is right in all circumstances to praise what is praiseworthy and blame what is blameworthy.

(2) It belongs to the same man both to speak the truth and to refute falsehood. Helen is universally condemned and regarded as the symbol of disasters; I wish to subject her story to critical examination, and so rescue her from ignorant calumny.

(3) She was of the highest parentage: her reputed father Tyndareus was the most powerful of men; her real father, Zeus, was king of all.

(4) From these origins she obtained her divine beauty, by the display

of which she inspired love in countless men, and caused the assemblage of a great number of ambitious suitors, some endowed with wealth, others with ancestral fame, others with personal prowess, others with accumulated wisdom.

(5) I shall not relate the story of who won Helen or how: to tell an audience what it knows wins belief but gives no pleasure. I shall pass over this period and come to the beginning of my defence, setting out the probable reasons for her journey to Troy.

(6) She acted as she did either through Fate and the will of the gods and the decrees of Necessity, or because she was seized by force, or won over by persuasion (*or captivated by love*). If the first, it is her accuser who deserves blame; for no human foresight can hinder the will of God: the stronger cannot be hindered by the weaker, and God is stronger than man in every way. Therefore if the cause was Fate, Helen cannot be blamed.

(7) If she was carried off by force, clearly her abductor wronged her and she was unfortunate. He, a barbarian, committed an act of barbarism, and should receive blame, disgrace and punishment; she, being robbed of her country and friends, deserves pity rather than obloquy.

(8) If it was speech that persuaded her and deceived her soul, her defence remains easy. Speech is a great power, which achieves the most divine works by means of the smallest and least visible form; for it can even put a stop to fear, remove grief, create joy, and increase pity. This I shall now prove:

(9) All poetry can be called speech in metre. Its hearers shudder with terror, shed tears of pity, and yearn with sad longing; the soul, affected by the words, feels as its own an emotion aroused by the good and ill fortunes of other people's actions and lives.

(10) The inspired incantations of words can induce pleasure and avert grief; for the power of the incantations, uniting with the feeling in the soul, soothes and persuades and transports by means of its wizardry. Two types of wizardry and magic have been invented, which are errors in the soul and deceptions in the mind.

(11) Their persuasions by means of fictions are innumerable; for if everyone had recollection of the past, knowledge of the present, and foreknowledge of the future, the power of speech would not be so great. But as it is, when men can neither remember the past nor observe the present nor prophesy the future, deception is easy; so that most men offer opinion as advice to the soul. But opinion, being unreliable, involves those who accept it in equally uncertain fortunes.

(12) (*Text corrupt*) Thus, persuasion by speech is equivalent to abduction by force, as she was compelled to agree to what was said, and consent to what was done. It was therefore the persuader, not Helen, who did wrong and should be blamed.

(13) That persuasion, when added to speech, can also make any impression it wishes on the soul, can be shown, firstly, from the arguments of the meteorologists, who by removing one opinion and implanting an-

other, cause what is incredible and invisible to appear before the eyes of the mind; secondly, from legal contests, in which a speech can sway and persuade a crowd, by the skill of its composition, not by the truth of its statements; thirdly, from the philosophical debates, in which quickness of thought is shown easily altering opinion.

(14) The power of speech over the constitution of the soul can be compared with the effect of drugs on the bodily state: just as drugs by driving out different humours from the body can put an end either to the disease or to life, so with speech: different words can induce grief, pleasure or fear; or again, by means of a harmful kind of persuasion, words can drug and bewitch the soul.

(15) If Helen was persuaded by love, defence is equally easy. What we see has its own nature, not chosen by us; and the soul is impressed through sight.

(16) For instance, in war, the sight of enemy forms wearing hostile array is so disturbing to the soul that often men flee in terror as if the coming danger were already present. The powerful habit induced by custom is displaced by the fear aroused by sight, which causes oblivion of what custom judges honourable and of the advantage derived from victory.

(17) People who have seen a frightful sight have been driven out of their minds, so great is the power of fear; while many have fallen victims to useless toils, dreadful diseases and incurable insanity, so vivid are the images of the things seen which vision engraves on the mind.

(18) Painters, however, when they create one shape from many colours, give pleasure to sight; and the pleasure afforded by sculpture to the eyes is divine; many objects engender in many people a love of many actions and forms.

(19) If therefore Helen's eye, delighted with Paris's form, engendered the passion of love in her soul, this is not remarkable; for if a god is at work with divine power, how can the weaker person resist him? And if the disease is human, due to the soul's ignorance, it must not be condemned as a crime but pitied as a misfortune, for it came about through the snares of Fate, not the choice of the will; by the compulsion of love, not by the plottings of art.

(20) Therefore, whichever of the four reasons caused Helen's action, she is innocent.

(21) I have expunged by my discourse this woman's ill fame, and have fulfilled the object set forth at the outset. I have tried to destroy the unjust blame and the ignorant opinion, and have chosen to write this speech as an Encomium on Helen and an amusement for myself.

· · ·

15. Beggarly toadying bards, who swear a false oath and swear it well.

· · ·

23. Tragedy, by means of legends and emotions, creates a deception in which the deceiver is more honest than the non-deceiver, and the deceived is wiser than the non-deceived.

.   .   .

26. Being is unrecognisable unless it succeeds in seeming, and seeming is weak unless it succeeds in being.

.   .   .

ANTIPHON

Of the many ancient Greeks who bore this name, at least three were put to death. One, a poet of Attica who wrote tragedies, epics, and speeches, defied Dionysius the tyrant, answering the question, what brass is best, by saying, "that of which the statues of Harmodius and Aristogiton are made," they being the men who in 510 B.C. had delivered Athens from tyranny; and when this Antiphon also refused to praise the compositions of Dionysius, the tyrant had him executed. Another Antiphon, an orator, promised Philip of Macedonia, the father of Alexander the Great, that he would set fire to the citadel of Athens; for this promise he was put to death at the instigation of Demosthenes.

A third Antiphon, born at Rhamnus in Attica about 480 B.C., was one of the great orators of the 5th Century. During the Peloponnesian War, he helped set up the oligarchy of the 400 in 411 B.C., and was condemned to death after the restoration of the democracy. Thucydides calls him "a man inferior in virtue to none of his contemporaries, and possessed of remarkable powers of thought and gifts of speech. He did not like to come forward in the assembly, or in any other public arena. To the multitude, who were suspicious of his great abilities, he was an object of dislike; but there was no man who could do more for any who consulted him, whether their business lay in the courts of justice or in the assembly. And when the government of the Four Hundred was overthrown and became exposed to the vengeance of the people, and he being accused of taking part in the plot had to speak in his own case, his defense was undoubtedly the best ever made by any man on a capital charge down to my time" (VIII. 68; Jowett's translation).

Most writers distinguish between Antiphon, the orator and Antiphon, the Sophist, but it is by no means certain that the two were not identical. (Detailed arguments for identifying them may be found in Karl Joel's *Geschichte der antiken Philosophie*, 1921, p. 663, and

A. E. Taylor leans the same way in his standard work on Plato, p. 102 of the Meridian paperback ed.) Among those who distinguish the orator and the Sophist, Karl Popper in *The Open Society and Its Enemies* (Princeton University Press) and R. B. Levinson in *In Defense of Plato* (Harvard University Press) arrive at opposite evaluations of Antiphon the Sophist: Popper sings his praises as a deeply humane thinker, while Levinson condemns him roundly as an enemy of civilization. It is generally admitted that at least some of his ideas are reencountered in, and presumably greatly influenced, first the Cynic school of philosophy and later the Stoics. Some of the material cited below was discovered only in the 20th Century, on Egyptian papyri. The translations are Freeman's. (For the Sophists generally, see the preface to the selections from Protagoras.)

. . .

10. (*From 'Truth'*): Hence he (*God*) needs nothing and receives no addition from anywhere, but is infinite and lacking nothing.

. . .

(*Oxyrhynchus papyrus. From 'Truth'*)
44. Justice, then, is not to transgress that which is the law of the city in which one is a citizen. A man therefore can best conduct himself in harmony with justice, if when in the company of witnesses he upholds the laws, and when alone without witnesses he upholds the edicts of nature. For the edicts of the laws are imposed artificially, but those of nature are compulsory. And the edicts of the laws are arrived at by consent, not by natural growth, whereas those of nature are not a matter of consent.

So, if the man who transgresses the legal code evades those who have agreed to these edicts, he avoids both disgrace and penalty; otherwise not. But if a man violates against possibility any of the laws which are implanted in nature, even if he evades all men's detection, the ill is no less, and even if all see, it is no greater. For he is not hurt on account of an opinion, but because of truth. The examination of these things is in general for this reason, that the majority of just acts according to law are prescribed contrary to nature. For there is legislation about the eyes, what they must see and what not; and about the ears, what they must hear and what not; and about the tongue, what it must speak and what not; and about the hands, what they must do and what not; and about the feet, where they must go and where not. Now the law's prohibitions are in no way more agreeable to nature and more akin than the law's injunctions. But life belongs to nature, and death too, and life for them is derived from advantages, and death from disadvantages. And the advantages laid down by the laws are chains upon nature, but those laid down by nature are free. So that the things which hurt, according to true reasoning, do not benefit nature more than those which delight; and things which grieve are not more advantageous than those which please;

for things truly advantageous must not really harm, but must benefit. The naturally advantageous things from among these ...

(*According to law, they are justified*) who having suffered defend themselves and do not themselves begin action; and those who treat their parents well, even though their parents have treated them badly; and those who give the taking of an oath to others and do not themselves swear. Of these provisions, one could find many which are hostile to nature; and there is in them the possibility of suffering more when one could suffer less; and enjoying less when one could enjoy more; and faring ill when one need not. Now if the person who adapted himself to these provisions received support from the laws, and those who did not, but who opposed them, received damage, obedience to the laws would not be without benefit; but as things are, it is obvious that for those who adapt themselves to these things the justice proceeding from law is not strong enough to help, seeing that first of all it allows him who suffers to suffer, and him who does, to do, and does not prevent the sufferer from suffering or the doer from doing. And if the case is brought up for punishment, there is no advantage peculiar to the sufferer rather than to the doer. For the sufferer must convince those who are to inflict the punishment, that he has suffered; and he needs the ability to win his case. And it is open to the doer to deny, by the same means ... and he can defend himself no less than the accuser can accuse, and persuasion is open to both parties, being a matter of technique. ...

We revere and honour those born of noble fathers, but those who are not born of noble houses we neither revere nor honour. In this we are, in our relations with one another, like barbarians, since we are all by nature born the same in every way, both barbarians and Hellenes. And it is open to all men to observe the laws of nature, which are compulsory. Similarly all of these things can be acquired by all, and in none of these things is any of us distinguished as barbarian or Hellene. We all breathe into the air through mouth and nostrils, and we all eat with hands. ...

.   .   .

49. Now let life proceed, and let him desire marriage and a wife. This day, this night begin a new destiny; for marriage is a great contest for mankind. If the woman turns out to be incompatible, what can one do about the disaster? Divorce is difficult: it means to make enemies of friends, who have the same thoughts, the same breath, and had been valued and had regarded one with esteem. And it is hard if one gets such a possession, that is, if when thinking to get pleasure, one brings home pain.

However, not to speak of malevolence: let us assume the utmost compatibility. What is pleasanter to a man than a wife after his own heart? What is sweeter, especially to a young man? But in the very pleasure lies near at hand the pain; pleasures do not come alone, but are attended by griefs and troubles. Olympic and Pythian victories and all pleasures are apt to be won by great pains. Honours, prizes, delights, which God has given to men, depend necessarily on great toils and exertions. For my part, if I had another body which was as much trouble to me as I am to myself, I could not live, so great is the trouble I give myself for the sake of health, the acquisition of a livelihood, and for fame, respectability, glory and a good reputation. What then, if I acquired another body which was as much trouble? Is it not clear that a wife, if she is to his mind, gives her husband no less cause for love and pain than he does to himself, for the health of two bodies, the acquisition of two livelihoods, and for respectability and honour? Suppose children are born: then all is full of anxiety, and the youthful spring goes out of the mind, and the countenance is no longer the same.

.   .   .

51. The whole of life is wonderfully open to complaint, my friend; it has nothing remarkable, great or noble, but all is petty, feeble, brief-lasting, and mingled with sorrows.

.   .   .

53a. There are some who do not live the present life, but prepare with great diligence as if they were going to live another life, not the present one. Meanwhile time, being neglected, deserts them.

54. There is a story that a man seeing another man earning much money begged him to lend him a sum at interest. The other refused; and being of a mistrustful nature, unwilling to help anyone, he carried it off and hid it somewhere. Another man, observing him, filched it. Later, the man who had hidden it returning, could not find it; and being very grieved at the disaster—especially that he had not lent to the man who had asked him, because then it would have been safe and would have earned increment—he went to see the man who had asked for a loan, and bewailed his misfortune, saying that he had done wrong and was sorry not to have granted his request but to have refused it, as his money was completely lost. The other man told him to hide a stone in the same place, and think of his money as his and not lost: 'For even when you had it you completely failed to use it; so that now too you can think you have lost nothing.' For when a person has not used and will not use anything, it makes no difference to him either whether he has it or not. For when God does not wish to give a man complete good fortune—when he has given him material wealth but made him poor in right thinking—in taking away one he has deprived him of both.

.   .   .

56. He is cowardly who is bold in speech concerning absent and future dangers, and hurries on in resolve, but shrinks back when the fact is upon him.

.   .   .

58. Whoever, when going against his neighbour with the intention of harming him, is afraid lest by failing to achieve his wishes he may get what he does not wish, is wiser. For his fear means hesitation, and his hesitation means an interval in which often his mind is deflected from his purpose. There can be no reversal of a thing that has happened: it is possible only for what is in the future not to happen. Whoever thinks he will illtreat his neighbours and not suffer himself is unwise. Hopes are not altogether a good thing; such hopes have flung down many into intolerable disaster, and what they thought to inflict on their neighbours, they have suffered themselves for all to see. Prudence in another man can be judged correctly by no one more than him who fortifies his soul against immediate pleasures and can conquer himself. But whoever wishes to gratify his soul immediately, wishes the worse instead of the better.

59. Whoever has not desired or touched the base and the bad, is not self-restrained; for there is nothing over which he has gained the mastery and proved himself well-behaved.

60. The first thing, I believe, for mankind is education. For whenever anyone does the beginning of anything correctly, it is likely that the end also will be right. As one sows, so can one expect to reap. And if in a young body one sows a noble education, this lives and flourishes through the whole of his life, and neither rain nor drought destroys it.

· · ·

62. One's character must necessarily grow like that with which one spends the greater part of the day.

· · ·

PERICLES (AS REPORTED BY THUCYDIDES)

Neither Pericles, the great statesman, who succumbed to the pestilence that struck Athens in 429 B.C., nor Thucydides, the great historian, who died about thirty years later was a philosopher. The plain fact that they were among the greatest minds produced by the 5th Century would not ensure their inclusion here; else, Aeschylus, Sophocles, and Euripides would have to be introduced, too. For a number of reasons, however, it is eminently worthwhile to bring in at this point the great speech which Pericles delivered in 431 B.C. at the funeral of those who had been killed in the war.

First, it is important to recall that the Greek philosophers did not think and write in ivory towers, but as men deeply involved in the public and cultural life of their day. Therefore it is desirable, if only it were possible, to bring to life, in a few pages, 5th Century Athens. That is precisely what Pericles succeeded in doing inimitably in his funeral speech.

Then one also wants something to which one might compare the *Apology* of Socrates, as reported by Plato; and one wonders about Alcibiades' remark, near the end of the *Symposium,* that even Pericles' speeches had not moved him the way Socrates' did, making him angry at the thought of his own slavish state. There are other references to Pericles both in the preceding pages and in the selections that follow. Moreover—and this is decisive—this speech, unlike anything in the great tragedies of the 5th Century, is a self-contained unit that does not suffer too greatly from being read out of context. Some of Sophocles' great choruses, on the other hand, are seen to be pregnant with irony when they are considered in relation to the action of the plays.

Finally, it is often said that Plato's critique of democracy, especially in Book VIII of the *Republic,* was entirely fitting in relation to Athenian democracy though, of course, not applicable to modern democracy. This is not the place to discuss the second point, but it is interesting to read the classical defense of Athenian democracy at its best, while keeping in mind that the democracy that put Socrates to death, 30 years after Pericles had died, was emphatically not democracy at its best, but rather an early and hideous example of what sometimes happens in democracies, especially after great wars. In this context, the first selection about Anaxagoras should be reread; also the end of the preface to the selections from Protagoras.

The first of our three selections from Thucydides' history of the Peloponnesian War comprises I. 22; the second runs from II. 34 through II. 46; the last comes from II. 65. All are offered in Benjamin Jowett's magnificent translation.

· · ·

22. As to the speeches which were made either before or during the war, it was hard for me, and for others who reported them to me, to recollect the exact words. I have therefore put into the mouth of each speaker the sentiments proper to the occasion, expressed as I thought he would be likely to express them, while at the same time I endeavored, as nearly as I could, to give the general purport of what was actually said. Of the events of the war I have not ventured to speak from any chance information, nor according to any notion of my own; I have described nothing but what I either saw myself, or learned from others of whom I made the most careful and particular inquiry. The task was a laborious one, because eye-witnesses of the same occurrences gave different accounts of them, as they remembered or were interested in the actions of one side or the other. And very likely the strictly historical character of my narrative may be disappointing to the ear. But if he who desires to have before his eyes a true picture of the events which have happened, and of the like events which may be expected to happen hereafter in the order of human

things, shall pronounce what I have written to be useful, then I shall be satisfied. My history is an everlasting possession, not a prize composition which is heard and forgotten.

. . .

When the remains have been laid in the earth, some man of known ability and high reputation, chosen by the city, delivers a suitable oration over them; after which the people depart. Such is the manner of interment; and the ceremony was repeated from time to time throughout the war. Over those who were the first buried Pericles was chosen to speak. At the fitting moment he advanced from the sepulchre to a lofty stage, which had been erected in order that he might be heard as far as possible by the multitude, and spoke as follows:—

[FUNERAL ORATION]

35. "Most of those who have spoken here before me have commended the lawgiver who added this oration to our other funeral customs; it seemed to them a worthy thing that such an honor should be given at their burial to the dead who have fallen on the field of battle. But I should have preferred that, when men's deeds have been brave, they should be honored in deed only, and with such an honor as this public funeral, which you are now witnessing. Then the reputation of many would not have been imperilled on the eloquence or want of eloquence of one, and their virtues believed or not as he spoke well or ill. For it is difficult to say neither too little nor too much; and even moderation is apt not to give the impression of truthfulness. The friend of the dead who knows the facts is likely to think that the words of the speaker fall short of his knowledge and of his wishes; another who is not so well informed, when he hears of anything which surpasses his own powers, will be envious and will suspect exaggeration. Mankind are tolerant of the praises of others so long as each hearer thinks that he can do as well or nearly as well himself, but, when the speaker rises above him, jealousy is aroused and he begins to be incredulous. However, since our ancestors have set the seal of their approval upon the practice, I must obey, and to the utmost of my power shall endeavor to satisfy the wishes and beliefs of all who hear me.

36. "I will speak first of our ancestors, for it is right and becoming that now, when we are lamenting the dead, a tribute should be paid to their memory. There has never been a time when they did not inhabit this land, which by their valor they have handed down from generation to generation, and we have received from them a free state. But if they were worthy of praise, still more were our fathers, who added to their inheritance, and after many a struggle transmitted to us their sons this great empire. And we ourselves assembled here to-day, who are still most of us in the vigor of life, have chiefly done the work of improvement, and have richly endowed our city with all things, so that she is sufficient for

herself both in peace and war. Of the military exploits by which our various possessions were acquired, or of the energy with which we or our fathers drove back the tide of war, Hellenic or Barbarian, I will not speak; for the tale would be long and is familiar to you. But before I praise the dead, I should like to point out by what principles of action we rose to power, and under what institutions and through what manner of life our empire became great. For I conceive that such thoughts are not unsuited to the occasion, and that this numerous assembly of citizens and strangers may profitably listen to them.

37. "Our form of government does not enter into rivalry with the institutions of others. We do not copy our neighbors, but are an example to them. It is true that we are called a democracy, for the administration is in the hands of the many and not of the few. But while the law secures equal justice to all alike in their private disputes, the claim of excellence is also recognized; and when a citizen is in any way distinguished, he is preferred to the public service, not as a matter of privilege, but as the reward of merit. Neither is poverty a bar, but a man may benefit his country whatever be the obscurity of his condition. There is no exclusiveness in our public life, and in our private intercourse we are not suspicious of one another, nor angry with our neighbor if he does what he likes; we do not put on sour looks at him which, though harmless, are not pleasant. While we are thus unconstrained in our private intercourse, a spirit of reverence pervades our public acts; we are prevented from doing wrong by respect for authority and for the laws, having an especial regard to those which are ordained for the protection of the injured as well as to those unwritten laws which bring upon the transgressor of them the reprobation of the general sentiment.

38. "And we have not forgotten to provide for our weary spirits many relaxations from toil; we have regular games and sacrifices throughout the year; at home the style of our life is refined; and the delight which we daily feel in all these things helps to banish melancholy. Because of the greatness of our city the fruits of the whole earth flow in upon us; so that we enjoy the goods of other countries as freely as of our own.

39. "Then, again, our military training is in many respects superior to that of our adversaries. Our city is thrown open to the world, and we never expel a foreigner or prevent him from seeing or learning anything of which the secret if revealed to an enemy might profit him. We rely not upon management or trickery, but upon our own hearts and hands. And in the matter of education, whereas they from early youth are always undergoing laborious exercises which are to make them brave, we live at ease, and yet are equally ready to face the perils which they face. And here is the proof. The Lacedaemonians come into Attica not by themselves, but with their whole confederacy following; we go alone into a neighbor's country; and although our opponents are fighting for their homes and we on a foreign soil, we have seldom any difficulty in overcoming them. Our enemies have never yet felt our united strength; the care of a navy divides our attention, and on land we are obliged to send

our own citizens everywhere. But they, if they meet and defeat a part of our army, are as proud as if they had routed us all, and when defeated they pretend to have been vanquished by us all.

"If then we prefer to meet danger with a light heart but without laborious training, and with a courage which is gained by habit and not enforced by law, are we not greatly the gainers? Since we do not anticipate the pain, although, when the hour comes, we can be as brave as those who never allow themselves to rest; and thus too our city is   [40] equally admirable in peace and in war. For we are lovers of the beautiful, yet simple in our tastes, and we cultivate the mind without loss of manliness. Wealth we employ, not for talk and ostentation, but when there is a real use for it. To avow poverty with us is no disgrace: the true disgrace is in doing nothing to avoid it. An Athenian citizen does not neglect the state because he takes care of his own household; and even those of us who are engaged in business have a very fair idea of politics. We alone regard a man who takes no interest in public affairs, not as a harmless, but as a useless character; and if few of us are originators, we are all sound judges of a policy. The great impediment to action is, in our opinion, not discussion, but the want of that knowledge which is gained by discussion preparatory to action. For we have a peculiar power of thinking before we act and of acting too, whereas other men are courageous from ignorance but hesitate upon reflection. And they are surely to be esteemed the bravest spirits who, having the clearest sense both of the pains and pleasures of life, do not on that account shrink from danger. In doing good, again, we are unlike others; we make our friends by conferring, not by receiving favors. Now he who confers a favor is the firmer friend, because he would fain by kindness keep alive the memory of an obligation; but the recipient is colder in his feelings, because he knows that in requiting another's generosity he will not be winning gratitude, but only paying a debt. We alone do good to our neighbors not upon a calculation of interest, but in the confidence of freedom and in a frank and fearless spirit. To sum up: I say that Athens is the school of Hellas, and that   [41] the individual Athenian in his own person seems to have the power of adapting himself to the most varied forms of action with the utmost versatility and grace. This is no passing and idle word, but truth and fact; and the assertion is verified by the position to which these qualities have raised the state. For in the hour of trial Athens alone among her contemporaries is superior to the report of her. No enemy who comes against her is indignant at the reverses which he sustains at the hands of such a city; no subject complains that his masters are unworthy of him. And we shall assuredly not be without witnesses; there are mighty monuments of our power which will make us the wonder of this and of succeeding ages; we shall not need the praises of Homer or of any other panegyrist whose poetry may please for the moment, although his representation of the facts will not bear the light of day. For we have compelled every land and every sea to open a path for our valor, and have everywhere planted eternal memorials of our friendship and of our enmity. Such is the city for whose sake these men nobly fought and died; they could not bear the thought that she might be taken from them; and every one of us who survive should gladly toil on her behalf.

42. "I have dwelt upon the greatness of Athens because I want to show you that we are contending for a higher prize than those who enjoy none of these privileges, and to establish by manifest proof the merit of these men whom I am now commemorating. Their loftiest praise has been already spoken. For in magnifying the city I have magnified them, and men like them whose virtues made her glorious. And of how few Hellenes can it be said as of them, that their deeds when weighed in the balance have been found equal to their fame! Methinks that a death such as theirs has been gives the true measure of a man's worth; it may be the first revelation of his virtues, but is at any rate their final seal. For even those who come short in other ways may justly plead the valor with which they have fought for their country; they have blotted out the evil with the good, and have benefited the state more by their public services than they have injured her by their private actions. None of these men were enervated by wealth or hesitated to resign the pleasures of life; none of them put off the evil day in the hope, natural to poverty, that a man, though poor, may one day become rich. But, deeming that the punishment of their enemies was sweeter than any of these things, and that they could fall in no nobler cause, they determined at the hazard of their lives to be honorably avenged, and to leave the rest. They resigned to hope their unknown chance of happiness; but in the face of death they resolved to rely upon themselves alone. And when the moment came they were minded to resist and suffer, rather than to fly and save their lives; they ran away from the word of dishonor, but on the battle-field their feet stood fast, and in an instant, at the height of their fortune, they passed away from the scene, not of their fear, but of their glory.

43. "Such was the end of these men; they were worthy of Athens, and the living need not desire to have a more heroic spirit, although they may pray for a less fatal issue. The value of such a spirit is not to be expressed in words. Any one can discourse to you for ever about the advantages of a brave defence which you know already. But instead of listening to him I would have you day by day fix your eyes upon the greatness of Athens, until you become filled with the love of her; and when you are impressed by the spectacle of her glory, reflect that this empire has been acquired by men who knew their duty and had the courage to do it, who in the hour of conflict had the fear of dishonor always present to them, and who, if ever they failed in an enterprise, would not allow their virtues to be lost to their country, but freely gave their lives to her as the fairest offering which they could present at her feast. The sacrifice which they collectively made was individually repaid to them; for they received again each one for himself a praise which grows not old, and the noblest of all sepulchres —I speak not of that in which their remains are laid, but of that in which their glory survives, and is proclaimed always and on every fitting occasion both in word and deed. For the whole earth is the sepulchre of

famous men; not only are they commemorated by columns and inscriptions in their own country, but in foreign lands there dwells also an unwritten memorial of them, graven not on stone but in the hearts of men. Make them your examples, and, esteeming courage to be freedom and freedom to be happiness, do not weigh too nicely the perils of war. The unfortunate who has no hope of a change for the better has less reason to throw away his life than the prosperous who, if he survive, is always liable to a change for the worse, and to whom any accidental fall makes the most serious difference. To a man of spirit, cowardice and disaster coming together are far more bitter than death, striking him unperceived at a time when he is full of courage and animated by the general hope. 44. "Wherefore I do not now commiserate the parents of the dead who stand here; I would rather comfort them. You know that your life has been passed amid manifold vicissitudes; and that they may be deemed fortunate who have gained most honor, whether an honorable death like theirs, or an honorable sorrow like yours, and whose days have been so ordered that the term of their happiness is likewise the term of their life. I know how hard it is to make you feel this, when the good fortune of others will too often remind you of the gladness which once lightened your hearts. And sorrow is felt at the want of those blessings, not which a man never knew, but which were a part of his life before they were taken from him. Some of you are of an age at which they may hope to have other children, and they ought to bear their sorrow better; not only will the children who may hereafter be born make them forget their own lost ones, but the city will be doubly a gainer. She will not be left desolate, and she will be safer. For a man's counsel cannot have equal weight or worth, when he alone has no children to risk in the general danger. To those of you who have passed their prime, I say; 'Congratulate yourselves that you have been happy during the greater part of your days; remember that your life of sorrow will not last long, and be comforted by the glory of those who are gone. For the love of honor alone is ever young, and not riches, as some say, but honor is the delight of men when they are old and useless.'

45. "To you who are the sons and brothers of the departed, I see that the struggle to emulate them will be an arduous one. For all men praise the dead, and, however pre-eminent your virtue may be, hardly will you be thought, I do not say to equal, but even to approach them. The living have their rivals and detractors, but when a man is out of the way, the honor and good-will which he receives is unalloyed. And, if I am to speak of womanly virtues to those of you who will henceforth be widows, let me sum them up in one short admonition: To a woman not to show more weakness than is natural to her sex is a great glory, and not to be talked about for good or for evil among men.

46. "I have paid the required tribute, in obedience to the law, making use of such fitting words as I had. The tribute of deeds has been paid in part; for the dead have been honorably interred, and it remains only that their children should be maintained at the public charge until

they are grown up; this is the solid prize with which, as with a garland, Athens crowns her sons living and dead, after a struggle like theirs. For where the rewards of virtue are greatest, there the noblest citizens are enlisted in the service of the state. And now, when you have duly lamented, every one his own dead, you may depart."

.   .   .

In private they felt their sufferings keenly; the common people had been deprived even of the little which they possessed, while the upper class had lost fair estates in the country with all their houses and rich furniture. Worst of all, instead of enjoying peace, they were now at war. The popular indignation was not pacified until they had fined Pericles; but, soon afterwards, with the usual fickleness of the multitude, they elected him general and committed all their affairs to his charge. Their private sorrows were beginning to be less acutely felt, and for a time of public need they thought that there was no man like him. During the peace while he was at the head of affairs he ruled with prudence; under his guidance Athens was safe, and reached the height of her greatness in his time. When the war began he showed that here too he had formed a true estimate of the Athenian power. He survived the commencement of hostilities two years and six months; and, after his death, his foresight was even better appreciated than during his life. For he had told the Athenians, that if they would be patient and would attend to their navy, and not seek to enlarge their dominion while the war was going on, nor imperil the existence of the city, they would be victorious; but they did all that he told them not to do, and in matters which seemingly had nothing to do with the war, from motives of private ambition and private interest they adopted a policy which had disastrous effects in respect both of themselves and of their allies; their measures, had they been successful, would only have brought honor and profit to individuals, and, when unsuccessful, crippled the city in the conduct of the war. The reason of the difference was that he, deriving authority from his capacity and acknowledged worth, being also a man of transparent integrity, was able to control the multitude in a free spirit; he led them rather than was led by them; for, not seeking power by dishonest arts, he had no need to say pleasant things, but, on the strength of his own high character, could venture to oppose and even to anger them. When he saw them unseasonably elated and arrogant, his words humbled and awed them; and, when they were depressed by groundless fears, he sought to reanimate their confidence. Thus Athens, though still in name a democracy, was in fact ruled by her greatest citizen. But his successors were more on an equality with one another, and, each one struggling to be first himself, they were ready to sacrifice the whole conduct of affairs to the whims of the people. Such weakness in a great and imperial city led to many errors, of which the greatest was the Sicilian expedition; not that the Athenians miscalculated their enemy's power, but they themselves, instead of consulting for the interests of the expedition which they had sent out, were occupied in intriguing against one another for the leadership of the democracy, and not only grew remiss in the management of the army, but became embroiled, for the first time, in civil strife. And yet after they had lost in the Sicilian expedition the greater part of their fleet and army, and were distracted by revolution at home, still they held out three years not only against their former enemies, but against the Sicilians who had combined with them, and against most of their own allies who had risen in revolt. Even when Cyrus the son of the King joined in the war and supplied the Peloponnesian fleet with money, they continued to resist, and were at last overthrown, not by their enemies, but by themselves and their own internal dissensions. So that at the time Pericles was more than justified in the conviction at which his foresight had arrived, that the Athenians would win an easy victory over the unaided forces of the Peloponnesians.

PART TWO

SOCRATES AND PLATO

I

Socrates is widely considered one of the greatest human beings of all time—largely on the basis of some of the texts that follow. He is known to us mainly through the works of Plato, his pupil; but we have some other sources of information about him, too.

Aristophanes (455-375 B.C.) made fun of Socrates in one of his comedies, *The Clouds*. First performed in 423, it received only the third prize, which is said to have galled the poet, who considered the play one of his best. He subsequently undertook, but did not complete, a revision. It is the revised version, never performed in the poet's lifetime, that has survived.

Xenophon, the general, known to elementary students of Greek as the author of *Anabasis,* recorded his memories of Socrates, his friend and master, in *Memorabilia,* in an *Apology of Socrates,* and in a *Symposium.* He wrote these works after the death of Socrates in an effort to defend him, and it is a commonplace that his Socrates is more innocuous and less exciting than Plato's.

Aristotle, Plato's great pupil, who was born 15 years after the death of Socrates, makes many interesting statements about Socrates in his philosophic works, and there is no reason to believe that he relied solely on Plato's testimony.

Socrates was the son of Sophroniscus, a sculptor, and Phaenarete, a midwife. He is said to have done some sculpting in his youth and to have fashioned some impressively simple and elegant statues of the Graces. About his adult life and his death nothing could be said that has not been said better in the *Apology*, in the closing pages of the *Phaedo*, and in Alcibiades' great speech about him at the end of the *Symposium*. It is above all in these three works that Plato has borne witness of the man who first taught him philosophy. If Plato had never written anything else, his place would still be secure as one of the world's greatest writers; and if we knew nothing else about Socrates, his place, too, would be assured.

Plato's *Apology* is generally held to be eminently faithful to what Socrates actually said when tried in 399 B.C., at the age of 70, on charges of impiety and corruption of the youth. The speech was delivered in public and heard by a large audience; Plato has Socrates mention that Plato was present; and there is no need to doubt the historical veracity of the speech, at least in essentials.

In the *Crito*, not reprinted here, Plato has Crito visit Socrates in prison to assure him that his escape from Athens has been well prepared and to persuade him to consent to leave. That Socrates, in fact, refused to leave is certain; whether he used the arguments Plato ascribes to him is much less certain. In any case, anyone who has read the *Apology* will agree that, after delivering that speech, Socrates could not very well have escaped.

The *Meno* is one of several early Platonic dialogues that gives, at least in a general way, a very fine and faithful picture of the manner in which Socrates liked to practice the art of dialogue. The work has the added advantage of being both very brief and philosophically interesting.

That the account of Socrates' death at the very end of the *Phaedo* is historically accurate is a matter of common agreement. It is almost as widely agreed that in the preceding conversation Plato has put his own views into the mouth of Socrates—views significantly different from those held by the real Socrates. A generation or more ago, John Burnet and A. E. Taylor, two scholars of repute, argued that the real Socrates did hold the views which Plato here ascribes to him. However, by the middle of the 20th Century, there was a virtual unanimity among scholars that the views which the historic Socrates held about life after death are correctly represented at the end of the *Apology*, while the arguments for immortality which Plato introduces in the *Phaedo* owe a great deal to Pythagoreanism, which exerted an increasingly deep influence on Plato's thought. (See the preface to the Pythagorean selections, above.)

The *Symposium* certainly makes no claim to historic accuracy, except for the contents of Alcibiades' speech on Socrates: what is there said is, no doubt, true. As for the rest, we need not believe that Aristophanes, the comic poet, really told the moving myth ascribed to him, or that the others ever said what Plato makes them say. The *Symposium* is not history but a work of art, and it shows us Plato's literary powers at their peak. Even those not interested in philosophy can read and reread and enjoy it; and chances are that it may lead at least some to develop a strong feeling for, if not to fall in love with, philosophy. This dialogue represents the most perfect blend ever achieved of philosophy and poetry.

Only one other dialogue comes close to it in this respect, the *Phaedrus*. It, too, is reprinted without omission. One or another professional philosopher may wonder why two dialogues that deal with love had to be included. In the first place, a volume of this sort is not intended primarily for professional philosophers, but rather for those seeking an approach to philosophy; and from that point of view the *Apology, Meno, Symposium*, and *Phaedrus*, all of which are offered complete, can hardly be rivalled. Secondly, both the *Symposium* and the *Phaedrus* involve a great deal besides love, and are of the utmost philosophic interest. Finally, these dialogues help to balance the selections from the later Plato, which are rather difficult and possibly discouraging for many a beginner.

II

Plato was probably born in 428/7 B.C. He had two older brothers, Adimantus and Glaucon, who appear in Plato's *Republic*, and a sister, Potone. Plato was still a child when his father, Ariston, died, and his mother, Perictione remarried—her uncle, Pyrilampes, who is said to have been a close friend of Pericles. From a previous marriage, Plato's stepfather had a son, Demus, famous for his good looks; and from the second marriage, to Plato's mother, another boy was born, Antiphon, who appears in Plato's *Parmenides*.

Plato's mother had a brother, Charmides, and a cousin, Critias, who were prominent in politics in the days of the oligarchy that ruled Athens at the end of the Peloponnesian War. One of Plato's early dialogues bears the name of *Charmides*, and from this dialogue it appears that Charmides knew Socrates quite well even before Plato was born. It is therefore possible that Plato knew Socrates from his childhood. But Plato may well have been close to twenty when he first came under the spell of Socrates and, as an ancient story has it, tore up the poetry he had written hitherto and resolved to devote his life to philosophy. Certainly, the death of Socrates made an enormous impression on Plato, who appears to have felt the call to bear witness for posterity of "the finest man"—to cite Plato's *Phaedo*— "of all whom we came to know in his generation; the wisest too, and the most righteous." Plato's early dialogues are as wonderful a monument as any man ever constructed for his teacher.

It was the restored democracy that put to death Socrates, and animosity against Socrates had certainly been nourished by his friendship with some of the oligarchs. Still, there is no need to suppose that this was the "real" reason, and that the charge of impiety and the corruption of the youth was a mere pretext for this political animus. The account Socrates gives of himself in the *Apology* fully accounts for the hatred which many must have felt against him. It also explains why Plato should have been almost as disillusioned with oligarchy (Socrates incriminates the oligarchs in no uncertain terms) as with democracy (seeing that the democracy put Socrates to death). Though Plato came from a most distinguished family and might have been fairly expected to follow the example of some of his relatives by going into politics, he decided definitely to abandon any such ambition in favor of philosophy.

His *Republic,* which contains lengthy criticisms of oligarchy and democracy and pictures only despotism as a still worse form of government, belongs to the same period of Plato's life as the *Phaedrus*, though the *Phaedrus* may have been written a little later. The *Republic* is entirely omitted here, because it would be a shame to excerpt it. Those who want to supplement the present volume with one further text could hardly do better than to turn to F. M. Cornford's translation, with commentary, of Plato's *Republic* (Oxford University Press, both in hard covers and in paperback). The English name of this dialogue is most unfortunate. Its Greek name is *politeia,* which means citizenship, civic life, politics, state, or commonwealth; and in Latin this was rendered as *res publica.* In German, it is called, with reasonable accuracy, *Der Staat.* The ideal city it describes is emphatically no republic. Rather, it is ruled by philosopher kings, and among its prominent features are censorship and a system of education which would probably make it impossible for any Socrates either to develop or to live there. Yet the arguments for this ideal are put into the mouth of Socrates. No irony appears to be intended. In the *Republic* and in those other late dialogues in which he appears, Socrates generally voices Plato's views, not those of the historic Socrates. And if occasionally Plato's own views are in doubt in some of the late dialogues, which are impassioned invitations to reflection rather than straightforward expositions of some doctrine, it is still agreed that what is said by Socrates is not to be ascribed to the historic Socrates.

Of Plato's late dialogues, five are here represented by long selections. The *Parmenides* marks a crisis in the development of Plato's thought. This is discussed briefly above, in the preface to the selections from Parmenides. The last part of the dialogue is omitted here because it is the most abstruse and difficult thing Plato ever wrote, and interpretations of it differ widely.

The *Theaetetus* deals with the problem of knowledge and contains an interesting discussion of some of the ideas of Protagoras, the Sophist. Besides much technical philosophy, it also offers some very charming digressions, and the conclusion of the dialogue, with its genuinely Socratic spirit, represents one of the highlights in Plato's works.

The selections from the *Sophist*, a fine example of Plato's later dialectic, is probably the most difficult thing in this part of the book, but rewarding for the serious student.

The passages from the *Timaeus* and the *Laws* summarize some of Plato's theology, though they deal with other things as well. Although Socrates appears in the *Timaeus*, most of the talking is done, not by him, but by the man whose name the dialogue bears. Timaeus tells how the world was created, and his account is heavily influenced by Pythagorean doctrines. In the early Middle Ages this was the only Platonic dialogue known, and it exerted an enormous influence.

The *Laws* was Plato's last work, written when he was eighty. Among his other dialogues, only the *Republic* equals it in length. The city described in the *Republic* is said in a famous passage to be an ideal—"a pattern set up in the heavens . . . But whether it exists anywhere or ever will exist, is no matter" (592). This ideal city is governed by ideally wise men, without the benefit of laws. In the *Laws*, Plato outlines the best feasible city, and this is ruled by laws. For that reason, some interpreters consider it a significant step in the direction of democracy. But the selection offered here from the justly famous tenth book (there are twelve books in all) shows how far Plato was from the spirit of Jeffersonian, and by no means only Jeffersonian, democracy.

It was Plato who first introduced into Western thought—along with a great deal else—the twin notions of dogma and heresy. It was he who first tried to offer precise formulations of central and indispensable doctrines; and it was he, too, who first proposed a painstakingly graduated penal code for dealing with all those who might differ with one or another of these dogmas. Aquinas' ideas about the treatment of heretics are better understood against the background of Plato's. And Aquinas' theology as well as Aristotle's is also best considered against the background of Plato's.

In addition to the dialogues, we have a number of letters which are said to have been written by Plato. There has been a good deal of controversy about their authenticity, but the seventh letter, which is at least as interesting and significant as any, is generally conceded to be genuine. When Plato wrote it, he was about 75.

The major events of his later life, alluded to in the seventh letter, revolve around two cities: Syracuse, in Sicily, and Athens. In 367 B.C., Dionysius I, tyrant of Syracuse, died and was succeeded by Dionysius II. Years before, Plato had gained the friendship and devotion of Dion, son-in-law of Dionysius I and brother-in-law of his successor. Dion called Plato to Syracuse to train Dionysius II, then 30 and unprepared for the tasks that suddenly confronted him. After a few months, however, the young tyrant sent away Dion as well as Plato, who returned to Athens. Plato's attempts to reconcile the brothers-in-law failed; but in 361/60, Plato made a second voyage to Syracuse. The tyrant had kept up a correspondence with him, and Plato thought it possible at this time to draft a constitution for a federation of Greek cities. At that time, Sicily was colonized not only by the Greeks but also by the Carthaginians, and the Greeks felt threatened by their rivals. Again there were intrigues, and Plato returned to Athens in 360. Three years later, Dion "liberated" Syracuse, but was later murdered. Plato still wrote two further letters to the remnants of Dion's party, and the "seventh letter" is one of these. It seems to have been written in 353 B.C.

In another great project, Plato succeeded. He founded a school in Athens, which came to be known as the Academy. One might call it the world's first university, and it endured as a center of higher learning for about 1,000 years, until a Christian emperor closed it in 529 A.D. In 367 B.C., young Aristotle entered the Academy and stayed on until after Plato died at eighty in 348/7 B.C.

III

The following translations have been used: for the *Apology, Meno, Symposium,* and *Laws,* those of Benjamin Jowett; for the *Phaedo* and *Phaedrus,* those of R. Hackforth (Cambridge University Press); and for the *Parmenides, Theaetetus, Sophist,* and *Timaeus* those of F. M. Cornford (Routledge & Kegan Paul).

Jowett's translations are of the highest literary quality: they have some of the magnificence of the King James Bible without imposing any comparable difficulties on the modern reader. In fact, neither

Cornford's versions nor Hackforth's are so immensely readable. In the earlier dialogues, where Plato's literary art is at its height, Jowett's beautiful translations appear most appropriate. But in most of the *Phaedo* and in the later dialogues, literary genius, though by no means altogether absent, tends to recede in importance; arguments become more and more central, the precise rendering of various concepts is frequently crucial, and it becomes essential to take into account the latest research. In this field, F. M. Cornford established himself as far and away the commanding figure. His translations, with commentary, of the *Parmenides*, (in *Plato and Parmenides*, 1939), of the *Theaetetus and Sophist* (in *Plato's Theory of Knowledge*, 1934), and of the *Timaeus* (in *Plato's Cosmology*, 1937) are models of graceful, lucid, and informative scholarship; it is a delight to be able to offer his translations here.

After Cornford's death, R. Hackforth undertook the task of dealing similarly with some of the other dialogues, and his versions of the *Phaedo* and *Phaedrus* have met with the same kind of acclaim. Permission to use them here greatly enhances the value of the present volume.

A few of Cornford's and Hackforth's footnotes have been retained, some because they are so very helpful, others to give at least some idea of the difficulties with which Plato scholars have to contend. Most of the footnotes and all of the commentary have been omitted. The marginal page numbers are the same in all scholarly editions, whether Greek, English, German, or French and are used in citing Plato in scholarly works. They are therefore indispensable for serious students.

Plato's letters are most conveniently consulted in the bilingual edition (Greek text and English translation on facing pages) in The Loeb Classical Library (Harvard University Press). All the translations in this series are very scholarly, and for the portions selected from the seventh letter that of the Rev. R. G. Bury has been used.

Those seeking further help with the dialogues translated by Cornford and Hackforth could not do better than to turn to the original editions, which feature excellent commentaries. These commentaries are not written primarily for beginners, but rather for serious students and fellow scholars.

Books about Plato are, of course, legion. Those seeking a relatively simple, comprehensive, but high-level volume to assist them will find help aplenty in A. E. Taylor's *Plato* (Meridian Books, paperback), to which I am indebted for some of the material in Section II of this preface. Taylor's little book on *Socrates* is less good: the author tends to make an Anglican of Socrates.

IV

Any detailed commentary on the following selections is impossible in the confines of the present volume. The point here is to offer the texts.

But what of Plato's influence? At this point, a single sentence may suffice: Alfred North Whitehead, one of the outstanding philosophers of the 20th Century, once remarked that the whole history of Western philosophy is but a series of footnotes on Plato.

SOCRATES
AND THE
EARLIER
PLATO

APOLOGY (*complete*)

How you, O Athenians, have been affected by my accusers, I cannot tell; but I know that they almost made me forget who I was—so persuasively did they speak; and yet they have hardly uttered a word of truth. But of the many falsehoods told by them, there was one which quite amazed me; —I mean when they said that you should be upon your guard and not allow yourselves to be deceived by the force of my eloquence. To say this, when they were certain to be detected as soon as I opened my lips and proved myself to be anything but a great speaker, did indeed appear to me most shameless—unless by the force of eloquence they mean the force of truth; for if such is their meaning, I admit that I am eloquent. But in how different a way from theirs! Well, as I was saying, they have scarcely spoken the truth at all; but from me you shall hear the whole truth: not, however, delivered after their manner in a set oration duly ornamented with words and phrases. No, by heaven! but I shall use the words and arguments which occur to me at the moment; for I am confident in the justice of my cause [1]: at my time of life I ought not to be appearing before you, O men of Athens, in the character of a juvenile orator—let no one expect it of me. And I must beg of you to grant me a favour:—If I defend myself in my accustomed manner, and you hear me using the

---

[1] Or, I am certain that I am right in taking this course.

words which I have been in the habit of using in the agora, at the tables
of the money-changers, or anywhere else, I would ask you not to be
surprised, and not to interrupt me on this account. For I am more than
seventy years of age, and appearing now for the first time in a court of
law, I am quite a stranger to the language of the place; and therefore I
would have you regard me as if I were really a stranger, whom you would
excuse if he spoke in his native tongue, and after the fashion of his   [18]
country: —Am I making an unfair request of you? Never mind the
manner, which may or may not be good; but think only of the truth of
my words, and give heed to that: let the speaker speak truly and the judge
decide justly.

And first, I have to reply to the older charges and to my first accusers,
and then I will go on to the later ones. For of old I have had many accusers, who have accused me falsely to you during many years; and I am
more afraid of them than of Anytus and his associates, who are dangerous,
too, in their own way. But far more dangerous are the others, who began
when you were children, and took possession of your minds with their
falsehoods, telling of one Socrates, a wise man, who speculated about
the heaven above, and searched into the earth beneath, and made the
worse appear the better cause. The disseminators of this tale are the accusers whom I dread; for their hearers are apt to fancy that such en-
quirers do not believe in the existence of the gods. And they are many,
and their charges against me are of ancient date, and they were made by
them in the days when you were more impressible than you are now—in
childhood, or it may have been in youth—and the cause when heard
went by default, for there was none to answer. And hardest of all, I do
not know and cannot tell the names of my accusers; unless in the chance
case of a Comic poet. All who from envy and malice have persuaded
you—some of them having first convinced themselves—all this class of
men are most difficult to deal with, for I cannot have them up here, and
cross-examine them, and therefore I must simply fight with shadows in
my own defence, and argue when there is no one who answers. I will ask
you then to assume with me, as I was saying, that my opponents are of
two kinds; one recent, the other ancient: and I hope that you will see the
propriety of my answering the latter first, for these accusations you heard
long before the others, and much oftener.

Well, then, I must make my defence, and endeavour to clear   [19]
away in a short time, a slander which has lasted a long time. May I succeed, if to succeed be for my good and yours, or likely to avail me in my
cause! The task is not an easy one; I quite understand the nature of it.
And so leaving the event with God, in obedience to the law I will now
make my defence.

I will begin at the beginning, and ask what is the accusation which has
given rise to the slander of me, and in fact has encouraged Meletus to
prefer this charge against me. Well, what do the slanderers say? They
shall be my prosecutors, and I will sum up their words in an affidavit:
'Socrates is an evil-doer, and a curious person, who searches into things

under the earth and in heaven, and he makes the worse appear the better cause; and he teaches the aforesaid doctrines to others.' Such is the nature of the accusation: it is just what you have yourselves seen in the comedy of Aristophanes [2], who has introduced a man whom he calls Socrates, going about and saying that he walks in air, and talking a deal of nonsense concerning matters of which I do not pretend to know either much or little—not that I mean to speak disparagingly of any one who is a student of natural philosophy. I should be very sorry if Meletus could bring so grave a charge against me. But the simple truth is, O Athenians, that I have nothing to do with physical speculations. Very many of those here present are witnesses to the truth of this, and to them I appeal. Speak then, you who have heard me, and tell your neighbours whether any of you have ever known me hold forth in few words or in many upon such matters. . . . You hear their answer. And from what they say of this part of the charge you will be able to judge of the truth of the rest.

As little foundation is there for the report that I am a teacher, and take money; this accusation has no more truth in it than the other. Although, if a man were really able to instruct mankind, to receive money for giving instruction would, in my opinion, be an honour to him. There is Gorgias of Leontium, and Prodicus of Ceos, and Hippias of Elis, who go the round of the cities, and are able to persuade the young men to leave their own citizens by whom they might be taught for nothing, and come to [20] them whom they not only pay, but are thankful if they may be allowed to pay them. There is at this time a Parian philosopher residing in Athens, of whom I have heard; and I came to hear of him in this way:—I came across a man who has spent a world of money on the Sophists, Callias, the son of Hipponicus, and knowing that he had sons, I asked him: 'Callias,' I said, 'if your two sons were foals or calves, there would be no difficulty in finding some one to put over them; we should hire a trainer of horses, or a farmer probably, who would improve and perfect them in their own proper virtue and excellence; but as they are human beings, whom are you thinking of placing over them? Is there any one who understands human and political virtue? You must have thought about the matter, for you have sons; is there any one?' 'There is,' he said. 'Who is he?' said I; 'and of what country? and what does he charge?' 'Evenus the Parian,' he replied; 'he is the man, and his charge is five minae.' Happy is Evenus, I said to myself, if he really has this wisdom, and teaches at such a moderate charge. Had I the same, I should have been very proud and conceited; but the truth is that I have no knowledge of the kind.

I dare say, Athenians, that some one among you will reply, 'Yes, Socrates, but what is the origin of these accusations which are brought against you; there must have been something strange which you have been doing? All these rumours and this talk about you would never have arisen if you had been like other men: tell us, then, what is the cause of them, for we should be sorry to judge hastily of you.' Now I regard this as a fair

[2] Aristoph., Clouds, 225 ff.

challenge, and I will endeavour to explain to you the reason why I am called wise and have such an evil fame. Please to attend then. And although some of you may think that I am joking, I declare that I will tell you the entire truth. Men of Athens, this reputation of mine has come of a certain sort of wisdom which I possess. If you ask me what kind of wisdom, I reply, wisdom such as may perhaps be attained by man, for to that extent I am inclined to believe that I am wise; whereas the persons of whom I was speaking have a superhuman wisdom, which I may fail to describe, because I have it not myself; and he who says that I have, speaks falsely, and is taking away my character. And here, O men of Athens, I must beg you not to interrupt me, even if I seem to say something extravagant. For the word which I will speak is not mine. I will refer you to a witness who is worthy of credit; that witness shall be the God of Delphi—he will tell you about my wisdom, if I have any, and of what sort it is. You must have known Chaerephon; he was early a friend of mine, and also a friend of yours, for he shared in the recent exile of   [21] the people, and returned with you. Well, Chaerephon, as you know, was very impetuous in all his doings, and he went to Delphi and boldly asked the oracle to tell him whether—as I was saying, I must beg you not to interrupt—he asked the oracle to tell him whether any one was wiser than I was, and the Pythian prophetess answered, that there was no man wiser. Chaerephon is dead himself; but his brother, who is in court, will confirm the truth of what I am saying.

Why do I mention this? Because I am going to explain to you why I have such an evil name. When I heard the answer, I said to myself, What can the god mean? and what is the interpretation of his riddle? for I know that I have no wisdom, small or great. What then can he mean when he says that I am the wisest of men? And yet he is a god, and cannot lie; that would be against his nature. After long consideration, I thought of a method of trying the question. I reflected that if I could only find a man wiser than myself, then I might go to the god with a refutation in my hand. I should say to him, 'Here is a man who is wiser than I am; but you said that I was the wisest.' Accordingly I went to one who had the reputation of wisdom, and observed him—his name I need not mention; he was a politician whom I selected for examination—and the result was as follows: When I began to talk with him, I could not help thinking that he was not really wise, although he was thought wise by many, and still wiser by himself; and thereupon I tried to explain to him that he thought himself wise, but was not really wise; and the consequence was that he hated me, and his enmity was shared by several who were present and heard me. So I left him, saying to myself, as I went away: Well, although I do not suppose that either of us knows anything really beautiful and good, I am better off than he is,—for he knows nothing, and thinks that he knows; I neither know nor think that I know. In this latter particular, then, I seem to have slightly the advantage of him. Then I went to another who had still higher pretensions to wisdom, and my conclusion was exactly the same. Whereupon I made another enemy of him, and of many others besides him.

Then I went to one man after another, being not unconscious of the enmity which I provoked, and I lamented and feared this: but necessity was laid upon me,—the word of God, I thought, ought to be considered first. And I said to myself, Go I must to all who appear to know, and find out the meaning of the oracle. And I swear to you, Athenians, by the [22] dog I swear!—for I must tell you the truth—the result of my mission was just this: I found that the men most in repute were all but the most foolish; and that others less esteemed were really wiser and better. I will tell you the tale of my wanderings and of the 'Herculean' labours, as I may call them, which I endured only to find at last the oracle irrefutable. After the politicians, I went to the poets; tragic, dithyrambic, and all sorts. And there, I said to myself, you will be instantly detected; now you will find out that you are more ignorant than they are. Accordingly, I took them some of the most elaborate passages in their own writings, and asked what was the meaning of them—thinking that they would teach me something. Will you believe me? I am almost ashamed to confess the truth, but I must say that there is hardly a person present who would not have talked better about their poetry than they did themselves. Then I knew that not by wisdom do poets write poetry, but by a sort of genius and inspiration; they are like diviners or soothsayers who also say many fine things, but do not understand the meaning of them. The poets appeared to me to be much in the same case; and I further observed that upon the strength of their poetry they believed themselves to be the wisest of men in other things in which they were not wise. So I departed, conceiving myself to be superior to them for the same reason that I was superior to the politicians.

At last I went to the artisans, for I was conscious that I knew nothing at all, as I may say, and I was sure that they knew many fine things; and here I was not mistaken, for they did know many things of which I was ignorant, and in this they certainly were wiser than I was. But I observed that even the good artisans fell into the same error as the poets;—because they were good workmen they thought that they also knew all sorts of high matters, and this defect in them overshadowed their wisdom; and therefore I asked myself on behalf of the oracle, whether I would like to be as I was, neither having their knowledge nor their ignorance, or like them in both; and I made answer to myself and to the oracle that I was better off as I was.

This inquisition has led to my having many enemies of the worst and most dangerous kind, and has given occasion also to many calumnies. [23] And I am called wise, for my hearers always imagine that I myself possess the wisdom which I find wanting in others: but the truth is, O men of Athens, that God only is wise; and by his answer he intends to show that the wisdom of men is worth little or nothing; he is not speaking of Socrates, he is only using my name by way of illustration, as if he said, He, O men, is the wisest, who, like Socrates, knows that his wisdom is in truth worth nothing. And so I go about the world, obedient to the god, and search and make enquiry into the wisdom of any one, whether citizen or stranger, who appears to be wise; and if he is not wise, then in vindication of the oracle I show him that he is not wise; and my occupation quite absorbs me, and I have no time to give either to any public matter of interest or to any concern of my own, but I am in utter poverty by reason of my devotion to the god.

There is another thing:—young men of the richer classes, who have not much to do, come about me of their own accord; they like to hear the pretenders examined, and they often imitate me, and proceed to examine others; there are plenty of persons, as they quickly discover, who think that they know something, but really know little or nothing; and then those who are examined by them instead of being angry with themselves are angry with me: This confounded Socrates, they say; this villainous misleader of youth!—and then if somebody asks them, Why, what evil does he practise or teach? they do not know, and cannot tell; but in order that they may not appear to be at a loss, they repeat the ready-made charges which are used against all philosophers about teaching things up in the clouds and under the earth, and having no gods, and making the worse appear the better cause; for they do not like to confess that their pretence of knowledge has been detected—which is the truth; and as they are numerous and ambitious and energetic, and are drawn up in battle array and have persuasive tongues, they have filled your ears with their loud and inveterate calumnies. And this is the reason why my three accusers, Meletus and Anytus and Lycon, have set upon me; Meletus, who has a quarrel with me on behalf of the poets; Anytus, on behalf of the craftsmen and politicians; Lycon, on behalf of the rhetoricians: [24] and as I said at the beginning, I cannot expect to get rid of such a mass of calumny all in a moment. And this, O men of Athens, is the truth and the whole truth; I have concealed nothing, I have dissembled nothing. And yet, I know that my plainness of speech makes them hate me, and what is their hatred but a proof that I am speaking the truth?—Hence has arisen the prejudice against me; and this is the reason of it, as you will find out either in this or in any future enquiry.

I have said enough in my defence against the first class of my accusers; I turn to the second class. They are headed by Meletus, that good man and true lover of his country, as he calls himself. Against these, too, I must try to make a defence. Let their affidavit be read; it contains something of this kind: It says that Socrates is a doer of evil, who corrupts the youth; and who does not believe in the gods of the state, but has other new divinities of his own. Such is the charge; and now let us examine the particular counts. He says that I am a doer of evil, and corrupt the youth; but I say, O men of Athens, that Meletus is a doer of evil, in that he pretends to be in earnest when he is only in jest, and is so eager to bring men to trial from a pretended zeal and interest about matters in which he really never had the smallest interest. And the truth of this I will endeavour to prove to you.

Come hither, Meletus, and let me ask a question of you. You think a great deal about the improvement of youth?

Yes, I do.

Tell the judges, then, who is their improver; for you must know, as you have taken the pains to discover their corrupter, and are citing and accusing me before them. Speak, then, and tell the judges who their improver is.—Observe, Meletus, that you are silent, and have nothing to say. But is not this rather disgraceful, and a very considerable proof of what I was saying, that you have no interest in the matter. Speak up, friend, and tell us who their improver is.

The laws.

But that, my good sir, is not my meaning. I want to know who the person is, who, in the first place, knows the laws.

The judges, Socrates, who are present in court.

What, do you mean to say, Meletus, that they are able to instruct and improve youth?

Certainly they are.

What, all of them, or some only and not others?

All of them.

By the goddess Herè, that is good news! There are plenty of improvers, then. And what do you say of the audience,—do they improve them?   [25]

Yes, they do.

And the senators?

Yes, the senators improve them.

But perhaps the members of the assembly corrupt them?—or do they too improve them?

They improve them.

Then every Athenian improves and elevates them; all with the exception of myself; and I alone am their corrupter? Is that what you affirm?

That is what I stoutly affirm.

I am very unfortunate if you are right. But suppose I ask you a question: How about horses? Does one man do them harm and all the world good? Is not the exact opposite the truth? One man is able to do them good, or at least not many;—the trainer of horses, that is to say, does them good, and others who have to do with them rather injure them? Is not that true, Meletus, of horses, or of any other animals? Most assuredly it is; whether you and Anytus say yes or no. Happy indeed would be the condition of youth if they had one corrupter only, and all the rest of the world were their improvers. But you, Meletus, have sufficiently shown that you never had a thought about the young: your carelessness is seen in your not caring about the very things which you bring against me.

And now, Meletus, I will ask you another question—by Zeus I will: Which is better, to live among bad citizens, or among good ones? Answer, friend, I say; the question is one which may be easily answered. Do not the good do their neighbours good, and the bad do them evil?

Certainly.

And is there any one who would rather be injured than benefited by those who live with him? Answer, my good friend, the law requires you to answer—does any one like to be injured?

Certainly not.

And when you accuse me of corrupting and deteriorating the youth, do you allege that I corrupt them intentionally or unintentionally?

Intentionally, I say.

But you have just admitted that the good do their neighbours good, and the evil do them evil. Now, is that a truth which your superior wisdom has recognized thus early in life, and am I, at my age, in such darkness and ignorance as not to know that if a man with whom I have to live is corrupted by me, I am very likely to be harmed by him; and yet I corrupt him, and intentionally, too—so you say, although neither I nor any other human being is ever likely to be convinced by you. But either I do [26] not corrupt them, or I corrupt them unintentionally; and on either view of the case you lie. If my offence is unintentional, the law has no cognizance of unintentional offences: you ought to have taken me privately, and warned and admonished me; for if I had been better advised, I should have left off doing what I only did unintentionally—no doubt I should; but you would have nothing to say to me and refused to teach me. And now you bring me up in this court, which is a place not of instruction, but of punishment.

It will be very clear to you, Athenians, as I was saying, that Meletus has no care at all, great or small, about the matter. But still I should like to know, Meletus, in what I am affirmed to corrupt the young. I suppose you mean, as I infer from your indictment, that I teach them not to acknowledge the gods which the state acknowledges, but some other new divinities or spiritual agencies in their stead. These are the lessons by which I corrupt the youth, as you say.

Yes, that I say emphatically.

Then, by the gods, Meletus, of whom we are speaking, tell me and the court, in somewhat plainer terms, what you mean! for I do not as yet understand whether you affirm that I teach other men to acknowledge some gods, and therefore that I do believe in gods, and am not an entire atheist—this you do not lay to my charge,—but only you say that they are not the same gods which the city recognizes—the charge is that they are different gods. Or, do you mean that I am an atheist simply, and a teacher of atheism?

I mean the latter—that you are a complete atheist.

What an extraordinary statement! Why do you think so, Meletus? Do you mean that I do not believe in the godhead of the sun or moon, like other men?

I assure you, judges, that he does not: for he says that the sun is stone, and the moon earth.

Friend Meletus, you think that you are accusing Anaxagoras: and you have but a bad opinion of the judges, if you fancy them illiterate to such a degree as not to know that these doctrines are found in the books of Anaxagoras the Clazomenian, which are full of them. And so, forsooth, the youth are said to be taught them by Socrates, when there are not unfrequently exhibitions of them at the theatre [3] (price of admission one drachma at the most); and they might pay their money, and laugh at Socrates if he pretends to father these extraordinary views. And so, Meletus, you really think that I do not believe in any god?

I swear by Zeus that you believe absolutely in none at all.

Nobody will believe you, Meletus, and I am pretty sure that you do not believe yourself. I cannot help thinking, men of Athens, that Meletus is reckless and impudent, and that he has written this indictment in a spirit of mere wantonness and youthful bravado. Has he not com- [27] pounded a riddle, thinking to try me? He said to himself:—I shall see whether the wise Socrates will discover my facetious contradiction, or whether I shall be able to deceive him and the rest of them. For he certainly does appear to me to contradict himself in the indictment as much as if he said that Socrates is guilty of not believing in the gods, and yet of believing in them—but this is not like a person who is in earnest.

I should like you, O men of Athens, to join me in examining what I conceive to be his inconsistency; and do you, Meletus, answer. And I must remind the audience of my request that they would not make a disturbance if I speak in my accustomed manner:

Did ever man, Meletus, believe in the existence of human things, and not of human beings? . . . I wish, men of Athens, that he would answer, and not be always trying to get up an interruption. Did ever any man believe in horsemanship, and not in horses? or in flute-playing, and not in flute-players? No, my friend; I will answer to you and to the court, as you refuse to answer for yourself. There is no man who ever did. But now please to answer the next question: Can a man believe in spiritual and divine agencies, and not in spirits or demigods?

He cannot.

How lucky I am to have extracted that answer, by the assistance of the court! But then you swear in the indictment that I teach and believe in divine or spiritual agencies (new or old, no matter for that); at any rate, I believe in spiritual agencies,—so you say and swear in the affidavit; and yet if I believe in divine beings, how can I help believing in spirits or demigods;—must I not? To be sure I must; and therefore I may assume that your silence gives consent. Now what are spirits or demigods? are they not either gods or the sons of gods?

Certainly they are.

But this is what I call the facetious riddle invented by you: the demi-gods or spirits are gods, and you say first that I do not believe in gods, and then again that I do believe in gods; that is, if I believe in demigods. For if the demigods are the illegitimate sons of gods, whether by the nymphs or by any other mothers, of whom they are said to be the sons— what human being will ever believe that there are no gods if they are the

---

[3] Probably in allusion to Aristophanes who caricatured, and to Euripides who borrowed the notions of Anaxagoras, as well as to other dramatic poets.

sons of gods? You might as well affirm the existence of mules, and deny that of horses and asses. Such nonsense, Meletus, could only have been intended by you to make trial of me. You have put this into the indictment because you had nothing real of which to accuse me. But no one who has a particle of understanding will ever be convinced by you that the same men can believe in divine and superhuman things, and yet not believe that there are gods and demigods and heroes.   [28]

I have said enough in answer to the charge of Meletus: any elaborate defence is unnecessary; but I know only too well how many are the enmities which I have incurred, and this is what will be my destruction if I am destroyed;—not Meletus, nor yet Anytus, but the envy and detraction of the world, which has been the death of many good men, and will probably be the death of many more; there is no danger of my being the last of them.

Some one will say: And are you not ashamed, Socrates, of a course of life which is likely to bring you to an untimely end? To him I may fairly answer: There you are mistaken: a man who is good for anything ought not to calculate the chance of living or dying; he ought only to consider whether in doing anything he is doing right or wrong—acting the part of a good man or of a bad. Whereas, upon your view, the heroes who fell at Troy were not good for much, and the son of Thetis above all, who altogether despised danger in comparison with disgrace; and when he was so eager to slay Hector, his goddess mother said to him, that if he avenged his companion Patroclus, and slew Hector, he would die himself —'Fate,' she said, in these or the like words, 'waits for you next after Hector;' he, receiving this warning, utterly despised danger and death, and instead of fearing them, feared rather to live in dishonour, and not to avenge his friend. 'Let me die forthwith,' he replies, 'and be avenged of my enemy, rather than abide here by the beaked ships, a laughing-stock and a burden of the earth.' Had Achilles any thought of death and danger? For wherever a man's place is, whether the place which he has chosen or that in which he has been placed by a commander, there he ought to remain in the hour of danger; he should not think of death or of anything but of disgrace. And this, O men of Athens, is a true saying.

Strange, indeed, would be my conduct, O men of Athens, if I who, when I was ordered by the generals whom you chose to command me at Potidaea and Amphipolis and Delium, remained where they placed me, like any other man, facing death—if now, when, as I conceive and imagine, God orders me to fulfil the philosopher's mission of searching into myself and other men, I were to desert my post through fear of death,   [29] or any other fear; that would indeed be strange, and I might justly be arraigned in court for denying the existence of the gods, if I disobeyed the oracle because I was afraid of death, fancying that I was wise when I was not wise. For the fear of death is indeed the pretence of wisdom, and not real wisdom, being a pretence of knowing the unknown; and no one knows whether death, which men in their fear apprehend to be the greatest evil, may not be the greatest good. Is not this ignorance of a disgraceful sort, the ignorance which is the conceit that a man knows what he does not know? And in this respect only I believe myself to differ from men in general, and may perhaps claim to be wiser than they are: —that whereas I know but little of the world below, I do not suppose that I know: but I do know that injustice and disobedience to a better, whether God or man, is evil and dishonourable, and I will never fear or avoid a possible good rather than a certain evil. And therefore if you let me go now, and are not convinced by Anytus, who said that since I had been prosecuted I must be put to death: (or if not that I ought never to have been prosecuted at all); and that if I escape now, your sons will all be utterly ruined by listening to my words—if you say to me, Socrates, this time we will not mind Anytus, and you shall be let off, but upon one condition, that you are not to enquire and speculate in this way any more, and that if you are caught doing so again you shall die;— if this was the condition on which you let me go, I should reply: Men of Athens, I honour and love you; but I shall obey God rather than you, and while I have life and strength I shall never cease from the practice and teaching of philosophy, exhorting any one whom I meet any saying to him after my manner: You, my friend,—a citizen of the great and mighty and wise city of Athens,—are you not ashamed of heaping up the greatest amount of money and honour and reputation, and caring so little about wisdom and truth and the greatest improvement of the soul, which you never regard or heed at all? And if the person with whom I am arguing, says: Yes, but I do care; then I do not leave him or let him go at once; but I proceed to interrogate and examine and cross-examine him, and if I think that he has no virtue in him, but only says that he has, I reproach him with undervaluing the greater, and overvaluing the less. And I   [30] shall repeat the same words to every one whom I meet, young and old, citizen and alien, but especially to the citizens inasmuch as they are my brethren. For know that this is the command of God; and I believe that no greater good has ever happened in the state than my service to the God. For I do nothing but go about persuading you all, old and young alike, not to take thought for your persons or your properties, but first and chiefly to care about the greatest improvement of the soul. I tell you that virtue is not given by money, but that from virtue comes money and every other good of man, public as well as private. This is my teaching, and if this is the doctrine which corrupts the youth, I am a mischievous person. But if any one says that this is not my teaching, he is speaking an untruth. Wherefore, O men of Athens, I say to you, do as Anytus bids or not as Anytus bids, and either acquit me or not; but whichever you do, understand that I shall never alter my ways, not even if I have to die many times.

Men of Athens, do not interrupt, but hear me; there was an understanding between us that you should hear me to the end: I have something more to say, at which you may be inclined to cry out; but I believe that to hear me will be good for you, and therefore I beg that you will not cry out. I would have you know, that if you kill such an one as I am, you will injure yourselves more than you will injure me. Nothing will injure me, not Meletus nor yet Anytus—they cannot, for a bad man is not permitted to injure a better than himself. I do not deny that Anytus may, perhaps, kill him, or drive him into exile, or deprive him of civil rights; and he may imagine, and others may imagine, that he is inflicting a great injury upon him: but there I do not agree. For the evil of doing as he is doing—the evil of unjustly taking away the life of another—is greater far.

And now, Athenians, I am not going to argue for my own sake, as you may think, but for yours, that you may not sin against the God by condemning me, who am his gift to you. For if you kill me you will not easily find a successor to me, who, if I may use such a ludicrous figure of speech, am a sort of gadfly, given to the state by God; and the state is a great and noble steed who is tardy in his motions owing to his very size, and requires to be stirred into life. I am that gadfly which God has   [31] attached to the state, and all day long and in all places am always fastening upon you, arousing and persuading and reproaching you. You will not easily find another like me, and therefore I would advise you to spare me. I dare say that you may feel out of temper (like a person who is suddenly awakened from sleep), and you think that you might easily strike me dead as Anytus advises, and then you would sleep on for the remainder of your lives, unless God in his care of you sent you another gadfly. When I say that I am given to you by God, the proof of my mission is this:—if I had been like other men, I should not have neglected all my own concerns or patiently seen the neglect of them during all these years, and have been doing yours, coming to you individually like a father or elder brother, exhorting you to regard virtue; such conduct, I say, would be unlike human nature. If I had gained anything, or if my exhortations had been paid, there would have been some sense in my doing so, but now, as you will perceive, not even the impudence of my accusers dares to say that I have ever exacted or sought pay of any one; of that they have no witness. And I have a sufficient witness to the truth of what I say—my poverty.

Some one may wonder why I go about in private giving advice and busying myself with the concerns of others, but do not venture to come forward in public and advise the state. I will tell you why. You have heard me speak at sundry times and in divers places of an oracle or sign which comes to me, and is the divinity which Meletus ridicules in the indictment. This sign, which is a kind of voice, first began to come to me when I was a child; it always forbids but never commands me to do anything which I am going to do. This is what deters me from being a politician. And rightly, as I think. For I am certain, O men of Athens, that if I had engaged in politics, I should have perished long ago, and done no good either to you or to myself. And do not be offended at my telling you the truth: for the truth is, that no man who goes to war with you or any other multitude, honestly striving against the many lawless and unrighteous deeds which are done in a state, will save his life; he   [32] who will fight for the right, if he would live even for a brief space, must have a private station and not a public one.

I can give you convincing evidence of what I say, not words only, but what you value far more—actions. Let me relate to you a passage of my own life which will prove to you that I should never have yielded to injustice from any fear of death, and that 'as I should have refused to yield' I must have died at once. I will tell you a tale of the courts, not very interesting perhaps, but nevertheless true. The only office of state which I ever held, O men of Athens, was that of senator: the tribe Antiochis, which is my tribe, had the presidency at the trial of the generals who had not taken up the bodies of the slain after the battle of Arginusae; and you proposed to try them in a body, contrary to law, as you all thought afterwards; but at the time I was the only one of the Prytanes who was opposed to the illegality, and I gave my vote against you; and when the orators threatened to impeach and arrest me, and you called and shouted, I made up my mind that I would run the risk, having law and justice with me, rather than take part in your injustice because I feared imprisonment and death. This happened in the days of the democracy. But when the oligarchy of the Thirty was in power, they sent for me and four others into the rotunda, and bade us bring Leon the Salaminian from Salamis, as they wanted to put him to death. This was a specimen of the sort of commands which they were always giving with the view of implicating as many as possible in their crimes; and then I showed, not in word only but in deed, that, if I may be allowed to use such an expression, I cared not a straw for death, and that my great and only care was lest I should do an unrighteous or unholy thing. For the strong arm of that oppressive power did not frighten me into doing wrong; and when we came out of the rotunda the other four went to Salamis and fetched Leon, but I went quietly home. For which I might have lost my life, had not the power of the Thirty shortly afterwards come to an end. And many will witness to my words.

Now do you really imagine that I could have survived all these years, if I had led a public life, supposing that like a good man I had always maintained the right and had made justice, as I ought, the first thing? No indeed, men of Athens, neither I nor any other man. But I have [33] been always the same in all my actions, public as well as private, and never have I yielded any base compliance to those who are slanderously termed my disciples, or to any other. Not that I have any regular disciples. But if any one likes to come and hear me while I am pursuing my mission, whether he be young or old, he is not excluded. Nor do I converse only with those who pay; but any one, whether he be rich or poor, may ask and answer me and listen to my words; and whether he turns out to be a bad man or a good one, neither result can be justly imputed to me; for I never taught or professed to teach him anything. And if any one says that he has ever learned or heard anything from me in private which all the world has not heard, let me tell you that he is lying.

But I shall be asked, Why do people delight in continually conversing with you? I have told you already, Athenians, the whole truth about this matter: they like to hear the cross-examination of the pretenders to wisdom; there is amusement in it. Now this duty of cross-examining other men has been imposed upon me by God; and has been signified to me by oracles, visions, and in every way in which the will of divine power was ever intimated to any one. This is true, O Athenians; or, if not true, would be soon refuted. If I am or have been corrupting the youth, those of them who are now grown up and have become sensible that I gave them bad advice in the days of their youth should come forward as accusers, and take their revenge; or if they do not like to come themselves, some of their relatives, fathers, brothers, or other kinsmen, should say what evil their families have suffered at my hands. Now is their time. Many of them I see in the court. There is Crito, who is of the same age and of the same deme with myself, and there is Critobulus his son, whom I also see. Then again there is Lysanias of Sphettus, who is the father of Aeschines—he is present; and also there is Antiphon of Cephisus, who is the father of Epigenes; and there are the brothers of several who have associated with me. There is Nicostratus the son of Theosdotides, and the brother of Theodotus (now Theodotus himself is dead, and therefore he, at any rate, will not seek to stop him); and there is Paralus the son of Demodocus, who had a brother Theages; and Adeimantus the son [34] of Ariston, whose brother Plato is present; and Aeantodorus, who is the brother of Apollodorus, whom I also see. I might mention a great many others, some of whom Meletus should have produced as witnesses in the course of his speech; and let him still produce them, if he has forgotten—I will make way for him. And let him say, if he has any testimony of the sort which he can produce. Nay, Athenians, the very opposite is the truth. For all these are ready to witness on behalf of the corrupter, of the injurer of their kindred, as Meletus and Anytus call me; not the corrupted youth only—there might have been a motive for that—but their uncorrupted elder relatives. Why should they too support me with their testimony? Why, indeed, except for the sake of truth and justice, and because they know that I am speaking the truth, and that Meletus is a liar.

Well, Athenians, this and the like of this is all the defence which I have to offer. Yet a word more. Perhaps there may be some one who is offended at me, when he calls to mind how he himself on a similar, or even a less serious occasion, prayed and entreated the judges with many tears, and how he produced his children in court, which was a moving spectacle, together with a host of relations and friends; whereas I, who am probably in danger of my life, will do none of these things. The contrast may occur to his mind, and he may be set against me, and vote in anger because he is displeased at me on this account. Now if there be such a person among you,—mind, I do not say that there is,—to him I may fairly reply: My friend, I am a man, and like other men, a creature of flesh and blood, and not 'of wood or stone,' as Homer says; and I have a family, yes, and sons, O Athenians, three in number, one almost a man, and two others who are still young; and yet I will not bring any of them hither in order to petition you for an acquittal. And why not? Not from any self-assertion or want of respect for you. Whether I am or am not afraid of death is another question, of which I will not now speak. But, having regard to public opinion, I feel that such conduct would be discreditable to myself, and to you, and to the whole state. One who has reached my years, and who has a name for wisdom, ought not to demean himself. Whether this opinion of me be deserved or not, at any rate the world has decided that Socrates is in some way superior to other [35] men. And if those among you who are said to be superior in wisdom and courage, and any other virtue, demean themselves in this way, how shameful is their conduct! I have seen men of reputation, when they have been condemned, behaving in the strangest manner: they seemed to fancy that they were going to suffer something dreadful if they died, and that they could be immortal if you only allowed them to live; and I think that such are a dishonour to the state, and that any stranger coming in would have said of them that the most eminent men of Athens, to whom the Athenians themselves give honour and command, are no better than women. And I say that these things ought not to be done by those of us who have a reputation; and if they are done, you ought not to permit them; you ought rather to show that you are far more disposed to condemn the man who gets up a doleful scene and makes the city ridiculous, than him who holds his peace.

But, setting aside the question of public opinion, there seems to be something wrong in asking a favour of a judge, and thus procuring an acquittal, instead of informing and convincing him. For his duty is, not to make a present of justice, but to give judgment; and he has sworn that he will judge according to the laws, and not according to his own good pleasure; and we ought not to encourage you, nor should you allow yourselves to be encouraged, in this habit of perjury—there can be no piety in that. Do not then require me to do what I consider dishonourable and impious and wrong, especially now, when I am being tried for impiety on the indictment of Meletus. For if, O men of Athens, by force of persuasion and entreaty I could overpower your oaths, then I should be teaching you to believe that there are no gods, and in defending should simply convict myself of the charge of not believing in them. But that is not so—far otherwise. For I do believe that there are gods, and in a sense higher than that in which any of my accusers believe in them. And to you and to God I commit my cause, to be determined by you as is best for you and me.

There are many reasons why I am not grieved, O men of Athens, [36] at the vote of condemnation. I expected it, and am only surprised that the votes are so nearly equal; for I had thought that the majority against me would have been far larger; but now, had thirty votes gone over to the other side, I should have been acquitted. And I may say, I think, that I have escaped Meletus. I may say more; for without the assistance of

Anytus and Lycon, any one may see that he would not have had a fifth part of the votes, as the law requires, in which case he would have incurred a fine of a thousand drachmae.

And so he proposes death as the penalty. And what shall I propose on my part, O men of Athens? Clearly that which is my due. And what is my due? What return shall be made to the man who has never had the wit to be idle during his whole life; but has been careless of what the many care for—wealth, and family interests, and military offices, and speaking in the assembly, and magistracies, and plots, and parties. Reflecting that I was really too honest a man to be a politician and live, I did not go where I could do no good to you or to myself; but where I could do the greatest good privately to every one of you, thither I went, and sought to persuade every man among you that he must look to himself, and seek virtue and wisdom before he looks to his private interests, and look to the state before he looks to the interests of the state; and that this should be the order which he observes in all his actions. What shall be done to such an one? Doubtless some good thing, O men of Athens, if he has his reward; and the good should be of a kind suitable to him. What would be a reward suitable to a poor man who is your benefactor, and who desires leisure that he may instruct you? There can be no reward so fitting as maintenance in the Prytaneum, O men of Athens, a reward which he deserves far more than the citizen who has won the prize at Olympia in the horse or chariot race, whether the chariots were drawn by two horses or by many. For I am in want, and he has enough; and he only gives you the appearance of happiness, and I give you the reality. And if I am to estimate the penalty fairly, I should [37] say that maintenance in the Prytaneum is the just return.

Perhaps you think that I am braving you in what I am saying now, as in what I said before about the tears and prayers. But this is not so. I speak rather because I am convinced that I never intentionally wronged any one, although I cannot convince you—the time has been too short; if there were a law at Athens, as there is in other cities, that a capital cause should not be decided in one day, then I believe that I should have convinced you. But I cannot in a moment refute great slanders; and, as I am convinced that I never wronged another, I will assuredly not wrong myself. I will not say of myself that I deserve any evil, or propose any penalty. Why should I? Because I am afraid of the penalty of death which Meletus proposes? When I do not know whether death is a good or an evil, why should I propose a penalty which would certainly be an evil? Shall I say imprisonment? And why should I live in prison, and be the slave of the magistrates of the year—of the Eleven? Or shall the penalty be a fine, and imprisonment until the fine is paid? There is the same objection. I should have to lie in prison, for money I have none, and cannot pay. And if I say exile (and this may possibly be the penalty which you will affix), I must indeed be blinded by the love of life, if I am so irrational as to expect that when you, who are my own citizens, cannot endure my discourses and words, and have found them so grievous and odious that you will have no more of them, others are likely to endure me. No indeed, men of Athens, that is not very likely. And what a life should I lead, at my age, wandering from city to city, ever changing my place of exile, and always being driven out! For I am quite sure that wherever I go, there, as here, the young men will flock to me; and if I drive them away, their elders will drive me out at their request; and if I let them come, their fathers and friends will drive me out for their sakes.

Some one will say: Yes, Socrates, but cannot you hold your tongue, and then you may go into a foreign city, and no one will interfere with you? Now I have great difficulty in making you understand my answer to this. For if I tell you that to do as you say would be a disobedience to the God, and therefore that I cannot hold my tongue, you will not believe that I am serious; and if I say again that daily to discourse [38] about virtue, and of those other things about which you hear me examining myself and others, is the greatest good of man, and that the unexamined life is not worth living, you are still less likely to believe me. Yet I say what is true, although a thing of which it is hard for me to persuade you. Also, I have never been accustomed to think that I deserve to suffer any harm. Had I money I might have estimated the offence at what I was able to pay, and not have been much the worse. But I have none, and therefore I must ask you to proportion the fine to my means. Well, perhaps I could afford a mina, and therefore I propose that penalty: Plato, Crito, Critobulus, and Apollodorus, my friends here, bid me say thirty minae, and they will be the sureties. Let thirty minae be the penalty; for which sum they will be ample security to you.

Not much time will be gained, O Athenians, in return for the evil name which you will get from the detractors of the city, who will say that you killed Socrates, a wise man; for they will call me wise, even although I am not wise, when they want to reproach you. If you had waited a little while, your desire would have been fulfilled in the course of nature. For I am far advanced in years, as you may perceive, and not far from death. I am speaking now not to all of you, but only to those who have condemned me to death. And I have another thing to say to them: You think that I was convicted because I had no words of the sort which would have procured my acquittal—I mean if I had thought fit to leave nothing undone or unsaid. Not so; the deficiency which led to my conviction was not of words—certainly not. But I had not the boldness or impudence or inclination to address you as you would have liked me to do, weeping and wailing and lamenting, and saying and doing many things which you have been accustomed to hear from others, and which, as I maintain, are unworthy of me. I thought at the time that I ought not to do anything common or mean when in danger: nor do I now repent of the style of my defence; I would rather die having spoken after my manner, than speak in your manner and live. For neither in war nor yet at law ought I or any man to use every way of escaping [39] death. Often in battle there can be no doubt that if a man will throw away his arms, and fall on his knees before his pursuers, he may escape death; and in other dangers there are other ways of escaping death, if a man is willing to say and do anything. The difficulty, my friends, is not to avoid death, but to avoid unrighteousness; for that runs faster than death. I am old and move slowly, and the slower runner has overtaken me, and my accusers are keen and quick, and the faster runner, who is unrighteousness, has overtaken them. And now I depart hence condemned by you to suffer the penalty of death,—they too go their ways condemned by the truth to suffer the penalty of villainy and wrong; and I must abide by my reward—let them abide by theirs. I suppose that these things may be regarded as fated,—and I think that they are well.

And now, O men who have condemned me, I would fain prophesy to you; for I am about to die, and in the hour of death men are gifted with prophetic power. And I prophesy to you who are my murderers, that immediately after my departure punishment far heavier than you have inflicted on me will surely await you. Me you have killed because you wanted to escape the accuser, and not to give an account of your lives. But that will not be as you suppose: far otherwise. For I say that there will be more accusers of you than there are now; accusers whom hitherto I have restrained: and as they are younger they will be more inconsiderate with you, and you will be more offended at them. If you think that by killing men you can prevent some one from censuring your evil lives, you are mistaken; that is not a way of escape which is either possible or honourable; the easiest and the noblest way is not to be disabling others, but to be improving yourselves. This is the prophecy which I utter before my departure to the judges who have condemned me.

Friends, who would have acquitted me, I would like also to talk with you about the thing which has come to pass, while the magistrates are busy, and before I go to the place at which I must die. Stay then a little, for we may as well talk with one another while there is time. You are my friends, and I should like to show you the meaning of this [40] event which has happened to me. O my judges—for you I may truly call judges—I should like to tell you of a wonderful circumstance. Hitherto the divine faculty of which the internal oracle is the source has constantly been in the habit of opposing me even about trifles, if I was going to make a slip or error in any matter; and now as you see there has come upon me that which may be thought, and is generally believed to be, the last and worst evil. But the oracle made no sign of opposition, either when I was leaving my house in the morning, or when I was on my way to the court, or while I was speaking, at anything which I was going to say; and yet I have often been stopped in the middle of a speech, but now in nothing I either said or did touching the matter in hand has the oracle opposed me. What do I take to be the explanation of this silence? I will tell you. It is an intimation that what has happened to me is a good, and that those of us who think that death is an evil are in error. For the customary sign would surely have opposed me had I been going to evil and not to good.

Let us reflect in another way, and we shall see that there is great reason to hope that death is a good; for one of two things—either death is a state of nothingness and utter unconsciousness, or, as men say, there is a change and migration of the soul from this world to another. Now if you suppose that there is no consciousness, but a sleep like the sleep of him who is undisturbed even by dreams, death will be an unspeakable gain. For if a person were to select the night in which his sleep was undisturbed even by dreams, and were to compare with this the other days and nights of his life, and then were to tell us how many days and nights he had passed in the course of his life better and more pleasantly than this one, I think that any man, I will not say a private man, but even the great king will not find many such days or nights, when compared with the others. Now if death be of such a nature, I say that to die is gain; for eternity is then only a single night. But if death is the journey to another place, and there, as men say, all the dead abide, what good, O my friends and judges, can be greater than this? If indeed when the pilgrim arrives in the world below, he is delivered from the pro- [41] fessors of justice in this world, and finds the true judges who are said to give judgment there, Minos and Rhadamanthus and Aeacus and Triptolemus, and other sons of God who were righteous in their own life, that pilgrimage will be worth making. What would not a man give if he might converse with Orpheus and Musaeus and Hesiod and Homer? Nay, if this be true, let me die again and again. I myself, too, shall have a wonderful interest in there meeting and conversing with Palamedes, and Ajax the son of Telamon, and any other ancient hero who has suffered death through an unjust judgment; and there will be no small pleasure, as I think, in comparing my own sufferings with theirs. Above all, I shall then be able to continue my search into true and false knowledge; as in this world, so also in the next; and I shall find out who is wise, and who pretends to be wise, and is not. What would not a man give, O judges, to be able to examine the leader of the great Trojan expedition; or Odysseus or Sisyphus, or numberless others, men and women too! What infinite delight would there be in conversing with them and asking them questions! In another world they do not put a man to death for asking questions: assuredly not. For besides being happier than we are, they will be immortal, if what is said is true.

Wherefore, O judges, be of good cheer about death, and know of a certainty, that no evil can happen to a good man, either in life or after death. He and his are not neglected by the gods; nor has my own approaching end happened by mere chance. But I see clearly that the time had arrived when it was better for me to die and be released from trouble; wherefore the oracle gave no sign. For which reason, also, I am not angry with my condemners, or with my accusers; they have done me no harm, although they did not mean to do me any good; and for this I may gently blame them.

Still I have a favour to ask of them. When my sons are grown up, I would ask you, O my friends, to punish them; and I would have you trouble them, as I have troubled you, if they seem to care about riches, or anything, more than about virtue; or if they pretend to be something when they are really nothing,—then reprove them, as I have reproved you, for not caring about that for which they ought to care, and thinking that they are something when they are really nothing. And if you do　[42] this, both I and my sons will have received justice at your hands.

The hour of departure has arrived, and we go our ways—I to die, and you to live. Which is better God only knows.

MENO (*complete*)

PERSONS OF THE DIALOGUE

Meno　　A slave of Meno

Socrates　*Anytus*

Meno. Can you tell me, Socrates, whether virtue is acquired by teaching or by practice; or if neither by teaching nor practice, then whether it comes to man by nature, or in what other way?

Socrates. O Meno, there was a time when the Thessalians were famous among the other Hellenes only for their riches and their riding; but now, if I am not mistaken, they are equally famous for their wisdom, especially at Larisa, which is the native city of your friend Aristippus. And this is Gorgias' doing; for when he came there, the flower of the Aleuadae, among them your admirer Aristippus, and the other chiefs of the Thessalians, fell in love with his wisdom. And he has taught you the habit of answering questions in a grand and bold style, which becomes those who know, and is the style in which he himself answers all comers; and any Hellene who likes may ask him anything. How different is our lot! my dear Meno. Here at Athens there is a dearth of the commodity,　[71] and all wisdom seems to have emigrated from us to you. I am certain that if you were to ask any Athenian whether virtue was natural or acquired, he would laugh in your face, and say: 'Stranger, you have far too good an opinion of me, if you think that I can answer your question. For I literally do not know what virtue is, and much less whether it is acquired by teaching or not.' And I myself, Meno, living as I do in this region of poverty, am as poor as the rest of the world; and I confess with shame that I know literally nothing about virtue; and when I do not know the 'quid' of anything how can I know the 'quale'? How, if I knew nothing at all of Meno, could I tell if he was fair, or the opposite of fair; rich and noble, or the reverse of rich and noble? Do you think that I could?

Men. No, indeed. But are you in earnest, Socrates, in saying that you do not know what virtue is? And am I to carry back this report of you to Thessaly?

Soc. Not only that, my dear boy, but you may say further that I have never known of any one else who did, in my judgment.

Men. Then you have never met Gorgias when he was at Athens?

Soc. Yes, I have.

Men. And did you not think that he knew?

Soc. I have not a good memory, Meno, and therefore I cannot now tell what I thought of him at the time. And I dare say that he did know, and that you know what he said: please, therefore, to remind me of what he said; or, if you would rather, tell me your own view; for I suspect that you and he think much alike.

Men. Very true.

Soc. Then as he is not here, never mind him, and do you tell me: By the gods, Meno, be generous, and tell me what you say that virtue is; for I shall be truly delighted to find that I have been mistaken, and that you and Gorgias do really have this knowledge; although I have been just saying that I have never found anybody who had.

Men. There will be no difficulty, Socrates, in answering your question. Let us take first the virtue of a man—he should know how to administer the state, and in the administration of it to benefit his friends and harm his enemies; and he must also be careful not to suffer harm himself. A woman's virtue, if you wish to know about that, may also be easily described: her duty is to order her house, and keep what is indoors, and obey her husband. Every age, every condition of life, young or old, male or female, bond or free, has a different virtue: there are virtues [72] numberless, and no lack of definitions of them; for virtue is relative to the actions and ages of each of us in all that we do. And the same may be said of vice, Socrates.[1]

Soc. How fortunate I am, Meno! When I ask you for one virtue, you present me with a swarm of them,[2] which are in your keeping. Suppose that I carry on the figure of the swarm, and ask of you, What is the nature of the bee? and you answer that there are many kinds of bees, and I reply: But do bees differ as bees, because there are many and different kinds of them; or are they not rather to be distinguished by some other quality, as for example beauty, size, or shape? How would you answer me?

Men. I should answer that bees do not differ from one another, as bees.

Soc. And if I went on to say: That is what I desire to know, Meno; tell me what is the quality in which they do not differ, but are all alike;— would you be able to answer?

Men. I should.

---

[1] Cp. Arist. Pol. i. 13, §10.
[2] Cp. Theaet. 146 D.

Soc. And so of the virtues, however many and different they may be, they have all a common nature which makes them virtues; and on this he who would answer the question, 'What is virtue?' would do well to have his eye fixed: Do you understand?

Men. I am beginning to understand; but I do not as yet take hold of the question as I could wish.

Soc. When you say, Meno, that there is one virtue of a man, another of a woman, another of a child, and so on, does this apply only to virtue, or would you say the same of health, and size, and strength? Or is the nature of health always the same, whether in man or woman?

Men. I should say that health is the same, both in man and woman.

Soc. And is not this true of size and strength? If a woman is strong, she will be strong by reason of the same form and of the same strength subsisting in her which there is in the man. I mean to say that strength, as strength, whether of man or woman, is the same. Is there any difference?

Men. I think not.

Soc. And will not virtue, as virtue, be the same, whether in a [73] child or in a grown-up person, in a woman or in a man?

Men. I cannot help feeling, Socrates, that this case is different from the others.

Soc. But why? Were you not saying that the virtue of a man was to order a state, and the virtue of a woman was to order a house?

Men. I did say so.

Soc. And can either house or state or anything be well ordered without temperance and without justice?

Men. Certainly not.

Soc. Then they who order a state or a house temperately or justly order them with temperance and justice?

Men. Certainly.

Soc. Then both men and women, if they are to be good men and women, must have the same virtues of temperance and justice?

Men. True.

Soc. And can either a young man or an elder one be good, if they are intemperate and unjust?

Men. They cannot.

Soc. They must be temperate and just?

Men. Yes.

Soc. Then all men are good in the same way, and by participation in the same virtues?

Men. Such is the inference.

Soc. And they surely would not have been good in the same way, unless their virtue had been the same?

Men. They would not.

Soc. Then now that the sameness of all virtue has been proven, try and remember what you and Gorgias say that virtue is.

Men. Will you have one definition of them all?

Soc. That is what I am seeking.

Men. If you want to have one definition of them all, I know not what to say, but that virtue is the power of governing mankind.

Soc. And does this definition of virtue include all virtue? Is virtue the same in a child and in a slave, Meno? Can the child govern his father, or the slave his master; and would he who governed be any longer a slave?

Men. I think not, Socrates.

Soc. No, indeed; there would be small reason in that. Yet once more, fair friend; according to you, virtue is 'the power of governing;' but do you not add 'justly and not unjustly'?

Men. Yes, Socrates; I agree there; for justice is virtue.

Soc. Would you say 'virtue,' Meno, or 'a virtue'?

Men. What do you mean?

Soc. I mean as I might say about anything; that a round, for example, is 'a figure' and not simply 'figure,' and I should adopt this mode of speaking, because there are other figures.

Men. Quite right; and that is just what I am saying about virtue—that there are other virtues as well as justice.

Soc. What are they? tell me the names of them, as I would tell [74] you the names of the other figures if you asked me.

Men. Courage and temperance and wisdom and magnanimity are virtues; and there are many others.

Soc. Yes, Meno; and again we are in the same case: in searching after one virtue we have found many, though not in the same way as before; but we have been unable to find the common virtue which runs through them all.

Men. Why, Socrates, even now I am not able to follow you in the attempt to get at one common notion of virtue as of other things.

Soc. No wonder; but I will try to get nearer if I can, for you know that all things have a common notion. Suppose now that some one asked you the question which I asked before: Meno, he would say, what is figure? And if you answered 'roundness,' he would reply to you, in my way of speaking, by asking whether you would say that roundness is 'figure' or 'a figure;' and you would answer 'a figure.'

Men. Certainly.

Soc. And for this reason—that there are other figures?

Men. Yes.

Soc. And if he proceeded to ask, What other figures are there? you would have told him.

Men. I should.

Soc. And if he similarly asked what colour is, and you answered whiteness, and the questioner rejoined, Would you say that whiteness is colour or a colour? you would reply, A colour, because there are other colours as well.

Men. I should.

Soc. And if he had said, Tell me what they are?—you would have told him of other colours which are colours just as much as whiteness.

Men. Yes.

Soc. And suppose that he were to pursue the matter in my way, he would say: Ever and anon we are landed in particulars, but this is not what I want; tell me then, since you call them by a common name, and say that they are all figures, even when opposed to one another, what is that common nature which you designate as figure—which contains straight as well as round, and is no more one than the other—that would be your mode of speaking?

Men. Yes.

Soc. And in speaking thus, you do not mean to say that the round is round any more than straight, or the straight any more straight than round?

Men. Certainly not.

Soc. You only assert that the round figure is not more a figure than the straight, or the straight than the round?

Men. Very true.

Soc. To what then do we give the name of figure? Try and answer. Suppose that when a person asked you this question either about figure or colour, you were to reply, Man, I do not understand what you want, or know what you are saying; he would look rather astonished [75] and say: Do you not understand that I am looking for the 'simile in multis'? And then he might put the question in another form: Meno, he might say, what is that 'simile in multis' which you call figure, and which includes not only round and straight figures, but all? Could you not answer that question, Meno? I wish that you would try; the attempt will be good practice with a view to the answer about virtue.

Men. I would rather that you should answer, Socrates.

Soc. Shall I indulge you?

Men. By all means.

Soc. And then you will tell me about virtue?

Men. I will.

Soc. Then I must do my best, for there is a prize to be won.

Men. Certainly.

Soc. Well, I will try and explain to you what figure is. What do you say to this answer?—Figure is the only thing which always follows colour. Will you be satisfied with it, as I am sure that I should be, if you would let me have a similar definition of virtue?

Men. But, Socrates, it is such a simple answer.

Soc. Why simple?

Men. Because, according to you, figure is that which always follows colour.

(*Soc.* Granted.)

Men. But if a person were to say that he does not know what colour is, any more than what figure is—what sort of answer would you have given him?

Soc. I should have told him the truth. And if he were a philosopher of the eristic and antagonistic sort, I should say to him: You have my answer, and if I am wrong, your business is to take up the argument and refute me. But if we were friends, and were talking as you and I are now, I should reply in a milder strain and more in the dialectician's vein; that is to say, I should not only speak the truth, but I should make use of premisses which the person interrogated would be willing to admit. And this is the way in which I shall endeavour to approach you. You will acknowledge, will you not, that there is such a thing as an end, or termination, or extremity?—all which words I use in the same sense, although I am aware that Prodicus might draw distinctions about them: but still you, I am sure, would speak of a thing as ended or terminated— that is all which I am saying—not anything very difficult.

Men. Yes, I should; and I believe that I understand your meaning.

Soc. And you would speak of a surface and also of a solid, as for [76] example in geometry.

Men. Yes.

Soc. Well then, you are now in a condition to understand my definition of figure. I define figure to be that in which the solid ends; or, more concisely, the limit of solid.

Men. And now, Socrates, what is colour?

Soc. You are outrageous, Meno, in thus plaguing a poor old man to give you an answer, when you will not take the trouble of remembering what is Gorgias' definition of virtue.

Men. When you have told me what I ask, I will tell you, Socrates.

Soc. A man who was blindfolded has only to hear you talking, and he would know that you are a fair creature and have still many lovers.

Men. Why do you think so?

Soc. Why, because you always speak in imperatives: like all beauties when they are in their prime, you are tyrannical; and also, as I suspect, you have found out that I have a weakness for the fair, and therefore to humour you I must answer.

Men. Please do.

Soc. Would you like me to answer you after the manner of Gorgias, which is familiar to you?

Men. I should like nothing better.

Soc. Do not he and you and Empedocles say that there are certain effluences of existence?

Men. Certainly.

Soc. And passages into which and through which the effluences pass?

Men. Exactly.

Soc. And some of the effluences fit into the passages, and some of them are too small or too large?

Men. True.

Soc. And there is such a thing as sight?

Men. Yes.

Soc. And now, as Pindar says, 'read my meaning:'—colour is an effluence of form, commensurate with sight, and palpable to sense.

Men. That, Socrates, appears to me to be an admirable answer.

Soc. Why, yes, because it happens to be one which you have been in the habit of hearing: and your wit will have discovered, I suspect, that you may explain in the same way the nature of sound and smell, and of many other similar phenomena.

Men. Quite true.

Soc. The answer, Meno, was in the orthodox solemn vein, and therefore was more acceptable to you than the other answer about figure.

Men. Yes.

Soc. And yet, O son of Alexidemus, I cannot help thinking that the other was the better; and I am sure that you would be of the same opinion, if you would only stay and be initiated, and were not compelled, as you said yesterday, to go away before the mysteries.

Men. But I will stay, Socrates, if you will give me many such answers.   [77]

Soc. Well then, for my own sake as well as for yours, I will do my very best; but I am afraid that I shall not be able to give you very many as good: and now, in your turn, you are to fulfil your promise, and tell me what virtue is in the universal; and do not make a singular into a plural, as the facetious say of those who break a thing, but deliver virtue to me whole and sound, and not broken into a number of pieces: I have given you the pattern.

Men. Well then, Socrates, virtue, as I take it, is when he, who desires the honourable, is able to provide it for himself; so the poet says, and I say too—

'Virtue is the desire of things honourable and the power of attaining them.'

Soc. And does he who desires the honourable also desire the good?

Men. Certainly.

Soc. Then are there some who desire the evil and others who desire the good? Do not all men, my dear sir, desire good?

Men. I think not.

Soc. There are some who desire evil?

Men. Yes.

Soc. Do you mean that they think the evils which they desire, to be good; or do they know that they are evil and yet desire them?

Men. Both, I think.

Soc. And do you really imagine, Meno, that a man knows evils to be evils and desires them notwithstanding?

Men. Certainly I do.

Soc. And desire is of possession?

Men. Yes, of possession.

Soc. And does he think that the evils will do good to him who possesses them, or does he know that they will do him harm?

Men. There are some who think that the evils will do them good, and others who know that they will do them harm.

Soc. And, in your opinion, do those who think that they will do them good know that they are evils?

Men. Certainly not.

Soc. Is it not obvious that those who are ignorant of their nature do not desire them; but they desire what they suppose to be goods although they are really evils; and if they are mistaken and suppose the evils to be goods they really desire goods?

Men. Yes, in that case.

Soc. Well, and do those who, as you say, desire evils, and think that evils are hurtful to the possessor of them, know that they will be hurt by them?

Men. They must know it.

Soc. And must they not suppose that those who are hurt are mis-   [78] erable in proportion to the hurt which is inflicted upon them?

Men. How can it be otherwise?

Soc. But are not the miserable ill-fated?

Men. Yes, indeed.

Soc. And does any one desire to be miserable and ill-fated?

Men. I should say not, Socrates.

Soc. But if there is no one who desires to be miserable, there is no one, Meno, who desires evil; for what is misery but the desire and possession of evil?

Men. That appears to be the truth, Socrates, and I admit that nobody desires evil.

Soc. And yet, were you not saying just now that virtue is the desire and power of attaining good?

Men. Yes, I did say so.

Soc. But if this be affirmed, then the desire of good is common to all, and one man is no better than another in that respect?

Men. True.

Soc. And if one man is not better than another in desiring good, he must be better in the power of attaining it?

Men. Exactly.

Soc. Then, according to your definition, virtue would appear to be the power of attaining good?

Men. I entirely approve, Socrates, of the manner in which you now view this matter.

Soc. Then let us see whether what you say is true from another point of view; for very likely you may be right:—You affirm virtue to be the power of attaining goods?

Men. Yes.

Soc. And the goods which you mean are such as health and wealth and the possession of gold and silver, and having office and honour in the state—those are what you would call goods?

Men. Yes, I should include all those.

Soc. Then, according to Meno, who is the hereditary friend of the great king, virtue is the power of getting silver and gold; and would you add that they must be gained piously, justly, or do you deem this to be of no consequence? And is any mode of acquisition, even if unjust and dishonest, equally to be deemed virtue?

Men. Not virtue, Socrates, but vice.

Soc.   Then justice or temperance or holiness, or some other part of virtue, as would appear, must accompany the acquisition, and without them the mere acquisition of goods will not be virtue.

Men.   Why, how can there be virtue without these?

Soc.   And the non-acquisition of gold and silver in a dishonest manner for oneself or another, or in other words the want of them, may be equally virtue?

Men.   True.

Soc.   Then the acquisition of such goods is no more virtue than the non-acquisition and want of them, but whatever is accompanied by justice or honesty is virtue, and whatever is devoid of justice is vice.   [79]

Men.   It cannot be otherwise, in my judgment.

Soc.   And were we not saying just now that justice, temperance, and the like, were each of them a part of virtue?

Men.   Yes.

Soc.   And so, Meno, this is the way in which you mock me.

Men.   Why do you say that, Socrates?

Soc.   Why, because I asked you to deliver virtue into my hands whole and unbroken, and I gave you a pattern according to which you were to frame your answer; and you have forgotten already, and tell me that virtue is the power of attaining good justly, or with justice; and justice you acknowledge to be a part of virtue.

Men.   Yes.

Soc.   Then it follows from your own admissions, that virtue is doing what you do with a part of virtue; for justice and the like are said by you to be parts of virtue.

Men.   What of that?

Soc.   What of that! Why, did not I ask you to tell me the nature of virtue as a whole? And you are very far from telling me this; but declare every action to be virtue which is done with a part of virtue; as though you had told me and I must already know the whole of virtue, and this too when frittered away into little pieces. And, therefore, my dear Meno, I fear that I must begin again and repeat the same question: What is virtue? for otherwise, I can only say, that every action done with a part of virtue is virtue; what else is the meaning of saying that every action done with justice is virtue? Ought I not to ask the question over again; for can any one who does not know virtue know a part of virtue?

Men.   No; I do not say that he can.

Soc.   Do you remember how, in the example of figure, we rejected any answer given in terms which were as yet unexplained or unadmitted?

Men.   Yes, Socrates; and we were quite right in doing so.

Soc.   But then, my friend, do not suppose that we can explain to any one the nature of virtue as a whole through some unexplained portion of virtue, or anything at all in that fashion; we should only have to ask over again the old question, What is virtue? Am I not right?

Men.   I believe that you are.

Soc. Then begin again, and answer me. What, according to you and your friend Gorgias, is the definition of virtue?

DOUBT AND RECOLLECTION

Men. O Socrates, I used to be told, before I knew you, that you were always doubting yourself and making others doubt; and now [80] you are casting your spells over me, and I am simply getting bewitched and enchanted, and am at my wits' end. And if I may venture to make a jest upon you, you seem to me both in your appearance and in your power over others to be very like the flat torpedo fish, who torpifies those who come near him and touch him, as you have now torpified me, I think. For my soul and my tongue are really torpid, and I do not know how to answer you; and though I have been delivered of an infinite variety of speeches about virtue before now, and to many persons—and very good ones they were, as I thought—at this moment I cannot even say what virtue is. And I think that you are very wise in not voyaging and going away from home, for if you did in other places as you do in Athens, you would be cast into prison as a magician.

Soc. You are a rogue, Meno, and had all but caught me.

Men. What do you mean, Socrates?

Soc. I can tell why you made a simile about me.

Men. Why?

Soc. In order that I might make another simile about you. For I know that all pretty young gentlemen like to have pretty similes made about them—as well they may—but I shall not return the compliment. As to my being a torpedo, if the torpedo is torpid as well as the cause of torpidity in others, then indeed I am a torpedo, but not otherwise; for I perplex others, not because I am clear, but because I am utterly perplexed myself. And now I know not what virtue is, and you seem to be in the same case, although you did once perhaps know before you touched me. However, I have no objection to join with you in the enquiry.

Men. And how will you enquire, Socrates, into that which you do not know? What will you put forth as the subject of enquiry? And if you find what you want, how will you ever know that this is the thing which you did not know?

Soc. I know, Meno, what you mean; but just see what a tiresome dispute you are introducing. You argue that a man cannot enquire either about that which he knows, or about that which he does not know; for if he knows, he has no need to enquire; and if not, he cannot; for he does not know the very subject about which he is to enquire.[3]

Men. Well, Socrates, and is not the argument sound? [81]

Soc. I think not.

Men. Why not?

Soc. I will tell you why: I have heard from certain wise men and women who spoke of things divine that—

---

[3] Cp. Aristot. Post. Anal. I. i. 6.

Men.   What did they say?

Soc.   They spoke of a glorious truth, as I conceive.

Men.   What was it? and who were they?

Soc.   Some of them were priests and priestesses, who had studied how they might be able to give a reason of their profession: there have been poets also, who spoke of these things by inspiration, like Pindar, and many others who were inspired. And they say—mark, now, and see whether their words are true—they say that the soul of man is immortal, and at one time has an end, which is termed dying, and at another time is born again, but is never destroyed. And the moral is, that a man ought to live always in perfect holiness. '*For in the ninth year Persephone sends the souls of those from whom she has received the penalty of ancient crime back again from beneath into the light of the sun above, and these are they who become noble kings and mighty men and great in wisdom and are called saintly heroes in after ages.*' The soul, then, as being immortal, and having been born again many times, and having seen all things that exist, whether in this world or in the world below, has knowledge of them all; and it is no wonder that she should be able to call to remembrance all that she ever knew about virtue, and about everything; for as all nature is akin, and the soul has learned all things, there is no difficulty in her eliciting or as men say learning, out of a single recollection all the rest, if a man is strenuous and does not faint; for all enquiry and all learning is but recollection. And therefore we ought not to listen to this sophistical argument about the impossibility of enquiry: for it will make us idle and is sweet only to the sluggard; but the other saying will make us active and inquisitive. In that confiding, I will gladly enquire with you into the nature of virtue.

Men.   Yes, Socrates; but what do you mean by saying that we do not learn, and that what we call learning is only a process of recollection? Can you teach me how this is?

Soc.   I told you, Meno, just now that you were a rogue, and now you ask whether I can teach you, when I am saying that there is no teaching, but only recollection; and thus you imagine that you will involve   [82] me in a contradiction.

Men.   Indeed, Socrates, I protest that I had no such intention. I only asked the question from habit; but if you can prove to me that what you say is true, I wish that you would.

Soc.   It will be no easy matter, but I will try to please you to the utmost of my power. Suppose that you call one of your numerous attendants, that I may demonstrate on him.

Men.   Certainly. Come hither, boy.

Soc.   He is Greek, and speaks Greek, does he not?

Men.   Yes, indeed; he was born in the house.

Soc.   Attend now to the questions which I ask him, and observe whether he learns of me or only remembers.

Men.   I will.

Soc.   Tell me, boy, do you know that a figure like this is a square?

Boy. I do.

Soc. And you know that a square figure has these four lines equal?

Boy. Certainly.

Soc. And these lines which I have drawn through the middle of the square are also equal?

Boy. Yes.

Soc. A square may be of any size?

Boy. Certainly.

Soc. And if one side of the figure be of two feet, and the other side be of two feet, how much will the whole be? Let me explain: if in one direction the space was of two feet, and in the other direction of one foot, the whole would be of two feet taken once?

Boy. Yes.

Soc. But since this side is also of two feet, there are twice two feet?

Boy. There are.

Soc. Then the square is of twice two feet?

Boy. Yes.

Soc. And how many are twice two feet? count and tell me.

Boy. Four, Socrates.

Soc. And might there not be another square twice as large as this, and having like this the lines equal?

Boy. Yes.

Soc. And of how many feet will that be?

Boy. Of eight feet.

Soc. And now try and tell me the length of the line which forms the side of that double square: this is two feet—what will that be?

Boy. Clearly, Socrates, it will be double.

Soc. Do you observe, Meno, that I am not teaching the boy anything, but only asking him questions; and now he fancies that he knows how long a line is necessary in order to produce a figure of eight square feet; does he not?

Men. Yes.

Soc. And does he really know?

Men. Certainly not.

Soc. He only guesses that because the square is double, the line is double.

Men. True.

Soc. Observe him while he recalls the steps in regular order. (*To the boy.*) Tell me, boy, do you assert that a double space comes [83] from a double line? Remember that I am not speaking of an oblong, but of a figure equal every way, and twice the size of this—that is to say of eight feet; and I want to know whether you still say that a double square comes from a double line?

Boy. Yes.

Soc. But does not this line become doubled if we add another such line here?

Boy. Certainly.

Soc. And four such lines will make a space containing eight feet?

Boy. Yes.

Soc. Let us describe such a figure: Would you not say that this is the figure of eight feet?

Boy. Yes.

Soc. And are there not these four divisions in the figure, each of which is equal to the figure of four feet?

Boy. True.

Soc. And is not that four times four?

Boy. Certainly.

Soc. And four times is not double?

Boy. No, indeed.

Soc. But how much?

Boy. Four times as much.

Soc. Therefore the double line, boy, has given a space, not twice, but four times as much.

Boy. True.

Soc. Four times four are sixteen—are they not?

Boy. Yes.

Soc. What line would give you a space of eight feet, as this gives one of sixteen feet;—do you see?

Boy. Yes.

Soc. And the space of four feet is made from this half line?

Boy. Yes.

Soc. Good; and is not a space of eight feet twice the size of this, and half the size of the other?

Boy. Certainly.

Soc. Such a space, then, will be made out of a line greater than this one, and less than that one?

Boy. Yes; I think so.

Soc. Very good; I like to hear you say what you think. And now tell me, is not this a line of two feet and that of four?

Boy. Yes.

Soc. Then the line which forms the side of eight feet ought to be more than this line of two feet, and less than the other of four feet?

Boy. It ought.

Soc. Try and see if you can tell me how much it will be.

Boy. Three feet.

Soc. Then if we add a half to this line of two, that will be the line of three. Here are two and there is one; and on the other side, here are two also and there is one: and that makes the figure of which you speak?

Boy. Yes.

Soc. But if there are three feet this way and three feet that way, the whole space will be three times three feet?

Boy. That is evident.

Soc. And how much are three times three feet?

Boy. Nine.

Soc. And how much is the double of four?

Boy. Eight.

Soc. Then the figure of eight is not made out of a line of three?

Boy. No.

Soc. But from what line?—tell me exactly; and if you would [84] rather not reckon, try and show me the line.

Boy. Indeed, Socrates, I do not know.

Soc. Do you see, Meno, what advances he has made in his power of recollection? He did not know at first, and he does not know now, what is the side of a figure of eight feet: but then he thought that he knew, and answered confidently as if he knew, and had no difficulty; now he has a difficulty, and neither knows nor fancies that he knows.

Men. True.

Soc. Is he not better off in knowing his ignorance?

Men. I think that he is.

Soc. If we have made him doubt, and given him the 'torpedo's shock,' have we done him any harm?

Men. I think not.

Soc. We have certainly, as would seem, assisted him in some degree to the discovery of the truth; and now he will wish to remedy his ignorance, but then he would have been ready to tell all the world again and again that the double space should have a double side.

Men. True.

Soc. But do you suppose that he would ever have enquired into or learned what he fancied that he knew, though he was really ignorant of it, until he had fallen into perplexity under the idea that he did not know, and had desired to know?

Men. I think not, Socrates.

Soc. Then he was the better for the torpedo's touch?

Men. I think so.

Soc. Mark now the farther development. I shall only ask him, and not teach him, and he shall share the enquiry with me: and do you watch and see if you find me telling or explaining anything to him, instead of eliciting his opinion. Tell me, boy, is not this a square of four feet which I have drawn?

Boy. Yes.

Soc. And now I add another square equal to the former one?

Boy. Yes.

Soc. And a third, which is equal to either of them?

Boy. Yes.

Soc. Suppose that we fill up the vacant corner?

Boy. Very good.

Soc. Here, then, there are four equal spaces?

Boy. Yes.

Soc. And how many times larger is this space than this other?

Boy. Four times.

Soc.   But it ought to have been twice only, as you will remember.

Boy.   True.

Soc.   And does not this line, reaching from corner to corner, bisect
each of these spaces?   [85]

Boy.   Yes.

Soc.   And are there not here four equal lines which contain this space?

Boy.   There are.

Soc.   Look and see how much this space is.

Boy.   I do not understand.

Soc.   Has not each interior line cut off half of the four spaces?

Boy.   Yes.

Soc.   And how many spaces are there in this section?

Boy.   Four.

Soc.   And how many in this?

Boy.   Two.

Soc.   And four is how many times two?

Boy.   Twice.

Soc.   And this space is of how many feet?

Boy.   Of eight feet.

Soc.   And from what line do you get this figure?

Boy.   From this.

Soc.   That is, from the line which extends from corner to corner of
the figure of four feet?

Boy.   Yes.

Soc.   And that is the line which the learned call the diagonal. And if
this is the proper name, then you, Meno's slave, are prepared to affirm
that the double space is the square of the diagonal?

Boy.   Certainly, Socrates.

Soc.   What do you say of him, Meno? Were not all these answers given
out of his own head?

Men.   Yes, they were all his own.

Soc.   And yet, as we were just now saying, he did not know?

Men.   True.

Soc.   But still he had in him those notions of his—had he not?

Men.   Yes.

Soc.   Then he who does not know may still have true notions of that
which he does not know?

Men.   He has.

Soc.   And at present these notions have just been stirred up in him,
as in a dream; but if he were frequently asked the same questions, in
different forms, he would know as well as any one at last?

Men.   I dare say.

Soc.   Without any one teaching him he will recover his knowledge
for himself, if he is only asked questions?

Men.   Yes.

Soc.   And this spontaneous recovery of knowledge in him is recollection?

Men. True.

Soc. And this knowledge which he now has must he not either have acquired or always possessed?

Men. Yes.

Soc. But if he always possessed this knowledge he would always have known; or if he has acquired the knowledge he could not have acquired it in this life, unless he has been taught geometry; for he may be made to do the same with all geometry and every other branch of knowledge. Now, has any one ever taught him all this? You must know about him, if, as you say, he was born and bred in your house.

Men. I am certain that no one ever did teach him.

Soc. And yet he has the knowledge?

Men. The fact, Socrates, is undeniable.

Soc. But if he did not acquire the knowledge in this life, then he must have had and learned it at some other time?   [86]

Men. Clearly he must.

Soc. Which must have been the time when he was not a man?

Men. Yes.

Soc. And if there have been always true thoughts in him, both at the time when he was and was not a man, which only need to be awakened into knowledge by putting questions to him, his soul must have always possessed this knowledge, for he always either was or was not a man?

Men. Obviously.

Soc. And if the truth of all things always existed in the soul, then the soul is immortal. Wherefore be of good cheer, and try to recollect what you do not know, or rather what you do not remember.

Men. I feel, somehow, that I like what you are saying.

Soc. And I, Meno, like what I am saying. Some things I have said of which I am not altogether confident. But that we shall be better and braver and less helpless if we think that we ought to enquire, than we should have been if we indulged in the idle fancy that there was no knowing and no use in seeking to know what we do not know;—that is a theme upon which I am ready to fight, in word and deed, to the utmost of my power.

Men. There again, Socrates, your words seem to me excellent.

CAN VIRTUE BE TAUGHT?

Soc. Then, as we are agreed that a man should enquire about that which he does not know, shall you and I make an effort to enquire together into the nature of virtue?

Men. By all means, Socrates. And yet I would much rather return to my original question, Whether in seeking to acquire virtue we should regard it as a thing to be taught, or as a gift of nature, or as coming to men in some other way?

Soc. Had I the command of you as well as of myself, Meno, I would not have enquired whether virtue is given by instruction or not, until we had first ascertained 'what it is.' But as you think only of controlling me who am your slave, and never of controlling yourself,—such being your notion of freedom, I must yield to you, for you are irresistible. And therefore I have now to enquire into the qualities of a thing of which I do not as yet know the nature. At any rate, will you condescend a little, and allow the question 'Whether virtue is given by instruction, or in any other way,' to be argued upon hypothesis? As the geometrician,   [87] when he is asked [4] whether a certain triangle is capable of being inscribed in a certain circle,[4] will reply: 'I cannot tell you as yet; but I will offer a hypothesis which may assist us in forming a conclusion: If the figure be such that [5] when you have produced a given side of it,[5] the given area of the triangle falls short by an area [6] corresponding to the part produced,[6] then one consequence follows, and if this is impossible then some other; and therefore I wish to assume a hypothesis before I tell you whether this triangle is capable of being inscribed in the circle:'—that is a geometrical hypothesis. And we too, as we know not the nature and qualities of virtue, must ask, whether virtue is or is not taught, under a hypothesis: as thus, if virtue is of such a class of mental goods, will it be taught or not? Let the first hypothesis be that virtue is or is not knowledge,—in that case will it be taught or not? or, as we were just now saying, 'remembered'? For there is no use in disputing about the name. But is virtue taught or not? or rather, does not every one see that knowledge alone is taught?

Men.   I agree.

Soc.   Then if virtue is knowledge, virtue will be taught?

Men.   Certainly.

Soc.   Then now we have made a quick end of this question: if virtue is of such a nature, it will be taught; and if not, not?

Men.   Certainly.

Soc.   The next question is, whether virtue is knowledge or of another species?

Men.   Yes, that appears to be the question which comes next in order.

Soc.   Do we not say that virtue is a good?—This is a hypothesis which is not set aside.

Men.   Certainly.

Soc.   Now, if there be any sort of good which is distinct from knowledge, virtue may be that good; but if knowledge embraces all good, then we shall be right in thinking that virtue is knowledge?

Men.   True.

Soc.   And virtue makes us good?

Men.   Yes.

Soc.   And if we are good, then we are profitable; for all good things are profitable?

Men.   Yes.

---

[4] Or, whether a certain area is capable of being inscribed as a triangle in a certain circle.

[5] Or, when you apply it to the given line, i.e. the diameter of the circle (αὐτοῦ)

[6] Or, similar to the area so applied.

Soc. Then virtue is profitable?

Men. That is the only inference.

Soc. Then now let us see what are the things which severally profit us. Health and strength, and beauty and wealth—these, and the like of these, we call profitable?

Men. True.

Soc. And yet these things may also sometimes do us harm: [88] would you not think so?

Men. Yes.

Soc. And what is the guiding principle which makes them profitable or the reverse? Are they not profitable when they are rightly used, and hurtful when they are not rightly used?

Men. Certainly.

Soc. Next, let us consider the goods of the soul: they are temperance, justice, courage, quickness of apprehension, memory, magnanimity, and the like?

Men. Surely.

Soc. And such of these as are not knowledge, but of another sort, are sometimes profitable and sometimes hurtful; as, for example, courage wanting prudence, which is only a sort of confidence? When a man has no sense he is harmed by courage, but when he has sense he is profited?

Men. True.

Soc. And the same may be said of temperance and quickness of apprehension; whatever things are learned or done with sense are profitable, but when done without sense they are hurtful?

Men. Very true.

Soc. And in general, all that the soul attempts or endures, when under the guidance of wisdom, ends in happiness; but when she is under the guidance of folly, in the opposite?

Men. That appears to be true.

Soc. If then virtue is a quality of the soul, and is admitted to be profitable, it must be wisdom or prudence, since none of the things of the soul are either profitable or hurtful in themselves, but they are all made profitable or hurtful by the addition of wisdom or of folly; and therefore if virtue is profitable, virtue must be a sort of wisdom or prudence?

Men. I quite agree.

Soc. And the other goods, such as wealth and the like, of which we were just now saying that they are sometimes good and sometimes evil, do not they also become profitable or hurtful, accordingly as the soul guides and uses them rightly or wrongly; just as the things of the soul herself are benefited when under the guidance of wisdom and harmed by folly?

Men. True.

Soc. And the wise soul guides them rightly, and the foolish soul wrongly.

Men. Yes.

Soc. And is not this universally true of human nature? All other things hang upon the soul, and the things of the soul herself hang upon wisdom, if they are to be good; and so wisdom is inferred to be that which profits—and virtue, as we say, is profitable?   [89]

Men. Certainly.

Soc. And thus we arrive at the conclusion that virtue is either wholly or partly wisdom?

Men. I think that what you are saying, Socrates, is very true.

Soc. But if this is true, then the good are not by nature good?

Men. I think not.

Soc. If they had been, there would assuredly have been discerners of characters among us who would have known our future great men; and on their showing we should have adopted them, and when we had got them, we should have kept them in the citadel out of the way of harm, and set a stamp upon them far rather than upon a piece of gold, in order that no one might tamper with them; and when they grew up they would have been useful to the state?

Men. Yes, Socrates, that would have been the right way.

Soc. But if the good are not by nature good, are they made good by instruction?

Men. There appears to be no other alternative, Socrates. On the supposition that virtue is knowledge, there can be no doubt that virtue is taught.

Soc. Yes, indeed; but what if the supposition is erroneous?

Men. I certainly thought just now that we were right.

Soc. Yes, Meno; but a principle which has any soundness should stand firm not only just now, but always.

Men. Well; and why are you so slow of heart to believe that knowledge is virtue?

Soc. I will try and tell you why, Meno. I do not retract the assertion that if virtue is knowledge it may be taught; but I fear that I have some reason in doubting whether virtue is knowledge: for consider now and say whether virtue, and not only virtue but anything that is taught, must not have teachers and disciples?

Men. Surely.

Soc. And conversely, may not the art of which neither teachers nor disciples exist be assumed to be incapable of being taught?

Men. True; but do you think that there are no teachers of virtue?

Soc. I have certainly often enquired whether there were any, and taken great pains to find them, and have never succeeded; and many have assisted me in the search, and they were the persons whom I thought the most likely to know. Here at the moment when he is wanted we fortunately have sitting by us Anytus, the very [90] person of whom we should make enquiry; to him then let us repair. In the first place, he is the son of a wealthy and wise father, Anthemion, who acquired his wealth, not by accident or gift, like Ismenias the Theban (who has recently made himself as rich as Polycrates), but by his own

skill and industry, and who is a well-conditioned, modest man, not insolent, or over-bearing, or annoying; moreover, this son of his has received
a good education, as the Athenian people certainly appear to think, for
they choose him to fill the highest offices. And these are the sort of men
from whom you are likely to learn whether there are any teachers of
virtue, and who they are. Please, Anytus, to help me and your friend
Meno in answering our question, Who are the teachers? Consider the
matter thus: If we wanted Meno to be a good physician, to whom should
we send him? Should we not send him to the physicians?

Any. Certainly.

Soc. Or if we wanted him to be a good cobbler, should we not send
him to the cobblers?

Any. Yes.

Soc. And so forth?

Any. Yes.

Soc. Let me trouble you with one more question. When we say that
we should be right in sending him to the physicians if we wanted him to
be a physician, do we mean that we should be right in sending him to
those who profess the art, rather than to those who do not, and to those
who demand payment for teaching the art, and profess to teach it to
any one who will come and learn? And if these were our reasons, should
we not be right in sending him?

Any. Yes.

Soc. And might not the same be said of flute-playing, and of the
other arts? Would a man who wanted to make another a flute-player
refuse to send him to those who profess to teach the art for money, and
be plaguing other persons to give him instruction, who are not professed
teachers and who never had a single disciple in that branch of knowledge
which he wishes him to acquire—would not such conduct be the height of
folly?

Any. Yes, by Zeus, and of ignorance too.

Soc. Very good. And now you are in a position to advise with me [91]
about my friend Meno. He has been telling me, Anytus, that he desires
to attain that kind of wisdom and virtue by which men order the state
or the house, and honour their parents, and know when to receive and
when to send away citizens and strangers, as a good man should. Now,
to whom should he go in order that he may learn this virtue? Does not
the previous argument imply clearly that we should send him to those
who profess and avouch that they are the common teachers of all Hellas,
and are ready to impart instruction to any one who likes, at a fixed price?

Any. Whom do you mean, Socrates?

Soc. You surely know, do you not, Anytus, that these are the people
whom mankind call Sophists?

Any. By Heracles, Socrates, forbear! I only hope that no friend or
kinsman or acquaintance of mine, whether citizen or stranger, will ever
be so mad as to allow himself to be corrupted by them; for they are a
manifest pest and corrupting influence to those who have to do with them.

Soc. What, Anytus? Of all the people who profess that they know how to do men good, do you mean to say that these are the only ones who not only do them no good, but positively corrupt those who are entrusted to them, and in return for this disservice have the face to demand money? Indeed, I cannot believe you; for I know of a single man, Protagoras, who made more out of his craft than the illustrious Pheidias, who created such noble works, or any ten other statuaries. How could that be? A mender of old shoes, or patcher up of clothes, who made the shoes or clothes worse than he received them, could not have remained thirty days undetected, and would very soon have starved; whereas during more than forty years, Protagoras was corrupting all Hellas, and sending his disciples from him worse than he received them, and he was never found out. For, if I am not mistaken, he was about seventy years old at his death, forty of which were spent in the practice of his profession; and during all that time he had a good reputation, which to this day he retains: and not only Protagoras, but many others are well spoken of; some who lived before him, and others who are still living. Now, when you say that they deceived and corrupted the [92] youth, are they to be supposed to have corrupted them consciously or unconsciously? Can those who were deemed by many to be the wisest men of Hellas have been out of their minds?

Any. Out of their minds! No, Socrates; the young men who gave their money to them were out of their minds, and their relations and guardians who entrusted their youth to the care of these men were still more out of their minds, and most of all, the cities who allowed them to come in, and did not drive them out, citizen and stranger alike.

Soc. Has any of the Sophists wronged you, Anytus? What makes you so angry with them?

Any. No, indeed, neither I nor any of my belongings has ever had, nor would I suffer them to have, anything to do with them.

Soc. Then you are entirely unacquainted with them?

Any. And I have no wish to be acquainted.

Soc. Then, my dear friend, how can you know whether a thing is good or bad of which you are wholly ignorant?

Any. Quite well; I am sure that I know what manner of men these are, whether I am acquainted with them or not.

Soc. You must be a diviner, Anytus, for I really cannot make out, judging from your own words, how, if you are not acquainted with them, you know about them. But I am not enquiring of you who are the teachers who will corrupt Meno (let them be, if you please, the Sophists); I only ask you to tell him who there is in this great city who will teach him how to become eminent in the virtues which I was just now describing. He is the friend of your family, and you will oblige him.

Any. Why do you not tell him yourself?

Soc. I have told him whom I supposed to be the teachers of these things; but I learn from you that I am utterly at fault, and I dare say that you are right. And now I wish that you, on your part, would tell me to whom among the Athenians he should go. Whom would you name?

Any. Why single out individuals? Any Athenian gentleman, taken at random, if he will mind him, will do far more good to him than the Sophists.

Soc. And did those gentlemen grow of themselves; and without having been taught by any one, were they nevertheless able to teach others that which they had never learned themselves? [93]

Any. I imagine that they learned of the previous generation of gentlemen. Have there not been many good men in this city?

Soc. Yes, certainly, Anytus; and many good statesmen also there always have been and there are still, in the city of Athens. But the question is whether they were also good teachers of their own virtue;—not whether there are, or have been, good men in this part of the world, but whether virtue can be taught, is the question which we have been discussing. Now, do we mean to say that the good men of our own and of other times knew how to impart to others that virtue which they had themselves; or is virtue a thing incapable of being communicated or imparted by one man to another? That is the question which I and Meno have been arguing. Look at the matter in your own way: Would you not admit that Themistocles was a good man?

Any. Certainly; no man better.

Soc. And must not he then have been a good teacher, if any man ever was a good teacher, of his own virtue?

Any. Yes, certainly,—if he wanted to be so.

Soc. But would he not have wanted? He would, at any rate, have desired to make his own son a good man and a gentleman; he could not have been jealous of him, or have intentionally abstained from imparting to him his own virtue. Did you never hear that he made his son Cleophantus a famous horseman; and had him taught to stand upright on horseback and hurl a javelin, and to do many other marvellous things; and in anything which could be learned from a master he was well trained? Have you not heard from our elders of him?

Any. I have.

Soc. Then no one could say that his son showed any want of capacity?

Any. Very likely not.

Soc. But did any one, old or young, ever say in your hearing that Cleophantus, son of Themistocles, was a wise or good man, as his father was?

Any. I have certainly never heard any one say so.

Soc. And if virtue could have been taught, would his father Themistocles have sought to train him in these minor accomplishments, and allowed him who, as you must remember, was his own son, to be no better than his neighbours in those qualities in which he himself excelled?

Any. Indeed, indeed, I think not.

Soc. Here was a teacher of virtue whom you admit to be among the best men of the past. Let us take another,—Aristides, the son [94] of Lysimachus: would you not acknowledge that he was a good man?

Any. To be sure I should.

Soc. And did not he train his son Lysimachus better than any other Athenian in all that could be done for him by the help of masters? But what has been the result? Is he a bit better than any other mortal? He is an acquaintance of yours, and you see what he is like. There is Pericles, again, magnificent in his wisdom; and he, as you are aware, had two sons, Paralus and Xanthippus.

Any. I know.

Soc. And you know, also, that he taught them to be unrivalled horsemen, and had them trained in music and gymnastics and all sorts of arts—in these respects they were on a level with the best—and had he no wish to make good men of them? Nay, he must have wished it. But virtue, as I suspect, could not be taught. And that you may not suppose the incompetent teachers to be only the meaner sort of Athenians and few in number, remember again that Thucydides had two sons, Melesias and Stephanus, whom, besides giving them a good education in other things, he trained in wrestling, and they were the best wrestlers in Athens: one of them he committed to the care of Xanthias, and the other of Eudorus, who had the reputation of being the most celebrated wrestlers of that day. Do you remember them?

Any. I have heard of them.

Soc. Now, can there be a doubt that Thucydides, whose children were taught things for which he had to spend money, would have taught them to be good men, which would have cost him nothing, if virtue could have been taught? Will you reply that he was a mean man, and had not many friends among the Athenians and allies? Nay, but he was of a great family, and a man of influence at Athens and in all Hellas, and, if virtue could have been taught, he would have found out some Athenian or foreigner who would have made good men of his sons, if he could not himself spare the time from cares of state. Once more, I suspect, friend Anytus, that virtue is not a thing which can be taught?

Any. Socrates, I think that you are too ready to speak evil of men: and, if you will take my advice, I would recommend you to be careful. Perhaps there is no city in which it is not easier to do men harm than to do them good, and this is certainly the case at Athens, as I [95] believe that you know.

Soc. O Meno, I think that Anytus is in a rage. And he may well be in a rage, for he thinks, in the first place, that I am defaming these gentlemen; and in the second place, he is of opinion that he is one of them himself. But some day he will know what is the meaning of defamation, and if he ever does, he will forgive me. Meanwhile I will return to you, Meno; for I suppose that there are gentlemen in your region too?

Men. Certainly there are.

Soc. And are they willing to teach the young? and do they profess to be teachers? and do they agree that virtue is taught?

Men. No indeed, Socrates, they are anything but agreed; you may hear them saying at one time that virtue can be taught, and then again the reverse.

Soc. Can we call those teachers who do not acknowledge the possibility of their own vocation?

Men. I think not, Socrates.

Soc. And what do you think of these Sophists, who are the only professors? Do they seem to you to be teachers of virtue?

Men. I often wonder, Socrates, that Gorgias is never heard promising to teach virtue: and when he hears others promising he only laughs at them; but he thinks that men should be taught to speak.

Soc. Then do you not think that the Sophists are teachers?

Men. I cannot tell you, Socrates; like the rest of the world, I am in doubt, and sometimes I think that they are teachers and sometimes not.

Soc. And are you aware that not you only and other politicians have doubts whether virtue can be taught or not, but that Theognis the poet says the very same thing?

Men. Where does he say so?

Soc. In these elegiac verses [7]:—

'Eat and drink and sit with the mighty, and make yourself agreeable to them; for from the good you will learn what is good, but if you mix with the bad you will lose the intelligence which you already have.'

Do you observe that here he seems to imply that virtue can be taught?

Men. Clearly.

Soc. But in some other verses he shifts about and says [8]:—

'If understanding could be created and put into a man, then they' [who were able to perform this feat] 'would have obtained great rewards.'

And again:—

'Never would a bad son have sprung from a good sire, for he would have [96] heard the voice of instruction; but not by teaching will you ever make a bad man into a good one.'

And this, as you may remark, is a contradiction of the other.

Men. Clearly.

Soc. And is there anything else of which the professors are affirmed not only not to be teachers of others, but to be ignorant themselves, and bad at the knowledge of that which they are professing to teach? or is there anything about which even the acknowledged 'gentlemen' are sometimes saying that 'this thing can be taught,' and sometimes the opposite? Can you say that they are teachers in any true sense whose ideas are in such confusion?

Men. I should say, certainly not.

---

[7] Theog. 33 ff.
[8] Theog. 435 ff.

Soc. But if neither the Sophists nor the gentlemen are teachers, clearly there can be no other teachers?

Men. No.

Soc. And if there are no teachers, neither are there disciples?

Men. Agreed.

Soc. And we have admitted that a thing cannot be taught of which there are neither teachers nor disciples?

Men. We have.

Soc. And there are no teachers of virtue to be found anywhere?

Men. There are not.

Soc. And if there are no teachers, neither are there scholars?

Men. That, I think, is true.

Soc. Then virtue cannot be taught?

Men. Not if we are right in our view. But I cannot believe, Socrates, that there are no good men: And if there are, how did they come into existence?

KNOWLEDGE AND RIGHT OPINION

Soc. I am afraid, Meno, that you and I are not good for much, and that Gorgias has been as poor an educator of you as Prodicus has been of me. Certainly we shall have to look to ourselves, and try to find some one who will help in some way or other to improve us. This I say, because I observe that in the previous discussion none of us remarked that right and good action is possible to man under other guidance than that of knowledge ($\grave{\epsilon}\pi\iota\sigma\tau\acute{\eta}\mu\eta$);—and indeed if this be denied, there is no seeing how there can be any good men at all.

Men. How do you mean, Socrates?

Soc. I mean that good men are necessarily useful or profitable. Were we not right in admitting this? It must be so.   [97]

Men. Yes.

Soc. And in supposing that they will be useful only if they are true guides to us of action—there we were also right?

Men. Yes.

Soc. But when we said that a man cannot be a good guide unless he have knowledge ($\varphi\varrho\acute{o}\nu\eta\sigma\iota\varsigma$), in this we were wrong.

Men. What do you mean by the word 'right'?

Soc. I will explain. If a man knew the way to Larisa, or anywhere else, and went to the place and led others thither, would he not be a right and good guide?

Men. Certainly.

Soc. And a person who had a right opinion about the way, but had never been and did not know, might be a good guide also, might he not?

Men. Certainly.

Soc. And while he has true opinion about that which the other knows, he will be just as good a guide if he thinks the truth, as he who knows the truth?

Men. Exactly.

Soc. Then true opinion is as good a guide to correct action as knowledge; and that was the point which we omitted in our speculation about the nature of virtue, when we said that knowledge only is the guide of right action; whereas there is also right opinion.

Men. True.

Soc. Then right opinion is not less useful than knowledge?

Men. The difference, Socrates, is only that he who has knowledge will always be right; but he who has right opinion will sometimes be right, and sometimes not.

Soc. What do you mean? Can he be wrong who has right opinion, so long as he has right opinion?

Men. I admit the cogency of your argument, and therefore, Socrates, I wonder that knowledge should be preferred to right opinion—or why they should ever differ.

Soc. And shall I explain this wonder to you?

Men. Do tell me.

Soc. You would not wonder if you had ever observed the images of Daedalus [9]; but perhaps you have not got them in your country?

Men. What have they to do with the question?

Soc. Because they require to be fastened in order to keep them, and if they are not fastened they will play truant and run away.

Men. Well, what of that?

Soc. I mean to say that they are not very valuable possessions if they are at liberty, for they will walk off like runaway slaves; but when fastened, they are of great value, for they are really beautiful works of art. Now this is an illustration of the nature of true opinions: [98] while they abide with us they are beautiful and fruitful, but they run away out of the human soul, and do not remain long, and therefore they are not of much value until they are fastened by the tie of the cause; and this fastening of them, friend Meno, is recollection, as you and I have agreed to call it. But when they are bound, in the first place, they have the nature of knowledge; and, in the second place, they are abiding. And this is why knowledge is more honourable and excellent than true opinion, because fastened by a chain.

Men. What you are saying, Socrates, seems to be very like the truth.

Soc. I too speak rather in ignorance; I only conjecture. And yet that knowledge differs from true opinion is no matter of conjecture with me. There are not many things which I profess to know, but this is most certainly one of them.

Men. Yes, Socrates; and you are quite right in saying so.

Soc. And am I not also right in saying that true opinion leading the way perfects action quite as well as knowledge?

Men. There again, Socrates, I think you are right.

Soc. Then right opinion is not a whit inferior to knowledge, or less

---

[9] Cp. Euthyphro 11 B.

useful in action; nor is the man who has right opinion inferior to him who has knowledge?

Men. True.

Soc. And surely the good man has been acknowledged by us to be useful?

Men. Yes.

Soc. Seeing then that men become good and useful to states, not only because they have knowledge, but because they have right opinion, and that neither knowledge nor right opinion is given to man by nature or acquired by him—(do you imagine either of them to be given by nature?

Men. Not I.)

Soc. Then if they are not given by nature, neither are the good by nature good?

Men. Certainly not.

Soc. And nature being excluded, then came the question whether virtue is acquired by teaching?

Men. Yes.

Soc. If virtue was wisdom [or knowledge], then, as we thought, it was taught?

Men. Yes.

Soc. And if it was taught it was wisdom?

Men. Certainly.

Soc. And if there were teachers, it might be taught; and if there were no teachers, not?

Men. True.

Soc. But surely we acknowledged that there were no teachers of virtue?

Men. Yes.

Soc. Then we acknowledged that it was not taught, and was not wisdom?

Men. Certainly.

Soc. And yet we admitted that it was a good?

Men. Yes.

Soc. And the right guide is useful and good?   [99]

Men. Certainly.

Soc. And the only right guides are knowledge and true opinion— these are the guides of man; for things which happen by chance are not under the guidance of man: but the guides of man are true opinion and knowledge.

Men. I think so too.

Soc. But if virtue is not taught, neither is virtue knowledge.

Men. Clearly not.

Soc. Then of two good and useful things, one, which is knowledge, has been set aside, and cannot be supposed to be our guide in political life.

Men. I think not.

Soc. And therefore not by any wisdom, and not because they were wise, did Themistocles and those others of whom Anytus spoke govern states. This was the reason why they were unable to make others like themselves—because their virtue was not grounded on knowledge.

Men. That is probably true, Socrates.

Soc. But if not by knowledge, the only alternative which remains is that statesmen must have guided states by right opinion, which is in politics what divination is in religion; for diviners and also prophets say many things truly, but they know not what they say.

Men. So I believe.

Soc. And may we not, Meno, truly call those men 'divine' who, having no understanding, yet succeed in many a grand deed and word?

Men. Certainly.

Soc. Then we shall also be right in calling divine those whom we were just now speaking of as diviners and prophets, including the whole tribe of poets. Yes, and statesmen above all may be said to be divine and illumined, being inspired and possessed of God, in which condition they say many grand things, not knowing what they say.

Men. Yes.

Soc. And the women too, Meno, call good men divine—do they not? and the Spartans, when they praise a good man, say 'that he is a divine man.'

Men. And I think, Socrates, that they are right; although very likely our friend Anytus may take offence at the word

Soc. I do not care; as for Anytus, there will be another opportunity of talking with him. To sum up our enquiry—the result seems to be, if we are at all right in our view, that virtue is neither natural nor acquired, but an instinct given by God to the virtuous. Nor is the instinct [100] accompanied by reason, unless there may be supposed to be among statesmen some one who is capable of educating statesmen. And if there be such an one, he may be said to be among the living what Homer says that Tiresias was among the dead, 'he alone has understanding; but the rest are flitting shades;' and he and his virtue in like manner will be a reality among shadows.

Men. That is excellent, Socrates.

Soc. Then, Meno, the conclusion is that virtue comes to the virtuous by the gift of God. But we shall never know the certain truth until, before asking how virtue is given, we enquire into the actual nature of virtue. I fear that I must go away, but do you, now that you are persuaded yourself, persuade our friend Anytus. And do not let him be so exasperated; if you can conciliate him, you will have done good service to the Athenian people.

PHAEDO (*in part: 72-82, 113-end*)

72E-77A A COMPLEMENTARY ARGUMENT • THE THEORY OF
RECOLLECTION

Cebes rejoined: 'There is also another theory which, if true, [72E]
points the same way, Socrates: the one that you are constantly asserting,
namely that learning is really just recollection, from which it follows
presumably that what we now call to mind we have learnt at some
previous time; which would not be possible unless our souls existed [73]
somewhere before being born in this human frame. Hence we seem to
have another indication that the soul is something immortal.'

Simmias now intervened to ask: 'But how is that proved, Cebes?
Please remind me, as I can't quite remember at the moment.'[1]

'First,' replied Cebes, 'by the excellent argument that when people
are asked questions they can produce the right answers to anything of
their own accord, provided that the questioning is done properly. Of
course they wouldn't be able to do so unless they had knowledge and
correct views within them. Secondly, if you confront people with anything
in the nature of a diagram, you have the plainest proof of the point [B]
in question.'

'And if that doesn't convince you, Simmias,' said Socrates, 'I will
suggest another consideration to which you may perhaps agree. You
are evidently sceptical about the possibility of what is called learning
being recollection.'

'Not sceptical,' said Simmias: 'what I need is just what we are talking
about, namely to recollect. In point of fact, thanks to Cebes's setting
out of the arguments I do already almost remember, and am almost
convinced; all the same, I should like now to hear how you yourself
have set them out.'

'I will tell you. We agree, I take it, that to be reminded of some- [c]
thing implies having at some previous time known it?'

'Certainly.'

'And can we further agree that recollection may take the form of
acquiring knowledge in a particular way, I mean like this: a man who
has seen or heard or by some other sense perceived something may
come to know something other than that, may think of something else
besides that, something that is the object of a different knowledge.
When this happens are we not justified in saying that he recollects or is
reminded of the new object that he has thought of?' [D]

---

[1] Simmias's defective memory is doubtless no more than a device to make it
more natural for Socrates to expound and defend a theory which, if it had in
fact been his own, would presumably have been quite familiar to his present
audience.

'How do you mean?'

'To give an example, the knowledge of a man is different from that of a lyre.'

'Of course.'

'Well, you know how a lover feels when he sees a lyre or a cloak or some other object commonly used by his beloved: he apprehends the lyre, but he also conceives in his mind the form of the boy to whom it belongs; and that is reminder. Similarly one who sees Simmias is often reminded of Cebes, and we could think of any number of similar cases.'

'Yes indeed, any number,' agreed Simmias emphatically.

'Reminder then may take that form: but it is most apt to occur in [E] connexion with things that we have forgotten owing to the lapse of time and our not having thought about them. Isn't that so?'

'Yes, certainly.'

'Another point: is it possible to see the picture of a horse or a lyre and be reminded of their owner: or again to see a picture of Simmias and be reminded of Cebes?'

'Certainly.'

'Or alternatively to see a picture of Simmias and be reminded of Simmias?'

'Yes, that is possible.'   [74]

'And from all this it follows, doesn't it, that we may be reminded of things either by something like them or by something unlike them?'

'It does.'

'Moreover, when it is by something like the other thing, are we not certain to find ourselves doing something else besides, namely asking ourselves whether the similarity between the object and the thing it reminds us of is defective or not?'

'Certainly we shall.'

'Well now, see if you agree with my next point. We maintain, do we not, that there is such a thing as equality, not the equality of one log to another, or one stone to another, but something beyond all these cases, something different, equality itself. May we maintain that that exists, or may we not?'

'Most assuredly we may', answered Simmias: 'not a doubt of it.'   [B]

'And have we knowledge of it, in and by itself?'

'Certainly we have.'

'Then where do we get that knowledge from? Mustn't it be from the objects we mentioned just now, the equal logs or stones or whatever they were that we saw? Didn't they lead us to conceive of that other something? You do regard it as something other than those things, don't you? Look at it like this: two stones or two logs equal in length sometimes seem equal to one man, but not to another, though they haven't changed.'

'Yes certainly.'

'But now, what about equals themselves? Have they ever [C] appeared to you to be unequal, or equality to be inequality?'

'Never, Socrates.'

'Then those equal objects are not the same as the equal itself.'

'Far from it, I should say.'

'And yet it is from those equal objects, different as they are from this equal, that you have conceived and acquired knowledge of the latter?'

'That is perfectly true.'

'This latter being either like those others or unlike?'

'Just so.'

'However, that point is immaterial; but so long as the sight of one thing leads you to conceive another, whether like it or unlike, a case   [D] of reminder must have occurred.'

'Yes, to be sure.'

'And to continue: in the instance of those equal logs and other equal objects that we mentioned just now, is it our experience that they appear equal to the same degree as the equal itself? Is there some deficiency in respect of the likeness of the former to the latter, or is there none?'

'Yes, a considerable deficiency.'

'Then when someone sees a certain object and says to himself "The thing I am looking at wants to be like something else, but can resemble that other thing only defectively, as an inferior copy", may we agree   [E] that what he is saying necessarily implies a previous knowledge of that which he finds the object seen to resemble thus defectively?'

'That is necessarily implied.'

'Well then, is our own experience of the equal objects and the equal itself that just described, or is it not?'

'Undoubtedly it is.'

'So it necessarily follows that we knew the equal at a time previous to that first sight of equal objects which led us to conceive all these   [75] as striving to be like *the* equal, but defectively succeeding.'

'That is so.'

'And we agree moreover on a further point, that the conception referred to has arisen only, and could have arisen only, from seeing or touching, or some other form of sense-perception: what I am saying applies to them all alike.'

'And alike they are, Socrates, in respect of the point that our argument seeks to establish.'

'But the fact is that these very sense-perceptions must lead us to conceive that all those objects of perception are striving for that   [B] which *is* equal, but defectively attaining it. Is that right?'

'Yes.'

'Hence before we ever began to see or hear or otherwise perceive things we must, it seems, have possessed knowledge of the equal itself, if we were going to refer the equal things of our sense-perceptions to that standard, conceiving that all such objects are doing their best to resemble it, yet are in fact inferior to it.'

'That must follow from what we said before, Socrates.'

'Well, we have been seeing and hearing things, and employing our other senses from the very moment we were born, have we not?'

'Certainly.'

'And before doing so we must, so we maintain, have possessed [c] knowledge of the equal?'

'Yes.'

'Then it seems that we must have possessed it before we were born.'

'It does.'

'Then if we were born with this knowledge,[2] having acquired it before birth, must we not have had knowledge, both before birth and immediately afterwards, not only of the equal, the greater and the smaller, but of all things of that sort? For our argument applies not merely to the equal, but with the same force to the beautiful itself, the good itself, the just, the holy, in fact, as I have just said, to every- [d] thing upon which we affix our seal and mark as being "the thing itself", when we put our questions and give our answers.[3] Of all these then we must have possessed the knowledge before we were born.'

'That is so.'

'And if we do not each time forget what we have acquired, we must be possessed of knowledge always, we must have it throughout our whole life; for to know means to have acquired knowledge of something and not have lost it. The losing of knowledge is what we mean by forgetting, isn't it, Simmias?'

'Undoubtedly, Socrates.' [e]

'But if on the other hand we lost at the moment of birth what we had acquired before birth, but afterwards by directing our senses to the relevant object recover that old knowledge, then, I take it, what is called learning will consist in recovering a knowledge which belongs to us; and should we not be right in calling this recollection?'

'Certainly.'

'The reason being that we found that it was possible for a person [76] who had seen or heard or otherwise perceived an object to go on to conceive another object which he had forgotten, something with which the first object was connected, whether by resemblance or contrast. Hence my two alternatives: either we are all of us born knowing the things in question, and retain the knowledge throughout our life, or else those who are said to learn are simply recollecting, and learning will consist in recollection.'

'I am quite sure you are right, Socrates.'

'Then which do you choose, Simmias? Are we born with that [b] knowledge, or do we recollect a knowledge which we once possessed?'

---

[2] It is important to realise that both the introductory clause of this paragraph οὐκοῦν εἰ μέν ... τὰ τοιαῦτα and the second εἰ μέν clause at d7 put forward hypotheses which Socrates does *not* accept; that which he does accept comes at e2 with the εἰ δέ clause.

[3] I.e. in philosophical dialogue or dialectic.

'At the moment, Socrates, I don't know which to choose.'

'Well, here is something about which perhaps you can choose, and give me your view. If a man knows certain things, will he be able to give an account of them, or will he not?'

'Unquestionably he will, Socrates.'

'And do you think that everybody could give an account of those objects we were speaking of just now?'

'I only wish I did', replied Simmias; 'alas, on the contrary I fear that by this time to-morrow there will be no man left alive capable of doing so adequately.'

'So you don't think that everybody knows those objects, Simmias.' [c]

'By no means.'

'Can they then recollect what they once learnt?'

'It must be so.'

'But when did our souls acquire this knowledge? Evidently not since our birth as human beings.'

'No indeed.'

'Before that, then?'

'Yes.'

'Then, Simmias, our souls did exist before they were within this human form, apart from our bodies and possessed of intelligence.'

"Unless possibly it was at the actual moment of birth that we acquired the knowledge in question, Socrates; there is that moment still left.'

'Yes yes, my friend; but at what moment, may I ask, do we lose it? [d] We are not born with the knowledge: that we agreed a moment ago: do we then lose it at the very moment that we acquire it, or is there some other moment that you can suggest?'

'No indeed, Socrates; I see now that I was talking nonsense.'

'Then may our position be put like this, Simmias? If those objects exist which are always on our lips, a beautiful and a good and all reality of that sort, and if it is to that that we refer the content of our sense-perceptions, thereby recovering what was ours aforetime, and com- [e] pare our percepts thereto, it must follow that as surely as those objects exist so surely do our souls exist before we are born; but if the former do not exist, all our argument will have gone for nothing. Is that our position? Does the existence of our souls before birth stand or fall with the existence of those objects?'

'I am utterly convinced, Socrates,' replied Simmias, 'that it does so stand or fall: our argument is happily reduced to this, that it is equally certain that our souls exist before birth as that the reality of which [77] you now speak exists. I say happily, because there is nothing so plainly true to my mind as that all that sort of thing most assuredly does exist, a beautiful and a good and all those other things that you were speaking of just now. So I think we have had a satisfactory proof.' [4]

---

[4] *Sc.* of the pre-natal existence of the soul; not, of course, of the existence of the Forms, which has been a premiss of the proof.

77A-78B COMBINED RESULTS OF THE TWO PRECEDING
ARGUMENTS • SOCRATES AS CHARMER

'And what about Cebes?' asked Socrates; 'we must convince him too.'   [77A]

'He is satisfied, I think,' said Simmias, 'though indeed he is the most obstinate sceptic in the world. I think he is fully persuaded that our souls existed before we were born; but will they still exist after we die? [B] That I myself don't think we have proved; we are still left with the ordinary man's misgiving which Cebes voiced a while ago, that when a man dies his soul is simultaneously dissipated and thus comes to the end of its existence. May it not be that, deriving its origin and construction from some external source, it exists before entering into a human body, yet when it quits the body it has entered it too comes to an end and is destroyed?'

'You are right, Simmias', said Cebes. 'We seem to have proved half   [C] of what we want, namely that our souls existed before we were born; but we have yet to prove that they will equally exist after we die; only then will our proof be complete.'

'But you have the complete proof already, my friends,' said Socrates, 'if you will combine the present argument with that which we agreed upon previously, that is to say the principle that everything that lives comes from what is dead. For if the soul exists before birth, and if its entry into life, its being born, must necessarily have one and only one   [D] origin, namely death or the state of being dead, must it not follow, seeing that it is to be born again, that it still exists after it has died? So your point is indeed proved already. Nevertheless I fancy you and Simmias would like to have further discussion of this point too; you seem to have a childish fear that the wind literally blows a soul to   [E] bits when it quits the body, and scatters it in all directions, more especially if one happens to die when it's blowing a full gale.'

'Then, Socrates,' replied Simmias with a smile, 'see if you can argue us out of our fear. Or rather, not so much us as the child, maybe, within us that is given to such fears. See if you can persuade him to abandon his fear of this bogy called death.'

'Well,' said Socrates, 'you will have to pronounce charms over him every day until you have charmed the bogy away.'

'And where, Socrates,' said Cebes, 'are we going to find an expert   [78] at such charms, now that you are leaving us?'

'There is a wide field in Greece, Cebes, which must surely contain experts, and a wide field also in the world outside Greece, the whole of which you ought to explore in quest of your charmer; and you should spare neither money nor trouble, for you couldn't spend your money on a more pressing object. But you should search amongst yourselves too: I daresay you won't easily find anyone better at this task than you are.'

'Very well,' said Cebes, 'we will see to that. But let us now, if it suits you, go back to the point at which we broke off.'   [B]

'Why, of course it suits me; what do you expect?'

'Excellent.'

78B-80C   THIRD ARGUMENT · THE KINSHIP OF SOULS AND FORMS

Socrates then resumed: 'Now the sort of question that we ought   [78B] to put to ourselves is this: what kind of thing is in fact liable to undergo this dispersal that you speak of? For what kind of thing should we fear that it may be dispersed, and for what kind should we not? And next we should consider to which kind the soul belongs, and so find some ground for confidence or for apprehension about our own souls. Am I right?'

'Yes, you are.'

'Well now, isn't anything that has been compounded or has a com-   [C] posite nature liable to be split up into its component parts? Isn't it incomposite things alone that can possibly be exempt from that?'

'I agree that that is so', replied Cebes.

'And isn't it most probable that the incomposite things are those that are always constant and unchanging, while the composite ones are those that are different at different times and never constant?'

'I agree.'

'Then let us revert to those objects which we spoke of earlier. What of that very reality of whose existence we give an account when we   [D] question and answer each other? [5] Is that always unchanging and constant, or is it different at different times? Can the equal itself, the beautiful itself, the being itself whatever it may be, ever admit any sort of change? Or does each of these real beings, uniform [6] and independent, remain unchanging and constant, never admitting any sort of alteration whatever?'

'They must be unchanging and constant', Cebes replied.

'But what about the many beautiful things, beautiful human beings, say, or horses or garments or anything else you like? What about the   [E] many equal things? What about all the things that are called by the same name as those real beings? Are *they* constant, or in contrast to those is it too much to say that they are never identical with themselves nor identically related to one another?'

---

[5] I.e. in philosophical discussions; cf. 75D2.

[6] The term μονοειδές recurs at 80B in close conjunction with ἀδιάλυτον, and it is used of the Form of beauty at *Symp.* 211B. It has the same force as πᾶν ὅμοιον which Parmenides asserts of his ἕν ὄν, viz. the denial of internal difference or distinction of unlike parts.

'You are right about them too,' said Cebes, 'they are never constant.'

'Then again, you can touch them and see them or otherwise per- [79] ceive them with your senses, whereas those unchanging objects cannot be apprehended save by the mind's reasoning. Things of that sort are invisible, are they not?'

'That is perfectly true.'

'Then shall we say there are two kinds of thing, the visible and the invisible?'

'Very well.'

'The invisible being always constant, the visible never?'

'We may agree to that too.'

'To proceed: we ourselves are partly body, partly soul, are we not?' [B]

'Just so.'

'Well, which kind of thing shall we say the body tends to resemble and be akin to?'

'The visible kind; anyone can see that.'

'And the soul? Is that visible or invisible?'

'Not visible to the human eye, at all events, Socrates.'

'Oh well, we were speaking of what is or is not visible to mankind: or are you thinking of some other sort of being?'

'No: of a human being.'

'Then what is our decision about the soul, that it can be seen, or cannot?'

'That it cannot.'

'In fact it is invisible?'

'Yes.'

'Hence soul rather than body is like the invisible, while body rather than soul is like the visible.'

'Unquestionably, Socrates.' [C]

'Now were we not saying some time ago that when the soul makes use of the body to investigate something through vision or hearing or some other sense—of course investigating by means of the body is the same as investigating by sense—it is dragged by the body towards objects that are never constant, and itself wanders in a sort of dizzy drunken confusion, inasmuch as it is apprehending confused objects?'

'Just so.'

'But when it investigates by itself alone, it passes to that other [D] world of pure, everlasting, immortal, constant being, and by reason of its kinship thereto abides ever therewith, whensoever it has come to be by itself and is suffered to do so; and then it has rest from wandering and ever keeps close to that being, unchanged and constant, inasmuch as it is apprehending unchanging objects. And is not the experience which it then has called intelligence?'

'All you have said, Socrates, is true and admirably put.'

'Once again, then, on the strength of our previous arguments as well as of this last, which of the two kinds of thing do you find that soul resembles and is more akin to?' [E]

'On the strength of our present line of inquiry, Socrates, I should think that the veriest dullard would agree that the soul has a far and away greater resemblance to everlasting, unchanging being than to its opposite.'

'And what does the body resemble?'

'The other kind.'

'Now consider a further point. When soul and body are conjoined, Nature prescribes that the latter should be slave and subject, the [80] former master and ruler. Which of the two, in your judgment, does that suggest as being like the divine, and which like the mortal? Don't you think it naturally belongs to the divine to rule and lead, and to the mortal to be ruled and subjected?'

'Yes, I do.'

'Then which is soul like?'

'Of course it is obvious, Socrates, that soul is like the divine, and body like the mortal.'

'Would you say then, Cebes, that the result of our whole discussion amounts to this: on the one hand we have that which is divine, im- [B] mortal, indestructible, of a single form, accessible to thought, ever constant and abiding true to itself; and the soul is very like it: on the other hand we have that which is human, mortal, destructible, of many forms, inaccessible to thought, never constant nor abiding true to itself; and the body is very like that. Is there anything to be said against that, dear Cebes?'

'Nothing.'

'Well then, that being so, isn't it right and proper for the body to be quickly destroyed, but for the soul to be altogether indestructible, or nearly so?'

'Certainly.' [c]

80c-82d THE AFTER-LIFE OF UNPURIFIED SOULS

'Now you are aware that when a man dies his body, the visible [80c] part of him which belongs to the visible world, the corpse as we call it, which in the natural course is destroyed, falling to pieces and scattered to the winds, does not undergo any part of this fate immediately, but survives for quite a considerable time, indeed for a very long time if death finds the body in favourable condition and comes at a favourable season: for that matter, a corpse that has been shrunk and embalmed, in the Egyptian fashion, will remain almost entire for ages and ages; and some parts of the body, such as bones, sinews and so forth, even [D] when decomposition has occurred, are virtually immortal. Isn't that so?'

'Yes.'

'What then of the soul, the invisible thing which passes to an invisible region, a region of splendour and purity, literally the "unseen" world of Hades,[7] into the presence of the good and wise god,[8] whither, if god will, my own soul must shortly pass? Having found what its nature is like, are we going to say that when it quits the body it is immediately blown to pieces and annihilated, as most people maintain?[9] Far from it, my friends: the truth of the matter is very different. Let us suppose [E] that a soul departs in a state of purity, trailing nothing bodily after it inasmuch as during life it has had as little connexion as possible with the body, has shunned it and gathered itself together to be by itself—a state it has always been training for, training itself, in fact, to die readily: which is precisely what true philosophy consists in, as I think you would [81] agree?'

'I agree entirely.'

'Well, will not a soul in such condition depart into the world of the invisible which it resembles, where all is divine, immortal and wise, and having come thither attain happiness, released from its wanderings and follies and fears, its wild desires and all the other ills that beset mankind? Will it not truly dwell, as the initiated are alleged to dwell, in the company of the gods for all time to come?[10] May we say that, Cebes, or may we not?'

'Yes, indeed we may', replied Cebes.

'But now let us suppose that another soul departs polluted, un- [B] cleansed of the body's taint, inasmuch as it has always associated with the body and tended it, filled with its lusts and so bewitched by its passions and pleasures as to think nothing real save what is bodily, what can be touched and seen and eaten and made to serve sexual enjoyment; while it has grown to hate and shun with terror the things that are invisible, obscure to the eyes but to be seized by philosophic

---

[7] Plato is ready to accept or reject popular etymologies according as they do or do not suit his momentary purpose. The etymology of 'Hades' here accepted is rejected at *Cratylus* 404B.

[8] I doubt whether any allusion is intended to εὐβουλεύς as an epithet of Hades, as Burnet suggests. Socrates has spoken earlier (63B) of his going to join θεοὺς ἄλλους σοφούς τε καὶ ἀγαθούς—in the plural, which he again uses at 81A9. Plato is notoriously indifferent about speaking of 'god' or 'gods' (see Cornford, *Plato's Cosmology*, p. 280), and Hades is brought in here simply for the sake of the etymology.

[9] This is a noteworthy assertion, but perhaps 'most people' (οἱ πολλοὶ ἄνθρωποι) should not be taken too literally; there was, no doubt, much variety of belief or half-belief about the soul's fate in the fourth century. 'The Classical Age', writes Prof. Dodds (*op. cit.* p. 179), 'inherited a whole series of inconsistent pictures of the "soul" or "self"—the living corpse in the grave, the shadowy image in Hades, the perishable breath that is spilt in the air or absorbed in the aether, the daemon that is reborn in other bodies.'

[10] According to this passage the philosopher's soul can escape from the 'wheel of birth' after a single incarnation; herein our dialogue differs from the *Phaedrus* (249A), where it can only do so after three times choosing the philosophic life: cf. Pindar, *Ol.* II, 68 ff. ὅσοι δ' ἐτόλμασαν ἐστρὶς ἑκατέρωθι μείναντες ἀπὸ πάμπαν ἀδίκων ἔχειν ψυχάν κ.τ.λ. The discrepancy may be due to Plato's closer adherence in the later dialogue to the details of Orphic eschatology.

thought. Do you believe that a soul in such condition as that will depart unsullied, alone by itself?'   [c]

'That could never be so.'

'No: it would be interspersed, I think, with a bodily element which had been worked into its substance by unceasing commerce and association with the body, and by long training.'

'Just so.'

'Yes, my friend; and we must think of that element as a ponderous, heavy, earthy and visible substance; and the soul that carries it is weighed down and dragged back into the visible world; you know the stories about souls which, in their dread of the invisible that is called Hades, roam about tombs and burying-places, in the neighbourhood   [D] of which, it is alleged, ghostly phantoms of souls have actually been seen—just the sort of wraiths that souls like that would produce, souls which are not pure when they are released but still retain some of that visible substance, which is just why they can be seen.'

'It may well be so, Socrates.'

'It may indeed, Cebes, and it is certainly not the souls of the righteous, but those of the wicked that are compelled to wander about such places, as the penalty for bad nurture in the past. And they must continue to wander until they are once more chained up in a body, by reason of the desires of that bodily attendant which is ever at their side; and nat-   [E] urally they will be chained to the type of character that they have trained themselves to exhibit in their lifetime.'

'What types have you in mind, Socrates?'

'I mean, for example, that those who have trained themselves in gluttony, unchastity and drunkenness, instead of carefully avoiding them, will naturally join the company of donkeys or some such creatures,   [82] will they not?'

'Yes, very naturally.'

'Whereas those who have set more value upon injuring and plundering and tyrannising over their fellows will join the wolves and hawks and kites. Or should we give such souls as these some other destination?'

'By no means', said Cebes; 'leave them where you have put them.'

'Then it is obvious, I take it, where all the other types will go conformably to the roles in which they have severally trained themselves.'

'Quite obvious, I agree.'

'Now if we may call any of these happy, the happiest, who pass to the most favoured region, are they that have practised the common virtues of social life, what are called temperance and justice, virtues   [B] which spring from habit and training devoid of philosophic wisdom.'

'Why are they the happiest?'

'Because they will naturally find themselves in another well-conducted society resembling their old one, a society of bees, perhaps, or wasps or ants; and later on they may rejoin the human race they have left, and turn into respectable men.'

'Naturally enough.'

'But the society of gods none shall join who has not sought wisdom and departed wholly pure; only the lover of knowledge may go [c] thither. And that is the reason, dear friends, why true philosophers abstain from the desires of the body, standing firm and never surrendering to them; they are not troubled about poverty and loss of estate like the common lover of riches, nor yet is their abstinence due to fear of the dishonour and disgrace that attach to an evil life, the fear felt by the lovers of power and position.'

'No, that would be unworthy of them, Socrates', remarked Cebes.

'Most certainly it would', he replied. 'And that of course, Cebes, is [D] why one who is concerned about his own soul, instead of spending his life getting his body into good shape, says good-bye to all that sort of thing; and while the rest follow a road which leads them they know not whither, he takes another one: holding that he must never act against philosophy and that deliverance and purification which philosophy achieves, he proceeds in the direction whither philosophy points him.'

. . .

113D-115A   THE MYTH CONCLUDED · ITS TRUTH AND VALUE

'Such then is the nature of the earth's interior. Now when the dead [D] are come to that place whither their several guardian spirits bring them, they that have lived well and righteously submit themselves to judgements, and likewise they that have not so lived. And such as are deemed to have lived indifferently well set off for Acheron, embarking on certain vessels appointed for them, which bring them to the lake; and while they dwell there they are purged and absolved from their evil deeds by making atonement therefor, and are rewarded for their good deeds, each according to his desert.

'But some there be who because of the enormity of their sins are [E] deemed incurable: such as have stolen much and often from the temples, or wrought wicked murder time and again, or committed other such crimes; these their due portion befalls, to be hurled into Tartarus, never to escape.

'Others there be whose sins are accounted curable, yet heinous: such as have been moved by anger to lay violent hands upon father or [114] mother, yet have lived thereafter a life of repentance; or such as have slaughtered a man in some similar condition, all these must be cast into Tartarus, but after abiding there for the space of a year the surging waters throw the parricides and matricides out by way of Pyriphlegethon, and the others by way of Cocytus. And when they have been swept along to a point near the Acherusian Lake, then do they cry aloud and call to those whom they have slain or despitefully used, begging and beseeching them that they would suffer them to come forth into the [B] lake and give them hearing. If they can prevail, they do come forth, and find an end to their trouble; but if not, they are swept back into Tartarus, and thence into the rivers again; nor can they ever have respite from their woes until they prevail upon those whom they have injured; for such is the penalty appointed by their judges.

'But lastly there are those that are deemed to have made notable progress on the road to righteous living; and these are they that are freed and delivered from the prison-houses of this interior of the   [c] earth, and come to make their habitation in the pure region above ground. And those of their number who have attained full purity through philosophy live for evermore without any bodies at all, and attain to habitations even fairer than those others; but the nature of these it would not be easy to reveal, even were time enough now left me.

'But now, Simmias, having regard to all these matters of our tale, we must endeavour ourselves to have part in goodness and intelligence while this life is ours; for the prize is glorious, and great is our hope thereof.

'Now to affirm confidently that these things are as I have told them   [d] would not befit a man of good sense; yet seeing that the soul is found to be immortal, I think it is befitting to affirm that this or something like it is the truth about our souls and their habitations. I think too that we should do well in venturing—and a glorious venture it is—to believe it to be so. And we should treat such tales as spells to pronounce over ourselves, as in fact has been my own purpose all this while in telling my long story.

'And now surely, by reason of all this, no anxiety ought to be felt about his own soul by a man who all his lifetime has renounced the   [e] pleasures of the body and its adornments as alien to him, and likely to do him more harm than good, and has pursued the pleasures of learning; who has adorned his soul with no alien adornment, but with its own, even with temperance and justice and courage and freedom and   [115] truth, and thus adorned awaits that journey to Hades which he is ready to make whensoever destiny calls him.

'Well, Simmias, you and Cebes and the others will make the journey some day later on; but now " 'tis I am called", as a tragic hero might say, by destiny; and it is just about time [11] I made my way to the bath; I really think it is better to have a bath before drinking the poison rather than give the women the trouble of washing a dead body.'

115B-118 SOCRATES' DEATH

To this Crito replied, 'Very well, Socrates; but what instruc-   [115B] tions have you for our friends here or for me about the children, or about any other matter? We want to do just what would be of most service to you.'

---

[11] The abrupt way in which Socrates 'comes down to earth' is perhaps intended to suggest his characteristic avoidance of pomposity and staginess.

'Only what I am always telling you, Crito, nothing very new. Look after yourselves: then anything you do will be of service to me and mine, and to yourselves too, even if at this moment you make no promises to that effect, but if you neglect yourselves, and refuse to follow that path of life which has been traced out in this present conversation and in others that we have had before, then, plentiful and vehement though your present promises may be, all you do will be fruitless.'   [c]

'Then,' said Crito, 'we shall strive to do as you bid us. But how are we to bury you?'

'However you like,' said Socrates, 'provided you can catch me and prevent my escaping you.' Then with a quiet laugh and a look in our direction he remarked, 'You know, I can't persuade Crito that I am the Socrates here present, the person who is now talking to you and arranging the topics of our conversation; he imagines that I am the dead body which he will shortly be looking at, and so he asks how he is to bury   [D] me. As for all I have been maintaining this long while, to wit that when I have drunk the poison I shall no longer be with you, but shall have taken my departure to some happy land of the blest, that, I suppose, he regards as idle talk, intended to console you all and myself as well. That being so, I want you to stand surety for me with Crito, but for the precise opposite of that for which he sought to stand surety with the court. His pledge then, offered under oath, was that I would stay where I was; but I want you to pledge yourselves under oath that I will not stay where I am after I have died, but will take my departure; that   [E] will make it easier for Crito: when he sees my body being burnt or put under ground he won't have to distress himself on my behalf, as though I were being outraged, and won't have to say at the funeral that it is Socrates whom he is laying out or carrying to the grave or burying.'

Then turning to Crito, 'My best of friends,' he continued, 'I would assure you that misuse of language is not only distasteful in itself, but actually harmful to the soul. So you must be of good cheer, and say that you are burying my body; and do that in whatever fashion you   [116] please and deem to be most conformable to custom.'

With these words he rose and went into another room to take his bath. Crito went with him, and told us to stay where we were. This we did, discussing amongst ourselves and meditating upon all that had been said, or sometimes talking of the great sorrow that had come upon us; for truly we felt like children who had lost a father, condemned to live henceforth as orphans. However, when Socrates had had his bath   [B] his children—two little boys and one bigger—were brought in to him, and those women relatives of his appeared; to these he addressed some words in the presence of Crito, with certain directions as to his wishes. He then told the women and children to withdraw, and himself came over to us.

By this time it was near to sunset, for he had spent a long time in the inner room. So he came and sat with us after his bath, and did not talk much more. And now the agent of the prison authorities had ar-   [C] rived, and stepping up to him said, 'Socrates, I shan't have my usual ground for complaint in your case; many people get angry and abusive when I instruct them, at the behest of the authorities, to drink the poison; but I have always known you, while you have been here, for the most generous, the best tempered and the finest man of any that have entered this place; and in particular I feel sure now that you are not angry with me, but with those whom you know to be responsible for this. Well, you know what I have come to tell you: so now good-bye, and try to [D] bear as best you may what must be borne.' As he said this, he burst into tears, and turned to leave us. Socrates looked up at him and said, 'Good-bye to you: I will do as you say'; and then to us, 'What a delightful person! All these weeks he has been coming to see me, and talking with me now and then, like the excellent fellow he is; and now see how generously he weeps for me! Well, come now, Crito, let us do his bidding. If the draught has been prepared, will someone please bring it me; if not, tell the man to prepare it.'

'Oh, but I think, Socrates,' said Crito, 'that the sun is still upon the [E] mountains; it has not set yet. Besides, I know of people who have taken the draught long after they were told to do so, and had plenty to eat and drink, and even in some cases had intercourse with those whom they desired. Don't hurry: there is still plenty of time.'

'It is quite natural, Crito,' he replied, 'that the people you speak of should do that: they think it brings them some advantage; and it is equally natural that I should not do so: I don't think I should get any advantage out of taking the poison a little later on; I should [117] merely make myself ridiculous in my own eyes by clinging to life and eking out its last dregs. No, no: don't hamper me: do as I say.'

At this Crito nodded to his slave who stood close by; whereupon the latter went out, and after a considerable time came back with the man who was to administer the poison, which he was carrying in a cup ready to drink. On seeing him Socrates exclaimed, 'All right, good sir: you know about this business: what must I do?'

'Simply drink it,' he replied, 'and then walk about until you have a feeling of heaviness in your legs; then lie down, and it will act of [B] itself.' And as he spoke he offered Socrates the cup. And I tell you, Echecrates, he took it quite calmly, without a tremor or any change of complexion or expression. He just fixed the man with his well-known glare and asked, 'What do you say to using the drink for a libation? Or is that not allowed?' The man replied, 'We only mix what we judge to be the right dose, Socrates.'

'I see', he rejoined. 'Well, at all events it is allowed to pray to the [C] gods, as indeed we must, for a happy journey to our new dwelling-place; and that is my prayer: so may it be.' With these words he put the cup to his lips and drained it with no difficulty or distaste whatever.

So far most of us had more or less contrived to hold back our tears, but now, when we saw him drinking, and the cup emptied, it became impossible; for myself, despite my efforts the tears were pouring down

my cheeks, so that I had to cover my face; but I was weeping not for
him, no, but for myself and my own misfortune in losing such a [D]
friend. Crito had got up and withdrawn already, finding that he could
not restrain his tears; as for Apollodorus, he had even before this been
weeping continuously, and at this last moment he burst into sobs, and
his tears of distress were heart-breaking to all of us, except to Socrates
himself, who exclaimed, 'My dear good people, what a way to behave!
Why, it was chiefly to avoid such a lapse that I sent the women [E]
away; for I was always told that a man ought to die in peace and quiet.
Come, calm yourselves and do not give way.'

At that we felt ashamed, and ceased to weep. He walked round the
room until, as he told us, his legs came to feel heavy, and then lay on
his back, as he had been bidden. Thereupon the man who had brought
the poison felt his body, and after a while examined his feet and legs,
and then squeezed his foot tightly, asking if he felt anything. [118]
Socrates said no; next he felt his legs again, and moving his hand gradually up he showed us that he was becoming cold and rigid. Touching
him once more, he told us that when the cold reached the heart all
would be over.

By this time it had reached somewhere about the pit of the stomach,
when he removed the covering which he had put over his face, and
uttered his final words: 'Crito, we owe a cock to Asklepios, pray do not
forget to pay the debt.' 'It shall be done', said Crito. 'Is there anything
else you can think of?' There was no reply to this question; a moment
afterwards he shuddered; the attendant uncovered his face again, and
his gaze had become rigid; seeing which Crito closed his mouth and
his eyes.

And that, Echecrates, was the end of our friend, the finest man—so
we should say—of all whom we came to know in his generation; the
wisest too, and the most righteous.'

SYMPOSIUM (*complete*)

PERSONS OF THE DIALOGUE

Apollodorus, *who repeats to his
companion the dialogue which
he had heard from Aristodemus,
and had already once narrated
to Glaucon*
Phaedrus

Pausanias
Eryximachus
Aristophanes
Agathon
Socrates
Alcibiades
A troop of revellers

SCENE:—*The House of Agathon*

Concerning the things about which you ask to be informed I believe that I am not ill-prepared with an answer. For the day before yes- [172] terday I was coming from my own home at Phalerum to the city, and one of my acquaintance, who had caught a sight of me from behind, calling out playfully in the distance, said: Apollodorus, O thou Phalerian [1] man, halt! So I did as I was bid; and then he said, I was looking for you, Apollodorus, only just now, that I might ask you about the speeches in praise of love, which were delivered by Socrates, Alcibiades, and others, at Agathon's supper. Phoenix, the son of Philip, told another person who told me of them; his narrative was very indistinct, but he said that you knew, and I wish that you would give me an account of them. Who, if not you, should be the reporter of the words of your friend? And first tell me, he said, were you present at this meeting?

Your informant, Glaucon, I said, must have been very indistinct indeed, if you imagine that the occasion was recent; or that I could have been of the party.

Why, yes, he replied, I thought so.

Impossible: I said. Are you ignorant that for many years Agathon has not resided at Athens; and not three have elapsed since I became acquainted with Socrates, and have made it my daily business to know all that he says and does. There was a time when I was running [173] about the world, fancying myself to be well employed, but I was really a most wretched being, no better than you are now. I thought that I ought to do anything rather than be a philosopher.

Well, he said, jesting apart, tell me when the meeting occurred.

In our boyhood, I replied, when Agathon won the prize with his first tragedy, on the day after that on which he and his chorus offered the sacrifice of victory.

Then it must have been a long while ago, he said; and who told you— did Socrates?

No indeed, I replied, but the same person who told Phoenix;—he was a little fellow, who never wore any shoes, Aristodemus, of the deme of Cydathenaeum. He had been at Agathon's feast; and I think that in those days there was no one who was a more devoted admirer of Socrates. Moreover, I have asked Socrates about the truth of some parts of his narrative, and he confirmed them. Then, said Glaucon, let us have the tale over again; is not the road to Athens just made for conversation? And so we walked, and talked of the discourses on love; and therefore, as I said at first, I am not ill-prepared to comply with your request, and will have another rehearsal of them if you like. For to speak or to hear others speak of philosophy always gives me the greatest pleasure, to say nothing of the profit. But when I hear another strain, especially that of you rich men and traders, such conversation displeases me; and I pity you who are my companions, because you think that you are doing something when in reality you are doing nothing. And I dare say that you pity me

---

[1] Probably a play of words on φαλαρὸς, 'bald-headed.'

in return, whom you regard as an unhappy creature, and very probably you are right. But I certainly know of you what you only think of me—there is the difference.

Companion. I see, Apollodorus, that you are just the same—always speaking evil of yourself, and of others; and I do believe that you pity all mankind, with the exception of Socrates, yourself first of all, true in this to your old name, which, however deserved, I know not how you acquired, of Apollodorus the madman; for you are always raging against yourself and everybody but Socrates.

Apollodorus. Yes, friend, and the reason why I am said to be mad, and out of my wits, is just because I have these notions of myself and you; no other evidence is required.

Com. No more of that, Apollodorus; but let me renew my request that you would repeat the conversation.

Apoll. Well, the tale of love was on this wise:—But perhaps I [174] had better begin at the beginning, and endeavour to give you the exact words of Aristodemus:

He said that he met Socrates fresh from the bath and sandalled; and as the sight of the sandals was unusual, he asked him whither he was going that he had been converted into such a beau:—

To a banquet at Agathon's, he replied, whose invitation to his sacrifice of victory I refused yesterday, fearing a crowd, but promising that I would come to-day instead; and so I have put on my finery, because he is such a fine man. What say you to going with me unasked?

I will do as you bid me, I replied.

Follow then, he said, and let us demolish the proverb:—

'To the feasts of inferior men the good unbidden go;'

instead of which our proverb will run:—

'To the feasts of the good the good unbidden go;'

and this alteration may be supported by the authority of Homer himself, who not only demolishes but literally outrages the proverb. For, after picturing Agamemnon as the most valiant of men, he makes Menelaus, who is but a faint-hearted warrior, come unbidden [2] to the banquet of Agamemnon, who is feasting and offering sacrifices, not the better to the worse, but the worse to the better.

I rather fear, Socrates, said Aristodemus, lest this may still be my case; and that, like Menelaus in Homer, I shall be the inferior person, who

'To the feasts of the wise unbidden goes.'

But I shall say that I was bidden of you, and then you will have to make an excuse.

'Two going together,'

---

[2] Iliad ii. 408, and xvii. 588.

he replied, in Homeric fashion, one or other of them may invent an excuse by the way.³

This was the style of their conversation as they went along. Socrates dropped behind in a fit of abstraction, and desired Aristodemus, who was waiting, to go on before him. When he reached the house of Agathon he found the doors wide open, and a comical thing happened. A servant coming out met him, and led him at once into the banqueting-hall in which the guests were reclining, for the banquet was about to begin. Welcome, Aristodemus, said Agathon, as soon as he appeared—you are just in time to sup with us; if you come on any other matter put it off, and make one of us, as I was looking for you yesterday and meant to have asked you, if I could have found you. But what have you done with Socrates?

I turned round, but Socrates was nowhere to be seen; and I had to explain that he had been with me a moment before, and that I came by his invitation to the supper.

You were quite right in coming, said Agathon; but where is he himself?

He was behind me just now, as I entered, he said, and I cannot   [175] think what has become of him.

Go and look for him, boy, said Agathon, and bring him in; and do you, Aristodemus, meanwhile take the place by Eryximachus.

The servant then assisted him to wash, and he lay down, and presently another servant came in and reported that our friend Socrates had retired into the portico of the neighbouring house. 'There he is fixed,' said he, 'and when I call to him he will not stir.'

How strange, said Agathon; then you must call him again, and keep calling him.

Let him alone, said my informant; he has a way of stopping anywhere and losing himself without any reason. I believe that he will soon appear; do not therefore disturb him.

Well, if you think so, I will leave him, said Agathon. And then, turning to the servants, he added, 'Let us have supper without waiting for him. Serve up whatever you please, for there is no one to give you orders; hitherto I have never left you to yourselves. But on this occasion imagine that you are our hosts, and that I and the company are your guests; treat us well, and then we shall commend you.' After this, supper was served, but still no Socrates; and during the meal Agathon several times expressed a wish to send for him, but Aristodemus objected; and at last when the feast was about half over—for the fit, as usual, was not of long duration—Socrates entered. Agathon, who was reclining alone at the end of the table, begged that he would take the place next to him; that 'I may touch you,' he said, 'and have the benefit of that wise thought which came into your mind in the portico, and is now in your possession; for I am certain that you would not have come away until you had found what you sought.'

³ Iliad x. 224.

How I wish, said Socrates, taking his place as he was desired, that wisdom could be infused by touch, out of the fuller into the emptier man, as water runs through wool out of a fuller cup into an emptier one; if that were so, how greatly should I value the privilege of reclining at your side! For you would have filled me full with a stream of wisdom plenteous and fair; whereas my own is of a very mean and questionable sort, no better than a dream. But yours is bright and full of promise, and was manifested forth in all the splendour of youth the day before yesterday, in the presence of more than thirty thousand Hellenes.

You are mocking, Socrates, said Agathon, and ere long you and I will have to determine who bears off the palm of wisdom—of this Dionysus shall be the judge; but at present you are better occupied with supper.

Socrates took his place on the couch, and supped with the rest;   [176] and then libations were offered, and after a hymn had been sung to the god, and there had been the usual ceremonies, they were about to commence drinking, when Pausanias said, And now, my friends, how can we drink with least injury to ourselves? I can assure you that I feel severely the effect of yesterday's potations, and must have time to recover; and I suspect that most of you are in the same predicament, for you were of the party yesterday. Consider then: How can the drinking be made easiest?

I entirely agree, said Aristophanes, that we should, by all means, avoid hard drinking, for I was myself one of those who were yesterday drowned in drink.

I think that you are right, said Eryximachus, the son of Acumenus; but I should still like to hear one other person speak: Is Agathon able to drink hard?

I am not equal to it, said Agathon.

Then, said Eryximachus, the weak heads like myself, Aristodemus, Phaedrus, and others who never can drink, are fortunate in finding that the stronger ones are not in a drinking mood. (I do not include Socrates, who is able either to drink or to abstain, and will not mind, whichever we do.) Well, as none of the company seem disposed to drink much, I may be forgiven for saying, as a physician, that drinking deep is a bad practice, which I never follow, if I can help, and certainly do not recommend to another, least of all to any one who still feels the effects of yesterday's carouse.

I always do what you advise, and especially what your prescribe as a physician, rejoined Phaedrus the Myrrhinusian, and the rest of the company, if they are wise, will do the same.

It was agreed that drinking was not to be the order of the day, but that they were all to drink only so much as they pleased.

Then, said Eryximachus, as you are all agreed that drinking is to be voluntary, and that there is to be no compulsion, I move, in the next place, that the flute-girl, who has just made her appearance, be told to go away and play to herself, or, if she likes, to the women who are within.[4] To-day let us have conversation instead; and, if you will allow me, I will tell you what sort of conversation. This proposal having [177] been accepted, Eryximachus proceeded as follows:—

I will begin, he said, after the manner of Melanippe in Euripides,

'Not mine the word'

which I am about to speak, but that of Phaedrus. For often he says to me in an indignant tone:—'What a strange thing it is, Eryximachus, that, whereas other gods have poems and hymns made in their honour, the great and glorious god, Love, has no encomiast among all the poets who are so many. There are the worthy sophists too—the excellent Prodicus for example, who have descanted in prose on the virtues of Heracles and other heroes; and, what is still more extraordinary, I have met with a philosophical work in which the utility of salt has been made the theme of an eloquent discourse; and many other like things have had a like honour bestowed upon them. And only to think that there should have been an eager interest created about them, and yet that to this day no one has ever dared worthily to hymn Love's praises! So entirely has this great diety been neglected.' Now in this Phaedrus seems to me to be quite right, and therefore I want to offer him a contribution; also I think that at the present moment we who are here assembled cannot do better than honour the god Love. If you agree with me, there will be no lack of conversation; for I mean to propose that each of us in turn, going from left to right, shall make a speech in honour of Love. Let him give us the best which he can; and Phaedrus, because he is sitting first on the left hand, and because he is the father of the thought, shall begin.

No one will vote against you, Eryximachus, said Socrates. How can I oppose your motion, who profess to understand nothing but matters of love; nor, I presume, will Agathon and Pausanias; and there can be no doubt of Aristophanes, whose whole concern is with Dionysus and Aphrodite; nor will any one disagree of those whom I see around me. The proposal, as I am aware, may seem rather hard upon us whose place is last; but we shall be contented if we hear some good speeches first. Let Phaedrus begin the praise of Love, and good luck to him. All the company expressed their assent, and desired him to do as Socrates bade him. [178]

Aristodemus did not recollect all that was said, nor do I recollect all that he related to me; but I will tell you what I thought most worthy of remembrance, and what the chief speakers said.

THE SPEECH OF PHAEDRUS

Phaedrus began by affirming that Love is a mighty god, and wonderful among gods and men, but especially wonderful in his birth. For he is the eldest of the gods, which is an honour to him; and a proof of his claim to this honour is, that of his parents there is no memorial; neither

---

[4] Cp. Prot. 347.

poet nor prose-writer has ever affirmed that he had any. As Hesiod says:—

'First Chaos came, and then broad-bosomed Earth,
The everlasting seat of all that is,
And Love.'

In other words, after Chaos, the Earth and Love, these two, came into being. Also Parmenides sings of Generation:

'First in the train of gods, he fashioned Love.'

And Acusilaus agrees with Hesiod. Thus numerous are the witnesses who acknowledge Love to be the eldest of the gods. And not only is he the eldest, he is also the source of the greatest benefits to us. For I know not any greater blessing to a young man who is beginning life than a virtuous lover, or to the lover than a beloved youth. For the principle which ought to be the guide of men who would nobly live—that principle, I say, neither kindred, nor honour, nor wealth, nor any other motive is able to implant so well as love. Of what am I speaking? Of the sense of honour and dishonour, without which neither states nor individuals ever do any good or great work. And I say that a lover who is detected in doing any dishonourable act, or submitting through cowardice when any dishonour is done to him by another, will be more pained at being detected by his beloved than at being seen by his father, or by his companions, or by any one else. The beloved too, when he is found in any disgraceful situation, has the same feeling about his lover. And if there were only some way of contriving that a state or an army should be made up of lovers and their loves [5], they would be the very best governors of their own city, abstaining from all dishonour, and emulating one another in honour; and when fighting at each other's side, although a mere [179] handful, they would overcome the world. For what lover would not choose rather to be seen by all mankind than by his beloved, either when abandoning his post or throwing away his arms? He would be ready to die a thousand deaths rather than endure this. Or who would desert his beloved or fail him in the hour of danger? The veriest coward would become an inspired hero, equal to the bravest, at such a time; Love would inspire him. That courage which, as Homer says, the god breathes into the souls of some heroes, Love of his own nature infuses into the lover.

Love will make men dare to die for their beloved—love alone; and women as well as men. Of this, Alcestis, the daughter of Pelias, is a monument to all Hellas; for she was willing to lay down her life on behalf of her husband, when no one else would, although he had a father and mother; but the tenderness of her love so far exceeded theirs, that she made them seem to be strangers in blood to their own son, and in name only related to him; and so noble did this action of hers appear to the gods, as well as to men, that among the many who have done virtuously she is one of the very few to whom, in admiration of her noble

---

[5] Cp. Rep. v. 468 D.

action, they have granted the privilege of returning alive to earth; such exceeding honour is paid by the gods to the devotion and virtue of love. But Orpheus, the son of Oeagrus, the harper, they sent empty away, and presented to him an apparition only of her whom he sought, but herself they would not give up, because he showed no spirit; he was only a harp-player, and did not dare like Alcestis to die for love, but was contriving how he might enter Hades alive; moreover, they afterwards caused him to suffer death at the hands of women, as the punishment of his coward-liness. Very different was the reward of the true love of Achilles towards his lover Patroclus—his lover and not his love (the notion that Patroclus was the beloved one is a foolish error into which Aeschylus has fallen, for Achilles was surely the fairer of the two, fairer also than all the other heroes; and, as Homer informs us, he was still beardless, and younger far). And greatly as the gods honour the virtue of love, still the re- [180] turn of love on the part of the beloved to the lover is more admired and valued and rewarded by them, for the lover is more divine; because he is inspired by God. Now Achilles was quite aware, for he had been told by his mother, that he might avoid death and return home, and live to a good old age, if he abstained from slaying Hector. Nevertheless he gave his life to revenge his friend, and dared to die, not only in his defence, but after he was dead. Wherefore the gods honoured him even above Alcestis, and sent him to the Islands of the Blest. These are my reasons for affirming that Love is the eldest and noblest and mightiest of the gods, and the chiefest author and giver of virtue in life, and of happiness after death.

THE SPEECH OF PAUSANIAS

This, or something like this, was the speech of Phaedrus; and some other speeches followed which Aristodemus did not remember; the next which he repeated was that of Pausanias. Phaedrus, he said, the argument has not been set before us, I think, quite in the right form;—we should not be called upon to praise Love in such an indiscriminate manner. If there were only one Love, then what you said would be well enough; but since there are more Loves than one, you should have begun by determining which of them was to be the theme of our praises. I will amend this defect; and first of all I will tell you which Love is deserving of praise, and then try to hymn the praiseworthy one in a manner worthy of him. For we all know that Love is inseparable from Aphrodite, and if there were only one Aphrodite there would be only one Love; but as there are two goddesses there must be two Loves. And am I not right in asserting that there are two goddesses? The elder one, having no mother, who is called the heavenly Aphrodite—she is the daughter of Uranus; the younger, who is the daughter of Zeus and Dione—her we call common; and the Love who is her fellow-worker is rightly named common, as the other love is called heavenly. All the gods ought to have praise given to them, but not without distinction of their natures; and therefore I must try to distinguish the characters of the two Loves. Now actions vary according to the manner of their performance. Take, for example, that which we are now doing, [181] drinking, singing and talking—these actions are not in themselves either good or evil, but they turn out in this or that way according to the mode of performing them; and when well done they are good, and when wrongly done they are evil; and in like manner not every love, but only that which has a noble purpose, is noble and worthy of praise. The Love who is the offspring of the common Aphrodite is essentially common, and has no discrimination, being such as the meaner sort of men feel, and is apt to be of women as well as of youths, and is of the body rather than of the soul—the most foolish beings are the objects of this love which desires only to gain an end, but never thinks of accomplishing the end nobly, and therefore does good and evil quite indiscriminately. The goddess who is his mother is far younger than the other, and she was born of the union of the male and female, and partakes of both. But the off-spring of the heavenly Aphrodite is derived from a mother in whose birth the female has no part,—she is from the male only; this is that love which is of youths, and the goddess being older, there is nothing of wantonness in her. Those who are inspired by this love turn to the male, and delight in him who is the more valiant and intelligent nature; any one may recognise the pure enthusiasts in the very character of their attachments. For they love not boys, but intelligent beings whose reason is beginning to be developed, much about the time at which their beards begin to grow. And in choosing young men to be their companions, they mean to be faithful to them, and pass their whole life in company with them, not to take them in their inexperience, and deceive them, and play the fool with them, or run away from one to another of them. But the love of young boys should be forbidden by law, because their future is uncertain; they may turn out good or bad, either in body or soul, and much noble enthusiasm may be thrown away upon them; in this matter the good are a law to themselves, and the coarser sort of lovers ought to be restrained by force, as we restrain or attempt to restrain them from fixing their affections on women of free birth. [182] These are the persons who bring a reproach on love; and some have been led to deny the lawfulness of such attachments because they see the impropriety and evil of them; for surely nothing that is decorously and lawfully done can justly be censured. Now here and in Lacedaemon the rules about love are perplexing, but in most cities they are simple and easily intelligible; in Elis and Boeotia, and in countries having no gifts of eloquence, they are very straightforward; the law is simply in favour of these connexions, and no one, whether young or old, has anything to say to their discredit; the reason being, as I suppose, that they are men of few words in those parts, and therefore the lovers do not like the trouble of pleading their suit. In Ionia and other places, and generally in countries which are subject to the barbarians, the custom is held to be dishonourable; loves of youths share the evil repute in which

philosophy and gymnastics are held, because they are inimical to tyranny;
for the interests of rulers require that their subjects should be poor in
spirit [6] and that there should be no strong bond of friendship or society
among them, which love, above all other motives, is likely to inspire, as
our Athenian tyrants learned by experience; for the love of Aristogeiton
and the constancy of Harmodius had a strength which undid their power.
And, therefore, the ill-repute into which these attachments have fallen
is to be ascribed to the evil condition of those who make them to be ill-
reputed; that is to say, to the self-seeking of the governors and the cowardice of the governed; on the other hand, the indiscriminate honour
which is given to them in some countries is attributable to the laziness of
those who hold this opinion of them. In our own country a far better
principle prevails, but, as I was saying, the explanation of it is rather
perplexing. For, observe that open loves are held to be more honourable
than secret ones, and that the love of the noblest and highest, even if
their persons are less beautiful than others, is especially honourable.
Consider, too, how great is the encouragement which all the world gives
to the lover; neither is he supposed to be doing anything dishonourable;
but if he succeeds he is praised, and if he fail he is blamed. And in the
pursuit of his love the custom of mankind allows him to do many strange
things, which philosophy would bitterly censure if they were done   [183]
from any motive of interest, or wish for office or power. He may pray,
and entreat, and supplicate, and swear, and lie on a mat at the door, and
endure a slavery worse than that of any slave—in any other case friends and
enemies would be equally ready to prevent him, but now there is no friend
who will be ashamed of him and admonish him, and no enemy will
charge him with meanness or flattery; the actions of a lover have a grace
which ennobles them; and custom has decided that they are highly com-
mendable and that there is no loss of character in them; and, what is
strangest of all, he only may swear and forswear himself (so men say),
and the gods will forgive his transgression, for there is no such thing as
a lover's oath. Such is the entire liberty which gods and men have
allowed the lover, according to the custom which prevails in our part of
the world. From this point of view a man fairly argues that in Athens to
love and to be loved is held to be a very honourable thing. But when
parents forbid their sons to talk with their lovers, and place them under
a tutor's care, who is appointed to see to these things, and their companions and equals cast in their teeth anything of the sort which they
may observe, and their elders refuse to silence the reprovers and do not
rebuke them—any one who reflects on all this will, on the contrary, think
that we hold these practices to be most disgraceful. But, as I was saying
as first, the truth as I imagine is, that whether such practices are honourable or whether they are dishonourable is not a simple question; they are
honourable to him who follows them honourably, dishonourable to him
who follows them dishonourably. There is dishonour in yielding to the

---

[6] Cp. Arist. Politics, v. II. §15.

evil, or in an evil manner; but there is honour in yielding to the good, or in an honourable manner. Evil is the vulgar lover who loves the body rather than the soul, inasmuch as he is not even stable, because he loves a thing which is in itself unstable, and therefore when the bloom of youth which he was desiring is over, he takes wing and flies away, in spite of all his words and promises; whereas the love of the noble disposition is life-long, for it becomes one with the everlasting. The custom of our country would have both of them proven well and truly, and would have   [184] us yield to the one sort of lover and avoid the other, and therefore encourages some to pursue, and others to fly; testing both the lover and beloved in contests and trials, until they show to which of the two classes they respectively belong. And this is the reason why, in the first place, a hasty attachment is held to be dishonourable, because time is the true test of this as of most other things; and secondly there is a dishonour in being overcome by the love of money, or of wealth, or of political power, whether a man is frightened into surrender by the loss of them, or, having experienced the benefits of money and political corruption, is unable to rise above the seductions of them. For none of these things are of a permanent or lasting nature; not to mention that no generous friendship ever sprang from them. There remains, then, only one way of honourable attachment which custom allows in the beloved, and this is the way of virtue; for as we admitted that any service which the lover does to him is not to be accounted flattery or a dishonour to himself, so the beloved has one way only of voluntary service which is not dishonourable, and this is virtuous service.

For we have a custom, and according to our custom any one who does service to another under the idea that he will be improved by him either in wisdom, or in some other particular of virtue—such a voluntary service, I say, is not to be regarded as a dishonour, and is not open to the charge of flattery. And these two customs, one the love of youth, and the other the practice of philosophy and virtue in general, ought to meet in one, and then the beloved may honourably indulge the lover. For when the lover and beloved come together, having each of them a law, and the lover thinks that he is right in doing any service which he can to his gracious loving one; and the other that he is right in showing any kindness which he can to him who is making him wise and good; the one capable of communicating wisdom and virtue, the other seeking to acquire them with a view to education and wisdom; when the two laws of love are fulfilled and meet in one—then, and then only, may the beloved yield with honour to the lover. Nor when love is of this disinterested sort is there any disgrace in being deceived, but in every other case there is equal disgrace in being or not being deceived. For he who is gracious to his lover under the impression that he is rich, and is   [185] disappointed of his gains because he turns out to be poor, is disgraced all the same: for he has done his best to show that he would give himself up to any one's 'uses base' for the sake of money; but this is not honourable. And on the same principle he who gives himself to a lover because he is a good man, and in the hope that he will be improved by his company, shows himself to be virtuous, even though the object of his affection turn out to be a villain, and to have no virtue; and if he is deceived he has committed a noble error. For he has proved that for his part he will do anything for anybody with a view to virtue and improvement, than which there can be nothing nobler. Thus noble in every case is the acceptance of another for the sake of virtue. This is that love which is the love of the heavenly goddess, and is heavenly, and of great price to individuals and cities, making the lover and the beloved alike eager in the work of their own improvement. But all other loves are the offspring of the other, who is the common goddess. To you, Phaedrus, I offer this my contribution in praise of love, which is as good as I could make extempore.

Pāusănĭās cāme tŏ ă pāuse—this is the balanced way in which I have been taught by the wise to speak; and Aristodemus said that the turn of Aristophanes was next, but either he had eaten too much, or from some other cause he had the hiccough, and was obliged to change turns with Eryximachus the physician, who was reclining on the couch below him. Eryximachus, he said, you ought either to stop my hiccough, or to speak in my turn until I have left off.

I will do both, said Eryximachus: I will speak in your turn, and do you speak in mine; and while I am speaking let me recommend you to hold your breath, and if after you have done so for some time the hiccough is no better, then gargle with a little water; and if it still continues, tickle your nose with something and sneeze; and if you sneeze once or twice, even the most violent hiccough is sure to go. I will do as you prescribe, said Aristophanes, and now get on.

THE SPEECH OF ERYXIMACHUS

Eryximachus spoke as follows: Seeing that Pausanias made a fair beginning, and but a lame ending, I must endeavour to supply [186] his deficiency. I think that he has rightly distinguished two kinds of love. But my art further informs me that the double love is not merely an affection of the soul of man towards the fair, or towards anything, but is to be found in the bodies of all animals and in productions of the earth, and I may say in all that is; such is the conclusion which I seem to have gathered from my own art of medicine, whence I learn how great and wonderful and universal is the deity of love, whose empire extends over all things, divine as well as human. And from medicine I will begin that I may do honour to my art. There are in the human body these two kinds of love, which are confessedly different and unlike, and being unlike, they have loves and desires which are unlike; and the desire of the healthy is one, and the desire of the diseased is another; and as Pausanias was just now saying that to indulge good men is honourable, and bad men dishonourable:—so too in the body the good and healthy elements are to be indulged, and the bad elements and the elements of disease are not to be indulged, but discouraged. And this is what the physician has to do, and in this the art of medicine consists: for medicine may be regarded generally as the knowledge of the loves and desires of the body, and how to satisfy them or not; and the best physician is he who is able to separate fair love for foul, or to convert one into the other; and he who knows how to eradicate and how to implant love, whichever is required, and can reconcile the most hostile elements in the constitution and make them loving friends, is a skilful practitioner. Now the most hostile are the most opposite, such as hot and cold, bitter and sweet, moist and dry, and the like. And my ancestor, Asclepius, knowing how to implant friendship and accord in these elements, was the creator of our art, as our friends the poets here tell us, and I believe them; and not only medicine in every branch, but the arts of gymnastic and husbandry are under his dominion. Any one who pays the least attention to the subject will also per- [187] ceive that in music there is the same reconciliation of opposites; and I suppose that this must have been the meaning of Heracleitus, although his words are not accurate; for he says that The One is united by dis-union, like the harmony of the bow and the lyre. Now there is an absurdity in saying that harmony is discord or is composed of elements which are still in a state of discord. But what he probably meant was, that harmony is composed of differing notes of higher or lower pitch which disagreed once, but are now reconciled by the art of music; for if the higher and lower notes still disagreed, there could be no harmony,— clearly not. For harmony is a symphony, and symphony is an agreement; but an agreement of disagreements while they disagree there cannot be; you cannot harmonize that which disagrees. In like manner rhythm is com-pounded of elements short and long, once differing and now in accord; which accordance, as in the former instance, medicine, so in all these other cases, music implants, making love and unison to grow up among them; and thus music, too, is concerned with the principles of love in their application to harmony and rhythm. Again, in the essential nature of harmony and rhythm there is no difficulty in discerning love which has not yet become double. But when you want to use them in actual life, either in the composition of songs or in the correct performance of airs or metres composed already, which latter is called education, then the difficulty begins, and the good artist is needed. Then the old tale has to be repeated of fair and heavenly love—the love of Urania the fair and heavenly muse, and of the duty of accepting the temperate, and those who are as yet intemperate only that they may become temperate, and of preserving their love; and again, of the vulgar Polyhymnia, who must be used with circumspection that the pleasure be enjoyed, but may not generate licentiousness; just as in my own art it is a great matter so to regulate the desires of the epicure that he may gratify his tastes without the attendant evil of disease. Whence I infer that in music, in medicine, in all other things human as well as divine, both loves ought to be noted as far as may be, for they are both present.   [188]

The course of the seasons is also full of both these principles; and when, as I was saying, the elements of hot and cold, moist and dry, attain the harmonious love of one another and blend in temperance and harmony, they bring to men, animals, and plants health and plenty, and do them no harm; whereas the wanton love, getting the upper hand and affecting the seasons of the year, is very destructive and injurious, being the source of pestilence, and bringing many other kinds of diseases on animals and plants; for hoar-frost and hail and blight spring from the excesses and disorders of these elements of love, which to know in relation to the revolutions of the heavenly bodies and the seasons of the year is termed astronomy. Furthermore all sacrifices and the whole province of divination, which is the art of communion between gods and men—these, I say, are concerned only with the preservation of the good and the cure of the evil love. For all manner of impiety is likely to ensue if, instead of accepting and honouring and reverencing the harmonious love in all his actions, a man honours the other love, whether in his feelings towards gods or parents, towards the living or the dead. Wherefore the business of divination is to see to these loves and to heal them, and divination is the peacemaker of gods and men, working by a knowledge of the religious or irreligious tendencies which exist in human loves. Such is the great and mighty, or rather omnipotent force of love in general. And the love, more especially, which is concerned with the good, and which is perfected in company with temperance and justice, whether among gods or men, has the greatest power, and is the source of all our happiness and harmony, and makes us friends with the gods who are above us, and with one another. I dare say that I too have omitted several things which might be said in praise of Love, but this was not intentional, and you, Aristophanes, may now supply the omission or take some other line of commendation; for I perceive that you are rid of the hiccough.

Yes, said Aristophanes, who followed, the hiccough is gone; not, [189] however, until I applied the sneezing; and I wonder whether the harmony of the body has a love of such noises and ticklings, for I no sooner applied the sneezing than I was cured.

Eryximachus said: Beware, friend Aristophanes, although you are going to speak, you are making fun of me; and I shall have to watch and see whether I cannot have a laugh at your expense, when you might speak in peace.

You are quite right, said Aristophanes, laughing. I will unsay my words; but do you please not to watch me, as I fear that in the speech which I am about to make, instead of others laughing with me, which is to the manner born of our muse and would be all the better, I shall only be laughed at by them.

Do you expect to shoot your bolt and escape, Aristophanes? Well, perhaps if you are very careful and bear in mind that you will be called to account, I may be induced to let you off.

THE SPEECH OF ARISTOPHANES

Aristophanes professed to open another vein of discourse; he had a mind to praise Love in another way, unlike that either of Pausanias or Eryximachus. Mankind, he said, judging by their neglect of him, have never, as I think, at all understood the power of Love. For if they had understood him they would surely have built noble temples and altars, and offered solemn sacrifices in his honour; but this is not done, and most certainly ought to be done: since of all the gods he is the best friend of men, the helper and the healer of the ills which are the great impediment to the happiness of the race. I will try to describe his power to you, and you shall teach the rest of the world what I am teaching you. In the first place, let me treat of the nature of man and what has happened to it; for the original human nature was not like the present, but different. The sexes were not two as they are now, but originally three in number; there was man, woman, and the union of the two, having a name corresponding to this double nature, which had once a real existence, but is now lost, and the word 'Androgynous' is only preserved as a term of reproach. In the second place, the primeval man was round, his back and sides forming a circle; and he had four hands and four feet, one head with two faces, looking opposite ways, set on a round neck and precisely alike; also four ears, two privy members, and the remainder to   [190] correspond. He could walk upright as men now do, backwards or forwards as he pleased, and he could also roll over and over at a great pace, turning on his four hands and four feet, eight in all, like tumblers going over and over with their legs in the air; this was when he wanted to run fast. Now the sexes were three, and such as I have described them; because the sun, moon, and earth are three; and the man was originally the child of the sun, the woman of the earth, and the man-woman of the moon, which is made up of sun and earth, and they were all round and moved round and round like their parents. Terrible was their might and strength, and the thoughts of their hearts were great, and they made an attack upon the gods; of them is told the tale of Otys and Ephialtes who, as Homer says, dared to scale heaven, and would have laid hands upon the gods. Doubt reigned in the celestial councils. Should they kill them and annihilate the race with thunderbolts, as they had done the giants, then there would be an end of the sacrifices and worship which men offered to them; but, on the other hand, the gods could not suffer their insolence to be unrestrained. At last, after a good deal of reflection, Zeus discovered a way. He said: 'Methinks I have a plan which will humble their pride and improve their manners; men shall continue to exist, but I will cut them in two and then they will be diminished in strength and increased in numbers; this will have the advantage of making them more profitable to us. They shall walk upright on two legs, and if they continue insolent and will not be quiet, I will split them again and they shall hop about on a single leg.' He spoke and cut men in two, like a sorb-apple which is halved for pickling, or as you might divide an egg with a hair;

and as he cut them one after another, he bade Apollo give the face and the half of the neck a turn in order that the man might contemplate the section of himself: he would thus learn a lesson of humility. Apollo was also bidden to heal their wounds and compose their forms. So he gave a turn to the face and pulled the skin from the sides all over that which in our language is called the belly, like the purses which draw in, and he made one mouth at the centre, which he fastened in a knot (the same which is called the navel); he also moulded the breast and took out most   [191] of the wrinkles, much as a shoemaker might smooth leather upon a last; he left a few, however, in the region of the belly and navel, as a memorial of the primeval state. After the division the two parts of man, each desiring his other half, came together, and throwing their arms about one another, entwined in mutual embraces, longing to grow into one, they were on the point of dying from hunger and self-neglect, because they did not like to do anything apart; and when one of the halves died and the other survived, the survivor sought another mate, man or woman as we call them,—being the sections of entire men or women,—and clung to that. They were being destroyed, when Zeus in pity of them invented a new plan: he turned the parts of generation round to the front, for this had not been always their position, and they sowed the seed no longer as hitherto like grasshoppers in the ground, but in one another; and after the transposition the male generated in the female in order that by the mutual embraces of man and woman they might breed, and the race might continue; or if man came to man they might be satisfied, and rest, and go their ways to the business of life: so ancient is the desire of one another which is implanted in us, reuniting our original nature, making one of two, and healing the state of man. Each of us when separated, having one side only, like a flat fish, is but the indenture of a man, and he is always looking for his other half. Men who are a section of that double nature which was once called Androgynous are lovers of women; adulterers are generally of this breed, and also adulterous women who lust after men: the women who are a section of the woman do not care for men, but have female attachments; the female companions are of this sort. But they who are a section of the male follow the male, and while they are young, being slices of the original man, they hang about men and embrace them, and they are themselves the best of boys and   [192] youths, because they have the most manly nature. Some indeed assert that they are shameless, but this is not true; for they do not act thus from any want of shame, but because they are valiant and manly, and have a manly countenance, and they embrace that which is like them. And these when they grow up become our statesmen, and these only, which is a great proof of the truth of what I am saying. When they reach manhood they are lovers of youth, and are not naturally inclined to marry or beget children,—if at all, they do so only in obedience to the law; but they are satisfied if they may be allowed to live with one another unwedded; and such a nature is prone to love and ready to return love, always embracing that which is akin to him. And when one of them meets with his other half, the actual half of himself, whether he be a lover of youth or a lover of another sort, the pair are lost in an amazement of love and friendship and intimacy, and will not be out of the other's sight, as I may say, even for a moment: these are the people who pass their whole lives together; yet they could not explain what they desire of one another. For the intense yearning which each of them has towards the other does not appear to be the desire of lover's intercourse, but of something else which the soul of either evidently desires and cannot tell, and of which she has only a dark and doubtful presentiment. Suppose Hephaestus, with his instruments, to come to the pair who are lying side by side and to say to them, 'What do you people want of one another?' they would be unable to explain. And suppose further, that when he saw their perplexity he said: 'Do you desire to be wholly one; always day and night to be in one another's company? for if this is what you desire, I am ready to melt you into one and let you grow together, so that being two you shall become one, and while you live a common life as if you were a single man, and after your death in the world below still be one departed soul instead of two—I ask whether this is what you lovingly desire, and whether you are satisfied to attain this?'—there is not a man of them who when he heard the proposal would deny or would not acknowledge that this meeting and melting into one another, this becoming one instead of two, was the very expression of his ancient need [7]. And the reason is that human nature was originally one and we were a whole, and the desire and pursuit of the whole is called love. [193] There was a time, I say, when we were one, but now because of the wickedness of mankind God has dispersed us, as the Arcadians were dispersed into villages by the Lacedaemonians [8]. And if we are not obedient to the gods, there is a danger that we shall be split up again and go about in basso-relievo, like the profile figures having only half a nose which are sculptured on monuments, and that we shall be like tallies. Wherefore let us exhort all men to piety, that we may avoid evil, and obtain the good, of which Love is to us the lord and minister; and let no one oppose him—he is the enemy of the gods who oppose him. For if we are friends of the God and at peace with him we shall find our own true loves, which rarely happens in this world at present. I am serious, and therefore I must beg Eryximachus not to make fun or to find any allusion in which I am saying to Pausanias and Agathon, who, as I suspect, are both of the manly nature, and belong to the class which I have been describing. But my words have a wider application—they include men and women everywhere; and I believe that if our loves were perfectly accomplished, and each one returning to his primeval nature had his original true love, then our race would be happy. And if this would be best of all, the best in the next degree and under present circumstances must be the nearest approach to such an union; and that will be the at-

---

[7] Cp. Arist. Pol. ii. 4, §6.
[8] Cp. Arist. Pol. ii. 2, §3.

tainment of a congenial love. Wherefore, if we would praise him who has given to us the benefit, we must praise the god Love, who is our greatest benefactor, both leading us in this life back to our own nature, and giving us high hopes for the future, for he promises that if we are pious, he will restore us to our original state, and heal us and make us happy and blessed. This, Eryximachus, is my discourse of love, which, although different to yours, I must beg you to leave unassailed by the shafts of your ridicule, in order that each may have his turn; each, or rather either, for Agathon and Socrates are the only ones left.

Indeed, I am not going to attack you, said Eryximachus, for I thought your speech charming, and did I not know that Agathon and Socrates are masters in the art of love, I should be really afraid that they would have nothing to say, after the world of things which have been said already. But, for all that, I am not without hopes.

Socrates said: You played your part well, Eryximachus; but if [194] you were as I am now, or rather as I shall be when Agathon has spoken, you would, indeed, be in a great strait.

You want to cast a spell over me, Socrates, said Agathon, in the hope that I may be disconcerted at the expectation raised among the audience that I shall speak well.

I should be strangely forgetful, Agathon, replied Socrates, of the courage and magnanimity which you showed when your own compositions were about to be exhibited, and you came upon the stage with the actors and faced the vast theatre altogether undismayed, if I thought that your nerves could be fluttered at a small party of friends.

Do you think, Socrates, said Agathon, that my head is so full of the theatre as not to know how much more formidable to a man of sense a few good judges are than many fools?

Nay, replied Socrates, I should be very wrong in attributing to you, Agathon, that or any other want of refinement. And I am quite aware that if you happened to meet with any whom you thought wise, you would care for their opinion much more than for that of the many. But then we, having been a part of the foolish many in the theatre, cannot be regarded as the select wise; though I know that if you chanced to be in the presence, not of one of ourselves, but of some really wise man, you would be ashamed of disgracing yourself before him—would you not?

Yes, said Agathon.

But before the many you would not be ashamed, if you thought that you were doing something disgraceful in their presence?

Here Phaedrus interrupted them, saying: Do not answer him, my dear Agathon; for if he can only get a partner with whom he can talk, especially a good-looking one, he will no longer care about the completion of our plan. Now I love to hear him talk; but just at present I must not forget the encomium on Love which I ought to receive from him and from every one. When you and he have paid your tribute to the god, then you may talk.

THE SPEECH OF AGATHON

Very good, Phaedrus, said Agathon; I see no reason why I should not proceed with my speech, as I shall have many other opportunities of conversing with Socrates. Let me say first how I ought to speak, and then speak:—

The previous speakers, instead of praising the god Love, or unfolding his nature, appear to have congratulated mankind on the benefits which he confers upon them. But I would rather praise the [195] god first, and then speak of his gifts; this is always the right way of praising everything. May I say without impiety or offence, that of all the blessed gods he is the most blessed because he is the fairest and best? And he is the fairest: for, in the first place, he is the youngest, and of his youth he is himself the witness, fleeing out of the way of age, who is swift enough, swifter truly than most of us like:—Love hates him and will not come near him; but youth and love live and move together—like to like, as the proverb says. Many things were said by Phaedrus about Love in which I agree with him; but I cannot agree that he is older than Iapetus and Kronos:—not so; I maintain him to be the youngest of the gods, and youthful ever. The ancient doings among the gods of which Hesiod and Parmenides spoke, if the tradition of them be true, were done of Necessity and not of Love; had Love been in those days, there would have been no chaining or mutilation of the gods, or other violence, but peace and sweetness, as there is now in heaven, since the rule of Love began. Love is young and also tender; he ought to have a poet like Homer to describe his tenderness, as Homer says of Ate, that she is a goddess and tender:—

> 'Her feet are tender, for she sets her steps,
> Not on the ground but on the heads of men:'

herein is an excellent proof of her tenderness,—that she walks not upon the hard but upon the soft. Let us adduce a similar proof of the tenderness of Love; for he walks not upon the earth, nor yet upon the skulls of men, which are not so very soft, but in the hearts and souls of both gods and men, which are of all things the softest: in them he walks and dwells and makes his home. Not in every soul without exception, for where there is hardness he departs, where there is softness there he dwells; and nestling always with his feet and in all manner of ways in the softest of soft places, how can he be other than the softest of [196] all things? Of a truth he is the tenderest as well as the youngest, and also he is of flexile form; for if he were hard and without flexure he could not enfold all things, or wind his way into and out of every soul of man undiscovered. And a proof of his flexibility and symmetry of form is his grace, which is universally admitted to be in an especial manner the attribute of Love; ungrace and love are always at war with one another. The fairness of his complexion is revealed by his habitation among the flowers; for he dwells not amid bloomless or fading beauties, whether of body or soul or aught else, but in the place of flowers and scents, there he sits and abides. Concerning the beauty of the god I have said enough; and yet there remains much more which I might say. Of his virtue I have now to speak: his greatest glory is that he can neither do nor suffer wrong to or from any god or any man; for he suffers not by force if he suffers; force comes not near him, neither when he acts does he act by force. For all men in all things serve him of their own free will, and where there is voluntary agreement, there, as the laws which are the lords of the city say, is justice. And not only is he just but exceedingly temperate, for Temperance is the acknowledged ruler of the pleasures and desires, and no pleasure ever masters Love; he is their master and they are his servants; and if he conquers them he must be temperate indeed. As to courage, even the God of War is no match for him; he is the captive and Love is the lord, for love, the love of Aphrodite, masters him, as the tale runs; and the master is stronger than the servant. And if he conquers the bravest of all others, he must be himself the bravest. Of his courage and justice and temperance I have spoken, but I have yet to speak of his wisdom; and according to the measure of my ability I must try to do my best. In the first place he is a poet (and here, like Eryximachus, I magnify my art), and he is also the source of poesy in others, which he could not be if he were not himself a poet. And at the touch of him every one becomes a poet,[9] even though he had no music in him before; [9] this also is a proof that Love is a good poet and accomplished in all the fine arts; for no one can give to another that which he has not himself, or teach that of which he has no knowledge. Who will deny that the creation of the animals is his doing? Are they not all the works of [197] his wisdom, born and begotten of him? And as to the artists, do we not know that he only of them whom love inspires has the light of fame?— he whom Love touches not walks in darkness. The arts of medicine and archery and divination were discovered by Apollo, under the guidance of love and desire; so that he too is a disciple of Love. Also the melody of the Muses, the metallurgy of Hephaestus, the weaving of Athene, the empire of Zeus over gods and men, are all due to Love, who was the inventor of them. And so Love set in order the empire of the gods—the love of beauty, as is evident, for with deformity Love has no concern. In the days of old, as I began by saying, dreadful deeds were done among the gods, for they were ruled by Necessity; but now since the birth of Love, and from the Love of the beautiful, has sprung every good in heaven and earth. Therefore, Phaedrus, I say of Love that he is the fairest and best in himself, and the cause of what is fairest and best in all other things. And there comes into my mind a line of poetry in which he is said to be the god who

'Gives peace on earth and calms the stormy deep,
Who stills the winds and bids the sufferer sleep.'

---

[9] A fragment of the Sthenoboea of Euripides.

This is he who empties men of disaffection and fills them with affection, who makes them to meet together at banquets such as these: in sacrifices, feasts, dances, he is our lord—who sends courtesy and sends away discourtesy, who gives kindness ever and never gives unkindness; the friend of the good, the wonder of the wise, the amazement of the gods; desired by those who have no part in him, and precious to those who have the better part in him; parent of delicacy, luxury, desire, fondness, softness, grace; regardful of the good, regardless of the evil: in every word, work, wish, fear—saviour, pilot, comrade, helper; glory of gods and men, leader best and brightest: in whose footsteps let every man follow, sweetly singing in his honour and joining in that sweet strain with which love charms the souls of gods and men. Such is the speech, Phaedrus, halfplayful, yet having a certain measure of seriousness, which, according to my ability, I dedicate to the god.

When Agathon had done speaking, Aristodemus said that there [198] was a general cheer; the young man was thought to have spoken in a manner worthy of himself, and of the god. And Socrates, looking at Eryximachus, said: Tell me, son of Acumenus, was there not reason in my fears? and was I not a true prophet when I said that Agathon would make a wonderful oration, and that I should be in a strait?

The part of the prophecy which concerns Agathon, replied Eryximachus, appears to me to be true; but not the other part—that you will be in a strait.

THE SPEECH OF SOCRATES

Why, my dear friend, said Socrates, must not I or any one be in a strait who has to speak after he has heard such a rich and varied discourse? I am especially struck with the beauty of the concluding words—who could listen to them without amazement? When I reflected on the immeasurable inferiority of my own powers, I was ready to run away for shame, if there had been a possibility of escape. For I was reminded of Gorgias, and at the end of his speech I fancied that Agathon was shaking at me the Gorginian or Gorgonian head of the great master of rhetoric, which was simply to turn me and my speech into stone, as Homer says,[10] and strike me dumb. And then I perceived how foolish I had been in consenting to take my turn with you in praising love, and saying that I too was a master of the art, when I really had no conception how anything ought to be praised. For in my simplicity I imagined that the topics of praise should be true, and that this being presupposed, out of the true the speaker was to choose the best and set them forth in the best manner. And I felt quite proud, thinking that I knew the nature of true praise, and should speak well. Whereas I now see that the intention was to attribute to Love every species of greatness and glory, whether really belonging to him or not, without regard to truth or

---

[10] *Odyssey*, λ. 632.

falsehood—that was no matter; for the original proposal seems to have been not that each of you should really praise Love, but only that you should appear to praise him. And so you attribute to Love every imaginable form of praise which can be gathered anywhere; and you say that 'he is all this,' and 'the cause of all that,' making him appear the   [199] fairest and best of all to those who know him not, for you cannot impose upon those who know him. And a noble and solemn hymn of praise have you rehearsed. But as I misunderstood the nature of the praise when I said that I would take my turn, I must beg to be absolved from the promise which I made in ignorance, and which (as Euripides would say[11]) was a promise of the lips and not of the mind. Farewell then to such a strain: for I do not praise in that way; no, indeed, I cannot. But if you like to hear the truth about love, I am ready to speak in my own manner, though I will not make myself ridiculous by entering into any rivalry with you. Say then, Phaedrus, whether you would like to have the truth about love, spoken in any words and in any order which may happen to come into my mind at the time. Will that be agreeable to you?

Aristodemus said that Phaedrus and the company bid him speak in any manner which he thought best. Then, he added, let me have your permission first to ask Agathon a few more questions, in order that I may take his admissions as the premises of my discourse.

I grant the permission, said Phaedrus: put your questions. Socrates then proceeded as follows:—

In the magnificent oration which you have just uttered, I think that you were right, my dear Agathon, in proposing to speak of the nature of Love first and afterwards of his works—that is a way of beginning which I very much approve. And as you have spoken so eloquently of his nature, may I ask you further, Whether love is the love of something or of nothing? And here I must explain myself: I do not want you to say that love is the love of a father or the love of a mother—that would be ridiculous; but to answer as you would, if I asked is a father a father of something? to which you would find no difficulty in replying, of a son or daughter: and the answer would be right.

Very true, said Agathon.

And you would say the same of a mother?

He assented.

Yet let me ask you one more question in order to illustrate my meaning: Is not a brother to be regarded essentially as a brother of something?

Certainly, he replied.

That is, of a brother or sister?

Yes, he said.

And now, said Socrates, I will ask about Love:—Is Love of something or of nothing?

---

11 Eurip. Hyppolytus, l. 612.

Of something, surely, he replied.   [200]

Keep in mind what this is, and tell me what I want to know—
whether Love desires that of which love is.

Yes, surely.

And does he possess, or does he not possess, that which he loves and
desires?

Probably not, I should say.

Nay, replied Socrates, I would have you consider whether 'necessarily'
is not rather the word. The inference that he who desires something is
in want of something, and that he who desires nothing is in want of
nothing, is in my judgment, Agathon, absolutely and necessarily true.
What do you think?

I agree with you, said Agathon.

Very good. Would he who is great, desire to be great, or he who is
strong, desire to be strong?

That would be inconsistent with our previous admissions.

True. For he who is anything cannot want to be that which he is?

Very true.

And yet, added Socrates, if a man being strong desired to be strong,
or being swift desired to be swift, or being healthy desired to be healthy,
in that case he might be thought to desire something which he already
has or is. I give the example in order that we may avoid misconception.
For the possessors of these qualities, Agathon, must be supposed to have
their respective advantages at the time, whether they choose or not;
and who can desire that which he has? Therefore, when a person says, I
am well and wish to be well, or I am rich and wish to be rich, and I
desire simply to have what I have—to him we shall reply: 'You, my
friend, having wealth and health and strength, want to have the con-
tinuance of them; for at this moment, whether you choose or no, you
have them. And when you say, I desire that which I have and nothing
else, is not your meaning that you want to have what you now have in
the future?' He must agree with us—must he not?

He must, replied Agathon.

Then, said Socrates, he desires that what he has at present may
be preserved to him in the future, which is equivalent to saying that
he desires something which is non-existent to him, and which as yet
he has not got.

Very true, he said.

Then he and every one who desires, desires that which he has not
already, and which is future and not present, and which he has not,
and is not, and of which he is in want;—these are the sort of things
which love and desire seek?

Very true, he said.

Then now, said Socrates, let us recapitulate the argument. First, is
not love of something, and of something too which is wanting to a man?

Yes, he replied.   [201]

Remember further what you said in your speech, or if you do not remember I will remind you: you said that the love of the beautiful set in order the empire of the gods, for that of deformed things there is no love—did you not say something of that kind?

Yes, said Agathon.

Yes, my friend, and the remark was a just one. And if this is true, Love is the love of beauty and not of deformity?

He assented.

And the admission has been already made that Love is of something which a man wants and has not?

True, he said.

Then Love wants and has not beauty?

Certainly, he replied.

And would you call that beautiful which wants and does not possess beauty?

Certainly not.

Then would you still say that love is beautiful?

Agathon replied: I fear that I did not understand what I was saying.

You made a very good speech, Agathon, replied Socrates; but there is yet one small question which I would fain ask:—Is not the good also the beautiful?

Yes.

Then in wanting the beautiful, love wants also the good?

I cannot refute you, Socrates, said Agathon:—Let us assume that what you say is true.

Say rather, beloved Agathon, that you cannot refute the truth; for Socrates is easily refuted.

And now, taking my leave of you, I will rehearse a tale of love which I heard from Diotima of Mantineia,[12] a woman wise in this and in many other kinds of knowledge, who in the days of old, when the Athenians offered sacrifice before the coming of the plague, delayed the disease ten years. She was my instructress in the art of love, and I shall repeat to you what she said to me, beginning with the admissions made by Agathon, which are nearly if not quite the same which I made to the wise woman when she questioned me: I think that this will be the easiest way, and I shall take both parts myself as well as I can.[13] As you, Agathon, suggested,[14] I must speak first of the being and nature of Love, and then of his works. First I said to her in nearly the same words which he used to me, that Love was a mighty god, and likewise fair; and she proved to me as I proved to him that, by my own showing, Love was neither fair nor good. 'What do you mean, Diotima,' I said, 'is love then evil and foul?' 'Hush,' she cried; 'must that be foul which is not fair?' 'Certainly,' I said. 'And is that which is not wise, ig-   [202] norant? do you not see that there is a mean between wisdom and igno-

---

12 Cp. I. Alcibiades.
13 Cp. Gorgias, 505 E.
14 Supra, 195 A.

rance?' 'And what may that be?' I said. 'Right opinion,' she replied; 'which, as you know, being incapable of giving a reason, is not knowledge (for how can knowledge be devoid of reason? nor again, ignorance, for neither can ignorance attain the truth), but is clearly something which is a mean between ignorance and wisdom.' 'Quite true,' I replied. 'Do not then insist,' she said, 'that what is not fair is of necessity foul, or what is not good evil; or infer that because love is not fair and good he is therefore foul and evil; for he is in a mean between them.' 'Well,' I said, 'Love is surely admitted by all to be a great god.' 'By those who know or by those who do not know?' 'By all.' 'And how, Socrates,' she said with a smile, 'can Love be acknowledged to be a great god by those who say that he is not a god at all?' 'And who are they?' I said. 'You and I are two of them,' she replied. 'How can that be?' I said. 'It is quite intelligible,' she replied; 'for you yourself would acknowledge that the gods are happy and fair—of course you would—would you dare to say that any god was not?' 'Certainly not,' I replied. 'And you mean by the happy, those who are the possessors of things good or fair?' 'Yes.' 'And you admitted that Love, because he was in want, desires those good and fair things of which he is in want?' 'Yes, I did.' 'But how can he be a god who has no portion in what is either good or fair?' 'Impossible.' 'Then you see that you also deny the divinity of Love.'

'What then is Love?' I asked; 'Is he mortal?' 'No.' 'What then?' 'As in the former instance, he is neither mortal nor immortal, but in a mean between the two.' 'What is he, Diotima?' 'He is a great spirit ($\delta\alpha\acute{\iota}\mu\omega\nu$), and like all spirits he is intermediate between the divine and the mortal.' 'And what,' I said, 'is his power?' 'He interprets,' she replied, 'between gods and men, conveying and taking across to the gods the prayers and sacrifices of men, and to men the commands and replies of the gods; he is the mediator who spans the chasm which divides them, and therefore in him all is bound together, and through him the arts of the prophet and the priest, their sacrifices and mysteries and [203] charms, and all prophecy and incantation, find their way. For God mingles not with man; but through Love all the intercourse and converse of god with man, whether awake or asleep, is carried on. The wisdom which understands this is spiritual; all other wisdom, such as that of arts and handicrafts, is mean and vulgar. Now these spirits or intermediate powers are many and diverse, and one of them is Love.' 'And who,' I said, 'was his father, and who his mother?' 'The tale,' she said, 'will take time; nevertheless I will tell you. On the birthday of Aphrodite there was a feast of the gods, at which the god Poros or Plenty, who is the son of Metis or Discretion, was one of the guests. When the feast was over, Penia or Poverty, as the manner is on such occasions, came about the doors to beg. Now Plenty, who was the worse for nectar (there was no wine in those days), went into the garden of Zeus and fell into a heavy sleep; and Poverty considering her own straitened circumstances, plotted to have a child by him, and accordingly she lay down at his side and conceived Love, who partly because he is naturally a lover of the beautiful, and because Aphrodite is herself beautiful, and also because he was born on her birthday, is her follower and attendant. And as his parentage is, so also are his fortunes. In the first place he is always poor, and anything but tender and fair, as the many imagine him; and he is rough and squalid, and has no shoes, nor a house to dwell in; on the bare earth exposed he lies under the open heaven, in the streets, or at the doors of houses, taking his rest; and like his mother he is always in distress. Like his father too, whom he also partly resembles, he is always plotting against the fair and good; he is bold, enterprising, strong, a mighty hunter, always weaving some intrigue or other, keen in the pursuit of wisdom, fertile in resources; a philosopher at all times, terrible as an enchanter, sorcerer, sophist. He is by nature neither mortal nor immortal, but alive and flourishing at one moment when he is in plenty, and dead at another moment, and again alive by reason of his father's nature. But that which is always flowing in is always flowing out, and so he is never in want and never in wealth; and, further, he is in a mean between ignorance and knowledge. The truth of the matter is this: No god is a philosopher or seeker after wisdom, for he is wise already; nor does any man who is wise seek after wisdom. Neither do the ignorant seek after wisdom. For herein is the evil of ignorance, that he who is neither [204] good nor wise is nevertheless satisfied with himself: he has no desire for that of which he feels no want.' 'But who then, Diotima,' I said, 'are the lovers of wisdom, if they are neither the wise nor the foolish?' 'A child may answer that question,' she replied; 'they are those who are in a mean between the two; Love is one of them. For wisdom is a most beautiful thing, and Love is of the beautiful; and therefore Love is also a philosopher or lover of wisdom, and being a lover of wisdom is in a mean between the wise and the ignorant. And of this too his birth is the cause; for his father is wealthy and wise, and his mother poor and foolish. Such, my dear Socrates, is the nature of the spirit Love. The error in your conception of him was very natural, and as I imagine from what you say, has arisen out of a confusion of love and the beloved, which made you think that love was all beautiful. For the beloved is the truly beautiful, and delicate, and perfect, and blessed; but the principle of love is of another nature, and is such as I have described.'

I said: 'O thou stranger woman, thou sayest well; but, assuming Love to be such as you say, what is the use of him to men?' 'That, Socrates,' she replied, 'I will attempt to unfold: of his nature and birth I have already spoken; and you acknowledge that love is of the beautiful. But some one will say: Of the beautiful in what, Socrates and Diotima?—or rather let me put the question more clearly, and ask: When a man loves the beautiful, what does he desire?' I answered her 'That the beautiful may be his.' 'Still,' she said, 'the answer suggests a further question: What is given by the possession of beauty?' 'To what you have asked,' I replied, 'I have no answer ready.' 'Then,' she said, 'let me put the word "good" in the place of the beautiful, and repeat the question once more: If he who loves loves the good, what is it then that he loves?' 'The possession of the good,' I said.

'And what does he gain who possesses the good?' 'Happiness,' I replied; 'there is less difficulty in answering that question.' 'Yes,' she said, 'the happy are made happy by the acquisition of good things. [205] Nor is there any need to ask why a man desires happiness; the answer is already final.' 'You are right,' I said. 'And is this wish and this desire common to all? and do all men always desire their own good, or only some men?—what say you?' 'All men,' I replied; 'the desire is common to all.' 'Why, then,' she rejoined, 'are not all men, Socrates, said to love, but only some of them? whereas you say that all men are always loving the same things.' 'I myself wonder,' I said, 'why this is.' 'There is nothing to wonder at,' she replied; 'the reason is that one part of love is separated off and receives the name of the whole, but the other parts have other names.' 'Give an illustration,' I said. She answered me as follows: 'There is poetry, which, as you know, is complex and manifold. All creation or passage of non-being into being is poetry or making, and the processes of all art are creative; and the masters of art are all poets or makers.' 'Very true.' 'Still,' she said, 'you know that they are not called poets, but have other names; only that portion of the art which is separated off from the rest, and is concerned with music and metre, is termed poetry, and they who possess poetry in this sense of the word are called poets.' 'Very true,' I said. 'And the same holds of love. For you may say generally that all desire of good and happiness is only the great and subtle power of love; but they who are drawn towards him by any other path, whether the path of money-making or gymnastics or philosophy, are not called lovers—the name of the whole is appropriated to those whose affection takes one form only—they alone are said to love, or to be lovers.' 'I dare say,' I replied, 'that you are right.' 'Yes,' she added, 'and you hear people say that lovers are seeking for their other half; but I say that they are seeking neither for the half of themselves, nor for the whole, unless the half or the whole be also a good. And they will cut off their own hands and feet and cast them away, if they are evil; for they love not what is their own, unless perchance there be some one who calls what belongs to him the good, and what belongs to another the evil. For there is nothing which men love but the [206] good. Is there anything?' 'Certainly, I should say, that there is nothing.' 'Then,' she said, 'the simple truth is, that men love the good.' 'Yes,' I said. 'To which must be added that they love the possession of the good?' 'Yes, that must be added.' 'And not only the possession, but the everlasting possession of the good?' 'That must be added too.' 'Then love,' she said, 'may be described generally as the love of the everlasting possession of the good?' 'That is most true.'

'Then if this be the nature of love, can you tell me further,' she said, 'what is the manner of the pursuit? what are they doing who show all this eagerness and heat which is called love? and what is the object which they have in view? Answer me.' 'Nay, Diotima,' I replied, 'if I had known, I should not have wondered at your wisdom, neither should I have come to learn from you about this very matter.' 'Well,' she said, 'I will teach you:—The object which they have in view is birth in beauty, whether of body or soul.' 'I do not understand you,' I said; 'the oracle requires an explanation.' 'I will make my meaning clearer,' she replied. 'I mean to say, that all men are bringing to the birth in their bodies and in their souls. There is a certain age at which human nature is desirous of procreation—procreation which must be in beauty and not in deformity; and this procreation is the union of man and woman, and is a divine thing; for conception and generation are an immortal principle in the mortal creature, and in the inharmonious they can never be. But the deformed is always inharmonious with the divine, and the beautiful harmonious. Beauty, then, is the destiny or goddess of parturition who presides at birth, and therefore, when approaching beauty, the conceiving power is propitious, and diffusive, and benign, and begets and bears fruit: at the sight of ugliness she frowns and contracts and has a sense of pain, and turns away, and shrivels up, and not without a pang refrains from conception. And this is the reason why, when the hour of conception arrives, and the teeming nature is full, there is such a flutter and ecstasy about beauty whose approach is the alleviation of the pain of travail. For love, Socrates, is not, as you imagine, the love of the beautiful only.' 'What then?' 'The love of generation and of birth in beauty.' 'Yes,' I said. 'Yes, indeed,' she replied. 'But why of generation?' 'Because to the mortal creature, generation is a sort of eternity and immortality,' she replied; 'and if, as has been already admitted, love is of the everlasting possession of the good, all men will necessarily desire immortality together with good: Wherefore love [207] is of immortality.'

All this she taught me at various times when she spoke of love. And I remember her once saying to me, 'What is the cause, Socrates, of love, and the attendant desire? See you not how all animals, birds, as well as beasts, in their desire of procreation, are in agony when they take the infection of love, which begins with the desire of union; whereto is added the care of offspring, on whose behalf the weakest are ready to battle against the strongest even to the uttermost, and to die for them, and will let themselves be tormented with hunger or suffer anything in order to maintain their young. Man may be supposed to act thus from reason; but why should animals have these passionate feelings? Can you tell me why?' Again I replied that I did not know. She said to me: 'And do you expect ever to become a master in the art of love, if you do not know this?' 'But I have told you already, Diotima, that my ignorance is the reason why I come to you; for I am conscious that I want a teacher; tell me then the cause of this and of the other mysteries of love.' 'Marvel not,' she said, 'if you believe that love is of the immortal, as we have several times acknowledged; for here again, and on the same principle too, the mortal nature is seeking as far as is possible to be everlasting and immortal: and this is only to be attained by generation, because generation always leaves behind a new existence in the place of the old. Nay even in the life of the same individual there is succession and not absolute unity: a man is called the same, and yet in the short interval which elapses between youth and age, and in which every animal is said to have life and identity, he is undergoing a perpetual process of loss and reparation—hair, flesh, bones, blood, and the whole body are always changing. Which is true not only of the body, but also of the soul, whose habits, tempers, opinions, desires, pleasures, pains, fears, never remain the same in any one of us, but are always coming and going; and equally true of knowledge, and what is still more surprising to us mortals, not only do the sciences   [208] in general spring up and decay, so that in respect of them we are never the same; but each of them individually experiences a like change. For what is implied in the word "recollection," but the departure of knowledge, which is ever being forgotten, and is renewed and preserved by recollection, and appears to be the same although in reality new, according to that law of succession by which all mortal things are preserved, not absolutely the same, but by substitution, the old worn-out mortality leaving another new and similar existence behind—unlike the divine, which is always the same and not another? And in this way, Socrates, the mortal body, or mortal anything, partakes of immortality; but the immortal in another way. Marvel not then at the love which all men have of their offspring; for that universal love and interest is for the sake of immortality.'

I was astonished at her words, and said: 'Is this really true, O thou wise Diotima?' And she answered with all the authority of an accomplished sophist: 'Of that, Socrates, you may be assured;—think only of the ambition of men, and you will wonder at the senselessness of their ways, unless you consider how they are stirred by the love of an immortality of fame. They are ready to run all risks greater far than they would have run for their children, and to spend money and undergo any sort of toil, and even to die, for the sake of leaving behind them a name which shall be eternal. Do you imagine that Alcestis would have died to save Admetus, or Achilles to avenge Patroclus, or your own Codrus in order to preserve the kingdom for his sons, if they had not imagined that the memory of their virtues, which still survives among us, would be immortal? Nay,' she said, 'I am persuaded that all men do all things, and the better they are the more they do them, in hope of the glorious fame of immortal virtue; for they desire the immortal.

'Those who are pregnant in the body only, betake themselves to women and beget children—this is the character of their love; their offspring, as they hope, will preserve their memory and give them the blessedness and immortality which they desire in the future. But souls which are pregnant —for there certainly are men who are more creative in their souls   [209] than in their bodies—conceive that which is proper for the soul to conceive or contain. And what are these conceptions?—wisdom and virtue in general. And such creators are poets and all artists who are deserving of the name inventor. But the greatest and fairest sort of wisdom by far is that which is concerned with the ordering of states and families, and which is called temperance and justice. And he who in youth has the seed of these implanted in him and is himself inspired, when he comes to maturity desires to beget and generate. He wanders about seeking beauty that he may beget offspring—for in deformity he will beget nothing—and naturally embraces the beautiful rather than the deformed body; above all when he finds a fair and noble and well-nurtured soul, he embraces the two in one person, and to such an one he is full of speech about virtue and the nature and pursuits of a good man; and he tries to educate him; and at the touch of the beautiful which is ever present to his memory, even when absent, he brings forth that which he had conceived long before, and in company with him tends that which he brings forth; and they are married by a far nearer tie and have a closer friendship than those who beget mortal children, for the children who are their common offspring are fairer and more immortal. Who, when he thinks of Homer and Hesiod and other great poets, would not rather have their children than ordinary human ones? Who would not emulate them in the creation of children such as theirs, which have preserved their memory and given them everlasting glory? Or who would not have such children as Lycurgus left behind him to be the saviours, not only of Lacedaemon, but of Hellas, as one may say? There is Solon, too, who is the revered father of Athenian laws; and many others there are in many other places, both among Hellenes and barbarians, who have given to the world many noble works, and have been the parents of virtue of every kind; and many temples have been raised in their honour for the sake of children such as theirs; which were never raised in honour of any one, for the sake of his mortal children.

'These are the lesser mysteries of love, into which even you, Socrates, may enter; to the greater and more hidden ones which are the   [210] crown of these, and to which, if you pursue them in a right spirit, they will lead, I know not whether you will be able to attain. But I will do my utmost to inform you, and do you follow if you can. For he who would proceed aright in this matter should begin in youth to visit beautiful forms; and first, if he be guided by his instructor aright, to love one such form only—out of that he should create fair thoughts; and soon he will of himself perceive that the beauty of one form is akin to the beauty of another; and then if beauty of form in general is his pursuit, how foolish would he be not to recognize that the beauty in every form is one and the same! And when he perceives this he will abate his violent love of the one, which he will despise and deem a small thing, and will become a lover of all beautiful forms; in the next stage he will consider that the beauty of the mind is more honourable than the beauty of the outward form. So that if a virtuous soul have but a little comeliness, he will be content to love and tend him, and will search out and bring to the birth thoughts which may improve the young, until he is compelled to contemplate and see the beauty of institutions and laws, and to understand that the beauty of them all is of one family, and that personal beauty is a trifle; and after laws and institutions he will go on to the sciences, that he may see their beauty, being not like a servant in love with the beauty of one youth or man or institution, himself a slave mean and narrow-minded, but drawing towards and contemplating the vast sea of beauty, he will create many fair and noble thoughts and notions in boundless love of wisdom; until on that shore he grows and waxes strong, and at last the vision is revealed to him of a single science, which is the science of beauty everywhere. To this I will proceed; please to give me your very best attention:

'He who has been instructed thus far in the things of love, and who has learned to see the beautiful in due order and succession, when he comes toward the end will suddenly perceive a nature of wondrous beauty (and this, Socrates, is the final cause of all our former toils) [211] —a nature which in the first place is everlasting, not growing and decaying, or waxing and waning; secondly, not fair in one point of view and foul in another, or at one time or in one relation or at one place fair, at another time or in another relation or at another place foul, as if fair to some and foul to others, or in the likeness of a face or hands or any other part of the bodily frame, or in any form of speech or knowledge, or existing in any other being, as for example, in an animal, or in heaven, or in earth, or in any other place; but beauty absolute, separate, simple, and everlasting, which without diminution and without increase, or any change, is imparted to the ever-growing and perishing beauties of all other things. He who from these ascending under the influence of true love, begins to perceive that beauty, is not far from the end. And the true order of going, or being led by another, to the things of love, is to begin from the beauties of earth and mount upwards for the sake of that other beauty, using these as steps only, and from one going on to two, and from two to all fair forms, and from fair forms to fair practices, and from fair practices to fair notions, until from fair notions he arrives at the notion of absolute beauty, and at last knows what the essence of beauty is. This, my dear Socrates,' said the stranger of Mantineia, 'is that life above all others which man should live, in the contemplation of beauty absolute; a beauty which if you once beheld, you would see not to be after the measure of gold, and garments, and fair boys and youths, whose presence now entrances you; and you and many a one would be content to live seeing them only and conversing with them without meat or drink, if that were possible—you only want to look at them and to be with them. But what if man had eyes to see the true beauty—the divine beauty, I mean, pure and clear and unalloyed, not clogged with the pollutions of mortality and all the colours and vanities of human life—thither looking, and holding converse with the true beauty simple and divine? [212] Remember how in that communion only, beholding beauty with the eye of the mind, he will be enabled to bring forth, not images of beauty, but realities (for he has hold not of an image but of a reality), and bringing forth and nourishing true virtue to become the friend of God and be immortal, if mortal man may. Would that be an ignoble life?'

Such, Phaedrus—and I speak not only to you, but to all of you—were the words of Diotima; and I am persuaded of their truth. And being persuaded of them, I try to persuade others, that in the attainment of this end human nature will not easily find a helper better than love. And therefore, also, I say that every man ought to honour him as I myself honour him, and walk in his ways, and exhort others to do the same, and praise the power and spirit of love according to the measure of my ability now and ever.

The words which I have spoken, you, Phaedrus, may call an encomium of love, or anything else which you please.

When Socrates had done speaking, the company applauded, and Aristophanes was beginning to say something in answer to the allusion which Socrates had made to his own speech [15], when suddenly there was a great knocking at the door of the house, as of revellers, and the sound of a flute-girl was heard. Agathon told the attendants to go and see who were the intruders. 'If they are friends of ours,' he said, 'invite them in, but if not, say that the drinking is over.' A little while afterwards they heard the voice of Alcibiades resounding in the court; he was in a great state of intoxication, and kept roaring and shouting 'Where is Agathon? Lead me to Agathon,' and at length, supported by the flute-girl and some of his attendants, he found his way to them. 'Hail, friends,' he said, appearing at the door crowned with a massive garland of ivy and violets, his head flowing with ribands. 'Will you have a very drunken man as a companion of your revels? Or shall I crown Agathon, which was my intention in coming, and go away? For I was unable to come yesterday, and therefore I am here to-day, carrying on my head these ribands, that taking them from my own head, I may crown the head of this fairest and wisest of men, as I may be allowed to call him. Will you laugh at me because I am drunk? Yet I know very well that I am speaking the truth, although [213] you may laugh. But first tell me; if I come in shall we have the understanding of which I spoke [16] ? Will you drink with me or not?'

THE SPEECH OF ALCIBIADES

The company were vociferous in begging that he would take his place among them, and Agathon specially invited him. Thereupon he was led in by the people who were with him; and as he was being led, intending to crown Agathon, he took the ribands from his own head and held them in front of his eyes; he was thus prevented from seeing Socrates, who made way for him, and Alcibiades took the vacant place between Agathon and Socrates, and in taking the place he embraced Agathon and crowned him. Take off his sandals, said Agathon, and let him make a third on the same couch.

By all means; but who makes the third partner in our revels? said Alcibiades, turning round and starting up as he caught sight of Socrates. By Heracles, he said, what is this? here is Socrates always lying in wait for me, and always, as his way is, coming out at all sorts of unsuspected places: and now, what have you to say for yourself, and why are you lying here, where I perceive that you have contrived to find a place, not

---

15 p. 205 E.
16 Supra 212 D. Will you have a very drunken man? etc.

by a joker or lover of jokes, like Aristophanes, but by the fairest of the company?

Socrates turned to Agathon and said: I must ask you to protect me, Agathon; for the passion of this man has grown quite a serious matter to me. Since I became his admirer I have never been allowed to speak to any other fair one, or so much as to look at them. If I do, he goes wild with envy and jealousy, and not only abuses me but can hardly keep his hands off me, and at this moment he may do me some harm. Please to see to this, and either reconcile me to him, or, if he attempts violence, protect me, as I am in bodily fear of his mad and passionate attempts.

There can never be reconciliation between you and me, said Alcibiades; but for the present I will defer your chastisement. And I must beg you, Agathon, to give me back some of the ribands that I may crown the marvellous head of this universal despot—I would not have him complain of me for crowning you, and neglecting him, who in conversation is the conqueror of all mankind; and this not only once, as you were the day before yesterday, but always. Whereupon, taking some of the ribands, he crowned Socrates, and again reclined.

Then he said: You seem, my friends, to be sober, which is a thing not to be endured; you must drink—for that was the agreement under which I was admitted—and I elect myself master of the feast until you are well drunk. Let us have a large goblet, Agathon, or rather, he said, addressing the attendant, bring me that wine-cooler. The wine-cooler which had caught his eye was a vessel holding more than two quarts—this he filled and emptied, and bade the attendant fill it again for Socrates. [214] Observe, my friends, said Alcibiades, that this ingenious trick of mine will have no effect on Socrates, for he can drink any quantity of wine and not be at all nearer being drunk. Socrates drank the cup which the attendant filled for him.

Eryximachus said: What is this, Alcibiades? Are we to have neither conversation nor singing over our cups; but simply to drink as if we were thirsty?

Alcibiades replied: Hail, worthy son of a most wise and worthy sire!

The same to you, said Eryximachus; but what shall we do?

That I leave to you, said Alcibiades.

'The wise physician skilled our wounds to heal' [17]

shall prescribe and we will obey. What do you want?

Well, said Eryximachus, before you appeared we had passed a resolution that each one of us in turn should make a speech in praise of love, and as good a one as he could: the turn was passed round from left to right; and as all of us have spoken, and you have not spoken but have well drunken, you ought to speak, and then impose upon Socrates any task which you please, and he on his right hand neighbour, and so on.

That is good, Eryximachus, said Alcibiades; and yet the comparison of

---

[17] From Pope's Homer, Il. xi. 514,

a drunken man's speech with those of sober men is hardly fair; and I should like to know, sweet friend, whether you really believe what Socrates was just now saying; for I can assure you that the very reverse is the fact, and that if I praise any one but himself in his presence, whether God or man, he will hardly keep his hands off me.

For shame, said Socrates.

Hold your tongue, said Alcibiades, for by Poseidon, there is no one else whom I will praise when you are of the company.

Well then, said Eryximachus, if you like praise Socrates.

What do you think, Eryximachus? said Alcibiades: shall I attack him and inflict the punishment before you all?

What are you about? said Socrates; are you going to raise a laugh at my expense? Is that the meaning of your praise?

I am going to speak the truth, if you will permit me.

I not only permit, but exhort you to speak the truth.

Then I will begin at once, said Alcibiades, and if I say anything which is not true, you may interrupt me if you will, and say 'that is a lie,' though my intention is to speak the truth. But you must not wonder if I speak any how as things come into my mind; for the fluent and orderly enumeration of all your singularities is not a task which is easy to a man in my condition.

And now, my boys, I shall praise Socrates in a figure which will   [215] appear to him to be a caricature, and yet I speak, not to make fun of him, but only for the truth's sake. I say, that he is exactly like the busts of Silenus, which are set up in the statuaries' shops, holding pipes and flutes in their mouths; and they are made to open in the middle, and have images of gods inside them. I say also that he is like Marsyas the satyr. You yourself will not deny, Socrates, that your face is like that of a satyr. Aye, and there is a resemblance in other points too. For example, you are a bully, as I can prove by witnesses, if you will not confess. And are you not a flute-player? That you are, and a performer far more wonderful than Marsyas. He indeed with instruments used to charm the souls of men by the powers of his breath, and the players of his music do so still: for the melodies of Olympus [18] are derived from Marsyas who taught them, and these, whether they are played by a great master or by a miserable flute-girl, have a power which no others have; they alone possess the soul and reveal the wants of those who have need of gods and mysteries, because they are divine. But you produce the same effect with your words only, and do not require the flute; that is the difference between you and him. When we hear any other speaker, even a very good one, he produces absolutely no effect upon us, or not much, whereas the mere fragments of you and your words, even at second-hand, and however imperfectly repeated, amaze and possess the souls of every man, woman, and child who comes within hearing of them. And if I were not afraid that you would think me hopelessly drunk, I would have sworn as well as spoken to the

---

[18] Cp. Arist. Pol. viii. 5. 16.

influence which they have always had and still have over me. For my heart leaps within me more than that of any Corybantian reveller, and my eyes rain tears when I hear them. And I observe that many others are affected in the same manner. I have heard Pericles and other great orators, and I thought that they spoke well, but I never had any similar feeling; my soul was not stirred by them, nor was I angry at the thought of my own slavish state. But this Marsyas has often brought me to such a pass, that I have felt as if I could hardly endure the life which I am [216] leading (this, Socrates, you will admit); and I am conscious that if I did not shut my ears against him, and fly as from the voice of the siren, my fate would be like that of others,—he would transfix me, and I should grow old sitting at his feet. For he makes me confess that I ought not to live as I do, neglecting the wants of my own soul, and busying myself with the concerns of the Athenians; therefore I hold my ears and tear myself away from him. And he is the only person who ever made me ashamed, which you might think not to be in my nature, and there is no one else who does the same. For I know that I cannot answer him or say that I ought not to do as he bids, but when I leave his presence the love of popularity gets the better of me. And therefore I run away and fly from him, and when I see him I am ashamed of what I have confessed to him. Many a time have I wished that he were dead, and yet I know that I should be much more sorry than glad, if he were to die: so that I am at my wit's end.

And this is what I and many others have suffered from the flute-playing of this satyr. Yet hear me once more while I show you how exact the image is, and how marvellous his power. For let me tell you; none of you know him; but I will reveal him to you; having begun, I must go on. See you how fond he is of the fair? He is always with them and is always being smitten by them, and then again he knows nothing and is ignorant of all things—such is the appearance which he puts on. Is he not like a Silenus in this? To be sure he is: his outer mask is the carved head of the Silenus; but, O my companions in drink, when he is opened, what temperance there is residing within! Know you that beauty and wealth and honour, at which the many wonder, are of no account with him, and are utterly despised by him: he regards not at all the persons who are gifted with them; mankind are nothing to him; all his life is spent in mocking and flouting at them. But when I opened him, and looked within at his serious purpose, I saw in him divine and golden images of such fascinating beauty that I was ready to do in a [217] moment whatever Socrates commanded: they may have escaped the observation of others, but I saw them. Now I fancied that he was seriously enamoured of my beauty, and I thought that I should therefore have a grand opportunity of hearing him tell what he knew, for I had a wonderful opinion of the attractions of my youth. In the prosecution of this design, when I next went to him, I sent away the attendant who usually accompanied me (I will confess the whole truth, and beg you to listen; and if I speak falsely, do you, Socrates, expose the falsehood).

Well, he and I were alone together, and I thought that when there was nobody with us, I should hear him speak the language which lovers use to their loves when they are by themselves, and I was delighted. Nothing of the sort; he conversed as usual, and spent the day with me and then went away. Afterwards I challenged him to the palaestra; and he wrestled and closed with me several times when there was no one present; I fancied that I might succeed in this manner. Not a bit; I made no way with him. Lastly, as I had failed hitherto, I thought that I must take stronger measures and attack him boldly, and, as I had begun, not give him up, but see how matters stood between him and me. So I invited him to sup with me, just as if he were a fair youth, and I a designing lover. He was not easily persuaded to come; he did, however, after a while accept the invitation, and when he came the first time, he wanted to go away at once as soon as supper was over, and I had not the face to detain him. The second time, still in pursuance of my design, after we had supped, I went on conversing far into the night, and when he wanted to go away, I pretended that the hour was late and that he had much better remain. So he lay down on the couch next to me, the same on which he had supped, and there was no one but ourselves sleeping in the apartment. All this may be told without shame to any one. But what follows I could hardly tell you if I were sober. Yet as the proverb says, 'In vino veritas,' whether with boys, or without them [19]; and therefore I must speak. Nor, again, should I be justified in concealing the lofty actions of Socrates when I come to praise him. Moreover I have felt the serpent's sting; and he who has suffered, as they say, is willing to tell his fellow-sufferers only, as they alone will be likely to understand him, and will not be ex-   [218] treme in judging of the sayings or doings which have been wrung from his agony. For I have been bitten by a more than viper's tooth; I have known in my soul, or in my heart, or in some other part, that worst of pangs, more violent in ingenuous youth than any serpent's tooth, the pang of philosophy, which will make a man say or do anything. And you whom I see around me, Phaedrus and Agathon and Eryximachus and Pausanias and Aristodemus and Aristophanes, all of you, and I need not say Socrates himself, have had experience of the same madness and passion in your longing after wisdom. Therefore listen and excuse my doings then and my sayings now. But let the attendants and other profane and unmannered persons close up the doors of their ears.

When the lamp was put out and the servants had gone away, I thought that I must be plain with him and have no more ambiguity. So I gave him a shake, and I said: 'Socrates, are you asleep?' 'No,' he said. 'Do you know what I am meditating?' 'What are you meditating?' he said. 'I think,' I replied, 'that of all the lovers whom I have ever had you are the only one who is worthy of me, and you appear to be too modest to speak. Now I feel that I should be a fool to refuse you this or any other favour, and therefore I come to lay at your feet all that I have and all that my

---

[19] In allusion to the two proverbs, οἶνος καὶ παῖδες ἀληθεῖς, and οἶνος καὶ ἀλήθεια.

friends have, in the hope that you will assist me in the way of virtue, which I desire above all things, and in which I believe that you can help me better than any one else. And I should certainly have more reason to be ashamed of what wise men would say if I were to refuse a favour to such as you, than of what the world, who are mostly fools, would say of me if I granted it.' To these words he replied in the ironical manner which is so characteristic of him:—'Alcibiades, my friend, you have indeed an elevated aim if what you say is true, and if there really is in me any power by which you may become better; truly you must see in me some rare beauty of a kind infinitely higher than any which I see in you. And therefore, if you mean to share with me and to exchange beauty for beauty, you will have greatly the advantage of me; you will gain true beauty in return for appearance—like Diomede, gold in exchange [219] for brass. But look again, sweet friend, and see whether you are not deceived in me. The mind begins to grow critical when the bodily eye fails, and it will be a long time before you get old.' Hearing this, I said: 'I have told you my purpose, which is quite serious, and do you consider what you think best for you and me.' 'That is good,' he said; 'at some other time then we will consider and act as seems best about this and about other matters.' Whereupon, I fancied that he was smitten, and that the words which I had uttered like arrows had wounded him, and so without waiting to hear more I got up, and throwing my coat about him crept under his threadbare cloak, as the time of year was winter, and there I lay during the whole night having this wonderful monster in my arms. This again, Socrates, will not be denied by you. And yet, notwithstanding all, he was so superior to my solicitations, so contemptuous and derisive and disdainful of my beauty—which really, as I fancied, had some attractions—hear, O judges; for judges you shall be of the haughty virtue of Socrates—nothing more happened, but in the morning when I awoke (let all the gods and goddesses be my witnesses) I arose as from the couch of a father or an elder brother.

What do you suppose must have been my feelings, after this rejection, at the thought of my own dishonour? And yet I could not help wondering at his natural temperance and self-restraint and manliness. I never imagined that I could have met with a man such as he is in wisdom and endurance. And therefore I could not be angry with him or renounce his company, any more than I could hope to win him. For I well knew that if Ajax could not be wounded by steel, much less he by money; and my only chance of captivating him by my personal attractions had failed. So I was at my wit's end; no one was ever more hopelessly enslaved by another. All this happened before he and I went on the expedition to Potidaea; there we messed together, and I had the opportunity of observing his extraordinary power of sustaining fatigue. His endurance was simply marvellous when, being cut off from our supplies, [220] we were compelled to go without food—on such occasions, which often happen in time of war, he was superior not only to me but to everybody; there was no one to be compared to him. Yet at a festival he was the only person who had any real powers of enjoyment; though not willing to drink, he could if compelled beat us all at that,—wonderful to relate! no human being had ever seen Socrates drunk; and his powers, if I am not mistaken, will be tested before long. His fortitude in enduring cold was also surprising. There was a severe frost, for the winter in that region is really tremendous, and everybody else either remained indoors, or if they went out had on an amazing quantity of clothes, and were well shod, and had their feet swathed in felt and fleeces: in the midst of this, Socrates with his bare feet on the ice and in his ordinary dress marched better than the other soldiers who had shoes, and they looked daggers at him because he seemed to despise them.

I have told you one tale, and now I must tell you another, which is worth hearing,

'Of the doings and sufferings of the enduring man'

while he was on the expedition. One morning he was thinking about something which he could not resolve; he would not give it up, but continued thinking from early dawn until noon—there he stood fixed in thought; and at noon attention was drawn to him, and the rumour ran through the wondering crowd that Socrates had been standing and thinking about something ever since the break of day. At last, in the evening after supper, some Ionians out of curiosity (I should explain that this was not in winter but in summer), brought out their mats and slept in the open air that they might watch him and see whether he would stand all night. There he stood until the following morning; and with the return of light he offered up a prayer to the sun, and went his way.[20] I will also tell, if you please—and indeed I am bound to tell—of his courage in battle; for who but he saved my life? Now this was the engagement in which I received the prize of valour: for I was wounded and he would not leave me, but he rescued me and my arms; and he ought to have received the prize of valour which the generals wanted to confer on me partly on account of my rank, and I told them so (this, again, Socrates will not impeach or deny), but he was more eager than the generals that I and not he should have the prize. There was another occasion on which his behaviour was very remarkable—in the [221] flight of the army after the battle of Delium, where he served among the heavy-armed,—I had a better opportunity of seeing him than at Potidaea, for I was myself on horseback, and therefore comparatively out of danger. He and Laches were retreating, for the troops were in flight, and I met them and told them not to be discouraged, and promised to remain with them; and there you might see him, Aristophanes, as you describe [21], just as he is in the streets of Athens, stalking like a pelican, and rolling his eyes, calmly contemplating enemies as well as friends, and making very intelligible to anybody, even from a distance,

---

20 Cp. supra, 175 B.
21 Aristoph. Clouds, 362.

that whoever attacked him would be likely to meet with a stout resistance; and in this way he and his companion escaped—for this is the
sort of man who is never touched in war; those only are pursued who are
running away headlong. I particularly observed how superior he was to
Laches in presence of mind. Many are the marvels which I might narrate
in praise of Socrates; most of his ways might perhaps be paralleled in
another man, but his absolute unlikeness to any human being that is or
ever has been is perfectly astonishing. You may imagine Brasidas and
others to have been like Achilles; or you may imagine Nestor and Antenor
to have been like Pericles; and the same may be said of other famous
men, but of this strange being you will never be able to find any likeness, however remote, either among men who now are or who ever have
been—other than that which I have already suggested of Silenus and the
satyrs; and they represent in a figure not only himself, but his words.
For, although I forgot to mention this to you before, his words are like
the images of Silenus which open; they are ridiculous when you first hear
them; he clothes himself in language that is like the skin of the wanton
satyr—for his talk is of pack-asses and smiths and cobblers and curriers,
and he is always repeating the same things in the same words [22], so that
any ignorant or inexperienced person might feel disposed to laugh [222]
at him; but he who opens the bust and sees what is within will find that
they are the only words which have a meaning in them, and also the
most divine, abounding in fair images of virtue, and of the widest
comprehension, or rather extending to the whole duty of a good and
honourable man.

This, friends, is my praise of Socrates. I have added my blame of
him for his ill-treatment of me; and he has ill-treated not only me, but
Charmides the son of Glaucon, and Euthydemus the son of Diocles, and
many others in the same way—beginning as their lover he has ended by
making them pay their addresses to him. Wherefore I say to you, Agathon,
'Be not deceived by him; learn from me and take warning, and do not
be a fool and learn by experience, as the proverb says.'

When Alcibiades had finished, there was a laugh at his outspokenness;
for he seemed to be still in love with Socrates. You are sober, Alcibiades,
said Socrates, or you would never have gone so far about to hide the
purpose of your satyr's praises, for all this long story is only an ingenious
circumlocution, of which the point comes in by the way at the end; you
want to get up a quarrel between me and Agathon, and your notion is
that I ought to love you and nobody else, and that you and you only
ought to love Agathon. But the plot of this Satyric or Silenic drama has
been detected, and you must not allow him, Agathon, to set us at variance.

I believe you are right, said Agathon, and I am disposed to think
that his intention in placing himself between you and me was only
to divide us; but he shall gain nothing by that move; for I will go and
lie on the couch next to you.

---

[22] Cp. Gorg. 490, 491, 517.

Yes, yes, replied Socrates, by all means come here and lie on the couch below me.

Alas, said Alcibiades, how I am fooled by this man; he is determined to get the better of me at every turn. I do beseech you, allow Agathon to lie between us.

Certainly not, said Socrates, as you praised me, and I in turn ought to praise my neighbour on the right, he will be out of order in praising me again when he ought rather to be praised by me, and I must entreat you to consent to this, and not be jealous, for I have a great desire to praise the youth.   [223]

Hurrah! cried Agathon, I will rise instantly, that I may be praised by Socrates.

The usual way, said Alcibiades; where Socrates is, no one else has any chance with the fair; and now how readily has he invented a specious reason for attracting Agathon to himself.

Agathon arose in order that he might take his place on the couch by Socrates, when suddenly a band of revellers entered, and spoiled the order of the banquet. Some one who was going out having left the door open, they had found their way in, and made themselves at home; great confusion ensued, and every one was compelled to drink large quantities of wine. Aristodemus said that Eryximachus, Phaedrus, and others went away—he himself fell asleep, and as the nights were long took a good rest: he was awakened towards daybreak by a crowing of cocks, and when he awoke, the others were either asleep, or had gone away; there remained only Socrates, Aristophanes, and Agathon, who were drinking out of a large goblet which they passed round, and Socrates was discoursing to them. Aristodemus was only half awake, and he did not hear the beginning of the discourse; the chief thing which he remembered was Socrates compelling the other two to acknowledge that the genius of comedy was the same with that of tragedy, and that the true artist in tragedy was an artist in comedy also. To this they were constrained to assent, being drowsy, and not quite following the argument. And first of all Aristophanes dropped off, then, when the day was already dawning, Agathon. Socrates, having laid them to sleep, rose to depart; Aristodemus, as his manner was, following him. At the Lyceum he took a bath, and passed the day as usual. In the evening he retired to rest at his own home.

PHAEDRUS (*complete*)

I

227A-230E INTRODUCTORY CONVERSATION • THE SCENE ON
THE BANK OF THE ILISSUS

Socrates. Where do you come from, Phaedrus my friend, and [227]
where are you going?

Phaedrus. I've been with Lysias, Socrates, the son of Cephalus, and
I'm off for a walk outside the wall, after a long morning's sitting there.
On the instructions of our common friend Acumenus [1] I take my walks
on the open roads; he tells me that is more invigorating than walking in
the colonnades.

Soc. Yes, he's right in saying so. But Lysias, I take it, was in town. [B]

Ph. Yes, staying with Epicrates, in that house where Morychus used
to live, close to the temple of Olympian Zeus.

Soc. Well, how were you occupied? No doubt Lysias was giving
the company a feast of eloquence.

Ph. I'll tell you, if you can spare time to come along with me and
listen.

Soc. What? Don't you realise that I should account it, in Pindar's
words,[2] 'above all business' to hear how you and Lysias passed your
time?

Ph. Lead on then. [C]

Soc. Please tell me.

Ph. As a matter of fact the topic is appropriate for your ears, Socrates;
for the discussion that engaged us may be said to have concerned love.
Lysias, you must know, has described how a handsome boy was tempted,
but not by a lover: that's the clever part of it: he maintains that surrender should be to one who is not in love rather than to one who is.

Soc. Splendid! I wish he would add that it should be to a poor man
rather than a rich one, an elderly man rather than a young one, and, in
general, to ordinary folk like myself. What an attractive democratic [D]
theory that would be! However, I'm so eager to hear about it that I vow
I won't leave you even if you extend your walk as far as Megara, up to
the walls and back again as recommended by Herodicus.[3]

Ph. What do you mean, my good man? Do you expect an [228]
amateur like me to repeat by heart, without disgracing its author, the work

---

[1] A well-known physician, father of Eryximachus, the physician who is one of
the speakers in the *Symposium*.

[2] *Isthm.* 1, 2.

[3] Another physician, mentioned in *Protag.* 316D as a Megarian who afterwards
settled at Selymbria in Thrace.

of the ablest writer of our day, which it took him weeks to compose at his leisure? That is far beyond me; though I'd rather have had the ability than come into a fortune.

Soc. I know my Phaedrus; yes indeed, I'm as sure of him as of my own identity. I'm certain that the said Phaedrus didn't listen just once to Lysias's speech: time after time he asked him to repeat it to him, and Lysias was very ready to comply. Even that would not content him: [B] in the end he secured the script and began poring over the parts that specially attracted him; and thus engaged he sat there the whole morning, until he grew weary and went for a walk. Upon my word, I believe he had learnt the whole speech by heart, unless it was a very long one; and he was going into the country to practise declaiming it. Then he fell in with one who has a passion for listening to discourses; and when he saw him he was delighted to think he would have someone to share his frenzied enthusiasm; so he asked him to join him on his way. But when the lover of discourses begged him to discourse, he [C] became difficult, pretending he didn't want to, though he meant to do so ultimately, even if he had to force himself on a reluctant listener. So beg him, Phaedrus, to do straightway what he will soon do in any case.

Ph. Doubtless it will be much my best course to deliver myself to the best of my ability, for I fancy you will never let me go until I have given you some sort of a speech.

Soc. You are quite right about my intention.

Ph. Then here's what I will do: it really is perfectly true, [D] Socrates, that I have not got the words by heart; but I will sketch the general purport of the several points in which the lover and the non-lover were contrasted, taking them in order one by one, and beginning at the beginning.

Soc. Very well, my dear fellow: but you must first show me what it is that you have in your left hand under your cloak; for I surmise that it is the actual discourse. If that is so, let me assure you of this, that much as I love you I am not altogether inclined to let you practice [E] your oratory on me when Lysias himself is here present. Come now, show it me.

Ph. Say no more, Socrates; you have dashed my hope of trying out my powers on you. Well, where would you like us to sit for our reading?

Soc. Let us turn off here and walk along the Ilissus: then we [229] can sit down in any quiet spot you choose.

Ph. It's convenient, isn't it, that I chance to be bare-footed: you of course always are so. There will be no trouble in wading in the stream, which is especially delightful at this hour of a summer's day.

Soc. Lead on then, and look out for a place to sit down.

Ph. You see that tall plane-tree over there?

Soc. To be sure.

Ph. There's some shade, and a little breeze, and grass to sit down [B] on, or lie down if we like.

Soc. Then make for it.

Ph. Tell me, Socrates, isn't it somewhere about here that they say Boreas seized Oreithuia from the river?

Soc. Yes, that is the story.

Ph. Was this the actual spot? Certainly the water looks charmingly pure and clear, it's just the place for girls to be playing beside the stream.

Soc. No, it was about a quarter of a mile lower down, where you [c] cross to the sanctuary of Agra: there is, I believe, an altar dedicated to Boreas close by.

Ph. I have never really noticed it; but pray tell me, Socrates, do you believe that story to be true?

Soc. I should be quite in the fashion if I disbelieved it, as the men of science do: I might proceed to give a scientific account of how the maiden, while at play with Pharmaceia, was blown by a gust of Boreas down from the rocks hard by, and having thus met her death was said to have been seized by Boreas: though it may have happened on the [D] Areopagus, according to another version of the occurrence. For my part, Phaedrus, I regard such theories as no doubt attractive, but as the invention of clever, industrious people who are not exactly to be envied, for the simple reason that they must then go on and tell us the real truth about the appearance of Centaurs and the Chimaera, not to mention a whole host of such creatures, Gorgons and Pegasuses and countless other remarkable monsters of legend flocking in on them. [E] If our sceptic, with his somewhat crude science, means to reduce every one of them to the standard of probability, he'll need a deal of time for it. I myself have certainly no time for the business: and I'll tell you why, my friend: I can't as yet 'know myself', as the inscription at [230] Delphi enjoins; and so long as that ignorance remains it seems to me ridiculous to inquire into extraneous matters. Consequently I don't bother about such things, but accept the current beliefs about them, and direct my inquiries, as I have just said, rather to myself, to discover whether I really am a more complex creature and more puffed up with pride than Typhon,[4] or a simpler, gentler being whom heaven has blessed with a quiet, un-Typhonic nature. By the way, isn't this the tree we were making for? [B]

Ph. Yes, that's the one.

Soc. Upon my word, a delightful resting-place, with this tall, spreading plane, and a lovely shade from the high branches of the agnus: now that it's in full flower, it will make the place ever so fragrant. And what a lovely stream under the plane-tree, and how cool to the feet! Judging by the statuettes and images I should say it's consecrated to Achelous and some of the Nymphs. And then too, isn't the freshness of the [c] air most welcome and pleasant: and the shrill summery music of the cicada-choir! And as crowning delight the grass, thick enough on a gentle

---

[4] Socrates connects the name of this hundred-headed monster with the verb τύφω, *to smoke,* and perhaps also with the noun τῦφος, *vanity, humbug.*

slope to rest your head on most comfortably. In fact, my dear Phaedrus, you have been the stranger's perfect guide.

Ph.   Whereas you, my excellent friend, strike me as the oddest of men. Anyone would take you, as you say, for a stranger being shown the country by a guide instead of a native: never leaving town to cross   [D] the frontier nor even, I believe, so much as setting foot outside the walls.

Soc.   You must forgive me, dear friend; I'm a lover of learning, and trees and open country won't teach me anything, whereas men in the town do. Yet you seem to have discovered a recipe for getting me out. A hungry animal can be driven by dangling a carrot or a bit of green stuff in front of it: similarly if you proffer me volumes of speeches I don't doubt you can cart me all round Attica, and anywhere else   [E] you please. Anyhow, now that we've got here I propose for the time being to lie down, and you can choose whatever posture you think most convenient for reading, and proceed.

Ph.   Here you are then.

II

230E-234C   THE SPEECH OF LYSIAS

You know how I am situated, and I have told you that I think it to our advantage that this should happen. Now I claim that I should not be refused what I ask simply because I am not your lover. Lovers,   [231] when their craving is at an end, repent of such benefits as they have conferred: but for the other sort no occasion arises for regretting what has passed; for being free agents under no constraint, they regulate their services by the scale of their means, with an eye to their own personal interest. Again, lovers weigh up profit and loss accruing to their account by reason of their passion, and with the extra item of labour expended decide that they have long since made full payment   [B] for favours received; whereas the non-lovers cannot allege any consequential neglect of their personal affairs, nor record any past exertions on the debit side, nor yet complain of having quarrelled with their relatives; hence, with all these troubles removed, all they have left to do is to devote their energies to such conduct as they conceive likely to gratify the other party.

Again, it is argued that a lover ought to be highly valued because   [C] he professes to be especially kind towards the loved one, and ready to gratify him in words and deeds while arousing the dislike of everyone else. If this is true, however, it is obvious that he will set greater store by the loved one of to-morrow than by that of to-day, and will doubtless do an injury to the old love if required by the new.

And really, what sense is there in lavishing what is so precious upon one labouring under an affliction which nobody who knew anything   [D] of it would even attempt to remove? Why, the man himself admits that he is not sound, but sick; that he is aware of his folly, but cannot control himself; how then, when he comes to his senses, is he likely to approve of the intentions that he formed in his aberration?

And observe this: if you are to choose the best of a number of lovers, your choice will be only amongst a few; whereas a general choice of the person who most commends himself to you gives you a wide field, so that in that wide field you have a much better prospect of finding [E] someone worthy of your friendship.

Now maybe you respect established conventions, and anticipate odium if people get to hear about you; if so, it may be expected that a lover, conceiving that everyone will admire him as he admires [232] himself, will be proud to talk about it and flatter his vanity by declaring to all and sundry that his enterprise has been successful; whereas the other type, who can control themselves, will prefer to do what is best rather than shine in the eyes of their neighbours.

Again, a lover is bound to be heard about and seen by many people, consorting with his beloved and caring about little else; so that when they are observed talking to one another, the meeting is taken to [B] imply the satisfaction, actual or prospective, of their desires; whereas, with the other sort, no one ever thinks of putting a bad construction on their association, realising that a man must have someone to talk to by way of friendship or gratification of one sort or another.

And observe this: perhaps you feel troubled by the reflection that it is hard for friendship to be preserved, and that whereas a quarrel arising from other sources will be a calamity shared by both parties, one that follows the sacrifice of your all will involve a grievous hurt to your- [c] self; in that case it is doubtless the lover who should cause you the more alarm, for he is very ready to take offence, and thinks the whole affair is to his own hurt. Hence he discourages his beloved from consorting with anyone else, fearing that a wealthy rival may overreach him with his money, or a cultured one outdo him with his intelligence: and he is perpetually on guard against the influence of those who possess other advantages. So by persuading you to become estranged [D] from such rivals he leaves you without a friend in the world; alternatively, if you look to your own interest and show more good sense than your lover, you will find yourself quarrelling with him. On the other hand, one who is not a lover, but has achieved what he asked of you by reason of his merit, will not be jealous of others who seek your society, but will rather detest those who avoid it, in the belief that the latter look down on him, whereas the former are serving his turn. Consequently the object of his attentions is far more likely to make friends [E] than enemies out of the affair.

And observe this: a lover more often than not wants to possess you before he has come to know your character or become familiar with your general personality; and that makes it uncertain whether he will still want to be your friend when his desires have waned; whereas [233] in the other case, the fact that the pair were already friends before the affair took place makes it probable that instead of friendship diminishing as the result of favours received, these favours will abide as a memory and promise of more to come.

And observe this: it ought to be for your betterment to listen to me rather than to a lover; for a lover commends anything you say or do even when it is amiss, partly from fear that he may offend you, partly because his passion impairs his own judgment. For the record of [B] Love's achievement is, first that, when things go badly, he makes a man count that an affliction which normally causes no distress: secondly that, when things go well, he compels his subjects to extol things that ought not to gratify them: which makes it fitting that they should be pitied far more than admired by the objects of their passion. On the other hand, if you listen to me, my intercourse with you will be a matter of ministering not to your immediate pleasure but to your future advantage; for I am the master of myself, rather than the victim [C] of love; I do not bring bitter enmity upon myself by resenting trifling offences: on the contrary it is only on account of serious wrongs that I am moved, and that but slowly, to mild indignation, pardoning what is done unintentionally, and endeavouring to hinder what is done of intent: for these are the tokens of lasting friendship. If however you are disposed to think that there can be no firm friendship save with a lover, you should reflect that in that case we should not set store by [D] sons, or fathers, or mothers, nor should we possess any trustworthy friends: no, it is not to erotic passion that we owe these, but to conduct of a different order.

Again, if we ought to favour those who press us most strongly, then in other matters too we should give our good offices not to the worthiest people but to the most destitute; for since their distress is the greatest, they will be the most thankful to us for relieving them. And observe this further consequence: when we give private banquets, the [E] right people to invite will be not our friends but beggars and those in need of a good meal: for it is they that will be fond of us and attend upon us and flock to our doors: it is they that will be most delighted and most grateful and call down blessings on our heads. No: the proper course, surely, is to show favour not to the most importunate but to those most able to make us a return; not to mere beggars, but to the deserving; not to those who will regale themselves with your youthful [234] beauty, but to those who will let you share their prosperity when you are older; not to those who, when they have had their will of you, will flatter their vanity by telling the world, but to those who will keep a strict and modest silence; not to those who are devoted to you for a brief period, but to those who will continue to be your friends as long as you live; not to those who, when their passion is spent, will look for an excuse to turn against you, but to those who, when your beauty is past, will make that the time for displaying their own goodness.

Do you therefore be mindful of what I have said and reflect that, [B] while lovers are admonished by their friends and relatives for the wrongness of their conduct, the other sort have never been reproached by one of their family on the score of behaving to the detriment of their own interest.

Perhaps you will ask me whether I recommend you to accord your favours to all and sundry of this sort. Well, I do not suppose that even a lover would bid you to be favourable towards all and sundry lovers; in the first place a recipient would not regard it as meriting so much [c] gratitude, and in the second you would find it more difficult if you wished to keep your affairs concealed; and what is wanted is that the business should involve no harm, but mutual advantage.

And now I think I have said all that is needed; if you think I have neglected anything, and want more, let me know.

III

234c-237b CRITICISM OF LYSIA'S SPEECH · SOCRATES IS INDUCED TO TREAT THE THEME HIMSELF

Ph. What do you think of the speech, Socrates? Isn't it extraordinarily fine, especially in point of language?

Soc. Amazingly fine indeed, my friend: I was thrilled by it. And [D] it was you, Phaedrus, that made me feel as I did: I watched your apparent delight in the words as you read. And as I'm sure that you understand such matters better than I do, I took my cue from you, and therefore joined in the ecstasy of my right worshipful companion.

Ph. Come, come! Do you mean to make a joke of it?

Soc. Do you think I am joking, and don't mean it seriously?

Ph. No more of that, Socrates: tell me truly, as one friend to [E] another, do you think there is anyone in Greece who could make a finer and more exhaustive speech on the same subject?

Soc. What? Are you and I required to extol the speech not merely on the score of its author's lucidity and terseness of expression, and his consistently precise and well-polished vocabulary, but also for his having said what he ought? If we are, we shall have to allow it only on your account, for my feeble intelligence failed to appreciate it; I was only attending to it as a piece of rhetoric, and as such I couldn't think [235] that even Lysias himself would deem it adequate. Perhaps you won't agree with me, Phaedrus, but really it seemed to me that he said the same things several times over: maybe he's not very clever at expatiating at length on a single theme, or possibly he has no interest in such topics. In fact it struck me as an extravagant performance, to demonstrate his ability to say the same thing twice, in different words but with equal success.

Ph. Not a bit of it, Socrates: the outstanding feature of the dis- [B] course is just this, that it has not overlooked any important aspect of the subject, so making it impossible for anyone else to outdo what he has said with a fuller or more satisfactory oration.

Soc. If you go as far as that I shall find it impossible to agree with you; if I were to assent out of politeness, I should be confuted by the wise men and women who in past ages have spoken and written on this theme.

Ph. To whom do you refer? Where have you heard anything [c] better than this?

Soc. I can't tell you off-hand; but I'm sure I have heard something better, from the fair Sappho maybe, or the wise Anacreon, or perhaps some prose writer. What ground, you may ask, have I for saying so? Good sir, there is something welling up within my breast, which makes me feel that I could find something different, and something better, to say. I am of course well aware it can't be anything originating in my own mind, for I know my own ignorance; so I suppose it can only be that it has been poured into me, through my ears, as into a vessel, [D] from some external source; though in my stupid fashion I have actually forgotten how, and from whom, I heard it.

Ph. Well said! You move me to admiration. I don't mind your not telling me, even though I should press you, from whom and how you heard it, provided you do just what you say: you have undertaken to make a better speech than that in the book here and one of not less length which shall owe nothing to it; I in my turn undertake like the nine Archons to set up at Delphi a golden life-size statue, not only of [E] myself but of you also.

Soc. How kind you are, Phaedrus, and what a pattern of golden-age simplicity, in supposing me to mean that Lysias has wholly missed the mark and that another speech could avoid all his points! Surely that couldn't be so even with the most worthless of writers. Thus, as regards the subject of the speech, do you imagine that anybody could argue that the non-lover should be favoured, rather than the lover, without praising the wisdom of the one and censuring the folly of the other? That he could dispense with these essential points, and then bring [236] up something different? No, no: surely we must allow such arguments, and forgive the orator for using them; and in that sort of field what merits praise is not invention, but arrangement; but when it comes to non-essential points, that are difficult to invent, we should praise arrangement and invention too.

Ph. I agree: what you say seems fair enough. For my part, this is what I will do: I will allow you to take it for granted that the lover is [B] less sane than the non-lover: and for the rest, if you can replace what we have here by a fuller speech of superior merit, up with your statue in wrought gold beside the offering of the Cypselids at Olympia.

Soc. Have you taken me seriously, Phaedrus, for teasing you with an attack on your darling Lysias? Can you possibly suppose that I shall make a real attempt to rival his cleverness with something more ornate?

Ph. As to that, my friend, I've got you where I can return your fire. Assuredly you must do what you can in the way of a speech, or [c] else we shall be driven, like vulgar comedians, to capping each other's remarks. Beware: do not deliberately compel me to utter the words 'Don't I know my Socrates? If not, I've forgotten my own identity', or 'He wanted to speak, but made difficulties about it'. No: make up your mind that we're not going to leave this spot until you have delivered yourself of what you told me you had within your breast. We are by ourselves in a lonely place, and I am stronger and younger than you: for all which reasons 'mistake not thou my bidding' [5] and please don't make [D] me use force to open your lips.

Soc. But, my dear good Phaedrus, it will be courting ridicule for an amateur like me to improvise on the same theme as an accomplished writer.

Ph. Look here, I'll have no more of this affectation; for I'm pretty sure I have something to say which will compel you to speak.

Soc. Then please don't say it.

Ph. Oh, but I shall, here and now; and what I say will be on oath. I swear to you by—but by whom, by what god? Or shall it be by this [E] plane-tree? I swear that unless you deliver your speech here in its very presence, I will assuredly never again declaim nor report any other speech by any author whatsoever.

Soc. Aha, you rogue! How clever of you to discover the means of compelling a lover of discourse to do your bidding!

Ph. Then why all this twisting?

Soc. I give it up, in view of what you've sworn. For how could I possibly do without such entertainment?

Ph. Then proceed.   [237]

Soc. Well, do you know what I'm going to do?

Ph. Do about what?

Soc. I shall cover my head before I begin: then I can rush through my speech at top speed without looking at you and breaking down for shame.[6]

Ph. You can do anything else you like, provided you make your speech.

Soc. Come then, ye clear-voiced Muses, whether it be from the nature of your song, or from the musical people of Liguria that ye came to be so styled,[7] 'assist the tale I tell' under compulsion by my good friend here, to the end that he may think yet more highly of one dear to [B] him, whom he already accounts a man of wisdom.

---

[5] Pindar, *frag.* 94 (Bowra).

[6] To Phaedrus Socrates's words here doubtless express apprehension that he will disgrace himself by an inferior performance, but the shame that Socrates really feels is, as transpires later (243B), due to his having been forced to adopt an unworthy conception of Eros.

[7] The suggested connexion between λιγύς (*clear-voiced*) and the Ligurian people is one of those etymological jests in which Plato often, and sometimes rather pointlessly, indulges.

IV

237B-238C SOCRATES BEGINS HIS SPEECH · A DEFINITION
OF LOVE

Soc. Well then, once upon a time there was a very handsome boy,
or rather young man, who had a host of lovers; and one of them was
wily, and had persuaded the boy that he was not in love with him,
though really he was, quite as much as the others. And on one occasion,
in pressing his suit he actually sought to convince him that he ought
to favour a non-lover rather than a lover. And this is the purport of
what he said:

My boy, if anyone means to deliberate successfully about anything,
there is one thing he must do at the outset: he must know what it is   [c]
he is deliberating about; otherwise he is bound to go utterly astray. Now
most people fail to realise that they don't know what this or that really
is: consequently when they start discussing something, they dispense
with any agreed definition, assuming that they know the thing; then
later on they naturally find, to their cost, that they agree neither with
each other nor with themselves. That being so, you and I would do
well to avoid what we charge against other people; and as the question
before us is whether one should preferably consort with a lover or a
non-lover, we ought to agree upon a definition of love which shows its
nature and its effects, so that we may have it before our minds as
something to refer to while we discuss whether love is beneficial   [D]
or injurious.

Well now, it is plain to everyone that love is some sort of desire; and
further we know that men desire that which is fair without being lovers.
How then are we to distinguish one who loves from one who does not?
We must go on to observe that within each one of us there are two sorts
of ruling or guiding principle that we follow: one is an innate desire for
pleasure, the other an acquired judgment that aims at what is best.
Sometimes these internal guides are in accord, sometimes at variance:
now one gains the mastery, now the other. And when judgment   [E]
guides us rationally towards what is best, and has the mastery,
that mastery is called temperance; but when desire drags us   [238]
irrationally towards pleasure, and has come to rule within us, the name
given to that rule is wantonness. But in truth wantonness itself has
many names, as it has many branches or forms, and when one of these
forms is conspicuously present in a man it makes that man bear its
name, a name that it is no credit or distinction to possess. If it be in the
matter of food that desire has the mastery over judgment of what is for the
best, and over all other desires, it is called gluttony, and the person   [B]
in question will be called a glutton; or again if desire has achieved
domination in the matter of drink, it is plain what term we shall apply
to its subject who is led down that path; and no less plain what are the

appropriate names in the case of other such persons and of other such desires, according as this one or that holds sway.

Now the reason for saying all this can hardly remain in doubt; yet even so a statement of it will be illuminating. When irrational desire, pursuing the enjoyment of beauty, has gained the mastery over judgment that prompts to right conduct, and has acquired from other [c] desires, akin to it, fresh strength to strain towards bodily beauty, that very strength provides it with its name: it is the strong passion called Love.

V

238c-241d SOCRATES CONCLUDES HIS FIRST SPEECH

Soc. Well, Phaedrus my friend, do you think, as I do, that I am divinely inspired?

Ph. Undoubtedly, Socrates, you have been vouchsafed a quite unusual eloquence.

Soc. Then listen to me in silence. For truly there seems to be a divine presence in this spot, so that you must not be surprised if, as [d] my speech proceeds, I become as one possessed; already my style is not far from dithyrambic.

Ph. Very true.

Soc. But for that you are responsible. Still, let me continue; possibly the menace may be averted. However, that must be as God wills: our business is to resume our address to the boy:—

Very well then, my good friend: the true nature of that on which we have to deliberate has been stated and defined; and so, with that definition in mind, we may go on to say what advantage or detriment [e] may be expected to result to one who accords his favour to a lover and a non-lover respectively.

Now a man who is dominated by desire and enslaved to pleasure is of course bound to aim at getting the greatest possible pleasure out of his beloved; and what pleases a sick man [8] is anything that does not thwart him, whereas anything that is as strong as, or stronger than, himself gives him offence. Hence he will not, if he can avoid it, put up with a favourite that matches or outdoes him in strength, but will [239] always seek to make him weaker and feebler: and weakness is found in the ignorant, the cowardly, the poor speaker, the slow thinker, as against the wise, the brave, the eloquent, the quick-minded. All these defects of mind and more in the beloved are bound to be a source of pleasure to the lover: if they do not exist already as innate qualities, he will cultivate them, for not to do so means depriving himself of immediate pleasure. And of course he is bound to be jealous, constantly

---

[8] cf. 231d, 236a.

debarring the boy not only, to his great injury, from the advantages [B]
of consorting with others, which would make a real man of him, but,
greatest injury of all, from consorting with that which would most
increase his wisdom; by which I mean divine philosophy: no access to
that can possibly be permitted by the lover, for he dreads becoming
thereby an object of contempt. And in general he must aim at making
the boy totally ignorant and totally dependent on his lover, by way of
securing the maximum of pleasure for himself, and the maximum of
damage to the other.

Hence in respect of the boy's mind it is anything but a profitable [C]
investment to have as guardian or partner a man in love.

After the mind, the body; we must see what sort of physical condition will be fostered, and how it will be fostered, in the boy that has
become the possession of one who is under compulsion to pursue pleasure
instead of goodness. We shall find him, of course, pursuing a weakling
rather than a sturdy boy, one who has had a cosy, sheltered upbringing
instead of being exposed to the open air, who has given himself up to
a soft unmanly life instead of the toil and sweat of manly exercise, [D]
who for lack of natural charm tricks himself out with artificial cosmetics,
and resorts to all sorts of other similar practices which are too obvious
to need further enumeration; yet before leaving the topic we may
sum it up in a sentence: the boy will be of that physical type which
in wartime, and other times that try a man's mettle, inspires confidence in
his enemies and alarm in his friends, aye and in his very lovers too.

And now let us pass from these obvious considerations and raise [E]
the next question: what advantage or detriment in respect of property and
possessions shall we find resulting from the society and guardianship of
a lover? Well, one thing is plain enough to anyone, and especially to
the lover, namely that his foremost wish will be for the boy to be bereft
of his dearest possessions, his treasury of kindness and ideal affection:
father and mother, kinsmen and friends—he will want him to be robbed
of them all, as likely to make difficulties and raise objections to the [240]
intercourse which he finds so pleasant. If however the boy possessess
property, in money or whatever it may be, he will reckon that he will not
be so easy to capture, or if captured to manage; hence a lover is bound
to nurse a grudge against one who possesses property, and to rejoice
when he loses it. Furthermore he will want his beloved to remain as
long as possible without wife or child or home, so as to enjoy for as long
as may be his own delights.

There are, to be sure, other evils in life, but with most of them heaven
has mixed some momentary pleasure: thus in the parasite, a fear- [B]
some and most pernicious creature, nature has mingled a dash of
pleasing wit or charm; a courtesan may well be branded as pernicious,
not to mention many other similar creatures with their respective callings,
yet in everyday life they can be very agreeable; but a lover, besides
being pernicious, is the most disagreeable of all men for a boy to spend
his days with. There's an old saying about 'not matching May [C]

with December', based, I suppose, on the idea that similarity of age tends to similarity of pleasures and consequently makes a couple good friends: still even with such a couple the association is apt to pall. Then again, in addition to the dissimilarity of age, there is that compulsion which is burdensome for anybody in any circumstances, but especially so in the relations of such a pair.

The elderly lover will not, if he can help it, suffer any desertion by his beloved by day or by night; he is driven on by a compelling, [D] goading power, lured by the continual promise of pleasure in the sight, hearing, touching or other physical experience of the beloved; to minister unfailingly to the boy's needs is his delight. But what pleasure or what solace will he have to offer to the beloved? How will he save him from experiencing the extremity of discomfort in those long hours at his lover's side, as he looks upon a face which years have robbed of its beauty, together with other consequences which it is unpleasant [E] even to hear mentioned, let alone to have continually to cope with in stark reality. And what of the suspicious precautions with which he is incessantly guarded, with whomsoever he associates, the unseasonable fulsome compliments to which he has to listen, alternating with reproaches which when uttered in soberness are hard to endure, but coming from one in his cups, in language of unlimited, undisguised coarseness, are both intolerable and disgusting?

To continue: if while his love lasts he is harmful and offensive, in later days, when it is spent, he will show his bad faith. He was lavish with promises, interspersed amongst his vows and entreaties, regarding those later days, contriving with some difficulty to secure his partner's endurance of an intercourse which even then was burdensome, by [241] holding out hopes of benefits to come. But when the time comes for fulfilling the promises, a new authority takes the place within him of the former ruler: love and passion are replaced by wisdom and temperance: he has become a different person. But the boy does not realise it, and demands a return for what he gave in the past, reminding him of what had been done and said, as though he were talking to the same person; while the erstwhile lover, who has now acquired wisdom and temperance, cannot for very shame bring himself to declare that he has become a new man, nor yet see his way to redeeming the solemn [B] assurances and promises made under the old régime of folly; he fears that if he were to go on acting as before he would revert to his old character, his former self. So he runs away from his obligations as one compelled to default; it's 'tails' this time instead of 'heads',[9] and he has to turn tail and rush away. But the boy must needs run after him, crying indignantly to high heaven: though from start to finish he has never understood that he ought not to have yielded to a lover in-

---

[9] An allusion to the game called ὀστρακίνδα in which a shell was thrown into the air between two opposing sides, and according as it fell white or dark side uppermost one side had to run and the other to catch them.

evitably devoid of reason, but far rather to one possessed of reason
and not in love. He should have known that the wrong choice [c]
must mean surrendering himself to a faithless, peevish, jealous and
offensive captor, to one who would ruin his property, ruin his physique,
and above all ruin his spiritual development, which is assuredly and
ever will be of supreme value in the sight of gods and men alike.[10]

Let that then, my boy, be your lesson: be sure that the attentions of
a lover carry no goodwill: they are no more than a glutting of his
appetite, for

As wolf to lamb, so lover to his lad.   [D]

There, I knew I should,[11] Phaedrus. Not a word more shall you have
from me: let that be the end of my discourse.

VI

241D-243E   INTERLUDE, LEADING TO SOCRATES'S RECANTATION

Ph. Why, I thought you were only half-way through and would
have an equal amount to say about the non-lover, enumerating his good
points and showing that he should be the favoured suitor. Why is it,
Socrates, that instead of that you break off?

Soc. My dear good man, haven't you noticed that I've got beyond [E]
dithyramb, and am breaking out into epic verse, despite my fault-
finding? What do you suppose I shall do if I start extolling the other
type? Don't you see that I shall clearly be possessed by those nymphs
into whose clutches you deliberately threw me? I therefore tell you,
in one short sentence, that to each evil for which I have abused the one
party there is a corresponding good belonging to the other. So why
waste words? All has been said that needs saying about them both.
And that being so, my story can be left to the fate appropriate to it,
and I will take myself off across the river here before you drive me [242]
to greater lengths.

Ph. Oh, but you must wait until it gets cooler, Socrates. Don't you
realise that it's just about the hour of 'scorching noonday', as the phrase
goes? Let us wait and discuss what we've heard; when it has got cool
perhaps we will go.

Soc. Phaedrus, your enthusiasm for discourse is sublime, and really
moves me to admiration. Of the discourses pronounced during your
lifetime no one, I fancy, has been responsible for more than you, [B]
whether by delivering them yourself or by compelling others to do so

---

10 cf. *Apol.* 29E, 30A-B.
11 Socrates had feared that he would break out into inspired verse, 238D.

by one means or another—with one exception, Simmias of Thebes: you are well ahead of all the rest. And now it seems that once more you are the cause of my having to deliver myself.

Ph. It might be a lot worse! But how so? To what do you refer?

Soc. At the moment when I was about to cross the river, dear friend, there came to me my familiar divine sign—which always checks me when on the point of doing something or other—and all at once [c] I seemed to hear a voice, forbidding me to leave the spot until I had made atonement for some offence to heaven. Now, you must know, I am a seer; not a very good one, it's true, but, like a poor scholar, good enough for my own purposes; hence I understand already well enough what my offence was. The fact is, you know, Phaedrus, the mind itself has a kind of divining power; for I felt disturbed some while ago as I was delivering that speech, and had a misgiving lest I might, in the words of Ibycus

> By sinning in the sight of God win high renown from man. [D]

But now I realise my sin.

Ph. And what is it?

Soc. That was a terrible theory, Phaedrus, a terrible theory that you introduced and compelled me to expound.

Ph. How so?

Soc. It was foolish, and somewhat blasphemous; and what could be more terrible than that?

Ph. I agree, if it merits your description.

Soc. Well, do you not hold Love to be a god, the child of Aphrodite?

Ph. He is certainly said to be.

Soc. But not according to Lysias, and not according to that discourse of yours which you caused my lips to utter by putting a spell on [E] them. If Love is, as he is indeed, a god or a divine being, he cannot be an evil thing: yet this pair of speeches treated him as evil. That then was their offence towards Love, to which was added the most exquisite folly of parading their pernicious rubbish as though it were good sense because it might deceive a few miserable people and win their [243] applause.

And so, my friend, I have to purify myself. Now for such as offend in speaking of gods and heroes there is an ancient mode of purification, which was known to Stesichorus, though not to Homer. When Stesichorus lost the sight of his eyes because of his defamation of Helen, he was not, like Homer, at a loss to know why: as a true artist he understood the reason, and promptly wrote the lines:

> False, false the tale:
> Thou never didst sail in the well-decked ships
> Nor come to the towers of Troy. [B]

And after finishing the composition of his so-called Palinode he straightway recovered his sight. Now it's here that I shall show greater wisdom than these poets: I shall attempt to make my due palinode to Love before any harm comes to me for my defamation of him, and no longer veiling my head for shame, but uncovered.

Ph. Nothing you could say, Socrates, would please me more.

Soc. Yes, dear Phaedrus: you understand how irreverent the two [c] speeches were, the one in the book and that which followed. Suppose we were being listened to by a man of generous and humane character, who loved or had once loved another such as himself: suppose he heard us saying that for some trifling cause lovers conceive bitter hatred and a spirit of malice and injury towards their loved ones; wouldn't he be sure to think that we had been brought up among the scum of the people and had never seen a case of noble love? Wouldn't he utterly refuse to accept our vilification of Love? [D]

Ph. Indeed, Socrates, he well might.

Soc. Then out of respect for him, and in awe of Love himself, I should like to wash the bitter taste out of my mouth with a draught of wholesome discourse; and my advice to Lysias is that he should lose no time in telling us that, other things being equal, favour should be accorded to the lover rather than to the non-lover.

Ph. Rest assured, that will be done. When you have delivered your encomium of the lover, I shall most certainly make Lysias compose [E] a new speech to the same purport.

Soc. I'm sure of that, so long as you continue to be the man you are.

Ph. Then you may confidently proceed.

Soc. Where is that boy I was talking to? He must listen to me once more, and not rush off to yield to his non-lover before he hears what I have to say.

Ph. Here he is, quite close beside you, whenever you want him.

VII

243E-245C SOCRATES BEGINS HIS SECOND SPEECH • THREE TYPES OF DIVINE MADNESS

Soc. Now you must understand, fair boy, that whereas the preceding discourse was by Phaedrus, son of Pythocles, of Myrrinous, that [244] which I shall now pronounce is by Stesichorus, son of Euphemus, of Himera.[12] This then is how it must run:

'False is the tale' that when a lover is at hand favour ought rather to be accorded to one who does not love, on the ground that the former

---

12 Thompson and, as we should expect, Hermeias before him, regard all these proper names as significant. Doubtless the last two are so: the speech will be εὔφημος, as opposed to κακήγορος, and Ἱμέραιος anticipates the 'flood of passion' (ἵμερος) of 251c. But to find significance in the other four is a task best left to Neoplatonic subtlety.

is mad, and the latter sound of mind. That would be right if it were an invariable truth that madness is an evil: but in reality, the greatest blessings come by way of madness, indeed of madness that is heaven-sent. It was when they were mad that the prophetess at Delphi and [B] the priestesses at Dodona achieved so much for which both states and individuals in Greece are thankful: when sane they did little or nothing. As for the Sibyl and others who by the power of inspired prophecy have so often foretold the future to so many, and guided them aright, I need not dwell on what is obvious to everyone. Yet it is in place to appeal to the fact that madness was accounted no shame nor disgrace by the men of old who gave things their names: otherwise they would not have connected that greatest of arts, whereby the future is dis- [C] cerned, with this very word 'madness', and named it accordingly. No, it was because they held madness to be a valuable gift, when due to divine dispensation, that they named that art as they did, though the men of to-day, having no sense of values, have put in an extra letter, making it not *manic* but *mantic*. That is borne out by the name they gave to the art of those sane prophets who inquire into the future by means of birds and other signs: the name was 'oionoistic', which by its components indicated that the prophet attained understanding and information by a purely human activity of thought belonging to his own intelligence; though a younger generation has come to call it 'oionistic', lengthening the quantity of the *o* to make it sound impressive. You [D] see then what this ancient evidence attests: corresponding to the superior perfection and value of the prophecy of inspiration over that of omen-reading, both in name and in fact, is the superiority of heaven-sent madness over man-made sanity.

And in the second place, when grievous maladies and afflictions have beset certain families by reason of some ancient sin, madness has appeared amongst them, and breaking out into prophecy has secured [E] relief by finding the means thereto, namely by recourse to prayer and worship; and in consequence thereof rites and means of purification were established, and the sufferer was brought out of danger, alike for the present and for the future. Thus did madness secure, for him that was maddened aright and possessed, deliverance from his troubles.

There is a third form of possession or madness, of which the [245] Muses are the source. This seizes a tender, virgin soul and stimulates it to rapt passionate expression, especially in lyric poetry, glorifying the countless mighty deeds of ancient times for the instruction of posterity. But if any man come to the gates of poetry without the madness of the Muses, persuaded that skill alone will make him a good poet, then shall he and his works of sanity with him be brought to naught by the poetry of madness, and behold, their place is nowhere to be found.

Such then is the tale, though I have not told it fully, of the achieve- [B] ments wrought by madness that comes from the gods. So let us have no fears simply on that score; let us not be disturbed by an argument that seeks to scare us into preferring the friendship of the sane to that of the passionate. For there is something more that it must prove if it is to carry the day, namely that love is not a thing sent from heaven for the advantage both of lover and beloved. What we have to prove is the opposite, namely that this sort of madness is a gift of the gods, [c] fraught with the highest bliss. And our proof assuredly will prevail with the wise, though not with the learned.

Now our first step towards attaining the truth of the matter is to discern the nature of soul, divine and human, its experiences and its activities. Here then our proof begins.

VIII

245c-246a THE IMMORTALITY OF SOUL

All soul is immortal; for that which is ever in motion is immortal. But that which while imparting motion is itself moved by something else can cease to be in motion, and therefore can cease to live; it is only that which moves itself that never intermits its motion, inasmuch as it cannot abandon its own nature; moreover this self-mover is the source and first principle of motion for all other things that are moved. Now a first principle cannot come into being: for while anything that [d] comes to be must come to be from a first principle, the latter itself cannot come to be from anything whatsoever: if it did, it would cease any longer to be a first principle. Furthermore, since it does not come into being, it must be imperishable: for assuredly if a first principle were to be destroyed, nothing could come to be out of it, nor could anything bring the principle itself back into existence, seeing that a first principle is needed for anything to come into being.

The self-mover, then, is the first principle of motion: and it is as impossible that it should be destroyed as that it should come into being: were it otherwise, the whole universe, the whole of that which comes to be, would collapse into immobility, and never find another source of [e] motion to bring it back into being.

And now that we have seen that that which is moved by itself is immortal, we shall feel no scruple in affirming that precisely that is the essence and definition of soul, to wit self-motion. Any body that has an external source of motion is soulless; but a body deriving its motion from a source within itself is animate or *besouled*, which implies that the nature of soul is what has been said.

And if this last assertion is correct, namely that 'that which moves itself' is precisely identifiable with soul, it must follow that soul is [246] not born and does not die.

IX

246A-247C MYTH OF THE SOUL • THE CHARIOTEER AND
TWO HORSES • THE PROCESSION OF SOULS

As to soul's immortality then we have said enough, but as to its
nature there is this that must be said: what manner of thing it is would
be a long tale to tell, and most assuredly a god alone could tell it; but
what it resembles, that a man might tell in briefer compass: let this
therefore be our manner of discourse. Let it be likened to the union of
powers in a team of winged steeds and their winged charioteer. Now
all the gods' steeds and all their charioteers are good, and of good
stock; but with other beings it is not wholly so. With us men, in the [B]
first place, it is a pair of steeds that the charioteer controls; moreover
one of them is noble and good, and of good stock, while the other has
the opposite character, and his stock is opposite. Hence the task of our
charioteer is difficult and troublesome.

And now we must essay to tell how it is that living beings are called
mortal and immortal. All soul has the care of all that is inanimate, and
traverses the whole universe, though in ever-changing forms. Thus
when it is perfect and winged it journeys on high and controls the [C]
whole world; but one that has shed its wings sinks down until it can
fasten on something solid, and settling there it takes to itself an earthy
body which seems by reason of the soul's power to move itself. This
composite structure of soul and body is called a living being, and is
further termed 'mortal': 'immortal' is a term applied on no basis of
reasoned argument at all, but our fancy pictures the god whom we have
never seen, nor fully conceived, as an immortal living being, pos- [D]
sessed of a soul and a body united for all time. Howbeit let these matters,
and our account thereof, be as god pleases; what we must understand
is the reason why the soul's wings fall from it, and are lost. It is on this
wise.

The natural property of a wing is to raise that which is heavy and
carry it aloft to the region where the gods dwell; and more than any
other bodily part it shares in the divine nature, which is fair, wise [E]
and good, and possessed of all other such excellences. Now by these
excellences especially is the soul's plumage nourished and fostered,
while by their opposites, even by ugliness and evil, it is wasted and
destroyed. And behold, there in the heaven Zeus, mighty leader, drives
his winged team: first of the host of gods and daemons he proceeds,
ordering all things and caring therefor: and the host follows after him,
marshalled in eleven companies. For Hestia abides alone in [247]
the gods' dwelling-place; but for the rest, all such as are ranked in the
number of the twelve as ruler gods lead their several companies, each
according to his rank.

Now within the heavens are many spectacles of bliss upon the highways whereon the blessed gods pass to and fro, each doing his own work; and with them are all such as will and can follow them: for jealousy has no place in the choir divine. But at such times as they go to their feasting and banquet, behold they climb the steep ascent even unto the summit of the arch that supports the heavens; and easy is [B] that ascent for the chariots of the gods, for that they are well-balanced and readily guided; but for the others it is hard, by reason of the heaviness of the steed of wickedness, which pulls down his driver with his weight, except that driver have schooled him well.

And now there awaits the soul the extreme of her toil and struggling. For the souls that are called immortal, so soon as they are at the summit, come forth and stand upon the back of the world: and straight-way the revolving heaven carries them round, and they look upon [C] the regions without.

X

247C-248E THE SOUL'S VISION OF TRUE BEING · ITS FALL
AND INCARNATION

Of that place beyond the heavens none of our earthly poets has yet sung, and none shall sing worthily. But this is the manner of it, for assuredly we must be bold to speak what is true, above all when our discourse is upon truth. It is there that true Being dwells, without colour or shape, that cannot be touched; reason alone, the soul's pilot, can behold it, and all true knowledge is knowledge thereof. Now even as the mind of a god is nourished by reason and knowledge, so also is [D] it with every soul that has a care to receive her proper food; wherefore when at last she has beheld Being she is well content, and contemplating truth she is nourished and prospers, until the heaven's revolution brings her back full circle. And while she is borne round she discerns justice, its very self, and likewise temperance, and knowledge, not the knowledge that is neighbour to Becoming and varies with the various objects to which we commonly ascribe being, but the veritable [E] knowledge of Being that veritably is. And when she has contemplated likewise and feasted upon all else that has true being, she descends again within the heavens and comes back home. And having so come, her charioteer sets his steeds at their manger, and puts ambrosia before them and draught of nectar to drink withal.

Such is the life of gods: of the other souls that which best fol- [248] lows a god and becomes most like thereunto raises her charioteer's head into the outer region, and is carried round with the gods in the revo-lution, but being confounded by her steeds she has much ado to discern the things that are; another now rises, and now sinks, and by reason of her unruly steeds sees in part, but in part sees not. As for the rest, though all are eager to reach the heights and seek to follow, they are not able: sucked down as they travel they trample and tread upon one another, this one striving to outstrip that. Thus confusion ensues, and [B] conflict and grievous sweat: whereupon, with their charioteers powerless, many are lamed, and many have their wings all broken; and for all their toiling they are baulked, every one, of the full vision of Being, and departing therefrom, they feed upon the food of semblance.

Now the reason wherefore the souls are fain and eager to behold the Plain of Truth, and discover it, lies herein: to wit, that the pasturage that is proper to their noblest part comes from that Meadow, and the [c] plumage by which they are borne aloft is nourished thereby.

Hear now the ordinance of Necessity. Whatsoever soul has followed in the train of a god, and discerned something of truth, shall be kept from sorrow until a new revolution shall begin; and if she can do this always, she shall remain always free from hurt. But when she is not able so to follow, and sees none of it, but meeting with some mischance comes to be burdened with a load of forgetfulness and wrongdoing, and because of that burden sheds her wings and falls to the earth, then thus runs the law: in her first birth she shall not be planted in any [D] brute beast, but the soul that hath seen the most of Being shall enter into the human babe that shall grow into a seeker after wisdom or beauty, a follower of the Muses and a lover; the next, having seen less, shall dwell in a king that abides by law, or a warrior and ruler; the third in a statesman, a man of business or a trader; the fourth in an athlete, or physical trainer or physician; the fifth shall have the life of a prophet [E] or a mystery-priest; to the sixth that of a poet or other imitative artist shall be fittingly given; the seventh shall live in an artisan or farmer, the eighth in a sophist or demagogue, the ninth in a tyrant.

XI

248E-249D REINCARNATION AND FINAL LIBERATION OF THE SOUL · THE PHILOSOPHER'S PRIVILEGE

Now in all these incarnations he who lives righteously has a better lot for his portion, and he who lives unrighteously a worse.[13] For a soul does not return to the place whence she came for ten thousand years, since in no lesser time can she regain her wings, save only his soul who [249] has sought after wisdom unfeignedly, or has conjoined his passion for a loved one with that seeking. Such a soul, if with three revolutions of a thousand years she has thrice chosen this philosophic life, regains thereby her wings, and speeds away after three thousand years; but the

---

[13] These words refer, not to the final destiny of the souls, but to the period of reward or punishment between two incarnations.

rest, when they have accomplished their first life, are brought to judgment, and after the judgment some are taken to be punished in places of chastisement beneath the earth, while others are borne aloft by Justice to a certain region of the heavens, there to live in such manner as is [B] merited by their past life in the flesh. And after a thousand years these and those alike come to the allotment and choice of their second life, each choosing according to her will; then does the soul of a man enter into the life of a beast, and the beast's soul that was aforetime in a man goes back to a man again. For only the soul that has beheld truth may enter into this our human form: seeing that man must needs understand the language of Forms, passing from a plurality of perceptions to [C] a unity gathered together by reasoning; and such understanding is a recollection of those things which our souls beheld aforetime as they journeyed with their god, looking down upon the things which now we suppose to be, and gazing up to that which truly is.

Therefore is it meet and right that the soul of the philosopher alone [14] should recover her wings: for she, so far as may be, is ever near in memory to those things a god's nearness whereunto makes him truly god. Wherefore if a man makes right use of such means of remembrance, and ever approaches to the full vision of the perfect mysteries, he and he alone becomes truly perfect. Standing aside from the busy doings of mankind, and drawing nigh to the divine, he is rebuked by the [D] multitude as being out of his wits, for they know not that he is possessed by a deity.

XII

249D-250D THE SOUL'S RECOLLECTION OF IDEAL BEAUTY

Mark therefore the sum and substance of all our discourse touching the fourth sort of madness: to wit, that this is the best of all forms of divine possession, both in itself and in its sources, both for him that has it and for him that shares therein; and when he that loves beauty is touched [E] by such madness he is called a lover. Such an one, as soon as he beholds the beauty of this world, is reminded of true beauty, and his wings begin to grow; then is he fain to lift his wings and fly upward; yet he has not the power, but inasmuch as he gazes upward like a bird, and cares nothing for the world beneath, men charge it upon him that he is demented.

Now, as we have said, every human soul has, by reason of her nature, had contemplation of true Being: else would she never have entered into this human creature; but to be put in mind thereof by things here [250]

---

[14] The word 'alone' is strictly inconsistent with 248E 5-7, where it is implied that all souls ultimately regain their wings. But in the present sentence Plato is thinking only of events within a 10,000-year period, and giving the ground for his assertion that the philosopher alone can shorten the period of πτέρωσις.

is not easy for every soul; some, when they had the vision, had it but for a moment; some when they had fallen to earth consorted unhappily with such as led them to deeds of unrighteousness, wherefore they forgot the holy objects of their vision. Few indeed are left that can still remember much: but when these discern some likeness of the things yonder, they are amazed, and no longer masters of themselves, and know not what is come upon them by reason of their perception being dim. [B]

Now in the earthly likenesses of justice and temperance and all other prized possessions of the soul there dwells no lustre; nay, so dull are the organs wherewith men approach their images that hardly can a few behold that which is imaged; but with beauty it is otherwise. Beauty it was ours to see in all its brightness in those days when, amidst that happy company, we beheld with our eyes that blessed vision, ourselves in the train of Zeus, others following some other god; then were we all initiated into that mystery which is rightly accounted blessed beyond all others; whole and unblemished were we that did celebrate it, [c] untouched by the evils that awaited us in days to come; whole and unblemished likewise, free from all alloy, steadfast and blissful were the spectacles on which we gazed in the moment of final revelation; pure was the light that shone around us, and pure were we, without taint of that prison-house which now we are encompassed withal, and call a body, fast bound therein as an oyster in its shell.

There let it rest then, our tribute to a memory that has stirred us to linger awhile on those former joys for which we yearn. Now beauty, [D] as we said, shone bright amidst these visions, and in this world below we apprehend it through the clearest of our senses, clear and resplendent. For sight is the keenest mode of perception vouchsafed us through the body; wisdom, indeed, we cannot see thereby—how passionate had been our desire for her, if she had granted us so clear an image of herself to gaze upon—nor yet any other of those beloved objects, save only beauty; for beauty alone this has been ordained, to be most manifest to sense and most lovely of them all.

XIII

250E-252C LOVE AS THE REGROWING OF THE SOUL'S WINGS

Now he whose vision of the mystery is long past, or whose purity [E] has been sullied, cannot pass swiftly hence to see Beauty's self yonder, when he beholds that which is called beautiful here; wherefore he looks upon it with no reverence, and surrendering to pleasure he essays to go after the fashion of a four-footed beast, and to beget offspring of the flesh; or consorting with wantonness he has no fear nor shame in running after unnatural pleasure. But when one who is fresh from the [251] mystery, and saw much of the vision, beholds a godlike face or bodily form that truly expresses beauty, first there comes upon him a shuddering and a measure of that awe which the vision inspired, and then reverence as at the sight of a god: and but for fear of being deemed a very madman he would offer sacrifice to his beloved, as to a holy image of deity. Next, with the passing of the shudder, a strange sweating and fever seizes him: for by reason of the stream of beauty [B] entering in through his eyes there comes a warmth, whereby his soul's plumage is fostered; and with that warmth the roots of the wings are melted, which for long had been so hardened and closed up that nothing could grow; then as the nourishment is poured in the stump of the wing swells and hastens to grow from the root over the whole substance of the soul: for aforetime the whole soul was furnished with wings. Meanwhile she throbs with ferment in every part, and even as [C] a teething child feels an aching and pain in its gums when a tooth has just come through, so does the soul of him who is beginning to grow his wings feel a ferment and painful irritation. Wherefore as she gazes upon the boy's beauty, she admits a flood of particles streaming therefrom—that is why we speak of a 'flood of passion' [15]—whereby she is warmed and fostered; then has she respite from her anguish, and is filled with joy. But when she has been parted from him and become [D] parched, the openings of those outlets at which the wings are sprouting dry up likewise and are closed, so that the wing's germ is barred off; and behind its bars, together with the flood aforesaid, it throbs like a fevered pulse, and pricks at its proper outlet; and thereat the whole soul round about is stung and goaded into anguish; howbeit she remembers the beauty of her beloved, and rejoices again. So between joy and anguish she is distraught at being in such strange case, perplexed and frenzied; with madness upon her she can neither sleep by night [E] nor keep still by day, but runs hither and thither, yearning for him in whom beauty dwells, if haply she may behold him. At last she does behold him, and lets the flood pour in upon her, releasing the imprisoned waters; then has she refreshment and respite from her stings and sufferings, and at that moment tastes a pleasure that is sweet beyond compare. Nor will she willingly give it up: above all others does [252] she esteem her beloved in his beauty: mother, brother, friends, she forgets them all: naught does she reck of losing worldly possessions through neglect: all the rules of conduct, all the graces of life, of which aforetime she was proud, she now disdains, welcoming a slave's estate and any couch where she may be suffered to lie down close beside her darling; for besides her reverence for the possessor of beauty she has found in him the only physician for her grievous suffering. [B]

Hearken, fair boy to whom I speak: this is the experience that men term love (ἔρως), but when you hear what the gods call it, you will probably smile at its strangeness. There are a couple of verses on love quoted by certain Homeric scholars from the unpublished works, the

---

[15] The suggestion is that ἵμερος is derived from ἱέναι + μέρη + ῥοή.

second of which is remarkably bold and a trifle astray in its quantities: they run as follows:

> Eros, cleaver of air, in mortals' speech is he named;
> But, since he must grow wings, Pteros the celestials call him.[16]

You may believe that or not, as you please; at all events the cause [c] and the nature of the lover's experience are in fact what I have said.

XIV

252C-253C THE VARIOUS TYPES OF LOVER

Now if he whom Love has caught be amongst the followers of Zeus, he is able to bear the burden of the winged one with some constancy; but they that attend upon Ares, and did range the heavens in his train, when they are caught by Love and fancy that their beloved is doing them some injury, will shed blood and not scruple to offer both themselves and their loved ones in sacrifice. And so does each lover live, after the manner of the god in whose company he once was, honour- [D] ing him and copying him so far as may be, so long as he remains uncorrupt and is still living in his first earthly period; and in like manner does he comport himself towards his beloved and all his other associates. And so each selects a fair one for his love after his disposition, and even as if the beloved himself were a god he fashions for himself as it were an image, and adorns it to be the object of his veneration and worship.

Thus the followers of Zeus seek a beloved who is Zeus-like in soul; [E] wherefore they look for one who is by nature disposed to the love of wisdom and the leading of men, and when they have found him and come to love him they do all in their power to foster that disposition. And if they have not aforetime trodden this path, they now set out upon it, learning the way from any source that may offer or finding it for themselves; and as they follow up the trace within themselves of the nature of their own god their task is made easier, inasmuch as [253] they are constrained to fix their gaze upon him, and reaching out after him in memory they are possessed by him, and from him they take their ways and manners of life, in so far as a man can partake of a god. But all this, mark you, they attribute to the beloved, and the draughts which they draw from Zeus they pour out, like Bacchants, into the soul of the beloved, thus creating in him the closest possible likeness to the god they worship. [B]

Those who were in the train of Hera look for a royal nature, and when

---

[16] For such double names cf. *Iliad* I, 404; XIV, 291; XX, 74. The name given by the gods is normally the more significant. It is uncertain whether the two lines are simply invented by Plato or modified from existing lines fathered upon Homer, perhaps by some Orphic writer. See Thompson's note.

they have found him they do unto him all things in like fashion. And so it is with the followers of Apollo and each other god: every lover is fain that his beloved should be of a nature like to his own god; and when he has won him, he leads him on to walk in the ways of their god, and after his likeness, patterning himself thereupon and giving counsel and discipline to the boy. There is no jealousy nor petty spitefulness in his dealings, but his every act is aimed at bringing the beloved to be every whit like unto himself and unto the god of their [c] worship.

So therefore glorious and blissful is the endeavour of true lovers in that mystery-rite, if they accomplish that which they endeavour after the fashion of which I speak, when mutual affection arises through the madness inspired by love. But the beloved must needs be captured: and the manner of that capture I will now tell.

XV

253C-256E THE SUBJUGATION OF LUST • LOVE AND
COUNTER-LOVE

In the beginning of our story we divided each soul into three parts, two being like steeds and the third like a charioteer. Well and good. Now of the steeds, so we declare, one is good and the other is not; [D] but we have not described the excellence of the one nor the badness of the other, and that is what must now be done. He that is on the more honourable side is upright and clean-limbed, carrying his neck high, with something of a hooked nose: in colour he is white, with black eyes: a lover of glory, but with temperance and modesty: one that consorts with genuine renown, and needs no whip, being driven by the word of command alone. The other is crooked of frame, a massive [E] jumble of a creature, with thick short neck, snub nose, black skin, and grey eyes; hot-blooded, consorting with wantonness and vainglory; shaggy of ear, deaf, and hard to control with whip and goad.

Now when the driver beholds the person of the beloved, and causes a sensation of warmth to suffuse the whole soul, he begins to experience a tickling or pricking of desire; and the obedient steed, con- [254] strained now as always by modesty, refrains from leaping upon the beloved; but his fellow, heeding no more the driver's goad or whip, leaps and dashes on, sorely troubling his companion and his driver, and forcing them to approach the loved one and remind him of the delights of love's commerce. For a while they struggle, indignant that he should force [B] them to a monstrous and forbidden act; but at last, finding no end to their evil plight, they yield and agree to do his bidding. And so he draws them on, and now they are quite close and behold the spectacle of the beloved flashing upon them. At that sight the driver's memory goes back to that form of Beauty, and he sees her once again enthroned by the side of Temperance upon her holy seat; then in awe and reverence he falls upon his back, and therewith is compelled to pull the reins so violently that he brings both steeds down on their haunches, [c] the good one willing and unresistant, but the wanton sore against his will. Now that they are a little way off, the good horse in shame and horror drenches the whole soul with sweat, while the other, contriving to recover his wind after the pain of the bit and his fall, bursts into angry abuse, railing at the charioteer and his yoke-fellow as cowardly treacherous deserters. Once again he tries to force them to advance, [d] and when they beg him to delay awhile he grudgingly consents. But when the time appointed is come, and they feign to have forgotten, he reminds them of it, struggling and neighing and pulling until he compels them a second time to approach the beloved and renew their offer; and when they have come close, with head down and tail stretched out he takes the bit between his teeth and shamelessly plunges on. But the driver, with resentment even stronger than before, like a racer [e] recoiling from the starting-rope, jerks back the bit in the mouth of the wanton horse with an even stronger pull, bespatters his railing tongue and his jaws with blood, and forcing him down on legs and haunches delivers him over to anguish.

And so it happens time and again, until the evil steed casts off his wantonness; humbled in the end, he obeys the counsel of his driver, and when he sees the fair beloved is like to die of fear. Wherefore at long last the soul of the lover follows after the beloved with reverence and awe.

Thus the loved one receives all manner of service, as peer of the [255] gods, from a lover that is no pretender but loves in all sincerity; of his own nature, too, he is kindly disposed to him who pays such service. Now it may be that in time past he has been misled, by his schoolfellows or others, who told him that it is shameful to have commerce with a lover, and by reason of this he may repel his advances; nevertheless as time goes on ripening age and the ordinance of destiny together lead him to welcome the other's society; for assuredly fate does not [b] suffer one evil man to be friend to another, nor yet one good man to lack the friendship of another.

And now that he has come to welcome his lover and to take pleasure in his company and converse, it comes home to him what a depth of kindliness he has found, and he is filled with amazement, for he perceives that all his other friends and kinsmen have nothing to offer in comparison with this friend in whom there dwells a god. So as he continues in this converse and society, and comes close to his lover in the gymnasium and elsewhere, that flowing stream which Zeus, as [c] the lover of Ganymede, called the 'flood of passion', pours in upon the lover; and part of it is absorbed within him, but when he can contain no more the rest flows away outside him; and as a breath of wind or an echo, rebounding from a smooth hard surface, goes back to its place of origin, even so the stream of beauty turns back and re-enters the eyes of the fair beloved; and so by the natural channel it reaches his soul and gives it fresh vigour, watering the roots of the wings and quickening them to growth: whereby the soul of the beloved, in its [D] turn, is filled with love. So he loves, yet knows not what he loves: he does not understand, he cannot tell what has come upon him; like one that has caught a disease of the eye from another, he cannot account for it, not realising that his lover is as it were a mirror in which he beholds himself. And when the other is beside him, he shares his respite from anguish; when he is absent, he likewise shares his longing and being longed for; since he possesses that counter-love which is the image of love, though he supposes it to be friendship rather than love, and [E] calls it by that name. He feels a desire, like the lover's yet not so strong, to behold, to touch, to kiss him, to share his couch: and now ere long the desire, as one might guess, leads to the act.

So when they lie side by side, the wanton horse of the lover's soul would have a word with the charioteer, claiming a little guerdon for all his trouble. The like steed in the soul of the beloved has no word to [256] say, but swelling with desire for he knows not what embraces and kisses the lover, in grateful acknowledgment of all his kindness. And when they lie by one another, he is minded not to refuse to do his part in gratifying his lover's entreaties; yet his yoke-fellow in turn, being moved by reverence and heedfulness, joins with the driver in resisting. And so, if the victory be won by the higher elements of mind guiding them into the ordered rule of the philosophic life, their days on earth will be blessed with happiness and concord; for the power of evil in [B] the soul has been subjected, and the power of goodness liberated: they have won self-mastery and inward peace. And when life is over, with burden shed and wings recovered they stand victorious in the first of the three rounds in that truly Olympic struggle; nor can any nobler prize be secured whether by the wisdom that is of man or by the madness that is of god.

But if they turn to a way of life more ignoble and unphilosophic, [C] yet covetous of honour, then mayhap in a careless hour, or when the wine is flowing, the wanton horses in their two souls will catch them off their guard, bring the pair together, and choosing that part which the multitude account blissful achieve their full desire. And this once done, they continue therein, albeit but rarely, seeing that their minds are not wholly set thereupon. Such a pair as this also are dear friends, but not so dear as that other pair, one to another, both in the time of their love and when love is past; for they feel that they have exchanged [D] the most binding pledges, which it were a sin to break by becoming enemies. When death comes they quit the body wingless indeed, yet eager to be winged, and therefore they carry off no mean reward for their lovers' madness: for it is ordained that all such as have taken the first steps on the celestial highway shall no more return to the dark pathways beneath the earth, but shall walk together in a life of shining

bliss, and be furnished in due time with like plumage the one to the [E]
other, because of their love.

XVI

256E-257B THE SPEECH CONCLUDED · A PRAYER FOR
LYSIAS AND PHAEDRUS

These then, my boy, are the blessings great and glorious which will
come to you from the friendship of a lover. He who is not a lover can
offer a mere acquaintance flavoured with worldly wisdom, dispensing
a niggardly measure of worldly goods; in the soul to which he is
attached he will engender an ignoble quality extolled by the multitude
as virtue, and condemn it to float for nine thousand years hither [257]
and thither, around the earth and beneath it, bereft of understanding.

Thus then, dear God of Love, I have offered the fairest recantation
and fullest atonement that my powers could compass; some of its
language, in particular, was perforce poetical, to please Phaedrus. Grant
me thy pardon for what went before, and thy favour for what ensued:
be merciful and gracious, and take not from me the lover's talent wherewith thou hast blest me, neither let it wither by reason of thy displeasure,
but grant me still to increase in the esteem of the fair. And if anything
that Phaedrus and I said earlier sounded discordant to thy ear, [B]
set it down to Lysias, the only begetter of that discourse; and staying
him from discourses after this fashion turn him towards the love of
wisdom, even as his brother Polemarchus has been turned. Then will
his loving disciple here present no longer halt between two opinions,
as now he does, but live for Love in singleness of purpose with the aid
of philosophical discourse.

XVII

257B-258E PRELIMINARY CONSIDERATION OF SPEECH-WRITING

Ph. If that be for our good, Socrates, I join in your prayer for it. And
I have this long while been filled with admiration for your speech [C]
as a far finer achievement than the one you made before. It makes me
afraid that I shall find Lysias cutting a poor figure, if he proves to be
willing to compete with another speech of his own. The fact is that only
the other day, my dear good sir, one of our politicians was railing at him
and reproaching him on this very score, constantly dubbing him a 'speech-
writer'; so possibly we shall find him desisting from further composition
to preserve his reputation.

Soc. What a ridiculous line to take, young man! And how utterly you misjudge our friend, if you suppose him to be such a timid creature!   [D] Am I to believe you really do think that the person you speak of meant his raillery as a reproach?

Ph. He gave me that impression, Socrates; and of course you know as well as I do that the men of greatest influence and dignity in political life are reluctant to write speeches and bequeath to posterity compositions of their own, for fear of the verdict of later ages, which might pronounce them Sophists.[17]

Soc. Phaedrus, you are unaware that the expression 'Pleasant Bend' comes from the long bend in the Nile: and besides the matter of the   [E] Bend you are unaware that the proudest of politicians have the strongest desire to write speeches and bequeath compositions; why, whenever they write a speech, they are so pleased to have admirers that they put in a special clause at the beginning with the names of the persons who admire the speech in question.

Ph. What do you mean? I don't understand.

Soc. You don't understand that when a politician begins a   [258] composition the first thing he writes is the name of his admirer.

Ph. Is it?

Soc. Yes, he says maybe 'Resolved by the Council' or 'by the People' or by both: and then 'Proposed by so-and-so'—a pompous piece of self-advertisement on the part of the author; after which he proceeds with what he has to say, showing off his own wisdom to his admirers, sometimes in a very lengthy composition. This sort of thing amounts, don't you think, to composing a speech?

Ph. Yes, I think it does.   [B]

Soc. Then if the speech holds its ground, the author quits the scene rejoicing; but if it is blotted out, and he loses his status as a recognised speech-writer, he goes into mourning, and his friends with him.

Ph. Quite so.

Soc. Which clearly implies that their attitude to the profession is not one of disdain, but of admiration.

Ph. To be sure.

Soc. Tell me then: when an orator, or a king, succeeds in acquiring the power of a Lycurgus, a Solon or a Darius, and so winning im-   [c] mortality among his people as a speech-writer, doesn't he deem himself a peer of the gods while still living, and do not people of later ages hold the same opinion of him when they contemplate his writings?

Ph. Yes, indeed.

Soc. Then do you suppose that anyone of that type, whoever he might be, and whatever his animosity towards Lysias, could reproach him simply on the ground that he writes?

---

17 The implication is that most prose works hitherto had come from the pens of Sophists; and a glance at the relevant *testimonia* in Diels-Kranz, *Vors.* II, makes this easy to believe.

Ph. What you say certainly makes that improbable; for apparently he would be reproaching what he wanted to do himself.

Soc. Then the conclusion is obvious, that there is nothing shame- [D] ful in the mere writing of speeches.

Ph. Of course.

Soc. But in speaking and writing shamefully and badly, instead of as one should, that is where the shame comes in, I take it.

Ph. Clearly.

Soc. Then what is the nature of good writing and bad? Is it incumbent on us, Phaedrus, to examine Lysias on this point, and all such as have written or mean to write anything at all, whether in the field of public affairs or private, whether in the verse of the poet or the plain speech of prose?

Ph. Is it incumbent! Why, life itself would hardly be worth living [E] save for pleasures like this: certainly not for those pleasures that involve previous pain, as do almost all concerned with the body, which for that reason are rightly called slavish.

XVIII

258E-259D INTERLUDE · THE MYTH OF THE CICADAS

Soc. Well, I suppose we can spare the time; and I think too that the cicadas overhead, singing after their wont in the hot sun and conversing with one another, don't fail to observe us as well. So if they were to [259] see us two behaving like ordinary folk at midday, not conversing but dozing lazy-minded under their spell, they would very properly have the laugh of us, taking us for a pair of slaves that had invaded their retreat like sheep, to have their midday sleep beside the spring. If however they see us conversing and steering clear of their bewitching siren-song, they might feel respect for us and grant us that boon [B] which heaven permits them to confer upon mortals.

Ph. Oh, what is that? I don't think I have heard of it.

Soc. Surely it is unbecoming in a devotee of the Muses not to have heard of a thing like that! The story is that once upon a time these creatures were men—men of an age before there were any Muses: and that when the latter came into the world, and music made its appearance, some of the people of those days were so thrilled with pleasure that they went on singing, and quite forgot to eat and drink until [C] they actually died without noticing it. From them in due course sprang the race of cicadas, to which the Muses have granted the boon of needing no sustenance right from their birth, but of singing from the very first, without food or drink, until the day of their death: after which they go and report to the Muses how they severally are paid honour amongst mankind, and by whom. So for those whom they report as having honoured Terpsichore in the dance they win that Muse's favour; [D] for those that have worshipped in the rites of love the favour of Erato; and so with all the others, according to the nature of the worship paid to each. To the eldest, Calliope, and to her next sister Urania, they tell of those who live a life of philosophy and so do honour to the music of those twain whose theme is the heavens and all the story of gods and men, and whose song is the noblest of them all.

Thus there is every reason for us not to yield to slumber in the noontide, but to pursue our talk.

Ph. Of course we must pursue it.

XIX

259E-261A RHETORIC AND KNOWLEDGE

Soc. Well, the subject we proposed for inquiry just now was the nature of good and bad speaking and writing: so we are to inquire into that.

Ph. Plainly.

Soc. Then does not a good and successful discourse presuppose a knowledge in the mind of the speaker of the truth about his subject?

Ph. As to that, dear Socrates, what I have heard is that the intending orator is under no necessity of understanding what is truly just, [260] but only what is likely to be thought just by the body of men who are to give judgment; nor need he know what is truly good or noble, but what will be thought so; since it is on the latter, not the former, that persuasion depends.

Soc. 'Not to be lightly rejected',[18] Phaedrus, is any word of the wise; perhaps they are right: one has to see. And in particular this present assertion must not be dismissed.

Ph. I agree.

Soc. Well, here is my suggestion for discussion.

Ph. Yes?

Soc. Suppose I tried to persuade you to acquire a horse to use in [B] battle against the enemy, and suppose that neither of us knew what a horse was, but I knew this much about you, that Phaedrus believes a horse to be that tame animal which possesses the largest ears.

Ph. A ridiculous thing to suppose, Socrates.

Soc. Wait a moment: suppose I continued to urge upon you in all seriousness, with a studied encomium of a donkey, that it was what

---

[18] A quotation from *Iliad* II, 361.

I called it, a horse: that it was highly important for you to possess the creature, both at home and in the field: that it was just the animal to ride on into battle, and that it was handy, into the bargain, for [c] carrying your equipment and so forth.

Ph. To go to that length would be utterly ridiculous.

Soc. Well, isn't it better to be a ridiculous friend than a clever enemy? [19]

Ph. I suppose it is.

Soc. Then when a master of oratory, who is ignorant of good and evil, employs his power of persuasion on a community as ignorant as himself, not by extolling a miserable donkey as being really a horse, but by extolling evil as being really good: and when by studying the beliefs of the masses he persuades them to do evil instead of good, what kind of crop do you think his oratory is likely to reap from the seed [d] thus sown?

Ph. A pretty poor one.

Soc. Well now, my good friend, have we been too scurrilous in our abuse of the art of speech? Might it not retort: 'Why do you extraordinary people talk such nonsense? I never insist on ignorance of the truth on the part of one who would learn to speak; on the contrary, if my advice goes for anything, it is that he should only resort to me after he has come into possession of truth; what I do however pride myself on is that without my aid knowledge of what is true will get a man no nearer to mastering the art of persuasion.'

Ph. And will not such a retort be just? [e]

Soc. Yes, if the arguments advanced against oratory sustain its claim to be an art. In point of fact, I fancy I can hear certain arguments advancing, and protesting that the claim is false, that it is no art, but a knack that has nothing to do with art: inasmuch as there is, as the Spartans put it, no 'soothfast' art of speech, nor assuredly will there ever be one, without a grasp of truth.[20]

Ph. We must have these arguments, Socrates. Come, bring [261] them up before us, and examine their purport.

Soc. Come hither then, you worthy creatures, and impress upon Phaedrus, who is so blessed in his offspring,[21] that unless he gets on with his philosophy he will never get on as a speaker on any subject; and let Phaedrus be your respondent.

Ph. I await their questions.

---

[19] The meaning is that the obviously ridiculous mistakes of a well-intentioned speaker are likely to do less harm than the mistakes of an ill-intentioned one who is clever enough to disguise his ignorance and so escape ridicule.

[20] The point urged here is that knowledge of truth must be part and parcel of the art of rhetoric, if it is really to be an art: knowledge cannot be something preliminary or extraneous which the orator can presume in his audience to start with, as had just been suggested by the apologist of rhetoric.

[21] The allusion is to Phaedrus as begetter of discourses: cf. 242A-B.

XX

261A-264E KNOWLEDGE OF RESEMBLANCES AND DIFFERENCES

Soc. Must not the art of rhetoric, taken as a whole, be a kind of influencing of the mind by means of words, not only in courts of law and other public gatherings, but in private places also? And must it not be the same art that is concerned with great issues and small, its right employment commanding no more respect when dealing with [B] important matters than with unimportant? Is that what you have been told about it?

Ph. No indeed, not exactly that: it is principally, I should say, to lawsuits that an art of speaking and writing is applied—and of course to public harangues also. I know of no wider application.

Soc. What? Are you acquainted only with the 'Arts' or manuals of oratory by Nestor and Odysseus, which they composed in their leisure hours at Troy? Have you never heard of the work of Palamedes?

Ph. No, upon my word, nor of Nestor either; unless you are cast- [c] ing Gorgias for the role of Nestor, with Odysseus played by Thrasymachus, or maybe Theodorus.

Soc. Perhaps I am. But anyway we may let them be, and do you tell me, what is it that the contending parties in lawcourts do? Do they not in fact contend with words, or how else should we put it?

Ph. That is just what they do.

Soc. About what is just and unjust?

Ph. Yes.

Soc. And he who possesses the art of doing this can make the same thing appear to the same people now just, now unjust, at will? [D]

Ph. To be sure.

Soc. And in public harangues, no doubt, he can make the same things seem to the community now good, and now the reverse of good?

Ph. Just so.

Soc. Then can we fail to see that the Palamedes of Elea [22] has an art of speaking, such that he can make the same things appear to his audience like and unlike, or one and many, or again at rest and in motion?

Ph. Indeed he can.

Soc. So contending with words is a practice found not only in lawsuits and public harangues but, it seems, wherever men speak [E] we find this single art, if indeed it is an art, which enables people to make out everything to be like everything else, within the limits of possible comparison, and to expose the corresponding attempts of others who disguise what they are doing.

---

[22] i.e. Zeno, whose method of argument was to show that an opponent's thesis led to two contradictory consequences. For the contradictory pairs here mentioned cf. *Parm.* 127E 6, 129B 5 and 129E 1; and see F. M. Cornford, *Plato and Parmenides*, pp. 57-9.

Ph. How so, pray?

Soc. I think that will become clear if we put the following question. Are we misled when the difference between two things is wide, or narrow?

Ph. When it is narrow. [262]

Soc. Well then, if you shift your ground little by little, you are more likely to pass undetected from so-and-so to its opposite than if you do so at one bound.

Ph. Of course.

Soc. It follows that anyone who intends to mislead another, without being misled himself, must discern precisely the degree of resemblance and dissimilarity between this and that.

Ph. Yes, that is essential.

Soc. Then if he does not know the truth about a given thing, how is he going to discern the degree of resemblance between that unknown thing and other things?

Ph. It will be impossible. [B]

Soc. Well now, when people hold beliefs contrary to fact, and are misled, it is plain that the error has crept into their minds through the suggestion of some similarity or other.

Ph. That certainly does happen.

Soc. But can anyone possibly master the art of using similarities for the purpose of bringing people round, and leading them away from the truth about this or that to the opposite of the truth, or again can anyone possibly avoid this happening to himself, unless he has knowledge of what the thing in question really is?

Ph. No, never.

Soc. It would seem to follow, my friend, that the art of speech [c] displayed by one who has gone chasing after beliefs, instead of knowing the truth, will be a comical sort of art, in fact no art at all.

Ph. I dare say.

Soc. Then would you like to observe some instances of what I call the presence and absence of art in that speech of Lysias which you are carrying, and in those which I have delivered?

Ph. Yes, by all means: at present our discussion is somewhat abstract, for want of adequate illustrations.

Soc. Why, as to that it seems a stroke of luck that in the two speeches we have a sort of illustration of the way in which one who knows [D] the truth can mislead his audience by playing an oratorical joke on them. I myself, Phaedrus, put that down to the local deities, or perhaps those mouthpieces of the Muses that are chirping over our heads have vouchsafed us their inspiration; for of course I don't lay claim to any oratorical skill myself.

Ph. I dare say that is so: but please explain your point.

Soc. Well, come along: read the beginning of Lysias's speech.

Ph. 'You know how I am situated, and I have told you that I [E] think it to our advantage that the thing should be done. Now I claim that

I should not be refused what I ask simply because I am not your lover. Lovers repent when—'

Soc. Stop. Our business is to indicate where the speaker is at fault, and shows absence of art, isn't it?

Ph. Yes.   [263]

Soc. Well now, is not the following assertion obviously true, that there are some words about which we all agree, and others about which we are at variance?

Ph. I think I grasp your meaning, but you might make it still plainer.

Soc. When someone utters the word 'iron' or 'silver', we all have the same object before our minds, haven't we?

Ph. Certainly.

Soc. But what about the words 'just' and 'good'? Don't we diverge, and dispute not only with one another but with our own selves?

Ph. Yes indeed.

Soc. So in some cases we agree, and in others we don't.   [b]

Ph. Quite so.

Soc. Now in which of the cases are we more apt to be misled, and in which is rhetoric more effective?

Ph. Plainly in the case where we fluctuate.

Soc. Then the intending student of the art of rhetoric ought, in the first place, to make a systematic division of words, and get hold of some mark distinguishing the two kinds of words, those namely in the use of which the multitude are bound to fluctuate, and those in which they are not.

Ph. To grasp that, Socrates, would certainly be an excellent piece   [c] of discernment.

Soc. And secondly, I take it, when he comes across a particular word he must realise what it is, and be swift to perceive which of the two kinds the thing he proposes to discuss really belongs to.

Ph. To be sure.

Soc. Well then, shall we reckon love as one of the disputed terms, or as one of the other sort?

Ph. As a disputed term, surely. Otherwise can you suppose it would have been possible for you to say of it what you said just now, namely that it is harmful both to the beloved and the lover, and then to turn round and say that it is really the greatest of goods?

Soc. An excellent point. But now tell me this, for thanks to my   [d] inspired condition I can't quite remember: did I define love at the beginning of my speech?

Ph. Yes indeed, and immensely thorough you were about it.

Soc. Upon my word, you rate the Nymphs of Achelous and Pan, son of Hermes, much higher as artists in oratory than Lysias, son of Cephalus. Or am I quite wrong? Did Lysias at the beginning of his discourse on love compel us to conceive of it as a certain definite entity, with a meaning he had himself decided upon? And did he proceed to bring all [E] his subsequent remarks, from first to last, into line with that meaning? Shall we read his first words once again?

Ph. If you like; but what you are looking for isn't there.

Soc. Read it out, so that I can listen to the author himself.

Ph. 'You know how I am situated, and I have told you that I think it to our advantage that the thing should be done. Now I claim that I should not be refused what I ask simply because I am not your lover. [264] Lovers, when their craving is at an end, repent of such benefits as they have conferred.'

Soc. No: he doesn't seem to get anywhere near what we are looking for: he goes about it like a man swimming on his back, in reverse, and starts from the end instead of the beginning; his opening words are what the lover would naturally say to his boy only when he had finished. Or am I quite wrong, dear Phaedrus?

Ph. I grant you, Socrates, that the substance of his address is [B] really a peroration.

Soc. And to pass to other points: doesn't his matter strike you as thrown out at haphazard? Do you find any cogent reason for his next remark, or indeed any of his remarks, occupying the place it does? I myself, in my ignorance, thought that the writer, with a fine abandon, put down just what came into his head. Can you find any cogent principle of composition which he observed in setting down his observations in this particular order?

Ph. You flatter me in supposing that I am competent to see into his mind with all that accuracy. [C]

Soc. Well, there is one point at least which I think you will admit, namely that any discourse ought to be constructed like a living creature, with its own body, as it were; it must not lack either head or feet; it must have a middle and extremities so composed as to suit each other and the whole work.

Ph. Of course.

Soc. Then ask yourself whether that is or is not the case with your friend's speech. You will find that it is just like the epitaph said to have been carved on the tomb of Midas the Phrygian.

Ph. What is that, and what's wrong with it? [D]

Soc. It runs like this:

> A maid of bronze I stand on Midas' tomb,
> So long as waters flow and trees grow tall,
> Abiding here on his lamented grave,
> I tell the traveller Midas here is laid.

I expect you notice that it makes no difference what order the lines [E] come in.

Ph. Socrates, you are making a joke of our speech!

XXI

264E-266B DIALECTIC METHOD AS EXHIBITED IN PRECEDING SPEECHES

Soc. Well, to avoid distressing you, let us say no more of that—though indeed I think it provides many examples which it would be profitable to notice, provided one were chary of imitating them—and let us pass to the other speeches; for they, I think, presented a certain feature which everyone desirous of examining oratory would do well to observe.

Ph. To what do you refer? [265]

Soc. They were of opposite purport, one maintaining that the lover should be favoured, the other the non-lover.

Ph. Yes, they did so very manfully.

Soc. I thought you were going to say—and with truth—madly; but that reminds me of what I was about to ask. We said, did we not, that love is a sort of madness?

Ph. Yes.

Soc. And that there are two kinds of madness, one resulting from human ailments, the other from a divine disturbance of our conventions of conduct.

Ph. Quite so. [B]

Soc. And in the divine kind we distinguished four types, ascribing them to four gods: the inspiration of the prophet to Apollo, that of the mystic to Dionysus, that of the poet to the Muses, and a fourth type which we declared to be the highest, the madness of the lover, to Aphrodite and Eros; moreover we painted, after a fashion, a picture of the lover's experience, in which perhaps we attained some degree of truth, though we may well have sometimes gone astray; the blend resulting in a discourse which had some claim to plausibility, or shall we say a mythical hymn of praise, in due religious language, a festal [C] celebration of my master and yours too, Phaedrus, that god of love who watches over the young and fair.

Ph. It certainly gave me great pleasure to listen to it.

Soc. Then let us take one feature of it, the way in which the discourse contrived to pass from censure to encomium.

Ph. Well now, what do you make of that?

Soc. For the most part I think our festal hymn has really been just a festive entertainment; but we did casually allude to a certain pair of procedures, and it would be very agreeable if we could seize their [D] significance in a scientific fashion.

Ph. What procedures do you mean?

Soc. The first is that in which we bring a dispersed plurality under a single form, seeing it all together: the purpose being to define so-and-so, and thus to make plain whatever may be chosen as the topic for exposition. For example, take the definition given just now of love: whether it was right or wrong, at all events it was that which enabled our discourse to achieve lucidity and consistency.

Ph. And what is the second procedure you speak of, Socrates?

Soc. The reverse of the other, whereby we are enabled to divide [E] into forms, following the objective articulation; we are not to attempt to hack off parts like a clumsy butcher, but to take example from our two recent speeches. The single general form which they postulated was irrationality; next, on the analogy of a single natural body with its [266] pairs of like-named members, right arm or leg, as we say, and left, they conceived of madness as a single objective form existing in human beings: wherefore the first speech divided off a part on the left, and continued to make divisions, never desisting until it discovered one particular part bearing the name of 'sinister' love, on which it very properly poured abuse. The other speech conducted us to the forms of madness which lay on the right-hand side, and upon discovering a type of love that shared its name with the other but was divine, displayed it to our view and extolled it as the source of the greatest goods that [B] can befall us.[23]

Ph. That is perfectly true.

Soc. Believe me, Phaedrus, I am myself a lover of these divisions and collections, that I may gain the power to speak and to think; and whenever I deem another man able to discern an objective unity and plurality, I follow 'in his footsteps where he leadeth as a god'. Furthermore—whether I am right or wrong in doing so, God alone knows—it is those that have this ability whom for the present I call dialecticians.

---

[23] There are serious difficulties in this paragraph. Socrates speaks as though the generic concept of madness (τὸ ἄφρον, παράνοια, μανία) had been common to his two speeches, and there had been a formal divisional procedure followed in both of them. Neither of these things is true. . . .

It must therefore be admitted that Socrates's account of the dialectical procedure followed in his speeches is far from exact. Nevertheless it may be said to be substantially true: for it is true to the spirit and implication of what has happened: it describes how the two speeches might naturally be schematised when taken together as part of a design which has gradually unfolded itself. A writer with more concern for exact statement than Plato had, would have made Socrates say something to the following effect: 'I can illustrate these two procedures, Collection and Division, by reference to my two speeches; if you think of them together, you will agree that I was in fact, though not explicitly, operating with a generic concept, μανία, under which I contrived to subsume two sorts of ἔρως: though I grant you that my actual procedure was very informal, and in particular that I tended to leap from genus to *infima species*, without any clear indication of intermediate species.'

It should further be remembered that the word μανία did occur in Socrates's first speech, although more or less casually . . .

XXII

266c-269c THE TECHNIQUE OF EXISTING RHETORIC

Soc. But now tell me what we ought to call them if we take instruction from Lysias and yourself. Or is what I have been describing precisely that art of oratory thanks to which Thrasymachus and the rest of them have not only made themselves masterly orators, but can do the same for anyone else who cares to bring offerings to these princes amongst men?

Ph. Doubtless they behave like princes, but assuredly they do not possess the kind of knowledge to which you refer. No, I think you are right in calling the procedure that you have described dialectical; but we still seem to be in the dark about rhetoric.

Soc. What? Can there really be anything of value that admits of [D] scientific acquisition despite the lack of that procedure? If so, you and I should certainly not disdain it, but should explain what this residuum of rhetoric actually consists in.

Ph. Well, Socrates, of course there is plenty of matter in the rhetorical manuals.

Soc. Thank you for the reminder. The first point, I suppose, is that a speech must begin with a Preamble. You are referring, are you not, to such niceties of the art?

Ph. Yes.   [E]

Soc. And next comes Exposition accompanied by Direct Evidence; thirdly Indirect Evidence, fourthly Probabilities; besides which there are the Proof and Supplementary Proof mentioned by the Byzantine master of rhetorical artifice.

Ph. You mean the worthy Theodorus?

Soc. Of course; and we are to have a Refutation and Supple- [267] mentary Refutation both for prosecution and defence. And can we leave the admirable Evenus of Paros out of the picture, the inventor of Covert Allusion and Indirect Compliment and (according to some accounts) of the Indirect Censure in mnemonic verse? A real master, that. But we won't disturb the rest of Tisias and Gorgias, who realised that probability deserves more respect than truth, who could make trifles seem important and important points trifles by the force of their language, who dressed up novelties as antiques and vice versa, and [B] found out how to argue concisely or at interminable length about anything and everything. This last accomplishment provoked Prodicus once to mirth when he heard me mention it: he remarked that he and he alone had discovered what sort of speeches the art demands: to wit, neither long ones nor short, but of fitting length.

Ph. Masterly, Prodicus!

Soc. Are we forgetting Hippias? I think Prodicus's view would be supported by the man of Elis.

Ph. No doubt.

Soc. And then Polus: what are we to say of his *Muses' Treasury of Phrases* with its Reduplications and Maxims and Similes, and of [c] words *à la* Licymnius which that master made him a present of as a contribution to his fine writing?

Ph. But didn't Protagoras in point of fact produce some such works, Socrates?

Soc. Yes, my young friend: there is his *Correct Diction,* and many other excellent works. But to pass now to the application of pathetic language to the poor and aged, the master in that style seems to me to be the mighty man of Chalcedon, who was also expert at rousing a crowd to anger and then soothing them down again with his spells, [d] to quote his own saying; while at casting aspersions and dissipating them, whatever their source, he was unbeatable.

But to resume: on the way to conclude a speech there seems to be general agreement, though some call it Recapitulation and others by some other name.

Ph. You mean the practice of reminding the audience towards the end of a speech of its main points?

Soc. Yes. And now if you have anything further to add about the art of rhetoric—

Ph. Only a few unimportant points.

Soc. If they are unimportant, we may pass them over. But let [268] us look at what we have got in a clearer light, to see what power the art possesses, and when.

Ph. A very substantial power, Socrates, at all events in large assemblies.

Soc. Yes indeed. But have a look at it, my good sir, and see whether you discern some holes in the fabric, as I do.

Ph. Do show them me.

Soc. Well, look here: Suppose someone went up to your friend Eryximachus, or his father Acumenus, and said 'I know how to apply such treatment to a patient's body as will induce warmth or coolness, as I choose: I can make him vomit, if I see fit, or go to stool, and so [b] on and so forth. And on the strength of this knowledge I claim to be a competent physician, and to make a competent physician of anyone to whom I communicate this knowledge.' What do you imagine they would have to say to that?

Ph. They would ask him, of course, whether he also knew which patients ought to be given the various treatments, and when, and for how long.

Soc. Then what if he said 'Oh, no: but I expect my pupils to manage what you refer to by themselves'?   [c]

Ph. I expect they would say 'The man is mad: he thinks he has made himself a doctor by picking up something out of a book, or coming across some common drug or other, without any real knowledge of medicine.'

Soc. Now suppose someone went up to Sophocles or Euripides and said he knew how to compose lengthy dramatic speeches about a trifling matter, and quite short ones about a matter of moment; that he could write pathetic passages when he chose, or again passages of intimidation and menace, and so forth; and that he considered that by [D] teaching these accomplishments he could turn a pupil into a tragic poet.

Ph. I imagine that they too would laugh at anyone who supposed that you could make a tragedy otherwise than by so arranging such passages as to exhibit a proper relation to one another and to the whole of which they are parts.

Soc. Still I don't think they would abuse him rudely, but rather treat him as a musician would treat a man who fancied himself to be a master of harmony simply because he knew how to produce the highest possible note and the lowest possible on his strings. The musician would not be so rude as to say 'You miserable fellow, you're off your [E] head': but rather, in the gentler language befitting his profession 'My good sir, it is true that one who proposes to become a master of harmony must know the things you speak of: but it is perfectly possible for one who has got at far as yourself to have not the slightest real knowledge of harmony. You are acquainted with what has to be learnt before studying harmony: but of harmony itself you know nothing.

Ph. Perfectly true.

Soc. Similarly then Sophocles would tell the man who sought [269] to show off to himself and Euripides that what he knew was not tragic composition but its antecedents; and Acumenus would make the same distinction between medicine and the antecedents of medicine.

Ph. I entirely agree.

Soc. And if 'mellifluous' Adrastus, or shall we say Pericles, were to hear of those admirable artifices that we were referring to just now—the Brachylogies and Imageries and all the rest of them, which we enumerated and deemed it necessary to examine in a clear light—are we to suppose that they would address those who practise and teach this sort of thing, under the name of the art of rhetoric, with the severity you and I displayed, and in rude, coarse language? Or would [B] they, in their ampler wisdom, actually reproach us and say 'Phaedrus and Socrates, you ought not to get angry, but to make allowances for such people; it is because they are ignorant of dialectic that they are incapable of properly defining rhetoric, and that in turn leads them to imagine that by possessing themselves of the requisite antecedent learning they have discovered the art itself. And so they teach these anteced- [C] ents to their pupils, and believe that that constitutes a complete instruction in rhetoric; they don't bother about employing the various artifices in such a way that they will be effective, or about organising a work as a whole: that is for the pupils to see to for themselves when they come to make speeches.'

XXIII

269c-272b PHILOSOPHY AND RHETORIC · PERICLES'S DEBT
TO ANAXAGORAS

Ph. Well yes, Socrates: I dare say that does more or less describe
what the teachers and writers in question regard as the art of rhetoric;
personally I think what you say is true. But now by what means and
from what source can one attain the art of the true rhetorician, the [D]
real master of persuasion?

Soc. If you mean how can one become a finished performer, then
probably—indeed I might say undoubtedly—it is the same as with anything else: if you have an innate capacity for rhetoric, you will become
a famous rhetorician, provided you also acquire knowledge and practice;
but if you lack any of these three you will be correspondingly un-
finished. As regards the art itself (as distinct from the artist) I fancy
that the line of approach adopted by Lysias and Thrasymachus is not
the one I have in view.

Ph. Then what is?

Soc. I am inclined to think, my good friend, that it was not [E]
surprising that Pericles became the most finished exponent of rhetoric
there has ever been.

Ph. Why so?

Soc. All the great arts need supplementing by a study of Nature: your
artist must cultivate garrulity and high-flown speculation; from [270]
that source alone can come the mental elevation and thoroughly finished
execution of which you are thinking; and that is what Pericles acquired
to supplement his inborn capacity. He came across the right sort of
man, I fancy, in Anaxagoras, and by enriching himself with high speculation and coming to recognise the nature of wisdom and folly—on which
topics of course Anaxagoras was always discoursing—he drew from
that source and applied to the art of rhetoric what was suitable thereto.

Ph. How do you mean?

Soc. Rhetoric is in the same case as medicine, don't you think? [B]

Ph. How so?

Soc. In both cases there is a nature that we have to determine, the
nature of body in the one, and of soul in the other, if we mean to be
scientific and not content with mere empirical routine when we apply
medicine and diet to induce health and strength, or words and rules
of conduct to implant such convictions and virtues as we desire.

Ph. You are probably right, Socrates.

Soc. Then do you think it possible to understand the nature of [C]
the soul satisfactorily without taking it as a whole?

Ph. If we are to believe Hippocrates the Asclepiad, we can't understand even the body without such a procedure.

Soc. No, my friend, and he is right. But we must not just rely on Hippocrates: we must examine the assertion and see whether it accords with the truth.

Ph. Yes.

Soc. Then what is it that Hippocrates and the truth have to say on this matter of nature? I suggest that the way to reflect about the [D] nature of anything is as follows: first, to decide whether the object in respect of which we desire to have scientific knowledge, and to be able to impart it to others, is simple or complex; secondly, if it is simple, to inquire what natural capacity it has of acting upon another thing, and through what means; or by what other thing, and through what means, it can be acted upon; or, if it is complex, to enumerate its parts and observe in respect of each what we observe in the case of the simple object, to wit what its natural capacity, active or passive, consists in.

Ph. Perhaps so, Socrates.

Soc. Well, at all events, to pursue an inquiry without doing so would be like a blind man's progress. Surely we mustn't make out [E] that any sort of scientific inquirer resembles a blind or deaf person. No, it is plain that if we are to address people scientifically, we shall show them precisely what is the real and true nature of that object on which our discourse is brought to bear. And that object, I take it, is the soul.

Ph. To be sure.

Soc. Hence the speaker's whole effort is concentrated on that, [271] for it is there that he is attempting to implant conviction. Isn't that so?

Ph. Yes.

Soc. Then it is plain that Thrasymachus, or anyone else who seriously proffers a scientific rhetoric, will, in the first place, describe the soul very precisely, and let us see whether it is single and uniform in nature or, analogously to the body, complex; for to do that is, we maintain, to show a thing's nature.

Ph. Yes, undoubtedly.

Soc. And secondly he will describe what natural capacity it has to act upon what, and through what means, or by what it can be acted upon.

Ph. Quite so.

Soc. Thirdly, he will classify the types of discourse and the types [B] of soul, and the various ways in which souls are affected, explaining the reasons in each case, suggesting the type of speech appropriate to each type of soul, and showing what kind of speech can be relied on to create belief in one soul and disbelief in another, and why.

Ph. I certainly think that would be an excellent procedure.

Soc. Yes: in fact I can assure you, my friend, that no other scientific method of treating either our present subject or any other will ever [C] be found, whether in the models of the schools or in speeches actually delivered. But the present-day authors of manuals of rhetoric, of whom you have heard, are cunning folk who know all about the soul but keep their knowledge out of sight. So don't let us admit their claim to write scientifically until they compose their speeches and writings in the way we have indicated.

Ph. And what way is that?

Soc. To give the actual words would be troublesome; but I am quite ready to say how one ought to compose if he means to be as scientific as possible.

Ph. Then please do.

Soc. Since the function of oratory is in fact to influence men's souls, the intending orator must know what types of soul there are. Now [D] these are of a determinate number, and their variety results in a variety of individuals. To the types of soul thus discriminated there corresponds a determinate number of types of discourse. Hence a certain type of hearer will be easy to persuade by a certain type of speech to take such-and-such action for such-and-such reason, while another type will be hard to persuade. All this the orator must fully understand; and next he must watch it actually occurring, exemplified in men's conduct, and must cultivate a keenness of perception in following it, if he is going [E] to get any advantage out of the previous instruction that he was given in the school. And when he is competent to say what type of man is susceptible to what kind of discourse; when, further, he can, on catching sight of so-and-so, tell himself 'That is the man, that character [272] now actually before me is the one I heard about in school, and in order to persuade him of so-and-so I have to apply *these* arguments in *this* fashion'; and when, on top of all this, he has further grasped the right occasions for speaking and for keeping quiet, and has come to recognise the right and the wrong time for the Brachylogy, the Pathetic Passage, the Exacerbation and all the rest of his accomplishments, then and not till then has he well and truly achieved the art. But if in his speaking or teaching or writing he fails in any of these requirements, he may tell you that he has the art of speech, but one mustn't believe [B] all one is told.

And now maybe our author will say 'Well, what of it, Phaedrus and Socrates? Do you agree with me, or should we accept some other account of the art of speech?'

Ph. Surely we can't accept any other, Socrates; still it does seem a considerable business.

XXIV

272B-274B THE TRUE METHOD OF RHETORIC · ITS DIFFICULTY
AND ITS JUSTIFICATION

Soc. You are right, and that makes it necessary thoroughly to overhaul all our arguments, and see whether there is some easier and shorter way of arriving at the art; we don't want to waste effort in [C] going off on a long rough road, when we might take a short smooth one. But if you can help us at all through what you have heard from Lysias or anyone else, do try to recall it.

Ph. As far as trying goes, I might; but I can suggest nothing on the spur of the moment.

Soc. Then would you like me to tell you something I have heard from those concerned with these matters?

Ph. Why, yes.

Soc. Anyhow, Phaedrus, we are told that even the devil's advocate ought to be heard.

Ph. Then you can put his case.   [D]

Soc. Well, they tell us that there is no need to make such a solemn business of it, or fetch such a long compass on an uphill road. As we remarked at the beginning of this discussion, there is, they maintain, absolutely no need for the budding orator to concern himself with the truth about what is just or good conduct, nor indeed about who are just and good men whether by nature or education. In the lawcourts nobody cares a rap for the truth about these matters, but only about what is plausible. And that is the same as what is probable, and is   [E] what must occupy the attention of the would-be master of the art of speech. Even actual facts ought sometimes not to be stated, if they don't tally with probability; they should be replaced by what is probable, whether in prosecution or defence; whatever you say, you simply must pursue this probability they talk of, and can say good-bye to the truth for ever. Stick to that all through your speech, and you are equipped   [273] with the art complete.

Ph. Your account, Socrates, precisely reproduces what is said by those who claim to be experts in the art of speech. I remember that we did touch briefly on this sort of contention a while ago; and the professionals regard it as a highly important point.

Soc. Very well then, take Tisias himself; you have thumbed him carefully, so let Tisias tell us this: does he maintain that the probable is anything other than that which commends itself to the multitude?   [B]

Ph. How could it be anything else?

Soc. Then in consequence, it would seem, of that profound scientific discovery he laid down that if a weak but brave man is arrested for assaulting a strong but cowardly one, whom he has robbed of his cloak or some other garment, neither of them ought to state the true facts; the coward should say that the brave man didn't assault him single-handed, and the brave man should contend that there were only the two of them, and then have recourse to the famous plea 'How could a little fellow like me have attacked a big fellow like him?' Upon which   [C] the big fellow will not avow his own poltroonery but will try to invent some fresh lie which will probably supply his opponent with a means of refuting him. And similar 'scientific' rules are given for other cases of the kind. Isn't that so, Phaedrus?

Ph. To be sure.

Soc. Bless my soul! It appears that he made a brilliant discovery of a buried art, your Tisias, or whoever it really was and whatever he is pleased to be called after. But, my friend, shall we or shall we not say to him—

Ph. Say what? [D]

Soc. This: 'In point of fact, Tisias, we have for some time before you came on the scene been saying that the multitude get their notion of probability as the result of a likeness to truth; and we explained just now that these likenesses can always be best discovered by one who knows the truth. Therefore if you have anything else to say about the art of speech, we should be glad to hear it; but if not we shall adhere to the point we made just now, namely that unless the aspirant to oratory can on the one hand list the various natures amongst his prospective audiences, and on the other divide things into their kinds and em- [E] brace each individual thing under a single form, he will never attain such success as is within the grasp of mankind. Yet he will assuredly never acquire such competence without considerable diligence, which the wise man should exert not for the sake of speaking to and dealing with his fellow-men, but that he may be able to speak what is pleasing to the gods, and in all his dealings to do their pleasure to the best of his ability. For you see, Tisias, what we are told by those wiser than ourselves is true, that a man of sense ought never to study the gratification [274] of his fellow-slaves, save as a minor consideration, but that of his most excellent masters. So don't be surprised that we have to make a long detour: it is because the goal is glorious, though not the goal you think of.' Not but what those lesser objects also, if you would have them, can best be attained (so our argument assures us) as a consequence of the greater.

Ph. Your project seems to be excellent, Socrates, if only one could carry it out.

Soc. Well, when a man sets his hand to something good, it is good that he should take what comes to him. [B]

Ph. Yes, of course.

Soc. Then we may feel that we have said enough about the art of speech, both the true art and the false?

Ph. Certainly.

XXV

274B-278B THE SUPERIORITY OF THE SPOKEN WORD · MYTH OF THE INVENTION OF WRITING

Soc. But there remains the question of propriety and impropriety in writing, that is to say the conditions which make it proper or improper. Isn't that so?

Ph. Yes.

Soc. Now do you know how we may best please God, in practice and in theory, in this matter of words?

Ph. No indeed. Do you?

Soc. I can tell you the tradition that has come down from our [c] forefathers, but they alone know the truth of it. However, if we could discover that for ourselves, should we still be concerned with the fancies of mankind?

Ph. What a ridiculous question! But tell me the tradition you speak of.

Soc. Very well. The story is that in the region of Naucratis in Egypt there dwelt one of the old gods of the country, the god to whom the bird called Ibis is sacred, his own name being Theuth. He it was that invented number and calculation, geometry and astronomy, not to [d] speak of draughts and dice, and above all writing. Now the king of the whole country at that time was Thamus, who dwelt in the great city of Upper Egypt which the Greeks call Egyptian Thebes, while Thamus they call Ammon. To him came Theuth, and revealed his arts, saying that they ought to be passed on to the Egyptians in general. Thamus asked what was the use of them all: and when Theuth explained, he condemned what he thought the bad points and praised what he [e] thought the good. On each art, we are told, Thamus had plenty of views both for and against; it would take too long to give them in detail, but when it came to writing Theuth said 'Here, O king, is a branch of learning that will make the people of Egypt wiser and improve their memories: my discovery provides a recipe for memory and wisdom'. But the king answered and said 'O man full of arts, to one is it given to create the things of art, and to another to judge what measure of harm and of profit they have for those that shall employ them. And so it is that you, by reason of your tender regard for the writing that [275] is your offspring, have declared the very opposite of its true effect. If men learn this, it will implant forgetfulness in their souls: they will cease to exercise memory because they rely on that which is written, calling things to remembrance no longer from within themselves, but by means of external marks; what you have discovered is a recipe not for memory, but for reminder. And it is no true wisdom that you offer your disciples, but only its semblance; for by telling them of many things without teaching them you will make them seem to know much, while for the most part they know nothing; and as men filled, not [b] with wisdom, but with the conceit of wisdom, they will be a burden to their fellows.'

Ph. It is easy for you, Socrates, to make up tales from Egypt or anywhere else you fancy.[24]

---

24 The little myth of Theuth and Thamus is, like that of the cicadas, apparently Plato's own invention, though of course the personages belong to Egyptian history or legend. The inventor of writing in Greek legend was Prometheus; but he was unsuitable for Plato's purpose, since it would have been difficult to make anyone play against him the part that Thamus plays against Theuth. And in any case it was natural enough for Plato to go to Egypt for a tale of pre-history, just as in a later dialogue he goes to an Egyptian priest for his story of Atlantis.

Soc. Oh, but the authorities of the temple of Zeus at Dodona, my friend, said that the first prophetic utterances came from an oak-tree. In fact the people of those days, lacking the wisdom of you young people, were content in their simplicity to listen to trees or rocks, provided these told the truth. For you apparently it makes a difference [c] who the speaker is, and what country he comes from: you don't merely ask whether what he says is true or false.

Ph. I deserve your rebuke, and I agree that the man of Thebes is right in what he said about writing.

Soc. Then anyone who leaves behind him a written manual, and likewise anyone who takes it over from him, on the supposition that such writing will provide something reliable and permanent, must be exceedingly simple-minded; he must really be ignorant of Ammon's utterance, if he imagines that written words can do anything more than remind one who knows that which the writing is concerned with. [D]

Ph. Very true.

Soc. You know, Phaedrus, that's the strange thing about writing, which makes it truly analogous to painting. The painter's products stand before us as though they were alive: but if you question them, they maintain a most majestic silence. It is the same with written words: they seem to talk to you as though they were intelligent, but if you ask them anything about what they say, from a desire to be instructed, they go on telling you just the same thing for ever. And once a thing is put in writing, the composition, whatever it may be, drifts all over the [E] place, getting into the hands not only of those who understand it, but equally of those who have no business with it; it doesn't know how to address the right people, and not address the wrong. And when it is ill-treated and unfairly abused it always needs its parent to come to its help, being unable to defend or help itself.

Ph. Once again you are perfectly right.

Soc. But now tell me, is there another sort of discourse, that is [276] brother to the written speech, but of unquestioned legitimacy? Can we see how it originates, and how much better and more effective it is than the other?

Ph. What sort of discourse have you now in mind, and what is its origin?

Soc. The sort that goes together with knowledge, and is written in the soul of the learner: that can defend itself, and knows to whom it should speak and to whom it should say nothing.

Ph. You mean no dead discourse, but the living speech, the original of which the written discourse may fairly be called a kind of image.

Soc. Precisely. And now tell me this: if a sensible farmer had [B] some seeds to look after and wanted them to bear fruit, would he with serious intent plant them during the summer in a garden of Adonis,[25] and enjoy watching it producing fine fruit within eight days? If he did so

---

[25] A pot or window-box for forcing plants at the festival of Adonis.

at all, wouldn't it be in a holiday spirit, just by way of pastime? For serious purposes wouldn't he behave like a scientific farmer, sow his seeds in suitable soil, and be well content if they came to maturity within eight months?

Ph. I think we may distinguish as you say, Socrates, between [c] what the farmer would do seriously and what he would do in a different spirit.

Soc. And are we to maintain that he who has knowledge of what is just, honourable and good has less sense than the farmer in dealing with his seeds?

Ph. Of course not.

Soc. Then it won't be with serious intent that he 'writes them in water' [26] or that black fluid we call ink, using his pen to sow words that can't either speak in their own defence or present the truth adequately.

Ph. It certainly isn't likely.

Soc. No, it is not. He will sow his seed in literary gardens, I take [D] it, and write when he does write by way of pastime, collecting a store of refreshment both for his own memory, against the day 'when age oblivious comes', and for all such as tread in his footsteps; and he will take pleasure in watching the tender plants grow up. And when other men resort to other pastimes, regaling themselves with drinking-parties and such like, he will doubtless prefer to indulge in the recreation I refer to.

Ph. And what an excellent one it is, Socrates! How far superior [E] to the other sort is the recreation that a man finds in words, when he discourses about justice and the other topics you speak of.

Soc. Yes indeed, dear Phaedrus. But far more excellent, I think, is the serious treatment of them, which employs the art of dialectic. The dialectician selects a soul of the right type, and in it he plants and sows his words founded on knowledge, words which can defend both themselves and him who planted them, words which instead of remain- [277] ing barren contain a seed whence new words grow up in new characters; whereby the seed is vouchsafed immortality, and its possessor the fullest measure of blessedness that man can attain unto.

Ph. Yes, that is a far more excellent way.

Soc. Then now that that has been settled, Phaedrus, we can proceed to the other point.

Ph. What is that?

Soc. The point that we wanted to look into before we arrived at our present conclusion. Our intention was to examine the reproach levelled against Lysias on the score of speech-writing, and therewith the general question of speech-writing and what does and does not [B] make it an art. Now I think we have pretty well cleared up the question of art.

---

[26] A proverbial phrase for useless labour.

Ph. Yes, we did think so, but please remind me how we did it.

Soc. The conditions to be fulfilled are these: first, you must know the truth about the subject that you speak or write about: that is to say, you must be able to isolate it in definition, and having so defined it you must next understand how to divide it into kinds, until you reach the limit of division; secondly, you must have a corresponding discernment of the nature of the soul, discover the type of speech appro- [c] priate to each nature, and order and arrange your discourse accordingly, addressing a variegated soul in a variegated style that ranges over the whole gamut of tones, and a simple soul in a simple style. All this must be done if you are to become competent, within human limits, as a scientific practitioner of speech, whether you propose to expound or to persuade. Such is the clear purport of all our foregoing discussion.

Ph. Yes, that was undoubtedly how we came to see the matter.

Soc. And now to revert to our other question, whether the de- [D] livery and composition of speeches is honourable or base, and in what circumstances they may properly become a matter of reproach, our earlier conclusions have, I think, shown—

Ph. Which conclusions?

Soc. They have shown that any work, in the past or in the future, whether by Lysias or anyone else, whether composed in a private capacity or in the role of a public man who by proposing a law becomes the author of a political composition, is a matter of reproach to its author (whether or no the reproach is actually voiced) if he regards it as containing important truth of permanent validity. For ignorance of what is a waking vision and what is a mere dream-image of justice and injustice, good and evil, cannot truly be acquitted of involving [E] reproach, even if the mass of men extol it.

Ph. No indeed.

Soc. On the other hand, if a man believes that a written discourse on any subject is bound to contain much that is fanciful: that nothing that has ever been written whether in verse or prose merits much serious attention—and for that matter nothing that has ever been spoken in the declamatory fashion which aims at mere persuasion without any questioning or exposition: that in reality such compositions are, at the best, a means of reminding those who know the truth: [278] that lucidity and completeness and serious importance belong only to those lessons on justice and honour and goodness that are expounded and set forth for the sake of instruction, and are veritably written in the soul of the listener: and that such discourses as these ought to be accounted a man's own legitimate children—a title to be applied primarily to such as originate within the man himself, and secondarily to such of their sons and brothers as have grown up aright in the souls [B] of other men: the man, I say, who believes this, and disdains all manner of discourse other than this, is, I would venture to affirm, the man whose example you and I would pray that we might follow.

Ph. My own wishes and prayers are most certainly to that effect.

XXVI

278B-279C MESSAGES TO LYSIAS AND ISOCRATES

Soc. Then we may regard our literary pastime [27] as having reached
a satisfactory conclusion. Do you now go and tell Lysias that we two
went down to the stream where is the holy place of the Nymphs, and
there listened to words which charged us to deliver a message, first to
Lysias and all other composers of discourses, secondly to Homer [c]
and all others who have written poetry whether to be read or sung, and
thirdly to Solon and all such as are authors of political compositions
under the name of laws: to wit, that if any of them has done his work
with a knowledge of the truth, can defend his statements when challenged, and can demonstrate the inferiority of his writings out of his
own mouth, he ought not to be designated by a name drawn from those
writings, but by one that indicates his serious pursuit.   [D]

Ph. Then what names would you assign him?

Soc. To call him wise, Phaedrus, would, I think, be going too far: the
epithet is proper only to a god; a name that would fit him better, and
have more seemliness, would be 'lover of wisdom', or something similar.

Ph. Yes, that would be quite in keeping.

Soc. On the other hand, one who has nothing to show of more value
than the literary works on whose phrases he spends hours, twisting them
this way and that, pasting them together and pulling them apart,[28] [E]
will rightly, I suggest, be called a poet or speech-writer or law-writer.

Ph. Of course.

Soc. Then that is what you must tell your friend.

Ph. But what about yourself? What are you going to do? You too
have a friend who should not be passed over.

Soc. Who is that?

Ph. The fair Isocrates. What will be your message to him, Socrates,
and what shall we call him?

Soc. Isocrates is still young, Phaedrus, but I don't mind telling you
the future I prophesy for him.   [279]

Ph. Oh, what is that?

Soc. It seems to me that his natural powers give him a superiority
over anything that Lysias has achieved in literature, and also that in
point of character he is of a nobler composition; hence it would not

---

27 The reference is probably not to the whole dialogue, but to the discussion
   from 274A 6 onwards.
28 Dionysius of Halicarnassus (*de comp. verb.* p. 208, Reiske) tells us that Plato
   continued throughout his life 'combing and curling' (κτενίζων καὶ βοστρυχίζων)
   his dialogues, and that at his death a tablet was found with numerous variants
   of the opening sentence of the *Republic;* cf. also Diog. Laert. III, 37. It is possible that the present sentence reflects the impatience of Plato the philosopher
   with Plato the meticulous literary artist.

surprise me if with advancing years he made all his literary predecessors look like very small fry; that is, supposing him to persist in the actual type of writing in which he engages at present; still more so, if he should become dissatisfied with such work, and a sublimer impulse lead him to do greater things. For that mind of his, Phaedrus, contains an innate tincture of philosophy.

Well then, there's the report I convey from the gods of this place [B] to Isocrates my beloved, and there's yours for your beloved Lysias.

Ph. So be it. But let us be going, now that it has become less oppressively hot.

Soc. Oughtn't we first to offer a prayer to the divinities here?

Ph. To be sure.

Soc. Dear Pan, and all ye other gods that dwell in this place, grant that I may become fair within, and that such outward things as I have may not war against the spirit within me. May I count him rich who [C] is wise; and as for gold, may I possess so much of it as only a temperate man might bear and carry with him.

Is there anything more we can ask for, Phaedrus? The prayer contents me.

Ph. Make it a prayer for me too, since friends have all things in common.

Soc. Let us be going.

THE
LATER
PLATO

PARMENIDES (*in part:* 127-136)

127A-D ANTIPHON REPEATS PYTHODORUS' ACCOUNT OF THE MEETING

According to Antiphon, then, this was Pythodorus' account. Zeno and Parmenides once came to Athens for the Great Panathenaea. Par- [B] menides was a man of distinguished appearance. By that time he was well advanced in years, with hair almost white; he may have been sixty-five. Zeno was nearing forty, a tall and attractive figure. It was said that he had been Parmenides' favourite. They were staying with Pythodorus outside the walls in the Ceramicus. Socrates and a few others came [C] there, anxious to hear a reading of Zeno's treatise, which the two visitors had brought for the first time to Athens. Socrates was then quite young. Zeno himself read it to them; Parmenides at the moment had gone out. The reading of the arguments was very nearly over when Pythodorus himself came in, accompanied by Parmenides and Aristoteles, the [D] man who was afterwards one of the Thirty; so they heard only a small part of the treatise. Pythodorus himself, however, had heard it read by Zeno before.

127D-128E THE CONTENTS AND CHARACTER OF ZENO'S TREATISE

When Zeno had finished, Socrates asked him to read once more the first hypothesis of the first argument. He did so, and Socrates asked: What does this statement mean, Zeno? 'If things are many,' you say, [E]

254

'they must be both like and unlike. But that is impossible: unlike things cannot be like, nor like things unlike.' That is what you say, isn't it?

Yes, replied Zeno.

And so, if unlike things cannot be like or like things unlike, it is also impossible that things should be a plurality; if many things did exist, they would have impossible attributes. Is this the precise purpose of your arguments—to maintain, against everything that is commonly said, that things are not a plurality? Do you regard every one of your arguments as evidence of exactly that conclusion, and so hold that, in each argument in your treatise, you are giving just one more proof that a plurality does not exist? Is that what you mean, or am I understanding you [128] wrongly?

No, said Zeno, you have quite rightly understood the purpose of the whole treatise.

I see, Parmenides, said Socrates, that Zeno's intention is to associate himself with you by means of his treatise no less intimately than by his personal attachment. In a way, his book states the same position as your own; only by varying the form he tries to delude us into thinking that his thesis is a different one. You assert, in your poem, that the All is one; and for this you advance admirable proofs. Zeno, for his part, asserts that it is not a plurality; and he too has many weighty proofs to bring forward. You assert unity, he asserts no plurality; each expresses himself in such a way that your arguments seem to have nothing in common, though really they come to very much the same thing. That is why your exposition and his seem to be rather over the heads of outsiders like ourselves.

Yes, Socrates, Zeno replied; but you have not quite seen the real [c] character of my book. True, you are as quick as a Spartan hound to pick up the scent and follow the trail of the argument; but there is a point you have missed at the outset. The book makes no pretence of disguising from the public the fact that it was written with the purpose you describe, as if such deception were something to be proud of. What you have pointed out is only incidental; the book is in fact a sort of defence of Parmenides' argument against those who try to make fun of it by [d] showing that his supposition, that there is a One, leads to many absurdities and contradictions. This book, then, is a retort against those who assert a plurality. It pays them back in the same coin with something to spare, and aims at showing that, on a thorough examination, their own supposition that there is a plurality leads to even more absurd consequences than the hypothesis of the One. It was written in that controversial spirit in my young days; and someone copied it surreptitiously, so that I had not even the chance to consider whether it should see the light or not. That is [e] where you are mistaken Socrates; you imagine it was inspired, not by a youthful eagerness for controversy, but by the more dispassionate aims of an older man; though, as I said, your description of it was not far wrong.

128E-130A SOCRATES OFFERS THE THEORY OF SEPARATE FORMS
AS EXPLAINING HOW ONE THING CAN HAVE TWO CONTRARY
CHARACTERS

I accept that, said Socrates, and I have no doubt it is as you say.
But tell me this. Do you not recognise that there exists, just by [129]
itself, a Form of Likeness and again another contrary Form, Unlikeness
itself, and that of these two Forms you and I and all the things we speak
of as 'many' come to partake? Also, that things which come to partake of
Likeness come to be alike in that respect and just in so far as they do
come to partake of it, and those that come to partake of Unlikeness come
to be unlike, while those which come to partake of both come to be both?
Even if all things come to partake of both, contrary as they are, and by
having a share in both are at once like and unlike one another, what
is there surprising in that? If one could point to things which are
simply 'alike' or 'unlike' proving to be unlike or alike, that no doubt would
be a portent; but when things which have a share in both are shown to
have both characters, I see nothing strange in that, Zeno; nor yet in a
proof that all things are one by having a share in unity and at the same
time many by sharing in plurality. But if anyone can prove that what is
simply Unity itself is many or that Plurality itself is one, then I shall [c]
begin to be surprised.

And so in all other cases; if the kinds or Forms themselves were shown
to have these contrary characters among themselves, there would be good
ground for astonishment; but what is there surprising in someone pointing
out that I am one thing and also many? When he wants to show that I
am many things, he can say that my right side is a different thing from
my left, my front from my back, my upper parts from my lower, since
no doubt I do partake of plurality. When he wants to prove that I am
one thing, he will say that I am one person among the seven of us, [D]
since I partake also of unity. So both statements are true. Accordingly, if
anyone sets out to show about things of this kind—sticks and stones, and
so on—that the same thing is many and one, we shall say that what he is
proving is that *something* is many and one, not that Unity is many or that
Plurality is one; he is not telling us anything wonderful, but only what
we should all admit. But, as I said just now, if he begins by distinguishing
the Forms apart just by themselves—Likeness, for instance, and Unlikeness, Plurality and Unity, Rest and Motion, and all the rest—and [E]
then shows that these Forms among themselves can be combined with,
or separate from, one another, then, Zeno, I should be filled with admiration. I am sure you have dealt with this subject very forcibly; but, as I
say, my admiration would be much greater if anyone could show that
these same perplexities are everywhere involved in the Forms themselves
—among the objects we apprehend in reflection, just as you and [130]
Parmenides have shown them to be involved in the things we see.

130A-E PARMENIDES CRITICISES THE THEORY OF FORMS

(1) *What classes of things have Forms?*

While Socrates was speaking, Pythodorus said he was expecting every moment that Parmenides and Zeno would be annoyed; but they listened very attentively and kept on exchanging glances and smiles in admiration of Socrates. When he ended, Parmenides expressed this feeling: Socrates, he said, your eagerness for discussion is admirable. And now tell me: have you yourself drawn this distinction you speak of and separated apart on the one side Forms themselves and on the other the things that share in them? Do you believe that there is such a thing as Likeness itself apart from the likeness that we possess, and so on with Unity and Plurality and all the terms in Zeno's argument that you have just been listening to?

Certainly I do, said Socrates.

And also in cases like these, asked Parmenides: is there, for example, a Form of Rightness or of Beauty or of Goodness, and all of such things?

Yes.

And again, a Form of Man, apart from ourselves and all other men like us—a Form of Man as something by itself? Or a Form of Fire or of Water?

I have often been puzzled about those things, Parmenides, whether one should say that the same thing is true in their case or not.

Are you also puzzled, Socrates, about cases that might be thought absurd, such as hair or mud or dirt or any other trivial and undignified objects? Are you doubtful whether or not to assert that each of these has a separate Form distinct from things like those we handle?   [D]

Not at all, said Socrates; in these cases, the things are just the things we see; it would surely be too absurd to suppose that they have a Form. All the same, I have sometimes been troubled by a doubt whether what is true in one case may not be true in all. Then, when I have reached that point, I am driven to retreat, for fear of tumbling into a bottomless pit of nonsense. Anyhow, I get back to the things which we were just now speaking of as having Forms, and occupy my time with thinking about them.

That, replied Parmenides, is because you are still young, Socrates,   [E] and philosophy has not yet taken hold of you so firmly as I believe it will some day. You will not despise any of these objects then; but at present your youth makes you still pay attention to what the world will think.

(2) *Objections to Participation.*   [130E-131E]

(a) *A thing cannot contain either the Form as a whole or a part of it.*

(*Parmenides continues*) However that may be, tell me this. You say you hold that there exist certain Forms, of which these other things come to partake and so to be called after their names: by coming to

partake of Likeness or Largeness or Beauty or Justice, they be-   [131]
come like or large or beautiful or just?

Certainly, said Socrates.

Then each thing that partakes receives as its share either the Form as
a whole or a part of it? Or can there be any other way of partaking
besides this?

No, how could there be?

Do you hold, then, that the Form as a whole, a single thing, is in each
of the many, or how?

Why should it not be in each, Parmenides?

If so, a Form which is one and the same will be at the same time,   [B]
as a whole, in a number of things which are separate, and consequently
will be separate from itself.

No, it would not, replied Socrates, if it were like one and the same day,
which is in many places at the same time and nevertheless is not separate
from itself. Suppose any given Form is in them all at the same time as one
and the same thing in that way.

I like the way you make out that one and the same thing is in many
places at once, Socrates. You might as well spread a sail over a number
of people and then say that the one sail as a whole was over them all.
Don't you think that is a fair analogy?

Perhaps it is.   [C]

Then would the sail as a whole be over each man, or only a part over
one, another part over another?

Only a part.

In that case, Socrates, the Forms themselves must be divisible into
parts, and the things which have a share in them will have a part for their
share. Only a part of any given Form, and no longer the whole of it, will
be in each thing.

Evidently, on that showing.

Are you, then, prepared to assert that we shall find the single Form
actually being divided? Will it still be one?

Certainly not.

No, for consider this. Suppose it is Largeness itself that you are going
to divide into parts, and that each of the many large things is to be   [D]
large by virtue of a part of Largeness which is smaller than Largeness
itself. Will not that seem unreasonable?

It will indeed.

And again, if it is Equality that a thing receives some small part of,
will that part, which is less than Equality itself, make its possessor equal
to something else?

No, that is impossible.

Well, take Smallness: is one of us to have a portion of Smallness, and
is Smallness to be larger than that portion, which is a part of it? On this
supposition again Smallness itself will be larger, and anything to which
the portion taken is added will be smaller, and not larger, than it   [E]
was before.

That cannot be so.

Well then, Socrates, how are the other things going to partake of your Forms, if they can partake of them neither in part nor as wholes?

Really, said Socrates, it seems no easy matter to determine in any way.

(b) *The Third Man* [131E-132B]

Again, there is another question.

What is that?

How do you feel about this? I imagine your ground for believing [132] in a single Form in each case is this: when it seems to you that a number of things are large, there seems, I suppose, to be a certain single character which is the same when you look at them all; hence you think that Largeness is a single thing.

True, he replied.

But now take Largeness itself and the other things which are large. Suppose you look at all these in the same way in your mind's eye, will not yet another unity make its appearance—a Largeness by virtue of which they all appear large?

So it would seem.

If so, a second Form of Largeness will present itself, over and above Largeness itself and the things that share in it; and again, covering all these, yet another, which will make all of them large. So each of [B] your Forms will no longer be one, but an indefinite number.

These objections cannot be met by making the Form a thought in a mind [132B-C]

But, Parmenides, said Socrates, may it not be that each of these Forms is a thought, which cannot properly exist anywhere but in a mind. In that way each of them can be one and the statements that have just been made would no longer be true of it.

Then, is each Form one of these thoughts and yet a thought of nothing?

No, that is impossible.

So it is a thought of something?

Yes.

Of something that is, or of something that is not? [C]

Of something that is.

In fact, of some *one* thing which that thought observes to cover all the cases, as being a certain single character?

Yes.

Then will not this thing that is thought of as being one and always the same in all cases be a Form?

That again seems to follow.

And besides, said Parmenides, according to the way in which you assert that the other things have a share in the Forms, must you not hold either that each of those things consists of thoughts, so that all things think, or else that they are thoughts which nevertheless do not think?

That too is unreasonable, replied Socrates.

Can the objections be met by making the Forms patterns of which there are likenesses in things?   [132c-133a]

(*Socrates continues.*) But, Parmenides, the best I can make of the matter is this: that these Forms are as it were patterns fixed in the nature of things; the other things are made in their image and are likenesses; and this participation they come to have in the Forms is nothing but their being made in their image.

Well, if a thing is made in the image of the Form, can that Form fail to be like the image of it, in so far as the image was made in its likeness? If a thing is like, must it not be like something that is like it?

It must.

And must not the thing which is like share with the thing that is   [E] like it in one and the same thing (character)?

Yes.

And will not that in which the like things share, so as to be alike, be just the Form itself that you spoke of?

Certainly.

If so, nothing can be like the Form, nor can the Form be like anything. Otherwise a second Form will always make its appearance over and above the first Form; and if that second Form is like anything,   [133] yet a third; and there will be no end to this emergence of fresh Forms, if the Form is to be like the thing that partakes of it.

Quite true.

It follows that the other things do not partake of Forms by being like them; we must look for some other means by which they partake.

So it seems.

(3) *Will not the separate Forms be unknowable by us?*   [133a-134e]

You see then, Socrates, said Parmenides, what great difficulties there are in asserting their existence as Forms just by themselves?

I do indeed.

I assure you, then, you have as yet hardly a notion of how great   [B] they will be, if you are going to set up a single Form for every distinction you make among things.

How so?

The worst difficulty will be this, though there are plenty more. Suppose someone should say that the Forms, if they are such as we are saying they must be, cannot even be known. One could not convince him that he was mistaken in that objection, unless he chanced to be a man of wide experience and natural ability, and were willing to follow one through a long and remote train of argument. Otherwise there would be no way of convincing a man who maintained that the Forms were unknow-   [C] able.

Why so, Parmenides?

Because, Socrates, I imagine that you or anyone else who asserts that each of them has a real being 'just by itself', would admit, to begin with, that no such real being exists in our world.

True; for how could it then be just by itself?

Very good, said Parmenides. And further, those Forms which are what they are with reference to one another, have their being in such references among themselves, not with reference to those likenesses (or whatever we are to call them) in our world, which we possess and so come to [D] be called by their several names. And, on the other hand, these things in our world which bear the same names as the Forms are related among themselves, not to the Forms; and all the names of that sort that they bear have reference to one another, not to the Forms.

How do you mean? asked Socrates.

Suppose, for instance, one of us is master or slave of another; he is not, of course, the slave of Master itself, the essential Master, nor, if he is a master, is he master of Slave itself, the essential Slave, but, being a [E] man, is master or slave of another man; whereas Mastership itself is what it is (mastership) of Slavery itself, and Slavery itself is slavery to Mastership itself. The significance of things in our world is not with reference to things in that other world, nor have these their significance with reference to us; but as I say, the things in that world are what they are with reference to one another and towards one another; and so likewise are the things in our world. You see what I mean?

Certainly I do.

And similarly Knowledge itself, the essence of Knowledge, will [134] be knowledge of that Reality itself, the essentially real.

Certainly.

And again any given branch of Knowledge in itself will be knowledge of some department of real things as it is in itself, will it not?

Yes.

Whereas the knowledge in our world will be knowledge of the reality in our world; and it will follow again that each branch of knowledge in our world must be knowledge of some department of things that [B] exist in our world.

Necessarily.

But, as you admit, we do not possess the Forms themselves, nor can they exist in our world.

No.

And presumably the Forms, just as they are in themselves, are known by the Form of Knowledge itself?

Yes.

The Form which we do not possess.

True.

Then, none of the Forms is known by us, since we have no part in Knowledge itself.

Apparently not.

So Beauty itself or Goodness itself and all the things we take as Forms in themselves, are unknowable to us.

I am afraid that is so.

Then here is a still more formidable consequence for you to consider.

What is that?

You will grant, I suppose, that if there is such a thing as a Form, Knowledge itself, it is much more perfect than the knowledge in our world; and so with Beauty and all the rest.

Yes.

And if anything has part in this Knowledge itself, you would agree that a god has a better title than anyone else to possess the most perfect knowledge?

Undoubtedly.

Then will the god, who possesses Knowledge itself, be able to [D] know the things in our world?

Why not?

Because we have agreed that those Forms have no significance with reference to things in our world, nor have things in our world any significance with reference to them. Each set has it only among themselves.

Yes, we did.

Then if this most perfect Mastership and most perfect Knowledge are in the gods' world, the gods' Mastership can never be exercised over [E] us, nor their Knowledge know us or anything in our world. Just as we do not rule over them by virtue of rule as it exists in our world and we know nothing that is divine by our knowledge, so they, on the same principle, being gods, are not our masters nor do they know anything of human concerns.

But surely, said Socrates, an argument which would deprive the gods of knowledge, would be too strange.

The Forms are admitted to be necessary for all thought [134E-135C]
and discourse

And yet, Socrates, Parmenides went on, these difficulties and many more besides are inevitably involved in the Forms, if these char- [135] acters of things really exist and one is going to distinguish each Form as a thing just by itself. The result is that the hearer is perplexed and inclined either to question their existence, or to contend that, if they do exist, they must certainly be unknowable by our human nature. Moreover, there seems to be some weight in these objections, and, as we were saying, it is extraordinarily difficult to convert the objector. Only a man of exceptional gifts will be able to see that a Form, or essence just by itself, does exist in each case; and it will require someone still more remarkable [B] to discover it and to instruct another who has thoroughly examined all these difficulties.

I admit that, Parmenides; I quite agree with what you are [135B] saying.

But on the other hand, Parmenides continued, if, in view of all these difficulties and others like them, a man refuses to admit that Forms of things exist or to distinguish a definite Form in every case, he will have nothing on which to fix his thought, so long as he will not allow [c] that each thing has a character which is always the same; and in so doing he will completely destroy the significance of all discourse. But of that consequence I think you are only too well aware.

True.

135C-136E TRANSITION TO THE SECOND PART

What are you going to do about philosophy, then? Where will you turn while the answers to these questions remain unknown?

I can see no way out at the present moment.

That is because you are undertaking to define 'Beautiful', 'Just', 'Good', and other particular Forms, too soon, before you have had a [D] preliminary training. I noticed that the other day when I heard you talking here with Aristoteles. Believe me, there is something noble and inspired in your passion for argument; but you must make an effort and submit yourself, while you are still young, to a severer training in what the world calls idle talk and condemns as useless. Otherwise, the truth will escape you.

What form, then, should this exercise take, Parmenides?

The form that Zeno used in the treatise you have been listening to. With this exception: there was one thing you said to him which [E] impressed me very much: you would not allow the survey to be confined to visible things or to range only over that field; it was to extend to those objects which are specially apprehended by discourse and can be regarded as Forms.

Yes, because in that other field there seems to be no difficulty about showing that things are both like and unlike and have any other character you please.

You are right. But there is one thing more you must do. If you want to be thoroughly exercised, you must not merely make the supposition that such and such a thing *is* and then consider the consequences; you [136] must also take the supposition that that same thing *is not*.

How do you mean?

Take, if you like, the supposition that Zeno made: *'If there is a plurality of things'*. You must consider what consequences must follow both for those many things with reference to one another and to the One, and also for the One with reference to itself and to the many. Then again, on the supposition that *there is not a plurality*, you must consider what will follow both for the One and for the many, with reference to themselves and to each other. . . .

THEAETETUS (*in part*)

PERSONS OF THE DIALOGUE

Socrates   Theaetetus   Theodorus

·   ·   ·

SOCR.   Do you fancy it is a small matter to discover the nature of   [148c]
knowledge? Is it not one of the hardest questions?
THEAET.   One of the very hardest, I should say.
SOCR.   You may be reassured, then, about Theodorus' account of you,
and set your mind on finding a definition of knowledge, as of any-   [D]
thing else, with all the zeal at your command.
THEAET.   If it depends on my zeal, Socrates, the truth will come to light.
SOCR.   Forward, then, on the way you have just shown so well. Take as
a model your answer about the roots: just as you found a single character
to embrace all that multitude, so now try to find a single formula that
applies to the many kinds of knowledge.
THEAET.   But I assure you, Socrates, I have often set myself to   [E]
study that problem, when I heard reports of the questions you ask. But
I cannot persuade myself that I can give any satisfactory solution or
that anyone has ever stated in my hearing the sort of answer you require.
And yet I cannot get the question out of my mind.

Socrates' art of midwifery

SOCR.   My dear Theaetetus, that is because your mind is not empty or
barren. You are suffering the pains of travail.
THEAET.   I don't know about that, Socrates. I am only telling you how
I feel.
SOCR.   How absurd of you, never to have heard that I am the son   [149]
of a midwife, a fine buxom woman called Phaenarete!
THEAET.   I have heard that.
SOCR.   Have you also been told that I practise the same art?
THEAET.   No, never.
SOCR.   It is true, though; only don't give away my secret. It is not known
that I possess this skill; so the ignorant world describes me in other
terms as an eccentric person who reduces people to hopeless perplexity.
Have you been told that too?
THEAET.   I have.   [B]
SOCR.   Shall I tell you the reason?
THEAET.   Please do.
SOCR.   Consider, then, how it is with all midwives; that will help you to
understand what I mean. I dare say you know that they never attend other
women in childbirth so long as they themselves can conceive and bear
children, but only when they are too old for that.

THEAET. Of course.

SOCR. They say that is because Artemis, the patroness of childbirth, is herself childless; and so, while she did not allow barren women to be midwives, because it is beyond the power of human nature to achieve [C] skill without any experience, she assigned the privilege to women who were past child-bearing, out of respect to their likeness to herself.

THEAET. That sounds likely.

SOCR. And it is more than likely, is it not, that no one can tell so well as a midwife whether women are pregnant or not?

THEAET. Assuredly.

SOCR. Moreover, with the drugs and incantations they administer, midwives can either bring on the pains of travail or allay them at [D] their will, make a difficult labour easy, and at an early stage cause a miscarriage if they so decide.

THEAET. True.

SOCR. Have you also observed that they are the cleverest match-makers, having an unerring skill in selecting a pair whose marriage will produce the best children?

THEAET. I was not aware of that.

SOCR. Well, you may be sure they pride themselves on that more than on cutting the umbilical cord. Consider the knowledge of the sort [E] of plant or seed that should be sown in any given soil; does not that go together with skill in tending and harvesting the fruits of the earth? They are not two different arts?

THEAET. No, the same.

SOCR. And so with a woman; skill in the sowing is not to be separated from skill in the harvesting?

THEAET. Probably not.

SOCR. No; only, because there is that wrong and ignorant way of [150] bringing together man and woman which they call pandering, midwives, out of self-respect, are shy even of matchmaking, for fear of falling under the accusation of pandering. Yet the genuine midwife is the only successful matchmaker.

THEAET. That is clear.

SOCR. All this, then, lies within the midwife's province; but her performance falls short of mine. It is not the way of women sometimes to bring forth real children, sometimes mere phantoms, such that it is [B] hard to tell the one from the other. If it were so, the highest and noblest task of the midwife would be to discern the real from the unreal, would it not?

THEAET. I agree.

SOCR. My art of midwifery is in general like theirs; the only difference is that my patients are men, not women, and my concern is not with the body but with the soul that is in travail of birth. And the highest point of my art is the power to prove by every test whether the off- [C] spring of a young man's thought is a false phantom or instinct with life and truth. I am so far like the midwife, that I cannot myself give birth to wisdom; and the common reproach is true, that, though I question others, I can myself bring nothing to light because there is no wisdom in me. The reason is this: heaven constrains me to serve as a midwife, but has debarred me from giving birth. So of myself I have no sort of [D] wisdom, nor has any discovery ever been born to me as the child of my soul. Those who frequent my company at first appear, some of them, quite unintelligent; but, as we go further with our discussions, all who are favoured by heaven make progress at a rate that seems surprising to others as well as to themselves, although it is clear that they have never learnt anything from me; the many admirable truths they bring to birth have been discovered by themselves from within. But the delivery is heaven's work and mine.

The proof of this is that many who have not been conscious of my [E] assistance but have made light of me, thinking it was all their own doing, have left me sooner than they should, whether under others' influence or of their own motion, and thenceforward suffered miscarriage of their thoughts through falling into bad company; and they have lost the children of whom I had delivered them by bringing them up badly, caring more for false phantoms than for the true; and so at last their lack of understanding has become apparent to themselves and to [151] everyone else. Such a one was Aristides, son of Lysimachus, and there have been many more. When they come back and beg for a renewal of our intercourse with extravagant protestations, sometimes the divine warning that comes to me forbids it; with others it is permitted, and these begin again to make progress. In yet another way, those who seek my company have the same experience as a woman with child: they suffer the pains of labour and, by night and day, are full of distress far greater than a woman's; and my art has power to bring on these [B] pangs or to allay them. So it fares with these; but there are some, Theaetetus, whose minds, as I judge, have never conceived at all. I see that they have no need of me and with all goodwill I seek a match for them. Without boasting unduly, I can guess pretty well whose society will profit them. I have arranged many of these matches with Prodicus, and with other men of inspired sagacity.

And now for the upshot of this long discourse of mine. I suspect that, as you yourself believe, your mind is in labour with some thought it has conceived. Accept, then, the ministration of a midwife's son who [C] himself practises his mother's art, and do the best you can to answer the questions I ask. Perhaps when I examine your statements I may judge one or another of them to be an unreal phantom. If I then take the abortion from you and cast it away, do not be savage with me like a woman robbed of her first child. People have often felt like that towards me and been positively ready to bite me for taking away some foolish notion they have conceived. They do not see that I am doing them a kindness. They have not learnt that no divinity is ever ill-disposed [D] towards man, nor is such action on my part due to unkindness; it is only that I am not permitted to acquiesce in falsehood and suppress the truth.

So, Theaetetus, start again and try to explain what knowledge is. Never say it is beyond your power; it will not be so, if heaven wills and you take courage.

Theaetetus identifies knowledge with perception

THEAET. Well, Socrates, with such encouragement from a person like you, it would be a shame not to do one's best to say what one can. It seems to me that one who knows something is perceiving the thing [E] he knows, and, so far as I can see at present, knowledge is nothing but perception.

SOCR. Good; that is the right spirit in which to express one's opinion. But now suppose we examine your offspring together, and see whether it is a mere wind-egg or has some life in it. Perception, you say, is knowledge?

THEAET. Yes.

SOCR. The account you give of the nature of knowledge is not, by any means, to be despised. It is the same that was given by [152] Protagoras, though he stated it in a somewhat different way. He says, you will remember, that 'man is the measure of all things—alike of the being of things that are and of the not-being of things that are not'. No doubt you have read that.

THEAET. Yes, often.

SOCR. He puts it in this sort of way, doesn't he?—that any given thing 'is to me such as it appears to me, and is to you such as it appears to you,' you and I being men.

THEAET. Yes, that is how he puts it.

SOCR. Well, what a wise man says is not likely to be nonsense. So [B] let us follow up his meaning. Sometimes, when the same wind is blowing, one of us feels chilly, the other does not; or one may feel slightly chilly, the other quite cold.

THEAET. Certainly.

SOCR. Well, in that case are we to say that the wind in itself is cold or not cold? Or shall we agree with Protagoras that it is cold to the one who feels chilly, and not to the other?

THEAET. That seems reasonable.

SOCR. And further that it so 'appears' to each of us?

THEAET. Yes.

SOCR. And 'appears' means that he 'perceives' it so?

THEAET. True.

SOCR. 'Appearing', then, is the same thing as 'perceiving', in the [C] case of what is hot or anything of that kind. They *are* to each man such as he *perceives* them.

THEAET. So it seems.

SOCR. Perception, then, is always of something that *is*, and, as being knowledge, it is infallible.

THEAET. That is clear.

.   .   .

[155B]

Socr. ... When we say that I, being of the height you see, without gaining or losing in size, may within a year be taller (as I am now) than a youth like you, and later on be shorter, not because I have lost [c] anything in bulk, but because you have grown. For apparently I am later what I was not before, and yet have not become so; for without the process of becoming the result is impossible, and I could not be in process of becoming shorter without losing some of my bulk. I could give you countless other examples, if we are to accept these. For I think you follow me, Theaetetus; I fancy, at any rate, such puzzles are not altogether strange to you.

Theaet. No; indeed it is extraordinary how they set me wondering whatever they can mean. Sometimes I get quite dizzy with thinking of them.

Socr. That shows that Theodorus was not wrong in his estimate [D] of your nature. This sense of wonder is the mark of the philosopher. Philosophy indeed has no other origin, and he was a good genealogist who made Iris the daughter of Thaumas.[1] Do you now begin to see the explanation of all this which follows from the theory we are attributing to Protagoras? Or is it not yet clear?

Theaet. I can't say it is yet.

Socr. Then perhaps you will be grateful if I help you to penetrate to the truth concealed in the thoughts of a man—or, I should say, of men— of such distinction.[2]   [E]

Theaet. Of course I shall be very grateful.

Socr. Then just take a look round and make sure that none of the un-initiate overhears us. I mean by the uninitiate the people who believe that nothing is real save what they can grasp with their hands and do not admit that actions or processes or anything invisible can count as real.

Theaet. They sound like a very hard and repellent sort of people.[3]   [156]

. . .

Socr. You have an absolute passion for discussion, Theodorus. I   [161] like the way you take me for a sort of bag full or arguments, and imagine I can easily pull out a proof to show that our conclusion is wrong.   [B] You don't see what is happening: the arguments never come out of me, they always come from the person I am talking with. I am only at a slight advantage in having the skill to get some account of the matter

---

1 The *Cratylus* connects Iris with εἴρειν (408B), and εἴρειν (λέγειν) with dialectic (398D). So Iris (philosophy) is daughter of Thaumas (wonder).

2 Observe the hints that the coming theory is one that 'we are attributing' to Protagoras, and not to him alone.

3 Like the physical bodies in whose reality they believe, with their essential property of hardness and resistance to touch.

from another's wisdom and entertain it with fair treatment. So now, I shall not give any explanation myself, but try to get it out of our friend.

THEOD. That is better, Socrates; do as you say.

.   .   .

Objections to a simple identification of Perceiving and Knowing

.   .   .

SOCR. Let us look at it in this way, then—this question whether [163A] knowledge and perception are, after all, the same thing or not. For that, you remember, was the point to which our whole discussion was directed, and it was for its sake that we stirred up all this swarm of queer doctrines, wasn't it?

THEAET. Quite true.

SOCR. Well, are we going to agree that, whenever we perceive [B] something by sight or hearing, we also at the same time know it? Take the case of a foreign language we have not learnt. Are we to say that we do not hear the sounds that foreigners utter, or that we both hear and know what they are saying? Or again, when we don't know our letters, are we to maintain that we don't see them when we look at them, or that, since we see them, we do know them?

THEAET. We shall say, Socrates, that we know just so much of them as we do see or hear. The shape and colour of the letters we both see and know; we hear and at the same time know the rising and falling [C] accents of the voice; but we neither perceive by sight and hearing nor yet know what a schoolmaster or an interpreter could tell us about them.

SOCR. Well done, Theaetetus. I had better not raise objections to that, for fear of checking your growth. But look, here is another objection threatening. How are we going to parry it?

THEAET. What is that?

SOCR. It is this. Suppose someone to ask: 'Is it possible for a man [D] who has once come to know something and still preserves a memory of it, not to know just that thing that he remembers at the moment when he remembers it?' This is, perhaps, rather a long-winded way of putting the question. I mean: Can a man who has become acquainted with something and remembers it, not know it?

THEAET. Of course not, Socrates; the supposition is monstrous.

SOCR. Perhaps I am talking nonsense, then. But consider: you call seeing 'perceiving', and sight 'perception', don't you?

THEAET. I do.

SOCR. Then, according to our earlier statement, a man who sees [E] something acquires from that moment knowledge of the thing he sees?

THEAET. Yes.

SOCR. Again, you recognise such a thing as memory?

THEAET. Yes.

SOCR. Memory of nothing, or of something?

THEAET. Of something, surely.

SOCR.   Of what one has become acquainted with and perceived—that sort of things?

THEAET.   Of course.

SOCR.   So a man sometimes remembers what he has seen?

THEAET.   He does.

SOCR.   Even when he shuts his eyes? Or does he forget when he shuts them?

THEAET.   No, Socrates; that would be a monstrous thing to say.

SOCR.   All the same, we shall have to say it, if we are to save our   [164] former statement. Otherwise, it goes by the board.

THEAET.   I certainly have a suspicion that you are right, but I don't quite see how. You must tell me.

SOCR.   In this way. One who sees, we say, acquires knowledge of what he sees, because it is agreed that sight or perception and knowledge are the same thing.

THEAET.   Certainly.

SOCR.   But suppose this man who sees and acquires knowledge of what he has seen, shuts his eyes; then he remembers the thing, but does not see it. Isn't that so?

THEAET.   Yes.

SOCR.   But 'does not see it' means 'does not know it', since 'sees' and   [B] 'knows' mean the same.

THEAET.   True.

SOCR.   Then the conclusion is that a man who has come to know a thing and still remembers it does not know it, since he does not see it; and we said that would be a monstrous conclusion.

THEAET.   Quite true.

SOCR.   Apparently, then, if you say that knowledge and perception are the same thing, it leads to an impossibility.

THEAET.   So it seems.

SOCR.   Then we shall have to say they are different.

THEAET.   I suppose so.

.   .   .

Defence of Protagoras   [165E-168C]

SOCR.   . . . Now, perhaps, you may wonder what argument Protagoras will find to defend his position. Shall we try to put it into words?

THEAET.   By all means.

SOCR.   No doubt, then, Protagoras will make all the points we have put forward in our attempt to defend him, and at the same time will   [166] come to close quarters with the assailant, dismissing us with contempt.[4] 'Your admirable Socrates', he will say, 'finds a little boy who is scared at

---

4 Protagoras will both ($\tau\epsilon$) urge, as we have done for him, that we are talking clap-trap (162D), that verbal disputation is futile (164B) and we must use words more carefully (165A), and ($\kappa\alpha\iota$) will come to grips (not with us, but) with the sophistic skirmisher and his armoury of eristic cavils, despising us for our feeble surrender to such weapons.

being asked whether one and the same person can remember and at the same time not know one and the same thing. When the child is frightened into saying No, because he cannot foresee the consequence, Socrates turns the conversation so as to make a figure of fun of my unfortunate self. You take things much too easily, Socrates. The truth of the matter is this: when you ask someone questions in order to canvass some opinion of mine and he is found tripping, then I am refuted only if his answers are such as I should have given; if they are different, it is he who is [B] refuted, not I. For instance, do you think you will find anyone to admit that one's present memory of a past impression is an impression of the same character as one had during the original experience, which is now over? It is nothing of the sort. Or again, will anyone shrink from admitting that it is possible for the same person to know and not to know the same thing? Or, if he is frightened of saying that, will he ever allow that a person who is changed is the *same* as he was before the change occurred; or rather, that he is *one* person at all, and not several, indeed an infinite succession of persons, provided change goes on happening—if we are [C] really to be on the watch against one another's attempts to catch at words? 'No,' he will say; 'show a more generous spirit by attacking what I actually say; and prove, if you can, that we have not, each one of us, his peculiar perceptions, or that, granting them to be peculiar, it would not follow that what appears to each becomes—or is, if we may use the word 'is'—for him alone to whom it appears. With this talk of pigs and baboons, you are behaving like a pig yourself,[5] and, what is more, you tempt your hearers to treat my writings in the same way, which is [D] not fair.
'For I do indeed assert that the truth is as I have written: each one of us is a measure of what is and of what is not; but there is all the difference in the world between one man and another just in the very fact that what is and appears to one is different from what is and appears to the other. And as for wisdom and the wise man, I am very far from saying they do not exist. By a wise man I mean precisely a man who can change any one of us, when what is bad appears and is to him, and make what is good appear and be to him. In this statement, again, don't set off in chase of words, but let me explain still more clearly what I mean. Remember [E] how it was put earlier in the conversation: to the sick man his food appears sour and is so; to the healthy man it is and appears the opposite. Now there is no call to represent either of the two as wiser—that cannot be— nor is the sick man to be pronounced unwise because he thinks [6] [167]

---

[5] The pig, in Greek, is an emblem of stupidity (ἀμαθία). *Lach.* 169D: 'Would not any pig know . . .' Cic. *Ac. Post.* i, 5, 18: *non sus docet Minervam.* This remark is less offensive than the English sounds.

[6] 'Thinks', 'judges' (δοξάξει), here replaces 'appears' (φαίνεσθαι). What is meant is the judgment stating the fact of a sense-impression: 'This food seems and is to me sour.' If Socrates' earlier expression, 'what every man believes as the result of perception' (ἃ ἂν δι᾽ αἰσθήσεως δοξάξῃ, 161D) is restricted to such judgments, they are not ignorant or foolish judgments; nor are they false.

as he does, or the healthy man wise because he thinks differently. What is wanted is a change to the opposite condition, because the other state is better.

'And so too in education a change has to be effected from the worse condition to the better; only, whereas the physician produces a change by means of drugs, the sophist does it by discourse. It is not that a man makes someone who previously thought what is false think what is true (for it is not possible either to think the thing that is not or to think anything but what one experiences, and all experiences are true);   [B] rather, I should say, when someone by reason of a depraved condition of mind has thoughts of a like character, one makes him, by reason of a sound condition, think other and sound thoughts, which some people ignorantly call true, whereas I should say that one set of thoughts is better than the other, but not in any way truer.[7] And as for the wise, my dear Socrates, so far from calling them frogs, I call them, when they have to do with the body, physicians, and when they have to do with plants, husbandmen. For I assert that husbandmen too, when plants are sickly and have depraved sensations, substitute for these sensations that   [c] are sound and healthy [8]; and moreover that wise and honest public speakers substitute in the community sound for unsound views of what is right. For I hold that whatever practices seem right and laudable to any particular State are so, for that State, so long as it holds by them. Only, when the practices are, in any particular case, unsound for them, the wise man substitutes others that are and appear sound. On the same principle the sophist, since he can in the same manner guide his pupils in the way they should go, is wise and worth a considerable fee to them when their   [D] education is completed. In this way it is true both that some men are wiser than others and that no one thinks falsely; and you, whether you like it or not, must put up with being a measure, since by these considerations my doctrine is saved from shipwreck. Now if you can dispute this doctrine in principle, do so by argument stating the case on the other side, or by asking questions, if you prefer that method, which has no terrors for a man of sense; on the contrary it ought to be specially agreeable to him. Only there is this rule to be observed: do not conduct   [E] your questioning unfairly. It is very unreasonable that one who professes a concern for virtue should be constantly guilty of unfairness in argument. Unfairness here consists in not observing the distinction between a debate and a conversation. A debate need not be taken seriously and

---

[7] The text is doubtful. The best sense is obtained by taking τίς (167A, 7) as the subject of a single sentence from ἐπεὶ (A, 6) to οὐδέν (B, 4). Read πονηρᾷ and χρηστῇ (sc. ψυχῆς ἕξει, with W.) and omit τὰ φαντάσματα (with Diels, *Vors.*⁴ ii, 225). It is the sophist, not the χρηστὴ ἕξις, that 'makes' the change to sound thoughts. The reading χρηστὴ will then be explained as an attempt to provide the ἐποίησε following it with a subject, made by someone who did not see that τίς (governing the earlier ἐποίησε, A. 7) is still the subject.

[8] Omitting τε καὶ ἀληθεῖς. Diels' suggestion (*Vors.*⁴ ii, 225) ὥστε καὶ ἀληθεῖς gives a wrong sense, for the unhealthy sensations are also true. The conjectures ἀληθείας (Schleiermacher), ἕξεις (Diès), πάθας (Richards) are not convincing.

one may trip up an opponent to the best of one's power; but a conversation should be taken in earnest; one should help out the other party and bring home to him only those slips and fallacies that are due to [168] himself or to his earlier instructors. If you follow this rule, your associates will lay the blame for their confusions and perplexities on themselves and not on you; they will like you and court your society, and disgusted with themselves, will turn to philosophy, hoping to escape from their former selves and become different men. But if, like so many, you take the opposite course, you will reach the opposite result: instead of turning your companions to philosophy, you will make them hate the whole [B] business when they get older. So, if you will take my advice, you will meet us in the candid spirit I spoke of, without hostility or contentiousness, and honestly consider what we mean when we say that all things are in motion and that what seems also is, to any individual or community. The further question whether knowledge is, or is not, the same thing as perception, you will consider as a consequence of these principles, not (as you did just now) basing your argument on the com- [C] mon use of words and phrases, which the vulgar twist into any sense they please and so perplex one another in all sorts of ways.'

. . .

Criticism of Protagoras' doctrine as extended to all judgments

SOCR. Let us begin, then, by coming to grips with the doctrine [169D] at the same point as before. Let us see whether or not our discontent was justified, when we criticised it as making every individual self-sufficient in wisdom. Protagoras then conceded that some people were superior in the matter of what is better or worse, and these, he said, were wise. Didn't he?

THEOD. Yes.

SOCR. If he were here himself to make that admission, instead of our conceding it for him in our defence, there would be no need to [E] reopen the question and make sure of our ground; but, as things are, we might be said to have no authority to make the admission on his behalf. So it will be more satisfactory to come to a more complete and clear agreement on this particular point; for it makes a considerable difference, whether this is so or not.

THEOD. That is true.

SOCR. Let us, then, as briefly as possible, obtain his agreement, not through any third person, but from his own statement. [170]

THEOD. How?

SOCR. In this way. He says—doesn't he?—that what seems true [9] to anyone is true for him to whom it seems so?

THEOD. He does.

---

[9] τὸ δοκοῦν here, as the context shows, mean 'what seems true'. Since Protagoras' maxim covered judgment, the interpretation is perfectly fair.

SOCR. Well now, Protagoras, we are expressing what seems true to a man, or rather to all men, when we say that everyone without exception holds that in some respects he is wiser than his neighbours and in others they are wiser than he. For instance, in moments of great danger and distress, whether in war or in sickness or at sea, men regard as a god anyone who can take control of the situation and look to him as a [B] saviour, when his only point of superiority is his knowledge. Indeed, the world is full of people looking for those who can instruct and govern men and animals and direct their doings, and on the other hand of people who think themselves quite competent to undertake the teaching and governing. In all these cases what can we say, if not that men do hold that wisdom and ignorance exist among them?

THEOD. We must say that.

SOCR. And they hold that wisdom lies in thinking truly, and ignorance in false belief?

THEOD. Of course.   [c]

SOCR. In that case, Protagoras, what are we to make of your doctrine? Are we to say that what men think is always true, or that it is sometimes true and sometimes false? From either supposition it results that their thoughts are not always true, but both true and false. For consider, Theodorus. Are you, or is any Protagorean, prepared to maintain that no one regards anyone else as ignorant or as making false judgments?

THEOD. That is incredible, Socrates.

SOCR. That, however, is the inevitable consequence of the doctrine [D] which makes man the measure of all things.

THEOD. How so?

SOCR. When you have formed a judgment on some matter in your own mind and express an opinion about it to me, let us grant that, as Protagoras' theory says, it is true for you; but are we to understand that it is impossible for us, the rest of the company, to pronounce any judgment upon your judgment; or, if we can, that we always pronounce your opinion to be true? Do you not rather find thousands of opponents who set their opinion against yours on every occasion and hold that your judgment and belief are false?

THEOD. I should just think so, Socrates; thousands and tens of [E] thousands, as Homer says; and they give me all the trouble in the world.

SOCR. And what then? Would you have us say that in such a case the opinion you hold is true for yourself and false for these tens of thousands?

THEOD. The doctrine certainly seems to imply that.

SOCR. And what is the consequence for Protagoras himself? Is it not this: supposing that not even he believed in man being the measure and the world in general did not believe it either—as in fact it doesn't—then this Truth which he wrote would not be true for anyone? If, on [171] the other hand, he did believe it, but the mass of mankind does not agree with him, then, you see, it is more false than true by just so much as the unbelievers outnumber the believers.

THEOD. That follows, if its truth or falsity varies with each individual opinion.

SOCR. Yes, and besides that it involves a really exquisite conclusion.[10] Protagoras, for his part, admitting as he does that everybody's opinion is true, must acknowledge the truth of his opponents' belief about his own belief, where they think he is wrong.

THEOD. Certainly.

SOCR. That is to say, he would acknowledge his own belief to be [B] false, if he admits that the belief of those who think him wrong is true?

THEOD. Necessarily.

SOCR. But the others, on their side, do not admit to themselves that they are wrong.

THEOD. No.

SOCR. Whereas Protagoras, once more, according to what he has written, admits that this opinion of theirs is as true as any other.

THEOD. Evidently.

SOCR. On all hands, then, Protagoras included, his opinion will be disputed, or rather Protagoras will join in the general consent—when he admits to an opponent the truth of his contrary opinion, from that [C] moment Protagoras himself will be admitting that a dog or the man in the street is not a measure of anything whatever that he does not understand. Isn't that so?

THEOD. Yes.

SOCR. Then, since it is disputed by everyone, the Truth of Protagoras is true to nobody—to himself no more than to anyone else.

THEOD. We are running my old friend too hard, Socrates.

SOCR. But it is not clear that we are outrunning the truth, my friend. Of course it is likely that, as an older man, he was wiser than we are; [D] and if at this moment he could pop his head up through the ground there as far as to the neck, very probably he would expose me thoroughly for talking such nonsense and you for agreeing to it, before he sank out of sight and took to his heels. However, we must do our best with such lights as we have and continue to say what we think.

．　　．　　．

Digression: The Philosopher

THEOD. What do you mean, Socrates? [174]

SOCR. The same thing as the story about the Thracian maidservant who exercised her wit at the expense of Thales, when he was looking up to study the stars and tumbled down a well. She scoffed at him for being so eager to know what was happening in the sky that he could not see what lay at his feet. Anyone who gives his life to philosophy is open

---

[10] Sextus, *Math.* vii, 389, says that an argument of this form, known as 'turning the tables' (περιτροπή), was used against Protagoras by Democritus, as well as by Plato here.

to such mockery. It is true that he is unaware what his next-door　[B]
neighbour is doing, hardly knows, indeed, whether the creature is a
man at all; he spends all his pains on the question, what man is, and what
powers and properties distinguish such a nature from any other.[11] You
see what I mean, Theodorus?

THEOD.　Yes; and it is true.

SOCR.　And so, my friend, as I said at first, on a public occasion or in
private company, in a law court or anywhere else, when he is forced　[C]
to talk about what lies at his feet or is before his eyes, the whole rabble
will join the maid-servants in laughing at him, as from inexperience he
walks blindly and stumbles into every pitfall. His terrible clumsiness
makes him seem so stupid. He cannot engage in an exchange of abuse,[12]
for, never having made a study of anyone's peculiar weaknesses, he has
no personal scandals to bring up; so in his helplessness he looks a fool.
When people vaunt their own or other men's merits, his unaffected　[D]
laughter makes him conspicuous and they think he is frivolous. When
a despot or king is eulogised, he fancies he is hearing some keeper of
swine or sheep or cows being congratulated on the quantity of milk he has
squeezed out of his flock; only he reflects that the animal that princes tend
and milk is more given than sheep or cows to nurse a sullen grievance,
and that a herdsman of this sort, penned up in his castle, is doomed by
sheer press of work to be as rude and uncultivated as the shepherd　[E]
in his mountain fold. He hears of the marvellous wealth of some landlord
who owns ten thousand acres or more; but that seems a small matter to
one accustomed to think of the earth as a whole. When they harp upon
birth—some gentleman who can point to seven generations of wealthy
ancestors—he thinks that such commendation must come from men of
purblind vision, too uneducated to keep their eyes fixed on the　[175]
whole or to reflect that any man has had countless myriads of ancestors
and among them any number of rich men and beggars, kings and slaves,
Greeks and barbarians. To pride oneself on a catalogue of twenty-five
progenitors going back to Heracles, son of Amphitryon, strikes him as
showing a strange pettiness of outlook. He laughs at a man who cannot
rid his mind of foolish vanity by reckoning that before Amphitryon　[B]
there was a twenty-fifth ancestor, and before him a fiftieth, whose
fortunes were as luck would have it. But in all these matters the world
has the laugh of the philosopher, partly because he seems arrogant, partly
because of his helpless ignorance in matters of daily life.

THEOD.　Yes, Socrates, that is exactly what happens.

SOCR.　On the other hand, my friend, when the philosopher drags the
other upwards to a height at which he may consent to drop the　[C]
question 'What injustice have I done to you or you to me?' and to think
about justice and injustice in themselves, what each is, and how they differ

---

[11] A clear allusion to the theory of Forms. The real object of knowledge is the
Form 'Man', not individual men.
[12] A constant feature of forensic speeches at Athens.

from one another and from anything else [13]; or to stop quoting poetry about the happiness of kings or of men with gold in store and think about the meaning of kingship and the whole question of human happiness and misery, what their nature is, and how humanity can gain the one and escape the other—in all this field, when that small, shrewd, legal mind has to render an account, then the situation is reversed. Now [D] it is he who is dizzy from hanging at such an unaccustomed height and looking down from mid-air. Lost and dismayed and stammering, he will be laughed at, not by maidservants or the uneducated—they will not see what is happening—but by everyone whose breeding has been the antithesis of a slave's.

Such are the two characters, Theodorus. The one is nursed in freedom and leisure, the philosopher, as you call him. He may be excused if [E] he looks foolish or useless when faced with some menial task, if he cannot tie up bedclothes into a neat bundle or flavour a dish with spices and a speech with flattery. The other is smart in the dispatch of all such services, but has not learnt to wear his cloak like a gentleman, or caught the accent of discourse that will rightly celebrate the true life of [176] happiness for gods and men.

THEOD. If you could convince everyone, Socrates, as you convince me, there would be more peace and fewer evils in the world.

SOCR. Evils, Theodorus, can never be done away with, for the good must always have its contrary; nor have they any place in the divine world; but they must needs haunt this region of our mortal nature. That is why we should make all speed to take flight from this world to the other; and that means becoming like the divine so far as we can, [B] and that again is to become righteous with the help of wisdom. But it is no such easy matter to convince men that the reasons for avoiding wickedness and seeking after goodness are not those which the world gives. The right motive is not that one should seem innocent and good— that is no better, to my thinking, than an old wives' tale—but let us state the truth in this way. In the divine there is no shadow of un- [C] righteousness, only the perfection of righteousness; and nothing is more like the divine than any one of us who becomes as righteous as possible. It is here that a man shows his true spirit and power or lack of spirit and nothingness. For to know this is wisdom and excellence of the genuine sort; not to know it is to be manifestly blind and base. All other forms of seeming power and intelligence in the rulers of society are as mean and vulgar as the mechanic's skill in handicraft. If a man's words [D] and deeds are unrighteous and profane, he had best not persuade himself that he is a great man because he sticks at nothing, glorying in his shame as such men do when they fancy that others say of them: They are no fools, no useless burdens to the earth, but men of the right sort to weather the storms of public life. Let the truth be told: they are what

---

[13] The moral Forms are here openly mentioned, and there are allusions to the allegory of the Cave in *Rep.* vi.

they fancy they are not, all the more for deceiving themselves; for they are ignorant of the very thing it most concerns them to know—the penalty of injustice. This is not, as they imagine, stripes and death, which do not always fall on the wrong-doer, but a penalty that cannot be escaped. [E]

THEOD. What penalty is that?

SOCR. There are two patterns, my friend, in the unchangeable nature of things, one of divine happiness, the other of godless misery—a truth to which their folly makes them utterly blind, unaware that in [177] doing injustice they are growing less like one of these patterns and more like the other. The penalty they pay is the life they lead, answering to the pattern they resemble. But if we tell them that, unless they rid themselves of their superior cunning, that other region which is free from all evil will not receive them after death, but here on earth they will dwell for all time in some form of life resembling their own and in the society of things as evil as themselves, all this will sound like foolishness to such strong and unscrupulous minds.

THEOD. So it will, Socrates.

SOCR. I have good reason to know it, my friend. But there is one [B] thing about them: when you get them alone and make them explain their objections to philosophy, then, if they are men enough to face a long examination without running away, it is odd how they end by finding their own arguments unsatisfying; somehow their flow of eloquence runs dry, and they become as speechless as an infant.

All this, however, is a digression; we must stop now, and dam the flood of topics that threatens to break in and drown our original [C] argument. With your leave, let us go back to where we were before.

THEOD. For my part, I rather prefer listening to your digressions, Socrates; they are easier to follow at my time of life. However, let us go back, if you like.

· · ·

Thinking

SOCR. Do you accept my description of the process of thinking? [189E]

THEAET. How do you describe it?

SOCR. As a discourse that the mind carries on with itself about any subject it is considering. You must take this explanation as coming from an ignoramus; but I have a notion that, when the mind is thinking, it is simply talking to itself, asking questions and answering them, and saying Yes or No. When it reaches a decision—which may come slowly or [190] in a sudden rush—when doubt is over and the two voices affirm the same thing, then we call that its 'judgment'. So I should describe thinking as discourse, and judgment as a statement pronounced, not aloud to someone else, but silently to oneself.[14]

---

[14] This account of the process of thinking and judgment is repeated in the *Sophist* 263, see below.

THEAET. I agree.

SOCR. It seems, then, that when a person thinks of one thing as another, he is affirming to himself that the one is the other.

. . .

Conclusion [210]

SOCR. So, apparently, to the question, What is knowledge? our definition will reply: 'Correct belief together with knowledge of a differentness'; for, according to it, 'adding an account' will come to that.

THEAET. So it seems.

SOCR. Yes; and when we are inquiring after the nature of knowledge, nothing could be sillier than to say that it is correct belief together with a *knowledge* of differentness or of anything whatever.

So, Theaetetus, neither perception, nor true belief, nor the addition of an 'account' to true belief can be knowledge. [B]

THEAET. Apparently not.

SOCR. Are we in labour, then, with any further child, my friend, or have we brought to birth all we have to say about knowledge?

THEAET. Indeed we have; and for my part I have already, thanks to you, given utterance to more than I had in me.

SOCR. All of which our midwife's skill pronounces to be mere wind-eggs and not worth the rearing?

THEAET. Undoubtedly.

SOCR. Then supposing you should ever henceforth try to conceive afresh, Theaetetus, if you succeed, your embryo thoughts will be [C] the better as a consequence of to-day's scrutiny; and if you remain barren, you will be gentler and more agreeable to your companions, having the good sense not to fancy you know what you do not know. For that, and no more, is all that my art can effect; nor have I any of that knowledge possessed by all the great and admirable men of our own day or of the past. But this midwife's art is a gift from heaven; my mother had it for women, and I for young men of a generous spirit [D] and for all in whom beauty dwells.

Now I must go to the portico of the King Archon to meet the indictment which Meletus has drawn up against me. But to-morrow morning, Theodorus, let us meet here again.

THE SOPHIST (*in part:* 216-18, 234-*end*)

PERSONS OF THE DIALOGUE

Theodorus   A stranger from Elea
Socrates   *Theaetetus*

Introductory conversation

THEODORUS.   Here we are, Socrates, faithful to our appointment   [216]
of yesterday; and, what is more, we have brought a guest with us. Our
friend here is a native of Elea; he belongs to the school of Parmenides
and Zeno, and is devoted to philosophy.

SOCRATES.   Perhaps, Theodorus, it is no ordinary guest but some god that
you have brought us unawares. Homer [1] tells us that gods attend   [B]
upon the goings of men of mercy and justice; and not least among them
the God of Strangers comes to mark the orderly or lawless doings of
mankind. Your companion may be one of those higher powers, who
intends to observe and expose our weakness in philosophic discourse, like
a very spirit of refutation.

THEOD.   That is not our friend's way, Socrates; he is more reasonable than
the devotees of verbal dispute. I should not call him a god by any means;
but there is something divine about him: I would say that of any   [C]
philosopher.

SOCR.   And rightly, my friend; but one might almost say that the type
you mention is hardly easier to discern than the god. Such men—the
genuine, not the sham philosophers—as they go from city to city surveying
from a height the life beneath them, appear, owing to the world's blindness, to wear all sorts of shapes. To some they seem of no account, to
others above all worth; now they wear the guise of statesmen, now of
sophists; and sometimes they may give the impression of simply   [D]
being mad. But if our guest will allow me, I should like to ask him what
his countrymen thought and how they used these names.   [217]

THEOD.   What names?

SOCR.   Sophist, Statesman, Philosopher.

THEOD.   What is your question exactly? What sort of difficulty about
these names have you in mind?

SOCR.   This: did they think of all these as a single type, or as two, or
did they distinguish three types and attach one of the three corresponding
names to each?

THEOD.   I imagine you are quite welcome to the information. Is not that
so, sir?

STRANGER.   Yes, Theodorus, perfectly welcome; and the answer is   [B]

---

[1] *Odyssey* ix, 270, and xvii, 483.

not difficult. They thought of them as three different types; but it is not so short and easy a task to define each one of them clearly.

THEOD. As luck would have it, Socrates, you have hit upon a subject closely allied to one on which we were pressing him with questions before we came here. He tried to put us off with the same excuse he has just made to you, though he admits he has been thoroughly instructed and has not forgotten what he heard.

SOCR. Do not deny us, then, the first favour we ask. Tell us this [c] much: which do you commonly prefer—to discourse at length by yourself on any matter you wish to make clear, or to use the method of asking questions, as Parmenides himself did on one occasion in developing some magnificent arguments in my presence, when I was young and he quite an elderly man?

STR. When the other party to the conversation is tractable and [D] gives no trouble, to address him is the easier course; otherwise, to speak by oneself.

SOCR. Then you may choose any of the company you will; they will all follow you and respond amenably. But if you take my advice, you will choose one of the younger men—Theaetetus here or any other you may prefer.

STR. I feel some shyness, Socrates, at the notion that, at my first meeting with you and your friends, instead of exchanging our ideas in the give and take of ordinary conversation, I should spin out a long dis- [E] course by myself or even address it to another, as if I were giving a display of eloquence.[2] For indeed the question you have just raised is not so easy a matter as one might suppose, on hearing it so simply put, but it calls for a very long discussion. On the other hand, to refuse you and your friends a request, especially one put to me in such terms as you have used, strikes me as a breach of civility in a guest. That Theaetetus should be the other party to our conversation is a proposal which my [218] earlier talk with him, as well as your recommendation, makes exceedingly welcome.

THEAETETUS. Then do as you say, sir; you will, as Socrates said, be conferring a favour on us all.

STR. On this point, Theaetetus, no more need be said; the discussion from now onwards must, it seems, be carried on with you. But if the long task should after all weigh heavy on you, your friends here, not I, must bear the blame.

THEAET. I do not feel at this moment as if I should sink under it; [B] but should something of that sort happen, we will call in Socrates' name-

---

[2] Three alternative procedures are suggested: (1) an unbroken monologue, such as the rhetorical Sophists preferred; (2) an exposition 'addressed to another', *i.e.* cast in the form of questions, to which the respondent merely answers 'yes' or 'no' as required (ὑπακούειν), like the young Aristotle in the *Parmenides;* (3) a genuine conversation, to which the respondent makes a real contribution. The Stranger's preference for the third marks that he understands 'dialectic' as Plato understood it.

sake here, who is of my own age and shares my pursuits. He is quite used to working out most questions with me.

STR. A good suggestion: that shall be for you to consider as our conversation goes forward. What now concerns us both is our joint inquiry. We had better, I think, begin by studying the Sophist and try to bring his nature to light in a clear formula. [c]

. . .

STR. About the Sophist: tell me, is it now clear that he is a sort of wizard, an imitator of real things—or are we still uncertain whether [235] he may not possess genuine knowledge of all the things he seems capable of disputing about?

THEAET. He cannot, sir. It is clear enough from what has been said that he is one of those whose province is play.

STR. Then we may class him as a wizard and an imitator of some sort.

THEAET. Certainly.

Division of Image-making into two species [235A-236C]

STR. Come then, it is now for us to see that we do not again relax the pursuit of our quarry. We may say that we have him en- [B] veloped in such a net as argument provides for hunting of this sort. He cannot shuffle out of this.

THEAET. Out of what?

STR. Out of being somewhere within the class of illusionists.[3]

THEAET. So far I quite agree with you.

STR. Agreed then that we should at once quarter the ground by dividing the art of Image-making, and if, as soon as we descend into that enclosure, we meet with the Sophist at bay, we should arrest him on [c] the royal warrant of reason, report the capture, and hand him over to the sovereign.[4] But if he should find some lurking-place among the subdivisions of this art of imitation, we must follow hard upon him, constantly dividing the part that gives him shelter, until he is caught. It any event there is no fear that he or any other kind shall ever boast of having eluded a process of investigation so minute and so comprehensive.

THEAET. Good; that is the way to go to work.

---

[3] θαυματοποιῶν means specially the puppet-showman, but it is used here to cover all species of 'imitators'—artists and poets as well as Sophists (cf. 224A). They are all 'creators of *eidola*'.

[4] Apelt illustrates the allusion to the Persian method (called 'draw-netting', σαγηνεία) of sweeping up the whole population of a district by means of a line of soldiers holding hands and marching across it. It is several times mentioned by Herodotus (*e.g.* vi, 31); and Plato (*Laws* 698D) says that Datis, ten years before Salamis, sent word to Athens that he had captured all the Eretrians by this method, under Darius' orders (the 'royal warrant') to transport all Eretrians and Athenians to Persia. The method is an admirable image for the procedure of the last section which has drawn the notion of Image-making or Imitation like a net around all the types called 'Sophists' collected for review. The net also includes other 'imitators', all the varieties of artist.

STR. Following, then, the same method of division as before, I seem once more to make out two forms of imitation; but as yet I do not [D] feel able to discover in which of the two the type we are seeking is to be found.

THEAET. Make your division first, at any rate, and tell us what two forms you mean.

STR. One art that I see contained in it is the making of likenesses (*eikastiké*). The perfect example of this consists in creating a copy that conforms to the proportions of the original in all three dimensions and giving moreover the proper colour to every part. [E]

THEAET. Why, is not that what all imitators try to do?

STR. Not those sculptors or painters whose works are of colossal size. If they were to reproduce the true proportions of a well-made figure,[5] as you know, the upper parts would look too small, and the lower too large, because we see the one at a distance, the other close at hand. [236]

THEAET. That is true.

STR. So artists, leaving the truth to take care of itself, do in fact put into the images they make, not the real proportions, but those that will appear beautiful.

THEAET. Quite so.

STR. The first kind of image, then, being like the original, may fairly be called a likeness (*eikon*).

THEAET. Yes.

STR. And the corresponding subdivision of the art of imitation may [B] be called by the name we used just now—Likeness-making.

THEAET. It may.

STR. Now, what are we to call the kind which only appears to be a likeness of a well-made figure because it is not seen from a satisfactory point of view, but to a spectator with eyes that could fully take in so large an object would not be even like the original it professes to resemble? Since it seems to be a likeness, but is not really so, may we not call it a semblance (*phantasma*)?

THEAET. By all means.

STR. And this is a very extensive class, in painting and in imitation of all sorts. [C]

THEAET. True.

STR. So the best name for the art which creates, not a likeness, but a semblance will be Semblance-making (*phantastiké*).

THEAET. Quite so.

STR. These, then, are the two forms of image-making I meant—the making of likenesses and the making of semblances.

---

5 'Well-made' (καλῶν), because what is in question is not improving the proportions of an ill-made model to conform to canons of beauty, but altering the proportions which are really beautiful so as to keep the appearance of beauty. Apelt mentions that, in the Epicurean inscription on a wall at Oenoanda, the letters in the top lines are cut larger than those in the lower, so that all may look the same size from below.

THEAET.   Good.

*Statement of the problems of unreal appearances and of falsity in
speech and thought*   [236c-237b]

STR.   Yes; but even now I cannot see clearly how to settle the doubt
I then expressed: under which of the two arts (likeness-making and
semblance-making) we must place the Sophist. It is really surprising
how hard it is to get a clear view of the man. At this very moment   [D]
he has, with admirable cleverness, taken refuge in a class [6] which baffles
investigation.

THEAET.   So it seems.

STR.   You assent, but do you recognise the class I mean, or has the current
of the argument carried you along to agree so readily from force of habit?

THEAET.   How? What are you referring to?

STR.   The truth is, my friend, that we are faced with an extremely difficult question. This 'appearing' or 'seeming' without really 'being'   [E]
and the saying of something which yet is not true—all these expressions
have always been and still are deeply involved in perplexity. It is extremely hard, Theaetetus, to find correct terms in which one may say or
think that falsehoods have a real existence, without being caught in a
contradiction by the mere utterance of such words.[7]   [237]

THEAET.   Why?

STR.   The audacity of the statement lies in its implication that 'what is
not' has being; for in no other way could a falsehood come to have being.
But, my young friend, when we were of your age the great Parmenides
from beginning to end testified against this, constantly telling us what he
also says in his poem:

'Never shall this be proved—that things that are not are; but do thou, in
thy inquiry, hold back thy thought from this way.'[8]

So we have the great man's testimony, and the best way to obtain a   [B]
confession of the truth may be to put the statement itself to a mild degree
of torture.[9] So, if it makes no difference to you, let us begin by studying
it on its own merits.

THEAET.   I am at your disposal. As for the argument, you must consider
the way that will best lead to a conclusion, and take me with you along it.

STR.   It shall be done.

------

[6] Namely 'unreal appearance and falsity.'

[7] Falsehoods being 'things which are not', as the Stranger next remarks. A common equivalent of 'speaking falsely' is 'saying the thing that is not', see *Theaet.*
188D ff. (p. 114). Campbell correctly interprets the construction. ψευδῆ is
placed where it stands for emphasis.

[8] *Parmenides,* frag. 7.

[9] The statement itself (that falsehood, or what is not, really exists) is compared
to a slave belonging to the *other* party in the suit, against whom Parmenides
has borne witness. The immediate sequel submits this statement (not Parmenides) to examination. Parmenides' own statement will be put to the question later (τὸν τοῦ πατρὸς Παρμενίδου ἀναγκαῖον ... βασανίζειν, 241D).

I

THE WORLDS OF REALITY AND APPEARANCE

(a) The totally unreal [237B-239C]

STR. (*continues*). Now tell me: we do not hesitate to utter the phrase 'that which has no sort of being'? [10]

THEAET. Surely not.

STR. Then setting aside disputation for its own sake [11] and playing with words, suppose one of this company were seriously required to concentrate his mind and tell us to what this name can be applied—'that [C] which is not'. Of what thing or of what sort of thing should we expect him to use it himself, and what would he indicate by it to the inquirer?

THEAET. That is a hard question. It is scarcely for a person like me to find an answer at all.

STR. Well, this much is clear at any rate: that the term 'what is not' must not be applied to anything that exists.

THEAET. Certainly not.

STR. And since it cannot be applied to what exists, neither can it properly be applied to 'something'.

THEAET. How so?

STR. Surely we can see that this expression 'something' is always [D] used of a thing that exists. We cannot use it just by itself in naked isolation from everything that exists, can we?

THEAET. No.

STR. Is your assent due to the reflection that to speak of 'something' is to speak of 'some *one* thing'? [12]

THEAET. Yes.

STR. Because you will admit that 'something' stands for one thing, as 'some things' stands for two or more.

THEAET. Certainly.

STR. So it seems to follow necessarily that to speak of what is not [E] 'something' is to speak of no thing at all.

---

[10] τὸ μηδαμῶς ὄν, the 'totally unreal' or 'absolute nonentity'. We can 'utter this phrase' (φθέγγεσθαι), but it will be shown to have no meaning.

[11] The problems to be stated had figured in Eristic debate, but our purpose is to face the real difficulties seriously.

[12] The accident that English confines 'some *one*' and 'no *one*' to persons, 'something', 'nothing' to things, makes translation awkward. Greek has (1) τις, 'some' (masc. someone, neut. something) with (in poetry) its contradictory οὔτις, 'not-some' (masc. no-one, neut. nothing); and (2) οὐδείς 'not even one' (masc. no-one, neut. no-thing) with its regular contradictory εἶς γέ τις, at least *some* one' (masc. *some*one, neut. *some*thing), which is used here, and has to be rendered 'some *one* thing', in order to introduce the word 'one'.

THEAET. Necessarily.

STR. Must we not even refuse to allow that in such a case a person is *saying* something, though he may be speaking of nothing? Must we not assert that he is not even saying anything when he sets about uttering the sounds 'a thing that is not'?

THEAET. That would certainly bring the argument to the last pitch of perplexity.

STR. 'No time for boasting yet.' There is more to come, in fact [238] the chief of all the difficulties and the first, for it goes to the very root of the matter.

THEAET. How do you mean? Do not hesitate to state it.

STR. When a thing exists, I suppose something else that exists may be attributed to it.

THEAET. Certainly.

STR. But can we say it is possible for something that exists to be attributed to what has no existence?

THEAET. How could it be?

STR. Well, among things that exist we include number in general.

THEAET. Yes, number must exist, if anything does. [B]

STR. We must not, then, so much as attempt to attach either plurality or unity in number to the non-existent.

THEAET. That would certainly seem to be wrong, according to our argument.

STR. How then can anyone utter the words 'things which are not', or 'that which is not', or even conceive such things in his mind at all, apart from number?

THEAET. How do you mean?

STR. When we speak of '*things* that are not', are we not undertaking to attribute plurality to them? [C]

THEAET. Yes.

STR. And unity, when we speak of '*that* which is not'?

THEAET. Clearly.

STR. And yet we admit that it is not justifiable or correct to set about attaching something that exists to the non-existent.

THEAET. Quite true.

STR. You see the inference then: one cannot legitimately utter the words, or speak or think of that which just simply is not; it is unthinkable, not to be spoken of or uttered or expressed.[13]

THEAET. Quite true.

STR. Perhaps then I was mistaken in saying just now that I was [D]

---

13 ἄλογον, not 'irrational', but 'incapable of being expressed in discourse' (λόγος). There is no *meaning* conveyed (cf. *Parm.* 142A). ἄρρητον means that there is nothing for the words to *refer to*. Plato is echoing Parmenides' warning against the 'Way of Not-Being', 'to leave that way as unthinkable, unnameable; for it is no true way' (frag. 8, 15).

going to state the greatest difficulty it presents; whereas there is a worse one still that we can formulate.

THEAET. What is that?

STR. I am surprised you do not see from the very phrases I have just used that the non-existent reduces even one who is refuting its claims [14] to such straits that, as soon as he sets about doing so, he is forced to contradict himself.

THEAET. How? Explain more clearly.

STR. You must not look to me for illumination. I who laid it down that the non-existent could have neither unity nor plurality, have not [E] only just now but at this very moment spoken of it as one thing: for I am saying '*the* non-existent'. You see what I mean?

THEAET. Yes.

STR. And again a little while ago I was speaking of its *being* a thing not to be uttered or spoken of or expressed. Do you follow?

THEAET. Yes, of course.

STR. Well, then, in trying to apply that term 'being' to it, was I not contradicting what I said before? [15]   [239]

THEAET. Evidently.

STR. And again in applying the term 'the', was I not addressing it as singular? [16]

THEAET. Yes.

STR. And again in speaking of it as 'a thing not to be expressed or spoken of or uttered', I was using language as if referring to a single thing.

THEAET. Certainly.

STR. Whereas we are admitting that, if we are to speak strictly, we ought not to specify it as either one thing or many or even to call it 'it' at all; for even that appellation means ascribing to it the character of singleness.

THEAET. Quite so.

STR. In that case there is nothing to be said for me. I shall be [B] found to have had the worst of it, now and all along, in my criticism of the non-existent. Accordingly, as I said, we must not look to anything I have to say for the correct way of describing the non-existent; we must turn to you for that. Come along now.

THEAET. What do you mean?

STR. Come, you are young; show your spirit and make the best effort you can. Try, without attributing being or unity or plurality to the non-existent, to find some form of words describing it correctly.

THEAET. I should need an extraordinary zeal for such an enter- [C] prise in face of what has happened to you.

---

[14] Refuting any claim it might make to 'being'. I cannot even deny its existence without contradicting myself by speaking of it at all.

[15] The reference is to 238A: nothing that has existence must be attributed to the non-existent. 'Being' ($\tau\grave{o}$ $\epsilon\tilde{\iota}\nu\alpha\iota$) is something that exists, in the same sense that number exists.

[16] Read $\tau\grave{o}$ '$\tau\grave{o}$' for $\tauο\tilde{\upsilon}\tauο$.

(*b*) *Definition of* eidolon *and the problem of false state-*   [239c-242b]
ment and belief

STR.   Well, if you agree, we will leave ourselves out of account; and until we meet with someone who can perform this feat, let us say that the Sophist with extreme cunning has found an impenetrable lurking-place.[17]

THEAET.   It certainly seems so.

STR.   Accordingly, if we are going to say he possesses an art of creating 'semblances', he will readily take advantage of our handling our   [D] arguments in this way to grapple with us and turn them against ourselves. When we call him a maker of images, he will ask what on earth we mean in speaking of an 'image' at all. So we must consider, Theaetetus, how this truculent person's question is to be answered.

THEAET.   Clearly we shall say we mean images in water or in mirrors, and again images made by the draughtsman or the sculptor, and any other things of that sort.

STR.   It is plain, Theaetetus, that you have never seen a Sophist.   [E]

THEAET.   Why?

STR.   He will make as though his eyes were shut or he had no eyes at all.

THEAET.   How so?

STR.   When you offer him your answer in such terms, if you speak of something to be found in mirrors or in sculpture, he will laugh at your words, as implying that he can see. He will profess to know noth-   [240] ing about mirrors or water or even eyesight, and will confine his question to what can be gathered from discourse.

THEAET.   Namely?

STR.   The common character in all these things you mentioned and thought fit to call by a single name when you used the expression 'image' as one term covering them all. State it, then, and hold your ground against the man without yielding an inch.

THEAET.   Well, sir, what could we say an image was, if not another thing of the same sort, copied from the real thing?

STR.   'Of the same sort'? Do you mean another real thing, or what   [B] does 'of the same sort' signify?

THEAET.   Certainly not real, but like it.

STR.   Meaning by 'real' a thing that really exists.

THEAET.   Yes.

STR.   And by 'not real' the opposite of real?

THEAET.   Of course.

STR.   Then by what is 'like' you mean what has not real existence,[18] if you are going to call it 'not real'.

THEAET.   But it has some sort of existence.

---

[17] It must be remembered that the various senses of 'that which is not' are only gradually being disclosed. The Sophist does not lurk in the region of nonentity, above dealt with, but in the field of the not wholly real and the false which we are now entering.

[18] Reading οὐκ ὄντως [οὐκ] ὄν with Burnet and others.

STR. Only not real existence, according to you.

THEAET. No; except that it is really a likeness.

STR. So, not having real existence, it really is what we call a likeness? [19]

THEAET. Real and unreal do seem to be combined in that per- [c] plexing way, and very queer it is.

STR. Queer indeed. You see that now again by dovetailing them together in this way our hydra-headed Sophist has forced us against our will to admit that 'what is not' has some sort of being.

THEAET. Yes, I do.

STR. And what now? How can we define his art without contradicting ourselves?

THEAET. How do you mean? What sort of contradiction do you fear?

STR. When we say that he deceives with that semblance we spoke [D] of and that his art is a practice of deception, shall we be saying that, as the effect of his art, our mind thinks what is false, or what shall we mean?

THEAET. Just that. What else could we mean?

STR. And false thinking, again, will be thinking things contrary to the things that are? [20]

THEAET. Yes.

STR. You mean, then, by false thinking, thinking things that are not?

THEAET. Necessarily.

STR. Does that mean thinking that things that are not, are not, or [E] that things that are not in any way, in some way are?

THEAET. It must at least mean thinking that things that are not [21] are in some way, if anyone is ever to be in error even to the smallest extent.

STR. And also surely thinking that things which certainly [22] are, are not in any way at all?

THEAET. Yes.

STR. That also is error?

THEAET. Yes, that also.

STR. And a false statement, [23] I suppose, is to be regarded in the same

---

19 Reading οὐκ ὂν ἄρα [οὐκ] ὄντως. The subject 'it' is, as in the previous sentences, τὸ ἐοικός, *i.e.* εἴδωλον, the term we are defining. The paradox lies in saying that an εἴδωλον, which *is not real, really is* a likeness.

20 'The things that are.' 'The facts' would be a more natural translation, but at this stage it seems better to keep the vaguer expression. 'Things that are not' (falsehoods) are things which are contrary to the facts and yet must have some sort of being, for we have already said that we cannot think sheer nonentity.

21 Theaetetus does not repeat the Stranger's suggestion τὰ μηδαμῶς ὄντα, but correctly substitutes τὰ μὴ ὄντα, things which are *not the fact,* but are not (as μηδαμῶς might suggest) sheer nonentities.

22 πάντως, 'in any case': 'things which *certainly* have being' (not παντελῶς, 'things which have the *fullest* sort of being or reality'). The whole means 'denying any existence to facts which certainly do exist'.

23 'Statement' is the best rendering for λόγος, not 'proposition', because of its modern uses. For Plato a 'statement' is simply the utterance in speech of a judgment made by the mind in its silent dialogue with itself (263E, and *Theaet.* 189E, 206D, 208C).

light, as stating that things that are, are not, and that things that [241] are not, are.

THEAET. Yes. How else could it be false?

STR. Hardly in any other way. But the Sophist will deny that. How could a sensible man agree, when the admissions we made earlier are set beside this one? We understand, Theaetetus, what he is referring to?

THEAET. Of course we understand. He will say that we are contradicting what was said just now, when we have the face to say that false- [B] hoods exist in thoughts and in statements; for we are constantly being obliged to attribute what has being to what is not, after agreeing just now that this was altogether impossible.[24]

STR. Your recollection is correct. But you must now consider what we are to do about the Sophist; for if we pursue our search for him by ranking him under the art of the illusionists and creators of error, you see what an easy opening we offer to many perplexities and counter-attacks.

THEAET. I do.

STR. They are almost without number and we have stated only a [C] small fraction of them.

THEAET. If that is so, it looks as if it were impossible to catch the Sophist.

STR. What then? Are we to lose heart and give up now?

THEAET. I don't think we ought to, if we have the least chance of being able to lay hands on him somehow.

STR. Then I may count on your indulgence, and, as you now say, you will be content if we can by some twist free ourselves, even to the least extent, from the grip of so powerful an argument?

THEAET. By all means.

STR. Then I have another still more pressing request. [D]

THEAET. What is that?

STR. That you will not think I am turning into a sort of parricide.

THEAET. In what way?

STR. We shall find it necessary in self-defence to put to the question that pronouncement of father Parmenides, and establish by main force [25] that what is not, in some respect has being, and conversely that what is, in a way is not.

THEAET. It is plain that the course of the argument requires us to maintain that at all costs.

STR. Plain enough for the blind to see, as they say. Unless these [E] propositions are either refuted or accepted, anyone who talks of false statements or false judgment as being images or likenesses or copies or semblances, or of any of the arts concerned with such things, can hardly escape becoming a laughing-stock by being forced to contradict himself.

THEAET. Quite true.

---

[24] This is the 'earlier admission' referred to: 'Nothing that exists (such as 'Being') must be attributed to the non-existent' (238A), an admission already recalled at 238E.

[25] βιάζεσθαι may allude to Parmenides' own word δαμῇ (δαμάζω) in the lines quoted above.

STR. That is why we must now dare to lay unfilial hands on that [242]
pronouncement, or else, if some scruple holds us back, drop the matter
entirely.

THEAET. As for that, we must let no scruple hinder us.

STR. In that case, for the third time, I have a small favour to ask.

THEAET. You have only to mention it.

STR. I believe I confessed just now that on this point the task of refutation has always proved too much for my powers, and still does so.

THEAET. You did say that.

STR. Well, that confession, I am afraid, may make you think me scatter-
brained when at every turn I shift my position to and fro. It is for [B]
your satisfaction that we shall attempt to refute the pronouncement, if
we can refute it.

THEAET. Then you may take it that I shall never think you are overstep-
ping the limits by entering on your refutation and proof. So far as that
goes, you may proceed with an easy mind.

(c) *The perfectly Real. What does 'real' mean?* [26]   [242B-244B]

STR. Come then, where is one to make a start on so hazardous a theme?
I think I see the path we must inevitably follow.

THEAET. And that is——?

STR. To take first things that are now supposed to be quite clear [27] [C]
and see whether we are not in some confusion about them and too easily
reaching conclusions on the assumption that we understand them well
enough.

THEAET. Tell me more plainly what you mean.

STR. It strikes me that Parmenides and everyone else who has set out
to determine how many real things there are and what they are like, have
discoursed to us in rather an off-hand fashion.

THEAET. How so?

STR. They each and all seem to treat us as children to whom they are
telling a story. According to one there are three real things, some of which
now carry on a sort of warfare with one another, and then make [D]
friends and set about marrying and begetting and bringing up their children. Another tells us that there are two—Moist and Dry, or Hot and
Cold—whom he marries off, and makes them set up house together.[28] In
our part of the world the Eleatic set, who hark back to Xenophanes or even
earlier, unfold their tale on the assumption that what we call 'all things'

---

[26] In the coming section τὸ ὄν will be translated by 'the real' or 'reality'. This
sense of the word has emerged from the contrast between the 'sort of existence' belonging to an *eidolon*, and the real existence of the ὄντως ὄν.

[27] Namely, the meaning of 'real', a word we all use and imagine we understand.

[28] Plato recognises in the pre-Socratic systems the presence of mythical images,
especially the two most important: the sex-imagery of the cosmic Eros, and
the warfare of opposed 'powers' (such as Hot and Cold). These images of
Love and Strife can be traced all through the ancient science of nature, and
survive even in Atomism as the Venus and Mars of Lucretius.

are only one thing. Later, certain Muses in Ionia and Sicily perceived that safety lay rather in combining both accounts and saying that the real [E] is both many and one and is held together by enmity and friendship. 'In parting asunder it is always being drawn together' say the stricter [29] of these Muses. The milder [30] relax the rule that this should always be so and tell us of alternate states, in which the universe is now one and [243] at peace through the power of Love, and now many and at war with itself owing to some sort of Strife.

In all this, whether any one of them has told the truth or not is a hard question, and it is in bad taste to find fault so grossly with men of long-established fame. But one observation may be made without offence.

THEAET. And that is——?

STR. That they have shown too little consideration for ordinary people like ourselves in talking over our heads. Each school pursues its own [B] argument to the conclusion without caring whether we follow what they say or get left behind.

THEAET. How do you mean?

STR. When one or another of them in his discourse uses these expressions 'there really are' or 'have come to be' or 'are coming to be' 'many things' or 'one thing' or 'two', or again another speaks [31] of 'Hot being mixed with Cold', assuming 'combinations' and 'separations', do you, Theaetetus understand a single word they say? Speaking for myself, when I was younger I thought I understood quite clearly when someone spoke of this thing that is now puzzling us—'the unreal'. But now you see how completely perplexed we are about that.

THEAET. I do.   [C]

STR. Possibly, then, our minds are in the same state of confusion about reality. We profess to be quite at our ease about the real and to understand the word when it is spoken though we may not understand the unreal, when perhaps we are equally in the dark about both.

THEAET. Perhaps.

STR. And we may take it that the same is true of the other expressions I have just mentioned.

THEAET. Certainly.

STR. The general run of these expressions we will consider later, if we so decide. We must begin now with the chief and most important [D] of them all.

---

29 The stricter Muses of Ionia represent the philosophy of Heracleitus. It was a main point of his doctrine that the Harmony of Opposites essentially involves a tension or strife that is never resolved. There is no peace without war.

30 The milder Muses of Sicily (Empedocles) recognised a Reign of Love (without Strife) and, at the opposite pole, a Reign of Strife (without Love). Between these polar states, worlds come into being and pass away. In one half of the cycle a world is formed by Love gaining upon Strife, in the other, by Strife gaining upon Love.

31 Reading ἄλλος εἴπῃ (Rademacher, Diès) for ἄλλοθί πῃ, which is pointless, whether it means 'elsewhere in his discourse' or 'elsewhere in the universe'.

THEAET.   Which is that? Of course you mean we ought to begin by study-ing 'reality' and finding out what those who use the word think it stands for.

STR.   You have hit my meaning precisely, Theaetetus; I do mean that we must take this line. Imagine them here before us, and let us put this question: 'You who say that Hot and Cold or some such pair *really are* all things, what exactly does this expression convey that you apply   [E] to both when you say that they both are "real" or each of them is "real" ? How are we to understand this "reality" you speak of? Are we to suppose it is a third thing alongside the other two and that the All is no longer, as you say, two things, but three? For surely you do not give the name "reality" to one of the two and then say that both alike are real; for then there will be only one thing, whichever of the two it may be, and not two.'

THEAET.   True.

STR.   'Well then, do you intend to give the name "reality" to the pair of them?'

THEAET.   Perhaps.

STR.   'But that again', we shall object, 'will clearly be speaking of   [244] your two things as one.'

THEAET.   You are quite right.

STR.   'We are completely puzzled, then, and you must clear up the ques-tion for us, what you do intend to signify when you use the word "real". Obviously you must be quite familiar with what you mean, whereas we, who formerly imagined we knew, are now at a loss. First, then, enlighten us on just this point, so that we may not fancy we understand what you have to tell us, when in fact we are as far as possible from under-   [B] standing.'

If we put our case in that way to these people and to any others who say that the All is more than one thing, will there be anything unwarrant-able in our request?

THEAET.   Not at all.

Criticism of Parmenides' One Real Being   [244B-245E]

STR.   Again, there are those who say that the All is one thing. Must we not do our best to find out what they mean by 'reality'?

THEAET.   Surely.

STR.   Let them answer this question, then: 'You say, we understand, that there is only one thing?' 'We do', they will reply, won't they?

THEAET.   Yes.

STR.   'And there is something to which you give the name *real*?'

THEAET.   Yes.

STR.   'Is it the same thing as that to which you give the name *one*?   [C] Are you applying two names to the same thing, or what do you mean?'

THEAET.   What will their next answer be?

STR.   Obviously, Theaetetus, it is not so very easy for one who has laid down their fundamental assertion to answer this question or any other.

THEAET.   How so?

STR. In the first place, it is surely absurd for him to admit the existence of *two* names, when he has laid down that there is no more than one thing.

THEAET. Of course.

STR. And further, it is equally absurd to allow anyone to assert [D] that a name can have any existence, when that would be inexplicable.

THEAET. How is it inexplicable?

STR. If, on the one hand, he assumes that the name is different from the thing, he is surely speaking of *two* things.

THEAET. Yes.

STR. Whereas, if he assumes that the name is the same as the thing, either he will have to say it is not the name of anything, or if he says it is the name of something, it will follow that the name is merely a name of a name and of nothing else whatsoever.

THEAET. That is so.

STR. . . .[32]

THEAET. Necessarily.

STR. And what of 'the whole'? Will they say that this is other than their 'one real thing' or the same?

THEAET. Certainly that is the same. In fact they do say so. [E]

STR. Then if it is a whole—as indeed Parmenides says [33] :

> 'Every way like the mass of a well-rounded sphere, evenly balanced
> from the midst in every direction; for there must not be something more
> nor something less here than there'——

if the real is like that, it has a middle and extremities, and consequently it must have parts, must it not?

THEAET. It must.

STR. Well, if a thing is divided into parts, there is nothing against [245] its having the property of unity as applied to the aggregate of all the parts and being in that way one, as being a sum or whole.

---

[32] The dilemma stated in the Stranger's last two speeches is complete. It has been shown that the very existence of a name is inexplicable, whether it be distinct from the thing or identical with it. This argument applies equally to the name 'real' and to the name 'one', and there is no need for any special application of it to the name 'one'. The speech here omitted is corrupt. It looks as if it might be intended to make that special application; but since that is not wanted, it is impossible to restore the sense with any probability. The oldest evidence for the text is Simplicius, *Phys.* 89: καὶ τὸ ἕν γε ἑνὸς ἓν (ἓν om. D) ὂν μόνον καὶ τοῦ ὀνόματος αὐτὸ ἓν ὄν. This (including ἕν) agrees with the Bodleian (B) of Plato. The view that ἑνὸς ἕν can mean 'unity of a unity' is rightly rejected by Ritter (*N. Unters.* 15), who adopts the reading of T: καὶ τὸ ἕν γε ἑνὸς ὂν μόνον (sc. ὄνομα συμβήσεται), καὶ τοῦτο ὀνόματος, αὐτὸ <τὸ?> ἓν ὄν, 'And it will result too that the One (they talk of) will be the name of itself only, and *that* the name (not of a different objective reality, but) of a name (the name "one"), while yet it is the One itself.' The last words here are barely intelligible, and the whole statement seems to have no point. If the speech, together with Theaetetus' previous reply οὕτως, were simply omitted, it would not be missed.

[33] Frag. 8, 43.

THEAET. Of course.

STR. On the other hand, the thing which has these properties cannot be just Unity itself, can it?

THEAET. Why not?

STR. Surely Unity in the true sense and rightly defined must be altogether without parts.

THEAET. Yes, it must.

STR. Whereas a thing such as we described, consisting of several [B] parts, will not answer to that definition.

THEAET. I see.

STR. Then, (A) is the Real one and a whole in the sense that it has the property of unity, or (B) are we to say that the Real is not a whole at all?

THEAET. That is a hard choice.

STR. Quite true. For if (A) the real has the property of being in a sense one, it will evidently not be the same thing as Unity, and so all things will be more than one.

THEAET. Yes.

STR. And again (B) if the Real is not a whole by virtue of hav- [C] ing this property of unity while (a) at the same time Wholeness itself is real, it follows that the Real falls short of itself.

THEAET. Certainly.

STR. So, on this line of argument too, the Real will be deprived of reality and will not be a thing that is.

THEAET. Yes.

STR. And further, once more all things will be more than one, since Reality on the one side and Wholeness on the other have now each a distinct nature.

THEAET. Yes.

STR. But if, (b) on the other hand, there is no such thing as Wholeness at all, not only are the same things true of the Real, but also that, besides not being a thing that really is, it could never even become such.

THEAET. Why not? [D]

STR. Whenever a thing comes into being, at that moment it has come to be as a whole; accordingly, if you do not reckon unity or wholeness among real things, you have no right to speak of either being or coming-into-being as having any existence.

THEAET. That seems perfectly true.

STR. And further, what is not a whole cannot have any definite number either; for if a thing has a definite number, it must amount to that number, whatever it may be, as a whole.

THEAET. Assuredly.

STR. And countless other difficulties, each involved in measureless [E] perplexity, will arise, if you say that the real is either two things or only one.

THEAET. That is plain enough from those we have had a glimpse of now. One leads to another, and each carries us further into a wilderness of doubt about every theory as it is mentioned.

The Battle of Gods and Giants: Idealists and Materialists   [245E-246E]

STR.   So much, then, for those who give an exact account of what is real or unreal. We have not gone through them all, but let this suffice. Now we must turn to look at those who put the matter in a different way, so that, from a complete review of all, we may see that reality is just as hard to define as unreality.

THEAET.   We had better go on, then, to their position.

STR.   What we shall see [34] is something like a Battle of Gods and   [246A] Giants going on between them over their quarrel about reality.

THEAET.   How so?

STR.   One party is trying to drag everything down to earth out of heaven and the unseen, literally grasping rocks and trees in their hands; for they lay hold upon every stock and stone and strenuously affirm that real exist-ence belongs only to that which can be handled and offers resistance to the touch. They define reality as the same thing as body, and as soon   [B] as one of the opposite party asserts that anything without a body is real, they are utterly contemptuous and will not listen to another word.

THEAET.   The people you describe are certainly a formidable crew. I have met quite a number of them before now.

STR.   Yes, and accordingly their adversaries are very wary in defending their position somewhere in the heights of the unseen, maintaining with all their force that true reality consists in certain intelligible and bodiless Forms. In the clash of argument they shatter and pulverise those bodies which their opponents wield, and what those others allege to be true   [C] reality they call, not real being, but a sort of moving process of becoming. On this issue an interminable battle is always going on between the two camps.

THEAET.   True.

STR.   Suppose, then, we challenge each party in turn to render an account of the reality they assert.

THEAET.   How shall we do so?

STR.   It will be easier to obtain from those who place reality in Forms, because they are more civilised; harder, from those whose vio-   [D] lence would drag everything down to the level of body—perhaps, all but impossible. However, I think I see the right way to deal with them.

THEAET.   What is that?

STR.   Best of all, if it were anyhow possible, would be to bring about a real change of heart; but if that is beyond our power, to imagine them reformed and assume them willing to moderate their present lawlessness in answering our questions. The better a man's character is, the more force there will be in any agreement you make with him. However, we are not concerned with them so much as with our search for the truth.

THEAET.   You are quite right.   [E]

---

[34] καὶ μήν, as in tragedy, where a person on the stage calls attention to the entry of a fresh character.

A mark of the real is offered for the materialists' accept-   [246ᴇ-248ᴀ]
ance

STR. Well then, call upon these reformed characters to oblige you with an answer, and you shall act as their spokesman.

THEAET. I will.

STR. Let them tell us, then, whether they admit that there is such a thing as a mortal living creature.

THEAET. Of course they do.

STR. And they will agree that it is a body animated by a soul?

THEAET. Certainly.

STR. Taking a soul to be something real?

THEAET. Yes.   [247]

STR. Again, they allow that one soul may be just, another unjust, or one wise, another foolish?

THEAET. Naturally.

STR. And that any soul comes to be just or the reverse by possessing justice or the reverse, which is present in it?

THEAET. Yes, they agree to that too.

STR. But surely they will admit that whatever can come to be present in a thing or absent from it is certainly a real thing.

THEAET. Yes.

STR. Granted, then, that justice or wisdom or any other sort of [ʙ] goodness or badness is real, and moreover that a soul in which they come to exist is real, do they maintain that any one of these things is visible and tangible, or are they all invisible?

THEAET. They can hardly say that any one of them is visible.

STR. And do they really assert that something that is not visible has a body?

THEAET. That question they do not answer as a whole without a distinction. The soul itself, they think, does possess a sort of body [35]; but when it comes to wisdom or any of the other things you asked about, they have not the face either to accept the inference that they have no place [ᴄ] among real things or to persist in maintaining that they are all bodies.

STR. That shows, Theaetetus, that they are genuinely reformed characters. The Giants among them, of the true earth-born breed, would not stick at any point; they would hold out to the end, that whatever they cannot squeeze between their hands is just nothing at all.

THEAET. I dare say that describes their state of mind.

STR. Let us question them further, then; for it is quite enough for our purpose if they consent to admit that even a small part of reality is [ᴅ] bodiless. They must now tell us this: when they say that these bodiless things and the other things which have body are alike 'real', what common

---

[35] The soul had been regarded both popularly and by philosophers before Plato as consisting of a subtle and invisible kind of matter. The Atomists continued to maintain that it was composed of atoms, like everything else; only its atoms were round and so specially mobile.

character that emerges as covering both sets of things have they in view? It is possible they may be at a loss for an answer. If that is their state of mind, you must consider whether they would accept at our suggestion a description of the real and agree to it.

THEAET. What description? Perhaps we can tell, if you will state it.

STR. I suggest that anything has real being, that is so constituted [E] as to possess any sort of power either to affect anything else or to be affected, in however small a degree, by the most insignificant agent, though it be only once. I am proposing as a mark to distinguish real things, that they are nothing but power.[36]

THEAET. Well, they accept that, having for the moment no better suggestion of their own to offer.

STR. That will do; for later on both they and we perhaps may [248] change our minds. For the present, then, let us take it that this agreement stands between us and the one party.

THEAET. It does.

The Idealists must concede that reality includes some [248A-249D] *changing things*

STR. Let us turn, then, to the opposite party, the friends of Forms. Once more you shall act as their spokesman.

THEAET. I will.

STR. We understand that you make a distinction between 'Becoming' and 'Real being' and speak of them as separate. Is that so?

THEAET. Yes.

STR. And you say that we have intercourse with [37] Becoming by means of the body through sense, whereas we have intercourse with Real being by means of the soul through reflection. And Real being, you say, is always in the same unchanging state, whereas Becoming is variable.

THEAET. We do. [B]

STR. Admirable. But now what are we to take you as meaning by this

---

36 Τίθεμαι γὰρ ὅρον ὁρίζειν τὰ ὄντα ὡς ἔστιν οὐκ ἄλλο τι πλὴν δύναμις. The construction is difficult. I think the sentence ought to mean that the mark of real things (not the real things themselves) is nothing but power. This sense could be obtained if we could translate: 'I am proposing a mark to distinguish real things—that there is nothing else but power (to serve as such a mark)' or 'that *it* (the mark) is nothing but power.' But neither rendering seems defensible.

37 κοινωνεῖν ('are in touch with', Taylor) is chosen as a neutral word covering all forms of cognition, the usual words (εἰδέναι, γιγνώσκειν, ἐπίστασθαι, αἰσθάνεσθαι, etc.) being too much specialised and associated either with knowledge to the exclusion of sensation and perception or *vice versa*. κοινωνεῖν is 'to enter into relations with'. It is used of social and business intercourse, and also of sexual intercourse, a metaphor already used in the analysis of sensation in the *Theaetetus* (see p. 47). κοινωνεῖν here is a psychological term for cognition, and this use has no connection (such as Campbell imagines) with its use later to describe the 'combination' of Forms (κοινωνία εἰδῶν).

expression 'intercourse' which you apply to both? Don't you mean what we described a moment ago?

THEAET.   What was that?

STR.   The experiencing an effect or the production of one, arising, as the result of some power, from things that encounter one another. Perhaps, Theaetetus, you may not be able to catch their answer to this, but I, who am familiar with them, may be more successful.

THEAET.   What have they to say, then?

STR.   They do not agree to the proposition we put just now to the   [c]
earth-born Giants about reality.

THEAET.   You mean——?

STR.   We proposed as a sufficient mark of real things the presence in a thing of the power of being acted upon or of acting in relation to however insignificant a thing.

THEAET.   Yes.

STR.   Well, to that they reply that a power of acting and being acted upon belongs to Becoming, but neither of these powers is compatible with Real being.

THEAET.   And there is something in that answer?

STR.   Something to which we must reply by a request for more   [D]
enlightenment. Do they acknowledge further that the soul knows and Real being is known?

THEAET.   Certainly they agree to that.

STR.   Well, do you agree that knowing or being known is an action, or is it experiencing an effect, or both? Or is one of them experiencing an effect, the other an action? Or does neither of them come under either of these heads at all? [38]

THEAET.   Evidently neither; otherwise our friends would be contradicting what they said earlier.

STR.   I see what you mean. They would have to say this: [39] If know-   [E]
ing is to be acting on something, it follows that what is known must be acted upon [40] by it; and so, on this showing, Reality when it is being known by the act of knowledge must, in so far as it is known, be changed owing to being so acted upon; and that, we say, cannot happen to the changeless.

THEAET.   Exactly.

STR.   But tell me, in heaven's name: are we really to be so easily convinced that change, life, soul, understanding have no place in that which

---

[38] The Stranger puts all the possible ways of regarding knowing. He does not suggest that it must be an action, not a being-acted-upon, but that it may be either, or both, or neither. The Idealists in their next reply take up only one of these suggestions—that knowing is an action—and object to that.

[39] ΞΕ. μανθάνω· τόδε γε (sc. λέγοιεν ἄν). What follows is put into the mouths of the Idealists, who state their objection to regarding knowing as an action. They ignore the possibility that knowing is an affection of the soul, acted upon by the object.

[40] Or 'affected'—a rendering that more clearly implies suffering some change.

is perfectly real—that it has neither life nor thought, but stands im- [249]
mutable in solemn aloofness, devoid of intelligence?

THEAET. That, sir, would be a strange doctrine to accept.

STR. But can we say it has intelligence without having life?

THEAET. Surely not.

STR. But if we say it contains both, can we deny that it has soul in which
they reside?

THEAET. How else could it possess them?

STR. But then, if it has intelligence, life, and soul, can we say that a
living thing remains at rest in complete changelessness?

THEAET. All that seems to me unreasonable. [B]

STR. In that case we must admit that what changes and change itself
are real things.

THEAET. Certainly.

STR. From this, however, it follows, Theaetetus, first, that, if all things
are unchangeable [41] no intelligence can really exist anywhere in anything
with regard to any object.

THEAET. Quite so.

STR. And, on the other hand, if we allow that all things are moving and
changing, on that view equally we shall be excluding intelligence from
the class of real things.

THEAET. How so?

STR. Do you think that, without rest, there could ever be anything that
abides constant in the same condition and in the same respects? [C]

THEAET. Certainly not.

STR. And without such objects can you make out that intelligence exists
or could ever exist anywhere?

THEAET. It would be quite impossible.

STR. Well then, all the force of reasoning must be enlisted to oppose
anyone who tries to maintain any assertion about anything at the same
time that he suppresses knowledge or understanding or intelligence.

THEAET. Most certainly.

STR. On these grounds, then, it seems that only one course is open to
the philosopher who values knowledge and the rest above all else. He
must refuse to accept from the champions either of the One or of [D]
the many Forms [42] the doctrine that all Reality is changeless; and he must
turn a deaf ear to the other party who represent Reality as everywhere
changing. Like a child begging for 'both', he must declare that Reality or

---

41 The point is that, if the *whole* of Reality excludes change, intelligence (which
   involves life and therefore change) will have no real existence *anywhere*.

42 As Ritter (*Platon* ii, 132) remarks, no one could ever have doubted that the
   Friends of Forms include the Platonic Socrates of the *Phaedo* and *Republic*,
   if the temporal sequence of the dialogues had been correctly determined
   earlier than it was. Ritter himself identifies the Friends of Forms with members of the Academy who took the doctrines of personal immortality and of
   bodiless Forms, as set forth in the *Phaedo*, more seriously and literally than
   Plato himself intended.

the sum of things is both at once—all that is unchangeable and all that is in change.

THEAET.   Perfectly true.

Transition. What does the idealist mean by 'real'?   [249D-251A]

STR.   Well then, does it not look now as if we had fairly caught reality within the compass of our description?

THEAET.   Certainly it does.

STR.   And yet—oh dear, Theaetetus, what if I say after all that I think it is just at this point that we shall come to see how baffling this question of reality is?

THEAET.   How so? Why do you say that?   [E]

STR.   My good friend, don't you see that now we are wholly in the dark about it, though we fancy we are talking good sense?

THEAET.   I certainly thought so, and I don't at all understand how we can be deceived about our condition.

STR.   Then consider these last conclusions of ours more carefully, and whether, when we agree to them, we might not fairly be posed   [250] with the same question we put earlier to those who said that the sum of things 'really is' Hot and Cold.

THEAET.   You must remind me what that question was.

STR.   By all means; and I will try to do it by questioning you in the same way as I questioned them, so that we may get a little further at the same time.

THEAET.   Very good.

STR.   Come along then. When you speak of Movement and Rest, these are things completely opposed to one another, aren't they?

THEAET.   Of course.

STR.   At the same time you say of both and of each severally, that they are real?

THEAET.   I do.   [B]

STR.   And when you admit that they are real, do you mean that either or both are in movement?

THEAET.   Certainly not.

STR.   Then, perhaps, by saying both are real you mean they are both at rest?

THEAET.   No, how could I?

STR.   So, then, you conceive of reality (realness) as a third thing over and above these two; and when you speak of both as being real, you mean that you are taking both movement and rest together as embraced by reality and fixing your attention on their common association with reality?

THEAET.   It does seem as if we discerned reality as a third thing,   [C] when we say that movement and rest are real.

STR.   So reality is not motion and rest 'both at once', but something distinct from them.

THEAET.   Apparently.

Str. In virtue of its own nature, then, reality is neither at rest nor in movement.

Theaet. I suppose so.

Str. If so, where is the mind to turn for help if one wants to reach any clear and certain conclusion about reality?

Theaet. Where indeed?

Str. It seems hard to find help in any quarter. If a thing is not in [D] movement, how can it not be at rest? Or how can what is not in any way at rest fail to be in movement? Yet reality is now revealed to us as outside both alternatives. Is that possible?

Theaet. As impossible as anything could be.

Str. Then there is one thing that ought to be remembered at this point.

Theaet. And that is——?

Str. That we were completely puzzled when we were asked to what the name 'unreal' should be applied. You remember?

Theaet. Of course.

Str. And now we are in no less perplexity about reality? [E]

Theaet. In even greater, I should say, sir, if that be possible.

Str. Let us take it, then, that our difficulty is now completely stated. But since reality and unreality are equally puzzling, there is henceforward some hope that any light, whether dim or bright, thrown upon the one will illuminate the other to an equal degree; and if, on the other [251] hand, we cannot get sight of either, at any rate we will make the best we can of it under these conditions and force a passage through the argument with both elbows at once.

Theaet. Very good.

II

THE COMBINATION OF FORMS AND THE PROBLEM OF
NEGATIVE STATEMENTS

Exclusion of the trivial question, how one individual thing [251A-C]
can have many names

Str. Let us explain, then, how it is that we call the same thing—whatever is in question at the moment—by several names.

Theaet. For instance? Give me an example.

Str. Well, when we speak of a man we give him many additional names: we attribute to him colours and shapes and sizes and defects and good qualities; and in all these and countless other statements we say he is not merely a 'man' but also 'good' and any number of other things. [B] And so with everything else: we take any given thing as one and yet speak of it as many and by many names.

Theaet. True.

Str. And thereby, I fancy, we have provided a magnificent entertain-

ment for the young and for some of their elders who have taken to learning late in life. Anyone can take a hand in the game and at once object
that many things cannot be one, nor one thing many; indeed, they delight
in forbidding us to speak of a man as 'good'; we must only speak of [c]
a good as good, and of the man as man. I imagine, Theaetetus, you often
meet with these enthusiasts, sometimes elderly men who, being poorly
endowed with intelligence, gape with wonder at these discoveries and
fancy they have lighted here on the very treasure of complete wisdom.

THEAET. I have indeed.

Proof that some Forms will combine, others will not   [251c-252e]

STR. Well then, we want our argument to be addressed to all alike
who have ever had anything to say about existence; so let us [D]
take it that the questions we shall put now are intended not only for these
people but for all those others whom we have been conversing with
earlier.

THEAET. And what are the questions?

STR. Are we not to attach Existence to Motion and Rest, nor anything
else to anything else, but rather to treat them in our discourse as incapable of any blending or participation in one another? Or are we to
lump them all together as capable of association with one another? Or
shall we say that this is true of some and not of others? Which of these
possibilities shall we say they prefer, Theaetetus?   [E]

THEAET. I am not prepared to answer that on their behalf.

STR. Then why not answer the questions one at a time and see what are
the consequences in each case?

THEAET. Very good.

STR. And first, if you like, let us suppose them to say that nothing has
any capacity for combination with anything else for any purpose. Then
Movement and Rest will have no part in Existence.

THEAET. No.   [252]

STR. Well then, will either of them exist, if it has no association with
Existence?

THEAET. No, it will not exist.

STR. That admission seems to make short work of all theories; it upsets
at one blow those who have a universe in motion, and those who make it
a motionless unity, and all who say their realities exist in Forms that are
always the same in all respects [43]; for they all attribute existence to things,
some saying they really *are* in movement, some that they really *are* at rest.

THEAET. Quite so.

STR. And further, those who make all things come together at one [B]
time and separate at another, whether they bring innumerable things into
a unity and out of a unity, or divide things into and combine them out
of a limited set of elements; no matter whether they suppose this to

---

[43] The three classes mentioned above (249B) at the end of the argument with
the idealists. The earlier philosophers are recalled in the next speech.

happen in alternation or to be going on all the time—however it may be, all this would be meaningless if there is no blending at all.[44]

THEAET.   True.

STR.   Moreover, the greatest absurdity of all results from pursuing the theory of those very people who will not allow one thing to share in the quality of another and so be called by its name.

THEAET.   How so?   [c]

STR.   Why, in referring to anything they cannot help using the words 'being' and 'apart' and 'from the others' and 'by itself' and any number more. They cannot refrain from these expressions or from connecting them in their statements, and so need not wait for others to refute them; the foe is in their own household, as the saying goes, and, like that queer fellow Eurycles,[45] they carry about with them wherever they go a voice in their own bellies to contradict them.

THEAET.   True; your comparison is very much to the purpose.   [d]

STR.   Well, suppose we allow that all are capable of combining with one another.

THEAET.   Even I can dispose of that suggestion.

STR.   How?

THEAET.   Because then Movement itself would come to a complete standstill, and again Rest itself would be in movement, if each were to supervene upon the other.

STR.   And that is to the last degree impossible—that Movement should come to be at rest and Rest be in motion?

THEAET.   Surely.

STR.   Then only the third choice is left.

THEAET.   Yes.

STR.   And observe that one of these alternatives must be true: [e] either all will blend, or none, or some will and some will not.

THEAET.   Certainly.

STR.   And two of the three have been found impossible.

THEAET.   Yes.

STR.   Whoever, then, wishes to give a right answer will assert the remaining one.

THEAET.   Quite so.

The texture of philosophic discourse [46]   [252e-253c]

STR.   Then since some will blend, some not, they might be said to be in the same case with the letters of the alphabet. Some of   [253] these cannot be conjoined, others will fit together.

---

44 'No blending' means no blending of Forms. If no Form partakes of any other, the statements that 'Motion exists' and 'Rest exists' are either false or meaningless. If that is so, it follows that physical things cannot partake of Motion or of Rest; and this is fatal to all cosmologies.

45 A ventriloquist, mentioned by Aristophanes.

46 *Rep.* vi, 511B. The phrase 'texture of discourse' is based on Plato's later remark that 'all discourse depends on the weaving together (συμπλοκή) of Forms' (p. 300).

THEAET. Of course.

STR. And the vowels are specially good at combination—a sort of bond pervading them all, so that without a vowel the others cannot be fitted together.

THEAET. That is so.

STR. And does everyone [47] know which can combine with which, or does one need an art to do it rightly?

THEAET. It needs art.

STR. And that art is——?

THEAET. Grammar.

STR. Again, is it not the same with sounds of high or low pitch? [B] To possess the art of recognising the sounds that can or can not be blended is to be a musician; if one doesn't understand that, one is unmusical.

THEAET. True.

STR. And we shall find differences of the same sort between competence and incompetence in any other art.

THEAET. Of course.

STR. Well, now that we have agreed that the Kinds stand towards one another in the same way as regards blending, is not some science needed as a guide on the voyage of discourse, if one is to succeed in pointing out which Kinds are consonant, and which are incompatible with one [C] another; also, whether there are certain Kinds that pervade them all and connect them so that they can blend, and again, where there are divisions (separations), whether there are certain others that traverse wholes and are responsible for the division?

THEAET. Surely some science is needed—perhaps the most important of all.

Description of the science of Dialectic   [253C–254B]

STR. And what name shall we give to this science? Or—good gracious, Theaetetus, have we stumbled unawares upon the free man's knowledge and, in seeking for the Sophist, chanced to find the Philosopher first?

THEAET. How do you mean?

STR. Dividing according to Kinds, not taking the same Form for [D] a different one or a different one for the same—is not that the business of the science of Dialectic?

THEAET. Yes.

STR. And the man who can do that discerns clearly *one* Form everywhere extended throughout many, where each one lies apart, and *many* Forms, different from one another, embraced from without by one Form; and again *one* Form connected in a unity through many wholes, and *many* Forms, entirely marked off apart. That means knowing how to distinguish, Kind by Kind, in what ways the several Kinds can or [E] can not combine.

---

[47] In Burnet's text (1899) πῶς is misprinted for πᾶς.

THEAET.   Most certainly.

STR.   And the only person, I imagine, to whom you would allow this mastery of Dialectic is the pure and rightful lover of wisdom.

THEAET.   To whom else could it be allowed?

STR.   It is, then, in some such region as this that we shall find the Philosopher now or later, if we should look for him. He too may be diffi-   [254] cult to see clearly; but the difficulty in his case is not the same as in the Sophist's.

THEAET.   What is the difference?

STR.   The Sophist takes refuge in the darkness of Not-being, where he is at home and has the knack of feeling his way; and it is the darkness of the place that makes him so hard to perceive.

THEAET.   That may well be.

STR.   Whereas the Philosopher, whose thoughts constantly dwell upon the nature of reality, is difficult to see because his region is so bright; for the eye of the vulgar soul cannot endure to keep its gaze fixed on   [B] the divine.

THEAET.   That may well be no less true.

STR.   Then we will look more closely at the Philosopher presently, if we are still in the mind to do so; meanwhile clearly we must not loosen our grip on the Sophist until we have studied him thoroughly.

THEAET.   I entirely agree.

Three of the most important Forms, selected for purposes of illustration: Existence, Motion, Rest   [254B-D]

STR.   Now that we are agreed, then, that some of the Kinds will combine with one another and some will not, and that some combine to a small extent, others with a large number, while some pervade all and there is nothing against their being combined with everything,   [C] let us next follow up the argument in this way. We will not take all the Forms, for fear of getting confused in such a multitude, but choose out some of those that are recognised as most (*or* very) important, and consider first their several natures and then how they stand in respect of being capable of combination with one another. In this way, though we may not be able to conceive Being and Not-being with perfect clearness, we may at least give as satisfactory an account of them as we can under the conditions of our present inquiry,[48] and see if there is any open-   [D] ing allowing us to assert that what is not, *really is* what is not, and to escape unscathed.

THEAET.   Yes, we had better do that.

STR.   Now, among the Kinds, those we were just now discussing—Existence itself and Rest and Motion—are very important.[49]

---

48 Possibly a hint that in what follows we shall not draw all the distinctions that a complete account would require, or at least not emphasise those which do not directly bear on the conclusion desired.

49 This sentence is usually mistranslated, μέγιστα being rendered as if it were τὰ μέγιστα and taken as subject; e.g., Campbell: '*The most important kinds*

THEAET. Quite so.

STR. And observe, we say that two of the three will not blend with one another.[50]

THEAET. Certainly.

STR. Whereas Existence can be blended with both; for surely they both exist.

THEAET. Of course.

STR. So they make three in all.

Two further Forms, Sameness and Difference, distinct from these three and all-pervading [254D-255E]

STR. And each one of them (Existence, Motion, Rest) is *different* from the other two [51] and the *same* as itself.

THEAET. That is so. [E]

STR. But what do we mean by these words we have just used—'same' and 'different'? Are they a pair of Kinds distinct from those three, though always necessarily blending with them, so that we must consider the Forms as five in all, not three? Or, when we say 'same' or 'different', are we unconsciously using a name that belongs to one or another of [255] those three Kinds?

THEAET. Possibly.

STR. Well, Motion and Rest at any rate cannot be (identical with) Difference or Sameness.

THEAET. Why not?

STR. Neither Motion nor Rest can be (identical with) anything that we say of both of them in common.

THEAET. Why?

STR. Because Motion would then be at rest, and Rest in motion; for

---

are those which we have just been considering.' The point is important because all these renderings mean that Existence, Motion, and Rest are *the* most important kinds. Plato does not assert this. The previous speech said that we would select 'some of those that are recognised as most (or very) important'. The present speech tells us which these 'some' are; but they are only *some* of the most important, not *the* most important. The subject is ἃ νυνδὴ διῆμεν: μέγιστα is predicate, standing first for emphasis and because it provides the link with the former speech. We might translate: "Now this description 'most important' (or 'very important') among the Kinds does apply to those we have been discussing, namely Existence, Rest, Motion." Accordingly, we take those as the 'some' we said we would take. But there are others of the highest importance, as the earlier speech implied. Sameness and Difference, presently added, are equally important, and actually 'wider' than Motion and Rest, being 'all-pervading' like Existence. These speeches leave open the possibility that there may be any number of other μέγιστα γένη, which we do not require to mention for our purpose. The consequences of mistranslation will be noted presently.

50 That Motion will not blend with Rest was remarked at 252D. The point of these sentences is that Existence, Motion, Rest, are three distinct Forms, no one of them identical with any other.

51 This statement at once notes that Difference is distinct from Incompatibility; for Motion and Rest are not incompatible with Existence.

whichever of the two (Motion or Rest) becomes applicable to both (by being identified with either Sameness or Difference, which *are* applicable to both) will force the other (Rest or Motion) to change to the contrary of its own nature, as thus coming to partake of its contrary.   [B]

THEAET. Quite so.

STR. But both do partake of Sameness and Difference.

THEAET. Yes.

STR. Then we must not say that Sameness or Difference is (identical with) Motion, nor yet with Rest.[52]

THEAET. No.

STR. Are we, however, to think of Existence and Sameness as a single thing?

THEAET. Perhaps.

STR. But if 'Existence' and 'Sameness' have no difference in meaning, once more, when we say that Motion and Rest both 'exist', we shall   [c] thereby be speaking of them as being 'the same'.

THEAET. But that is impossible.

STR. Then Sameness and Existence cannot be one thing.

THEAET. Hardly.

STR. We may, then, set down Sameness as a fourth Form, additional to our three.

THEAET. Certainly.

STR. And are we to call Difference a fifth? Or must we think of Difference and Existence as two names for a single Kind?

THEAET. Perhaps.

STR. But I suppose you admit that, among things that exist, some are always spoken of as being what they are [53] just in themselves, others as being what they are with reference to other things.

---

52 This argument is highly compressed and somewhat obscure even with the additions I have interpolated in the translation. We want to prove that neither the word 'Motion' (or 'being in motion') nor the word 'Rest' (or 'being at rest') can mean the same thing as either the word 'Sameness' (or 'being the same') or the word 'Different' (or 'being different'). The proof is (1) We know that

Motion blends with		Sameness
Rest	"	"	Sameness
Motion	"	"	Difference
Rest	"	"	Difference.

(2) We now say: Anything that can be asserted of (blends with) both Motion and Rest—and Sameness and Difference do blend with both—cannot be identical with either. (3) For suppose (for example) that Motion is identical with Sameness. Then 'Motion' can be substituted for 'Sameness' in any statement. So the second statement above ('Rest blends with Sameness') becomes 'Rest blends with Motion'. But this is false. Therefore Motion is not identical with Sameness. The same proof holds of all the other identifications of Motion with Difference, Rest with Difference, Rest with Sameness.

53 The addition of the words 'being what they are' is justified by the statement below (D7) that what is different *is what it is* ($\tau o \hat{v} \theta$ ' $\ddot{o} \pi \epsilon \rho$ $\dot{\epsilon} \sigma \tau \dot{\iota} \nu$) with reference to another thing.

THEAET. Of course.

STR. And what is different is always so called with reference to [D] another thing, isn't it?

THEAET. That is so.

STR. It would not be so, if Existence and Difference were not very different things. If Difference partook of both characters [54] as Existence does, there would sometimes be, within the class of different things, something that was different not with reference to another thing. But in fact we undoubtedly find that whatever is different, as a necessary consequence, is what it is with reference to another.

THEAET. It is as you say.

STR. Then we must call the nature of Difference a fifth among the [E] Forms we are singling out.

THEAET. Yes.

STR. And moreover we shall say that this nature pervades all the Forms; for each one is different from the rest, not by virtue of its own nature, but because it partakes of the character of Difference.

THEAET. Quite so.

A review of true statements involving the five Forms shows that there are any number of true statements asserting that 'what is' in a sense 'is not'
[255E-257A]

STR. Now, then, taking our five Kinds one by one, let us make some statements about them.

THEAET. What statements?

STR. First about Motion: let us say that Motion is altogether different from Rest. Or is that not so?

THEAET. It is so.

STR. So Motion is not Rest.

THEAET. Not in any sense.[55]

STR. But Motion *is* (exists), by virtue of partaking of Existence. [256]

THEAET. Yes.

STR. And once more Motion is different from the Same (Sameness).[56]

THEAET. No doubt.

STR. So Motion is not the Same (Sameness).

THEAET. No.

STR. But on the other hand, Motion, we said, is the same as itself, because everything partakes of the Same (Sameness).[57]

---

[54] I.e. τὸ καθ' αὑτό and τὸ πρὸς ἄλλο. Note that Existence, which *includes* both these Forms, is said to *partake of* both. This is one of the places which show that 'partaking' is symmetrical in the case of Forms.

[55] Possibly 'altogether different' and 'not *in any sense*' mean that Motion and Rest are not only different but also incompatible.

[56] In Greek the appearance of contradiction is increased by ταὐτὸν meaning both 'Sameness' and 'the same'.

[57] Reading αὐτῇ ... πᾶν ταὐτοῦ with Madvig.

THEAET.   Certainly.

STR.   Motion, then, is both the same and not the Same: we must admit that without boggling at it. For when we say it is 'the same' and 'not the Same' we are not using the expression in the same sense: we   [B] call it 'the same' on account of its participation in the Same with reference to itself; but we call it 'not the Same' because of its combination with Difference, a combination that separates it off from the Same (Sameness) and makes it not the Same but different, so that we have the right to say this time that it is 'not the Same'.

THEAET.   Certainly.

STR.   So too, supposing Motion iteslf did in any way participate in Rest, there would be nothing outrageous in speaking of it as stationary. <But it does not in fact participate in Rest at all.

THEAET.   No, it does not.

STR.   Whereas it does participate both in Sameness and in Difference, so that it is correct to speak of it as both the same and not the Same.>

THEAET.   Perfectly correct, provided that we are to agree that some of the Kinds will blend with one another, some will not.

STR.   Well, that is a conclusion we proved at an earlier stage, when   [C] we showed that such was indeed their nature.

THEAET.   Of course.[58]

STR.   To go back to our statements, then: is Motion different from Different (Difference), just as it was other than the Same (Sameness) and other than Rest?

THEAET.   Necessarily.

STR.   Motion, then, in a sense is not Different, and also is different, in accordance with the argument we stated just now.

THEAET.   True.

STR.   What, then of the next point? Are we to say that Motion is different from three of the four, but not from the fourth, when we have   [D]

---

[58] I understand the argument here as follows. We have just said that Motion is the same and not the same (as partaking of Difference). This sounds like a contradiction: how can what is the same partake of Difference? 'Same' and 'Different' sound as if they were contraries and so incompatible, like Motion and Rest, which are contraries and incompatible. But suppose Motion and Rest were merely different, not incompatible: then Motion could partake of Rest and be called stationary. That is impossible because Motion and Rest are in fact incompatible. But the sameness which Motion has towards itself and the difference it has towards other things are not incompatible. So there is no contradiction in saying Motion is the same and not the same. (Cf. Brochard, *Études,* 143.)

If this is the meaning, the text is intolerably elliptical and obscure. . . .

Other critics suppose that Plato is suggesting that there is, after all, a sense in which Motion does partake of Rest, *e.g.* the uniform motion of a sphere in the same place (Diès), or because Motion partakes of stability in that it can be measured and described (Ritter, *N. Unt.* 61). But I agree with Brochard that the reference to earlier statements asserting that Motion and Rest are incompatible excludes such interpretations.

agreed that there were five Kinds in the field we set before us for examination?

THEAET. How can we? We cannot allow that their number is less than it was shown to be.

STR. So we may fearlessly contend that Motion is different from Existence.

THEAET. Without the smallest fear.

STR. In fact, it is clear that Motion really is a thing that is not (Existence) and a thing that is, since it partakes of Existence.

THEAET. Perfectly clear.

STR. It must, then, be possible for 'that which is not' (*i.e.* is different from Existence) to be (to exist), not only in the case of Motion but of all the other Kinds. For in the case of them all the nature of Differ- [E] ence makes each one of them different from Existence and so makes it a thing that 'is not'; and hence we shall be right to speak of them all on the same principle as things that in this sense '*are not*', and again, because they partake of Existence, to say that they '*are*' (exist) and call them things that have been (existence).

THEAET. No doubt.

STR. So, in the case of every one of the Forms there is much that it *is* and an indefinite number of things that it *is not.*[59]

THEAET. So it appears.

STR. And, moreover, Existence itself must be called different [257] from the rest.

THEAET. Necessarily.

STR. We find, then, that Existence likewise 'is not' in as many respects as there are other things; for, not being those others, while it *is* its single self, it *is not* all that indefinite number of other things.

THEAET. That is so.

STR. Then we must not boggle even at that conclusion, granted that Kinds are of a nature to admit combination with one another. If anyone denies that, he must win over our earlier arguments to his side before he tries to win over their consequences.

THEAET. That is a fair demand.

There are also any number of true statements asserting that 'what is not' in a sense 'is' [257B-258C]

STR. Now let us mark this.

THEAET. Yes?

STR. When we speak of 'that which is not', it seems that we do not mean something contrary to what exists but only something that is different.

THEAET. How?

STR. In the same way that when, for example, we speak of something as

---

[59] This means that many affirmative statements are true of any Form, and also any number of negative statements, expressing its difference from other Forms. This conclusion is next applied to Existence itself.

'not tall', we may just as well mean by that phrase 'what is equal' as 'what is short', mayn't we? [60]

THEAET. Certainly.

STR. So, when it is asserted that a negative signifies a contrary, we shall not agree, but admit no more than this: that the prefix 'not' indicates [c] something different from the words that follow—or rather from the things designated by the words pronounced after the negative.

THEAET. Exactly.

STR. And here, if you agree, is a point for us to consider.

THEAET. Namely?

STR. The nature of the Different (Difference) [61] appears to the parcelled out, in the same way as knowledge.

THEAET. How so?

STR. Knowledge also is surely one, but each part of it that commands a certain field is marked off and given a special name proper to itself. [D] Hence language recognises many arts and forms of knowledge.[62]

THEAET. Certainly.

STR. And the same thing is true of the parts of the single nature of the Different.

THEAET. Perhaps; but shall we explain how?

STR. There exists a part of the Different that is set in contrast to the Beautiful?

THEAET. Yes.

STR. Are we to say it is nameless, or has it a special name?

THEAET. It has. Whenever we use the expression 'not Beautiful', the thing we mean is precisely that which is different from the nature of the Beautiful.

STR. Then tell me this.

THEAET. What?   [E]

STR. May we not say that the *existence* of the not-Beautiful is constituted by its being marked off from a single definite Kind among existing things and again set in contrast with something that exists?

THEAET. Yes.

STR. So it appears that the not-Beautiful is an instance of something that exists being set in contrast to something that exists.

THEAET. Perfectly.

STR. What then? On this showing has the non-Beautiful any less claim than the Beautiful to be a thing that exists?

---

[60] 'Short' is the contrary of 'tall'; but 'equal' is not; so the equal is different from the tall, not contrary. Similarly 'the not-beautiful' is not necessarily 'the ugly'.

[61] The ambiguity of θάτερον in all this section—'the different' (that which is different) and 'Difference itself'—will be discussed below.

[62] Knowledge and its species are a mere illustration. There is no suggestion that the species of knowledge correspond to 'parts of the Different'. Every Form is a part of the Different, but there is not a species of knowledge for every Form.

THEAET. None whatever.

STR. And so the not-Tall must be said to exist just as much as the Tall itself. [258]

THEAET. Just as much.

STR. And we must also put the not-Just [63] on the same footing as the Just with respect to the fact that the one exists no less than the other.

THEAET. Certainly.

STR. And we shall say the same of all the rest, since we have seen that the nature of the Different is to be ranked among things that exist, and, once it exists, its parts also must be considered as existing just as much as anything else.

THEAET. Of course.

STR. So, it seems, when a part of the nature of the Different and a part of the nature of the Existent (Existence) are set in contrast to one [B] another, the contrast is, if it be permissible to say so, as much a reality as Existence itself; it does not mean what is contrary to 'existent', but only what is different from that Existent.

THEAET. That is quite clear.

STR. What name are we to give it, then?

THEAET. Obviously this is just that 'what-is-not' which we were seeking for the sake of the Sophist.

STR. Has it then, as you say, an existence inferior to none of the rest *in* reality? May we now be bold to say that 'that which is not' unquestionably *is* a thing that has a nature of its own—just as the Tall was tall and [C] the Beautiful was beautiful, so too with the not-Tall and the not-Beautiful—and in that sense 'that which is not' also, on the same principle, both was and *is* what-is-not, a single Form to be reckoned among the many realities? Or have we any further doubts with regard to it, Theaetetus?

THEAET. None at all.

Conclusion: We have refuted Parmenides' dogma that [258C-259D] *'what is' cannot in any sense not-be, and that 'what is not' cannot in any sense be*

STR. You see, then, that in our disobedience to Parmenides we have trespassed far beyond the limits of his prohibition.

THEAET. In what way?

STR. In pushing forward on our quest, we have shown him results in a field which he forbade us even to explore.

THEAET. How?

STR. He says, you remember, [D]

'Never shall this be proved, that things that are not, are; but keep back thy thought from this way of inquiry'.

THEAET. Yes, he does say that.

---

[63] The 'not-Just' is not 'the unjust', but any Form that is different from 'the Just'. . . . Note that the moral Forms (Beautiful, Just) once more appear alongside the rest.

STR.   Whereas we have not merely shown that things that are not, are, but we have brought to light the real character of 'not-being'. We have shown that the nature of the Different has existence and is parcelled   [E] out over the whole field of existent things with reference to one another; and of every part of it that is set in contrast to 'that which is' we have dared to say that precisely that *is really* 'that which is not'.

THEAET.   Yes, sir, and I think what we have said is perfectly true.

STR.   Then let no one say that it is the contrary of the existent that we mean by 'what is not', when we make bold to say that 'what is not' exists. So far as any contrary of the existent is concerned, we have long ago [64] said good-bye to the question whether there is such a thing or not   [259] and whether any account can be given of it or none whatsoever.

But with respect to the 'what-is-not' that we have now asserted to exist, an opponent must either convince us that our account is wrong by refuting it, or, so long as he proves unable to do that, he must accept our statements:

that the Kinds blend with one another;

that Existence and Difference pervade them all, and pervade one another;

that Difference (*or* the Different),[65] by partaking of Existence, *is* by virtue of that participation, but on the other hand *is not* that Existence of which it partakes, but is different; and since it is different from Existence (*or* an existent), quite clearly it must be possible [66] that it should *be* a thing that *is not* [67];

and again, Existence, have a part in Difference, will be differ-   [B] ent from all the rest of the Kinds; and, because it is different from them all, it *is not* any one of them nor yet all the others put together, but is only itself, [68] with the consequence, again indisputable, that Existence *is not* myriads upon myriads of things, and that all the other Kinds in the

---

[64] At 238C, where τὸ μηδαμῶς ὄν, 'the simply non-existent', was dismissed as not to be spoken or thought of. There are no true statements saying that any Form does not exist. But it is true of every Form other than Existence itself that it is not (identical with) Existence.

[65] As before, θάτερον is verbally ambiguous and the formula covers the two statements: (1) that the Form Difference *is not* (the same as) Existence, but *is* (exists); (2) that the different (that which is not so-and-so) *is not* (the same as) a thing that is (*viz.* a certain existent, the so-and-so differs from), but *is* a thing that is (an existent).

[66] ἔστιν ἐξ ἀνάγκης εἶναι, 'It is possible, necessarily, for it to be'. Cf 256D, ἔστιν ἐξ ἀνάγκης ...εἶναι in the same sense.

[67] *I.e.* (1) Difference is not Existence; and (2) the different is not some other definite existent with which it contrasted.

[68] Here the distinction between the Form Existence as discussed in all this section and the Existent (the Real, the whole world of real Forms) is clearly recognised. The corresponding statements are: (1) Existence *is not* (the same as any other Form), but *is* (the same as) itself; (2) the Existent (any Form or group of Forms) *is not* (the same as) any other existent, but *is* (exists).

same way, whether taken severally or all together, in many respects *are* and in many respects *are not*.

THEAET. True.

STR. And if anyone mistrusts these apparent contradictions, he should study the question and produce some better explanation that we [c] have now given; whereas if he imagines he has discovered an embarrassing puzzle and takes delight in reducing argument to a tug of war, he is wasting his pains on a triviality, as our present argument declares. There is nothing clever in such a discovery, nor is it hard to make; what is hard and at the same time worth the pains is something different.

THEAET. And that is—?

STR. What I said before: leaving such quibbling alone as leading nowhere,[69] to be able to follow our statements step by step and, in criticising the assertion that a different thing is the same or the same thing is [D] different in a certain sense, to take account of the precise sense and the precise respect in which they are said to be one or the other. Merely to show that in some unspecified way the same is different or the different is the same, the tall short, the like unlike, and to take pleasure in perpetually parading such contradictions in argument—that is not genuine criticism, but may be recognised as the callow offspring of a too recent contact with reality.

THEAET. I quite agree.

III

FALSE SPEAKING AND THINKING

Introductory statement of the problem [259D-261C]

STR. Yes, my friend, and the attempt to separate everything from every other thing not only strikes a discordant note but amounts to a [E] crude defiance of the philosophic Muse.

THEAET. Why?

STR. This isolation of everything from everything else means a complete abolition of all discourse; for any discourse we can have owes its existence to the weaving together of Forms.

THEAET. True.

STR. Observe, then, how opportune was our struggle with those [260] separatists, when we forced them to allow one Form to blend with another.

THEAET. In what respect?

STR. In respect of securing the position of discourse as one of the kinds

---

[69] ἀνήνυτα (Badham) seems to be the most probable correction of δυνατὰ yet proposed.

of things that exist. To rob us of discourse would be to rob us of philosophy. That would be the most serious consequence; but, besides that, we need at the present moment to come to an agreement about the nature of discourse, and if its very existence had been taken from us, we should naturally not be able to discourse any further. And that [B] would have happened, if we had yielded the point that there is no blending of any one Form with another.

THEAET.　That is certainly true. But I do not understand why we need an agreement about discourse at the present moment.

STR.　I may be able to suggest a line of thought that will help you to understand.

THEAET.　What is that?

STR.　We saw the 'not being' is a single kind among the rest, dispersed over the whole field of realities.

THEAET.　Yes.

STR.　We have next to consider whether it blends with thinking and discourse.

THEAET.　Why that?

STR.　If it does not blend with them, everything must be true; but [C] if it does, we shall have false thinking and discourse; for thinking or saying 'what is not' comes, I suppose, to the same thing as falsity in thought and speech.

THEAET.　Yes.

STR.　And if falsity exists, deception is possible.

THEAET.　Yes.

STR.　And once deception exists, images and likenesses and appearance will be everywhere rampant.

THEAET.　Of course.

STR.　And the Sophist, we said, had taken refuge somewhere in [D] that region, but then he had denied the very existence of falsity: no one could either think or say 'what is not', because what is not never has any sort of being.

THEAET.　So he said.

STR.　But now that 'what is not' has been found to have its share in existence, perhaps he will not fight with us further on that point. On the other hand, he may perhaps say that some things partake of not-being, some do not, and that speech and thinking are among those that do not; and so once more he might contend that the art of creating images [E] and semblances, where we say he is to be found, has no existence at all, since thought and speech have no share in not-being, and without that combination there is no such thing as falsity.

That is why we must begin by investigating the nature of discourse and thinking and appearance, in order that we may then make out their combination with not-being and so prove that falsity exists, and by [261] that proof pin down the Sophist there, if he is amenable to capture, or else let him go and pursue our search in some other Kind.

THEAET.　Certainly, sir, what we said at the outset about the Sophist seems true: that he is a hard sort of beast to hunt down. Evidently he possesses a whole armoury of problems, and every time that he puts one forward to shield him, we have to fight our way through it before we can get at him. So now, hardly have we got the better of his defence that 'what is not' cannot exist, when another obstacle is raised in our path: [B] we must, it seems, prove that falsity exists both in speech and thought, and after that perhaps something else, and so on. It looks as if the end would never be in sight.

STR. A man should be of good courage, Theaetetus, if he can make only a little headway at each step. If he loses heart then, what will he do in another case where he cannot advance at all or even perhaps loses ground? No city, as they say, will surrender to so faint a summons. And now [C] that we have surmounted the barrier you speak of, we may have already taken the highest wall and the rest may be easier to capture.

THEAET. That is encouraging.

Every statement is a complex of heterogeneous elements (name and verb) [261C-262E]

STR. Then, as I said, let us take first statement [70] and judgment, so as to establish clearly whether not-being has any point of contact with them, or both are altogether true and there is never falsity in either.

THEAET. Very good.

STR. Now, remembering what we said about Forms and letters,[71] [D] let us consider words in the same way. The solution of our present problem promises to lie in that quarter.

THEAET. What are you going to ask me about words?

STR. Whether they all fit together, or none of them, or some will and some will not.

THEAET. That is plain enough: some will, some will not.

STR. You mean perhaps something like this: words which, when spoken in succession, signify something, do fit together, while those which [E] mean nothing when they are strung together, do not.

THEAET. What do you mean?

STR. What I supposed you had in your mind when you gave your assent.[72] The signs we use in speech to signify being are surely of two kinds.

---

[70] 'Statement.' So far λόγος has been translated 'discourse'; but the following analysis is concerned with what Aristotle calls the ἀποφαντικὸς λόγος, a statement which can and must be either true or false, as distinct from questions, prayers, etc. A 'judgment' (as explained later) is here equivalent to an unspoken statement made by the mind in its internal dialogue with itself.

[71] At 253A (p. 260).

[72] Probably what Theaetetus had in mind was the combination of Forms in affirmative statements and the incompatibility of Forms expressed by negative statements, which was illustrated by the fitting-together (συναρμόττειν) or not fitting of vowels and consonants at 253A. But the Stranger is referring only to the illustration and is thinking of the fact that a statement cannot consist of a combination of two nouns only or of two verbs only, any more than a word can consist of two consonants without a vowel.

THEAET. How?

STR.   One kind called 'names', the other 'verbs'.   [262]

THEAET. Give me a description of each.

STR.   By 'verb' we mean an expression which is applied to actions.

THEAET. Yes.

STR.   And by a 'name' the spoken sign applied to what performs these actions.

THEAET. Quite so.

STR.   Now a statement never consists solely of names spoken in succession, nor yet of verbs apart from names.

THEAET. I don't follow that.

STR.   Evidently you had something else in mind when you agreed   [B] with me just now; because what I meant was just this: that these words spoken in a string in this way do not make a statement.

THEAET. In what way?

STR.   For example, 'walks runs sleeps',[73] and so on with all the other verbs signifying actions—you may utter them all one after another, but that does not make a statement.

THEAET. Naturally.

STR.   And again, if you say 'lion stag horse' and any other names given to things that perform actions, such a string never makes up a state-   [C] ment. Neither in this example nor in the other do the sounds uttered signify any action performed or not performed or nature of anything that exists or does not exist,[74] until you combine verbs with names. The moment you do that, they fit together and the simplest combination becomes a statement of what might be called the simplest and briefest kind.

THEAET. Then how do you make a statement of that kind?

STR.   When one says 'A man understands', do you agree that this is a statement of the simplest and shortest possible kind?

THEAET. Yes.   [D]

STR.   Because now it gives information about facts or events in the present or past or future: it does not merely name something but gets you somewhere by weaving together verbs with names. Hence we say it 'states' something, not merely 'names' something, and in fact it is this complex that we mean by the word 'statement'.

THEAET. True.

STR.   And so, just as some things fit together, some do not, so with the

---

[73] The inverted commas in Burnet's text between βαδίζει and καθεύδει (and below, between λέων and ἵπποι) should be omitted.

[74] πρᾶξιν οὐδ' ἀπραξίαν refers to the former example (ἐκείνως) of the string of verbs, which does not state that any action is actually performed, or not performed, by any agent. οὐδὲ οὐσίαν ὄντος οὐδὲ μὴ ὄντος refers to the latter example (οὕτως) of the string of names, which does not state that there actually exists (ὄντος), or does not exist, anything with the nature (οὐσία) expressed by any of the names. This does not mean that the words themselves have no meaning, and are senseless noises; but that such concatenations are not statements of fact, do not refer (or profess to refer) to any actual fact or event.

signs of speech: some do not fit, but those that do fit make a state- [E] ment.

THEAET. Quite so.

Every statement is about something and is either true or false [262E]

STR. Now another small point.

THEAET. Yes?

STR. Whenever there is a statement, it must be about something; it cannot be about nothing.

THEAET. That is so.

STR. And must it not have a certain character? [75]

THEAET. Of course.

The definition of true statement [262E-263B]

STR. Now let us fix our attention on ourselves.

THEAET. We will.

STR. I will make a statement to you, then, putting together a thing with an action by means of a name and a verb. You are to tell me what the statement is about.

THEAET. I will do my best. [263]

STR. 'Theaetetus sits'—not a lengthy statement, is it?

THEAET. No, of very modest length.

STR. Now it is for you to say what it is about—to whom it belongs.

THEAET. Clearly about me: it belongs to me.

STR. Now take another.

THEAET. Namely——?

STR. 'Theaetetus (whom I am talking to at this moment) [76] flies.'

THEAET. That too can only be described as belonging to me and about me.

STR. And moreover we agree that any statement must have a certain character.

THEAET. Yes. [B]

STR. Then what sort of character can we assign to each of these?

THEAET. One is false, the other true.

STR. And the true one states about you the things that are (or the facts) as they are.

THEAET. Certainly.

The definition of false statement [263B-D]

STR. Whereas the false statement states about you things *different* from the things that are.

THEAET. Yes.

STR. And accordingly states *things that are-not* as being.

---

[75] That 'character' or 'quality' means truth or falsity, here as at *Philebus* 37B, is obvious from what follows (263A, B).

[76] Not an imaginary Theaetetus or Theaetetus at some other moment, but the real Theaetetus here and now.

THEAET.   No doubt.

STR.   Yes, but things that *exist,* different from things that *exist* in your case. For we said that in the case of everything there are many things that are and also many that are not.

THEAET.   Quite so.

STR.   So the second statement I made about you, in the first place,   [c] according to our definition of the nature of a statement, must itself necessarily be one of the shortest possible.

THEAET.   So we agreed just now.

STR.   And secondly it must be about something.

THEAET.   Yes.

STR.   And if it is not about you, it is not about anything else.

THEAET.   Certainly.

STR.   And if it were about nothing, it would not be a statement at all; for we pointed out that there could not be a statement that was a statement about nothing.

THEAET.   Quite true.

STR.   So what is stated about you, but so that what is different is   [d] stated as the same or what is not as what is—a combination of verbs and names answering to that description finally seems to be really and truly a false statement.

THEAET.   Perfectly true.

Judgment being simply unspoken statement, false judg-   [263D-264B]
ment and false 'appearing' are possible

STR.   And next, what of thinking and judgment and appearing? Is it not now clear that all these things occur in our minds both as false and as true?

THEAET.   How so?

STR.   You will see more easily if you begin by letting me give you an account of their nature and how each differs from the others.   [E]

THEAET.   Let me have it.

STR.   Well, thinking and discourse [77] are the same thing, except that what we call thinking is, precisely, the inward dialogue carried on by the mind with itself without spoken sound.

THEAET.   Certainly.

STR.   Whereas the stream which flows from the mind through the lips with sound is called discourse.

THEAET.   True.

STR.   And further there is a thing [78] which we know occurs in discourse.

---

[77] Thinking ($\delta\iota\acute{a}\nu o\iota a$) and discourse ($\lambda\acute{o}\gamma o\varsigma$) are both used in the wide sense which includes, not only judgment ($\delta\acute{o}\xi a$) and statement ($\lambda\acute{o}\gamma o\varsigma$) which must be true or false, but all forms of thinking and speech, questions, commands, etc. The account of thinking as unspoken discourse at *Theaet.* 189E (p. 118) and 206D (p. 155), is here briefly repeated.

[78] $a\grave{v}\tau\grave{o}$, BT should be retained: 'a thing (presently to be mentioned)'. Cf. $a\grave{v}\tau\grave{a}$ at *Theaet.* 207D (Campbell).

THEAET. Namely?

STR. Assertion and denial.[79]

THEAET. Yes.

STR. Then when this occurs in the mind in the course of silent [264] thinking, can you call it anything but judgment?

THEAET. No.

STR. And suppose judgment occurs, not independently, but by means of perception, the only right name for such a state of mind is 'appearing'.

THEAET. Yes.

STR. Well then, since we have seen that there is true and false statement, and of these mental processes we have found thinking to be a dialogue of the mind with itself, and judgment to be the conclusion of think- [B] ing, and what we mean by 'it appears' a blend of perception and judgment, it follows that these also, being of the same nature as statement, must be, some of them and on some occasions, false.

THEAET. Of course.

STR. You see, then, that we have discovered the nature of false judgment and false statement sooner than we expected just now when we feared there would be no end to the task we were setting ourselves in the search for them.

THEAET. I do.

Transition, connecting these results with the interrupted [264B-D]
Division of Image-making

STR. Then let us not lose courage for what remains to be done. Now that these matters are cleared up, let us recall our earlier divisions [C] by forms.

THEAET. Which do you mean?

STR. We distinguished two forms of Image-making: the making of likenesses and the making of semblances.

THEAET. Yes.

STR. And we said we were puzzled to tell under which of these two we should place the Sophist.

THEAET. We did.

STR. And to increase our perplexity we were plunged in a whirl of confusion by the apparition of an argument that called in question all these terms and disputed the very existence of any copy or image or semblance, on the ground that falsity never has any sort of existence anywhere. [D]

THEAET. True.

STR. But now that we have brought to light the existence of false statement and of false judgment, it is possible that there should be imitations

---

[79] φάσις and ἀπόφασις cover (1) affirmation and negation, which appear in the affirmative or negative form of the spoken statement, and (2) the mental acts of assent and dissent—saying 'yes' and 'no'—to questions which the mind puts to itself, as described at *Theaet.* 190A, φάσκουσα καὶ οὐ φάσκουσα (p. 118). Judgment was there defined as the mind's final decision when all doubt and debate is over.

of real things and that this condition of mind (false judgment) should account for the existence of an art of deception.

THEAET. Yes, it is.

STR. And we agreed earlier that the Sophist does come under one or other of the two kinds mentioned.

THEAET. Yes.

The Sophist as a species of Image-maker [80]   [264D-268D]

STR. Now, then, let us set to work again and, as we divide the Kind proposed in two, keep to the right-hand section at each stage. [E] Holding fast to the characters of which the Sophist partakes until we have stripped off all that he has in common with others and left only the nature that is peculiar to him, let us so make that nature plain, in the first place to ourselves, and secondly to others whose temperament   [265] finds a procedure of this sort congenial.

THEAET. Very good.

STR. Well, we began by dividing Art into Productive and Acquisitive.

THEAET. Yes.

STR. And under the head of the Acquisitive we had glimpses of the Sophist in the arts of hunting, contention, trafficking, and other kinds of that sort.[81]

---

[80] The final Table of Division is as follows:

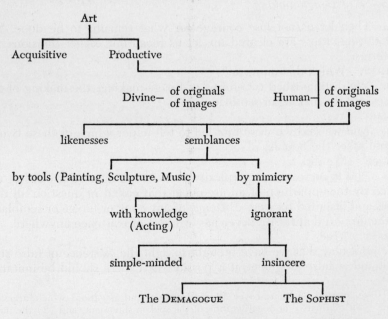

---

[81] This reference to the five tentative Divisions of the Acquisitive branch is significant. They only provided 'glimpses' or indistinct visions of various types called sophists, not the essential feature. With ἐφαντάζετο compare

THEAET. Certainly.

STR. But now that he has been included under an art of Imitation, clearly we must start by dividing into two the Productive branch of Art. [B] For Imitation is surely a kind of production, though it be only a production of images, as we say, not of originals of every sort. Is that not so?

THEAET. Assuredly.

STR. Let us begin, then, by recognising two kinds of Production.

THEAET. What are they?

STR. The one Divine, the other Human.

THEAET. I don't understand yet.

STR. Production—to recall what we said at the outset—we defined as any power that can bring into existence what did not exist before.

THEAET. I remember.

STR. Now take all mortal animals and also all things that grow— [C] plants that grow above the earth from seeds and roots, and lifeless bodies compacted beneath the earth, whether fusible or not fusible. Must we not attribute the coming into being of these things out of not-being to divine craftsmanship and nothing else? Or are we to fall in with the belief that is commonly expressed?

THEAET. What belief do you mean?

STR. That Nature gives birth to them as a result of some spontaneous cause that generates without intelligence. Or shall we say that they come from a cause which, working with reason and art, is divine and proceeds from divinity?

THEAET. Perhaps because I am young, I often shift from one belief to the other; but at this moment, looking at your face and believing you to hold that these things have a divine origin, I too am convinced.

STR. Well said, Theaetetus. If I thought you were the sort of person that might believe otherwise in the future, I should now try by force of persuasion to make you accept that account. But I can see clearly that, without any arguments of mine, your nature will come of itself to [E] the conclusion which you tell me attracts you at this moment. So I will let that pass: I should be wasting time. I will only lay it down that the products of Nature, as they are called, are works of divine art, as things made out of them by man are works of human art. Accordingly there will be two kinds of Production, one human, the other divine.

THEAET. Good.

STR. Once more, then, divide each of these two into two parts.

THEAET. How?

STR. As you have just divided the whole extent of Production [266] horizontally, now divide it vertically.

THEAET. Be it so.

φαντα£όμενον used of the figure indistinctly seen at a distance, *Philebus* 38c. The third main branch of Art, the Separative (διακριτική), from which was derived the Cathartic method of Socrates in Division VI, is here ignored. It gave us no glimpse of the Sophist.

STR. The result is four parts in all: two on our side, human; two on the side of the gods, divine.

THEAET. Yes.

STR. And taking the divisions made in the first way (horizontally: divine and human), one section of each part will be the production of originals, and the remaining two sections will be best described as production of images. So we have a second division of Production on that principle (originals and images).

THEAET. Explain once more how each of the two parts (divine [B] and human) is divided.

STR. Ourselves, I take it, and all other living creatures and the elements of natural things—fire, water, and their kindred—are all originals, the offspring, as we are well assured, of divine workmanship. Is it not so?

THEAET. Yes.

STR. And every one of these products is attended by images which are not the actual thing, and which also owe their existence to divine contrivance.

THEAET. You mean——?

STR. Dream images, and in daylight all those naturally produced semblances which we call 'shadow' when dark patches interrupt the [C] light, or a 'reflection' when the light belonging to the eye meets and coalesces with light belonging to something else on a bright and smooth surface and produces a form yielding a perception that is the reverse of the ordinary direct view.

THEAET. There are, indeed, these two products of divine workmanship: the original and the image that in every case accompanies it.[82]

STR. And what of our human art? Must we not say that in building it produces an actual house, and in painting a house of a different sort, as it were a man-made dream for waking eyes?

THEAET. Certainly. [D]

STR. And so in all cases, we find once more twin products of our own productive activity in pairs—one an actual thing, the other an image.

THEAET. I understand better now, and I recognise two forms of production, each of them twofold: divine and human according to one division, and according to the other a production of actual things and of some sort of likenesses.

STR. Let us remind ourselves, then, that of this production of images there were to be two kinds, one producing likenesses, the other [E] semblances, provided that falsity should be shown to be a thing that

---

[82] These originals and images make up the contents of the visible world (ὁρατά or δοξαστά of *Rep.* vi, where they are described in similar terms, 510A). They are the work of the divine craftsman of the *Timaeus*, who fashions the visible world after the pattern of the Forms. The Forms themselves, which are not created, are, of course, not mentioned here. But the Platonist will recall that the actual things here called originals are themselves only copies or images of the Forms. They are those *eidola* whose ambiguous existence still remains a problem.

really is false and of such a nature as to have a place among existing things.

THEAET. Yes, it was to be so.

STR. And that has now been shown; so on that ground shall we now reckon the distinction of these two forms as beyond dispute?

THEAET. Yes.

STR. Once more, then, let us divide in two the kind that pro- [267] duces semblances.

THEAET. How?

STR. There is the semblance produced by means of tools, and another sort where the producer of the semblance takes his own person as an instrument.

THEAET. How do you mean?

STR. When someone uses his own person or voice to counterfeit your traits or speech, the proper name for creating such a semblance is, I take it, Mimicry.

THEAET. Yes.

STR. Let us reserve that section, then, under the name of mimicry, and indulge ourselves so far as to leave all the rest for someone else to [B] collect into a unity and give it an appropriate name.

THEAET. So be it.

STR. But there is still ground for thinking that mimicry is of two sorts. Let me put it before you.

THEAET. Do.

STR. Some mimics know the thing they are impersonating, other do not; and could we find a more important distinction than that of knowing from not knowing?

THEAET. No.

STR. And the mimicry we have just mentioned goes with knowledge; for to impersonate you, one must be acquainted with you and your traits.

THEAET. Of course. [C]

STR. And what of the traits of Justice and of virtue generally? Are there not many who, having no knowledge of virtue but only some sort of opinion about it, zealously set about making it appear that they embody virtue as they conceive it, mimicking it as effectively as they can in their words and actions?

THEAET. Only too many.

STR. And are they always unsuccessful in appearing to be virtuous when they are not really virtuous at all? Do they not rather succeed perfectly?

THEAET. They do.

STR. We must, then, distinguish the ignorant mimic from the other, [D] who has knowledge.

THEAET. Yes.

STR. Where, then, must we look for a suitable name for each? No doubt it is hard to find one, because the ancients, it would seem, suffered from a certain laziness and lack of discrimination with regard to the division of Kinds by forms, and not one of them even tried to make such divisions, with the result that there is a serious shortage of names. However, though the expression may seem daring, for purposes of distinction let us call mimicry guided by opinion 'conceit-mimicry', and the sort that is   [E] guided by knowledge 'mimicry by acquaintance'.

THEAET.   So be it.

STR.   It is the former, then, that concerns us; for the Sophist was not among those who have knowledge, but he has a place among mimics.

THEAET.   Certainly.

STR.   Then let us take this conceit-mimic and see if his metal rings sound or there is still a crack in it somewhere.

THEAET.   Let us do so.

STR.   Well, there is a gaping crack. There is the simple-minded   [268] type who imagines that what he believes is knowledge, and an opposite type who is versed in discussion, so that his attitude betrays no little misgiving and suspicion that the knowledge he has the air of possessing in the eyes of the world is really ignorance.

THEAET.   Certainly both the types you describe exist.

STR.   We may, then, set down one of these mimics as sincere, the other as insincere.

THEAET.   So it appears.

STR.   And the insincere—is he of two kinds or only one?

THEAET.   That is for you to consider.

STR.   I will; and I can clearly make out a pair of them. I see one   [B] who can keep up his dissimulation publicly in long speeches to a large assembly. The other uses short arguments in private and forces others to contradict themselves in conversation.

THEAET.   Very true.

STR.   And with whom shall we identify the more long-winded type— with the Statesman or with the demagogue?

THEAET.   The demagogue.

STR.   And what shall we call the other—wise man or Sophist?

THEAET.   We cannot surely call him wise, because we set him down   [C] as ignorant; but as a mimic of the wise man he will clearly assume a title derived from his, and I now see that here at last is the man who must be truly described as the real and genuine Sophist.

STR.   Shall we, then, as before collect all the elements of his description, from the end to the beginning,[83] and draw our threads together in a knot?

THEAET.   By all means.

STR.   The art of contradiction-making, descended from an insincere kind of conceited mimicry, of the semblance-making breed, derived from im- age-making, distinguished as a portion, not divine but human, of   [D] production, that presents a shadow-play of words—such is the blood and

---

[83] The construction of the final definition is obscured by the effort to frame it so as to mention all the specific differences in order 'from the end to the beginning' (productive art).

lineage which can, with perfect truth, be assigned to the authentic Sophist.

THEAET. I entirely agree.

TIMAEUS (*in part*)

PERSONS OF THE DIALOGUE

Critias   *Socrates*   *Timaeus*

·   ·   ·

Crit. I will submit to you the plan we have arranged for your [27A] entertainment, Socrates. We decided that Timaeus shall speak first. He knows more of astronomy than the rest of us and has made knowledge of the nature of the universe his chief object; he will begin with the birth of the world and end with the nature of man.

·   ·   ·

Tim. We must in my judgment, first make this distinction: what is that which is always real and has no becoming, and what is that which is always becoming and is never real? That which is apprehensible by thought [28] with a rational account is the thing that is always unchangeably real; whereas that which is the object of belief together with unreasoning sensation is the thing that becomes and passes away, but never has real being. Again, all that becomes must needs become by the agency of some cause; for without a cause nothing can come to be. Now whenever the maker of anything looks to that which is always unchanging and uses a model of that description in fashioning the form and quality of his work, all that he thus accomplishes must be good. If he looks to something that has [B] come to be and uses a generated model, it will not be good.

So concerning the whole Heaven or World—let us call it by whatsoever name may be most acceptable to it [1]—we must ask the question which, it is agreed, must be asked at the outset of inquiry concerning anything: Has it always been, without any source of becoming; or has it come to be, starting from some beginning? It has come to be; for it can be seen and touched and it has body, and all such things are sensible; and as we saw, sensible things, that are to be apprehended by belief together with [C] sensation, are things that become and can be generated. But again, that which becomes, we say, must necessarily become by the agency of some cause. The maker and father of this universe it is a hard task to find, and having found him it would be impossible to declare him to all mankind.

---

[1] "Heaven" (οὐρανός) is used throughout the dialogue as a synonym of *cosmos*, the entire world, not the sky.

Be that as it may, we must go back to this question about the world: After
which of the two models did its builder frame it—after that which is
always in the same unchanging state, or after that which has come   [29]
to be? Now if this world is good and its maker is good, clearly he looked to
the eternal; on the contrary supposition (which cannot be spoken without
blasphemy), to that which has come to be. Everyone, then, must see that
he looked to the eternal; for the world is the best of things that have become, and he is the best of causes. Having come to be, then, in this way,
the world has been fashioned on the model of that which is comprehensible by rational discourse and understanding and is always in the
same state.

Again, these things being so, our world must necessarily be a like-   [B]
ness of something. Now in every matter it is of great moment to start at
the right point in accordance with the nature of the subject. Concerning
a likeness, then, and its model we must make this distinction: an account
is of the same order as the things which it sets forth—an account of that
which is abiding and stable and discoverable by the aid of reason will
itself be abiding and unchangeable (so far as it is possible and it lies in
the nature of an account to be incontrovertible and irrefutable, there must
be no falling short of that); while an account of what is made in the   [C]
image of that other, but is only a likeness, will itself be but likely, standing
to accounts of the former kind in a proportion: as reality is to becoming,
so is truth to disbelief. If then, Socrates, in many respects concerning
many things—the gods and the generation of the universe—we prove unable to render an account at all points entirely consistent with itself and
exact, you must not be surprised. If we can furnish accounts no less likely
than any other, we must be content, remembering that I who speak and
you my judges are only human, and consequently it is fitting that we   [D]
should, in these matters, accept the likely story and look for nothing
further.

Socr.   Excellent, Timaeus; we must certainly accept it as you say. Your
prelude we have found exceedingly acceptable; so now go on to develop
your main theme.

Tim.   Let us, then, state for what reason becoming and this universe
were framed by him who framed them. He was good; and in the   [E]
good no jealousy in any matter can ever arise. So, being without jealousy,
he desired that all things should come as near as possible to being like
himself. That this is the supremely valid principle of becoming and of
the order of the world, we shall most surely be right to accept from men
of understanding. Desiring, then, that all things should be good and,   [30]
so far as might be, nothing imperfect, the god took over all that is visible
—not at rest, but in discordant and unordered motion—and brought it from
disorder into order, since he judged that order was in every way the better.

Now it was not, nor can it ever be, permitted that the work of the
supremely good should be anything but that which is best. Taking
thought, therefore, he found that, among things that are by nature   [B]
visible, no work that is without intelligence will ever be better than one

that has intelligence, when each is taken as a whole, and moreover that intelligence cannot be present in anything apart from soul. In virtue of this reasoning, when he framed the universe, he fashioned reason within soul and soul within body, to the end that the work he accomplished might be by nature as excellent and perfect as possible. This, then, is how we must say, according to the likely account, that this world came to be, by the god's providence, in very truth a living creature with soul and   [c] reason.

This being premised, we have now to state what follows next: What was the living creature in whose likeness he framed the world? We must not suppose that it was any creature that ranks only as a species; for no copy of that which is incomplete can ever be good. Let us rather say that the world is like, above all things, to that Living Creature of which all other living creatures, severally and in their families, are parts. For that embraces and contains within itself all the intelligible living crea-   [d] tures, just as this world contains ourselves and all other creatures that have been formed as things visible. For the god, wishing to make this world most nearly like that intelligible thing which is best and in every way complete, fashioned it as a single visible living creature, containing within itself all living things whose nature is of the same order.

Have we, then, been right to call it one Heaven, or would it have   [31] been true rather to speak of many and indeed of an indefinite number? One we must call it, if we are to hold that it was made according to its pattern. For that which embraces all the intelligible living creatures that there are, cannot be one of a pair; for then there would have to be yet another Living Creature embracing those two, and they would be parts of it; and thus our world would be more truly described as a likeness, not of them, but of that other which would embrace them. Accordingly, to the end that this world may be like the completely Living Creature in respect of its uniqueness, for that reason its maker did not make two   [b] worlds nor yet an indefinite number; but this Heaven has come to be and is and shall be hereafter one and unique.

Now that which comes to be must be bodily, and so visible and tangible; and nothing can be visible without fire, or tangible without something solid, and nothing is solid without earth. Hence the god, when he began to put together the body of the universe, set about making it of fire and earth. But two things alone cannot be satisfactorily united without a third; for there must be some bond between them drawing them together.   [c] And of all bonds the best is that which makes itself and the terms it connects a unity in the fullest sense; and it is of the nature of a continued geometrical proportion to effect this most perfectly. For whenever, of three numbers, the middle one between any two that are either   [32] solids (cubes?) or squares is such that, as the first is to it, so is it to the last, and conversely as the last is to the middle, so is the middle to the first, then since the middle becomes first and last, and again the last and first becomes middle, in that way all will necessarily come to play the same part toward one another, and by so doing they will all make a unity.

Now if it had been required that the body of the universe should be a plane surface with no depth, a single mean would have been enough to connect its companions and itself; but in fact the world was to be [B] solid in form, and solids are always conjoined, not by one mean, but by two. Accordingly the god set water and air between fire and earth, and made them, so far as was possible, proportional to one another, so that as fire is to air, so is air to water, and as air is to water, so is water to earth, and thus he bound together the frame of a world visible and tangible.

For these reasons and from such constituents, four in number, the [c] body of the universe was brought into being, coming into concord by means of proportion, and from these it acquired Amity, so that coming into unity with itself it became indissoluble by any other save him who bound it together.

Now the frame of the world took up the whole of each of these four; he who put it together made it consist of all the fire and water and air and earth, leaving no part or power of any one of them outside. This was his intent: first, that it might be in the fullest measure a living being [D] whole and complete, of complete parts; next, that it might be single, nothing being left over, out of which such another might come into [33] being; and moreover that it might be free from age and sickness. For he perceived that, if a body be composite, when hot things and cold and all things that have strong powers beset that body and attack it from without, they bring it to untimely dissolution and cause it to waste away by bringing upon it sickness and age. For this reason and so considering, he fashioned it as a single whole consisting of all these wholes, complete and free from age and sickness.

And for shape he gave it that which is fitting and akin to its [B] nature. For the living creature that was to embrace all living creatures within itself, the fitting shape would be the figure that comprehends in itself all the figures there are; accordingly, he turned its shape rounded and spherical, equidistant every way from center to extremity—a figure the most perfect and uniform of all; for he judged uniformity to be immeasurably better than its opposite. And all round on the outside he made it perfectly smooth, for several reasons. It had no need of [c] eyes, for nothing visible was left outside; nor of hearing, for there was nothing outside to be heard. There was no surrounding air to require breathing, nor yet was it in need of any organ by which to receive food into itself or to discharge it again when drained of its juices. For nothing went out or came into it from anywhere, since there was nothing: it was designed to feed itself on its own waste and to act and be acted upon entirely by itself and within itself; because its framer thought that [D] it would be better self-sufficient, rather than dependent upon anything else.

It had no need of hands to grasp with or to defend itself, nor yet of feet or anything that would serve to stand upon; so he saw no need to attach to it these limbs to no purpose. For he assigned to it the motion proper to its bodily form, namely, that one of the seven which [34] above all belongs to reason and intelligence; accordingly, he caused it to turn about uniformly in the same place and within its own limits and made it revolve round and round; he took from it all the other six motions and gave it no part in their wanderings. And since for this revolution it needed no feet, he made it without feet or legs.

All this, then, was the plan of the god who is forever for the god who was sometime to be. According to this plan he made it smooth and [B] uniform, everywhere equidistant from its center, a body whole and complete, with complete bodies for its parts. And in the center he set a soul and caused it to extend throughout the whole and further wrapped its body round with soul on the outside; and so he established one world alone, round and revolving in a circle, solitary but able by reason of its excellence to bear itself company, needing no other acquaintance or friend but sufficient to itself. On all these accounts the world which he brought into being was a blessed god.

Now this soul, though it comes later in the account we are now attempting, was not made by the god younger than the body; for when he joined them together, he would not have suffered the elder to be [C] ruled by the younger. There is in us too much of the casual and random, which shows itself in our speech; but the god made soul prior to body and more venerable in birth and excellence, to be the body's mistress and governor.

. . .

When the father who had begotten it saw it set in motion and alive, a shrine brought into being for the everlasting gods, he rejoiced and being well pleased he took thought to make it yet more like its pattern. So as that pattern is the Living Being that is forever existent, he sought to make this universe also like it, so far as might be, in that respect. Now the [37D] nature of that Living Being was eternal, and this character it was impossible to confer in full completeness on the generated thing. But he took thought to make, as it were, a moving likeness of eternity; and, at the same time that he ordered the Heaven, he made, of eternity that abides in unity, an everlasting likeness moving according to number—that to which we have given the name Time.

For there were no days and nights, months and years, before the Heaven came into being; but he planned that they should now come [E] to be at the same time that the Heaven was framed. All these are parts of Time, and "was" and "shall be" are forms of time that have come to be; we are wrong to transfer them unthinkingly to eternal being. We say that it was and is and shall be; but "is" alone really belongs to it and describes it truly; "was" and "shall be" are properly used of becoming which [38] proceeds in time, for they are motions. But that which is forever in the same state immovably cannot be becoming older or younger by lapse of time, nor can it ever become so; neither can it now have been, nor will it be in the future; and in general nothing belongs to it of all that Becoming attaches to the moving things of sense; but these have come into being as forms of time, which images eternity and revolves according to number. And besides we make statements like these: that what is past *is* [B] past, what happens now *is* happening now, and again that what will happen *is* what will happen, and that the nonexistent *is* nonexistent: no one of these expressions is exact. But this, perhaps, may not be the right moment for a precise discussion of these matters.

Be that as it may, Time came into being together with the Heaven, in order that, as they were brought into being together, so they may be dissolved together, if ever their dissolution should come to pass; and it is made after the pattern of the ever-enduring nature, in order that it may be as like that pattern as possible; for the pattern is a thing that [C] has being for all eternity, whereas the Heaven has been and is and shall be perpetually throughout all time.

. . .

As concerning the other divinities, to know and to declare their generation is too high a task for us; we must trust those who have declared it in former times: being, as they said, descendants of gods, they must, no doubt, have had certain knowledge of their own ancestors. We cannot, then, mistrust the children of gods, though they speak without prob- [E] able or necessary proofs; when they profess to report their family history, we must follow established usage and accept what they say. Let us, then, take on their word this account of the generation of these gods. As children of Earth and Heaven were born Oceanus and Tethys; and of these Phorkys and Cronos and Rhea and all their company; and of Cronos and Rhea, Zeus and Hera and all their brothers and sisters whose names [41] we know; and of these yet other offspring.

Be that as it may, when all the gods had come to birth—both all that revolve before our eyes and all that reveal themselves in so far as they will—the author of this universe addressed them in these words:

"Gods, of gods whereof I am the maker and of works the father, those which are my own handiwork are indissoluble, save with my consent. Now, although whatsoever bond has been fastened may be unloosed, [B] yet only an evil will could consent to dissolve what has been well fitted together and is in a good state; therefore, although you, having come into being, are not immortal nor indissoluble altogether, nevertheless you shall not be dissolved nor taste of death, finding my will a bond yet stronger and more sovereign than those wherewith you were bound together when you came to be.

"Now, therefore, take heed to this that I declare to you. There are yet left mortal creatures of three kinds that have not been brought into being. If these be not born, the Heaven will be imperfect; for it will not contain all the kinds of living being, as it must if it is to be perfect and com- [C] plete. But if I myself gave them birth and life, they would be equal to gods. In order, then, that mortal things may exist and this All may be truly all, turn according to your own nature to the making of living creatures, imitating my power in generating you. In so far as it is fitting that something in them should share the name of the immortals, being called divine and ruling over those among them who at any time are willing to follow after righteousness and after you—that part, having sown it as seed and made a beginning, I will hand over to you. For the rest, do you, weaving mortal to immortal, make living beings; bring them to birth, [D] feed them, and cause them to grow; and when they fail, receive them back again."

Having said this, he turned once more to the same mixing bowl wherein he had mixed and blended the soul of the universe, and poured into it what was left of the former ingredients, blending them this time in somewhat the same way, only no longer so pure as before, but second or third in degree of purity. And when he had compounded the whole, he divided it into souls equal in number with the stars, and distributed them, each soul to its several star. There mounting them as it were in chariots, [E] he showed them the nature of the universe and declared to them the laws of Destiny. There would be appointed a first incarnation one and the same for all, that none might suffer disadvantage at his hands; and they were to be sown into the instruments of time, each one into that which was meet for it, and to be born as the most god-fearing of living [42] creatures; and human nature being twofold, the better sort was that which should thereafter be called "man."

Whensoever, therefore, they should of necessity have been implanted in bodies, and of their bodies some part should always be coming in and some part passing out, there must needs be innate in them, first, sensation, the same for all, arising from violent impressions; second, desire blended with pleasure and pain, and besides these fear and anger and all the feelings that accompany these and all that are of a contrary [B] nature: and if they should master these passions, they would live in righteousness; if they were mastered by them, in unrighteousness.

And he who should live well for his due span of time should journey back to the habitation of his consort star and there live a happy and congenial life; but failing of this, he should shift at his second birth into a woman; and if in this condition he still did not cease from wicked- [C] ness, then according to the character of his depravation, he should constantly be changed into some beast of a nature resembling the formation of that character, and should have no rest from the travail of these changes, until letting the revolution of the Same and uniform within himself draw into its train all that turmoil or fire and water and air and earth that had later grown about it, he should control its irrational tur- [D] bulence by discourse of reason and return once more to the form of his first and best condition.

When he had delivered to them all these ordinances, to the end that he might be guiltless of the future wickedness of any one of them, he sowed them, some in the Earth, some in the Moon, some in all the other instruments of time. After this sowing he left it to the newly made gods to mold mortal bodies, to fashion all that part of a human soul that there was still need to add and all that these things entail, and to govern [E] and guide the mortal creature to the best of their powers, save in so far as it should be a cause of evil to itself.

·　　·　　·

I will try to give an explanation of all these matters in detail, no less probable than another, but more so, starting from the beginning in the same manner as before. So now once again at the outset of our discourse let us call upon a protecting deity to grant us safe passage through a strange and unfamiliar exposition to the conclusion that probabil-　[48E] ity dictates; and so let us begin once more.

Our new starting point in describing the universe must, however, be a fuller classification than we made before. We then distinguished two things; but now a third must be pointed out. For our earlier discourse the two were sufficient: one postulated as model, intelligible and always unchangingly real; second, a copy of this model, which becomes　[49] and is visible. A third we did not then distinguish, thinking that the two would suffice; but now, it seems, the argument compels us to attempt to bring to light and describe a form difficult and obscure. What nature must we, then, conceive it to possess and what part does it play? This, more than anything else: that it is the Receptacle—as it were, the nurse—of all Becoming.

True, however, as this statement is, it needs to be put in clearer language; and that is hard, in particular because to that end it is neces-　[B] sary to raise a previous difficulty about fire and the things that rank with fire. It is hard to say, with respect to any one of these, which we ought to call really water rather than fire, or indeed which we should call by any given name rather than by all the names together or by each severally, so as to use language in a sound and trustworthy way. How, then, and in what terms are we to speak of this matter, and what is the previous difficulty that may be reasonably stated?

In the first place, take the thing we now call water. This, when it is compacted, we see (as we imagine) becoming earth and stones, and　[C] this same thing, when it is dissolved and dispersed, becoming wind and air; air becoming fire by being inflamed; and, by a reverse process, fire, when condensed and extinguished, returning once more to the form of air, and air coming together again and condensing as mist and cloud; and from these, as they are yet more closely compacted, flowing water; and from water once more earth and stones: and thus, as it appears, they transmit in a cycle the process of passing into one another. Since, then, in this way no one of these things ever makes its appearance as the *same*　[D] thing, which of them can we steadfastly affirm to be *this*—whatever it may be—and not something else, without blushing for ourselves? It cannot be done; but by far the safest course is to speak of them in the following terms. Whenever we observe a thing perpetually changing—fire, for example—in every case we should speak of fire not as "this," but as "what is of such and such a quality," nor of water as "this," but always as "what is of such and such a quality"; nor must we speak of anything else as

having some permanence, among all the things we indicate by the   [E]
expressions "this" or "that," imagining we are pointing out some definite
thing. For they slip away and do not wait to be described as "that" or
"this" or by any phrase that exhibits them as having permanent being.
We should not use these expressions of any of them, but "that which is
of a certain quality and has the same sort of quality as it perpetually
recurs in the cycle"—that is the description we should use in the case of
each and all of them. In fact, we must give the name "fire" to that which
is at all times of such and such a quality; and so with anything else that
is in process of becoming. Only in speaking of that *in* which all of them
are always coming to be, making their appearance and again vanishing
out of it, may we use the words "this" or "that"; we must not apply   [50]
any of these words to that which is of some quality—hot or cold or any
of the opposites—or to any combination of these opposites.

But I must do my best to explain this thing once more in still clearer
terms.

Suppose a man had molded figures of all sorts out of gold, and were
unceasingly to remold each into all the rest: then, if you should point to
one of them and ask what it was, much the safest answer in respect   [B]
of truth would be to say "gold," and never to speak of a triangle or any
of the other figures that were coming to be in it as things that have being,
since they are changing even while one is asserting their existence. Rather
one should be content if they so much as consent to accept the description
"what is of such and such a quality" with any certainty. Now the same
thing must be said of that nature which receives all bodies. It must be
called always the same; for it never departs at all from its own character;
since it is always receiving all things, and never in any way what-   [C]
soever takes on any character that is like any of the things that enter it:
by nature it is there as a matrix for everything, changed and diversified
by the things that enter it, and on their account it *appears* to have different qualities at different times; while the things that pass in and out are
to be called copies of the eternal things, impressions taken from them in a
strange manner that is hard to express: we will follow it up on another
occasion.

Be that as it may, for the present we must conceive three things: [D]
that which becomes; that in which it becomes; and the model in whose
likeness that which becomes is born. Indeed we may fittingly compare
the Recipient to a mother, the model to a father, and the nature that
arises between them to their offspring. Further we must observe that, if
there is to be an impress presenting all diversities of aspect, the thing
itself in which the impress comes to be situated, cannot have been duly
prepared unless it is free from all those characters which it is to receive
from elsewhere. For if it were like any one of the things that come   [E]
in upon it, then, when things of contrary or entirely different nature came,
in receiving them it would reproduce them badly, intruding its own features alongside. Hence that which is to receive in itself all kinds must
be free from all characters; just like the base which the makers of scented

ointments skillfully contrive to start with: they make the liquids that are to receive the scents as odorless as possible. Or again, anyone who sets about taking impressions of shapes in some soft substance allows no shape to show itself there beforehand, but begins by making the surface as smooth and level as he can. In the same way, that which is duly to [51] receive over its whole extent and many times over all the likenesses of the intelligible and eternal things ought in its own nature to be free of all the characters. For this reason, then, the mother and Receptacle of what has come to be visible and otherwise sensible must not be called earth or air or fire or water, nor any of their compounds or components; but we shall not be deceived if we call it a nature invisible and characterless, all-receiving, partaking in some very puzzling way of the intelligible [B] and very hard to apprehend. So far as its nature can be arrived at from what has already been said, the most correct account of it would be this: that part of it which has been made fiery appears at any time as fire; the part that is liquefied as water; and as earth or air such parts as receive likenesses of these.

But in pressing our inquiry about them, there is a question that must rather be determined by argument. Is there such a thing as "Fire just in itself" or any of the other things which we are always describing in such terms, as things that "are just in themselves"? Or are the things we [C] see or otherwise perceive by the bodily senses the only things that have such reality, and has nothing else, over and above these, any sort of being at all? Are we talking idly whenever we say that there is such a thing as an intelligible Form of anything? Is this nothing more than a word?

Now it does not become us either to dismiss the present question without trial or verdict, simply asseverating that it is so, nor yet to insert a lengthy digression into a discourse that is already long. If we could [D] see our way to draw a distinction of great importance in few words, that would best suit the occasion. My own verdict, then, is this. If intelligence and true belief are two different kinds, then these things—Forms that we cannot perceive but only think of—certainly exist in themselves; but if, as some hold, true belief in no way differs from intelligence, then all the things we perceive through the bodily senses must be taken as the most certain reality. Now we must affirm that they are two different things, [E] for they are distinct in origin and unlike in nature. The one is produced in us by instruction, the other by persuasion; the one can always give a true account of itself, the other can give none; the one cannot be shaken by persuasion, whereas the other can be won over; and true belief, we must allow, is shared by all mankind, intelligence only by the gods and a small number of men.

This being so, we must agree that there is, first, the unchanging Form, ungenerated and indestructible, which neither receives anything [52] else into itself from elsewhere nor itself enters into anything else anywhere, invisible and otherwise imperceptible; that, in fact, which thinking has for its object.

Second is that which bears the same name and is like that Form; is sensible; is brought into existence; is perpetually in motion, coming to be in a certain place and again vanishing out of it; and is to be apprehended by belief involving perception.

Third is Space, which is everlasting, not admitting destruction; providing a situation for all things that come into being, but itself appre- [B] hended without the senses by a sort of bastard reasoning, and hardly an object of belief.

This, indeed, is that which we look upon as in a dream and say that anything that is must needs be in some place and occupy some room, and that what is not somewhere in earth or heaven is nothing. Because of this dreaming state, we prove unable to rouse ourselves and to draw all these distinctions and others akin to them, even in the case of the [C] waking and truly existing nature, and so to state the truth: namely that, whereas for an image, since not even the very principle on which it has come into being belongs to the image itself, but it is the ever moving semblance of something else, it is proper that it should come to be *in* something else, clinging in some sort of existence on pain of being nothing at all, on the other hand that which has real being has the support of the exactly true account, which declares that, so long as the two things are different, neither can ever come to be in the other in such a way that [D] the two should become at once one and the same thing and two.

Let this, then, be given as the tale summed according to my judgment: that there are Being, Space, Becoming—three distinct things—even before the Heaven came into being. Now the nurse of Becoming, being made watery and fiery and receiving the characters of earth and air, and qualified by all the other affections that go with these, had every sort of [E] diverse appearance to the sight; but because it was filled with powers that were neither alike nor evenly balanced, there was no equipoise in any region of it; but it was everywhere swayed unevenly and shaken by these things, and by its motion shook them in turn. And they, being thus moved, were perpetually being separated and carried in different directions; just as when things are shaken and winnowed by means of winnowing baskets and other instruments for cleaning corn, the dense and [53] heavy things go one way, while the rare and light are carried to another place and settle there. In the same way at that time the four kinds were shaken by the Recipient, which itself was in motion like an instrument for shaking, and it separated the most unlike kinds farthest apart from one another, and thrust the most alike closest together; whereby the different kinds came to have different regions, even before the ordered whole [B] consisting of them came to be. Before that, all these kinds were without proportion or measure. Fire, water, earth, and air possessed indeed some vestiges of their own nature, but were altogether in such a condition as we should expect for anything when deity is absent from it. Such being their nature at the time when the ordering of the universe was taken in hand, the god then began by giving them a distinct configuration by means of shapes and numbers. That the god framed them with the greatest possible perfection, which they had not before, must be taken, above all, as a principle we constantly assert.

... But as it was, the artificers who brought us into being reckoned whether they should make a long-lived but inferior race or one with a shorter life but nobler, and agreed that everyone must on all [75c] accounts prefer the shorter and better life to the longer and worse.

· · ·

When the conjoined bonds of the triangles in the marrow no longer hold out under the stress, but part asunder, they let go in their turn the bonds of the soul; and she, when thus set free in the course of nature, finds pleasure in taking wing to fly away. For whereas all that is against nature is painful, what takes place in the natural way is pleasant. [81E] So death itself, on this principle, is painful and contrary to nature when it results from disease or wounds, but when it comes to close the natural course of old age, it is, of all deaths, the least distressing and is accompanied rather by pleasure than by pain.

· · ·

And now, it would seem, we have fairly accomplished the task laid [E] upon us at the outset: to tell the story of the universe so far as to the generation of man: For the manner in which the other living creatures have come into being, brief mention shall be enough, where there is no need to speak at length; so shall we, in our own judgment, rather preserve due measure in our account of them.

Let this matter, then, be set forth as follows. Of those who were born as men, all that were cowardly and spent their life in wrongdoing were, according to the probable account, transformed at the second birth [91] into women: for this reason it was at that time that the gods constructed the desire of sexual intercourse, fashioning one creature instinct with life in us, and another in women. The two were made by them in this way. From the conduit of our drink, where it receives liquid that has passed through the lungs by the kidneys into the bladder and ejects it with the air that presses upon it, they pierced an opening communicating with the compact marrow which runs from the head down the neck and along the spine and has, indeed, in our earlier discourse been called "seed." [B] This marrow, being instinct with life and finding an outlet, implanted in the part where this outlet was a lively appetite for egress and so brought it to completion as an Eros of begetting. Hence it is that in men the privy member is disobedient and self-willed, like a creature that will not listen to reason, and because of frenzied appetite bent upon carrying all before it. In women again, for the same reason, what is called the matrix or [c] womb, a living creature within them with a desire for childbearing, if it be left long unfruitful beyond the due season, is vexed and aggrieved, and wandering throughout the body and blocking the channels of the breath, by forbidding respiration brings the sufferer to extreme distress and causes all manner of disorders; until at last the Eros of the one and the Desire of the other bring the pair together, pluck as it were the fruit from [D] the tree and sow the plowland of the womb with living creatures still unformed and too small to be seen, and again differentiating their parts nourish them till they grow large within, and thereafter by bringing them to the light of day accomplish the birth of the living creature. Such is the origin of women and of all that is female.

Birds were made by transformation: growing feathers instead of hair, they came from harmless but light-witted men, who studied the heavens but imagined in their simplicity that the surest evidence in these matters comes through the eye. [E]

Land animals came from men who had no use for philosophy and paid no heed to the heavens because they had lost the use of the circuits in the head and followed the guidance of those parts of the soul that are in the breast. By reason of these practices they let their forelimbs and heads be drawn down to earth by natural affinity and there supported, and their heads were lengthened out and took any sort of shape into which [92] their circles were crushed together through inactivity. On this account their kind was born with four feet or with many, heaven giving to the more witless the greater number of points of support, that they might be all the more drawn earthward. The most senseless, whose whole bodies were stretched at length upon the earth, since they had no further need of feet, the gods made footless, crawling over the ground.

The fourth sort, that live in water, came from the most foolish and [B] stupid of all. The gods who remolded their form thought these unworthy any more to breathe the pure air, because their souls were polluted with every sort of transgression; and in place of breathing the fine and clean air, they thrust them down to inhale the muddy water of the depths. Hence came fishes and shellfish and all that lives in the water: in penalty for the last extreme of folly they are assigned the last and lowest habitation. These are the principles on which, now as then, all living creatures change one into another, shifting their place with the loss or gain [C] of understanding or folly.

Here at last let us say that our discourse concerning the universe has come to its end. For having received in full its complement of living creatures, mortal and immortal, this world has thus become a visible living creature embracing all that are visible and an image of the intelligible, a perceptible god, supreme in greatness and excellence, in beauty and perfection, this Heaven single in its kind and one.

LAWS, *Book X* (*in part*)

PERSONS OF THE DIALOGUE

An Athenian Stranger　　　　*Cleinias, a Cretan*

Athenian.　Now we have to determine what is to be the punishment of those who speak or act insolently toward the Gods. But first we must give them an admonition which may be in the following terms:—No one who in obedience to the laws believed that there were Gods, ever intentionally did any unholy act, or uttered any unlawful word; but he who did must have supposed one of three things,—either that they did not exist,—which is the first possibility, or secondly, that, if they did, they took no care of man, or thirdly, that they were easily appeased and turned aside from their purpose by sacrifices and prayers.

Cleinias.　What shall we say or do to these persons?

Ath.　My good friend, let us first hear the jests which I suspect that they in their superiority will utter against us.

Cle.　What jests?

Ath.　They will make some irreverent speech of this sort:—'O inhabitants of Athens, and Sparta, and Cnosus,' they will reply, 'in that you speak truly; for some of us deny the very existence of the Gods, while others, as you say, are of opinion that they do not care about us; and others that they are turned from their course by gifts. Now we have a right to claim, as you yourself allowed, in the matter of laws, that before you are hard upon us and threaten us, you should argue with us and convince us—you should first attempt to teach and persuade us that there are Gods by reasonable evidences, and also that they are too good to be unrighteous, or to be propitiated, or turned from their course by gifts. For when we hear such things said of them by those who are esteemed to be the best of poets, and orators, and prophets, and priests, and by innumerable others, the thoughts of most of us are not set upon abstaining from unrighteous acts, but upon doing them and atoning for them. When lawgivers profess that they are gentle and not stern, we think that they should first of all use persuasion to us, and show us the existence of Gods, if not in a better manner than other men, at any rate in a truer; and who knows but that we shall hearken to you? If then our request is a fair one, please to accept our challenge.'

Cle.　But is there any difficulty in proving the existence of the Gods?

Ath.　How would you prove it?　　　　　　　　　　　　　　　[886]

Cle.　How? In the first place, the earth and the sun, and the stars and the universe, and the fair order of the seasons, and the division of them into years and months, furnish proofs of their existence; and also there is the fact that all Hellenes and barbarians believe in them.

Ath. I fear, my sweet friend, though I will not say that I much regard, the contempt with which the profane will be likely to assail us. For you do not understand the nature of their complaint, and you fancy that they rush into impiety only from a love of sensual pleasure.

Cle. Why, Stranger, what other reason is there?

Ath. One which you who live in a different atmosphere would never guess.

Cle. What is it?

Ath. A very grievous sort of ignorance which is imagined to be the greatest wisdom.

Cle. What do you mean?

Ath. At Athens there are tales preserved in writing which the virtue of your state, as I am informed, refuses to admit. They speak of the Gods in prose as well as verse, and the oldest of them tell of the origin of the heavens and of the world, and not far from the beginning of their story they proceed to narrate the birth of the Gods, and how after they were born they behaved to one another. Whether these stories have in other ways a good or a bad influence, I should not like to be severe upon them, because they are ancient; but, looking at them with reference to the duties of children to their parents, I cannot praise them, or think that they are useful, or at all true. Of the words of the ancients I have nothing more to say; and I should wish to say of them only what is pleasing to the Gods. But as to our younger generation and their wisdom, I cannot let them off when they do mischief. For do but mark the effect of their words: when you and I argue for the existence of the Gods, and produce the sun, moon, stars, and earth, claiming for them a divine being, if we would listen to the aforesaid philosophers we should say that they are earth and stones only, which can have no care at all of human affairs, and that all religion is a cooking up of words and a make-believe.

Cle. One such teacher, O Stranger, would be bad enough, and you imply that there are many of them, which is worse.

Ath. Well, then; what shall we say or do?—Shall we assume [887] that some one is accusing us among unholy men, who are trying to escape from the effect of our legislation; and that they say of us—How dreadful that you should legislate on the supposition that there are Gods! Shall we make a defence of ourselves?

.   .   .

The duty of the legislator is and always will be to teach you the truth of these matters. [888]

.   .   .

I must repeat the singular argument of those who manufacture the soul according to their own impious notions; they affirm that which is the first cause of the generation and destruction of all things, to be not first, but last, and that which is last to be first, and hence they have fallen into error about the true nature of the Gods.

Cle.   Still I do not understand you.   [892]

Ath.   Nearly all of them, my friends, seem to be ignorant of the nature and power of the soul, especially in what relates to her origin: they do not know that she is among the first of things, and before all bodies, and is the chief author of their changes and transpositions. And if this is true, and if the soul is older than the body, must not the things which are of the soul's kindred be of necessity prior to those which appertain to the body?

Cle.   Certainly.

Ath.   Then thought and attention and mind and art and law will be prior to that which is hard and soft and heavy and light; and the great and primitive works and actions will be works of art; they will be the first, and after them will come nature and works of nature, which however is a wrong term for men to apply to them; these will follow, and will be under the government of art and mind.

Cle.   But why is the word 'nature' wrong?

Ath.   Because those who use the term mean to say that nature is the first creative power; but if the soul turn out to be the primeval element, and not fire or air, then in the truest sense and beyond other things the soul may be said to exist by nature; and this would be true if you proved that the soul is older than the body, but not otherwise.

.   .   .

Holding fast to the rope we will venture upon the depths of the argument. When questions of this sort are asked of me, my safest answer would appear to be as follows:—Some one says to me, 'O Stranger, are all things at rest and nothing in motion, or is the exact opposite of this true, or are some things in motion and others at rest?'—To this I shall reply that some things are in motion and others at rest. 'And do not things which move move in a place, and are not the things which are at rest at rest in a place?' Certainly. 'And some move or rest in one place and some in more places than one?' You mean to say, we shall rejoin, that those things which rest at the centre move in one place, just as the circumference goes round of globes which are said to be at rest? 'Yes.' And we observe that, in the revolution, the motion which carries round the larger and the lesser circle at the same time is proportionally distributed to greater and smaller, and is greater and smaller in a certain proportion. Here is a wonder which might be thought an impossibility, that the same motion should impart swiftness and slowness in due proportion to larger and lesser circles. 'Very true.' And when you speak of bodies moving in many places, you seem to me to mean those which move from one place to another, and sometimes have one centre of motion and sometimes more than one because they turn upon their axis; and whenever they meet anything, if it be stationary, they are divided by it; but if they get in the midst between bodies which are approaching and moving towards the same spot from opposite directions, they unite with them. 'I admit the truth of what you are saying.' Also when they unite they grow, and when they are divided they waste away,—that is, supposing the constitution of each to remain, or if that fails, then there is a second reason of their dissolution. 'And when are all things created and how?' Clearly, [894] they are created when the first principle receives increase and attains to the second dimension, and from this arrives at the one which is neighbour to this, and after reaching the third becomes perceptible to sense. Everything which is thus changing and moving is in process of generation; only when at rest has it real existence, but when passing into another state it is destroyed utterly. Have we not mentioned all motions that there are, and comprehended them under their kinds and numbered them with the exception, my friends, of two?

Cle. Which are they?

Ath. Just the two, with which our present enquiry is concerned.

Cle. Speak plainer.

Ath. I suppose that our enquiry has reference to the soul?

Cle. Very true.

Ath. Let us assume that there is a motion able to move other things, but not to move itself;—that is one kind; and there is another kind which can move itself as well as other things, working in composition and decomposition, by increase and diminution and generation and destruction, —that is also one of the many kinds of motion.

Cle. Granted.

Ath. And we will assume that which moves other, and is changed by other, to be the ninth, and that which changes itself and others, and is co-incident with every action and every passion, and is the true principle of change and motion in all that is,—that we shall be inclined to call the tenth.

Cle. Certainly.

Ath. And which of these ten motions ought we to prefer as being the mightiest and most efficient?

Cle. I must say that the motion which is able to move itself is ten thousand times superior to all the others.

Ath. Very good; but may I make one or two corrections in what I have been saying?

Cle. What are they?

Ath. When I spoke of the tenth sort of motion, that was not quite correct.

Cle. What was the error?

Ath. According to the true order, the tenth was really the first in generation and power; then follows the second, which was strangely enough termed the ninth by us.

Cle. What do you mean?

Ath. I mean this: when one thing changes another, and that another, of such will there be any primary changing element? How can a thing which is moved by another ever be the beginning of change? Impossible. But when the self-moved changes other, and that again other, and thus thousands upon tens of thousands of bodies are set in motion, must [895] not the beginning of all this motion be the change of the self-moving principle?

Cle. Very true, and I quite agree.

Ath. Or, to put the question in another way, making answer to ourselves:—If, as most of these philosophers have the audacity to affirm, all things were at rest in one mass, which of the above-mentioned principles of motion would first spring up among them?

Cle. Clearly the self-moving; for there could be no change in them arising out of any external cause; the change must first take place in themselves.

Ath. Then we must say that self-motion being the origin of all motions, and the first which arises among things at rest as well as among things in motion, is the eldest and mightiest principle of change, and that which is changed by another and yet moves other is second.

Cle. Quite true.

Ath. At this stage of the argument let us put a question.

Cle. What question?

Ath. If we were to see this power existing in any earthy, watery, or fiery substance, simple or compound—how should we describe it?

Cle. You mean to ask whether we should call such a self-moving power life?

Ath. I do.

Cle. Certainly we should.

Ath. And when we see soul in anything, must we not do the same—must we not admit that this is life?

Cle. We must.

Ath. And now, I beseech you, reflect;—you would admit that we have a threefold knowledge of things?

Cle. What do you mean?

Ath. I mean that we know the essence, and that we know the definition of the essence, and the name,—these are the three; and there are two questions which may be raised about anything.

Cle. How two?

Ath. Sometimes a person may give the name and ask the definition; or he may give the definition and ask the name. I may illustrate what I mean in this way.

Cle. How?

Ath. Number like some other things is capable of being divided into equal parts; when thus divided, number is named 'even,' and the definition of the name 'even' is 'number divisible into two equal parts?'

Cle. True.

Ath. I mean, that when we are asked about the definition and give the name, or when we are asked about the name and give the definition—in either case, whether we give name or definition, we speak of the same thing, calling 'even' the number which is divided into two equal parts.

Cle. Quite true.

Ath. And what is the definition of that which is named 'soul'? [896]

Can we conceive of any other than that which has been already given—the motion which can move itself?

Cle. You mean to say that the essence which is defined as the self-moved is the same with that which has the name soul?

Ath. Yes; and if this is true, do we still maintain that there is anything wanting in the proof that the soul is the first origin and moving power of all that is, or has become, or will be, and their contraries, when she has been clearly shown to be the source of change and motion in all things?

Cle. Certainly not; the soul as being the source of motion, has been most satisfactorily shown to be the oldest of all things.

Ath. And is not that motion which is produced in another, by reason of another, but never has any self-moving power at all, being in truth the change of an inanimate body, to be reckoned second, or by any lower number which you may prefer?

Cle. Exactly.

Ath. Then we are right, and speak the most perfect and absolute truth, when we say that the soul is prior to the body, and that the body is second and comes afterwards, and is born to obey the soul, which is the ruler?

Cle. Nothing can be more true.

Ath. Do you remember our old admission, that if the soul was prior to the body the things of the soul were also prior to those of the body?

Cle. Certainly.

Ath. Then characters and manners, and wishes and reasonings, and true opinions, and reflections, and recollections are prior to length and breadth and depth and strength of bodies, if the soul is prior to the body.

Cle. To be sure.

Ath. In the next place, must we not of necessity admit that the soul is the cause of good and evil, base and honourable, just and unjust, and of all other opposites, if we suppose her to be the cause of all things?

Cle. We must.

Ath. And as the soul orders and inhabits all things that move, however moving, must we not say that she orders also the heavens?

Cle. Of course.

Ath. One soul or more? More than one—I will answer for you;—at any rate, we must not suppose that there are less than two—one the author of good, and the other of evil.

Cle. Very true.

. . .

Ath. If, my friend, we say that the whole path and movement of heaven, and of all that is therein, is by nature akin to the movement and revolution and calculation of mind, and proceeds by kindred laws, then, as is plain, we must say that the best soul takes care of the world and guides it along the good path. [897]

. . .

Cle. And judging from what has been said, Stranger, there would be impiety in asserting that any but the most perfect soul or souls carries round the heavens. [898]

. . .

Ath. Either the soul which moves the sun this way and that, resides within the circular and visible body, like the soul which carries us about every way; or the soul provides herself with an external body of [899] fire or air, as some affirm, and violently propels body by body; or thirdly, she is without such a body, but guides the sun by some extraordinary and wonderful power.

Cle. Yes, certainly; the soul can only order all things in one of these three ways.

Ath. And this soul of the sun, which is therefore better than the sun, whether taking the sun about in a chariot to give light to men, or acting from without, or in whatever way, ought by every man to be deemed a God.

Cle. Yes, by every man who has the least particle of sense.

Ath. And of the stars too, and of the moon, and of the years and months and seasons, must we not say in like manner, that since a soul or souls having every sort of excellence are the causes of all of them, those souls are Gods, whether they are living beings and reside in bodies, and in this way order the whole heaven, or whatever be the place and mode of their existence;—and will any one who admits all this venture to deny that all things are full of Gods?

Cle. No one, Stranger, would be such a madman.

Ath. And now, Megillus and Cleinias, let us offer terms to him who has hitherto denied the existence of the Gods, and leave him.

Cle. What terms?

Ath. Either he shall teach us that we were wrong in saying that the soul is the original of all things, and arguing accordingly; or, if he be not able to say anything better, then he must yield to us and live for the remainder of his life in the belief that there are Gods.—Let us see, then, whether we have said enough or not enough to those who deny that there are Gods.

Cle. Certainly,—quite enough, Stranger.

Ath. Then to them we will say no more. And now we are to address him who, believing that there are Gods, believes also that they take no heed of human affairs: To him we say,—O thou best of men, in believing that there are Gods you are led by some affinity to them, which attracts you towards your kindred and makes you honour and believe in them. But the fortunes of evil and unrighteous men in private as well as public life, which, though not really happy, are wrongly counted happy in the judgment of men, and are celebrated both by poets and prose writers— these draw you aside from your natural piety. Perhaps you have [900] seen impious men growing old and leaving their children's children in high offices, and their prosperity shakes your faith—you have known or heard or been yourself an eyewitness of many monstrous impieties, and have beheld men by such criminal means from small beginnings attaining to sovereignty and the pinnacle of greatness; and considering all these things you do not like to accuse the Gods of them, because they are your relatives; and so from some want of reasoning power, and also from an unwillingness to find fault with them, you have come to believe that they exist indeed, but have no thought or care of human things. Now, that your present evil opinion may not grow to still greater impiety, and that we may if possible use arguments which may conjure away the evil before it arrives, we will add another argument to that originally addressed to him who utterly denied the existence of the Gods. And do you, Megillus and Cleinias, answer for the young man as you did before; and if any impediment comes in our way, I will take the word out of your mouths, and carry you over the river as I did just now.

Cle. Very good; do as you say, and we will help you as well as we can.

Ath. There will probably be no difficulty in proving to him that the Gods care about the small as well as about the great. For he was present and heard what was said, that they are perfectly good, and that the care of all things is most entirely natural to them.

Cle. No doubt he heard that.

Ath. Let us consider together in the next place what we mean by this virtue which we ascribe to them. Surely we should say that to be temperate and to possess mind belongs to virtue, and the contrary to vice?

Cle. Certainly.

Ath. Yes; and courage is a part of virtue, and cowardice of vice?

Cle. True.

Ath. And the one is honourable, and the other dishonourable?

Cle. To be sure.

Ath. And the one, like other meaner things, is a human quality, but the Gods have no part in anything of the sort?

Cle. That again is what everybody will admit.

Ath. But do we imagine carelessness and idleness and luxury to be virtues? What do you think?

Cle. Decidedly not.

Ath. They rank under the opposite class?

Cle. Yes.

Ath. And their opposites, therefore, would fall under the [901] opposite class?

Cle. Yes.

Ath. But are we to suppose that one who possesses all these good qualities will be luxurious and heedless and idle, like those whom the poet compares to stingless drones? [1]

Cle. And the comparison is a most just one.

Ath. Surely God must not be supposed to have a nature which He

---

[1] Hesiod, *Works and Days,* 307.

Himself hates?—he who dares to say this sort of thing must not be tolerated for a moment.

Cle.   Of course not. How could He have?

Ath.   Should we not on any principle be entirely mistaken in praising any one who has some special business entrusted to him, if he have a mind which takes care of great matters and no care of small ones? Reflect; he who acts in this way, whether he be God or man, must act from one of two principles.

Cle.   What are they?

Ath.   Either he must think that the neglect of the small matters is of no consequence to the whole, or if he knows that they are of consequence, and he neglects them, his neglect must be attributed to carelessness and indolence. Is there any other way in which his neglect can be explained? For surely, when it is impossible for him to take care of all, he is not negligent if he fails to attend to these things great or small, which a God or some inferior being might be wanting in strength or capacity to manage?

Cle.   Certainly not.

Ath.   Now, then, let us examine the offenders, who both alike confess that there are Gods, but with a difference,—the one saying that they may be appeased, and the other that they have no care of small matters: there are three of us and two of them, and we will say to them,—In the first place, you both acknowledge that the Gods hear and see and know all things, and that nothing can escape them which is matter of sense and knowledge:—do you admit this?

Cle.   Yes.

Ath.   And do you admit also that they have all power which mortals and immortals can have?

Cle.   They will, of course, admit this also.

.   .   .

Ath.   Let us say to the youth:—The ruler of the universe has or-   [903] dered all things with a view to the excellence and preservation of the whole, and each part, as far as may be, has an action and passion appropriate to it. Over these, down to the least fraction of them, ministers have been appointed to preside, who have wrought out their perfection with infinitesimal exactness. And one of these portions of the universe is thine own, unhappy man, which, however little, contributes to the whole; and you do not seem to be aware that this and every other creation is for the sake of the whole, and in order that the life of the whole may be blessed; and that you are created for the sake of the whole, and not the whole for the sake of you. For every physician and every skilled artist does all things for the sake of the whole, directing his effort towards the common good, executing the part for the sake of the whole, and not the whole for the sake of the part. And you are annoyed because you are ignorant how what is best for you happens to you and to the universe, as far as the laws of the common creation admit. Now, as the soul combining first with one body and then with another undergoes all sorts of changes, either of herself, or through the influence of another soul, all that remains to the player of the game is that he should shift the pieces; sending the better nature to the better place, and the worse to the worse, and so assigning to them their proper portion.

· · ·

The formation of qualities he left to the wills of individuals. For every one of us is made pretty much what he is by the bent of his desires and the nature of his soul.

Cle. Yes, that is probably true.

Ath. Then all things which have a soul change, and possess in themselves a principle of change, and in changing move according to law and to the order of destiny: natures which have undergone a lesser change move less and on the earth's surface, but those which have suffered more change and have become more criminal sink into the abyss, that is to say, into Hades and other places in the world below, of which the very names terrify men, and which they picture to themselves as in a dream, both while alive and when released from the body. And whenever the soul receives more of good or evil from her own energy and the strong influence of others—when she has communion with divine virtue and becomes divine, she is carried into another and better place, which is perfect in holiness; but when she has communion with evil, then she also changes the place of her life.

'This is the justice of the Gods who inhabit Olympus.' [2]

O youth or young man, who fancy that you are neglected by the Gods, know that if you become worse you shall go to the worse souls, or if better, and in every succession of life and death you will do and suffer what like may fitly suffer at the hands of like. This is the justice [905] of heaven, which neither you nor any other unfortunate will ever glory in escaping, and which the ordaining powers have specially ordained; take good heed thereof, for it will be sure to take heed of you. If you say:—I am small and will creep into the depths of the earth, or I am high and will fly up to heaven, you are not so small or so high but that you shall pay the fitting penalty, either here or in the world below or in some still more savage place whither you shall be conveyed. . . . For I think that we have sufficiently proved the existence of the Gods, and that they care for men:—The other notion that they are appeased by the wicked, and take gifts, is what we must not concede to any one, and what every man should disprove to the utmost of his power.

· · ·

Ath. And shall we say that those who guard our noblest interests, and are the best of guardians, are inferior in virtue to dogs, and to men even

---

[2] Hom. *Odyss.* xix. 43.

of moderate excellence, who would never betray justice for the sake of gifts which unjust men impiously offer them?

Cle. Certainly not; nor is such a notion to be endured, and he who holds this opinion may be fairly singled out and characterized as of all impious men the wickedest and most impious.

Ath. Then are the three assertions—that the Gods exist, and that they take care of men, and that they can never be persuaded to do injustice, now sufficiently demonstrated? May we say that they are?

Cle. You have our entire assent to your words.

Ath. I have spoken with vehemence because I am zealous against evil men; and I will tell you, dear Cleinias, why I am so. I would not have the wicked think that, having the superiority in argument, they may do as they please and act according to their various imaginations about the Gods; and this zeal has led me to speak too vehemently; but if we have at all succeeded in persuading the men to hate themselves and love their opposites, the prelude of our laws about impiety will not have been spoken in vain.

Cle. So let us hope; and even if we have failed, the style of our argument will not discredit the lawgiver.

Ath. After the prelude shall follow a discourse, which will be the interpreter of the law; this shall proclaim to all impious persons that they must depart from their ways and go over to the pious. And to those who disobey, let the law about impiety be as follows:—If a man be guilty of any impiety in word or deed, any one who happens to be present shall give information to the magistrates, in aid of the law; and if a magistrate, after receiving information, refuses to act, he shall be tried for impiety at the instance of any one who is willing to vindicate the laws; and if any one be cast, the court shall estimate the punishment of each act of impiety; and let all such criminals be imprisoned. There shall be [908] three prisons in the state: the first of them is to be the common prison in the neighborhood of the agora for the safe-keeping of the generality of offenders; another is to be in the neighborhood of the nocturnal council, and is to be called the 'House of Reformation'; another, to be situated in some wild and desolate region in the centre of the country, shall be called by some name expressive of retribution. Now, men fall into impiety from three causes, which have been already mentioned, and from each of these causes arise two sorts of impiety, in all six, which are worth distinguishing, and should not all have the same punishment. For he who does not believe in the Gods, and yet has a righteous nature, hates the wicked and dislikes and refuses to do injustice, and avoids unrighteous men, and loves the righteous. But they who besides believing that the world is devoid of Gods are intemperate, and have at the same time good memories and quick wits, are worse; although both of them are unbelievers, much less injury is done by the one than by the other. The one may talk loosely about the Gods and about sacrifices and oaths, and perhaps by laughing at other men he may make them like himself, if he be not punished. But the other who holds the same opinions and is called a clever man, is full of stratagem and deceit—men of this class deal in prophecy and jugglery of all kinds, and out of their ranks sometimes come tyrants and demagogues and generals and hierophants of private mysteries and the Sophists, as they are termed, with their ingenious devices. There are many kinds of unbelievers, but two only for whom legislation is required; one the hypocritical sort, whose crime is deserving of death many times over, while the other needs only bonds and admonition. In like manner also the notion that the Gods take no thought of men produces two other sorts of crimes, and the notion that they may be propitiated produces two more. Assuming these divisions, let those who have been made what they are only from want of understanding, and not from malice or an evil [909] nature, be placed by the judge in the House of Reformation, and ordered to suffer imprisonment during a period of not less than five years. And in the meantime let them have no intercourse with the other citizens, except with the members of the nocturnal council, and with them let them converse with a view to the improvement of their soul's health. And when the time of their imprisonment has expired, if any of them be of sound mind let him be restored to sane company, but if not, and if he be condemned a second time, let him be punished with death. As to that class of monstrous natures who not only believe that there are no Gods, or that they are negligent, or to be propitiated, but in contempt of mankind conjure the souls of the living and say that they can conjure the dead and promise to charm the Gods with sacrifices and prayers, and will utterly overthrow individuals and whole houses and states for the sake of money —let him who is guilty of any of these things be condemned by the court to be bound according to law in the prison which is in the centre of the land, and let no freeman ever approach him, but let him receive the rations of food appointed by the guardians of the law from the hands of the public slaves; and when he is dead let him be cast beyond the borders unburied, and if any freeman assist in burying him, let him pay the penalty of impiety to any one who is willing to bring a suit against him. But if he leaves behind him children who are fit to be citizens, let the guardians of orphans take care of them, just as they would of any other orphans, from the day on which their father is convicted.

In all these cases there should be one law, which will make men in general less liable to transgress in word or deed, and less foolish, because they will not be allowed to practise religious rites contrary to law. And let this be the simple form of the law:—No man shall have sacred rites in a private house. When he would sacrifice, let him go to the temples and hand over his offerings to the priests and priestesses, who see to the sanctity of such things, and let him pray himself, and let any one who pleases join with him in prayer. The reason of this is as follows:—Gods and temples are not easily instituted, and to establish them rightly is the work of a mighty intellect. And women especially, and men too, when they are sick or in danger, or in any sort of difficulty, or again on their receiving any good fortune, have a way of consecrating the occasion, vowing sacrifices, and promising shrines to Gods, demigods, and [910] sons of Gods; and when they are awakened by terrible apparitions and dreams or remember visions, they find in altars and temples the remedies of them, and will fill every house and village with them, placing them in the open air, or wherever they may have had such visions; and with a view to all these cases we should obey the law. The law has also regard to the impious, and would not have them fancy that by secret performance of these actions—by raising temples and by building altars in private houses, they can propitiate the God secretly with sacrifices and prayers, while they are really multiplying their crimes infinitely, bringing guilt from heaven upon themselves, and also upon those who permit them, and who are better men than they are; and the consequence is that the whole state reaps the fruit of their impiety, which, in a certain sense, is deserved. Assuredly God will not blame the legislator, who will enact the following law:—No one shall possess shrines of the Gods in private houses, and he who is found to possess them, and perform any sacred rites not publicly authorized,—supposing the offender to be some man or woman who is not guilty of any other great and impious crime,—shall be informed against by him who is acquainted with the fact, which shall be announced by him to the guardians of the law; and let them issue orders that he or she shall carry away their private rites to public temples, and if they do not persuade them, let them inflict a penalty on them until they comply. And if a person is proven guilty of impiety, not merely from childish levity, but such as grown-up men may be guilty of, whether he have sacrificed publicly or privately to any Gods, let him be punished with death, for his sacrifice is impure. Whether the deed has been done in earnest, or only from childish levity, let the guardians of the law determine, before they bring the matter into court and prosecute the offender for impiety.

EPILOGUE

EPISTLE VII (*in part:* 324-26, 330-31, 341)

In the days of my youth my experience was the same as that of many others. I thought that as soon as I should become my own master I would immediately enter into public life. But it so happened, I found, that the following changes occurred in the political situation.

In the government then existing, reviled as it was by many, a revolution took place; and the revolution was headed by fifty-one leaders, of whom eleven were in the City and ten in the Piraeus—each of these sections dealing with the market and with all municipal matters requiring management—and Thirty were established as irresponsible rulers of all. Now of these some were actually connexions and acquaintances of mine; and indeed they invited me at once to join their administration, thinking it would be congenial. The feelings I then experienced, owing to my youth, were in no way surprising: for I imagined that they would administer the State by leading it out of an unjust way of life into a just way, and consequently I gave my mind to them very diligently, to see what they would do. And indeed I saw how these men within a short time caused men to look back on the former government as a golden age; and above all how they treated my aged friend Socrates, whom I would hardly scruple to call the most just of men then living, when they tried to send him, along with others, after one of the citizens, to fetch him by force that he might be put to death—their object being that Socrates, whether he wished or no, might be made to share in their political actions; he, however, refused to obey and risked the uttermost penalties rather than be a partaker in their unholy deeds. So when I beheld all these actions and others of a similar grave kind, I was indignant, and I withdrew myself from the evil practices then going on. But in no long time the power of the Thirty was overthrown together with the whole of the government which then existed. Then once again I was really, though less urgently, impelled with

353

a desire to take part in public and political affairs. Many deplorable events, however, were still happening in those times, troublous as they were, and it was not surprising that in some instances, during these revolutions, men were avenging themselves on their foes too fiercely; yet, notwithstanding, the exiles who then returned exercised no little moderation. But, as ill-luck would have it, certain men of authority summoned our comrade Socrates before the law-courts, laying a charge against him which was most unholy, and which Socrates of all men least deserved; for it was on the charge of impiety that those men summoned him and the rest condemned and slew him—the very man who on the former occasion, when they themselves had the misfortune to be in exile, had refused to take part in the unholy arrest of one of the friends of the men then exiled.

When, therefore, I considered all this, and the type of men who were administering the affairs of State, with their laws too and their customs, the more I considered them and the more I advanced in years myself, the more difficult appeared to me the task of managing affairs of State rightly. For it was impossible to take action without friends and trusty companions; and these it was not easy to find ready to hand, since our State was no longer managed according to the principles and institutions of our forefathers; while to acquire other new friends with any facility was a thing impossible. Moreover, both the written laws and the customs were being corrupted, and that with surprising rapidity. Consequently, although at first I was filled with an ardent desire to engage in public affairs, when I considered all this and saw how things were shifting about anyhow in all directions, I finally became dizzy; and although I continued to consider by what means some betterment could be brought about not only in these matters but also in the government as a whole, yet as regards political action I kept constantly waiting for an opportune moment; until, finally, looking at all the States which now exist, I perceived that one and all they are badly governed; for the state of their laws is such as to be almost incurable without some marvellous overhauling and good-luck to boot. So in my praise of the right philosophy I was compelled to declare that by it one is enabled to discern all forms of justice both political and individual. Wherefore the classes of mankind (I said) will have no cessation from evils until either the class of those who are right and true philosophers attains political supremacy, or else the class of those who hold power in the States becomes, by some dispensation of Heaven, really philosophic. [cf. *Republic* 473]

. . .

Ought not the doctor that is giving counsel to a sick man who is indulging in a mode of life that is bad for his health to try first of all to change his life, and only proceed with the rest of his advice if the patient is willing to obey? But should he prove unwilling, then I would esteem him both manly and a true doctor if he withdraws from advising a patient of that description, and contrariwise unmanly and unskilled if he continues to advise.[1] So too with a State, whether it has one ruler or many, if so be that it asks for some salutary advice when its government is duly proceeding by the right road, then it is the act of a judicious man to give advice to such people. But in the case of those who altogether exceed the bounds of right government and wholly refuse to proceed in its tracks, and who warn their counsellor to leave the government alone and not disturb it, on pain of death if he does disturb it, while ordering him to advise as to how all that contributes to their desires and appetites may most easily and quickly be secured for ever and ever—then, in such a case, I should esteem unmanly the man who continued to engage in counsels of this kind, and the man who refused to continue manly.

This, then, being the view I hold, whenever anyone consults me concerning any very important affair relating to his life—the acquisition of wealth, for instance, or the care of his body or his soul,—if I believe that he is carrying on his daily life in a proper way, or that he will be willing to obey my advice in regard to the matters disclosed, then I give counsel readily and do not confine myself to some merely cursory reply. But if he does not ask my advice at all or plainly shows that he will in no wise obey his adviser, I do not of my own instance come forward to advise such an one, nor yet to compel him, not even were he my own son. To a slave, however, I would give advice, and if he refused it I would use compulsion. But to a father or mother I deem it impious to apply compulsion, unless they are in the grip of the disease of insanity; but if they are living a settled life which is pleasing to them, though not to me, I would neither irritate them with vain exhortations nor yet minister to them with flatteries by providing them with means to satisfy appetites of a sort such that I, were I addicted to them, would refuse to live. So likewise it behooves the man of sense to hold, while he lives, the same view concerning his own State: if it appears to him to be ill governed he ought to speak, if so be that his speech is not likely to prove fruitless nor to cause his death; but he ought not to apply violence to his fatherland in the form of a political revolution, whenever it is impossible to establish the best kind of polity without banishing and slaughtering citizens, but rather he ought to keep quiet and pray for what is good both for himself and for his State.

. . .

I know indeed that certain others have written about these same subjects; but what manner of men they are not even themselves know. But thus much I can certainly declare concerning all these writers, or prospective writers, who claim to know the subjects which I seriously study, whether as hearers of mine or of other teachers, or from their own discoveries; it is impossible, in my judgement at least, that these men should understand anything about this subject. There does not exist, nor will there ever exist, any treatise of mine dealing therewith. For it does not

---

[1] For the comparison of the political adviser to a physician *cf. Rep.* 425 E ff., *Laws* 720 A ff.

at all admit of verbal expression like other studies, but, as a result of continued application to the subject itself and communion therewith, it is brought to birth in the soul on a sudden, as light that is kindled by a leaping spark, and thereafter it nourishes itself. Notwithstanding, of thus much I am certain, that the best statement of these doctrines in writing or in speech would be my own statement; and further, that if they should be badly stated in writing, it is I who would be the person most deeply pained. And if I had thought that these subjects ought to be fully stated in writing or in speech to the public, what nobler action could I have performed in my life than that of writing what is of great benefit to mankind and bringing forth to the light for all men the nature of reality? But were I to undertake this task it would not, as I think, prove a good thing for men, save for some few who are able to discover the truth themselves with but little instruction; for as to the rest, some it would most unseasonably fill with a mistaken contempt, and others with an overweening and empty aspiration, as though they had learnt some sublime mysteries.

．　　．　　．

PART THREE

ARISTOTLE

I

Aristotle was born at Stagira, on the borders of Macedonia, in 384 B.C. For twenty years, beginning in 367, he was a student in Plato's Academy; but, as he said, he loved the truth more than he loved Plato, and he had no mind to remain a mere disciple. It is said that he left Athens when Plato made his nephew Speusippus his successor as head of the Academy, in 347. Around 343 he was called to Macedonia by king Philip to tutor the king's son, Alexander. Ten years later, Alexander had conquered all of Greece and overthrown the Persian Empire. By that time Aristotle had returned to Athens, where he presided over his own school, the so-called Lyceum. Because he liked to do some of his teaching while walking up and down under the colonnades with some of his more advanced students, his school and his philosophy were also called peripatetic. Charged with impiety when he was just over sixty, he fled Athens "lest," as he put it, "the Athenians sin twice against philosophy." A year later, in 322, he died.

There is no doubt that, after Plato, he was the most influential philosopher of all time. He dominated later medieval philosophy to such an extent that St. Thomas referred to him simply as *philosophus*, "the philosopher." Thomism and contemporary Catholic philosophy are unthinkable without him. Logic, as taught until about the time of the second World War, was essentially Aristotle's logic. His *Poetics* is still one of the classics of literary criticism, and his dicta about tragedy are still widely accepted. In metaphysics and ethics, criticism of his views has spread since Bacon and Descartes inaugurated modern philosophy, hurling their defiance at him; but for all that, the problems he saw, the distinctions he introduced, and the terms he defined are still central in many, if not most, discussions. His influence and prestige, like Plato's, are international and not confined to any school. Without him, Western philosophy might be very different.

His extant works lack the literary grace of Plato's. He, too, is said to have written dialogues, but they have not survived. What we have are often crabbed, extremely difficult, but generally highly interesting notes. There is a great deal of overlapping, repetition, and no dearth of apparent contradictions. Even one who is loath to violate the philosophic and artistic integrity of a complete work finds that we simply do not have works from Aristotle's hand that are complete in that sense. Still, there is no need to paste together snippets from here and there to piece together a system.

A little over half of the following selections comes from Aristotle's *Metaphysics:* four of its fourteen books are offered complete, and about half of Book V is included. In the first book (A), he introduces his conception of the four kinds of causes (formal, material, efficient, and final), and reviews the history of philosophy to his own time. In the fourth (Γ) he speaks of the study of being as such, of substance, of the law of contradiction and the law of excluded middle, and discusses and criticizes the teaching of Protagoras. In the fifth book (Δ) he furnishes a "Philosophical Lexicon" and defines thirty terms or groups of terms. Only half of this "dictionary" is offered here. Book nine (θ) is devoted to the distinction between potency and actuality. The twelfth book (Λ) has been called "in some ways the most impressive of all" by W. D. Ross. It employs many of the conceptions introduced previously, such as substance, actuality, and potency, and then argues to a first mover, to whom a large number of other unmoved movers are added in short order, before we are offered Aristotle's conception of the divine as contemplating itself.

Scholars agree that the books of the *Metaphysics* represent a collection of notes and treatises, not a finished work. Many of the best consider Book V (Δ) an independent work, earlier than most of the rest, and regard XII (Λ) as a separate treatise, too. XII.8, with its many unmoved movers, has been relegated to a later phase in Aristotle's development.

The first five chapters of Aristotle's *Categories* help to clear up all kinds of questions about his conception of substance; and they add a few other interesting points as well.

The *Posterior Analytics*, which deals with the forms of argument and inquiry, is divided into two books. From the first, Chapters 1-3,

8-10, and 31 are offered here. Of these three sections, the first deals with the need for pre-existent knowledge, the nature of scientific knowledge, the conditions of demonstration, and the meaning of contradiction, enunciation, proposition, basic truth, thesis, axiom, hypothesis, and definition. In Chapter 8, Aristotle argues that only eternal connections can be demonstrated; in Chapter 9, that demonstrations must proceed from the basic premises peculiar to each science, except in the case of subalternate sciences. In Chapter 10, he distinguishes the different kinds of basic truth. Chapters 1 and 2 of Book II, reproduced here, consider the four possible forms of inquiry and argue that they all concern the middle term. And in Chapter 19, the last Chapter of the whole work, he discusses how the individual mind comes to know the basic truths.

Of Aristotle's many works on science, two are represented in the following pages. From the *Physics,* three sections have been selected: In Book II, Chapter 8, Aristotle argues that nature is purposeful; in Book IV, Chapters 10 through 14, he offers a noteworthy discussion of time; and in Book VI, Chapter 9, he attempts to refute Zeno's arguments against the possibility of motion.

From the first book of On the Heavens (often cited as *De Caelo*), Chapters 2 and 3 are offered. Here the four elements which we know from the pre-Socratics—earth, water, air, and fire—are found insufficient, and Aristotle adds a fifth, sometimes called aither.

Next, we turn to Aristotle's work On the Soul (also known as *De Anima*). In the first three chapters of the second book, Aristotle defines the soul and distinguishes its faculties. In Chapters 4 and 5 of the third and last book, the passive and the active mind are discussed.

The *Nicomachean Ethics* is still considered one of the greatest works, if not the single most important one, in the whole field of ethics. The comprehensive selections from it include Aristotle's discussions of the subject matter and nature of ethics, of the good for man, of moral virtue, of the mean, of the conditions of responsibility for an action, of pride, vanity, humility, and the great-souled man (Aristotle's ideal), of the superiority of loving over being loved, of friendship and self-love, and finally of human happiness.

The last selection comprises the first fifteen (of 26) chapters of the famous *Poetics.* This is still a standard work of literary criticism, if not *the* standard work. This is not to say that everybody agrees with Aristotle, although it is astonishing how many critics do. But no other work in this field has elicited so much discussion. The discussion of diction in some of the later chapters, here omitted, is scarcely comprehensible in translation (at least the original Greek words or lines have to be furnished in parentheses or notes), and much of the rest abounds in brief allusions to a great number of plays: those who have read all of these plays will surely want to read the whole of the *Poetics,* while those who have not will not find the later chapters as rewarding as the fifteen reproduced here.

II

Most of the translations offered are taken from The Loeb Classical Library, founded by James Loeb and published by the Harvard University Press, in Cambridge, Massachusetts, and by William Heinemann Ltd., in London. In over two hundred volumes, which are available singly, The Loeb Classical Library offers scholarly editions of the original texts of the great Greek and Latin works of classical antiquity, with exceedingly faithful and readable English translations on facing pages. Top scholars have contributed translations with introductions and notes. The names of the translators of the selections offered here are as follows:

Metaphysics, Hugh Tredennick; *Categories,* Harold P. Cooke; *Physics,* Philip H. Wicksteed and Francis M. Cornford; *On the Heavens,* W. K. C. Guthrie; *On the Soul,* W. S. Hett; and *Nicomachean Ethics,* H. Rackham.

The translation of the *Posterior Analytics* used here is that of G. R. G. Mure; and this comes from *The Works of Aristotle,* translated into English under the editorship of W. D. Ross, and published by the Oxford University Press.

The translation of the *Poetics* is that of S. H. Butcher. Those who want to go on to read the whole work will find much helpful material in G. M. A. Grube's version.

The marginal page numbers, with their "a" and "b," are the same in all scholarly editions, regardless of language. They are therefore used in all scholarly citations of Aristotle. They will be found at the top of the following pages, as part of the running heads.

The student who seeks further guidance will find W. D. Ross's *Aristotle* (published in paperback by Meridian Books) particularly helpful.

CATEGORIES

I. Things are equivocally [1] named, when they have the name only in common, the definition (or statement of essence) corresponding with the name being different. For instance, while a man and a portrait can properly both be called 'animals,' these are equivocally named.[2] For they have the name only in common, the definitions (or statements of essence) corresponding with the name being different. For if you are asked to define what the being an ainmal means in the case of the man and the portrait, you give in either case a definition appropriate to that case alone.

Things are univocally named, when not only they bear the same name but the name means the same in each case—has the same definition corresponding. Thus a man and an ox are called 'animals.' The name is the same in both cases; so also the statement of essence. For if you are asked what is meant by their both of them being called 'animals,' you give that particular name in both cases the same definition.

Things are 'derivatively' named that derive their own name from some other, that is given a new verbal form, as, for instance, 'grammarian' from 'grammar,' from 'heroism,' 'hero,' and so on.[3]

II. We may or we may not combine what we call words, expressions and phrases. Combine them; you have propositions—for instance, 'man runs' or 'man wins'—while examples of uncombined forms are 'man,' 'ox,' 'runs' and 'wins' and the like.

But as for the things that are *meant,* when we thus speak of uncombined words, you can predicate some of a subject, but they never are present in one. You can predicate 'man,' for example, of this or that man as the subject, but man is not found in a subject. By 'in,' 'present,' 'found in a subject' I do not mean present or found as its parts are contained in a whole; I mean that it cannot exist as apart from the subject referred to. And then there is that class of things which are present or found in a subject, although they cannot be asserted of any known subject whatever. A piece of grammatical knowledge is there in the mind as a subject but cannot be predicated of any known subject whatever. Again, a particular whiteness is present or found in a body (all colour implies some such

---

[1] I retain the traditional renderings, 'univocal,' namely, and 'equivocal.' The ordinary reader, I suspect, will be little familiar with the former. He may, if he pleases, substitute such terms as 'ambiguous,' 'unambiguous.' 'Univocal' has the advantage of being a *positive* term.

[2] Ζῷον in Greek had two meanings, that is to say, living creature, and, secondly, a figure or image in painting, embroidery, sculpture. We have no ambiguous noun. However, we use the word 'living' of portraits to mean 'true to life.'

[3] 'Courageous man,' 'courage,' in Greek. But the former obscures the real point by consisting of two words in English. By 'a new verbal form' is intended a new termination or inflexion.

basis as what we intend by 'a body') but cannot itself be asserted of any known subject whatever. We find there are some things, moreover, not only affirmed of a subject but present also in a subject. Thus knowledge, for instance, while present in this or that mind as a subject, is also asserted of grammar. There is, finally, that class of things which can neither be found in a subject nor yet be asserted of one—this or that man or horse, for example. For nothing of that kind is in or is ever affirmed of a subject. More generally speaking, indeed, we can never affirm of a subject what is in its nature individual and also numerically one. Yet in some cases nothing prevents its being *present* or *found in* a subject. Thus a piece of grammatical knowledge is present, as we said, in a mind.

III. A word upon predicates here. When you predicate this thing or that of another thing as of a subject, the predicates then of the predicate will also hold good of the subject. We predicate 'man' of *a* man; so of 'man' do we predicate 'animal.' Therefore, of this or that man we can predicate 'animal' too. For a man is both 'animal' and 'man.'

When genera are co-ordinate and different, differentiae will differ in kind.[4] Take the genera, animal and knowledge. 'Footed,' 'two-footed,' 'winged,' 'aquatic' are among the differentiae of animal. But none will be found to distinguish a particular species of knowledge. No species of knowledge will differ from another in being 'two-footed.'

Where the genera, however, are subordinate, nothing whatever prevents them from having the same differentiae. For we predicate the higher or larger of the smaller or subordinate class. The differentiae, then, of the predicate will also belong to the subject.

IV. Each uncombined word or expression means one of the following things:—what (or Substance), how large (that is, Quantity), what sort of thing (that is, Quality), related to what (or Relation), where (that is, Place), when (or Time), in what attitude (Posture, Position), how circumstanced (State or Condition), how active, what doing (or Action), how passive, what suffering (Affection).[5] Examples, to speak but in outline, of Substance are 'man' and 'a horse,' of Quantity 'two cubits long,' 'three cubits in length' and the like, of Quality 'white' and 'grammatical.' Terms such as 'half,' 'double,' 'greater' are held to denote a Relation. 'In the market-place,' 'in the Lyceum' and similar phrases mean Place, while Time is intended by phrases like 'yesterday,' 'last year' and so on. 'Is lying' or 'sitting' means Posture, 'is shod' or 'is armed' means a State. 'Cuts' or 'burns,' again, indicates Action, 'is cut' or 'is burnt' an Affection.

Not one of these terms in itself will involve any positive statement. Affirmations, as also denials, can only arise when such terms are com-

---

4 'Co-ordinate' is literally in Greek 'not arranged the one under the other.' The differentia added to the genus constitutes what is known as the species. Supposing that 'building' is the genus and 'used for a dwelling' the difference, we then have the species called 'house.'

5 I give here two versions of each category. The Greek as a rule is more concrete than the customary English translations. The reader may here be referred to Theodor Gomperz, *Greek Thinkers* (translated by G. G. Berry), vol. iv. c. 4.

bined or united together. Each positive or negative statement must either be true or be false—that, at least, is allowed on all hands—but an uncombined word or expression (for instance, 'man,' 'white,' 'runs' or 'conquers') can neither be true nor be false.

V. Substance in the truest and strictest, the primary sense of that term, is that which is neither asserted of nor can be found in a subject.[6] We take as examples of this a particular man or a horse. But we *do* speak of secondary substances—those within which, being species, the primary or first are included, and those within which, being genera, the species themselves are contained. For instance, a particular man we include in the species called 'man' and the species itself in its turn is included in the genus called 'animal.' These, then, are secondary substances, that is to say, man and animal—otherwise, species and genus.

From what we have said it is plain that the name and definition of the predicates can both be affirmed of the subject. For instance, we predicate 'man' of an individual man as the subject. The name of the species called 'man' is asserted of each individual; you predicate 'man' of *a* man. The definition or meaning of 'man' will apply to *a* man, in like manner, for a man is both man and an animal. The name and definition of the species will thus both apply to the subject.

When we come, on the contrary, to things which are present or found in a subject, we find that their names and definitions we cannot, at least in most cases, affirm or predicate of that subject. Indeed, the definition itself will in no case whatever apply. But in some cases nothing prevents us from using the *name* of the subject. Suppose we take 'white' as an instance. Now 'white' is, no doubt, in a body and thus is affirmed of a body, for a body, of course, is called 'white.' The definition, however, of 'white'—of the colour, that is, we call 'white'—can never be predicated of any such body whatever.

Everything else but first substance is either affirmed of first substance or present in such as its subject. This is evident from particular instances taken by way of examples. We predicate 'animal' of 'man.' So we predicate 'animal' also of any particular man. Were there no individuals existing of whom it could thus be affirmed, it could not be affirmed of the species. Colour, again, is in body; so also in this or that body. For were there no bodies existing wherein it could also exist, it could not be in body at all. In fine, then, all things whatsoever, save what we call primary substances, are predicates of primary substances or present in such as their subjects. And were there no primary substance, nought else could so much as exist.

Of secondary substances species is better called substance than genus:

---

6 ' "Asserted of a subject" here refers to the relation of universal to particular, "present in a subject" to that of an attribute to its possessor' (W. D. Ross, *Aristotle*, p. 23). The distinction is the same as that into essential and accidental predicates. Aristotle under substance distinguishes, first of all, primary substance, that is to say, the individual (or this or that man, for example), and, secondly, secondary substances, that is, the species and genera in which the individuals are included.

it is nearer to primary substance, while genus is more removed from it. Suppose someone asks you 'what is it?' regarding a primary substance. Your answer is both more instructive and also more apt to the subject, provided you mention its species than if you should mention its genus. Take this or that man, for example. You would give a more instructive account, if you stated the species or 'man,' than you would, if you called him 'an animal.' The former belongs the more to him, the latter is somewhat too wide. Or, again, take an individual tree. By mentioning the species or 'tree' you will give a more instructive account than by giving the genus or 'plant.'

Moreover, the primary substances most of all merit that name, since they underlie all other things, which in turn will be either their predicates or present in such as their subjects. But exactly as primary substances stand to all else that exists, so also stands species to genus. Species is related to genus as subject is related to predicate. We predicate genus of species; but never, indeed, can we predicate species of genus conversely. On this further ground we may hold that of secondary substances species is more truly substance than genus.

If we turn to the species themselves, none, unless it is also a genus, is more of a substance than another. No apter description is 'man' of a concrete or individual man than is 'horse' of a concrete horse. So also of primary substances—none is more a substance than others. For this or that man, for example, could not well be *more truly* substance than, let us say, this or that ox.

Apart, then, from primary substances, species and genus alone of the things that will then remain over are rightly called secondary substance, for they of all possible predicates alone define primary substance. For only by species or genus can this or that man be defined in a fit or appropriate way; and we make our definition preciser by stating the species or 'man' than by stating the genus or 'animal.' Anything else we might state, as, for instance, 'he runs' or 'is white,' would be foreign from the purpose in hand. So species and genera only are rightly designated as substance, first substances only excepted.

'Substance,' again, strictly speaking, applies to first substances only, because they not only underlie but provide all things else with their subjects. Exactly as primary substance is related to all else whatever, so also are genus and species, in which is included that substance, related to all attributes not included in genus and species. For these are the subjects of such. You may call a man 'learned in grammar.' And, therefore, his species and genus, that is to say, man and animal, you may also call 'learned in grammar.' And this will be so in all cases.

That it never is present in a subject holds good of all substance whatever. For what we call primary substance can neither be present in a subject nor yet predicated of one. And as for the secondary substance, the following points, among others, will prove it is not in a subject. We predicate 'man' of a man; 'man,' however, is not *in* a subject. For manhood is not *in* a man. As the species, so also the genus. For 'animal' is also asserted of this or that man in particular but cannot be found present in him. Again, we may notice this point. When a thing can be found in a subject, then nothing prevents us from using its name of the subject in question; not so the definition, however. And yet of a secondary substance both name and definition hold good in the case of the subject as well. The definition of the species (or man) and that of the genus (or animal) are used of an individual man. Therefore, substance is not in a subject.

That they cannot be present in subjects is true not of substances only but holds of differentiae, too. Thus we can of the species called 'man' assert 'going on foot' and 'two-footed.' But these are not found present in it. For neither of these is *in* man. Where, again, you affirm the differentia, you also affirm its definition. Suppose of the species called 'man' you should predicate 'going on foot.' The definition also of that attribute then will apply to that species. For 'man' does, indeed, go on foot.

That the parts of the substances are present or found in the wholes as in subjects is a fact that need hardly disturb us or render us fearful of having to brand all such parts as no substances. Did we not qualify 'present in a subject' by 'not as the parts in a whole'?

Differentia and substance alike have this characteristic in common, that, wherever we predicate them, we predicate them univocally. For such propositions have always individuals or species for subjects. The primary substance, no doubt, being never predicated of anything, never itself can be predicate of any proposition whatever. Not so with the secondary substance. The species is predicated of all individual examples, the genus of these and the species. And so with differentiae also. Of species and individuals we predicate these in like manner. Both definitions, moreover, or those of the genus and species, apply to the primary substance and that of the genus to the species. For all we affirm of the predicate will also be affirmed of the subject. The definition of each differentia applies in a similar manner to both individuals and species. But, as we have already noticed, univocal is used of such things as not only possess the same name but are also defined the same way. Hence it follows that in all propositions having substance or difference for predicate that predicate is quite unequivocal.

All substance appears individual. And this is indisputably true in the case of the primary substances. What each denotes is a unit. In that of the secondary substances language may make it appear so, as when we say 'animal,' 'man.' This, however, is not really so, for a quality rather is meant. Second substance is not one and single, as, no doubt, the primary is; not of one but of many, indeed, do we predicate 'animal,' 'man.' Species and genus, however, do not merely indicate quality, as 'white' merely indicates quality. Accidents, that is, like 'white,' mean a quality simply and merely. But species and genus determine a quality in reference to substance. They tell you *what sort* of a substance. In the case of the genus, however, such determining qualification will cover a much wider field than it does in the case of the species. Say 'ainmal'; you comprehend more than you would, if instead you said 'man.'

Substances never have contraries. How could first substances have them—this man, for example, that animal? Nothing is contrary to them. And species and genus have none. This particular characteristic belongs not to substance alone. For it holds of a good many things and, among them, for instance, of quantity. 'Two cubits long' has no contrary; neither has 'three cubits long'; nor has 'ten' nor yet anything like it, unless, indeed, someone should say 'large' and 'small,' 'much' and 'little' are contraries. Definite quantities, however, can certainly never have contraries.

No substance, it seems, has degrees or admits of a more and a less. I do not mean here that one substance may not be more truly called substance, less truly called substance, than others; indeed, we have said that it may. But I mean that no substance as such can admit of degrees in itself. For example, the same substance, man, cannot really be more or less man as compared with himself or another. This man is not *more* man than that, as one white thing is more or less white than another white object may be or, again, as one beautiful object has more or less beauty than others. The same quality in the same object may vary at times in degree. For example, a body, if white, is called whiter just now than it was or, if warm, is called more or less warm. But a substance is not more or less of whatever, *qua* substance, it is. For a man is not more of a man than he was at some time in the past. And so of all substances else. Therefore, substance can have no degrees.

But what is most characteristic of substance appears to be this: that, although it remains, notwithstanding, numerically one and the same, it is capable of being the recipient of contrary qualifications. Of things that are other than substance we could hardly adduce an example possessed of this characteristic. For instance, a particular colour, numerically one and the same, can in no wise be both black and white, and an action, if one and the same, can in no wise be both good and bad. So of everything other than substance. But substance, remaining the same, yet admits of such contrary qualities. One and the same individual at one time is white, warm or good, at another time black, cold or bad. This is not so with anything else, though it might be maintained that assertions or opinions admitted of contraries. That is to say, the same statement may appear to be both true and false.[7] 'He sits' may, for instance, be true. If he rises, it then becomes false. And so with opinions as well. One may be of the opinion, and truly, that such or such person is sitting. And yet, when that person has risen, that opinion, if held still, is false. Even though we allow this exception, it would differ, in fact, from the rest in its manner of coming about. For whenever a substance admits of such contrary qualifications, it is by a change in itself. It is by a change in itself that a thing that was hot becomes cold (having passed from one state to another) or a thing that was white becomes black or a thing that was

---

[7] True at one time and false at another.

good becomes bad. And so, too, in all other cases where substance admits of such qualities. The statement or opinion, however, remains in itself quite unaltered in any and every respect. If it takes on the contrary quality, being now true and now false, then the facts of the case will have changed. For the statement 'he sits' is unchanged; but according to existing conditions we call it now true and now false. As with statements, so, too, with opinions. In its manner, then, of coming about it is really peculiar to substance to admit of the contrary qualities—to wit, by a change in itself.

If a man, then, should make an exception in favour of opinions and statements, maintaining that these admit also of contrary qualifications, his view would, in truth, be unsound. If opinions and statements are said to admit of such qualifications, the fact is that not they themselves but that *something else* undergoes change. For it is by the facts of the case, by their being or not being so, that a statement is called true or false. It is not that the statement itself can admit of such contrary qualities. For nothing, in one word, can alter the nature of opinions and statements, and, seeing no change occurs in them, they cannot admit of such contraries. But substance admits of such contraries by having received them itself: it alternately takes to itself health, disease, whiteness, blackness, the like. By receiving them into itself is it said to admit of such contraries. So, to conclude, we may call this above all distinctive of substance, that, remaining still one and the same, it may yet through a change in itself receive contrary qualifications. Let so much on substance suffice.

.   .   .

POSTERIOR ANALYTICS

Book I

1   All instruction given or received by way of argument proceeds   [71a] from pre-existent knowledge. This becomes evident upon a survey of all species of such instruction. The mathematical sciences and all other speculative disciplines are acquired in this way, and so are the two forms of dialectical reasoning, syllogistic and inductive: for each of these latter makes use of old knowledge to impart new, the syllogism assuming an audience that accepts its premises, induction exhibiting the universal as implicit in the clearly known particular. Again, the persuasion exerted by rhetorical arguments is in principle the same, since they use either example, a kind of induction, or enthymeme, a form of syllogism.

The pre-existent knowledge required is of two kinds. In some cases admission of the fact must be assumed, in others comprehension of the meaning of the term used, and sometimes both assumptions are essential.

Thus, we assume that every predicate can be either truly affirmed or truly denied of any subject, and that 'triangle' means so and so; as regards 'unit' we have to make the double assumption of the meaning of the word and the existence of the thing. The reason is that these several objects are not equally obvious to us. Recognition of a truth may in some cases contain as factors both previous knowledge and also knowledge acquired simultaneously with that recognition—knowledge, this latter, of the particulars actually falling under the universal and therein already virtually known. For example, the student knew beforehand that the angles of every triangle are equal to two right angles; but it was only at the actual moment at which he was being led on to recognize this as true in the instance before him that he came to know 'this figure inscribed in the semicircle' to be a triangle. For some things (viz. the singulars finally reached which are not predicable of anything else as subject) are only learnt in this way, i. e. there is here no recognition through a middle of a minor term as subject to a major. Before he was led on to recognition or before he actually drew a conclusion, we should perhaps say that in a manner he knew, in a manner not.

If he did not in an unqualified sense of the term *know* the existence of this triangle, how could he *know* without qualification that its angles were equal to two right angles? No: clearly he *knows* not without qualification but only in the sense that he *knows* universally. If this distinction is not drawn, we are faced with the dilemma in the *Meno*: either a man will learn nothing or what he already knows; for we cannot accept the solution which some people offer. A man is asked, 'Do you, or do you not, know that every pair is even?' He says he does know it. The questioner then produces a particular pair, of the existence, and so *a fortiori* of the evenness, of which he was unaware. The solution which some people offer is to assert that they do not know that every pair is even, but only that everything which they know to be a pair is even: yet what they [71b] know to be even is that of which they have demonstrated evenness, i. e. what they made the subject of their premiss, viz. not merely every triangle or number which they know to be such, but any and every number or triangle without reservation. For no premiss is ever couched in the form 'every number which you know to be such', or 'every rectilinear figure which you know to be such': the predicate is always construed as applicable to any and every instance of the thing. On the other hand, I imagine there is nothing to prevent a man in one sense knowing what he is learning, in another not knowing it. The strange thing would be, not if in some sense he knew what he was learning, but if he were to know it in that precise sense and manner in which he was learning it.

2   We suppose ourselves to possess unqualified scientific knowledge of a thing, as opposed to knowing it in the accidental way in which the sophist knows, when we think that we know the cause on which the fact depends, as the cause of that fact and of no other, and, further, that the fact could not be other than it is. Now that scientific knowing is some-

thing of this sort is evident—witness both those who falsely claim it and those who actually possess it, since the former merely imagine themselves to be, while the latter are also actually, in the condition described. Consequently the proper object of unqualified scientific knowledge is something which cannot be other than it is.

There may be another manner of knowing as well—that will be discussed later. What I now assert is that at all events we do know by demonstration. By demonstration I mean a syllogism productive of scientific knowledge, a syllogism, that is, the grasp of which is *eo ipso* such knowledge. Assuming then that my thesis as to the nature of scientific knowing is correct, the premisses of demonstrated knowledge must be true, primary, immediate, better known than and prior to the conclusion, which is further related to them as effect to cause. Unless these conditions are satisfied, the basic truths will not be 'appropriate' to the conclusion. Syllogism there may indeed be without these conditions, but such syllogism, not being productive of scientific knowledge, will not be demonstration. The premisses must be true: for that which is non-existent cannot be known—we cannot know, e. g., that the diagonal of a square is commensurate with its side. The premisses must be primary and indemonstrable; otherwise they will require demonstration in order to be known, since to have knowledge, if it be not accidental knowledge, of things which are demonstrable, means precisely to have a demonstration of them. The premisses must be the causes of the conclusion, better known than it, and prior to it; its causes, since we possess scientific knowledge of a thing only when we know its cause; prior, in order to be causes; antecedently known, this antecedent knowledge being not our mere understanding of the meaning, but knowledge of the fact as well. Now 'prior' and 'better known' are ambiguous terms, for there is a difference between what is prior and better known in the order of being and what is prior [72ᵃ] and better known to man. I mean that objects nearer to sense are prior and better known to man; objects without qualification prior and better known are those further from sense. Now the most universal causes are furthest from sense and particular causes are nearest to sense, and they are thus exactly opposed to one another. In saying that the premisses of demonstrated knowledge must be primary, I mean that they must be the 'appropriate' basic truths, for I identify primary premiss and basic truth. A 'basic truth' in a demonstration is an immediate proposition. An immediate proposition is one which has no other proposition prior to it. A proposition is either part of an enunciation, i. e. it predicates a single attribute of a single subject. If a proposition is dialectical, it assumes either part indifferently; if it is demonstrative, it lays down one part to the definite exclusion of the other because that part is true. The term 'enunciation' denotes either part of a contradiction indifferently. A contradiction is an opposition which of its own nature excludes a middle. The part of a contradiction which conjoins a predicate with a subject is an affirmation; the part disjoining them is a negation. I call an immediate basic truth of syllogism a 'thesis' when, though it is not susceptible of proof by the teacher, yet ignorance of it does not constitute a total bar to progress on the part of the pupil: one which the pupil must know if he is to learn anything whatever is an axiom. I call it an axiom because there are such truths and we give them the name of axioms *par excellence*. If a thesis assumes one part or the other of an enunciation, i. e. asserts either the existence or the non-existence of a subject, it is a hypothesis; if it does not so assert, it is a definition. Definition *is* a 'thesis' or a 'laying something down', since the arithmetician lays it down that to be a unit is to be quantitatively indivisible; but it is not a hypothesis, for to define what a unit is is not the same as to affirm its existence.

Now since the required ground of our knowledge—i. e. of our conviction —of a fact is the possession of such a syllogism as we call demonstration, and the ground of the syllogism is the facts constituting its premisses, we must not only know the primary premisses—some if not all of them— beforehand, but know them better than the conclusion: for the cause of an attribute's inherence in a subject always itself inheres in the subject more firmly than that attribute; e. g. the cause of our loving anything is dearer to us than the object of our love. So since the primary premisses are the cause of our knowledge—i. e. of our conviction—it follows that we know them better—that is, are more convinced of them—than their consequences, precisely because our knowledge of the latter is the effect of our knowledge of the premisses. Now a man cannot believe in anything more than in the things he knows, unless he has either actual knowledge of it or something better than actual knowledge. But we are faced with this paradox if a student whose belief rests on demonstration has not prior knowledge; a man must believe in some, if not in all, of the basic truths more than in the conclusion. Moreover, if a man sets out to acquire the scientific knowledge that comes through demonstration, he must not only have a better knowledge of the basic truths and a firmer conviction of them than of the connexion which is being demonstrated: more [72ᵇ] than this, nothing must be more certain or better known to him than these basic truths in their character as contradicting the fundamental premisses which lead to the opposed and erroneous conclusion. For indeed the conviction of pure science must be unshakable.

3 Some hold that, owing to the necessity of knowing the primary premisses, there is no scientific knowledge. Others think there is, but that all truths are demonstrable. Neither doctrine is either true or a necessary deduction from the premisses. The first school, assuming that there is no way of knowing other than by demonstration, maintain that an infinite regress is involved, on the ground that if behind the prior stands no primary, we could not know the posterior through the prior (wherein they are right, for one cannot traverse an infinite series): if on the other hand —they say—the series terminates and there are primary premisses, yet these are unknowable because incapable of demonstration, which according to them is the only form of knowledge. And since thus one cannot know the primary premisses, knowledge of the conclusions which follow

from them is not pure scientific knowledge nor properly knowing at all, but rests on the mere supposition that the premisses are true. The other party agree with them as regards knowing, holding that it is only possible by demonstration, but they see no difficulty in holding that all truths are demonstrated, on the ground that demonstration may be circular and reciprocal.

Our own doctrine is that not all knowledge is demonstrative: on the contrary, knowledge of the immediate premisses is independent of demonstration. (The necessity of this is obvious; for since we must know the prior premisses from which the demonstration is drawn, and since the regress must end in immediate truths, those truths must be indemonstrable.) Such, then, is our doctrine, and in addition we maintain that besides scientific knowledge there is its originative source which enables us to recognize the definitions.

Now demonstration must be based on premisses prior to and better known than the conclusion; and the same things cannot simultaneously be both prior and posterior to one another: so circular demonstration is clearly not possible in the unqualified sense of 'demonstration', but only possible if 'demonstration' be extended to include that other method of argument which rests on a distinction between truths prior to us and truths without qualification prior, i. e. the method by which induction produces knowledge. But if we accept this extension of its meaning, our definition of unqualified knowledge will prove faulty; for there seem to be two kinds of it. Perhaps, however, the second form of demonstration, that which proceeds from truths better known to us, is not demonstration in the unqualified sense of the term.

The advocates of circular demonstration are not only faced with the difficulty we have just stated: in addition their theory reduces to the mere statement that if a thing exists, then it does exist—an easy way of proving anything. That this is so can be clearly shown by taking three terms, for to constitute the circle it makes no difference whether many terms or few or even only two are taken. Thus by direct proof, if A is, B must be; if B is, C must be; therefore if A is, C must be. Since then—by the circular proof—if A is, B must be, and if B is, A must be, A may [73ᵃ] be substituted for C above. Then 'if B is, A must be' = 'if B is, C must be', which above gave the conclusion 'if A is, C must be': but C and A have been identified. Consequently the upholders of circular demonstration are in the position of saying that if A is, A must be—a simple way of proving anything. Moreover, even such circular demonstration is impossible except in the case of attributes that imply one another, viz. 'peculiar' properties.

Now, it has been shown that the positing of one thing—be it one term or one premiss—never involves a necessary consequent: two premisses constitute the first and smallest foundation for drawing a conclusion at all and therefore a fortiori for the demonstrative syllogism of science. If, then, A is implied in B and C, and B and C are reciprocally implied in one another and in A, it is possible, as has been shown in my writings on the syllogism, to prove all the assumptions on which the original conclusion rested, by circular demonstration in the first figure. But it has also been shown that in the other figures either no conclusion is possible, or at least none which proves both the original premisses. Propositions the terms of which are not convertible cannot be circularly demonstrated at all, and since convertible terms occur rarely in actual demonstrations, it is clearly frivolous and impossible to say that demonstration is reciprocal and that therefore everything can be demonstrated.

· · ·

8   It is also clear that if the premisses from which the syllogism proceeds are commensurately universal, the conclusion of such demonstration—demonstration, i. e., in the unqualified sense—must also be eternal. Therefore no attribute can be demonstrated nor known by strictly scientific knowledge to inhere in perishable things. The proof can only be accidental, because the attribute's connexion with its perishable subject is not commensurately universal but temporary and special. If such a demonstration is made, one premiss must be perishable and not commensurately universal (perishable because only if it is perishable will the conclusion be perishable; not commensurately universal, because the predicate will be predicable of some instances of the subject and not of others); so that the conclusion can only be that a fact is true at the moment—not commensurately and universally. The same is true of definitions, since a definition is either a primary premiss or a conclusion of a demonstration, or else only differs from a demonstration in the order of its terms. Demonstration and science of merely frequent occurrences—e. g. of eclipse as happening to the moon—are, as such, clearly eternal: whereas so far as they are not eternal they are not fully commensurate. Other subjects too have properties attaching to them in the same way as eclipse attaches to the moon.

9   It is clear that if the conclusion is to show an attribute inhering as such, nothing can be demonstrated except from its 'appropriate' basic truths. Consequently a proof even from true, indemonstrable, and immediate premisses does not constitute knowledge. Such proofs are like Bryson's method of squaring the circle; for they operate by taking as their middle a common character—a character, therefore, which [76a] the subject may share with another—and consequently they apply equally to subjects different in kind. They therefore afford knowledge of an attribute only as inhering accidentally, not as belonging to its subject as such: otherwise they would not have been applicable to another genus.

Our knowledge of any attribute's connexion with a subject is accidental unless we know that connexion through the middle term in virtue of which it inheres, and as an inference from basic premisses essential and 'appropriate' to the subject—unless we know, e. g., the property of possessing angles equal to two right angles as belonging to that subject in which it inheres essentially, and as inferred from basic premisses essential and 'appropriate' to that subject: so that if that middle term also belongs essentially to the minor, the middle must belong to the same kind as the major and minor terms. The only exceptions to this rule are such cases as theorems in harmonics which are demonstrable by arithmetic. Such theorems are proved by the same middle terms as arithmetical properties, but with a qualification—the fact falls under a separate science (for the subject genus is separate), but the reasoned fact concerns the superior science, to which the attributes essentially belong. Thus, even these apparent exceptions show that no attribute is strictly demonstrable except from its 'appropriate' basic truths, which, however, in the case of these sciences have the requisite identity of character.

It is no less evident that the peculiar basic truths of each inhering attribute are indemonstrable; for basic truths from which they might be deduced would be basic truths of all that is, and the science to which they belonged would possess universal sovereignty. This is so because he knows better whose knowledge is deduced from higher causes, for his knowledge is from prior premises when it derives from causes themselves uncaused: hence, if he knows better than others or best of all, his knowledge would be science in a higher or the highest degree. But, as things are demonstration is not transferable to another genus with such exceptions as we have mentioned of the application of geometrical demonstrations to theorems in mechanics or optics, or of arithmetical demonstrations to those of harmonics.

It is hard to be sure whether one knows or not; for it is hard to be sure whether one's knowledge is based on the basic truths appropriate to each attribute—the differentia of true knowledge. We think we have scientific knowledge if we have reasoned from true and primary premises. But that is not so: the conclusion must be homogeneous with the basic facts of the science.

10   I call the basic truths of every genus those elements in it the existence of which cannot be proved. As regards both these primary truths and the attributes dependent on them the meaning of the name is assumed. The fact of their existence as regards the primary truths must be assumed; but it has to be proved of the remainder, the attributes. Thus we assume the meaning alike of unity, straight, and triangular; but while as regards unity and magnitude we assume also the fact of their existence, in the case of the remainder proof is required.

Of the basic truths used in the demonstrative sciences some are peculiar to each science, and some are common, but common only in the sense of analogous, being of use only in so far as they fall within the genus constituting the province of the science in question.

Peculiar truths are, e. g., the definitions of line and straight; common truths are such as 'take equals from equals and equals remain'. Only so much of these common truths is required as falls within the genus [76^b] in question: for a truth of this kind will have the same force even if not used generally but applied by the geometer only to magnitudes, or by the arithmetician only to numbers. Also peculiar to a science are the subjects the existence as well as the meaning of which it assumes, and the essential attributes of which it investigates, e. g. in arithmetic units, in geometry points and lines. Both the existence and the meaning of the subjects are assumed by these sciences; but of their essential attributes only the meaning is assumed. For example arithmetic assumes the meaning of odd and even, square and cube, geometry that of incommensurable, or of deflection or verging of lines, whereas the existence of these attributes is demonstrated by means of the axioms and from previous conclusions as premisses. Astronomy too proceeds in the same way. For indeed every demonstrative science has three elements: (1) that which it posits, the subject genus whose essential attributes it examines; (2) the so-called axioms, which are primary premisses of its demonstration; (3) the attributes, the meaning of which it assumes. Yet some sciences may very well pass over some of these elements; e. g. we might not expressly posit the existence of the genus if its existence were obvious (for instance, the existence of hot and cold is more evident than that of number); or we might omit to assume expressly the meaning of the attributes if it were well understood. In the same way the meaning of axioms, such as 'Take equals from equals and equals remain', is well known and so not expressly assumed. Nevertheless in the nature of the case the essential elements of demonstration are three: the subject, the attributes, and the basic premisses.

That which expresses necessary self-grounded fact, and which we must necessarily believe, is distinct both from the hypotheses of a science and from illegitimate postulate—I say 'must believe', because all syllogism, and therefore *a fortiori* demonstration, is addressed not to the spoken word, but to the discourse within the soul, and though we can always raise objections to the spoken word, to the inward discourse we cannot always object. That which is capable of proof but assumed by the teacher without proof is, if the pupil believes and accepts it, hypothesis, though only in a limited sense hypothesis—that is, relatively to the pupil; if the pupil has no opinion or a contrary opinion on the matter, the same assumption is an illegitimate postulate. Therein lies the distinction between hypothesis and illegitimate postulate: the latter is the contrary of the pupil's opinion, demonstrable, but assumed and used without demonstration.

The definitions—viz. those which are not expressed as statements that anything is or is not—are not hypotheses: but it is in the premisses of a science that its hypotheses are contained. Definitions require only to be understood, and this is not hypothesis—unless it be contended that the pupil's hearing is also an hypothesis required by the teacher. Hypotheses, on the contrary, postulate facts on the being of which depends the being of the fact inferred. Nor are the geometer's hypotheses false, as some have held, urging that one must not employ falsehood and that the geometer is uttering falsehood in stating that the line which he draws is a foot long or straight, when it is actually neither. The truth is [77ᵃ] that the geometer does not draw any conclusion from the being of the particular line of which he speaks, but from what his diagrams symbolize. A further distinction is that all hypotheses and illegitimate postulates are either universal or particular, whereas a definition is neither.

.   .   .

31   Scientific knowledge is not possible through the act of perception. Even if perception as a faculty is of 'the such' and not merely of a 'this somewhat', yet one must at any rate actually perceive a 'this somewhat', and at a definite present place and time: but that which is commensurately universal and true in all cases one cannot perceive, since it is not 'this' and it is not 'now'; if it were, it would not be commensurately universal—the term we apply to what is always and everywhere. Seeing, therefore, that demonstrations are commensurately universal and universals imperceptible, we clearly cannot obtain scientific knowledge by the act of perception: nay, it is obvious that even if it were possible to perceive that a triangle has its angles equal to two right angles, we should still be looking for a demonstration—we should not (as some say) possess knowledge of it; for perception must be of a particular, whereas scientific knowledge involves the recognition of the commensurate universal. So if we were on the moon, and saw the earth shutting out the sun's light, we should not know the cause of the eclipse: we should perceive the present fact of the eclipse, but not the reasoned fact at all,   [88ª] since the act of perception is not of the commensurate universal. I do not, of course, deny that by watching the frequent recurrence of this event we might, after tracking the commensurate universal, possess a demonstration, for the commensurate universal is elicited from the several groups of singulars.

The commensurate universal is precious because it makes clear the cause; so that in the case of facts like these which have a cause other than themselves universal knowledge is more precious than sense-perceptions and than intuition. (As regards primary truths there is of course a different account to be given.) Hence it is clear that knowledge of things demonstrable cannot be acquired by perception, unless the term perception is applied to the possession of scientific knowledge through demonstration. Nevertheless certain points do arise with regard to connexions to be proved which are referred for their explanation to a failure in sense-perception: there are cases when an act of vision would terminate our inquiry, not because in seeing we should be knowing, but because we should have elicited the universal from seeing; if, for example, we saw pores in the glass and the light passing through, the reason of the kindling would be clear to us because we should at the same time see it in each instance and intuit that it must be so in all instances.

Book II

1 The kinds of question we ask are as many as the kinds of things which we know. They are in fact four:—(1) whether the connexion of an attribute with a thing is a fact, (2) what is the reason of the connexion, (3) whether a thing exists, (4) what is the nature of the thing. Thus, when our question concerns a complex of thing and attribute and we ask whether the thing is thus or otherwise qualified—whether, e. g., the sun suffers eclipse or not—then we are asking as to the fact of a connexion. That our inquiry ceases with the discovery that the sun does suffer eclipse is an indication of this; and if we know from the start that the sun suffers eclipse, we do not inquire whether it does so or not. On the other hand, when we know the fact we ask the reason; as, for example, when we know that the sun is being eclipsed and that an earthquake is in progress, it is the reason of eclipse or earthquake into which we inquire.

Where a complex is concerned, then, those are the two questions we ask; but for some objects of inquiry we have a different kind of question to ask, such as whether there is or is not a centaur or a God. (By 'is or is not' I mean 'is or is not, without further qualification'; as opposed to 'is or is not (e. g.) white'.) On the other hand, when we have ascertained the thing's existence, we inquire as to its nature, asking, for instance, 'what, then, is God? or 'what is man?'.

2 These, then, are the four kinds of question we ask, and it is in the answers to these questions that our knowledge consists.

Now when we ask whether a connexion is a fact, or whether a thing without qualification *is*, we are really asking whether the connexion or the thing has a 'middle'; and when we have ascertained either that the connexion is a fact or that the thing *is*—i. e. ascertained either the partial or the unqualified being of the thing—and are proceeding [90ᵃ] to ask the reason of the connexion or the nature of the thing, then we are asking what the 'middle' is.

(By distinguishing the fact of the connexion and the existence of the thing as respectively the partial and the unqualified being of the thing I mean that if we ask 'does the moon suffer eclipse?', or 'does the moon wax?', the question concerns a part of the thing's being; for what we are asking in such questions is whether a thing is this or that, i. e. has or has not this or that attribute: whereas, if we ask whether the moon or night exists, the question concerns the unqualified being of a thing.)

We conclude that in all our inquiries we are asking either whether there is a 'middle' or what the 'middle' is: for the 'middle' here is precisely the cause, and it is the cause that we seek in all our inquiries. Thus, 'Does the moon suffer eclipse?' means 'Is there or is there not a cause producing eclipse of the moon?', and when we have learnt that there is, our next question is, 'What, then, is this cause?'; for the cause through which a thing *is*—not *is this or that*, i. e. has this or that attribute, but without qualification *is*—and the cause through which it is—not *is* without qualification, but *is this or that* as having some essential attribute or some accident—are both alike the 'middle'. By that which *is* without qualification I mean the subject, e. g. moon or earth or sun or triangle; by that which a subject *is* (in the partial sense) I mean a property, e. g. eclipse, equality or inequality, interposition or non-interposition. For in all these examples it is clear that the nature of the thing and the reason of the fact are identical: the question 'What is eclipse?' and its answer 'The privation of the moon's light by the interposition of the earth' are identical with the question 'What is the reason of eclipse?' or 'Why does the moon suffer eclipse?' and the reply 'Because of the failure of light through the earth's shutting it out'. Again, for 'What is a concord? A commensurate numerical ratio of a high and a low note', we may substitute 'What reason makes a high and a low note concordant? Their relation according to a commensurate numerical ratio.' 'Are the high and the low note concordant?' is equivalent to 'Is their ratio commensurate?'; and when we find that it is commensurate, we ask 'What, then, is their ratio?'.

Cases in which the 'middle' is sensible show that the object of our inquiry is always the 'middle': we inquire, because we have not perceived it, whether there is or is not a 'middle' causing e. g. an eclipse. On the other hand, if we were on the moon we should not be inquiring either as to the fact or the reason, but both fact and reason would be obvious simultaneously. For the act of perception would have enabled us to know the universal too; since, the present fact of an eclipse being evident, perception would then at the same time give us the present fact of the earth's screening the sun's light, and from this would arise the universal.

Thus, as we maintain, to know a thing's nature is to know the reason why it is; and this is equally true of things in so far as they are said without qualification to *be* as opposed to being possessed of some attribute, and in so far as they are said to be possessed of some attribute such as equal to two right angles, or greater or less.

. . .

19 As regards syllogism and demonstration, the definition of, and the conditions required to produce each of them, are now clear, and with that also the definition of, and the conditions required to produce, demonstrative knowledge, since it is the same as demonstration. As to the basic premises, how they become known and what is the developed state of knowledge of them is made clear by raising some preliminary problems.

We have already said that scientific knowledge through demonstration is impossible unless a man knows the primary immediate premises. But there are questions which might be raised in respect of the apprehension of these immediate premisses: one might not only ask whether it is of the same kind as the apprehension of the conclusions, but also whether there is or is not scientific knowledge of both; or scientific knowledge of the latter, and of the former a different kind of knowledge; and, further, whether the developed states of knowledge are not innate but come to be in us, or are innate but at first unnoticed. Now it is strange if we possess them from birth; for it means that we possess apprehensions more accurate than demonstration and fail to notice them. If on the other hand we acquire them and do not previously possess them, how could we apprehend and learn without a basis of pre-existent knowledge? For that is impossible, as we used to find in the case of demonstration. So it emerges that neither can we possess them from birth, nor can they come to be in us if we are without knowledge of them to the extent of having no such developed state at all. Therefore we must possess a capacity of some sort, but not such as to rank higher in accuracy than these developed states. And this at least is an obvious characteristic of all animals, for they possess a congenital discriminative capacity which is called sense-perception. But though sense-perception is innate in all animals, in some the sense-impression comes to persist, in others it does not. So animals in which this persistence does not come to be have either no knowledge at all outside the act of perceiving, or no knowledge of objects of which no impression persists; animals in which it does come into being have perception and can continue to retain the sense-impression in the soul: and when such   [100ᵃ] persistence is frequently repeated a further distinction at once arises between those which out of the persistence of such sense-impressions develop a power of systematizing them and those which do not. So out of sense-perception comes to be what we call memory, and out of frequently repeated memories of the same thing develops experience; for a number of memories constitute a single experience. From experience again—i. e. from the universal now stabilized in its entirety within the soul, the one beside the many which is a single identity within them all —originate the skill of the craftsman and the knowledge of the man of science, skill in the sphere of coming to be and science in the sphere of being.

We conclude that these states of knowledge are neither innate in a determinate form, nor developed from other higher states of knowledge, but from sense-perception. It is like a rout in battle stopped by first one man making a stand and then another, until the original formation has been restored. The soul is so constituted as to be capable of this process.

Let us now restate the account given already, though with insufficient clearness. When one of a number of logically indiscriminable particulars has made a stand, the earliest universal is present in the soul: for though the act of sense-perception is of the particular, its content is universal—is man, for example, not the man Callias. A   [100ᵇ] fresh stand is made among these rudimentary universals, and the process does not cease until the indivisible concepts, the true universals, are established: e. g. such and such a species of animal is a step towards the genus animal, which by the same process is a step towards a further generalization.

Thus it is clear that we must get to know the primary premisses by induction; for the method by which even sense-perception implants the universal is inductive. Now of the thinking states by which we grasp truth, some are unfailingly true, others admit of error—opinion, for instance, and calculation, whereas scientific knowing and intuition are always true: further, no other kind of thought except intuition is more accurate than scientific knowledge, whereas primary premisses are more knowable than demonstrations, and all scientific knowledge is discursive. From these considerations it follows that there will be no scientific knowledge of the primary premisses, and since except intuition nothing can be truer than scientific knowledge, it will be intuition that apprehends the primary premisses—a result which also follows from the fact that demonstration cannot be the originative source of demonstration, nor, consequently, scientific knowledge of scientific knowledge. If, therefore, it is the only other kind of true thinking except scientific knowing, intuition will be the originative source of scientific knowledge. And the originative source of science grasps the original basic premiss, while science as a whole is similarly related as originative source to the whole body of fact.

THE METAPHYSICS

Book I (*complete*)

I. All men naturally desire knowledge. An indication of this is our esteem for the senses; for apart from their use we esteem them for their own sake, and most of all the sense of sight. Not only with a view to action, but even when no action is contemplated, we prefer sight, generally speaking, to all the other senses. The reason of this is that of all the senses sight best helps us to know things, and reveals many distinctions.

Now animals are by nature born with the power of sensation, and from this some acquire the faculty of memory, whereas others do not. Accordingly the former are more intelligent and capable of learning than those which cannot remember. Such as cannot hear sounds (as the bee, and any other similar type of creature) are intelligent, but cannot learn; those only are capable of learning which possess this sense in addition to the faculty of memory.

Thus the other animals live by impressions and memories, and have but a small share of experience; but the human race lives also by art and reasoning. It is from memory that men acquire experience, because the numerous memories of the same thing eventually produce the effect of a single experience. Experience seems very similar to science and art, but actually it is through experience that men acquire science and art; for as Polus rightly says, "experience produces art, but inexperience chance." Art is produced when from many notions of experience a single universal judgement is formed with regard to like objects. To have a judgement that when Callias was suffering from this or that disease this or that benefited him, and similarly with Socrates and various other individuals, is a matter of experience; but to judge that it benefits all persons of a certain type, considered as a class, who suffer from this or that disease (*e.g.* the phlematic or bilious when suffering from burning fever) is a matter of art.

It would seem that for practical purposes experience is in no way inferior to art; indeed we see men of experience succeeding more than those who have theory without experience. The reason of this is that experience is knowledge of particulars, but art of universals; and actions and the effects produced are all concerned with the particular. For it is not man that the physician cures, except incidentally, but Callias or Socrates or some other person similarly named, who is incidentally a man as well. So if a man has theory without experience, and knows the universal, but does not know the particular contained in it, he will often fail in his treatment; for it is the particular that must be treated. Nevertheless we consider that knowledge and proficiency belong to art rather than to experience, and we assume that artists are wiser than men of mere experience (which implies that in all cases wisdom depends rather upon knowledge); and this is because the former know the cause, whereas the latter do not. For the experienced know the fact, but not the wherefore; but the artists know the wherefore and the cause. For the same season we consider that the master craftsmen in every profession are more estimable and know more and are wiser than the artisans, because they know the reasons of the things which are done; but we think that the artisans, like certain inanimate objects, do things, but without knowing what they are doing (as, for instance, fire burns); only whereas inanimate objects perform all their actions in virtue of a certain natural quality, artisans perform theirs through habit. Thus the master craftsmen are superior in wisdom, not because they can do things, but because they possess a theory and know the causes.

In general the sign of knowledge or ignorance is the ability to teach, and for this reason we hold that art rather than experience is scientific knowledge; for the artists can teach, but the others cannot. Further, we do not consider any of the senses to be Wisdom. They are indeed our chief sources of knowledge about particulars, but they do not tell us the reason for anything, as for example why fire is hot, but only that it *is* hot.

It is therefore probable that at first the inventor of any art which went further than the ordinary sensations was admired by his fellow-men, not merely because some of his inventions were useful, but as being a wise and superior person. And as more and more arts were discovered, some relating to the necessities and some to the pastimes of life, the inventors of the latter were always considered wiser than those of the former, because their branches of knowledge did not aim at utility. Hence when all the discoveries of this kind were fully developed, the sciences which relate neither to pleasure nor yet to the necessities of life were invented, and first in those places where men had leisure. Thus the mathematical sciences originated in the neighbourhood of Egypt, because there the priestly class was allowed leisure.

The difference between art and science and the other kindred mental activities has been stated in the *Ethics;* the reason for our present discussion is that it is generally assumed that what is called Wisdom is concerned with the primary causes and principles, so that, as has been already stated, the man of experience is held to be wiser than the mere possessors of any power of sensation, the artist than the man of experience, the master craftsman than the artisan; and the speculative sciences to be more learned than the productive. Thus it is clear that Wisdom is knowledge of certain principles and causes.

II. Since we are investigating this kind of knowledge, we must consider what these causes and principles are whose knowledge is Wisdom. Perhaps it will be clearer if we take the opinions which we hold about the wise man. We consider first, then, that the wise man knows all things, so far as it is possible, without having knowledge of every one of them individually; next, that the wise man is he who can comprehend difficult things, such as are not easy for human comprehension (for sense-perception, being common to all, is easy, and has nothing to do with Wisdom); and further that in every branch of knowledge a man is wiser in proportion as he is more accurately informed and better able to expound the causes. Again among the sciences we consider that that science which is desirable in itself and for the sake of knowledge is more nearly Wisdom than that which is desirable for its results, and that the superior is more nearly Wisdom than the subsidiary; for the wise man should give orders, not receive them; nor should he obey others, but the less wise should obey him.

Such in kind and in number are the opinions which we hold with regard to Wisdom and the wise. Of the qualities there described the knowledge of everything must necessarily belong to him who in the highest degree possesses knowledge of the universal, because he knows in a sense all the particulars which it comprises. These things, viz. the most universal, are perhaps the hardest for man to grasp, because they are furthest removed from the senses. Again, the most exact of the sciences are those which are most concerned with the first principles; for those which are based on fewer principles are more exact than those which include additional principles; *e.g.*, arithmetic is more exact than geometry. Moreover, the science which investigates causes is more instructive than one which does not, for it is those who tell us the causes of any particular thing who instruct us. Moreover, knowledge and understanding which are desirable for their own sake are most attainable in the knowledge of that which is most knowable. For the man who desires knowledge for its own sake will most desire the most perfect knowledge, and this is the knowledge of the most knowable, and the things which are most knowable are first principles and causes; for it is through these and from these that other things come to be known, and not these through the particulars which fall under them. And that science is supreme, and superior to the subsidiary, which knows for what end each action is to be done; *i.e.* the Good in each particular case, and in general the highest Good in the whole of nature.

Thus as a result of all the above considerations the term which we are investigating falls under the same science, which must speculate about first principles and causes; for the Good, *i.e.* the *end,* is one of the causes.

That it is not a productive science is clear from a consideration of the first philosophers. It is through wonder that men now begin and originally began to philosophize; wondering in the first place at obvious perplexities, and then by gradual progression raising questions about the greater matters too, *e.g.* about the changes of the moon and of the sun, about the stars and about the origin of the universe. Now he who wonders and is perplexed feels that he is ignorant (thus the myth-lover is in a sense a philosopher, since myths are composed of wonders); therefore if it was to escape ignorance that men studied philosophy, it is obvious that they pursued science for the sake of knowledge, and not for any practical utility. The actual course of events bears witness to this; for speculation of this kind began with a view to recreation and pastime, at a time when practically all the necessities of life were already supplied. Clearly then it is for no extrinsic advantage that we seek this knowledge; for just as we call a man independent who exists for himself and not for another, so we call this the only independent science, since it alone exists for itself.

For this reason its acquisition might justly be supposed to be beyond human power, since in many respects human nature is servile; in which case, as Simonides says, "God alone can have this privilege," and man should only seek the knowledge which is within his reach. Indeed if the poets are right and the Deity is by nature jealous, it is probable that in this case He would be particularly jealous, and all those who excel in knowledge unfortunate. But it is impossible for the Deity to be jealous (indeed, as the proverb says, "poets tell many a lie"), nor must we suppose that any other form of knowledge is more precious than this; for what is most divine is most precious. Now there are two ways only in which it can be divine. A science is divine if it is peculiarly the possession of God, or if it is concerned with divine matters. And this science alone fulfils both these conditions; for (*a*) all believe that God is one of the causes and a kind of principle, and (*b*) God is the sole or chief possessor of this sort of knowledge. Accordingly, although all other sciences are more necessary than this, none is more excellent.

The acquisition of this knowledge, however, must in a sense result in something which is the reverse of the outlook with which we first approached the inquiry. All begin, as we have said, by wondering that things should be as they are, *e.g.* with regard to marionettes, or the solstices, or the incommensurability of the diagonal of a square; because it seems wonderful to everyone who has not yet perceived the cause that a thing should not be measurable by the smallest unit. But we must end with the contrary and (according to the proverb) the better view, as men do even in these cases when they understand them; for a geometrician would wonder at nothing so much as if the diagonal were to become measurable.

Thus we have stated what is the nature of the science which we are seeking, and what is the object which our search and our whole investigation must attain.

III. It is clear that we must obtain knowledge of the primary causes, because it is when we think that we understand its primary cause that we claim to know each particular thing. Now there are four recognized kinds of cause. Of these we hold that one is the essence or essential nature of the thing (since the "reason why" of a thing is ultimately reducible to its formula, and the ultimate "reason why" is a cause and principle); another is the matter or substrate; the third is the source of motion; and the fourth is the cause which is opposite to this, namely the purpose or "good"; for this is the end of every generative or motive process. We have investigated these sufficiently in the *Physics;* however, let us avail ourselves of the evidence of those who have before us approached the investigation of reality and philosophized about Truth. For clearly they too recognize certain principles and causes, and so it will be of some assistance to our present inquiry if we study their teaching; because we shall either discover some other kind of cause, or have more confidence in those which we have just described.

Most of the earliest philosophers conceived only of material principles as underlying all things. That of which all things consist, from which they first come and into which on their destruction they are ultimately resolved, of which the essence persists although modified by its affections —this, they say, is an element and principle of existing things. Hence they believe that nothing is either generated or destroyed, since this kind of primary entity always persists. Similarly we do not say that Socrates comes into being *absolutely* when he becomes handsome or cultured, nor that he is destroyed when he loses these qualities; because the substrate, Socrates himself, persists. In the same way nothing else is generated or destroyed; for these is some one entity (or more than one) which always persists and from which all other things are generated. All are not agreed, however, as to the number and character of these principles. Thales, the founder of this school of philosophy, says the permanent entity is water (which is why he also propounded that the earth floats on water). Presumably he derived this assumption from seeing that the nutriment of everything is moist, and that heat itself is generated from moisture and depends upon it for its existence (and that from which a thing is generated is always its first principle). He derived his assumption, then, from this; and also from the fact that the seeds of everything have a moist nature, whereas water is the first principle of the nature of moist things.

There are some who think that the men of very ancient times, long before the present era, who first speculated about the gods, also held this same opinion about the primary entity. For they represented Oceanus and Tethys to be the parents of creation and the oath of the gods to be by water—Styx, as they call it. Now what is most ancient is most revered, and what is most revered is what we swear by. Whether this view of the primary entity is really ancient and time-honoured may perhaps be considered uncertain; however, it is said that this was Thales' opinion concerning the first cause. (I say nothing of Hippo, because no one would presume to include him in this company, in view of the paltriness of his intelligence.)

Anaximenes and Diogenes held that air is prior to water, and is of all corporeal elements most truly the first principle. Hippasus of Metapontum and Heraclitus of Ephesus hold this of fire; and Empedocles—adding earth as a fourth to those already mentioned—takes all four. These, he says, always persist, and are only generated in respect of multitude and paucity, according as they are combined into unity or differentiated out of unity.

Anaxagoras of Clazomenae—prior to Empedocles in point of age, but posterior in his activities—says that the first principles are infinite in number. For he says that as a general rule all things which are, like fire and water, homoeomerous, are generated and destroyed in this sense only, by combination and differentiation; otherwise they are neither generated nor destroyed, but persist eternally.

From this account it might be supposed that the only cause is of the kind called "material." But as men proceeded in this way, the very circumstances of the case led them on and compelled them to seek further; because if it is really true that all generation and destruction is out of some one entity or even more than one, *why* does this happen, and what is the cause? It is surely not the substrate itself which causes itself to change. I mean, *e.g.*, that neither wood nor bronze is responsible for changing itself; wood does not make a bed, nor bronze a statue, but something else is the cause of the change. Now to investigate this is to investigate the second type of cause: the *source of motion*, as we should say.

Those who were the very first to take up this inquiry, and who maintained that the substrate is one thing, had no misgivings on the subject; but some of those who regard it as one thing, being baffled, as it were, by the inquiry, say that that one thing (and indeed the whole physical world) is immovable in respect not only of generation and destruction (this was a primitive belief and was generally admitted) but of all other change. This belief is peculiar to them.

None of those who maintained that the universe is a unity achieved any conception of this type of cause, except perhaps Parmenides; and him only in so far as he admits, in a sense, not one cause only but two. But those who recognize more than one entity, *e.g.* hot and cold, or fire and earth, are better able to give a systematic explanation, because they avail themselves of fire as being of a kinetic nature, and of water, earth, etc., as being the opposite.

After these thinkers and the discovery of these causes, since they were insufficient to account for the generation of the actual world, men were again compelled (as we have said) by truth itself to investigate the next first principle. For presumably it is unnatural that either fire or earth or any other such element should cause existing things to be or become well and beautifully disposed; or indeed that those thinkers should hold such a view. Nor again was it satisfactory to commit so important a matter to spontaneity and chance. Hence when someone said that there is Mind in nature, just as in animals, and that this is the cause of all order and arrangement, he seemed like a sane man in contrast with the haphazard statements of his predecessors. We know definitely that Anaxagoras adopted this view; but Hermotimus of Clazomenae is credited with having stated it earlier. Those thinkers, then, who held this view assumed a principle in things which is the cause of beauty, and the sort of cause by which motion is communicated to things.

IV. It might be inferred that the first person to consider this question was Hesiod, or indeed anyone else who assumed Love or Desire as a first principle in things; *e.g.* Parmenides. For he says, where he is describing the creation of the universe,

> Love she created first of all the gods.

And Hesiod says,

> First of all things was Chaos made, and then
> Broad-bosomed Earth . . .
> And Love, the foremost of immortal beings,

thus implying that there must be in the world some cause to move things and combine them.

The question of arranging these thinkers in order of priority may be decided later. Now since it was apparent that nature also contains the opposite of what is good, *i.e.* not only order and beauty, but disorder and ugliness; and that there are more bad and common things than there are good and beautiful: in view of this another thinker introduced Love and Strife as the respective causes of these things—because if one follows up and appreciates the statements of Empedocles with a view to his real meaning and not to his obscure language, it will be found that Love is the cause of good, and Strife of evil. Thus it would perhaps be correct to say that Empedocles in a sense spoke of evil and good as first principles, and was the first to do so—that is, if the cause of all good things is absolute good.

These thinkers then, as I say, down to the time of Empedocles, seem to have grasped two of the causes which we have defined in the *Physics:* the material cause and the source of motion; but only vaguely and indefinitely. They are like untrained soldiers in a battle, who rush about and often strike good blows, but without science; in the same way these thinkers do not seem to understand their own statements, since it is clear that upon the whole they seldom or never apply them. Anaxagoras avails himself of Mind as an artificial device for producing order, and drags it in whenever he is at a loss to explain some necessary result; but otherwise he makes anything rather than Mind the cause of what happens. Again, Empedocles does indeed use causes to a greater degree than Anaxagoras, but not sufficiently; nor does he attain to consistency in their use. At any rate Love often differentiates and Strife combines: because whenever the universe is differentiated into its elements by Strife, fire and each of the other elements are agglomerated into a unity; and whenever they are all combined together again by Love, the particles of each element are necessarily again differentiated.

Empedocles, then, differed from his predecessors in that he first introduced the division of this cause, making the source of motion not one but two contrary forces. Further, he was the first to maintain that the so-called material elements are four—not that he uses them as four, but as two only, treating fire on the one hand by itself, and the elements opposed to it—earth, air and water—on the other, as a single nature. This can be seen from a study of his writings. Such, then, as I say, is his account of the nature and number of the first principles.

Leucippus, however, and his disciple Democritus hold that the elements are the Full and the Void—calling the one "what is" and the other "what is not." Of these they identify the full or solid with "what is," and the void or rare with "what is not" (hence they hold that what is not is no less real than what is, because Void is as real as Body); and they say that these are the material causes of things. And just as those who make the underlying substance a unity generate all other things by means of its modifications, assuming rarity and density as first principles of these modifications, so these thinkers hold that the "differences" are the causes of everything else. These differences, they say, are three: shape, arrangement, and position; because they hold that what is differs only in *contour, inter-contact,* and *inclination.* (Of these contour means shape, inter-contact, arrangement, and inclination position.) Thus, *e.g.,* A differs from N in shape, AN from NA in arrangement, and Z from N in position. As for motion, whence and how it arises in things, they casually ignored this point, very much as the other thinkers did. Such, then, as I say, seems to be the extent of the inquiries which the earlier thinkers made into these two kinds of cause.

V. At the same time, however, and even earlier the so-called Pythagoreans applied themselves to mathematics, and were the first to develop this science; and through studying it they came to believe that its principles are the principles of everything. And since *numbers* are by nature first among these principles, and they fancied that they could detect in numbers, to a greater extent than in fire and earth and water, many analogues of what is and comes into being—such and such a property of number being *justice,* and such and such *soul* or *mind,* another *opportunity,* and similarly, more or less, with all the rest—and since they saw further that the properties and ratios of the musical scales are based on numbers, and since it seemed clear that all other things have their whole nature modelled upon numbers, and that numbers are the ultimate things in the whole physical universe, they assumed the elements of numbers to be the elements of everything, and the whole universe to be a proportion or number. Whatever analogues to the processes and parts of the heavens and to the whole order of the universe they could exhibit in numbers and proportions, these they collected and correlated; and if there was any deficiency anywhere, they made haste to supply it, in order to make their system a connected whole. For example, since the decad is considered to be a complete thing and to comprise the whole essential nature of the numerical system, they assert that the bodies which revolve in the heavens are ten; and there being only nine that are visible, they make the "antichthon" the tenth. We have treated this subject in greater detail elsewhere; but the object of our present review is to discover from these thinkers too what causes they assume and how these coincide with our list of causes. Well, it is obvious that these thinkers too consider number to be a first principle, both as the material of things and as constituting their properties and states. The elements of number, according to them, are the Even and the Odd. Of these the former is limited and the latter unlimited; Unity consists of both (since it is both odd and even); number is derived from Unity; and numbers, as we have said, compose the whole sensible universe.

Others of this same school hold that there are ten principles, which they enunciate in a series of corresponding pairs: (i.) Limit and the Unlimited; (ii.) Odd and Even; (iii.) Unity and Plurality; (iv.) Right and Left; (v.) Male and Female; (vi.) Rest and Motion; (vii.) Straight and Crooked; (viii.) Light and Darkness; (ix.) Good and Evil; (x.) Square and Oblong. Apparently Alcmaeon of Croton speculated along the same lines, and either he derived the theory from them or they from him; for [Alcmaeon was contemporary with the old age of Pythagoras, and] his doctrines were very similar to theirs. He says that the majority of things in the world of men are in pairs; but the contraries which he mentions are not, as in the case of the Pythagoreans, carefully defined, but are taken at random, *e.g.* white and black, sweet and bitter, good and bad, great and small. Thus Alcmaeon only threw out vague hints with regard to the other instances of contrariety, but the Pythagoreans pronounced how many and what the contraries are. Thus from both these authorities we can gather thus much, that the contraries are first principles of things; and from the former, how many and what the contraries are. How these can be referred to our list of causes is not definitely expressed by them, but they appear to reckon their elements as material; for they say that these are the original constituents of which Being is fashioned and composed.

From this survey we can sufficiently understand the meaning of those ancients who taught that the elements of the natural world are a plurality. Others, however, theorized about the universe as though it were a single entity; but their doctrines are not all alike either in point of soundness or in respect of conformity with the facts of nature. For the purposes of our present inquiry an account of their teaching is quite irrelevant, since they do not, while assuming a unity, at the same time make out that Being is generated from the unity as from matter, as do some physicists, but give a different explanation; for the physicists assume motion also, at any rate when explaining the generation of the universe; but these thinkers hold that it is immovable. Nevertheless thus much is pertinent to our present inquiry. It appears that Parmenides conceived of the Unity as one in definition, but Melissus as materially one. Hence the former says that it is finite, and the latter that it is infinite. But Xenophanes, the first exponent of the Unity (for Parmenides is said to have been his disciple), gave no definite teaching, nor does he seem to have grasped either of these conceptions of unity; but regarding the whole material universe he stated that the Unity is God. This school then, as we have said, may be disregarded for the purposes of our present inquiry; two of them, Xenophanes and Melissus, may be completely ignored, as being somewhat too crude in their views. Parmenides, however, seems to speak with rather more insight. For holding as he does that Not-being, as contrasted with Being, is nothing, he necessarily supposes that Being is one and that there is nothing else (we have discussed this point in greater detail in the *Physics*); but being compelled to accord with phenomena, and assuming that Being is one in definition but many in respect of sensation, he posits in his turn two causes, *i.e.* two first principles, Hot and Cold; or in other words, Fire and Earth. Of these he ranks Hot under Being and the other under Not-being.

From the account just given, and from a consideration of those thinkers who have already debated this question, we have acquired the following information. From the earliest philosophers we have learned that the first principle is corporeal (since water and fire and the like are bodies); some of them assume one and others more than one corporeal principle, but both parties agree in making these principles material. Others assume in addition to this cause the *source of motion*, which some hold to be one and others two. Thus down to and apart from the Italian philosophers the other thinkers have expressed themselves vaguely on the subject, except that, as we have said, they actually employ two causes, and one of these—the source of motion—some regard as one and others as two. The Pythagoreans, while they likewise spoke of two principles, made this further addition, which is peculiar to them: they believed, not that the Limited and the Unlimited are separate entities, like fire or water or some other such thing, but that the Unlimited itself and the One itself are the essence of those things of which they are predicated, and hence that

number is the essence of all things. Such is the nature of their pronouncements on this subject. They also began to discuss and define the "what"
of things; but their procedure was far too simple. They defined super-
ficially, and supposed that the essence of a thing is that to which the
term under consideration first applies—*e.g.* as if it were to be thought
that "double" and "2" are the same, because 2 is the first number which
is double another. But presumably "to be double a number" is not the
same as "to be the number 2." Otherwise, one thing will be many—a
consequence which actually followed in their system. This much, then,
can be learned from other and earlier schools of thought.

VI. The philosophies described above were succeeded by the system
of Plato, which in most respects accorded with them, but contained also
certain peculiar features distinct from the philosophy of the Italians.
In his youth Plato first became acquainted with Cratylus and the Hera-
clitean doctrines—that the whole sensible world is always in a state of
flux, and that there is no scientific knowledge of it—and in after years
he still held these opinions. And when Socrates, disregarding the physical
universe and confining his study to moral questions, sought in this sphere
for the universal and was the first to concentrate upon definition, Plato
followed him and assumed that the problem of definition is concerned
not with any sensible thing but with entities of another kind; for the
reason that there can be no general definition of sensible things which
are always changing. These entities he called "Ideas," [1] and held that all
sensible things are named after them and in virtue of their relation to
them; for the plurality of things which bear the same name as the Forms [1]
exist by participation in them. (With regard to the "participation," it
was only the term that he changed; for whereas the Pythagoreans say
that things exist by imitation of numbers, Plato says that they exist by
participation—merely a change of term. As to what this "participation"
or "imitation" may be, they left this an open question.)

Further, he states that besides sensible things and the Forms there
exists an intermediate class, the *objects of mathematics,* which differ
from sensible things in being eternal and immutable, and from the Forms
in that there are many similar objects of mathematics, whereas each Form
is itself unique.

Now since the Forms are the causes of everything else, he supposed
that their elements are the elements of all things. Accordingly the material
principle is the "Great and Small," and the essence <or formal principle>
is the One, since the numbers are derived from the "Great and Small"
by participation in the One. In treating the One as a substance instead
of a predicate of some other entity, his teaching resembles that of the
Pythagoreans, and also agrees with it in stating that the numbers are
the causes of Being in everything else; but it is peculiar to him to posit

---

[1] I have translated ἰδέα by Idea and εἶδος by Form wherever Aristotle uses
the words with reference to the Platonic theory. Plato apparently uses them
indifferently, and so does Aristotle in this particular connexion, but he also
uses εἶδος in the sense of form in general.

a duality instead of the single Unlimited, and to make the Unlimited consist of the "Great and Small." He is also peculiar in regarding the numbers as distinct from sensible things, whereas they hold that things themselves *are* numbers, nor do they posit an intermediate class of mathematical objects. His distinction of the One and the numbers from ordinary things (in which he differed from the Pythagoreans) and his introduction of the Forms were due to his investigation of logic (the earlier thinkers were strangers to Dialectic); his conception of the other principle as a duality to the belief that numbers other than primes can be readily generated from it, as from a matrix. The fact, however, is just the reverse, and the theory is illogical; for whereas the Platonists derive multiplicity from matter although their Form generates only once,[2] it is obvious that only one table can be made from one piece of timber, and yet he who imposes the form upon it, although he is but one, can make many tables. Such too is the relation of male to female: the female is impregnated in one coition, but one male can impregnate many females. And these relations are analogues of the principles referred to.

This, then, is Plato's verdict upon the question which we are investigating. From this account it is clear that he only employed two causes[3]: that of the essence, and the material cause; for the Forms are the cause of the essence in everything else, and the One is the cause of it in the Forms. He also tells us what the material substrate is of which the Forms are predicated in the case of sensible things, and the One in that of the Forms—that it is this duality, the "Great and Small." Further, he assigned to these two elements respectively the causation of good and of evil; a problem which, as we have said, had also been considered by some of the earlier philosophers, *e.g.* Empedocles and Anaxagoras.

VII. We have given only a concise and summary account of those thinkers who have expressed views about the causes and reality, and of their doctrines. Nevertheless we have learned thus much from them: that not one of those who discuss principle or cause has mentioned any other type than those which we have distinguished in the *Physics*. Clearly it is after these types that they are groping, however uncertainly. Some speak of the first principle as material, whether they regard it as one or several, as corporeal or incorporeal: *e.g.* Plato speaks of the "Great and Small"; the Italians of the Unlimited; Empedocles of Fire, Earth, Water and Air; Anaxagoras of the infinity of homoeomeries. All these have apprehended this type of cause; and all those too who make their first principle air or water or "something denser than fire but rarer than air" (for some have so described the primary element). These, then,

---

2 Aristotle's objection is that it is unreasonable that a single operation of the formal upon the material principle should result in more than one product; *i.e.* that the material principle should be in itself duplicative.

3 Plato refers several times in the dialogues to an efficient cause (*e.g.* the Demiurgus, *Sophist* 265 B-D, *Timaeus* 28 c ff.) and a final cause (*e.g. Philebus* 20 D, 53 E, *Timaeus* 29 D ff.); but Aristotle does not seem to take these allusions seriously.

apprehended this cause only, but others apprehended the *source of motion*—e.g. all such as make Love and Strife, or Mind, or Desire a first principle. As for the *essence* or *essential nature*, nobody has definitely introduced it; but the inventors of the Forms express it most nearly. For they do not conceive of the Forms as the *matter* of sensible things (and the One as the matter of the Forms), nor as producing the *source of motion* (for they hold that they are rather the cause of immobility and tranquillity); but they adduce the Forms as the *essential nature* of all other things, and the One as that of the Forms. The *end* towards which actions, changes and motions tend they do in a way treat as a cause, but not in this sense, *i.e.* not in the sense in which it is naturally a cause. Those who speak of Mind or Love assume these causes as being something *good;* but nevertheless they do not profess that anything exists or is generated *for the sake* of them, but only that motions originate from them. Similarly also those who hold that Unity or Being is an entity of this kind state that it is the same of existence, but not that things exist or are generated for the sake of it. So it follows that in a sense they both assert and deny that the Good is a cause; for they treat it as such not absolutely, but incidentally. It appears, then, that all these thinkers too (being unable to arrive at any other cause) testify that we have classified the causes rightly, as regards both number and nature. Further, it is clear that all the principles must be sought either along these lines or in some similar way.

Let us next examine the possible difficulties arising out of the statements of each of these thinkers, and out of his attitude to the first principles.

VIII. All those who regard the universe as a unity, and assume as its matter some one nature, and that corporeal and extended, are clearly mistaken in many respects. They only assume elements of corporeal things, and not of incorporeal ones, which also exist. They attempt to state the causes of generation and destruction, and investigate the nature of everything; and at the same time do away with the cause of motion. Then there is their failure to regard the *essence* or formula as a cause of anything; and further their readiness to call any one of the simple bodies—except earth—a first principle, without inquiring how their reciprocal generation is effected. I refer to fire, water, earth and air. Of these some are generated from each other by combination and others by differentiation; and this difference is of the greatest importance in deciding their relative priority. In one way it might seem that the most elementary body is that from which first other bodies are produced by combination; and this will be that body which is rarest and composed of the finest particles. Hence all who posit Fire as first principle will be in the closest agreement with this theory. However, even among the other thinkers everyone agrees that the primary corporeal element is of this kind. At any rate none of the Monists thought earth likely to be an element—obviously on account of the size of its particles—but each of the other three has had an advocate; for some name fire as the primary element, others water, and others air. And yet why do they not suggest earth too, as common opinion does? for people say "Everything is earth." And Hesiod too says that earth was generated first of corporeal things—so ancient and popular is the conception found to be. Thus according to this theory anyone who suggests any of these bodies other than fire, or who assumes something "denser than air but rarer than water," will be wrong. On the other hand if what is posterior in generation is prior in nature, and that which is developed and combined is posterior in generation, then the reverse will be the case; water will be prior to air, and earth to water. So much for those who posit *one* cause such as we have described.

The same will apply too if anyone posits more than one, as *e.g.* Empedocles says that matter consists of four bodies; objections must occur in his case also, some the same as before, and some peculiar to him. First, we can see things being generated from each other in a way which shows that fire and earth do *not* persist as the same corporeal entity. (This subject has been treated in my works on Natural Science.) Again with regard to the cause of motion in things, whether one or two should be assumed, it must not be thought that his account is entirely correct or even reasonable. And in general those who hold such views as these must of necessity do away with qualitative alteration; for on such a theory cold will not come from hot nor hot from cold, because to effect this there must be something which actually takes on these contrary qualities: some single element which becomes both fire and water— which Empedocles denies.

If one were to infer that Anaxagoras recognized two elements, the inference would accord closely with a view which, although he did not articulate it himself, he must have accepted as developed by others. To say that originally everything was a mixture is absurd for various reasons, but especially since (*a*) it follows that things must have existed previously in an unmixed state; (*b*) it is contrary to nature for *anything* to mix with *anything;* (*c*) moreover affections and attributes would then be separable from their substances (because what is mixed can also be separated). At the same time, if one were to follow his doctrine carefully and interpret its meaning, perhaps it would be seen to be more up-to-date; because when nothing was yet differentiated, obviously nothing could be truly predicated of that substance—*e.g.* that it was white or black or buff or any other colour. It must necessarily have been colourless, since otherwise it would have had one of these colours. Similarly by the same argument it had no taste or any other such attribute; for it cannot have had any quality or magnitude or individuality. Otherwise some particular form would have belonged to it; but this is impossible on the assumption that everything was mixed together, for then the form would have been already differentiated, whereas he says that everything was mixed together except Mind, which alone was pure and unmixed. It follows from this that he recognizes as principles the One (which is simple and unmixed) and the Other, which is such as we suppose the Indeterminate to be before it is determined and partakes of some form. Thus his account is neither correct nor clear, but his meaning approximates to more recent theories and what is now more obviously true.

However, these thinkers are really concerned only with the theories of generation and destruction and motion (for in general it is only with reference to this aspect of reality that they look for their principles and causes). Those, however, who make their study cover the whole of reality, and who distinguish between sensible and non-sensible objects, clearly give their attention to both kinds; hence in their case we may consider at greater length what contributions, valuable or otherwise, they make to the inquiry which is now before us.

The so-called Pythagoreans employ abstruser principles and elements than the physicists. The reason is that they did not draw them from the sensible world; for mathematical objects, apart from those which are connected with astronomy, are devoid of motion. Nevertheless all their discussions and investigations are concerned with the physical world. They account for the generation of the sensible universe, and observe what happens in respect of its parts and affections and activities, and they use up their principles and causes in this connexion, as though they agreed with the others—the physicists—that reality is just so much as is sensible and is contained in the so-called "heavens." All the same, as we have said, the causes and principles which they describe are capable of application to the remoter class of realities as well, and indeed are better fitted to these than to their physical theories. But as to how there is to be motion, if all that is premissed is Limit and the Unlimited, and Odd and Even, they do not even hint; nor how, without motion and change, there can be generation and destruction, or the activities of the bodies which traverse the heavens. And further, assuming that it be granted to them or proved by them that *magnitude* [4] is composed of these factors, yet how is it to be explained that some bodies are light, and others have weight? For in their premises and statements they are speaking just as much about sensible as about mathematical objects; and this is why they have made no mention of fire or earth or other similar bodies, because, I presume, they have no separate explanation of sensible things. Again, how are we to understand that number and the modifications of number are the causes of all being and generation, both in the beginning and now, and at the same time that there is no other number than the number of which the universe is composed? [5] Because when they make out that Opinion and Opportunity are in such and such a region, and a little above or below them Injustice and Separation or Mixture, and when they state as proof of this that each of these abstractions is a number; and that also in this region there is already a plurality of the magnitudes composed of number, inasmuch as these modifications

---

[4] Aristotle uses the word μέγεθος both of magnitude in general and of spatial magnitude or extension. Here the meaning seems to be the former. Numbers obviously have magnitude, and might be regarded as causing it; but they are no more the cause of extension than that of gravity.

[5] *i.e.,* how can number be both reality and the cause of reality?

of number correspond to these several regions,—is the number which we must understand each of these abstractions to be the same number which is present in the sensible universe, or another kind of number? [6] Plato at least says that it is another. It is true that he too supposes that numbers are both these magnitudes and their causes; but in his view the causative numbers are intelligible and the others sensible.

IX. The Pythagoreans, then, may be dismissed for the present, for it is enough to touch upon them thus briefly. As for those who posit the Forms as causes, in the first place in their attempt to find the causes of things in our sensible world, they introduced an equal number of other entities—as though a man who wishes to count things should suppose that it would be impossible when they are few, and should attempt to count them when he has added to them. For the Forms are as many as, or not fewer than, the things in search of whose causes these thinkers were led to the Forms; because corresponding to each thing there is a synonymous entity apart from the substances (and in the case of non-substantial things there is a One over the Many), both in our everyday world and in the realm of eternal entities.

Again, not one of the arguments by which we try to prove that the Forms exist demonstrates our point: from some of them no necessary conclusion follows, and from others it follows that there are Forms of things of which we hold that there are no Forms. For according to the arguments from the sciences there will be Forms of all things of which there· are sciences; and according to the "One-over-Many" argument, of negations too; and according to the argument that "we have some conception of what has perished," of perishable things; because we have a mental picture of these things. Again, of Plato's more exact arguments some establish Ideas of relations, which we do not hold to form a separate genus; and others state the "Third Man." [7] And in general the arguments for the Forms do away with things which are more important to us exponents of the Forms than the existence of the Ideas; for they imply that it is not the Dyad that is primary, but Number; and that the relative is prior to the absolute; and all the other conclusions in respect of which certain persons, by following up the views held about the Ideas, have gone against the principles of the theory.

Again, according to the assumption by which we hold that the Ideas

---

[6] The point seems to be this. The Pythagoreans say that Opinion is a number, 3 (or 2, according to another version), and is located in a certain region of the universe because that region is proper to a corporeal magnitude composed of the number 3 (air was so composed according to Syrianus). Are we to understand, says Aristotle, that the abstract number identified with Opinion is the same as the concrete number of which air consists? The difficulty is probably due to an attempt to combine two different Pythagorean views of number.

[7] Several arguments bore this name. Here the reference is probably to the following: If X is a man because he resembles the Idea of Man, there must be a third "man" in whom the humanity of these two is united. *Cf. Parmenides* 132 A-133 A.

exist, there will be Forms not only of substances but of many other things (since the concept is one not only in the case of substances, but also in the case of all other things; and there are sciences not only of substances but of other things as well; and there are a thousand other similar consequences); but according to logical necessity, and from the views generally held about them, it follows that if the Forms are participated in, then there can only be Ideas of substances. For they are not participated in *qua* accidents; each Form can only be participated in in so far as it is not predicated of a subject. I mean, *e.g.*, that if anything participates in "absolute Doubleness" it participates also in "eternal," but only accidentally; because it is an *accident* of Doubleness to be eternal. Thus the Forms must be substance. But the same names denote substance in the sensible as in the Ideal world; otherwise what meaning will there be in saying that something exists beside the particulars, *i.e.* the unity comprising their multiplicity? If the form of the Ideas and of the things which participate in them is the same, they will have something in common (for why should Duality mean one and the same thing in the case of perishable "twos" and the "twos" which are many but eternal, and not in the case of the Idea of Duality and a particular "two"?); but if the form is not the same, they will simply be homonyms; just as though one were to call both Callias and a piece of wood "man," without remarking any property common to them.

Above all we might examine the question what on earth the Forms contribute to sensible things, whether eternal or subject to generation and decay; for they are not the cause of any motion or change in them. Again, they are no help towards the *knowledge* of other things [8] (for they are not the substance of things, otherwise they would be *in* things), nor to their *existence,* since they are not present in the things which partake of them. If they were, it might perhaps seem that they are causes, in the sense in which the admixture of white causes a thing to be white; but this theory, which was first stated by Anaxagoras and later by Eudoxus and others, is very readily refutable, for it is easy to adduce plenty of impossibilities against such a view. Again, other things are not in any accepted sense *derived* from the Forms. To say that the Forms are patterns, and that other things participate in them, is to use empty phrases and poetical metaphors; for what is it that fashions things on the model of the Ideas? Besides, anything may both be and become like something else without being imitated from it; thus a man may become just like Socrates whether Socrates exists or not, and even if Socrates were eternal, clearly the case would be the same. Also there will be several "patterns," and hence Forms, of the same thing; *e.g.* "animal" and "two-footed" will be patterns of "man," and so too will the Idea of Man. Further, the Forms will be patterns not only of sensible things but of themselves (*e.g.* genus in the sense of genus of species), and thus the same thing will be both pattern

---

[8] This objection, like the next, is chiefly directed against the transcendence of the Ideas. It is anticipated by Plato in *Parmenides* 134 D.

and copy. Further, it would seem impossible that the substance and the thing of which it is the substance exist in separation; hence how can the Ideas, if they are the substances of things, exist in separation from them? It is stated in the *Phaedo* that the Forms are the causes both of existence and of generation. Yet, assuming that the Forms exist, still the things which participate in them are not generated unless there is something to impart motion; while many other things *are* generated (*e.g.* house, ring) of which we hold that there are no Forms. Thus it is clearly possible that all other things may both exist and be generated for the same causes as the things just mentioned.

Further, if the Forms are numbers, in what sense will they be causes? Is it because things are other numbers, *e.g.* such and such a number Man, such and such another Socrates, such and such another Callias? then why are those numbers the causes of these? Even if the one class is eternal and the other not, it will make no difference. And if it is because the things of our world are ratios of numbers (*e.g.* a musical concord), clearly there is some one class of things of which they are ratios. Now if there is this something, *i.e.* their *matter*, clearly the numbers themselves will be ratios of one thing to another. I mean, *e.g.*, that if Callias is a numerical ratio of fire, earth, water and air, the corresponding Idea too will be a number of certain other things which are its substrate. The Ideal of Man, too, whether it is in a sense a number or not, will yet be an arithmetical ratio of certain things, and not a mere number; nor, on these grounds, will any Idea be a number.

Again, one number can be composed of several numbers, but how can one Form be composed of several Forms? And if the one number is not composed of the other numbers themselves, but of their constituents (*e.g.* those of the number 10,000), what is the relation of the units? If they are specifically alike, many absurdities will result, and also if they are not (whether (*a*) the units in a given number are unlike, or (*b*) the units in each number are unlike those in every other number). For in what can they differ, seeing that they have no qualities? Such a view is neither reasonable nor compatible with our conception of units.

Further, it becomes necessary to set up another kind of number (with which calculation deals), and all the objects which are called "intermediate" by some thinkers. But how or from what principles can these be derived? or on what grounds are they to be considered intermediate between things *here* and Ideal numbers? Further, each of the units in the number 2 comes from a prior 2; but this is impossible.

Further, why should a number <of units>, taken together, be one thing? And further, in addition to the above objections, if the units are unlike, they should be treated as the thinkers who assume two or four elements treat those elements; for not one of them applies the term "element" to the common substrate, *e.g.* body, but to fire and earth—whether there is a common substrate (*i.e.* body) or not. As it is, the One is spoken of as though it were homogeneous, like fire or water. But if this is so, the numbers will not be substances. And if there is an absolute One which is a principle, clearly the term "one" is ambiguous; otherwise this is impossible.

When we wish to refer substances to their principles we derive lines from "Long and Short," a kind of "Great and Small"; and the plane from "Wide and Narrow," and the solid body from "Deep and Shallow." But in this case how can the plane contain a line, or the solid a line and a plane? for "Wide and Narrow" and "Deep and Shallow" are different genera. Nor is Number contained in these objects (because "Many and Few" is yet another class); and in the same way it is clear that none of the other higher genera will be contained in the lower. Nor, again, is the Broad the genus of which the Deep is a species; for then body would be a kind of plane. Further, how will it be possible for figures to contain points? Plato steadily rejected this class of objects as a geometrical fiction, but he recognized "the beginning of a line," and he frequently assumed this latter class, *i.e.* the "indivisible lines." But these must have some limit; and so by the same argument which proves the existence of the line, the point also exists.

In general, although Wisdom is concerned with the cause of visible things, we have ignored this question (for we have no account to give of the cause from which change arises), and in the belief that we are accounting for their substance we assert the existence of other substances; but as to *how* the latter are the substances of the former, our explanation is worthless—for "participation," as we have said before, means nothing. And as for that which we can see to be the cause in the sciences, and through which all mind and all nature works—this cause which we hold to be one of the first principles—the Forms have not the slightest bearing upon it either. Philosophy has become mathematics for modern thinkers, although they profess that mathematics is only to be studied as a means to some other end.

Further, one might regard the substance which they make the material substrate as too mathematical, and as being a predicate and differentia of substance or matter rather than as matter itself. I mean the "Great and Small," which is like the "Rare and Dense" of which the physicists speak, holding that they are the primary differentiae of the substrate; because these qualities are a species of excess and defect. Also with regard to motion, if the "Great and Small" is to constitute motion, obviously the Forms will be moved; if not, whence did it come? On this view the whole study of physics is abolished. And what is supposed to be easy, to prove that everything is One, does not follow; because from their exposition it does not follow, even if you grant them all their assumptions, that everything is One, but only that there is an absolute One—and not even this, unless you grant that the universal is a class; which is impossible in some cases. Nor is there any explanation of the lines, planes and solids which "come after" the Numbers: neither as to how they exist or can exist, nor as to what their importance is. They cannot be Forms (since they are not numbers) or Intermediates (which are the objects of mathematics) or perishables; clearly they form yet another fourth class.

In general, to investigate the elements of existing things without distinguishing the various senses in which things are said to exist is a hopeless task; especially when one inquires along these lines into the nature of the elements of which things are composed. For (*a*) we cannot surely conceive of the elements of activity or passivity or straightness; this is possible, if at all, only in the case of substances. Hence to look for, or to suppose that one has found, the elements of *everything* that exists, is a mistake. (*b*) How *can* one apprehend the elements of *everything?* Obviously one could not have any previous knowledge of anything; because just as a man who is beginning to learn geometry can have previous knowledge of other facts, but no previous knowledge of the principles of that science or of the things about which he is to learn, so it is in the case of all other branches of knowledge. Hence if there is a science which embraces everything (as some say), the student of it can have no previous knowledge at all. But all learning proceeds, wholly or in part, from what is already known; whether it is through demonstration or through definition—since the parts of the definition must be already known and familiar. The same is true of induction. On the other hand, assuming that this knowledge should turn out to be innate,[9] it is astonishing that we should possess unawares the most important of the sciences. Further, how is one to *know* of what elements things consist? how is it to be established? Even this presents a difficulty, because the facts might be disputed, as happens in the case of certain syllables—for some say that ZA is composed of S, D and A, while others say that it is a distinct sound and not any one of those which are familiar to us.

Further, how can one gain knowledge of the objects of a particular sense-perception without possessing that sense? Yet it should be possible, that is if the elements of which all things consist, as composite sounds consist of their peculiar elements, are the same.

X. Thus it is obvious, from the statements of earlier thinkers also, that all inquiry is apparently directed towards the causes described in the *Physics,* and that we cannot suggest any other cause apart from these. They were, however, only vaguely conceived; and although in one sense they have all been stated before, in another they have not been stated at all. For the earliest philosophy speaks falteringly, as it were, on all subjects; being new and in its infancy. Even Empedocles says that bone exists by virtue of its ratio, which is the definition or essence of a thing. But by similar reasoning both flesh and every other thing, or else nothing at all, must *be* ratio; for it must be because of this, and not because of their matter—which he calls fire, earth, water and air—that flesh and bone and every other thing exists. If anyone else had stated this, he would necessarily have agreed, but his own statement was not clear.

These and similar points have been explained already. We will now

---

9 *Cf.* the doctrine of ἀνάμνησις (recollection), Plato, *Meno* 81 c, *Phaedo* 72 ε.

return to the difficulties which might be raised about these same questions, for they may throw some light upon subsequent difficulties.

.   .   .

Book IV (*complete*)

I. There is a science which studies Being *qua* Being, and the properties inherent in it in virtue of its own nature. This science is not the same as any of the so-called particular sciences, for none of the others contemplates Being generally *qua* Being; they divide off some portion of it and study the attribute of this portion, as do for example the mathematical sciences. But since it is for the first principles and the most ultimate causes that we are searching, clearly they must belong to something in virtue of its own nature. Hence if these principles were investigated by those also who investigated the elements of existing things, the elements must be elements of Being not incidentally, but *qua* Being. Therefore it is of Being *qua* Being that we too must grasp the first causes.

II. The term "being" is used in various senses, but with reference to one central idea and one definite characteristic, and not as merely a common epithet. Thus as the term "healthy" always relates to health (either as preserving it or as producing it or as indicating it or as receptive of it), and as "medical" relates to the art of medicine (either as possessing it or as naturally adapted for it or as being a function of medicine)—and we shall find other terms used similarly to these—so "being" is used in various senses, but always with reference to one principle. For some things are said to "be" because they are substances; others because they are modifications of substance; others because they are a process towards substance, or destructions or privations or qualities of substance, or productive or generative of substance or of terms relating to substance, or negations of certain of these terms or of substance. (Hence we even say that not-being *is* not-being.) And so, just as there is one science of all healthy things, so it is true of everything else. For it is not only in the case of terms which express one common notion that the investigation belongs to one science, but also in the case of terms which relate to one particular characteristic; for the latter too, in a sense, express one common notion. Clearly then the study of things which *are*, *qua* being, also belongs to one science. Now in every case knowledge is principally concerned with that which is primary, *i.e.* that upon which all other things depend, and from which they get their names. If, then, substance is this primary thing, it is of substances that the philosopher must grasp the first principles and causes.

Now of every single class of things, as there is one perception, so there is one science: *e.g.*, grammar, which is one science, studies all articulate sounds. Hence the study of all the species of Being *qua* Being belongs to a science which is generically one, and the study of the several species of Being belongs to the specific parts of that science.

Now if Being and Unity are the same, *i.e.* a single nature, in the sense that they are associated as principle and cause are, and not as being denoted by the same definition (although it makes no difference but rather helps our argument if we understand them in the same sense), since "one man" and "man" and "existent man" and "man" are the same thing, *i.e.* the duplication in the statement "he is a man and an *existent* man" gives no fresh meaning (clearly the concepts of humanity and existence are not dissociated in respect of either coming to be or ceasing to be), and similarly in the case of the term "one," so that obviously the additional term in these phrases has the same significance, and Unity is nothing distinct from Being; and further if the substance of each thing is one in no accidental sense, and similarly is of its very nature something which *is*—then there are just as many species of Being as of Unity. And to study the essence of these species (I mean, *e.g.*, the study of Same and Other and all the other similar concepts—roughly speaking all the "contraries" are reducible to this first principle; but we may consider that they have been sufficiently studied in the "Selection of Contraries") is the province of a science which is generically one.

And there are just as many divisions of philosophy as there are kinds of substance; so that there must be among them a First Philosophy and one which follows upon it. For Being and Unity at once entail genera, and so the sciences will correspond to these genera. The term "philosopher" is like the term "mathematician" in its uses; for mathematics too has divisions,—there is a primary and a secondary science, and others successively, in the realm of mathematics.

Now since it is the province of one science to study opposites, and the opposite of unity is plurality, and it is the province of one science to study the negation and privation of Unity, because in both cases we are studying Unity, to which the negation (or privation) refers, stated either in the simple form that Unity is not present, or in the form that it is not present in a particular class; in the latter case Unity is modified by the differentia, apart from the content of the negation (for the negation of Unity is its absence); but in privation there is a substrate of which the privation is predicated.—The opposite of Unity, then, is Plurality; and so the opposites of the above-mentioned concepts—Otherness, Dissimilarity, Inequality and everything else which is derived from these or from Plurality or Unity —fall under the cognizance of the aforesaid science. And one of them is Oppositeness; for this is a form of Difference, and Difference is a form of Otherness. Hence since the term "one" is used in various senses, so too will these terms be used; yet it pertains to one science to take cognizance of them all. For terms fall under different sciences, not if they are used in various senses, but if their definitions are neither identical nor referable to a common notion. And since everything is referred to that which is primary, *e.g.* all things which are called "one" are referred to the primary "One," we must admit that this is also true of Identity and Otherness and the Contraries. Thus we must first distinguish all the senses in which each term is used, and then attribute them to the primary in the case of each predicate, and see how they are related to it; for some will derive their name from possessing and others from producing it, and others for similar reasons.

Thus clearly it pertains to one science to give an account both of these concepts and of substance (this was one of the questions raised in the "Difficulties"), and it is the function of the philosopher to be able to study all subjects. If this is not so, who is it who will investigate whether "Socrates" and "Socrates seated" are the same thing; or whether one thing has one contrary, or what the contrary is, or how many meanings it has? and similarly with all other such questions. Thus since these are the essential modifications of Unity *qua* Unity and of Being *qua* Being, and not *qua* numbers or lines or fire, clearly it pertains to that science to discover both the essence and the attributes of these concepts. And those who investigate them err, not in being unphilosophical, but because the substance, of which they have no real knowledge, is prior. For just as number *qua* number has its peculiar modifications, *e.g.* oddness and evenness, commensurability and equality, excess and defect, and these things are inherent in numbers both considered independently and in relation to other numbers; and as similarly other peculiar modifications are inherent in the solid and the immovable and the moving and the weightless and that which has weight; so Being *qua* Being has certain peculiar modifications, and it is about these that it is the philosopher's function to discover the truth. And here is evidence of this fact. Dialecticians and sophists wear the same appearance as the philosopher, for sophistry is Wisdom in appearance only, and dialecticians discuss all subjects, and Being is a subject common to them all; but clearly they discuss these concepts because they appertain to philosophy. For sophistry and dialectic are concerned with the same class of subjects as philosophy, but philosophy differs from the former in the nature of its capability and from the latter in its outlook on life. Dialectic treats as an exercise what philosophy tries to understand, and sophistry seems to be philosophy, but is not.

Further, the second column of contraries is privative, and everything is reducible to Being and Not-being, and Unity and Plurality; *e.g.* Rest falls under Unity and Motion under Plurality. And nearly everyone agrees that substance and existing things are composed of contraries; at any rate all speak of the first principles as contraries—some as Odd and Even, some as Hot and Cold, some as Limit and Unlimited, some as Love and Strife. And it is apparent that all other things also are reducible to Unity and Plurality (we may assume this reduction); and the principles adduced by other thinkers fall entirely under these as genera. It is clear, then, from these considerations also, that it pertains to a single science to study Being *qua* Being; for all things are either contraries or derived from contraries, and the first principles of the contraries are Unity and Plurality. And these belong to one science, whether they have reference to one common notion or not. Probably the truth is that they have not; but nevertheless even if the term "one" is used in various senses, the others will be related to the primary sense (and similarly with the contraries)—even if Being or Unity is not a universal and the same in all cases, or is not separable from particulars (as it presumably is not; the unity is in some cases one of reference and in others one of succession). For this very reason it is not the function of the geometrician to inquire what is Contrariety or Completeness or Being or Unity or Identity or Otherness, but to proceed from the assumption of them.

Clearly, then, it pertains to one science to study Being *qua* Being, and the attributes inherent in it *qua* Being; and the same science investigates, besides the concepts mentioned above, Priority and Posteriority, Genus and Species, Whole and Part, and all other such concepts.

III. We must pronounce whether it pertains to the same science to study both the so-called axioms in mathematics and substance, or to different sciences. It is obvious that the investigation of these axioms too pertains to one science, namely the science of the philosopher; for they apply to all existing things, and not to a particular class separate and distinct from the rest. Moreover all thinkers employ them—because they are axioms of Being *qua* Being, and every genus possesses Being—but employ them only in so far as their purposes require; *i.e.*, so far as the genus extends about which they are carrying out their proofs. Hence since these axioms apply to all things *qua* Being (for this is what is common to them), it is the function of him who studies Being *qua* Being to investigate them as well. For this reason no one who is pursuing a particular inquiry—neither a geometrician nor an arithmetician—attempts to state whether they are true or false; but some of the physicists did so, quite naturally; for they alone professed to investigate nature as a whole, and Being. But inasmuch as there is a more ultimate type of thinker than the natural philosopher (for nature is only a genus of Being), the investigation of these axioms too will belong to the universal thinker who studies the primary reality. Natural philosophy is a kind of Wisdom, but not the primary kind. As for the attempts of some of those who discuss how the truth should be received, they are due to lack of training in logic; for they should understand these things before they approach their task, and not investigate while they are still learning. Clearly then it is the function of the philosopher, *i.e.* the student of the whole of reality in its essential nature, to investigate also the principles of syllogistic reasoning. And it is proper for him who best understands each class of subject to be able to state the most certain principles of that subject; so that he who understands the modes of Being *qua* Being should be able to state the most certain principles of all things. Now this person is the philosopher, and the most certain principle of all is that about which one cannot be mistaken; for such a principle must be both the most familiar (for it is about the unfamiliar that errors are always made), and not based on hypothesis. For the principle which the student of any form of Being must grasp is no hypothesis; and that which a man must know if he knows anything he must bring with him to his task.

Clearly, then, it is a principle of this kind that is the most certain of all principles. Let us next state *what* this principle is. "It is impossible for the same attribute at once to belong and not to belong to the same thing and in the same relation"; and we must add any further qualifications that may be necessary to meet logical objections. This is the most certain of all principles, since it possesses the required definition; for it is impossible for anyone to suppose that the same thing is and is not, as some imagine that Heraclitus says—for what a man says does not necessarily represent what he believes. And if it is impossible for contrary attributes to belong at the same time to the same subject (the usual qualifications must be added to this premiss also), and an opinion which contradicts another is contrary to it, then clearly it is impossible for the same man to suppose at the same time that the same thing is and is not; for the man who made this error would entertain two contrary opinions at the same time. Hence all men who are demonstrating anything refer back to this as an ultimate belief; for it is by nature the starting-point of all the other axioms as well.

IV. There are some, however, as we have said, who both state themselves that the same thing can be and not be, and say that it is possible to hold this view. Many even of the physicists adopt this theory. But we have just assumed that it is impossible at once to be and not to be, and by this means we have proved that this is the most certain of all principles. Some, indeed, demand to have the law proved, but this is because they lack education; for it shows lack of education not to know of what we should require proof, and of what we should not. For it is quite impossible that everything should have a proof; the process would go on to infinity, so that even so there would be no proof. If on the other hand there are some things of which no proof need be sought, they cannot say what principle they think to be more self-evident. Even in the case of this law, however, we can demonstrate the impossibility by refutation, if only our opponent makes some statement. If he makes none, it is absurd to seek for an argument against one who has no arguments of his own about anything, in so far as he has none; for such a person, in so far as he is such, is really no better than a vegetable. And I say that proof by refutation differs from simple proof in that he who attempts to prove might seem to beg the fundamental question, whereas if the discussion is provoked thus by someone else, refutation and not proof will result. The starting-point for all such discussions is not the claim that he should state that something is or is not so (because this might be supposed to be a begging of the question), but that he should say something significant both to himself and to another (this is essential if any argument is to follow; for otherwise such a person cannot reason either with himself or with another); and if this is granted, demonstration will be possible, for there will be something already defined. But the person responsible is not he who demonstrates but he who acquiesces; for though he disowns reason he acquiesces to reason. Moreover, he who makes such an admission as this has admitted the truth of something apart from demonstration [so that not everything will be "so and not so"].

Thus in the first place it is obvious that this at any rate is true: that the term "to be" or "not to be" has a definite meaning; so that not everything can be "so and not so." Again, if "man" has one meaning, let this be "two-footed animal." By "has one meaning" I mean this: if X means "man," then if anything is a man, its humanity will consist in being X. And it makes no difference even if it be said that "man" has several meanings, provided that they are limited in number; for one could assign a different name to each formula. For instance, it might be said that "man" has not one meaning but several, one of which has the formula "two-footed animal," and there might be many other formulae as well, if they were limited in number; for a particular name could be assigned to each formula. If on the other hand it be said that "man" has an infinite number of meanings, obviously there can be no discourse; for not to have one meaning is to have no meaning, and if words have no meaning there is an end of discourse with others, and even, strictly speaking, with oneself; because it is impossible to think of anything if we do not think of one thing; and even if this were possible, one name might be assigned to that of which we think. Now let this name, as we said at the beginning, have a meaning; and let it have *one* meaning. Now it is impossible that "being man" should have the same meaning as "not being man," that is, if "man" is not merely predicable of one subject but has one meaning (for we do not identify "having one meaning" with "being predicable of one subject," since in this case "cultured" and "white" and "man" would have one meaning, and so all things would be one; for they would all have the same meaning). And it will be impossible for the same thing to be and not to be, except by equivocation, as *e.g.* one whom we call "man" others might call "not-man"; but the problem is whether the same thing can at once be and not be "man," not in *name*, but in *fact*. If "man" and "not-man" have not different meanings, clearly "not being a man" will mean nothing different from "being a man"; and so "being a man" will be "not being a man"; they will be one. For "to be one" means, as in the case of "garment" and "coat," that the formula is one. And if "being man" and "being not-man" are to be one, they will have the same meaning; but it has been proved above that they have different meanings. If then anything can be truly said to be "man," it must be "two-footed animal"; for this is what "man" was intended to mean. And if this is necessarily so, it is impossible that at the same time the same thing should *not* be "two-footed animal." For "to be necessarily so" means this: that it is impossible not to be so. Thus it cannot be true to say at the same time that the same thing is and is not man. And the same argument holds also in the case of not being man; because "being man" and "being not-man" have different meanings if "being white" and "being man" have different meanings (for the opposition is much stronger in the former case so as to produce different meanings). And if we are told that "white" too means one and the same thing, we shall say again just what we said before, that in that case all things, and not merely the opposites, will be one. But if this is impossible, what we have stated follows; that is, if our opponent answers our question; but if when asked the simple question he includes in his answer the negations, he is not answering our question. There is nothing to prevent the same thing from being "man" and "white" and a multitude of other things; but nevertheless when asked whether it is true to say that X is man, or not, one should return an answer that means one thing, and not add that X is white and large. It is indeed impossible to enumerate all the infinity of accidents; and so let him enumerate either all or none. Similarly therefore, even if the same thing is ten thousand times "man" and "not-man," one should not include in one's answer to the question whether it is "man" that it is at the same time also "not-man," unless one is also bound to include in one's answer all the other accidental things that the subject is or is not. And if one does this, he is not arguing properly.

In general those who talk like this do away with substance and essence, for they are compelled to assert that all things are accidents, and that there is no such thing as "being essentially man" or "animal." For if there is to be such a thing as "being essentially man," this will not be "being not-man" nor "not-being man" (and yet these are negations of it); for it was intended to have one meaning, *i.e.* the substance of something. But to denote a substance means that the essence is that and nothing else; and if for it "being essentially man" is the same as either "being essentially not-man" or "essentially not-being man," the essence will be something else. Thus they are compelled to say that nothing can have such a definition as this, but that all things are accidental; for this is the distinction between substance and accident: "white" is an accident of "man," because although he is white, he is not white in essence. And since the accidental always implies a predication about some subject, if all statements are accidental, there will be nothing primary about which they are made; so the predication must proceed to infinity. But this is impossible, for not even more than two accidents can be combined in predication. An accident cannot be an accident of an accident unless both are accidents of the same thing. I mean, *e.g.*, that "white" is "cultured" and "cultured" "white" merely because both are accidents of a man. But it is not in this sense—that both terms are accidents of something else—that Socrates is cultured. Therefore since some accidents are predicated in the latter and some in the former sense, such as are predicated in the way that "white" is of Socrates cannot be an infinite series in the upper direction; *e.g.* there cannot be another accident of "white Socrates," for the sum of these predications does not make a single statement. Nor can "white" have a further accident, such as "cultured"; for the former is no more an accident of the latter than *vice versa;* and besides we have distinguished that although some predicates are accidental in this sense, others are accidental in the sense that "cultured" is to Socrates; and whereas in the former case the accident is an accident of an accident, it is not so in the latter; and thus not all predications will be of accidents. Therefore even so there will be something which denotes substance. And if this is so, we have proved that contradictory statements cannot be predicated at the same time.

Again, if all contradictory predications of the same subject at the same time are true, clearly all things will be one. For if it is equally possible either to affirm or deny anything of anything, the same thing will be a trireme and a wall and a man; which is what necessarily follows for those who hold the theory of Protagoras.[10] For if anyone thinks that a man is not a trireme, he is clearly not a trireme; and so he also is a trireme if the contradictory statement is true. And the result is the dictum of Anaxagoras, "all things mixed together"; so that nothing truly exists. It seems, then, that they are speaking of the Indeterminate; and while they think that they are speaking of what exists, they are really speaking of what does not; for the Indeterminate is that which exists potentially but not actually. But indeed they must admit the affirmation or negation of any predicate of any subject, for it is absurd that in the case of each term its own negation should be true, and the negation of some other term which is not true of it should not be true. I mean, *e.g.,* that if it is true to say that a man is not a man, it is obviously also true to say that he is not a trireme. Then if the affirmation is true, so must the negation be true; but if the affirmation is not true the negation will be even truer than the negation of the original term itself. Therefore if the latter negation is true, the negation of "trireme" will also be true; and if this is true, the affirmation will be true too.

And not only does this follow for those who hold this theory, but also that it is not necessary either to affirm or to deny a statement. For if it is true that X is both man and not-man, clearly he will be neither man nor not-man; for to the two statements there correspond two negations, and if the former is taken as a single statement compounded out of two, the latter is also a single statement and opposite to it.

Again, either this applies to all terms, and the same thing is both white and not-white, and existent and non-existent, and similarly with all other assertions and negations; or it does not apply to all, but only to some and not to others. And if it does not apply to all, the exceptions will be admitted; but if it does apply to all, again either (*a*) the negation will be true wherever the affirmation is true, and the affirmation will be true wherever the negation is true, or (*b*) the negation will be true wherever the assertion is true, but the assertion will not always be true where the negation is true. And in the latter case there will be something which definitely is not, and this will be a certain belief; and if that it is not is certain and knowable, the opposite assertion will be still more knowable. But if what is denied can be equally truly asserted, it must be either true or false to state the predicates separately and say, *e.g.,* that a thing is white, and again that it is not-white. And if it is not-true to state them separately, our opponent does not say what he professes to say, and nothing exists; and how can that which does not exist speak or walk? And again all things will be one, as we said before, and the same thing will be "man" and "God" and "trireme" and the negations of these terms. For if it is equally possible to assert or deny anything of anything, one thing will not differ from another; for if anything does differ, it will be true and

---

10 *i.e.,* that all appearances and opinions are true.

unique. And similarly even if it is possible to make a true statement while separating the predicates, what we have stated follows. Moreover it follows that all statements would be true and all false; and that our opponent himself admits that what he says is false. Besides, it is obvious that discussion with him is pointless, because he makes no real statement. For he says neither "yes" nor "no," but "yes and no"; and again he denies both of these and says "neither yes nor no"; otherwise there would be already some definite statement.

Again, if when the assertion is true the negation is false, and when the latter is true the affirmation is false, it will be impossible to assert and deny with truth the same thing at the same time. But perhaps it will be said that this is the point at issue.

Again, is the man wrong who supposes that a thing is so or not so, and he who supposes both right? If he is right, what is the meaning of saying that "such is the nature of reality"? And if he is not right, but is more right than the holder of the first view, reality will at once have a definite nature, and this will be true, and not at the same time not-true. And if all men are equally right and wrong, an exponent of this view can neither speak nor mean anything, since at the same time he says both "yes" and "no." And if he forms no judgement, but "thinks" and "thinks not" indifferently, what difference will there be between him and the vegetables?

Hence it is quite evident that no one, either of those who profess this theory or of any other school, is really in this position. Otherwise, why does a man walk to Megara and not stay at home, when he thinks he ought to make the journey? Why does he not walk early one morning into a well or ravine, if he comes to it, instead of clearly guarding against doing so, thus showing that he does *not* think that it is equally good and not good to fall in? Obviously then he judges that the one course is better and the other worse. And if this is so, he must judge that one thing is man and another not man, and that one thing is sweet and another not sweet. For when, thinking that it is desirable to drink water and see a man, he goes to look for them, he does not look for and judge all things indifferently; and yet he should, if the same thing were equally man and not-man. But as we have said, there is no one who does not evidently avoid some things and not others. Hence, as it seems, all men form unqualified judgements, if not about all things, at least about what is better or worse. And if they do this by guesswork and without knowledge, they should be all the more eager for truth; just as a sick man should be more eager for health than a healthy man; for indeed the man who guesses, as contrasted with him who knows, is not in a healthy relation to the truth.

Again, however much things may be "so and not so," yet differences of degree are inherent in the nature of things. For we should not say that 2 and 3 are equally even; nor are he who thinks that 4 is 5, and he who thinks it is 1000, equally wrong: hence if they are not equally wrong, the one is clearly less wrong, and so more right. If then that which has more the nature of something is nearer to that something, there will be some truth to which the more true is nearer. And even if there is not, still there is now something more certain and true, and we shall be freed from the undiluted doctrine which precludes any mental determination.

V. From the same view proceeds the theory of Protagoras, and both alike must be either true or false. For if all opinions and appearances are true, everything must be at once true and false; for many people form judgements which are opposite to those of others, and imagine that those who do not think the same as themselves are wrong: hence the same thing must both be and not be. And if this is so, all opinions must be true; for those who are wrong and those who are right think contrarily to each other. So if reality is of this nature, everyone will be right.

Clearly then both these theories proceed from the same mental outlook. But the method of approach is not the same for all cases; for some require persuasion and others compulsion. The ignorance of those who have formed this judgement through perplexity is easily remedied, because we are dealing not with the theory but with their mental outlook; but those who hold the theory for its own sake can only be cured by refuting the theory as expressed in their own speech and words.

This view comes to those who are perplexed from their observation of sensible things. (i.) The belief that contradictions and contraries can be true at the same time comes to them from seeing the contraries generated from the same thing. Then if what is not cannot be generated, the thing must have existed before as both contraries equally—just as Anaxagoras says that everything is mixed in everything; and also Democritus, for he too says that Void and Plenum are present equally in any part, and yet the latter *is*, and the former *is not*. To those, then, who base their judgement on these considerations, we shall say that although in one sense their theory is correct, in another they are mistaken. For "being" has two meanings, so that there is a sense in which something can be generated from "not-being," and a sense in which it cannot; and a sense in which the same thing can at once be and not be; but not in the same respect. For the same thing can "be" contraries at the same time potentially, but not actually. And further, we shall request them to conceive another kind also of substance of existing things, in which there is absolutely no motion or destruction or generation.

And (ii.) similarly the theory that there is truth in appearance has come to some people from an observation of sensible things. They think that the truth should not be judged by the number or fewness of its upholders; and they say that the same thing seems sweet to some who taste it, and bitter to others; so that if all men were diseased or all insane, except two or three who were healthy or sane, the latter would seem to be diseased or insane, and not the others. And further they say that many of the animals as well get from the same things impressions which are contrary to ours, and that the individual himself does not always think the same in matters of sense-perception. Thus it is uncertain which of these impressions are true or false; for one kind is no more true than another, but equally so. And hence Democritus says that either there is no truth or we cannot discover it.

And in general it is because they suppose that thought is sense-perception, and sense-perception physical alteration, that they say that the impression given through sense-perception is necessarily true; for it is on these grounds that both Empedocles and Democritus and practically all the rest have become obsessed by such opinions as these. For Empedocles says that those who change their bodily condition change their thought:

For according to that which is present to them doth thought increase in men.

And in another passage he says:

And as they change into a different nature, so it ever comes to them to think differently.

And Parmenides too declares in the same way:

For as each at any time hath the temperament of his many-jointed limbs, so thought comes to men. For for each and every man the substance of his limbs is that very thing which thinks; for thought is that which preponderates.

There is also recorded a saying of Anaxagoras to some of his disciples, that things would be for them as they judged them to be. And they say that Homer too clearly held this view, because he made Hector, when he was stunned by the blow, lie with thoughts deranged—thus implying that even those who are "out of their minds" still think, although not the same thoughts. Clearly then, if both are kinds of thought, reality also will be "both so and not so." It is along this path that the consequences are most difficult; for if those who have the clearest vision of such truth as is possible (and these are they who seek and love it most) hold such opinions and make these pronouncements about the truth, surely those who are trying to be philosophers may well despair; for the pursuit of truth will be "chasing birds in the air."

But the reason why these men hold this view is that although they studied the truth about reality, they supposed that reality is confined to sensible things, in which the nature of the Indeterminate, *i.e.* of Being in the sense which we have explained, is abundantly present. (Thus their statements, though plausible, are not true; this form of the criticism is more suitable than that which Epicharmus applied to Xenophanes.) And further, observing that all this indeterminate substance is in motion, and that no true predication can be made of that which changes, they supposed that it is impossible to make any true statement about that which is in all ways and entirely changeable. For it was from this supposition that there blossomed forth the most extreme view of those which we have mentioned, that of the professed followers of Heraclitus, and such as Cratylus held, who ended by thinking that one need not say anything, and only moved his finger; and who criticized Heraclitus for saying that one cannot enter the same river twice, for he himself held that it cannot be done even once.

But we shall reply to this theory also that although that which is changeable supplies them, when it changes, with some real ground for supposing that it "is not," yet there is something debatable in this; for that which is shedding any quality retains something of that which is being shed, and something of that which is coming to be must already exist. And in general if a thing is ceasing to be, there will be something there which *is;* and if a thing is coming to be, that from which it comes and by which it is generated must *be;* and this cannot go on to infinity. But let us leave this line of argument and remark that quantitative and qualitative change are not the same. Let it be granted that there is nothing permanent in respect of quantity; but it is by the *form* that we recognize everything. And again those who hold the theory that we are attacking deserve censure in that they have maintained about the whole material universe what they have observed in the case of a mere minority of sensible things. For it is only the realm of sense around us which continues subject to destruction and generation, but this is a practically negligible part of the whole; so that it would have been fairer for them to acquit the former on the ground of the latter than to condemn the latter on account of the former.

Further, we shall obviously say to these thinkers too the same as we said some time ago; for we must prove to them and convince them that there is a kind of nature that is not moved (and yet those who claim that things can at once be and not be are logically compelled to admit rather that all things are at rest than that they are in motion; for there is nothing for them to change into, since everything exists in everything).

And as concerning reality, that not every appearance is real, we shall say, first, that indeed the perception, at least of the proper object of a sense, is not false, but the impression we get of it is not the same as the perception. And then we may fairly express surprise if our opponents raise the question whether magnitudes and colours are really such as they appear at a distance or close at hand, as they appear to the healthy or to the diseased; and whether heavy things are as they appear to the weak or to the strong; and whether truth is as it appears to the waking or to the sleeping. For clearly they do not really believe the latter alternative—at any rate no one, if in the night he thinks that he is at Athens whereas he is really in Africa, starts off to the Odeum. And again concerning the future (as indeed Plato says) the opinion of the doctor and that of the layman are presumably not equally reliable, *e.g.* as to whether a man will get well or not. And again in the case of the senses themselves, our perception of a foreign object and of an object proper to a given sense, or of a kindred object and of an actual object of that sense itself, is not equally reliable; but in the case of colours sight, and not taste, is authoritative, and in the case of flavour taste, and not sight. But not one of the senses ever asserts at the same time of the same object that it is "so and not so." Nor even at another time does it make a conflicting statement about the quality, but only about that to which the quality belongs. I mean, *e.g.*, that the same wine may seem, as the result of its own change or of that of one's body, at one time sweet and at another not; but sweetness, such as it is when it exists, has never yet changed, and there is no mistake about it, and that which is to be sweet is necessarily of such a nature. Yet all these theories destroy the possibility of anything's existing by necessity, inasmuch as they destroy the existence of its essence; for "the necessary" cannot be in one way and in another; and so if anything exists of necessity, it cannot be "both so and not so."

And in general, if only the sensible exists, without animate things there would be nothing; for there would be no sense-faculty. That there would be neither sensible qualities nor sensations is probably true (for these depend upon an effect produced in the percipient), but that the substrates which cause the sensation should not exist even apart from the sensation is impossible. For sensation is not of itself, but there is something else too besides the sensation, which must be prior to the sensation; because that which moves is by nature prior to that which is moved, and this is no less true if the terms are correlative.

VI. But there are some, both of those who really hold these convictions and of those who merely profess these views, who raise a difficulty; they inquire who is to judge of the healthy man, and in general who is to judge rightly in each particular case. But such questions are like wondering whether we are at any given moment asleep or awake; and all problems of this kind amount to the same thing. These people demand a reason for everything. They want a starting-point, and want to grasp it by demonstration; while it is obvious from their actions that they have no conviction. But their case is just what we have stated before; for they require a reason for things which have no reason, since the starting-point of a demonstration is not a matter of demonstration. The first class, then, may be readily convinced of this, because it is not hard to grasp. But those who look only for cogency in argument look for an impossibility, for they claim the right to contradict themselves, and lose no time in doing so. Yet if not everything is relative, but some things are self-existent, not every appearance will be true; for an appearance is an appearance to someone. And so he who says that all appearances are true makes everything relative. Hence those who demand something cogent in argument, and at the same time claim to make out a case, must guard themselves by saying that the appearance is true not in itself, but *for him to whom* it appears, and *at the time when* it appears, and in the *way* and *manner* in which it appears. And if they make out a case without this qualification, as a result they will soon contradict themselves; for it is possible in the case of the same man for a thing to appear honey to the sight, but not to the taste, and for things to appear different to the sight of each of his two eyes, if their sight is unequal. For to those who assert (for the reasons previously stated) that appearances are true, and that all things are therefore equally false and true, because they do not appear the same to all, nor always the same to the same person, but often have contrary appearances at the same time (since if one crosses the fingers touch says that an object is two, while sight says that it is only one), we shall say "but not to the same sense or to the same part of it in the same way and at the same time"; so that with this qualification the appearance will be true. But perhaps it is for this reason that those who argue not from a sense of difficulty but for argument's sake are compelled to say that the appearance is not true in itself, but true to the percipient; and, as we have said before, are compelled also to make every-thing relative and dependent upon opinion and sensation, so that nothing has happened or will happen unless someone has first formed an opinion about it; otherwise clearly all things would not be relative to opinion.

Further, if a thing is one, it is relative to one thing or to something de-terminate. And if the same thing is both a half and an equal, yet the equal is not relative to the double. If to the thinking subject "man" and the object of thought are the same, "man" will not be the thinking subject but the object of thought; and if each thing is to be regarded as relative to the thinking subject, the thinking subject will be relative to an infinity of specifically different things.

That the most certain of all beliefs is that opposite statements are not both true at the same time, and what follows for those who maintain that they are true, and why these thinkers maintain this, may be regarded as adequately stated. And since the contradiction of a statement cannot be true at the same time of the same thing, it is obvious that contraries can-not apply at the same time to the same thing. For in each pair of con-traries one is a privation no less than it is a contrary—a privation of sub-stance. And privation is the negation of a predicate to some defined genus. Therefore if it is impossible at the same time to affirm and deny a thing truly, it is also impossible for contraries to apply to a thing at the same time; either both must apply in a modified sense, or one in a modified sense and the other absolutely.

VII. Nor indeed can there be any intermediate between contrary state-ments, but of one thing we must either assert or deny one thing, whatever it may be. This will be plain if we first define truth and falsehood. To say that what is is not, or that what is not is, is false; but to say that what is is, and what is not is not, is true; and therefore also he who says that a thing is or is not will say either what is true or what is false. But neither what is nor what is not is said not to be *or* to be. Further, an intermediate be-tween contraries will be intermediate either as grey is between black and white, or as "neither man nor horse" is between man and horse. If in the latter sense, it cannot change (for change is from not-good to good, or from good to not-good); but in fact it is clearly always changing; for change can only be into the opposite and the intermediate. And if it is a true intermediate, in this case too there would be a kind of change into white not from not-white; but in fact this is not seen. Further, the under-standing either affirms or denies every object of understanding or thought (as is clear from the definition) whenever it is right or wrong. When, in asserting or denying, it combines the predicates in one way, it is right; when in the other, it is wrong.

Again, unless it is maintained merely for argument's sake, the inter-mediate must exist beside all contrary terms; so that one will say what is neither true nor false. And it will exist beside what is and what is not; so that there will be a form of change beside generation and destruction.

Again, there will also be an intermediate in all classes in which the negation of a term implies the contrary assertion; *e.g.*, among numbers there will be a number which is neither odd nor not-odd. But this is impossible, as is clear from the definition.

Again, there will be an infinite progression, and existing things will be not only half as many again, but even more. For again it will be possible to deny the intermediate in reference both to its assertion and to its negation, and the result will be something; for its essence is something distinct.

Again, when a man is asked whether a thing is white and says "no," he has denied nothing except that it is <white>, and its not-being <white> is a negation.

Now this view has occurred to certain people in just the same way as other paradoxes have also occurred; for when they cannot find a way out from eristic arguments, they submit to the argument and admit that the conclusion is true. Some, then, hold the theory for this kind of reason, and others because they require an explanation for everything. In dealing with all such persons the starting-point is from definition; and definition results from the necessity of their meaning something; because the formula, which their term implies, will be a definition. The doctrine of Heraclitus, which says that everything is and is not, seems to make all things true; and that of Anaxagoras seems to imply an intermediate in contradiction, so that all things are false; for when things are mixed, the mixture is neither good nor not-good; and so no statement is true.

VIII. It is obvious from this analysis that the one-sided and sweeping statements which some people make cannot be substantially true—some maintaining that nothing is true (for they say that there is no reason why the same rule should not apply to everything as applies to the commensurability of the diagonal of a square), and some that everything is true. These theories are almost the same as that of Heraclitus. For the theory which says that all things are true and all false also makes each of these statements separately; so that if they are impossible in combination they are also impossible individually. And again obviously there are contrary statements which cannot be true at the same time. Nor can they all be false, although from what we have said this might seem more possible. But in opposing all such theories we must demand, as was said in our discussion above, not that something should be or not be, but some significant statement; and so we must argue from a definition, having first grasped what "falsehood" or "truth" means. And if to assert what is true is nothing else than to deny what is false, everything cannot be false; for one part of the contradiction must be true. Further, if everything must be either asserted or denied, both parts cannot be false; for one and only one part of the contradiction is false. Indeed, the consequence follows which is notorious in the case of all such theories, that they destroy themselves; for he who says that everything is true makes the opposite theory true too, and therefore his own untrue (for the opposite theory says that his is not true); and he who says that everything is false makes himself a liar. And if they make exceptions, the one that the opposite theory alone is not true, and the other that his own theory alone is not false, it follows none the less that they postulate an infinite number of true and false statements. For the statement that the true statement is true is also true; and this will go on to infinity.

Nor, as is obvious, are those right who say that all things are at rest; nor those who say that all things are in motion. For if all things are at rest, the same things will always be true and false, whereas "this state of affairs" is obviously subject to change; for the speaker himself once did not exist, and again he will not exist. And if all things are in motion, nothing will be true, so everything will be false; but this has been proved to be impossible. Again, it must be that which *is* that changes, for change is from something into something. And further, neither it is true that all things are at rest or in motion sometimes, but nothing continuously; for there is something which always moves that which is moved, and the "prime mover" is itself unmoved.

Book V (*in part*)

II. "Cause" means: (*a*) in one sense, that as the result of whose presence something comes into being—*e.g.* the bronze of a statue and the silver of a cup, and the classes which contain these; (*b*) in another sense, the *form* or pattern; that is, the essential formula and the classes which contain it—*e.g.* the ratio 2:1 and number in general is the cause of the octave—and parts of the formula. (*c*) The source of the first beginning of change or rest; *e.g.* the man who plans is a cause, and the father is the cause of the child, and in general that which produces is the cause of that which is produced, and that which changes of that which is changed. (*d*) The same as "end"; *i.e.* the final cause; *e.g.*, as the "end" of walking is health. For why does a man walk? "To be healthy," we say, and by saying this we consider that we have supplied the cause. (*e*) All those means towards the end which arise at the instigation of something else; as, *e.g.* fat-reducing, purging, drugs and instruments are causes of health; for they all have the *end* as their object, although they differ from each other as being some instruments, others actions.

These are roughly all the meanings of "cause," but since causes are spoken of with various meanings, it follows that there are several causes (and that not in an accidental sense) of the same thing. *E.g.*, both *statuary* and *bronze* are causes of the statue; not in different connexions, but *qua* statue. However, they are not causes in the same way, but the one as *material* and the other as the *source of motion*. And things are causes of each other; as *e.g.* labour of vigour, and vigour of labour—but not in the same way; the one as an *end*, and the other as *source of motion*. And again the same thing is sometimes the cause of contrary results; because that which by its presence is the cause of so-and-so we sometimes accuse of being, by its absence, the cause of the contrary—as, *e.g.*, we say that the absence of the pilot is the cause of a capsize, whereas his presence was the cause of safety. And both, presence and privation, are *moving* causes.

Now there are four senses which are most obvious under which all the causes just described may be classed. The components of syllables; the material of manufactured articles; fire, earth and all such bodies; the parts of a whole; and the premisses of a syllogistic conclusion; are causes in the *material* sense. Of these some are causes as substrate: *e.g.* the parts; and others as *essence:* the whole, and the composition, and the form. The seed and the physician and the contriver and in general that which produces, all these are the source of change or stationariness. The remainder represent the *end* and *good* of the others; for the final cause tends to be the greatest good and *end* of the rest. Let it be assumed that it makes no difference whether we call it "good" or "apparent good." In *kind*, then, there are these four classes of cause.

The *modes* of cause are numerically many, although these too are fewer when summarized. For causes are spoken of in many senses, and even of those which are of the same kind, some are causes in a prior and some in a posterior sense; *e.g.*, the physician and the expert are both causes of health; and the ratio 2:1 and number are both causes of the octave; and the universals which include a given cause are causes of its particular effects. Again, a thing may be a cause in the sense of an accident, and the classes which contain accidents; *e.g.*, the cause of a statue is in one sense Polyclitus and in another a sculptor, because it is an accident of the sculptor to be Polyclitus. And the universal terms which include accidents are causes; *e.g.*, the cause of a statue is a man, or even, generally, an animal; because Polyclitus is a man, and man is an animal. And even of accidental causes some are remoter or more proximate than others; *e.g.*, the cause of the statue might be said to be "white man" or "cultured man," and not merely "Polyclitus" or "man."

And besides the distinction of causes as *proper* and *accidental,* some are termed causes in a *potential* and others in an *actual* sense; *e.g.*, the cause of building is either the builder or the builder who builds. And the same distinctions in meaning as we have already described will apply to the *effects* of the causes; *e.g.* to *this* statue, or *a* statue, or generally an image; and to *this* bronze, or bronze, or generally material. And it is the same with accidental effects. Again, the proper and accidental senses will be combined; *e.g.*, the cause is neither "Polyclitus" nor "a sculptor" but "the sculptor Polyclitus."

However, these classes of cause are in all six in number, each used in two senses. Causes are (i.) particular, (ii.) generic, (iii.) accidental, (iv.) generically accidental; and these may be either stated singly or (v., vi.) in combination; and further they are all either actual or potential. And there is this difference between them, that actual and particular causes coexist or do not coexist with their effects (*e.g. this* man giving medical treatment with *this* man recovering his health, and *this* builder with *this* building in course of erection); but potential causes do not always do so; for the house and the builder do not perish together.

．　．　．

IV. "Nature" means: (*a*) in one sense, the genesis of growing things—as would be suggested by pronouncing the v of φύσις long—and (*b*) in another, that immanent thing from which a growing thing first begins to grow. (*c*) The source from which the primary motion in every natural object is induced in that object as such. All things are said to grow which gain increase through something else by contact and organic unity (or adhesion, as in the case of embryos). Organic unity differs from contact; for in the latter case there need be nothing except contact, but in both the things which form an organic unity there is some one and the same thing which produces, instead of mere contact, a unity which is organic, continuous and quantitative (but not qualitative). Again, "nature" means (*d*) the primary stuff, shapeless and unchangeable from its own potency, of which any natural object consists or from which it is produced; *e.g.*, bronze is called the "nature" of a statue and of bronze articles, and wood that of wooden ones, and similarly in all other cases. For each article consists of these "natures," the primary material persisting. It is in this sense that men call the elements of natural objects the "nature," some calling it fire, others earth or air or water, others something else similar, others some of these, and others all of them. Again in another sense "nature" means (*e*) the substance of natural objects; as in the case of those who say that the "nature" is the primary composition of a thing, or as Empedocles says:

Of nothing that exists is there nature, but only mixture and separation of what has been mixed; nature is but a name given to these by men.

Hence as regards those things which exist or are produced by nature, although that from which they naturally are produced or exist is already present, we say that they have not their nature yet unless they have their form and shape. That which comprises both of these exists by nature; *e.g.* animals and their parts. And nature is both the primary matter (and this in two senses: either primary in relation to the thing, or primary in general; *e.g.*, in bronze articles the primary matter in relation to those articles is bronze, but in general it is perhaps water—that is if all things which can be melted are water) and the form or essence, *i.e.* the end of the process of generation. Indeed from this sense of "nature," by an extension of meaning, every essence in general is called "nature," because the nature of anything is a kind of essence.

From what has been said, then, the primary and proper sense of "nature" is the essence of those things which contain in themselves as such a source of motion; for the matter is called "nature" because it is capable of receiving the nature, and the processes of generation and growth are called "nature" because they are motions derived from it. And nature in this sense is the source of motion in natural objects, which is somehow inherent in them, either potentially or actually.

V. "Necessary" means: (*a*) That without which, as a concomitant condition, life is impossible; *e.g.*, respiration and food are necessary for an animal, because it cannot exist without them. (*b*) The conditions without which good cannot be or come to be, or without which one cannot get rid or keep free of evil—*e.g.*, drinking medicine is necessary to escape from ill-health, and sailing to Aegina is necessary to recover one's money. (*c*) The compulsory and compulsion; *i.e.* that which hinders and prevents, in opposition to impulse and purpose. For the compulsory is called necessary, and hence the necessary is disagreeable; as indeed Evenus says:

For every necessary thing is by nature grievous.

And compulsion is a kind of necessity, as Sophocles says:

Compulsion makes me do this of necessity.

And necessity is held, rightly, to be something inexorable; for it is opposed to motion which is in accordance with purpose and calculation. (*d*) Again, what cannot be otherwise we say is necessarily so. It is from this sense of "necessary" that all others are somehow derived; for the term "compulsory" is used of something which it is necessary for one to do or suffer only when it is impossible to act according to impulse, because of the compulsion: which shows that necessity is that because of which a thing cannot be otherwise; and the same is true of the concomitant conditions of living and of the good. For when in the one case good, and in the other life or existence, is impossible without certain conditions, these conditions are necessary, and the cause is a kind of necessity. (*e*) Again, demonstration is a "necessary" thing, because a thing cannot be otherwise if the demonstration has been absolute. And this is the result of the first premises, when it is impossible for the assumptions upon which the syllogism depends to be otherwise.

Thus of necessary things, some have an external cause of their necessity, and others have not, but it is through them that other things are of necessity what they are. Hence the "necessary" in the primary and proper sense is the *simple*, for it cannot be in more than one condition. Hence it cannot be in one state *and* in another; for if so it would *ipso facto* be in more than one condition. Therefore if there are certain things which are eternal and immutable, there is nothing in them which is compulsory or which violates their nature.

.   .   .

VII. "Being" means (i.) accidental being, (ii.) absolute being. (i.) *E.g.*, we say that the upright person "is" cultured, and that the man "is" cultured, and that the cultured person "is" a man; very much as we say that the cultured person builds, because the builder happens to be cultured, or the cultured person a builder; for in this sense "X is Y" means that Y is an accident of X. And so it is with the examples cited above; for when we say that "the man is cultured" and "the cultured person is a man" or "the white is cultured" or "the cultured is white," in the last two cases it is because both predicates are accidental to the same subject, and in the first case because the predicate is accidental to what *is;* and we say that "the cultured is a man" because "the cultured" is accidental to "a man." (Similarly "not-white" is said to "be," because the subject of which "not-white" is an accident, *is.*) These, then, are the senses in which things are said to "be" accidentally: either because both predicates belong to the same subject, which *is;* or because the predicate belongs to the subject, which *is;* or because the subject to which belongs that of which it is itself predicated itself *is.*

(ii.) The senses of essential being are those which are indicated by the figures of predication [11]; for "being" has as many senses as there are ways of predication. Now since some predicates indicate (*a*) what a thing is, and others its (*b*) quality, (*c*) quantity, (*d*) relation, (*e*) activity or passivity, (*f*) place, (*g*) time, to each of these corresponds a sense of "being." There is no difference between "the man is recovering" and "the man recovers"; or between "the man is walking" or "cutting" and "the man walks" or "cuts"; and similarly in the other cases.

(iii.) Again, "to be" and "is" mean that a thing is true, and "not to be" that it is false. Similarly too in affirmation and negation; *e.g.*, in "Socrates is cultured" "is" means that this is true; or in "Socrates is not-white" that this is true; but in "the diagonal is not commensurable" "is not" means that the statement is false.

(iv.) Again, "to be" <or "is"> means that some of these statements can be made in virtue of a potentiality and others in virtue of an actuality. For we say that both that which sees potentially and that which sees actually *is* "a seeing thing." And in the same way we call "understanding" both that which *can* use the understanding, and that which *does;* and we call "tranquil" both that in which tranquillity is already present, and that which is potentially tranquil. Similarly too in the case of substances. For we say that Hermes is in the stone, and the half of the line in the whole; and we call "corn" what is not yet ripe. But when a thing is potentially existent and when not, must be defined elsewhere.

VIII. "Substance" means (*a*) simple bodies, *e.g.* earth, fire, water and the like; and in general bodies, and the things, animal or divine, including their parts, which are composed of bodies. All these are called substances because they are not predicated of any substrate, but other things are predicated of them. (*b*) In another sense, whatever, being immanent in such things as are not predicated of a substrate, is the cause of their being; as, *e.g.*, the soul is the cause of being for the animal. (*c*) All parts immanent in things which define and indicate their individuality, and whose destruction causes the destruction of the whole; as, *e.g.*, the plane is essential to the body (as some hold) and the line to the plane. And

---

11 The categories. For the full list of these see *Categories* 1 b.

number in general is thought by some to be of this nature, on the ground that if it is abolished nothing exists, and that it determines everything. (*d*) Again, the *essence*, whose formula is the definition, is also called the substance of each particular thing.

Thus it follows that "substance" has two senses: the ultimate subject, which cannot be further predicated of something else; and whatever has an individual and separate existence. The shape and form of each particular thing is of this nature.

IX. "The same" means (*a*) accidentally the same. *E.g.*, "white" and "cultured" are the same because they are accidents of the same subject; and "man" is the same as "cultured," because one is an accident of the other; and "cultured" is the same as "man" because it is an accident of "man"; and "cultured man" is the same as each of the terms "cultured" and "man," and *vice versa*; for both "man" and "cultured" are used in the same way as "cultured man," and the latter in the same way as the former. Hence none of these predications can be made universally. For it is not true to say that every man is the same as "the cultured"; because universal predications are essential to things, but accidental predications are not so, but are made of individuals and with a single application. "Socrates" and "cultured Socrates" seem to be the same; but "Socrates" is not a class-name, and hence we do not say "every Socrates" as we say "every man." Some things are said to be "the same" in this sense, but (*b*) others in an essential sense, in the same number of senses as "the one" is essentially one; for things whose matter is formally or numerically one, and things whose substance is one, are said to be the same. Thus "sameness" is clearly a kind of unity in the being, either of two or more things, or of one thing treated as more than one; as, *e.g.*, when a thing is consistent with itself; for it is then treated as two.

Things are called "other" of which either the forms or the matter or the definition of essence is more than one; and in general "other" is used in the opposite senses to "same."

Things are called "different" which, while being in a sense the same, are "other" not only numerically, but formally or generically or analogically; also things whose genus is not the same; and contraries; and all things which contain "otherness" in their essence.

Things are called "like" which have the same attributes in all respects; or more of those attributes the same than different; or whose quality is one. Also that which has a majority or the more important of those attributes of something else in respect of which change is possible (*i.e.* the contraries) is like that thing. And "unlike" is used in the opposite senses to "like."

X. The term "opposite" is applied to (*a*) contradiction; (*b*) contraries; (*c*) relative terms; (*d*) privation; (*e*) state; (*f*) extremes; *e.g.* in the process of generation and destruction. And (*g*) all things which cannot be present at the same time in that which admits of them both are called opposites; either themselves or their constituents. "Grey" and "white" do not apply at the same time to the same thing, and hence their constituents are opposite.

"Contrary" means: (*a*) attributes, generically different, which cannot apply at the same time to the same thing. (*b*) The most different attributes in the same genus; or (*c*) in the same subject; or (*d*) falling under the same faculty. (*e*) Things whose difference is greatest absolutely, or in genus, or in species. Other things are called "contrary" either because they possess attributes of this kind, or because they are receptive of them, or because they are productive of or liable to them, or actually produce or incur them, or are rejections or acquisitions or possessions or privations of such attributes. And since "one" and "being" have various meanings, all other terms which are used in relation to "one" and "being" must vary in meaning with them; and so "same," "other" and "contrary" must so vary, and so must have a separate meaning in accordance with each category.

Things are called "other in species" (*a*) which belong to the same genus and are not subordinate one to the other; or (*b*) which are in the same genus and contain a differentia; or (*c*) which contain a contrariety in their essence. (*d*) Contraries, too (either all of them or those which are called so in a primary sense), are "other in species" than one another; and (*e*) so are all things of which the formulae are different in the final species of the genus (*e.g.*, "man" and "horse" are generically indivisible, but their formulae are different); and (*f*) attributes of the same substance which contain a difference. "The same in species" has the opposite meanings to these.

XI. "Prior" and "posterior" mean: (i.) (*a*) In one sense (assuming that there is in each genus some primary thing or starting-point) that which is nearer to some starting-point, determined either absolutely and naturally, or relatively, or locally, or by some agency; *e.g.*, things are prior in space because they are nearer either to some place naturally determined, such as the middle or the extreme, or to some chance relation; and that which is further is posterior. (*b*) In another sense, prior or posterior in *time*. Some things are prior as being further from the present, as in the case of past events (for the Trojan is prior to the Persian war, because it is further distant from the present); and others as being nearer the present, as in the case of future events (for the Nemean are prior to the Pythian games because they are nearer to the present, regarded as a starting-point and as primary). (*c*) In another sense, in respect of motion (for that which is nearer to the prime mover is prior; *e.g.*, the boy is prior to the man). This too is a kind of starting-point in an absolute sense. (*d*) In respect of potency; for that which is superior in potency, or more potent, is prior. Such is that in accordance with whose will the other, or posterior, thing must follow, so that according as the former moves or does not move, the latter is or is not moved. And the *will* is a "starting-point." (*e*) In respect of order; such are all things which are systematically arranged in relation to some one determinate object. *E.g.*, he who is next to the leader of the chorus is prior to him who is next but one, and the seventh string is prior to the eighth; for in one case the leader is the starting-point, and in the other the middle string.

In these examples "prior" has this sense; but (ii.) in another sense that which is prior in knowledge is treated as absolutely prior; and of things which are prior in this sense the prior in *formula* are different from the prior in *perception*. Universals are prior in formula, but particulars in perception. And in formula the attribute is prior to the concrete whole: *e.g.* "cultured" to "the cultured man"; for the formula will not be a whole without the part. Yet "cultured" cannot exist apart from some cultured person.

Again, (iii.) attributes of prior subjects are called prior; *e.g.*, straightness is prior to smoothness, because the former is an attribute of the line in itself, and the latter of a surface.

Some things, then, are called prior and posterior in this sense; but others (iv.) in virtue of their nature and substance, namely all things which can exist apart from other things, whereas other things cannot exist without them. This distinction was used by Plato. (And since "being" has various meanings, (*a*) the substrate, and therefore substance, is prior; (*b*) potential priority is different from actual priority. Some things are prior potentially, and some actually; *e.g.*, potentially the half-line is prior to the whole, or the part to the whole, or the matter to the substance; but actually it is posterior, because it is only upon dissolution that it will actually exist.) Indeed, in a sense all things which are called "prior" or "posterior" are so called in this connexion; for some things can exist apart from others in generation (*e.g.* the whole without the parts), and others in destruction (*e.g.* the parts without the whole). And similarly with the other examples.

XII. "Potency" means: (*a*) the source of motion or change which is in something other than the thing changed, or in it *qua* other. *E.g.*, the science of building is a potency which is not present in the thing built; but the science of medicine, which is a potency, may be present in the patient, although not *qua* patient. Thus "potency" means the source in general of change or motion in another thing, or in the same thing *qua* other; or the source of a thing's being moved or changed by another thing, or by itself *qua* other (for in virtue of that principle by which the passive thing is affected in any way we call it capable of being affected; sometimes if it is affected at all, and sometimes not in respect of every affection, but only if it is changed for the better). (*b*) The power of performing this well or according to intention; because sometimes we say that those who can merely take a walk, or speak, without doing it as well as they intended, *cannot* speak or walk. And similarly in the case of passivity. (*c*) All states in virtue of which things are unaffected generally, or are unchangeable, or cannot readily deteriorate, are called "potencies." For things are broken and worn out and bent and in general destroyed not through potency but through impotence and deficiency of some sort; and things are unaffected by such processes which are scarcely or slightly affected because they have a potency and are potent and are in a definite state.

Since "potency" has all these meanings, "potent" (or "capable") will mean (*a*) that which contains a source of motion or change (for even what is static is "potent" in a sense) which takes place in another thing, or in itself *qua* other. (*b*) That over which something else has a potency of this kind. (*c*) That which has the potency of changing things, either for the worse or for the better (for it seems that even that which perishes is "capable" of perishing; otherwise, if it had been incapable, it would not have perished. As it is, it has a kind of disposition or cause or principle which induces such an affection. Sometimes it seems to be such as it is because it *has* something, and sometimes because it is *deprived* of something; but if privation is in a sense a state or "habit," everything will be "potent" through *having* something; and so a thing is "potent" in virtue of having a certain "habit" or principle, and also in virtue of having the privation of that "habit," if it can *have* privation; and if privation is not in a sense "habit," the term "potent" is equivocal). (*d*) A thing is "potent" if neither any other thing nor itself *qua* other contains a potency or principle destructive of it. (*e*) All these things are "potent" either because they merely might chance to happen or not to happen, or because they might do so *well.* Even in inanimate things this kind of potency is found; *e.g.* in instruments; for they say that one lyre "can" be played, and another not at all, if it has not a good tone.

"Impotence" is a privation of potency—a kind of abolition of the principle which has been described—either in general or in something which would naturally possess that principle, or even at a time when it would naturally already possess it (for we should not use "impotence"—in respect of begetting—in the same sense of a boy, a man and a eunuch). Again, there is an "impotence" corresponding to each kind of potency; both to the kinetic and to the successfully kinetic.

Some things are said to be "impotent" in accordance with this meaning of "impotence," but others in a different sense, namely "possible" and "impossible." "Impossible" means: (*a*) that whose contrary is necessarily true; *e.g.*, it is impossible that the diagonal of a square should be commensurable with the sides, because such a thing is a lie, whose contrary is not only true but inevitable. Hence that it is commensurable is not only a lie but necessarily a lie. And the contrary of the impossible, *i.e.* the possible, is when the contrary is not necessarily a lie; *e.g.*, it is possible that a man should be seated, for it is not necessarily a lie that he should not be seated. "Possible," then, means in one sense, as we have said, that which is not necessarily a lie; in another, that which is true; and in another, that which may be true.

(The "power" in geometry is so called by an extension of meaning.)

These are the senses of "potent" which do not correspond to "potency." Those which do correspond to it all refer to the first meaning, *i.e.* "a source of change which exists in something other than that in which the change takes place, or in the same thing *qua* other." Other things are said to be "potent" because something else has such a potency over them; others because it does not possess it; others because it possesses it in a particular way. The term "impotent" is similarly used. Thus the authoritative definition of "potency" in the primary sense will be "a principle producing change, which is in something other than that in which the change takes place, or in the same thing *qua* other."

XIII. "Quantity" means that which is divisible into constituent parts, each or every one of which is by nature some one individual thing. Thus plurality, if it is numerically calculable, is a kind of quantity; and so is magnitude, if it is measurable. "Plurality" means that which is potentially divisible into non-continuous parts; and "magnitude" that which is potentially divisible into continuous parts. Of kinds of magnitude, that which is continuous in one direction is length; in two directions, breadth; in three, depth. And of these, plurality, when limited, is a number; length, a line; breadth, a plane; depth, a body. Again, some things are essentially quantitative, but others only accidentally; *e.g.* the line is essentially, but "cultured" accidentally quantitative. And of the former class some are quantitative in virtue of their substance, *e.g.* the line (because the definition which describes it is quantitative in some form); and others are attributes and conditions of a substance of this kind—*e.g.*, "much" and "little," "long" and "short," "broad" and "narrow," "deep" and "shallow," "heavy" and "light," etc. Moreover, "great" and "small," and "greater" and "smaller," whether used absolutely or relatively to one another, are essential attributes of quantity; by an extension of meaning, however, these terms are also applied to other things. Of things called quantitative in an accidental sense, one kind is so called in the sense in which we said above that "cultured" or "white" is quantitative—because the subject to which they belong is quantitative; and others in the sense that motion and time are so called—for these too are said in a sense to be quantitative and continuous, since the subjects of which they are attributes are divisible. I mean, not the thing moved, but that through or along which the motion has taken place; for it is because the latter is quantitative that the motion is quantitative, and because the motion is quantitative that the time is also.

XIV. "Quality" means (*a*) in one sense, the differentia of essence; *e.g.*, a man is an animal of a certain quality because he is two-footed; and so is a horse, because it is four-footed. Also a circle is a geometrical figure of a certain quality, because it has no angles; which shows that the essential differentia is quality. In this one sense, then, "quality" means differentia of essence; but (*b*) in another it is used as of immovable and mathematical objects, in the sense that numbers are in a way qualitative—*e.g.* such as are composite and are represented geometrically not by a line but by a plane or solid (these are products respectively of two and of three factors)—and in general means that which is present besides quantity in the essence. For the essence of each number is that which goes into it once; *e.g.* that of 6 is not what goes twice or three times, but what goes once; for 6 is once 6. (*c*) All affections of substance in motion in respect of which bodies become different when they (the affections) change—*e.g.* heat and cold, whiteness and blackness, heaviness and lightness, etc. (*d*) The term is used with reference to goodness and badness, and in general to good and bad.

Thus there are, roughly speaking, two meanings which the term "quality" can bear, and of these one is more fundamental than the other. Quality in the primary sense is the differentia of the essence; and quality in numbers falls under this sense, because it is a kind of differentia of essences, but of things either not in motion or not *qua* in motion. Secondly, there are the affections of things in motion *qua* in motion, and the differentiae of motions. Goodness and badness fall under these affections, because they denote differentiae of the motion or functioning in respect of which things in motion act or are acted upon well or badly. For that which can function or be moved in such-and-such a way is good, and that which can function in such-and-such a way *and* in the contrary way is bad. Quality refers especially to "good" and "bad" in the case of living things, and of these especially in the case of such as possess choice.

. . .

XVII. "Limit" means: (*a*) The furthest part of each thing, and the first point outside which no part of a thing can be found, and the first point within which all parts are contained. (*b*) Any form of magnitude or of something possessing magnitude. (*c*) The end of each thing. (This end is that *to* which motion and action proceed, and not the end *from* which. But sometimes it is both the end from which and the end to which, *i.e.* the final cause.) (*d*) The reality or essence of each thing; for this is the limit of our knowledge of it, and if it is a limit of the knowledge, it is also a limit of the thing. Thus it is obvious that "limit" has not only as many senses as "beginning" but even more; because the beginning is a kind of limit, but not every limit is a beginning.

. . .

XXI. "Affected" means (*a*) In one sense, a quality in virtue of which alteration is possible; *e.g.*, whiteness and blackness, sweetness and bitterness, heaviness and lightness, etc. (*b*) The actualizations of these qualities: *i.e.* the alterations already realized. (*c*) More particularly, hurtful alterations and motions, and especially hurts which cause suffering. (*d*) Extreme cases of misfortune and suffering are called "affections." [12]

XXII. We speak of "privation"; (*a*) In one sense, if a thing does not possess an attribute which is a natural possession, even if the thing itself would not naturally possess it [13]; *e.g.*, we say that a vegetable is is "deprived" of eyes. (*b*) If a thing does not possess an attribute which it

---

[12] The English equivalent for πάθος in this sense would be "calamity" or "disaster."

[13] This is not a proper sense of privation, as Aristotle implies by choosing an example from everyday speech.

or its genus would naturally possess. *E.g.*, a blind man is not "deprived" of sight in the same sense that a mole is; the latter is "deprived" in virtue of its genus, but the former in virtue of himself.[14] (*c*) If a thing has not an attribute which it would naturally possess, and when it would naturally possess it (for blindness is a form of privation; but a man is not blind at *any* age, but only if he lacks sight at the age when he would naturally possess it), and similarly if it lacks an attribute in the medium and organ and relation and manner in which it would naturally possess it. (*d*) The forcible removal of anything is called privation. (*e*) Privation has as many senses as there are senses of negation derived from the negative affix (*ă-*). For we call a thing "unequal" because it does not possess equality (though it would naturally do so); and "invisible" either because it has no colour at all or because it has only a faint one; and "footless" either because it has no feet at all or because it has rudimentary feet. Again, a negative affix may mean "having something in a small degree"—*e.g.* "stoneless"—that is, having it in some rudimentary manner. Again, it may mean having it "not easily" or "not well"; *e.g.*, "uncutable" means not only that which cannot be cut, but that which cannot be cut easily or well. And again, it may mean not having a thing at all; for it is not the one-eyed man, but the man who lacks sight in both eyes, who is called blind. Hence not every man is good or bad, moral or immoral; there is also the intermediate state.

. . .

Book IX (*complete*)

I. We have now dealt with Being in the primary sense, to which all the other categories of being are related; *i.e.* substance. For it is from the concept of substance that all the other modes of being take their meaning; both quantity and quality and all other such terms; for they will all involve the concept of substance, as we stated it in the beginning of our discussion. And since the senses of being are analysable not only into substance or quality or quantity, but also in accordance with potentiality and actuality and function, let us also gain a clear understanding about potentiality and actuality; and first about potentiality in the sense which is most proper to the word, but not most useful for our present purpose—for potentiality and actuality extend beyond the sphere of terms which only refer to motion. When we have discussed this sense of potentiality we will, in the course of our definitions of actuality, explain the others also.

We have made it plain elsewhere that "potentiality" and "can" have

---

[14] *i.e.*, a mole is blind as being a member of a blind genus, whereas a man is blind only as an individual. Of course moles are not really blind, but we still speak as though they were.

several senses. All senses which are merely equivocal may be dismissed; for some are used by analogy, as in geometry, and we call things possible or impossible because they "are" or "are not" in some particular way. But the potentialities which conform to the same type are all principles, and derive their meaning from one primary sense of potency, which is the source of change in some other thing, or in the same thing *qua* other.

One kind of potentiality is the power of being affected; the principle in the patient itself which initiates a passive change in it by the action of some other thing, or of itself *qua* other. Another is a positive state of impassivity in respect of deterioration or destruction by something else or by itself *qua* something else; *i.e.* by a transformatory principle—for all these definitions contain the formula of the primary sense of potentiality. Again, all these potentialities are so called either because they merely act or are acted upon in a particular way, or because they do so *well*. Hence in their formulae also the formulae of potentiality in the senses previously described are present in some degree.

Clearly, then, in one sense the potentiality for acting and being acted upon is one (for a thing is "capable" both because it itself possesses the power of being acted upon, and also because something else has the power of being acted upon by it); and in another sense it is not; for it is partly in the patient (for it is because it contains a certain principle, and because even the matter is a kind of principle, that the patient is acted upon; *i.e.*, one thing is acted upon by another: oily stuff is inflammable, and stuff which yields in a certain way is breakable, and similarly in other cases)—and partly in the agent; *e.g.* heat and the art of building: the former in that which produces heat, and the latter in that which builds. Hence in so far as it is a natural unity, nothing is acted upon by itself; because it is one, and not a separate thing. "Incapacity" and "the incapable" is the privation contrary to "capacity" in this sense; so that every "capacity" has a contrary incapacity for producing the same result in respect of the same subject.

Privation has several senses—it is applied (i.) to anything which does not possess a certain attribute; (ii.) to that which would naturally possess it, but does not; either (*a*) in general, or (*b*) when it would naturally possess it; and either (1) in a particular way, *e.g.* entirely, or (2) in any way at all. And in some cases if things which would naturally possess some attribute lack it as the result of constraint, we say that they are "deprived."

II. Since some of these principles are inherent in inanimate things, and others in animate things and in the soul and in the rational part of the soul, it is clear that some of the potencies also will be irrational and some rational. Hence all arts, *i.e.* the productive sciences, are potencies; because they are principles of change in another thing, or in the artist himself *qua* other.

Every rational potency admits equally of contrary results, but irrational potencies admit of one result only. *E.g.*, heat can only produce heat, but medical science can produce disease and health. The reason of this is that science is a rational account, and the same account explains both the thing and its privation, though not in the same way; and in one sense it applies to both, and in another sense rather to the actual fact. Therefore such sciences must treat of contraries—essentially of the one, and non-essentially of the other; for the rational account also applies essentially to the one, but to the other in a kind of accidental way, since it is by negation and removal that it throws light on the contrary. For the contrary is the primary privation, and this is the removal of that to which it is contrary. And since contrary attributes cannot be induced in the same subject, and science is a potency which depends upon the possession of a rational formula, and the soul contains a principle of motion, it follows that whereas "the salutary" can only produce health, and "the calefactory" only heat, and "the frigorific" only cold, the scientific man can produce both contrary results. For the rational account includes both, though not in the same way; and it is in the soul, which contains a principle of motion, and will therefore, by means of the same principle, set both processes in motion, by linking them with the same rational account. Hence things which have a rational potency produce results contrary to those of things whose potency is irrational; for the results of the former are included under one principle, the rational account. It is evident also that whereas the power of merely producing (or suffering) a given effect is implied in the power of producing that effect *well*, the contrary is not always true; for that which produces an effect well must also produce it, but that which merely produces a given effect does not necessarily produce it well.

III. There are some, *e.g.* the Megaric school, who say that a thing only has potency when it functions, and that when it is not functioning it has no potency. *E.g.*, they say that a man who is not building cannot build, but only the man who is building, and at the moment when he is building; and similarly in the other cases. It is not difficult to see the absurd consequences of this theory. Obviously a man will not be a builder unless he is building, because "to be a builder" is "to be capable of building"; and the same will be true of the other arts. If, therefore, it is impossible to possess these arts without learning them at some time and having grasped them, and impossible not to possess them without having lost them at some time (through forgetfulness or some affection or the lapse of time; not, of course, through the destruction of the object of the art, because it exists always), when the artist ceases to practise his art, he will not possess it; and if he immediately starts building again, how will he have re-acquired the art?

The same is true of inanimate things. Neither the cold nor the hot nor the sweet nor in general any sensible thing will exist unless we are perceiving it (and so the result will be that they are affirming Protagoras' theory). Indeed, nothing will have the faculty of sensation unless it is perceiving, *i.e.* actually employing the faculty. If, then, that is blind which has not sight, though it would naturally have it, and when it would naturally have it, and while it still exists, the same people will be blind many times a day; and deaf too.

Further, if that which is deprived of its potency is incapable, that which is not happening will be incapable of happening; and he who says that that which is incapable of happening *is* or *will be,* will be in error, for this is what "incapable" meant. Thus these theories do away with both motion and generation; for that which is standing will always stand, and that which is sitting will always sit; because if it is sitting it will not get up, since it is impossible that anything which is incapable of getting up should get up. Since, then, we cannot maintain this, obviously potentiality and actuality are different. But these theories make potentiality and actuality identical; hence it is no small thing that they are trying to abolish.

Thus it is possible that a thing may be capable of being and yet not be, and capable of not being and yet be; and similarly in the other categories that which is capable of walking may not walk, and that which is capable of not walking may walk. A thing is capable of doing something if there is nothing impossible in its having the actuality of that of which it is said to have the potentiality. I mean, *e.g.,* that if a thing is capable of sitting and is not prevented from sitting, there is nothing impossible in its actually sitting; and similarly if it is capable of being moved or moving or standing or making to stand or being or becoming or not being or not becoming.

The term "actuality," with its implication of "complete reality," has been extended from motions, to which it properly belongs, to other things; for it is agreed that actuality is properly motion. Hence people do not invest non-existent things with motion, although they do invest them with certain other predicates. *E.g.,* they say that non-existent things are conceivable and desirable, but not that they are in motion. This is because, although these things do not exist actually, they will exist actually; for some non-existent things exist potentially; yet they do not exist, because they do not exist in complete reality.

IV. Now if, as we have said, that is possible which does not involve an impossibility, obviously it cannot be true to say that so-and-so is possible, but will not be; this view entirely loses sight of the instances of impossibility. I mean, suppose that someone—*i.e.* the sort of man who does not take the impossible into account—were to say that it is possible to measure the diagonal of a square, but that it will not be measured, because there is nothing to prevent a thing which is capable of being or coming to be from neither being nor being likely ever to be. But from our premises this necessarily follows: that if we are to assume that which is not, but is possible, to be or to have come to be, nothing impossible must be involved. But in this case something impossible will take place; for the measuring of the diagonal is impossible.

The false is of course not the same as the impossible; for although it is false that you are now standing, it is not impossible. At the same time it is also clear that if B must be real if A is, then if it is possible for A to be real, it must also be possible for B to be real; for even if B is not necessarily possible, there is nothing to prevent its being possible. Let A, then, be possible. Then when A was possible, if A was assumed to be real, nothing impossible was involved; but B was necessarily real too. But *ex hypothesi* B was impossible. Let B be impossible. Then if B is impossible, A must also be impossible. But A was by definition possible. Therefore so is B.

If, therefore, A is possible, B will also be possible; that is if their relation was such that if A is real, B must be real. Then if, A and B being thus related, B is not possible on this condition, A and B will not be related as we assumed; and if when A is possible B is necessarily possible, then if A is real B must be real too. For to say that B must be possible if A is possible means that if A is real at the time when and in the way in which it was assumed that it was possible for it to be real, then B must be real at that time and in that way.

V. Since all potencies are either innate, like the senses, or acquired by practice, like flute-playing, or by study, as in the arts, some—such as are acquired by practice or a rational formula—we can only possess when we have first exercised them; in the case of others which are not of this kind and which imply passivity, this is not necessary.

Since anything which is possible is something possible at some time and in some way, and with any other qualifications which are necessarily included in the definition; and since some things can set up processes rationally and have rational potencies, while others are irrational and have irrational potencies; and since the former class can only belong to a living thing, whereas the latter can belong both to living and to inanimate things: it follows that as for potencies of the latter kind, when the agent and the patient meet in accordance with the potency in question, the one must act and the other be acted upon; but in the former kind of potency this is not necessary, for whereas each single potency of the latter kind is productive of a single effect, those of the former kind are productive of contrary effects, so that one potency will produce at the same time contrary effects. But this is impossible. Therefore there must be some other deciding factor, by which I mean *desire* or *conscious choice*. For whichever of two things an animal desires decisively it will do, when it is in circumstances appropriate to the potency and meets with that which admits of being acted upon. Therefore everything which is rationally capable, when it desires something of which it has the capability, and in the circumstances in which it has the capability, must do that thing. Now it has the capability when that which admits of being acted upon is present and is in a certain state; otherwise it will not be able to act. (To add the qualification "if nothing external prevents it" is no longer necessary; because the agent has the capability in so far as it is a capability of acting; and this is not in all, but in certain circumstances, in which external hindrances will be excluded; for they are precluded by some of the positive qualifications in the definition.) Hence even if it wishes or desires to do two things or contrary things simultaneously, it will not do them, for it has not the capability to do them under these conditions, nor has it the capability of doing things simultaneously, since it will only do the things to which the capability applies and under the appropriate conditions.

VI. Since we have now dealt with the kind of potency which is related to motion, let us now discuss actuality; what it is, and what its qualities are. For as we continue our analysis it will also become clear with regard to the potential that we apply the name not only to that whose nature it is to move or be moved by something else, either without qualification or in some definite way, but also in other senses; and it is on this account that in the course of our inquiry we have discussed these as well.

"Actuality" means the presence of the thing, not in the sense which we mean by "potentially." We say that a thing is present potentially as Hermes is present in the wood, or the half-line in the whole, because it can be separated from it; and as we call even a man who is not studying "a scholar" if he is capable of studying. That which is present in the opposite sense to this is present actually. What we mean can be plainly seen in the particular cases by induction; we need not seek a definition for every term, but must comprehend the analogy: that as that which is actually building is to that which is capable of building, so is that which is awake to that which is asleep; and that which is seeing to that which has the eyes shut, but has the power of sight; and that which is differentiated out of matter to the matter; and the finished article to the raw material. Let actuality to be defined by one member of this antithesis, and the potential by the other.

But things are not all said to exist actually in the same sense, but only by analogy—as A is in B or to B, so is C in or to D; for the relation is either that of motion to potentiality, or that of substance to some particular matter.

Infinity and void and other concepts of this kind are said to "be" potentially or actually in a different sense from the majority of existing things, *e.g.* that which sees, or walks, or is seen. For in these latter cases the predication may sometimes be truly made without qualification, since "that which is seen" is so called sometimes because it is seen and sometimes because it is capable of being seen; but the Infinite does not exist potentially in the sense that it will ever exist separately in actuality; it is separable only in knowledge. For the fact that the process of division never ceases makes this actuality exist potentially, but not separately.

Since no action which has a limit is an end, but only a means to the end, as, *e.g.*, the process of thinning; and since the parts of the body themselves, when one is thinning them, are in motion in the sense that they are not already that which it is the object of the motion to make them, this process is not an action, or at least not a complete one, since it is not an end; it is the process which includes the end that is an action. *E.g.*, at the same time we see and have seen, understand and have understood, think and have thought; but we cannot at the same time learn and have learnt, or become healthy and be healthy. We are living well and have lived well, we are happy and have been happy, at the same time; otherwise the process would have had to cease at some time, like the thinning-process; but it has not ceased at the present moment: we both are living and have lived.

Now of these processes we should call the one type motions, and the other actualizations. Every motion is incomplete—the processes of thinning, learning, walking, building—these are motions, and incomplete at that. For it is not the same thing which at the same time is walking and has walked, or is building and has built, or is becoming and has become, or is being moved and has been moved, but two different things; and that which is causing motion is different from that which has caused motion. But the same thing at the same time is seeing and has seen, is thinking and has thought. The latter kind of process, then, is what I mean by actualization, and the former what I mean by motion.

What the actual is, then, and what it is like, may be regarded as demonstrated from these and similar considerations.

VII. We must, however, distinguish when a particular thing exists potentially, and when it does not; for it does not so exist at any and every time. *E.g.*, is earth potentially a man? No, but rather when it has already become semen, and perhaps not even then; just as not *everything* can be healed by medicine, or even by chance, but there is some definite kind of thing which is capable of it, and this is that which is potentially healthy.

The definition of that which as a result of thought comes, from existing potentially, to exist actually, is that, when it has been willed, if no external influence hinders it, it comes to pass; and the condition in the case of the patient, *i.e.* in the person who is being healed, is that nothing in him should hinder the process. Similarly a house exists potentially if there is nothing in X, the matter, to prevent it from becoming a house, *i.e.*, if there is nothing which must be added or removed or changed; then X is potentially a house; and similarly in all other cases where the generative principle is external. And in all cases where the generative principle is contained in the thing itself, one thing is potentially another when, if nothing external hinders, it will of itself become the other. *E.g.*, the semen is not yet potentially a man; for it must further undergo a change in some other medium. But when, by its own generative principle, it has already come to have the necessary attributes, in this state it is now potentially a man, whereas in the former state it has need of another principle; just as earth is not yet potentially a statue, because it must undergo a change before it becomes bronze.

It seems that what we are describing is not a particular thing, but a definite material; *e.g.*, a box is not wood, but wooden material, and wood is not earth, but earthen material; and earth also is an illustration of our point if it is similarly not some other thing, but a definite material— it is always the latter term in this series which is, in the fullest sense, potentially something else. *E.g.*, a box is not earth, nor earthen, but wooden; for it is this that is potentially a box, and this is the matter of the box—that is, wooden material in general is the matter of "box" in general, whereas the matter of a particular box is a particular piece of wood.

If there is some primary stuff, which is not further called the material of some other thing, this is primary matter. *E.g.*, if earth is "made of air," and air is not fire, but "made of fire," then fire is primary matter, not being an individual thing. For the subject or substrate is distinguishable into two kinds by either being or not being an individual thing. Take for example as the subject of the attributes "man," or "body" or "soul," and as an attribute "cultured" or "white." Now the subject, when culture is induced in it, is called not "culture" but "cultured," and the man is called not whiteness but white; nor is he called "ambulation" or "motion," but "walking" or "moving"; just as we said that things are of a definite material. Thus where "subject" has this sense, the ultimate substrate is substance; but where it has not this sense, and the predicate is a form or individuality, the ultimate substrate is matter or material substance. It is quite proper that both matter and attributes should be described by a derivative predicate, since they are both indefinite.

Thus it has now been stated when a thing should be said to exist potentially, and when it should not.

VIII. Now since we have distinguished the several senses of priority, it is obvious that actuality is prior to potentiality. By potentiality I mean not that which we have defined as "a principle of change which is in something other than the thing changed, or in that same thing *qua* other," but in general any principle of motion or of rest; for nature also is in the same genus as potentiality, because it is a principle of motion, although not in some other thing, but in the thing itself *qua* itself. To every potentiality of this kind actuality is prior, both in formula and in substance; in time it is sometimes prior and sometimes not.

That actuality is prior in formula is evident; for it is because it can be actualized that the potential, in the primary sense, is potential, I mean, *e.g.*, that the potentially constructive is that which can construct, the potentially seeing that which can see, and the potentially visible that which can be seen. The same principle holds in all other cases too, so that the formula and knowledge of the actual must precede the knowledge of the potential.

In time it is prior in this sense: the actual is prior to the potential with which it is formally identical, but not to that with which it is identical numerically. What I mean is this: that the matter and the seed and the thing which is capable of seeing, which are potentially a man and corn and seeing, but are not yet so actually, are prior in time to the individual man and corn and seeing subject which already exist in actuality. But prior in time to these potential entities are other actual entities from which the former are generated; for the actually existent is always generated from the potentially existent *by* something which is actually existent— *e.g.*, man by man, cultured by cultured—there is always some prime mover; and that which initiates motion exists already in actuality.

We have said in our discussion of substance that everything which is generated is generated from something and by something; and by something formally identical with itself. Hence it seems impossible that a man can be a builder if he has never built, or a harpist if he has never played a harp; because he who learns to play the harp learns by playing it, and similarly in all other cases. This was the origin of the sophists' quibble that a man who does not know a given science will be doing that which is the object of that science, because the learner does not know the science. But since something of that which is being generated is already generated, and something of that which is being moved as a whole is already moved (this is demonstrated in our discussion on Motion), presumably the learner too must possess something of the science. At any rate from this argument it is clear that actuality is prior to potentiality in this sense too, *i.e.* in respect of generation and time.

But it is also prior in substantiality; (*a*) because things which are posterior in generation are prior in form and substantiality; *e.g.*, adult is prior to child, and man to semen, because the one already possesses the form, but the other does not; and (*b*) because everything which is generated moves towards a principle, *i.e.* its *end*. For the object of a thing is its principle; and generation has as its object the *end*. And the actuality is the end, and it is for the sake of this that the potentiality is acquired; for animals do not see in order that they may have sight, but have sight in order that they may see. Similarly men possess the art of building in order that they may build, and the power of speculation that they may speculate; they do not speculate in order that they may have the power of speculation—except those who are learning by practice; and they do not really speculate, but only in a limited sense, or about a subject about which they have no desire to speculate.

Further, matter exists potentially, because it may attain to the form; but when it exists actually, it is then *in* the form. The same applies in all other cases, including those where the end is motion. Hence, just as teachers think that they have achieved their end when they have exhibited their pupil performing, so it is with nature. For if this is not so, it will be another case of "Pauson's Hermes"; it will be impossible to say whether the knowledge is *in* the pupil or outside him, as in the case of the Hermes. For the activity is the end, and the actuality is the activity; hence the term "actuality" is derived from "activity," and tends to have the meaning of "complete reality."

Now whereas in some cases the ultimate thing is the use of the faculty, as, *e.g.*, in the case of sight seeing is the ultimate thing, and sight produces nothing else besides this; but in other cases something is produced, *e.g.* the art of building produces not only the act of building but a house; nevertheless in the one case the use of the faculty is the end, and in the other it is more truly the end than is the potentiality. For the act of building resides in the thing built; *i.e.*, it comes to be and exists simultaneously with the house.

Thus in all cases where the result is something other than the exercise of the faculty, the actuality resides in the thing produced; *e.g.* the act of building in the thing built, the act of weaving in the thing woven, and so on; and in general the motion resides in the thing moved. But where there is no other result besides the actualization, the actualization resides in the subject; *e.g.* seeing in the seer, and speculation in the speculator, and life in the soul (and hence also happiness, since happiness is a particular kind of life). Evidently, therefore, substance or form is actuality. Thus it is obvious by this argument that actuality is prior in substantiality to potentiality; and that in point of time, as we have said, one actuality presupposes another right back to that of the prime mover in each case.

It is also prior in a deeper sense; because that which is eternal is prior in substantiality to that which is perishable, and nothing eternal is potential. The argument is as follows. Every potentiality is at the same time a potentiality for the opposite. For whereas that which is incapable of happening cannot happen to anything, everything which is capable may fail to be actualized. Therefore that which is capable of being may both be and not be. Therefore the same thing is capable both of being and of not being. But that which is capable of not being may possibly not be; and that which may possibly not be is perishable; either absolutely, or in the particular sense in which it is said that it may possibly not be; that is, in respect either of place or of quantity or of quality. "Absolutely" means in respect of substance. Hence nothing which is absolutely imperishable is absolutely potential (although there is no reason why it should not be potential in some particular respect; *e.g.* of quality or place); therefore all imperishable things are actual. Nor can anything which is of necessity be potential; and yet these things are primary, for if they did not exist, nothing would exist. Nor can motion be potential, if there is any eternal motion. Nor, if there is anything eternally in motion, is it potentially in motion (except in respect of some starting-point or destination), and there is no reason why the matter of such a thing should not exist. Hence the sun and stars and the whole visible heaven are always active, and there is no fear that they will ever stop—a fear which the writers on physics entertain. Nor do the heavenly bodies tire in their activity; for motion does not imply for them, as it does for perishable things, the potentiality for the opposite, which makes the continuity of the motion distressing; this results when the substance is matter and potentiality, not actuality.

Imperishable things are resembled in this respect by things which are always undergoing transformation, such as earth and fire; for the latter too are always active, since they have their motion independently and in themselves. Other potentialities, according to the distinctions already made, all admit of the opposite result; for that which is capable of causing motion in a certain way can also cause it not in that way; that is if it acts rationally. The same irrational potentialities can only produce opposite results by their presence or absence.

Thus if there are any entities or substances such as the dialecticians describe the Ideas to be, there must be something which has much more knowledge than absolute knowledge, and much more mobility than motion; for they will be in a truer sense actualities, whereas knowledge and motion will be their potentialities. Thus it is obvious that actuality is prior both to potentiality and to every principle of change.

IX. That a good actuality is both better and more estimable than a good potentiality will be obvious from the following arguments. Everything of which we speak as capable is alike capable of contrary results; *e.g.*, that which we call capable of being well is alike capable of being ill, and has both potentialities at once; for the same potentiality admits of health and disease, or of rest and motion, or of building and of pulling down, or of being built and of falling down. Thus the capacity for two contraries can belong to a thing at the same time, but the contraries cannot belong at the same time; *i.e.*, the actualities, *e.g.* health and disease, cannot belong to a thing at the same time. Therefore one of them must be the good; but the potentiality may equally well be both or neither. Therefore the actuality is better.

Also in the case of evils the end or actuality must be worse than the potentiality; for that which is capable is capable alike of both contraries.

Clearly, then, evil does not exist apart from *things;* for evil is by nature posterior to potentiality. Nor is there in things which are original and eternal any evil or error, or anything which has been destroyed—for destruction is an evil.

Geometrical constructions, too, are discovered by an actualization, because it is by dividing that we discover them. If the division were already done, they would be obvious; but as it is the division is only there potentially. Why is the sum of the interior angles of a triangle equal to two right angles? Because the angles about one point <in a straight line> are equal to two right angles. If the line parallel to the side had been already drawn, the answer would have been obvious at sight. Why is the angle in a semicircle always a right angle? If three lines are equal, the two forming the base, and the one set upright from the middle of the base, the answer is obvious to one who knows the former proposition. Thus it is evident that the potential constructions are discovered by being actualized. The reason for this is that the actualization is an act of thinking. Thus potentiality comes from actuality (and therefore it is by constructive action that we acquire knowledge). <But this is true only in the abstract>, for the individual actuality is posterior in generation to its potentiality.

X. The terms "being" and "not-being" are used not only with reference to the types of predication, and to the potentiality or actuality, or nonpotentiality and non-actuality, of these types, but also (in the strictest sense) to denote truth and falsity. This depends, in the case of the objects, upon their being united or divided; so that he who thinks that what is divided is divided, or that what is united is united, is right; while he whose thought is contrary to the real condition of the objects is in error. Then *when* do what we call truth and falsity exist or not exist? We must consider what we mean by these terms.

It is not because we are right in thinking that you are white that you are white; it is because you are white that we are right in saying so. Now if whereas some things are always united and cannot be divided, and others are always divided and cannot be united, others again admit of both contrary states, then "to be" is to be united, *i.e.* a unity; and "not to be" is to be not united, but a plurality. Therefore as regards the class of things which admit of both contrary states, the same opinion or the same statement comes to be false and true, and it is possible at one time to be right and at another wrong; but as regards things which cannot be otherwise the same opinion is not sometimes true and sometimes false, but the same opinions are always true or always false.

But with regard to incomposite things, what is being or not-being, and truth or falsity? Such a thing is not composite, so as to be when it is united and not to be when it is divided, like the proposition that "the wood is white," or "the diagonal is incommensurable"; nor will truth and falsity apply in the same way to these cases as to the previous ones. In point of fact, just as truth is not the same in these cases, so neither is being. Truth and falsity are as follows: contact and assertion are truth (for assertion is not the same as affirmation), and ignorance is non-contact. I say ignorance, because it is impossible to be deceived with respect to what a thing is, except accidentally; and the same applies to incomposite substances, for it is impossible to be deceived about them. And they all exist actually, not potentially; otherwise they would be generated and destroyed; but as it is, Being itself is not generated (nor destroyed); if it were, it would be generated out of something. With respect, then, to all things which are essences and actual, there is no question of being mistaken, but only of thinking or not thinking them. Inquiry as to *what* they are takes the form of inquiring whether they are of such-and-such a nature or not.

As for being in the sense of truth, and not-being in the sense of falsity, a unity is true if the terms are combined, and if they are not combined it is false. Again, if the unity exists, it exists in a particular way, and if it does not exist in that way, it does not exist at all. Truth means to think these objects, and there is no falsity or deception, but only ignorance —not, however, ignorance such as blindness is; for blindness is like a total absence of the power of thinking. And it is obvious that with regard to immovable things also, if one assumes that there are immovable things, there is no deception in respect of time. *E.g.*, if we suppose that the triangle is immutable, we shall not suppose that it sometimes contains two right angles and sometimes does not, for this would imply that it changes; but we may suppose that one thing has a certain property and another has not; *e.g.*, that no even number is a prime, or that some are primes and others are not. But about a single number we cannot be mistaken even in this way, for we can no longer suppose that one instance is of such a nature, and another not, but whether we are right or wrong, the fact is always the same.

Book XII (*complete*)

I. Our inquiry is concerned with substance; for it is the principles and causes of substances that we are investigating. Indeed if the universe is to be regarded as a whole, substance is its first part; and if it is to be regarded as a succession, even so substance is first, then quality, then quantity. Moreover, the latter hardly exist at all in the full sense, but are merely qualifications and affections of Being. Otherwise "not-white" and "not-straight" would also exist; at any rate we say that they too "are," *e.g.*, "it is not white." Further, none of the other categories is separately existent. Even the ancients in effect testify to this, for it was of substance that they sought the principles and elements and causes. Present-day thinkers [15] tend to regard universals as substance, because genera are universal, and they hold that these are more truly principles and substances because they approach the question theoretically; but the ancients identified substance with particular things, *e.g.* fire and earth, and not with body in general.

Now there are three kinds of substance. One is *sensible* (and may be either eternal [16] or perishable; the latter, *e.g.* plants and animals, is universally recognized); of this we must apprehend the elements, whether they are one or many. Another is *immutable*, which certain thinkers hold to exist separately; some dividing it into two classes, others combining the Forms and the objects of mathematics into a single class, and others recognizing only the objects of mathematics as of this nature.[17] The first two kinds of substance come within the scope of physics, since they involve motion; the last belongs to some other science, if there is no principle common to all three.

Sensible substance is liable to change. Now if a change proceeds from opposites or intermediates—not however from all opposites (for speech is not white), but only from the contrary—then there must be something underlying which changes into the opposite contrary; for the contraries [18] do not change.

II. Further, something persists, whereas the contrary does not persist. Therefore besides the contraries there is some third thing, the *matter*. Now if change is of four kinds, in respect either of substance or of quality or of quantity or of place, and if change of substance is generation or destruction in the simple sense, and change of quantity is increase or decrease, and change of affection is alteration, and change of place is locomotion, then changes must be in each case into the corresponding contrary state. It must be the matter, then, which admits of both con-

---

[15] Platonists.

[16] *i.e.*, the celestial bodies.

[17] These three views were held respectively by Plato, Xenocrates and Speusippus.

[18] *i.e.*, contrary qualities.

traries, that changes. And since "that which is" is twofold, everything changes from that which is potentially to that which is actually; *e.g.* from potentially white to actually white. The same applies to increase and decrease. Hence not only may there be generation accidentally from that which is not, but also everything is generated from that which is, but is potentially and is not actually. And this is the "one" of Anaxagoras; for his "all things were together," and the "mixture" of Empedocles and Anaximander and the doctrine of Democritus would be better expressed as "all things were together potentially, but not actually." Hence these thinkers must have had some conception of matter. All things which change have matter, but different things have different kinds; and of eternal things such as are not generable but are movable by locomotion have matter; matter, however, which admits not of generation, but of motion from one place to another.

One might raise the question from what sort of "not-being" generation takes place; for not-being has three senses.[19] If a thing exists through a potentiality, nevertheless it is not through a potentiality for any chance thing; different things are derived from different things. Nor is it satisfactory to say that "all things were together," for they differ in their matter, since otherwise why did they become an infinity and not one? For Mind is one; so that if matter is also one, only that could have come to be in actuality whose matter existed potentially. The causes and principles, then, are three; two being the pair of contraries, of which one is the formula or form and the other the privation, and the third being the matter.

III. We must next observe that neither matter nor form (I mean in the proximate sense) is generated. All change is of some subject by some agent into some object. The agent is the immediate mover; the subject is the matter; and the object is the form. Thus the process will go on to infinity if not only the bronze comes to be round, but also roundness or bronze comes to be; there must, then, be some stopping-point.

We must next observe that every substance is generated from something which has the same name ("substances" including not only natural but all other products). Things are generated either by art or by nature or by chance or spontaneously. Art is a generative principle in something else; nature is a generative principle in the subject itself [20] (for man begets man); the other causes are privations of these.

There are three kinds of substance: (i.) matter, which exists individually in virtue of being apparent [21] (for everything which is character-

---

19 *i.e.*, (1) the negation of a category, (2) falsity, (3) unrealized potentiality.

20 In natural reproduction the generative principle is obviously in the parent. But the offspring is in a sense a part of the parent, and so Aristotle identifies the two.

21 Aristotle is contrasting proximate with primary matter. Fire, the primary matter of a man, is a simple undifferentiated element which cannot be perceived as such, and has no individuality. The head, and the other parts of the body, considered merely as in contact and not as forming an organic

ized by contact and not by coalescence is matter and substrate; *e.g.* fire, flesh and head; these are all matter, and the last is the matter of a substance in the strictest sense); (ii.) the "nature" [22] (existing individually) —*i.e.* a kind of positive state which is the terminus of motion; and (iii.) the particular combination of these, *e.g.* Socrates or Callias. In some cases the individuality does not exist apart from the composite substance (*e.g.*, the form of a house does not exist separately, except as the art of building; nor are these forms liable to generation and destruction; there is a distinct sense in which "house" and "health" and every artificial product, considered in the abstract, do or do not exist [23]); if it does so at all, it does so in the case of natural objects. Hence Plato was not far wrong in saying that there are as many Forms as there are kinds of natural objects; that is if there are Forms distinct from the things of our world.

Moving causes are causes in the sense of pre-existent things, but formal causes coexist with their effects. For it is when the man becomes healthy that health exists, and the shape of the bronze sphere comes into being simultaneously with the bronze sphere. Whether any form remains also afterwards is another question. In some cases there is nothing to prevent this, *e.g.* the soul may be of this nature [24] (not all of it, but the intelligent part; for presumably all of it cannot be). Clearly then there is no need on these grounds for the Ideas to exist; for man begets man, the individual begetting the particular person. And the same is true of the arts, for the art of medicine is the formula of health.

IV. In one sense the causes and principles are different for different things; but in another, if one speaks generally and analogically, they are the same for all. For the question might be raised whether the principles and elements of substances and of relations are the same or different; and similarly with respect to each of the other categories. But it is absurd that they should be the same for all; for then relations and substance would have the same constituents. What then can their common constituent be? For there is nothing common to and yet distinct from substance and the other predicable categories, yet the element is prior to that of which it is an element. Moreover substance is not an element of relations, nor is any of the latter an element of substance. Further, how can all the categories have the same elements? For no element can be the same as that which is composed of elements; *e.g.*, neither B nor A can be the same as BA (nor indeed can any of the "intelligibles," [25] *e.g.* Unity or Being, be an element; for these apply in every case, even to composite things); hence no element can be either substance or relation.

---

unity, are the proximate matter of a man; they are perceptible and individual. Flesh (in general) represents the matter in an intermediate stage.

[22] *i.e.*, form.

[23] *i.e.*, in the mind of the architect or doctor.

[24] *i.e.*, such as to survive after death.

[25] Unity and being are called intelligibles as being the most universal predicates and as contrasted with particulars, which are sensible.

But it must be one or the other. Therefore the categories have not all the same elements.

The truth is that, as we say, in one sense all things have the same elements and in another they have not. *E.g.*, the elements of sensible bodies are, let us say, (1) as form, the hot, and in another sense the cold, which is the corresponding privation; as matter, that which directly and of its own nature is potentially hot or cold. And not only these are substances, but so are (2) the compounds [26] of which they are principles, and (3) any unity which is generated from hot and cold, *e.g.* flesh or bone; for the product of hot and cold must be distinct from them. These things, then, have the same elements and principles, although specifically different things have specifically different elements; we cannot, however, say that all things have the same elements in this sense, but only by analogy: *i.e.*, one might say that there are three principles, form, privation and matter. But each of these is different in respect of each class of things, *e.g.*, in the case of colour they are white, black, surface; or again there is light, darkness and air, of which day and night are composed. And since not only things which are inherent in an object are its causes, but also certain external things, *e.g.* the moving cause, clearly "principle" and "element" are not the same; but both are causes. Principles are divided into these two kinds, and that which moves a thing or brings it to rest is a kind of principle and substance. Thus analogically there are three elements and four causes or principles; but they are different in different cases, and the proximate moving cause is different in different cases. Health, disease, body; and the moving cause is the art of medicine. Form, a particular kind of disorder, bricks; and the moving cause is the art of building. And since in the sphere of natural objects the moving cause of man is man, while in the sphere of objects of thought the moving cause is the form or its contrary, in one sense there are three causes and in another four. For in a sense the art of medicine is health, and the art of building is the form of a house, and man begets man; but besides these there is that which as first of all things moves all things.[27]

V. Now since some things can exist in separation and others cannot, it is the former that are substances. And therefore all things have the same causes, because without substance there can be no affections and motions. Next we shall see that these causes are probably soul and body, or mind, appetite and body.[28] Again, there is another sense in which by analogy the principles are the same, viz. actuality and potentiality; but these are different for different things, and apply to them in different ways. For in some cases the same thing exists now actually and now poten-

---

26 This apparently refers to the elements; fire and air are hot matter, water and earth cold matter.

27 For the first time the ultimate efficient cause is distinguished from the proximate. Aristotle is leading up to the description of the Prime Mover which occupies the latter half of the book.

28 Aristotle is thinking of animals and human beings, which are substances in the truest sense.

tially; *e.g.* wine or flesh or man (actuality and potentiality also fall under the causes as already described; for the form exists actually if it is separable, and so does the compound of form and matter, and the privation, *e.g.* darkness or disease; and the matter exists potentially, for it is this which has the potentiality of becoming both [29]); but the distinction in virtue of actuality and potentiality applies in a different sense to cases where the matter of cause and effect is not the same, in some of which the form is not the same but different. *E.g.*, the cause of a man is (i) his elements: fire and earth as matter, and the particular form; (ii) some external formal cause, viz. his father; and besides these (iii) the sun and the ecliptic,[30] which are neither matter nor form nor privation nor identical in form with him, but cause motion.

Further, we must observe that some causes can be stated universally, but others cannot. The proximate principles of all things are the proximate actual individual and another individual which exists potentially.[31] Therefore the proximate principles are not universal. For it is the particular that is the principle of particulars; "man" in general is the principle of "man" in general, but there is no such person as "man," whereas Peleus is the principle of Achilles and your father of you, and this particular B of this particular BA; but B in general is the principle of BA regarded absolutely. Again, even if the causes of substances are universal, still, as has been said, different things, *i.e.* things which are not in the same genus, as colours, sounds, substances and quantity, have different causes and elements, except in an analogical sense; and the causes of things which are in the same species are different, not in species, but because the causes of individuals are different: your matter and form and moving cause being different from mine, although in their universal formula they are the same.

As for the question what are the principles or elements of substances and relations and qualities, whether they are the same or different, it is evident that when the terms "principle" and "element" are used with several meanings they are the same for everything; but when the meanings are distinguished, they are not the same but different; except that in a certain sense they are the same for all. In a certain sense they are the same or analogous, because (*a*) everything has matter, form, privation and a moving cause; (*b*) the causes of substances may be regarded as the causes of all things, since if substances are destroyed everything is destroyed; and further (*c*) that which is first in complete reality [32] is the cause of all things. In another sense, however, proximate causes are different; there are as many proximate causes as there are contraries

---

[29] *i.e.*, of acquiring either of the contrary qualities distinguished by the form and the privation.

[30] The sun, moving in the ecliptic, approaches nearer to the earth in summer, causing generation, and recedes farther from the earth in winter, causing destruction.

[31] *i.e.*, the proximate efficient cause and proximate matter.

[32] *i.e.*, the prime mover.

which are predicated neither as genera nor with a variety of meanings [33]; and further the particular material causes are different.

Thus we have stated what the principles of sensible things are, and how many they are, and in what sense they are the same and in what sense different.

VI. Since we have seen that there are three kinds of substance, two of which are natural and one immutable, we must now discuss the last named and show that there must be some substance which is eternal and immutable. Substances are the primary reality, and if they are all perishable, everything is perishable. But motion cannot be either generated or destroyed, for it always existed; nor can time, because there can be no priority or posteriority if there is no time.[34] Hence as time is continuous, so too is motion; for time is either identical with motion or an affection of it. But there is no continuous motion except that which is spatial, and of spatial motion only that which is circular.[35]

But even if we are to suppose that there is something which is kinetic and productive although it does not actually move or produce, there will not necessarily be motion; for that which has a potentiality may not actualize it. Thus it will not help matters if we posit eternal substances, as do the exponents of the Forms, unless there is in them some principle which can cause change.[36] And even this is not enough, nor is it enough if there is another substance besides the Forms; for unless it actually functions there will not be motion. And it will still not be enough even if it does function, if its essence is potentiality; for there will not be eternal motion, since that which exists potentially may not exist. Therefore there must be a principle of this kind whose essence is actuality. Furthermore these substances [37] must be immaterial; for they must be eternal if anything is. Therefore they are actuality.

There is a difficulty, however; for it seems that everything which actually functions has a potentiality, whereas not everything which has a potentiality actually functions; so that potentiality is prior. But if this is so, there need be no reality; for everything may be capable of existing, but not yet existent. Yet if we accept the statements of the cosmologists who generate everything from Night, or the doctrine of the physicists that "all things were together," we have the same impossibility; for how can there be motion if there is no actual cause? Wood will not move itself—carpentry must act upon it; nor will the menses or the earth move themselves—the seeds must act upon the earth, and the semen on the menses. Hence some, *e.g.* Leucippus and Plato, posit an eternal actuality,

---

[33] *i.e.*, individual forms and privations of individual things.

[34] The argument seems to be: If we assume that time was generated, it follows that before that there was no time; but the very term "before" implies time. The same applies to the destruction of time.

[35] These statements are proved in *Physics* VIII. viii., ix.

[36] As there is not, according to Aristotle; *cf.* I. vii.

[37] Aristotle is now thinking not only of the prime mover (God or Mind) but also of the movers of the celestial spheres.

for they say that there is always motion; but why there is, and what it is, they do not say; nor, if it moves in this or that particular way, what the cause is. For nothing is moved at haphazard, but in every case there must be some reason present; as in point of fact things are moved in one way by nature, and in another by force or mind or some other agent. And further, what kind of motion is primary? For this is an extremely important point. Again, Plato at least cannot even explain what it is that he sometimes thinks to be the source of motion, *i.e.*, that which moves itself; for according to him the soul is posterior to motion and coeval with the sensible universe. Now to suppose that potentiality is prior to actuality is in one sense right and in another wrong; we have explained the distinction. But that actuality is prior is testified by Anaxagoras (since mind is actuality), and by Empedocles with his theory of Love and Strife, and by those who hold that motion is eternal, *e.g.* Leucippus.

Therefore Chaos or Night did not endure for an unlimited time, but the same things have always existed, either passing through a cycle or in accordance with some other principle—that is, if actuality is prior to potentiality. Now if there is a regular cycle, there must be something [38] which remains always active in the same way; but if there is to be generation and destruction, there must be something else [39] which is always active in two different ways. Therefore this must be active in one way independently, and in the other in virtue of something else, *i.e.* either of some third active principle or of the first. It must, then, be in virtue of the first; for this is in turn the cause both of the third and of the second. Therefore the first is preferable, since it was the cause of perpetual regular motion, and something else was the cause of variety; and obviously both together make up the cause of perpetual variety. Now this is just what actually characterizes motions; therefore why need we seek any further principles?

VII. Since (*a*) this is a possible explanation, and (*b*) if it is not true, we shall have to regard everything as coming from "Night" and "all things together" and "not-being," these difficulties may be considered to be solved. There is something which is eternally moved with an unceasing motion, and that circular motion. This is evident not merely in theory, but in fact. Therefore the "ultimate heaven" must be eternal. Then there is also something which moves it. And since that which is moved while it moves is intermediate, there is something which moves without being moved; something eternal which is both substance and actuality.

Now it moves in the following manner. The object of desire and the object of thought move without being moved. The primary objects of desire and thought are the same. For it is the apparent good that is the object of appetite, and the real good that is the object of the rational

---

[38] The sphere of the fixed stars.
[39] The sun, which has its own yearly orbit in the ecliptic, and a daily rotation round the earth, which is explained most economically with reference to the rotation of the sphere of the fixed stars.

will.[40] Desire is the result of opinion rather than opinion that of desire; it is the act of thinking that is the starting-point. Now thought is moved by the intelligible, and one of the series of contraries [41] is essentially intelligible. In this series substance stands first, and of substance that which is simple and exists actually. (The one and the simple are not the same; for one signifies a measure, whereas "simple" means that the subject itself is in a certain state.) But the Good, and that which is in itself desirable, are also in the same series; and that which is first in a class is always best or analogous to the best.

That the final cause may apply to immovable things is shown by the distinction of its meanings. For the final cause is not only "the good *for something*," but also "the good which is *the end of some action*." In the latter sense it applies to immovable things, although in the former it does not; and it causes motion as being an object of love, whereas all other things cause motion because they are themselves in motion. Now if a thing is moved, it can be otherwise than it is. Therefore if the actuality of "the heaven" is primary locomotion, then in so far as "the heaven" is moved, in this respect at least it is possible for it to be otherwise; *i.e.* in respect of place, even if not of substantiality. But since there is something —X—which moves while being itself unmoved, existing actually, X cannot be otherwise in any respect. For the primary kind of change is locomotion, and of locomotion circular locomotion; and this is the motion which X induces. Thus X is necessarily existent; and *qua* necessary it is good, and is in this sense a first principle.[42] For the necessary has all these meanings: that which is by constraint because it is contrary to impulse; and that without which excellence is impossible; and that which cannot be otherwise, but is absolutely necessary.

Such, then, is the first principle upon which depend the sensible universe and the world of nature. And its life is like the best which we temporarily enjoy. It must be in that state always (which for us is impossible), since its actuality is also pleasure. (And for this reason waking, sensation and thinking are most pleasant, and hopes and memories are pleasant because of them.) Now thinking in itself is concerned with that which is in itself best, and thinking in the highest sense with that which is in the highest sense best.[43] And thought thinks itself through partici-

---

40 This shows that desire in general (of which appetite and will are the irrational and rational aspects) has as its object the good.

41 Aristotle himself recognizes two series, lists or columns of contraries, similar to those of the Pythagoreans (I. v. 6). One, the positive, contains being, unity, substance, etc.; the other is negative and contains not-being, plurality, non-substance, etc. The negative terms are intelligible only in reference to the positive.

42 The argument is: X (the prime mover), since it imparts the primary motion, cannot be liable to motion (or change) of any kind. Therefore it exists of necessity, and must be good; and it is *qua* good, *i.e.*, the object of desire, that X is a first principle.

43 Since the prime mover is pure actuality, and has or rather is the highest form of life, Aristotle identifies it with the highest activity—pure thinking.

pation in the object of thought; for it becomes an object of thought by the act of apprehension and thinking, so that thought and the object of thought are the same, because that which is receptive of the object of thought, *i.e.* essence, is thought. And it actually functions when it possesses this object.[44] Hence it is actuality rather than potentiality that is held to be the divine possession of rational thought, and its active contemplation is that which is most pleasant and best. If, then, the happiness which God always enjoys is as great as that which we enjoy sometimes, it is marvellous; and if it is greater, this is still more marvellous. Nevertheless it is so. Moreover, life belongs to God. For the actuality of thought is life, and God is that actuality; and the essential actuality of God is life most good and eternal. We hold, then, that God is a living being, eternal, most good; and therefore life and a continuous eternal existence belong to God; for that is what God is.

Those who suppose, as do the Pythagoreans and Speusippus, that perfect beauty and goodness do not exist in the beginning (on the ground that whereas the first beginnings of plants and animals are causes, it is in the products of these that beauty and perfection are found) are mistaken in their views. For seed comes from prior creatures which are perfect, and that which is first is not the seed but the perfect creature. *E.g.*, one might say that prior to the seed is the man—not he who is produced from the seed, but another man from whom the seed comes.

Thus it is evident from the foregoing account that there is some substance which is eternal and immovable and separate from sensible things; and it has also been shown that this substance can have no magnitude, but is impartible and indivisible (for it causes motion for infinite time, and nothing finite has an infinite potentiality; and therefore since every magnitude is either finite or infinite, it cannot have finite magnitude, and it cannot have infinite magnitude because there is no such thing at all); and moreover that it is impassive and unalterable; for all the other kinds of motion are posterior to spatial motion. Thus it is clear why this substance has these attributes.

VIII. We must not disregard the question whether we should hold that there is one substance of this kind or more than one, and if more than one, how many; we must review the pronouncements of other thinkers and show that with regard to the number of the substances they have said nothing that can be clearly stated. The theory of the Ideas contains no peculiar treatment of the question; for the exponents of the theory call the Ideas numbers, and speak of the numbers now as though they were unlimited and now as though they were limited by the number 10; but as for why there should be just so many numbers, there is no explanation given with demonstrative accuracy. We, however, must discuss the question on the basis of the assumptions and distinctions which we have already made.

---

[44] In actualization the subject and object of thought are identical.

The first principle and primary reality is immovable, both essentially and accidentally, but it excites the primary form of motion, which is one and eternal. Now since that which is moved must be moved by something, and the prime mover must be essentially immovable, and eternal motion must be excited by something eternal, and one motion by some one thing; and since we can see that besides the simple spatial motion of the universe (which we hold to be excited by the primary immovable substances) there are other spatial motions—those of the planets—which are eternal (because a body which moves in a circle is eternal and is never at rest—this has been proved in our physical treatises); then each of these spatial motions must also be excited by a substance which is essentially immovable and eternal. For the nature of the heavenly bodies is eternal, being a kind of substance; and that which moves is eternal and prior to the moved; and that which is prior to a substance must be a substance. It is therefore clear that there must be an equal number of substances, in nature eternal, essentially immovable, and without magnitude; for the reason already stated.

Thus it is clear that the movers are substances, and that one of them is first and another second and so on in the same order as the spatial motions of the heavenly bodies. As regards the number of these motions, we have now reached a question which must be investigated by the aid of that branch of mathematical science which is most akin to philosophy, *i.e.* astronomy; for this has as its object a substance which is sensible but eternal, whereas the other mathematical sciences, *e.g.* arithmetic and geometry, do not deal with any substance. That there are more spatial motions than there are bodies which move in space is obvious to those who have even a moderate grasp of the subject, since each of the non-fixed stars has more than one spatial motion. As to how many these spatial motions actually are we shall now, to give some idea of the subject, quote what some of the mathematicians say, in order that there may be some definite number for the mind to grasp; but for the rest we must partly investigate for ourselves and partly learn from other investigators, and if those who apply themselves to these matters come to some conclusion which clashes with what we have just stated, we must appreciate both views, but follow the more accurate.

Eudoxus [45] held that the motion of the sun and moon involves in either case three spheres, of which the outermost is that of the fixed stars,[46] the second revolves in the circle which bisects the zodiac,[47] and the third revolves in a circle which is inclined across the breadth of the zodiac; [48] but the circle in which the moon moves is inclined at a greater angle than that in which the sun moves. And he held that the motion of the planets

---

[45] Of Cnidus (*circa* 408-355 B.C.). He was a pupil of Plato, and a distinguished mathematician.

[46] Not identical with that of the fixed stars, but having the same motion.

[47] *i.e.*, revolves with its equator in the ecliptic.

[48] *i.e.*, has the plane of its equator inclined to the plane of the ecliptic. This sphere carries the sun (or moon) fixed to a point in its equator.

involved in each case four spheres; and that of these the first and second are the same [49] as before (for the sphere of the fixed stars is that which carries round all the other spheres, and the sphere next in order, which has its motion in the circle which bisects the zodiac, is common to all the planets); the third sphere of all the planets has its poles in the circle which bisects the zodiac; and the fourth sphere moves in the circle inclined to the equator of the third. In the case of the third sphere, while the other planets have their own peculiar poles, those of Venus and Mercury are the same.

Callippus [50] assumed the same arrangement of the spheres as did Eudoxus (that is, with respect to the order of their intervals), but as regards their number, whereas he assigned to Jupiter and Saturn the same number of spheres as Eudoxus, he considered that two further spheres should be added both for the sun and for the moon, if the phenomena are to be accounted for, and one for each of the other planets.

But if all the spheres in combination are to account for the phenomena, there must be for each of the other planets other spheres, one less in number than those already mentioned, which counteract these and restore to the same position the first sphere of the star which in each case is next in order below.[51] In this way only can the combination of forces produce the motions of the planets. Therefore since the forces by which the planets themselves are moved are 8 for Jupiter and Saturn, and 25 for the others, and since of these the only ones which do not need to be counteracted are those by which the lowest planet [52] is moved, the counteracting spheres for the first two planets will be 6, and those of the remaining four will be 16; and the total number of spheres, both those which move the planets and those which counteract these, will be 55. If we do not invest the moon and the sun with the additional motions which we have mentioned, there will be 47 (?) [53] spheres in all.

This, then, may be taken to be the number of the spheres; and thus it is reasonable to suppose that there are as many immovable substances and principles,[54] the statement of logical necessity may be left to more competent thinkers.

If there can be no spatial motion which is not conducive to the motion of a star, and if moreover every entity and every substance which is impassive and has in itself attained to the highest good should be regarded

---

[49] Not the same, but having the same motion.

[50] Of Cyzicus (*fl.* 330 B.C.). Simplicius says (493. 5-8) that he corrected and elaborated Eudoxus's theory with Aristotle's help while on a visit to him at Athens.

[51] Aristotle is trying to establish a mechanical relation between the spheres, which Eudoxus and Callippus did not attempt to do.

[52] The moon.

[53] Either Aristotle has made a slip in his calculations, or we should read ἐννέα (Sosigenes) for ἑπτά; this would give 49, which appears to be the correct total. For alternative explanations of an error in calculation see Ross *ad loc.*

[54] *i.e.*, the movers of the spheres.

as an end, then there can be no other entity besides these,[55] and the number of the substances, they must move something, since they are the end of spatial motion. But there can be no other spatial motions besides those already mentioned. This is a reasonable inference from a general consideration of spatial motion. For if everything which moves exists for the sake of that which is moved, and every motion for the sake of something which is moved, no motion can exist for the sake of itself or of some other motion, but all motions must exist for the sake of the stars. For if we are to suppose that one motion is for the sake of another, the latter too must be for the sake of something else; and since the series cannot be infinite, the end of every motion must be one of the divine bodies which are moved through the heavens.

It is evident that there is only one heaven.[56] For if there is to be a plurality of heavens (as there is of men), the principle of each must be one in kind but many in number. But all things which are many in number have matter (for one and the same definition applies to many individuals, *e.g.* that of "man"; but Socrates is one [57]), but the primary essence has no matter, because it is complete reality. Therefore the prime mover, which is immovable, is one both in formula and in number; and therefore so also is that which is eternally and continuously in motion. Therefore there is only one heaven.

A tradition has been handed down by the ancient thinkers of very early times, and bequeathed to posterity in the form of a myth, to the effect that these heavenly bodies are gods,[58] and that the Divine pervades the whole of nature. The rest of their tradition has been added later in a mythological form to influence the vulgar and as a constitutional and utilitarian expedient; they say that these gods are human in shape or are like certain other animals,[59] and make other statements consequent upon and similar to those which we have mentioned. Now if we separate these statements and accept only the first, that they supposed the primary substances to be gods, we must regard it as an inspired saying; and reflect that whereas every art and philosophy has probably been repeatedly developed to the utmost and has perished again, these beliefs of theirs have been preserved as a relic of former knowledge. To this

---

[55] See previous note.

[56] This paragraph seems to belong to an earlier period of Aristotle's thought. At any rate the argument that plurality involves matter is inconsistent with the view that there are 55 immaterial movers.

[57] The definition or form is one and universal; it is the combination of form with matter that constitutes an individual. Thus a plurality of individuals is caused by the combination of the same form with different matter.

[58] This statement is not literally true. The planets do not seem to have been associated with the gods of popular mythology until the fourth century B.C. (see Burnet, *E.G.P.* p. 23 n.). But Aristotle's general meaning seems to be that the gods were identified with the primary natural forces; and this is substantially true.

[59] *e.g.* the Egyptian deities. Zoomorphism in Greek religion is a doubtful quantity.

extent only, then, are the views of our forefathers and of the earliest thinkers intelligible to us.

IX. The subject of Mind involves certain difficulties. Mind is held to be of all phenomena the most supernatural; but the question of how we must regard it if it is to be of this nature involves certain difficulties. If Mind thinks nothing, where is its dignity? It is in just the same state as a man who is asleep. If it thinks, but something else determines its thinking, then since that which is its essence is not thinking but potentiality,[60] it cannot be the best reality; because it derives its excellence from the act of thinking. Again, whether its essence is thought or thinking, what does it think? It must think either itself or something else; and if something else, then it must think either the same thing always, or different things at different times. Then does it make any difference, or not, whether it thinks that which is good or thinks at random? Surely it would be absurd for it to think about some subjects. Clearly, then, it thinks that which is most divine and estimable, and does not change; for the change would be for the worse, and anything of this kind would immediately imply some sort of motion. Therefore if Mind is not thinking but a potentiality, (a) it is reasonable to suppose that the continuity of its thinking is laborious; (b) clearly there must be something else which is more excellent than Mind; *i.e.* the object of thought; for both thought and the act of thinking will belong even to the thinker of the worst thoughts.[61] Therefore if this is to be avoided (as it is, since it is better not to see some things than to see them), thinking cannot be the supreme good. Therefore Mind thinks itself, if it is that which is best; and its thinking is a thinking of thinking.

Yet it seems that knowledge and perception and opinion and understanding are always of something else, and only incidentally of themselves. And further, if to think is not the same as to be thought, in respect of which does goodness belong to thought? for the act of thinking and the object of thought have not the same essence. The answer is that in some cases the knowledge is the object. In the productive sciences, if we disregard the matter, the substance, *i.e.* the essence, is the object; but in the speculative sciences the formula or the act of thinking is the object. Therefore since thought and the object of thought are not different in the case of things which contain no matter, they will be the same, and the act of thinking will be one with the object of thought.

There still remains the question whether the object of thought is composite; for if so, thought would change in passing from one part of the whole to another. The answer is that everything which contains no matter is indivisible. Just as the human mind, or rather the mind of

---

[60] *i.e.*, if its thinking is determined by something else, Mind is only a potentiality, and not (as described in ch. vii. 1-9) the highest actuality.

[61] If Mind is a potentiality, since a potentiality is of contraries, Mind may think that which is worst.

composite beings,[62] is in a certain space of time [63] (for it does not possess the good at this or at that moment, but in the course of a certain whole period it attains to the supreme good, which is other than itself), so is absolute self-thought throughout all eternity.

X. We must also consider in which sense the nature of the universe contains the good or the supreme good; whether as something separate and independent, or as the orderly arrangement of its parts. Probably in both senses, as an army does; for the efficiency of an army consists partly in the order and partly in the general; but chiefly in the latter, because he does not depend upon the order, but the order depends upon him. All things, both fishes and birds and plants, are ordered together in some way, but not in the same way; and the system is not such that there is no relation between one thing and another; there is a definite connexion. Everything is ordered together to one end; but the arrangement is like that in a household, where the free persons have the least liberty to act at random, and have all or most of their actions preordained for them, whereas the slaves and animals have little common responsibility and act for the most part at random; for the nature of each class is a principle such as we have described.[64] I mean, for example, that everything must at least come to dissolution; and similarly there are other respects in which everything contributes to the good of the whole.

We must not fail to observe how many impossibilities and absurdities are involved by other theories, and what views the more enlightened thinkers hold, and what views entail the fewest difficulties. All thinkers maintain that all things come from contraries; but they are wrong both in saying "all things" [65] and in saying that they come from contraries,[66] nor do they explain how things in which the contraries really are present come from the contraries; for the contraries cannot act upon each other. For us, however, this problem is satisfactorily solved by the fact that there is a third factor. Other thinkers make one of the two contraries matter; *e.g.*, this is done by those who make the Unequal matter for the Equal, or the Many matter for the One. But this also is disposed of in the same way; for the one matter of two contraries is contrary to nothing. Further, on their view everything except Unity itself will partake of evil; for "the Bad" [67] is itself one of the elements. The other school does

---

62 *i.e.*, beings composed of matter as well as form. Such beings are contrasted with the divine Mind, which is pure form.

63 The meaning of this sentence is shown by the definition of Happiness in *Eth. Nic.* 1098 a 16-20. It takes the human mind a lifetime of the highest intellectual activity of which it is capable to attain to happiness; but the divine Mind is always happy.

64 The free persons correspond to the heavenly bodies, whose movements are fixed by necessity; the servile class to human beings. Each class acts in accordance with its nature, a principle which "produces obedience to duty in the higher creatures, caprice in the lower" (Ross).

65 Because there is an eternal substance, which is not derived from contraries.

66 Things are derived from a substrate as well.

67 The "Bad" was identified with the unequal.

not even regard the Good and the Bad as principles; yet the Good is in the truest sense a principle in all things. The former school is right in holding that the Good is a principle, but they do not explain how it is a principle—whether as an end or as a moving cause or as form.

Empedocles' theory is also absurd, for he identifies the Good with Love. This is a principle both as causing motion (since it combines) and as matter (since it is part of the mixture). Now even if it so happens that the same thing is a principle both as matter and as causing motion, still the essence of the two principles is not the same. In which respect, then, is Love a principle? And it is also absurd that Strife should be imperishable; strife is the very essence of evil.

Anaxagoras makes the Good a principle as causing motion; for Mind moves things, but moves them for some end, and therefore there must be some other Good [68]—unless it is as we say; for on our view the art of medicine is in a sense health.[69] It is absurd also not to provide a contrary for the Good, *i.e.* for Mind.[70] But all those who recognize the contraries fail to make use of the contraries, unless we systematize their theories. And none of them explains why some things are perishable and others imperishable; for they make all existing things come from the same first principles. Again, some make existing things come from not-being, while others,[71] to avoid this necessity, make all things one. Again, no one explains why there must always be generation, and what the cause of generation is.

Moreover, those who posit two principles must admit another superior principle,[72] and so must the exponents of the Forms; for what made or makes particulars participate in the Forms? And on all other views it follows neessarily that there must be something which is contrary to Wisdom or supreme knowledge, but on ours it does not. For there is no contrary to that which is primary, since all contraries involve matter, and that which has matter exists potentially; and the ignorance which is contrary to Wisdom would tend towards the contrary of the object of Wisdom; but that which is primary has no contrary.

Further, if there is to be nothing else besides sensible things, there will be no first principle, no order, no generation, and no celestial motions, but every principle will be based upon another,[73] as in the accounts of all the cosmologists and physicists. And if the Forms or numbers are to

---

[68] Motion presupposes a final cause, which was not what Anaxagoras meant by "Mind."

[69] Aristotle identifies the efficient cause, in a sense, with the final cause.

[70] In I. vi. 10 Aristotle describes Anaxagoras as recognizing contrary principles of good and evil. Moreover, on Aristotle's own showing, evil cannot be a principle (IX. ix. 3).

[71] The Eleatics.

[72] *i.e.*, an efficient cause.

[73] If there is nothing but what is sensible or potential, there can be no prime mover (which is actuality) to excite motion in the universe, and no teleology in causation.

exist, they will be causes of nothing; or if not of nothing, at least not of motion.

Further, how can extension, *i.e.* a continuum, be produced from that which is unextended? Number cannot, either as a moving or as a formal cause, produce a continuum. Moreover, no contrary can be essentially productive and kinetic, for then it would be possible for it not to exist; and further, the act of production would in any case be posterior to the potentiality. Therefore the world of reality is not eternal. But there are real objects which are eternal. Therefore one of these premises must be rejected. We have described how this may be done.[74]

Further, in virtue of what the numbers, or soul and body, or in general the form and the object, are one, no one attempts to explain; nor is it possible to do so except on our theory, that it is the moving cause that makes them one. As for those [75] who maintain that mathematical number is the primary reality, and so go on generating one substance after another and finding different principles for each one, they make the substance of the universe incoherent (for one substance in no way affects another by its existence or non-existence) and give us a great many governing principles. But the world must not be governed badly:

> The rule of many is not good; let one be the ruler.[76]

PHYSICS

Book II (*Chapter VIII: On Purpose in Nature*)

CHAPTER VIII

We must now consider why Nature is to be ranked among causes that are final, that is to say purposeful; and further we must consider what is meant by 'necessity' when we are speaking of Nature. For thinkers are for ever referring things to necessity as a cause, and explaining that, since hot and cold and so forth are what they are, this or that exists or comes into being 'of necessity'; for even if one or another of them alleges some other cause, such as 'Sympathy and Antipathy' or 'Mind,' he straight away drops it again, after a mere acknowledgement.

So here the question rises whether we have any reason to regard Nature as making for any goal at all, or as seeking any one thing as preferable to any other. Why not say, it is asked, that Nature acts as

---

[74] By assuming an eternal actual mover.
[75] Speusippus and his followers.
[76] Homer, *Iliad* ii. 204.

Zeus drops the rain, not to make the corn grow, but of necessity (for the rising vapour must needs be condensed into water by the cold, and must then descend, and incidentally, when this happens, the corn grows), just as, when a man loses his corn on the threshing-floor, it did not rain on purpose to destroy the crop, but the result was merely incidental to the raining? So why should it not be the same with natural organs like the teeth? Why should it not be a coincidence that the front teeth come up with an edge, suited to dividing the food, and the back ones flat and good for grinding it, without there being any design in the matter? And so with all other organs that seem to embody a purpose. In cases where a coincidence brought about such a combination as might have been arranged on purpose, the creatures, it is urged, having been suitably formed by the operation of chance, survived; otherwise they perished, and still perish, as Empedocles says of his 'man-faced oxen.'

Such and suchlike are the arguments which may be urged in raising this problem; but it is impossible that this should really be the way of it. For all these phenomena and all natural things are either constant or normal, and this is contrary to the very meaning of luck or chance. No one assigns it to chance or to a remarkable coincidence if there is abundant rain in the winter, though he would if there were in the dog-days; and the other way about, if there were parching heat. Accordingly, if the only choice is to assign these occurrences either to coincidence or to purpose, and if in these cases chance coincidence is out of the question, then it must be purpose. But, as our opponents themselves would admit, these occurrences are all natural. There is purpose, then, in what is, and in what happens, in Nature.

Further, in any operation of human art, where there is an end to be achieved, the earlier and successive stages of the operation are performed for the purpose of realizing that end. Now, when a thing is produced by Nature, the earlier stages in every case lead up to the final development in the same way as in the operation of art, and *vice versa*, provided that no impediment balks the process. The operation is directed by a purpose; we may, therefore, infer that the natural process was guided by a purpose to the end that is realized. Thus, if a house were a natural product, the process would pass through the same stages that it in fact passes through when it is produced by art; and if natural products could also be produced by art, they would move along the same line that the natural process actually takes. We may therefore say that the earlier stages are for the purpose of leading to the later. Indeed, as a general proposition, the arts either, on the basis of Nature, carry things further than Nature can, or they imitate Nature. If, then, artificial processes are purposeful, so are natural processes too; for the relation of antecedent to consequent is identical in art and in Nature.

This principle comes out most clearly when we consider the other animals. For their doings are not the outcome of art (design) or of previous research or deliberation; so that some raise the question whether the works of spiders and ants and so on should be attributed to intelligence or to some similar faculty. And then, descending step by step, we find that plants too produce organs subservient to their perfect development—leaves, for instance, to shelter the fruit. Hence, if it is by nature and also for a purpose that the swallow makes her nest and the spider his web, and that plants make leaves for the sake of the fruit and strike down (and not up) with their roots in order to get their nourishment, it is clear that causality of the kind we have described is at work in things that come about or exist in the course of Nature.

Also, since the term 'nature' is applied both to material and to form, and since it is the latter that constitutes the goal, and all else is for the sake of that goal, it follows that the form is the final cause.

Now there are failures even in the arts (for writers make mistakes in writing and physicians administer the wrong dose); so that analogous failures in Nature may evidently be anticipated as possible. Thus, if in art there are cases in which the correct procedure serves a purpose, and attempts that fail are aimed at a purpose but miss it, we may take it to be the same in Nature, and monstrosities will be like failures of purpose in Nature. So if, in the primal combinations, such 'ox-creatures' as could not reach an equilibrium and goal, should appear, it would be by the miscarriage of some principle, as monstrous births are actually produced now by abortive developments of sperm. Besides, the sperm must precede the formation of the animal, and Empedocles' 'primal all-generative' is no other than such sperm.

In plants, too, though they are less elaborately articulated, there are manifest indications of purpose. Are we to suppose, then, that as there were 'ox-creatures man-faced' so also there were 'vine-growths olive-bearing'? Incongruous as such a thing seems, it ought to follow if we accept the principle in the case of animals. Moreover, it ought still to be a matter of chance what comes up when you sow this seed or that.

In general, the theory does away with the whole order of Nature, and indeed with Nature's self. For natural things are exactly those which do move continuouly, in virtue of a principle inherent in themselves, towards a determined goal; and the final development which results from any one such principle is not identical for any two species, nor yet is it any random result; but in each there is always a tendency towards an identical result, if nothing interferes with the process. A desirable result and the means to it may also be produced by chance, as for instance we say it was 'by luck' that the stranger came and ransomed the prisoner before he left, where the ransoming is done as if the man had come for that purpose, though in fact he did not. In this case the desirable result is incidental; for, as we have explained, chance is an incidental cause. But when the desirable result is effected invariably or normally, it is not an incidental or chance occurrence; and in the course of Nature the result always is achieved either invariably or normally, if nothing hinders. It is absurd to suppose that there is no purpose because in Nature we can never detect the moving power in the act of deliberation. Art, in fact, does not deliberate either, and if the shipbuilding art were incorporate in the timber, it would proceed by nature in the same way in which it now proceeds by art. If purpose, then, is inherent in art, so is it in Nature also. The best illustration is the case of a man being his own physician, for Nature is like that—agent and patient at once.

That Nature is a cause, then, and a goal-directed cause, is above dispute.

Book IV (*Chapters X-XIV: On Time*)

CHAPTER X

The subject of inquiry next in succession is 'time.' It will be well to begin with the questions which general reflections suggest as to its existence or non-existence and its nature.

The following considerations might make one suspect either that there is really no such thing as time, or at least that it has only an equivocal and obscure existence.

(1) Some of it is past and no longer exists, and the rest is future and does not yet exist; and time, whether limitless or any given length of time we take, is entirely made up of the no-longer and not-yet; and how can we conceive of that which is composed of non-existents sharing in existence in any way?

(2) Moreover, if anything divisible exists, then, so long as it is in existence, either all its parts or some of them must exist. Now time is divisible into parts, and some of these were in the past and some will be in the future, but none of them exists. The present 'now' is not part of time at all, for a part measures the whole, and the whole must be made up of the parts, but we cannot say that time is made up of 'nows.'

(3) Nor is it easy to see whether the 'now' that appears to divide the past and the future (*a*) is always one and the same or (*b*) is perpetually different.

(*b*) For if it is perpetually different, and if no two sectional parts of time can exist at once (unless one includes the other, the longer the shorter), and if the 'now' that is not, but was, must have ceased to be at *some* time or other, so also no two 'nows' can exist together, but the past 'now' must have perished before there was any other 'now.' Now it cannot have ceased to be when it was itself the 'now,' for that is just when it existed; but it is impossible that the past 'now' should have perished in any other 'now' but itself. For we must lay it down as an axiom that there can be no next 'now' to a given 'now', any more than a next point to a given point. So that if it did not perish in the next 'now,' but in some subsequent one, it would have been in existence coincidently with the countless 'nows' that lie between the 'now' in which it was and the subsequent 'now' in which we are supposing it to perish; which is impossible.

(*a*) But neither can it continuously persist in its identity. For nothing

which is finite and divisible is bounded by a single limit, whether it be
continuous in one dimension only or in more than one; but the 'now' is
a time limit, and if we take any limited period of time, it must be determined by two limits, which cannot be identical. Again, if simultaneity in
time, and not being before or after, means coinciding and being in the
very 'now' wherein they coincide, then, if the before and the after were
both in the persistently identical 'now' we are discussing, what happened
ten thousand years ago would be simultaneous with what is happening
to-day, and nothing would be before or after anything else.

Let this suffice as to the problems raised by considering the properties
of time.

But what time really is and under what category it falls, is no more
revealed by anything that has come down to us from earlier thinkers than
it is by the considerations that have just been urged. For (a) some have
identified time with the revolution of the all-embracing heaven, and (b)
some with that heavenly sphere itself. But (a) a partial revolution is time
just as much as a whole one is, but it is not just as much a revolution;
for any finite portion of time is a portion of a revolution, but is not a
revolution. Moreover, if there were more universes than one, the re-
entrant circumlation of each of them would be time, so that several different times would exist at once. And (b) as to those who declare the
heavenly sphere itself to be time, their only reason was that all things
are contained 'in the celestial sphere' and also occur 'in time,' which is
too childish to be worth reducing to absurdities more obvious than itself.

Now the most obvious thing about time is that it strikes us as some
kind of 'passing along' and changing; but if we follow this clue, we find
that, when any particular thing changes or moves, the movement or
change is in the moving or changing thing itself or occurs only where
that thing is; whereas 'the passage of time' is current everywhere alike
and is in relation with everything. And further, all changes may be faster
or slower, but not so time; for fast and slow are defined by time, 'faster'
being more change in less time, and 'slower' less in more. But time
cannot measure time thus, as though it were a distance (like the space
passed through in motion) or a qualitive modification, as in other kinds
of change. It is evident, therefore, that time is not identical with movement; nor, in this connexion, need we distinguish between movement and
other kinds of change.

CHAPTER XI

On the other hand, time cannot be disconnected from change; for
when we experience no changes of consciousness, or, if we do, are not
aware of them, no time seems to have passed, any more than it did
to the men in the fable who 'slept with the heroes' in Sardinia, when they
awoke; for under such circumstances we fit the former 'now' on to the
later, making them one and the same and eliminating the interval between

them, because we did not perceive it. So, just as there would be no time if there were no distinction between this 'now' and that 'now,' but it were always the same 'now'; in the same way there appears to be no time between two 'nows' when we fail to distinguish between them. Since, then, we are not aware of time when we do not distinguish any change (the mind appearing to abide in a single indivisible and undifferentiated state), whereas if we perceive and distinguish changes, then we say that time has elapsed, it is clear that time cannot be disconnected from motion and change.

Plainly, then, time is neither identical with movement nor capable of being separated from it.

In our attempt to find out what time is, therefore, we must start from the question, in what way it pertains to movement. For when we are aware of movement we are thereby aware of time, since, even if it were dark and we were conscious of no bodily sensations, but something were 'going on' in our minds, we should, from that very experience, recognize the passage of time. And conversely, whenever we recognize that there has been a lapse of time, we by that act recognize that something 'has been going on.' So time must either itself be movement, or if not, must pertain to movement; and since we have seen that it is not identical with movement, it must pertain to it in some way.

Well then, since anything that moves moves from a 'here' to a 'there,' and magnitude as such is continuous, movement is dependent on magnitude; for it is because magnitude is continuous that movement is so also, and because movement is continuous so is time; for (excluding differences of velocity) the time occupied is conceived as proportionate to the distance moved over. Now, the primary significance of before-and-afterness is the local one of 'in front of' and 'behind.' There it is applied to order of position; but since there is a before-and-after in magnitude, there must also be a before-and-after in movement in analogy with them. But there is also a before-and-after in time, in virtue of the dependence of time upon motion. Motion, then, is the objective seat of before-and-afterness both in movement and in time; but conceptually the before-and-afterness is distinguishable from movement. Now, when we determine a movement by defining its first and last limit, we also recognize a lapse of time; for it is when we are aware of the measuring of motion by a prior and posterior limit that we may say time has passed. And our determination consists in distinguishing between the initial limit and the final one, and seeing that what lies between them is distinct from both; for when we distinguish between the extremes and what is between them, and the mind pronounces the 'nows' to be two—an initial and a final one—it is then that we say that a certain time has passed; for that which is determined either way by a 'now' seems to be what we mean by time. And let this be accepted and laid down.

Accordingly, when we perceive a 'now' in isolation, that is to say not as one of two, an initial and a final one in the motion, nor yet as being a final 'now' of one period and at the same time the initial 'now' of a succeeding period, then no time seems to have elapsed, for neither has there been any corresponding motion. But when we perceive a distinct before and after, then we speak of time; for this is just what time is, the calculable measure or dimension of motion with respect to before-and-afterness.

Time, then, is not movement, but that by which movement can be numerically estimated. To see this, reflect that we estimate any kind of more-and-lessness by number; so, since we estimate all more-or-lessness on some numerical scale and estimate the more-or-lessness of motion by time, time is a scale on which something (to wit movement) can be numerically estimated. But now, since 'number' has two meanings (for we speak of the 'numbers' that are counted in the thing in question, and also of the 'numbers' by which we count them and in which we calculate), we are to note that time is the countable thing that we are counting, not the numbers we count in—which two things are different.

And as motion is a continuous flux, so is time; but at any given moment time is the same everywhere, for the 'now' itself is identical in its essence, but the relations into which it enters differ in different connexions, and it is the 'now' that marks off time as before and after. But this 'now,' which is identical everywhere, itself retains its identity in one sense, but does not in another; for inasmuch as the point in the flux of time which it marks is changing (and so to mark it is its essential function) the 'now' too differs perpetually, but inasmuch as at every moment it is performing its essential function of dividing the past and future it retains its identity. For there is a dependent sequence, as we have shown, of movement upon magnitude and (we may add) of time upon movement; and the moving object, by which we become aware of movement and its before-and-afterness, may be regarded as a point; and throughout its course this— whether point or stone or what you like—retains its identity, but its relations alter: as the Sophists distinguish between Koriscos in the Lyceum and Koriscos in the market-place, so this moving object also is different in so far as it is perpetually marking a different position. And as time follows the analogy of movement, so does the 'now' of time follow the analogy of the moving object, since it is by the moving object that we come to know the before-and-after in motion, and it is in virtue of the countableness of its before-and-afters that the 'now' exists; so that the 'now,' wherever found in the before-and-afters, is identical (for it is simply the mark of the before-and-afters in motion), but the before-and-afternesses it marks differ; though the nature of the 'now' depends on the markableness of any before-and-after in general, not on the specific before-and-after marked by it. And it is this specifically related 'now' that is nearest to our apprehension, just as motion-change is apprehended through the changing object, and translation through the translated object, for this object is a concrete thing, which motion is not. There is a sense, then, in which what we mean when we say 'now' is always the same, and a sense in which it is not, just as is the case with anything that is in motion.

It is evident, too, that neither would time be if there were no 'now,' nor would 'now' be if there were no time; for they belong to each other as the moving thing and the motion do, so that whatever ticks off the position of the one ticks off the other. For time is the dimension proper to motion, and the 'now' corresponds to the moving object as the numerical monad.

So, too, time owes its continuity to the 'now,' and yet is divided by reference to it, since in this respect also the analogy with the translation and the object translated holds good; for the movement or translation is one and continuous in virtue of the identity of the translated object—not its identity *qua* object (for it would preserve that if it stopped) but its unbroken identity *qua* 'the thing that is being moved'; and it is this that also marks the division between the movement before and the movement after. And there is an analogy also between such a 'body that is being moved' and a point; for it is a point that both constitutes (by its movement) the continuity of the line it traces and also marks the end of the line that is behind and the beginning of the line in front. If, however, one ascribes the latter function to it, regarding the one point in two capacities —as the end of one section of the line and the beginning of another—it must have been arrested, since its identity in this 'statical' relation must be preserved. But the 'now,' as it follows the object in motion, marks a perpetually different position, so that time is not counted as if by one and the same point,—since each point in it so counted is a double point, being end and beginning at once,—but rather as the two extremities of the line, and not as *parts* of it, for the reason already stated (that, if one were to count the dividing point in its two capacities that would involve a pause), and because it is obvious that the 'now' is not a portion of time, just as the division of motion is not part of motion any more than points are of a line; it is the two sections that are *parts* of the one line. The 'now,' therefore, as a limit is not time, but is incidental to time, while as the numerator it is a number; for limits are limits only of the particular thing they limit, whereas the number 10, for instance, pertains equally to the ten horses (say) the sum of which it has defined, and to anything else numerable.

That time, then, is the dimension of movement in its before-and-afterness, and is continuous (because movement is so), is evident.

CHAPTER XII

The dyad is the smallest possible *abstract number*. In one sense there is no smallest possible number, but in another sense there is; for, whatever line you take for the unit, two is the smallest number of such units, but in magnitude there is no minimum, for any line whatever may itself be divided into smaller lines. So too with time, 'two' is the smallest possible number of time units, but there is no smallest possible time unit itself that may be selected.

Observe too that we do not speak of time itself as 'swift or slow,' but as consisting of 'many or few' of the units in which it is counted, or as 'long and short' when we regard it as a continuum. It would not be swift or slow, even if we supposed it to be the counter that counts, not the dimension that is counted (which it really is); for abstract numbers are in no case swift or slow, though the counting of them may be.

Moreover, though time is identical everywhere simultaneously, it is not identical if taken twice successively; for the change it measures, likewise, is one when considered as present, but not one if considered as partly past and partly future. And time considered numerically is concrete, not abstract; whereby follows that it changes from the former to the latter 'now,' inasmuch as these 'nows' themselves are different; just as the number of a hundred horses is identical with that of a hundred men, but the horses enumerated are different from the men enumerated. Now note further that as there may be movemnt (of rotation to wit) that covers the same course over and over again, in like manner we mark off time by the year or by spring or autumn.

And not only do we measure the length of uniform movement by time, but also the length of time by uniform movement, since they mutually determine each other; for the time taken determines the length moved over (the time units corresponding to the space units), and the length moved over determines the time taken. And when we call time 'much' or 'little' we are estimating it in units of uniform motion, as we measure the 'number' of anything we count by the units we count it in—the number of horses, for example, by taking one horse as our unit. For when we are told the number of horses, we know how many there are in the troop; and by counting how many there are, horse by horse, we know their number. And so too with time and uniform motion, for we measure them by each other either way. And this is only natural, for movement corresponds to linear magnitude, and time to movement, in being a quantity, in being continuous, and in being divisible; for it is from linear magnitude that motion takes on these qualities, and from motion that time does. That we do measure linear magnitude by movement, and *vice versa*, is evidenced from our saying that it is a great 'way' if it is a great 'walk,' or *vice versa*. So too with time and movement: we speak of a 'long walk' taking a 'long time,' or *vice versa*.

It is by reference to the standard unit of time that we determine the relative velocity of two several motions. For we ask what distance either motion has covered during the lapse of the standard unit of time, and pronounce the motion itself fast or slow in proportion as that distance is great or small. But that same standard unit of time measures the duration of a motion. So the way in which a motion exists in time is by both itself and its duration being measured by time. For time measures both the motion and its duration by the same act, and its duration being so measured constitutes it as existing in time. But it is obvious that other things as well as motion exist in time because their existence too is measured by time.

For this phrase 'existing in time' is ambiguous. It may mean (1) existing when time also exists, or (2) it may mean 'in time' in a sense analogous to that in which we say that certain things exist 'in number'; and this phrase again is ambiguous, for it may mean (*a*) that they exist in number as parts or affections of it, or generally that they pertain to it in some way or other, or (*b*) it may mean that they themselves can be counted.

Now (2) taking time as a number scale, (*a*) the 'now' and the 'before' and suchlike exist in time as the monad and the odd and even exist in number (for these latter pertain to number just in the same way in which the former pertain to time); but (*b*) events have their places in time in a sense analogous to that in which any numbered group of things exist in number (*i.e.*, in such and such a definite number), and such things as these are *embraced* in number (*i.e.*, in time) as things that have locality are embraced in their places.

And it is further evident (1) that to be in existence while time is in existence does not constitute being 'in time,' just as neither is a thing constituted as in motion or in a place because a motion and place exist while it does. For if this constitutes being '*in*' a thing, everything would be in anything, and the universe in a grain of millet, because a grain of millet exists while the universe is in existence. But this latter is an incidental coincidence; whereas when a thing is said to exist in time, it follows of necessity that there should be time while this thing exists, and if it exists in motion, it follows of necessity that there should be motion while it exists.

And since what exists in time exists in it as number (that is to say, as countable), you can take a time longer than anything that exists in time. So we must add that for things to exist in time they must be embraced by time, just as with other cases of being 'in' something; for instance, things that are in places are embraced by place. And it will follow that they are in some respect affected by time, just as we are wont to say that time crumbles things, and that everything grows old under the power of time and is forgotten through the lapse of time. But we do not say that we have learnt, or that anything is made new or beautiful, by the mere lapse of time; for we regard time in itself as destroying rather than producing, for what is counted in time is movement, and movement dislodges whatever it affects from its present state. From all this it is clear that things which exist eternally, as such, are not in time; for they are not embraced by time, nor is their duration measured by time. This is indicated by their not suffering anything under the action of time as though they were within its scope.

And since time is the measure of a motion, it will also incidentally be the measure of rest; for all rest is in time. For a thing being in motion necessitates that it should be moving, but its being in time does not; for time is not identical with motion, but is that in terms of which motion is counted, and even if a thing is at rest, it may be countable by the same count as motion. For not everything that is unmoved is at rest, but that only which by its nature is capable of moving but now lacks its actual motion, as we have already noted. But a thing existing in number means that it 'has' a number and that its existence is measured by that number; and so too in the case of time. And time will measure that which is in motion and that which is at rest, *as such;* for it is their motion and their rest of which it determines the amount. So that the thing in motion is not measured by time in all respects in its capacity of a quantum, but in so far as its motion is defined in quantity; hence that which is neither in motion nor at rest is not in time, since to be 'in time' means to be measured by time, and it is motion and rest of which time is the measure.

Clearly, then, not all non-existences are in time, but only such as might exist; for instance, the commensurability of the diagonal and the side does not exist, but its non-existence is not temporal. For, as a general proposition, if time is the measure of motion on its own account and of anything else only by incidental coincidence, obviously everything whose existence it measures must have its existence in rest or in motion. Accordingly, whatever is destructible or generable, or (more broadly) sometimes existing and sometimes not, must be embraced by time; for there must be some time great enough to exceed the time of their duration and therefore the time which measures their being. Among non-existents, on the other hand, those which are embraced by time either once were (as Homer once existed) or will be (*e.g.*, some future event), according as they are embraced by time on one or the other side of the present moment, or, if they are embraced in both directions, they can be either past or future; whereas those which are not in any way embraced by time neither were nor are nor will be. Non-existents of this latter kind are all those things whose opposites eternally exist; for instance, the incommensurability of the diagonal eternally exists, and therefore is not in time. And it follows that neither is its commensurability in time; hence it is *eternally* non-existent, inasmuch as it is a contradiction of what is eternally existent; whereas things of which the opposite does not exist eternally may either be or not be, and so they can come into existence and vanish from it.

CHAPTER XIII

We have said that it is through the 'now' that time is continuous, for it holds time past and future time together; and in its general character of 'limit' it is at once the beginning of time to come and the end of time past. But in the case of the 'now' this is not so obvious as in that of the stationary point; for, as well as actually continuing, it potentially divides time. And in this potentiality one 'now' differs from another, but in its actual holding of time continuously together it always remains the same, as in the parallel case of mathematical lines traced by moving points, in which case the point too, if arrested as a divider, is not conceived as retaining its identity with the tracing point or another arrested point; for if we are dividing the line, the point differs at every division, but if we regard the line as a single undivided one, the point that traces it is the same all along. Thus too the 'now' of time is a divider in mental potentiality, but a continuing unifier as the coincident end-term and beginning-term of past and future time; and these two capacities of potential divider and actual uniter pertain to the same actual 'now' and on the same count of its being two limits at once, but its essential and defined functioning in the one capacity differs from that in the other.

This is one of the meanings of 'now,' but it is also used for 'not far off in time.' 'He will come now,' if he will come to-day; 'He has come but now,' if he came to-day. But we do not speak so of the Trojan war or Deucalion's flood; though time is continuous between us and these events, they are not near.

'Sometimes' is used when we wish to be no more definite than that the present 'now' comes after it or the reverse. When was Troy taken? 'Sometime' in the past. When will the flood be? 'Sometime' in the future. There will be a measurable stretch of time from now onwards to that, or there has been one from that to now.

And since there is no time-ago or time-to-come that was not, or will not be, 'some time' off, it would seem that all time is limited. Will it come to an end, then? Surely not; for if motion is everlasting, so is time. Is it, then, always a different stretch of time that continues the succession, or the same stretch of time taken repeatedly? As to this, evidently it must conform to motion; for whichever of these kinds of counting applies to motion must apply to time. And besides, since the 'now' is the final limit and the initial limit of time, but not of the same time, but the final limit of time past and the initial limit of time to come, it must present a relation analogous to the kind of identity between the convexity and the concavity of the same circumference, which necessitates a difference between that with respect to which it bears the one character and that with respect to which it bears the other. So too, since every 'now' is at once the initial limit and the final limit of a stretch of time, the two stretches must be different; for the same 'now' cannot be both the beginning and the end of the same thing, for, if so, it would be both of two contradictories in the same subject at once. Neither, then, will time ever come to an end, for it is always at a beginning.

We say 'already' (*ēdē*) for any time close enough to the indivisible 'now' of the absolute present. 'When do you take your walk?' 'I am starting already,' or 'I have already taken it.' But the phrase only applies to the near future or past; so that we should not say 'Troy has already fallen.' Another term for the near past is 'just now' (*arti*). 'When did you arrive?' 'Just now,' if it was near to the instantaneous 'now' at which you speak; but 'some time ago' (*palai*) if the interval is considerable; and 'suddenly' (*exaiphnēs*) if the passage of time is so short as to be imperceptible.

All change is in its nature a 'passing away.' And it is 'in time' that everything begins and ceases to be; so some have called it the wisest of things, because it brings all knowledge, but the Pythagorean Paron said it was the most ignorant, because it is in time too that everything is forgotten, and he was nearer the mark. Indeed, it is evident that the mere passage of time itself is destructive rather than generative, as we said earlier; because change is primarily a 'passing away.' So it is only incidentally that time is the cause of the things coming into being and existing. A sufficient indication of this may be found in the fact that nothing comes into being without being started by some cause and reacting to it, but things perish without anything being stirred, and it is a kind of perishing without apparent provocation that we especially attribute to time. But yet, after all, it is not really time itself that destroys things in this way, but the changes that do destroy take place concurrently with time.

That there is such a thing as time, therefore, and what it is, and in how many senses we speak of 'now,' and what 'sometime' and 'but now' and 'already' and 'some time ago' and 'suddenly' mean, has now been said.

CHAPTER XIV

All this being so established, it becomes clear that all changes and everything that moves are conditioned by time. For it is a patent fact that every change may be quicker or slower. And what I mean by one change being quicker than another is that, of two homogeneous change-movements (either both on a periphery, for instance, or both on a straight line, if it be a local movement, and *mutatis mutandis* in other kinds of change), that one is the quicker which reaches a certain determined stage or point in its course 'before' the other reaches the point at the same distance from the starting-point in its course. Now this 'before' means before 'in time,' for both 'before' and 'after' are expressions of an interval between the 'nows' of arrival; and since the 'now' is a boundary between past and future, it follows that the two 'nows' (of the former and latter arrival, namely) being both phenomena of time, so must their 'before' and 'after' be. For, whatever it be that the 'now' pertains to, to that must the interval determined by it pertain. (But note that 'before' has opposite meanings according to whether it refers to past or future time; for in the past we regard the event that is farther from the present as 'before' the other and the nearer event as 'after' it, but in the future the nearer as 'before' and the farther as 'after' the other.) So, inasmuch as 'before' pertains to time, and may be a 'before' of arrival at a point of any kind of change-movement, it follows that every change or movement occurs 'in time.'

The relation of time to consciousness deserves examination, and so does the question why we conceive of time as immanent in everything in earth and sea and sky. As to the latter point, it is because time, being the numerator of motion, pertains to such motion wherever it exists, as an affection or disposition of it (namely, that it is either actually counted in units or potentially countable in such); and all things in the material universe are susceptible of motion (for they can all change their positions), and time and movement run in pairs both potentially and actually.

The question remains, then, whether or not time would exist if there were no consciousness; for if it were impossible for there to be the factor that does the counting, it would be impossible that anything should be counted; so that evidently there could be no number, for a number is either that which has actually been counted or that which can be counted. And if nothing can count except consciousness, and consciousness only as intellect (not as sensation merely), it is impossible that time should exist if consciousness did not; unless as the 'objective thing' which is subjectively time to us, if we may suppose that movement could thus objectively exist without there being any consciousness. For 'before' and 'after' are objectively involved in motion, and these, *qua* capable of numeration, constitute time.

It may be asked further to what kind of motion-change time does pertain. We may answer, 'It does not matter.' For things begin and cease to be, and grow, and change their qualities and their places 'in time'; so far, then, as change can be regarded as movement, so far time must be a numerator of every such kind of movement. We conclude, then, that time is the numeration of continuous movement, without any qualification, not only of some particular kind.

But if we take one kind of change and say 'now' with respect to it, other kinds of change, each of which has a specifically different unit to be counted in, will be at a certain stage of their change at this same 'now.' Can each of them have a different time, and must there be more than one time running concurrently? No; for it is the same lapse of time that is counted by two 'nows,' everywhere at once, whatever the units of movement or change; whereas the one-and-sameness of the units is determined by their kind and not by their 'at-once-ness'; just as if there were dogs and horses, seven of each, the number would be the same, but the units numbered different. So, too, of all movement-changes determined simultaneously the time is the same; one may be quick and another slow, and one a change of place and the other of quality; the time, however, is the same, if the counting has reached the same number and been made simultaneously, whether of the qualitive modification or of the change of place. So the movements or changes are different and stand apart, but the time is the same everywhere, because the numeration, if made simultaneously and up to the same figure, is one and the same.

And now, keeping locomotion and especially rotation in mind, note that everything is counted by some unit of like nature to itself—monads monad by monad, for instance, and horses horse by horse—and so likewise time by some finite unit of time. But as we have said, motion and time mutually determine each other quantitively; and that because the standard of time established by the motion we select is the quantitive measure both of that motion and of time. If, then, the standard once fixed measures all dimensionality of its own order, a uniform rotation will be the best standard, since it is easiest to count.

Neither qualitive modification nor growth nor genesis had the kind of uniformity that rotation has; and so time is regarded as the rotation of the sphere, inasmuch as all other orders of motion are measured by it, and time itself is standardized by reference to it. And this is the reason of our habitual way of speaking; for we say that human affairs and those of all other things that have natural movement and become and perish seem to be in a way circular, because all these things come to pass in time and have their beginning and end as it were 'periodically'; for time itself is conceived as 'coming round'; and this again because time and such a standard rotation mutually determine each other. Hence, to call the happenings of a thing a circle is saying that there is a sort of circle of time; and that is because it is measured by a complete revolution, and the whole measurement of a thing is nought else but a defined number of the units of its measurements.

[It is correct to say that the number of sheep and of dogs is the same number, if that of the sheep and that of the dogs are equal; but it is not the same decad in each case, nor are the units of one the same as the units of the other, any more than a scalene and an isoscles are the same triangle, though they are the same figure, both being triangles; for things bear the same name if they do not differ as to the characteristic in virtue of which that name is borne, in this case the differentia of triangle. They are different as triangles, therefore, but not different as figures, since they belong to one and the same figure denomination. For, as a figure, this is a circle and that a triangle, but, as a triangle, this isosceles and that scalene. The two, then, have the same figure conformation (for both are triangular), but not the same triangle formation. So with the animals: the number of each ten-group is the same, for they do not differ in a numerical differentia; but the ten-groups themselves are not the same, for the ten-ness is predicated of different subjects—dogs in the one case and horses in the other.]

This closes our investigation of time and its properties, in so far as they are germane to our inquiry.

.   .   .

Book VI (*Chapter IX: Against Zeno*)*

CHAPTER IX

The fallacy of Zeno's argument is now obvious; for he says that since a thing is at rest when it has not shifted in any degree out of a place equal to its own dimensions, and since at any given instant during the whole of its

---

* This translation by P. H. Wicksteed, edited after his death by F. M. Cornford, should be compared with the section on Zeno, above, which embodies more recent research.

supposed motion the supposed moving thing is in the place it occupies at that instant, the arrow is not moving at *any time* during its flight. But this is a false conclusion; for time is not made up of atomic 'nows,' any more than any other magnitude is made up of atomic elements.

Of Zeno's arguments about motion, there are four which give trouble to those who try to solve the problems they raise. The first is the one which declares movement to be impossible because, however near the mobile is to any given point, it will always have to cover the half, and then the half of that, and so on without limit before it gets there. And this we have already taken to pieces.

The second is what is known as 'the Achilles,' which purports to show that the slowest will never be overtaken in its course by the swiftest, inasmuch as, reckoning from any given instant, the pursuer, before he can catch the pursued, must reach the point from which the pursued started at that instant, and so the slower will always be some distance in advance of the swifter. But this argument is the same as the former one which depends on bisection, with the difference that the division of the magnitudes we successively take is not a division into halves (but according to any ratio we like to assume between the two speeds). The conclusion of the argument is that the slower cannot be overtaken by the swifter, but it is reached by following the same lines as the 'bisection' argument of the first thesis; for the reason why neither supposed process lands us at the limit, is that the method of division is expressly so designed as not to get us there, only in this second thesis a declamatory intensification is introduced by representing the swiftest racer as unable to overtake the slowest. The solution then must be identical in both cases, and the claim that the thing that is ahead is not overtaken is false. It is not overtaken *while* it is ahead, but none the less it *is* overtaken if Zeno will allow it to traverse to the end its finite distance. So much for these two theses.

The third thesis is the one just mentioned, namely that the arrow is stationary while on its flight. The demonstration rests on the assumption that time is made up of 'nows,' and if this be not granted the inference fails.

The fourth thesis supposes a number of objects all equal with each other in dimensions, forming two equal trains and arranged so that one train stretches from one end of a racecourse to the middle of it, and the other from the middle to the other end. Then if you let the two trains, moving in opposite directions but at the same rate, pass each other, Zeno undertakes to show that half of the time they occupy in passing each other is equal to the whole of it. The fallacy lies in his assuming that a moving object takes an equal time in passing another object equal in dimensions to itself, whether that other object is stationary or in motion; which assumption is false. For this is his demonstration. Let there be a number of objects *AAAA*, equal in number and bulk to those that compose the two trains but stationary in the middle of the stadium. Then let the objects *BBBB*, in number and dimension equal to the *A*'s, form one of the trains stretching from the middle of the *A*'s in one direction; and from the inner end of the *B*'s let *CCCC* stretch in the opposite direction, being the equal in number, dimension, and rate of movement to the *B*'s.

Then when they cross, the first *B* and the first *C* will simultaneously reach the extreme *A*'s in contrary directions.

Now during this process the first *C* has passed all the *B*'s, whereas the first *B* has only passed half the *A*'s, and therefore only taken half the time; for it takes an equal time (the minimal time) for the *C* to pass one *B* as for the *B* to pass one *A*. But during this same half-time the first *B* has also passed all the *C*'s (though the first *B* takes as long, says Zeno, to pass a *C* as an *A*) because measured by their progress through the *A*'s the *B*'s and *C*'s have had the same time in which to cross each other. Such is his argument, but the result depends on the fallacy above mentioned.

Nor need we be troubled by any attack on the possibility of change based on the axiom that a thing 'must either be or not be' but cannot 'both be and not be' this or that at the same time. For, it is argued, if a thing is changing, for instance, from being not-white to being white and is on its way from one to the other, you can truly assert at the same time that it is neither white nor not-white. But this is not true, for we sometimes call a thing 'white' even if it is not entirely white, and we sometimes call a thing 'not-white' even if there is some trace of white in it; we speak of it according to its prevailing condition or the conditions of its most significant parts or aspects. For to say that a thing is not in a certain condition 'at all' and to say that it is not 'altogether,' in it are two different things. And so, too, in the case of being or not being or any other pair of contradictory opposites. For during the whole process of changing it must be prevailingly one or the other and can never be exclusively either.

Again it is said that a rotating circle or sphere or anything else that moves within its own dimensions is stationary because in itself and all its parts it will remain in the same place for the given time: so it will be in motion and at rest at the same time. But in the first place its parts are not in the same place during any space of time, and in the second place the whole is also continuously changing to a different (rotational) position;

for the circumference measured round from *A* to *A* again is not identical with the circumference as measured from *B* to *B* or from *C* to *C* or any other point, except by accidental concomitance, as the cultivated person is a man. Thus one circumference is ever succeeding another and it will never be at rest. So, too, with the sphere, and any other body that moves within fixed dimensions.

ON THE HEAVENS

Book I (*Chapters II-III: The Fifth Element*)

CHAPTER II

The question of the nature of this Whole, whether it is of infinite magnitude or its total bulk is limited, must be left until later. We have now to speak of its formally distinct parts, and we may start from this, that all natural bodies and magnitudes are capable of moving of themselves in space; for nature we have defined as the principle of motion in them. Now all motion in space (locomotion) is either straight or circular or a compound of the two, for these are the only simple motions, the reason being that the straight and circular lines are the only simple magnitudes. By "circular motion" I mean motion around the centre, by "straight," motion up and down. "Up" means away from the centre, "down" towards the centre. It follows that all simple locomotion is either away from the centre or towards the centre or around the centre. This appears to follow consistently on what was said at the beginning: body was completed by the number three, and so now is its motion.

Of bodies some are simple, and some are compounds of the simple. By "simple" I mean all bodies which contain a principle of natural motion, like fire and earth and their kinds, and the other bodies of the same order. Hence motions also must be similarly divisible, some simple and others compound in one way or another; simple bodies will have simple motions and composite bodies composite motions, though the movement may be according to the prevailing element in the compound.

If we take these premises, (*a*) that there is such a thing as simple motion, (*b*) that circular motion is simple, (*c*) that simple motion is the motion of a simple body (for if a composite body moves with a simple motion, it is only by virtue of a simple body prevailing and imparting its direction to the whole), than it follows that there exists a simple body naturally so constituted as to move in a circle in virtue of its own nature. By force it can be brought to move with the motion of another, different body, but not naturally, if it is true that each of the simple bodies has one natural motion only. Moreover, granted that (*a*) unnatural motion is the contrary of natural, (*b*) a thing can have only one contrary, then circular motion, seeing it is one of the simple motions, must, if it is not the motion natural to the moved body, be contrary to its nature. Suppose now that the body which is moving in a circle be fire or some other of the four elements, than its natural motion must be contrary to the circular. But a thing can have only one contrary, and the contrary of upward is downward, and *vice versa*. Suppose on the other hand that this body which is moving in a circle contrary to its own nature is something other than the elements, there must be some other motion which is natural to it. But that is impossible: for if the motion were upward, the body would be fire or air, if downward, water or earth.

Furthermore, circular motion must be primary. That which is complete is prior in nature to the incomplete, and the circle is a complete figure, whereas no straight line can be so. An infinite straight line cannot, for to be complete it would have to have an end or completion, nor yet a finite, for all finite lines have something beyond them: any one of them is capable of being extended. Now if (*a*) a motion which is prior to another is the motion of a body prior in nature, (*b*) circular motion is prior to rectilinear, (*c*) rectilinear motion is the motion of the simple bodies (as *e.g.* fire moves in a straight line upwards and earthy bodies move downwards towards the centre), then circular motion also must of necessity be the motion of some simple body. (We have already made the reservation that the motion of composite bodies is determined by whatever simple body predominates in the mixture.) From all these premises therefore it clearly follows that there exists some physical substance besides the four in our sublunary world, and moreover that it is more divine than, and prior to, all these. The same can also be proved on the further assumption that all motion is either natural or unnatural, and that motion which is unnatural to one body is natural to another, as the motions up and down are natural or unnatural to fire and earth respectively; from these it follows that circular motion too, since it is unnatural to these elements, is natural to some other. Moreover, if circular motion is natural to anything, it will clearly be one of the simple and primary bodies of such a nature as to move naturally in a circle, as fire moves upward and earth downward. If on the other hand it be maintained that the revolutionary motion of the body which is carried round in a circle is unnatural, it is strange, in fact quite absurd, that being unnatural it should yet be the only continuous and eternal motion, seeing that in the rest of nature what is unnatural is the quickest to fall into decay. And so, if fire be the body carried round, as some say, this motion will be no less unnatural to it than motion downwards; for we see the natural motion of fire to be in a straight line away from the centre.

Thus the reasoning from all our premises goes to make us believe that there is some other body separate from those around us here, and of a higher nature in proportion as it is removed from the sublunary world.

CHAPTER III

After what has been said, whether laid down as hypothesis or demonstrated in the course of the argument, it becomes clear that not every body has either lightness or weight. However, we must first lay down what we mean by heavy and light, at present only so far as it is necessary for the purpose in hand, but later with more precision, when we come to investigate the real nature of the two. Let "the heavy" then be that whose nature it is to move towards the centre, "the light" that whose nature it is to move away from the centre, "heaviest" that which sinks below all other bodies whose motion is downwards, and "lightest" that which rises to the top of the bodies whose motion is upwards. Thus every body which moves downwards or upwards must have either lightness or weight or both. (A body cannot of course be both heavy and light in relation to the same thing, but the elements are so in relation to each other, *e.g.* air is light in comparison with water, but water in comparison with earth.) Now the body whose motion is circular cannot have either weight or lightness, for neither naturally nor unnaturally can it ever move towards or away from the centre. (*a*) Naturally it cannot have rectilinear motion, because it was laid down that each simple body has only one natural motion, and therefore it would itself be one of the bodies whose natural motion is rectilinear. (*b*) But suppose it moves in a straight line contrary to its nature, then if the motion is downwards, upward motion will be its natural one, and *vice versa;* for it was one of our hypotheses that of two contrary motions, if one is unnatural the other is natural. Taking into account then the fact that a whole and its part move naturally in the same direction (as do *e.g.* all earth together and a small clod), we have established (*a*) that it has neither lightness nor weight, since otherwise it would have been able to move naturally either towards the centre or away from the centre, (*b*) that it cannot move locally by being violently forced either up or down, for it is impossible for it to move, either naturally or unnaturally, with any other motion but its own, either itself as a whole or any of its parts, seeing that the same argument applies to whole and part.

With equal reason we may regard it as ungenerated and indestructible, and susceptible neither to growth nor alteration. (*a*) Everything that is generated comes into being out of an opposite and a substrate, and is destroyed only if it has a substrate, and through the agency of an opposite, and passes into its opposite, as has been explained in our first discussions. (*b*) Opposites have opposite motions. (*c*) There cannot be an opposite to the body under discussion, because there cannot be an opposite motion to the circular. It looks then as if nature had providently abstracted from the class of opposites that which was to be ungenerated and indestructible, because generation and destruction take place among opposites. Moreover anything which is subject to growth [or diminution] grows [or diminishes] in consequence of substance of the same kind being added to it and dissolving into its matter; but this body has no such matter. And if it is subject neither to growth nor to destruction, the same train of thought leads us to suppose that it is not subject to alteration either. Alteration is movement in respect of quality, and the temporary or permanent states of quality, health and disease for example, do not come into being without changes of affection. But all physical bodies which possess changing affections may be seen to be subject also to growth and diminution. Such are, for example, the bodies of animals and plants and their parts, and also those of the elements. If then the body whose natural motion is circular cannot be subject to growth or diminution, it is a reasonable supposition that it is not subject to alteration either.

From what has been said it is clear why, if our hypotheses are to be trusted, the primary body of all is eternal, suffers neither growth nor diminution, but is ageless, unalterable and impassive. I think too that the argument bears out experience and is borne out by it. All men have a conception of gods, and all assign the highest place to the divine, both barbarians and Hellenes, as many as believe in gods, supposing, obviously, that immortal is closely linked with immortal. It could not, they think, be otherwise. If then—and it is true—there is something divine, what we have said about the primary bodily substance is well said. The truth of it is also clear from the evidence of the senses, enough at least to warrant the assent of human faith; for throughout all past time, according to the records handed down from generation to generation, we find no trace of change either in the whole of the outermost heaven or in any one of its proper parts. It seems too that the name of this first body has been passed down to the present time by the ancients, who thought of it in the same way as we do, for we cannot help believing that the same ideas recur to men not once nor twice but over and over again. Thus they, believing that the primary body was something different from earth and fire and air and water, gave the name *aither* to the uppermost region, choosing its title from the fact that it "runs always" ($\dot{\alpha}\varepsilon\grave{\iota}\ \theta\varepsilon\tilde{\iota}\nu$) and eternally. (Anaxagoras badly misapplies the word when he uses *aither* for fire.)

It is also clear from what has been said why the number of the simple bodies, as we call them, cannot be more than we have mentioned. A simple body must have a simple motion, and we hold that these are the only simple motions, circular and rectilinear, the latter of two sorts, away from the centre and towards the centre.

ON THE SOUL

Book II (*Chapters I-III: What Is a Soul?*)

I. The theories of the soul handed down by our predecessors have been sufficiently discussed; now let us start afresh, as it were, and try to determine what the soul is, and what definition of it will be most comprehensive. We describe one class of existing things as substance; and this we subdivide into three: (1) matter, which in itself is not an individual thing; (2) shape or form, in virtue of which individuality is directly attributed, and (3) the compound of the two. Matter is potentiality, while form is realization or actuality, and the word actuality is used in two senses, illustrated by the possession of knowledge and the exercise of it.[1] Bodies seem to be pre-eminently substances, and most particularly those which are of natural origin; for these are the sources from which the rest are derived. But of natural bodies some have life and some have not; by life we mean the capacity for self-sustenance, growth, and decay. Every natural body, then, which possesses life must be substance, and substance of the compound type. But since it is a body of a definite kind, *viz.*, having life, the body cannot be soul, for the body is not something predicated of a subject, but rather is itself to be regarded as a subject, *i.e.*, as matter.[2] So the soul must be substance in the sense of being the form of a natural body, which potentially has life. And substance in this sense is actuality. The soul, then, is the actuality of the kind of body we have described. But actuality has two senses, analogous to the possession of knowledge and the exercise of it. Clearly actuality in our present sense is analogous to the possession of knowledge; for both sleep and waking depend upon the presence of soul, and waking is analogous to the exercise of knowledge, sleep to its possession but not its exercise. Now in one and the same person the possession of knowledge comes first. The soul may therefore be defined as the first actuality of a natural body potentially possessing life; and such will be any body which possesses organs. (The parts of plants are organs too, though very simple ones: *e.g.*, the leaf protects the pericarp, and the pericarp protects the seed; the roots are analogous to the mouth, for both these absorb food.) If then

---

[1] If you have the capacity to acquire knowledge of a subject, you may be said to have potential knowledge of it, which will become actual by study. In another sense, if you possess knowledge which you are not using, it may be called potential, actual only when you are using it.

[2] Every "substance" is composed of two factors—matter and form; *e.g.* a billiard ball. Its matter is ivory, its form spherical. An animate body, then, as it is a substance, consists of matter and form. The body must be matter, for it is not itself an attribute, but has attributes. Therefore the soul is form.

one is to find a definition which will apply to every soul, it will be "the first actuality of a natural body possessed of organs." So one need no more ask whether body and soul are one than whether the wax and the impression it receives are one, or in general whether the matter of each thing is the same as that of which it is the matter; for admitting that the terms unity and being are used in many senses, the paramount sense is that of actuality.

We have, then, given a general definition of what the soul is: it is substance in the sense of formula; *i.e.*, the essence of such-and-such a body. Suppose [3] that an implement, *e.g.* an axe, were a natural body; the substance of the axe would be that which makes it an axe, and this would be its soul; suppose this removed, and it would be no longer be an axe, except equivocally. As it is, it remains an axe, because it is not of this kind of body that the soul is the essence or formula, but only of a certain kind of natural body which has in itself a principle of movement and rest. We must, however, investigate our definition in relation to the parts of the body. If the eye were a living creature, its soul would be its vision; for this is the substance in the sense of formula of the eye. But the eye is the matter of vision, and if vision fails there is no eye, except in an equivocal sense, as for instance a stone or painted eye. Now we must apply what we have found true of the part to the whole living body. For the same relation must hold good of the whole of sensation to the whole sentient body *qua* sentient as obtains between their respective parts. That which has the capacity to live is not the body which has lost its soul, but that which possesses its soul; so seed and fruit are potentially bodies of this kind. The waking state is actuality in the same sense as the cutting of the axe or the seeing of the eye, while the soul is actuality in the same sense as the faculty of the eye for seeing, or of the implement for doing its work. The body is that which exists potentially; but just as the pupil and the faculty of seeing make an eye, so in the other case the soul and body make a living creature. It is quite clear, then, that neither the soul nor certain parts of it, if it has parts, can be separated from the body; for in some cases the actuality belongs to the parts themselves. Not but what there is nothing to prevent some parts being separated, because they are not actualities of any body. It is also uncertain whether the soul as an actuality bears the same relation to the body as the sailor to the ship. This must suffice as an attempt to determine in rough outline the nature of the soul.

---

[3] A.'s argument in the rest of this chapter is not quite easy to follow. The introduction of the axe seems at first irrelevant, because, as A. afterwards explains, being inanimate, it is not really parallel to the living creature. But his point is clear, the axe consists of the matter (wood and metal) of which it is composed, and its form (*i.e.* what makes it an axe—cutting edge, weight, and so forth). If you take away (*e.g.*) its edge, what remains? Still an axe, although one that will not cut. But this is not true of the living creature. It has a body which is its matter, and a soul which is its form. Take away the latter and the body perishes, so that the whole is no longer a living creature; by removing the form of a living creature we destroy its identity.

II. But since the definite and logically more intelligible conception arises from the vague but more obvious data of sense, we must try to review the question of the soul in this light; for a definitive formula ought not merely to show the fact, as most definitions do, but to contain and exhibit the cause. But in practice the formulae of our definitions are like conclusions; for instance, what is squaring a rectangle? The construction of an equilateral rectangle equal to an oblong rectangle. Such a definition is merely a statement of the conclusion. But if a man says that squaring a rectangle is the finding of a mean proportional, he is giving the underlying cause of the thing to be defined.[4]

We say then, assuming a fresh starting-point for our inquiry, that that which has soul is distinguished from that which has not by living. But the word living is used in many senses, and we say that a thing lives if any one of the following is present in it—mind, sensation, movement or rest in space, besides the movement implied in nutrition and decay or growth. Consequently all plants are considered to live, for they evidently have in themselves a capacity and first principle by means of which they exhibit both growth and decay in opposite directions; for they do not grow up and not down, but equally in both directions, and in every direction, and they are nourished and continue to live, as long as they are able to absorb food. This capacity to absorb food may exist apart from all other powers, but the others cannot exist apart from this in mortal beings. This is evident in the case of plants; for they have no other capacity of the soul.

This, then, is the principle through which all living things have life, but the first characteristic of an animal is sensation; for even those which do not move or change their place, but have sensation, we call living creatures, and do not merely say that they live. The first essential factor of sensation, which we all share, is a sense of touch. Just as the merely nutritive faculty may exist apart from touch and from all sensation, so touch may exist apart from all other senses. (By "nutritive faculty" I mean

---

[4] AB is a straight line divided into two parts at C. On AB a semicircle ADB is described. CD is drawn at right angles to AB to meet the circumference in D. Two conclusions can be proved. (1) The square on CD is equal to the rectangle AC.CB. (2) CD is the mean proportional between AC and CB, or in other words AC:CD::CD:CB. For the proofs of these two propositions *cf.* Euclid ii. 14 and vi. 13.

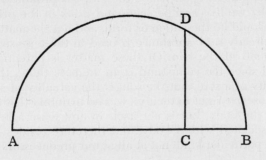

that part of the soul which even the plants share; all animals obviously possess the sense of touch.) Why each of these two facts is so, we shall explain later on.

But for the moment let us be satisfied with saying that the soul is the origin of the characteristics we have mentioned, and is defined by them, that is by the faculties of nutrition, sensation, thought and movement. The further questions, whether each of these faculties is a soul, or part of a soul, and, if a part, whether a part in the sense that it is only separable in thought or also in space, are in some cases easy of solution, but others involve difficulty. For just as in the case of plants some parts clearly live when divided and separated from each other, so that the soul in them appears to be one in actuality in each whole plant, but potentially more than one, so we can see that in other varieties of the soul the same thing happens, *e.g.*, in insects which are divided; for each of the parts has sensation and movement in space; and, if it has sensation, it must also have imagination and appetite; for, where sensation is, there is also pain and pleasure, and where these are there must also be desire. But in the case of the mind and the thinking faculty nothing is yet clear; it seems to be a distinct kind of soul, and it alone admits of being separated, as the immortal from the perishable. But it is quite clear from what we have said that the other parts of the soul are not separable, as some say; though it is obvious that they are theoretically different; for there is a difference between the abstract faculties of sensation and opinion, just as feeling is different from opining. The same is true of all the other faculties we have mentioned. Again, some animals have all these faculties, some only some of them, and others again only one. It is this which constitutes the differences between animals; the reason for it must be considered later. It is much the same with the senses; for some animals have all, some only some, and some again one only—the most indispensable—touch.

The phrase "that whereby we live and perceive" has two senses, as has "that whereby we know" (in the one sense we mean knowledge and in the other the soul; for we can say that we know by each of these); similarly we are healthy either by health or by part or the whole of the body. Now of these, knowledge and health are a kind of shape or form, or notion; an actuality, as it were, of the recipient, *i.e.* of that which is capable of knowledge or health (for the actualization of active processes appears to reside in the patient upon which the effect is produced), and the soul is that whereby we live and perceive and think in the primary sense; so that the soul would be the notion or form, and not the matter or substrate. As we have already said, substance is used in three senses, form, matter, and a compound of the two. Of these matter is potentiality, and form actuality; and since the compound is an animate thing, the body cannot be the actuality of a soul, but the soul is the actuality of some body. For this reason those are right in their view who maintain that the soul cannot exist without the body, but is not itself in any sense a body. It is not a body, it is associated with a body, and therefore resides in a body, and in a body of a particular kind; not at all as our predecessors supposed, who fitted it to any body, without adding any limitations as to what body or what kind of body, although it is unknown for any chance thing to admit any other chance thing. But our view explains the facts quite reasonably [5]; for the actuality of each thing is naturally inherent in its potentiality, that is in its own proper matter. From all this it is clear that the soul is a kind of actuality or notion of that which has the capacity of having a soul.

III. Now of the faculties of the soul which we have mentioned, some living things, as we have said, have all, others only some, and others again only one. Those which we have mentioned are the faculties for nourishment, for appetite, for sensation, for movement in space, and for thought. Plants have the nutritive faculty only, but other living things have the faculty for sensation too. But if for sensation then also for appetite; for appetite consists of desire, inclination, and wish, and all animals have at least one of the senses, that of touch; and that which has sensation knows pleasure and pain, the pleasant and the painful, and that which knows these has also desire; for desire is an appetite for what is pleasant. Again, they have a sense which perceives food; for touch is the sense which does this. All animals feed on what is dry or wet, hot or cold, and touch is the sense which apprehends these; the other objects of sense are only indirectly apprehended by touch. Neither sound, nor colour, nor smell contributes anything to nourishment; but flavour is one of the things apprehended by touch. Hunger and thirst are desire, the former for what is dry and hot, the latter for what is cold and wet; flavour is a kind of seasoning of these. We must be precise about these subjects later, but for the moment let it suffice to say that those animals which have a sense of touch have also appetite. The question of imagination is obscure, and must be considered later. In addition to these senses some also possess the power of movement in space, and others again—*viz.*, man, and any other being similar or superior to him—have the power of thinking and intelligence.

Thus it is clear that there must be a single definition of soul, just as there is of rectilinear figure; for as in the latter case there is no figure besides the triangle and those that follow it (*i.e.*, quadrilateral, pentagon, etc.), so there is no soul besides those we have mentioned. It would be possible in the case of figures to frame a common definition, which would fit them all, but would be descriptive of no particular figure; and similarly in the case of the kinds of soul we have mentioned. Hence it would be ridiculous, in this case as in others, to look for the common definition, which is the particular definition of no existing thing, and has no reference to any special or individual species, while we neglect such a particular definition.[6]

The facts regarding the soul are much the same as those relating to

---

[5] *i.e.* on general grounds we should expect a particular soul to belong to a particular body.

[6] The argument of this paragraph is as follows: Just as figure has a definition applicable to all varieties of figures, so soul has a similar "common" definition; but to understand individual types of soul, *e.g.*, of man, animal, and plant, we must study these types themselves.

figures; for both in figures and in things which possess soul, the earlier type always exists potentially in that which follows; e.g., the triangle is implied by the quadrilateral, and the nutritive faculty by the sensitive. We must then inquire in each several case, what is the soul of each individual, for instance of the plant, the man, and the beast. But we must also consider why they are thus arranged in a series. For without the nutritive faculty the sensitive does not exist, but in plants the nutritive is divorced from the sensitive faculty. Again, without the sense of touch none of the other senses exists, but touch may exist without any others; for many of the animals have neither vision nor hearing nor any sense of smell at all. Again, of those which have sensation, some have the locomotive faculty, and some have not. And lastly, and most rarely, living creatures have power of reasoning and thought. For those perishable creatures which have reasoning power have all the other powers as well, but not all those which have any one of them have reasoning power; some have not even imagination, while others live in virtue of this alone. The consideration of the speculative faculty is another question. It is clear, then, that the account of each of these faculties is also the most relevant account that can be given of the soul.

Book III (Chapters IV-V: Mind and Thinking)

IV. Concerning that part of the soul (whether it is separable in extended space, or only in thought) with which the soul knows and thinks, we have to consider what is its distinguishing characteristic, and how thinking comes about. If it is analogous to perceiving, it must be either a process in which the soul is acted upon by what is thinkable, or something else of a similar kind. This part, then, must (although impassive) be receptive of the form of an object, i.e., must be potentially the same as its object, although not identical with it: as the sensitive is to the sensible, so must mind be to the thinkable. It is necessary then that mind, since it thinks all things, should be uncontaminated, as Anaxagoras says, in order that it may be in control, that is, that it may know; for the intrusion of anything foreign hinders and obstructs it. Hence the mind, too, can have no characteristic except its capacity to receive. That part of the soul, then, which we call mind (by mind I mean that part by which the soul thinks and forms judgements) has no actual existence until it thinks. So it is unreasonable to suppose that it is mixed with the body; for in that case it would become somehow qualitative, e.g., hot or cold, or would even have some organ, as the sensitive faculty has; but in fact it has none. It has been well said that the soul is the place of forms, except that this does not apply to the soul as a whole, but only in its thinking capacity, and the forms occupy it not actually but only potentially. But that the perceptive and thinking faculties are not alike in their impassivity is obvious if we consider the sense organs and sensation. For the sense loses sensation under the stimulus of a too violent sensible object; *e.g.*, of sound immediately after loud sounds, and neither seeing nor smelling is possible just after strong colours and scents; but when mind thinks the highly intelligible, it is not less able to think of slighter things, but even more able; for the faculty of sense is not apart from the body, whereas the mind is separable. But when the mind has become the several groups of its objects, as the learned man when active is said to do (and this happens, when he can exercise his function by himself), even then the mind is in a sense potential, though not quite in the same way as before it learned and discovered; moreover the mind is then capable of thinking itself.

Since magnitude is not the same as the essence of magnitude, nor water the same as the essence of water (and so too in many other cases, but not in all, because in some cases there is no difference), we judge flesh and the essence of flesh either by different faculties, or by the same faculty in different relations; for flesh cannot exist without its matter, but like "snub-nosed" implies a definite form in a definite matter. Now it is by the sensitive faculty that we judge hot and cold, and all qualities whose due proportion constitutes flesh; but it is by a different sense, either quite distinct, or related to it in the same way as a bent line to itself when pulled out straight, that we judge the essence of flesh. Again, among abstract objects "straight" is like "snub-nosed," for it is always combined with extension; but its essence, if "straight" and "straightness" are not the same, is something different; let us call it duality. Therefore we judge it by another faculty, or by the same faculty in a different relation. And speaking generally, as objects are separable from their matter so also are the corresponding faculties of the mind.

One might raise the question: if the mind is a simple thing, and not liable to be acted upon, and has nothing in common with anything else, as Anaxagoras says, how will it think, if thinking is a form of being acted upon? For it is when two things have something in common that we regard one as acting and the other as acted upon. And our second problem is whether the mind itself can be an object of thought.[7] For either mind will be present in all other objects (if, that is, mind is an object of thought in itself and not in virtue of something else, and what is thought is always identical in form), or else it will contain some common element, which makes it an object of thought like other things. Or there is the explanation which we have given before of the phrase "being acted upon in virtue of some common element," that mind is potentially identical with the objects of thought but is actually nothing, until it thinks. What the mind thinks must be in it in the same sense as letters are on a tablet which bears no actual writing; this is just what happens in the case of the mind. It is also itself thinkable, just like other objects of

---

[7] This and the succeeding sentence are not very satisfactory; but A. is apparently arguing that if mind is *sui generis* it cannot be an object of thought, for this would put it in the same class as other objects of thought.

thought. For in the case of things without matter that which thinks and that which is thought are the same; for speculative knowledge is the same as its object. (We must consider why mind does not always think.) In things which have matter, each of the objects of thought is only potentially present. Hence while material objects will not have mind in them (for it is apart from their matter that mind is potentially identical with them) mind will still have the capacity of being thought.

V. Since in every class of objects, just as in the whole of nature, there is something which is their matter, *i.e.*, which is potentially all the individuals, and something else which is their cause or agent in that it makes them all—the two being related as an art to its material—these distinct elements must be present in the soul also. Mind in the passive sense is such because it becomes all things, but mind has another aspect in that it makes all things; this is a kind of positive state like light; for in a sense light makes potential into actual colours. Mind in this sense is separable, impassive and unmixed, since it is essentially an activity; for the agent is always superior to the patient, and the originating cause to the matter. Actual knowledge is identical with its object. Potential is prior in time to actual knowledge in the individual, but in general it is not prior in time. Mind does not think intermittently. When isolated it is its true self and nothing more, and this alone is immortal and everlasting (we do not remember [8] because, while mind in this sense cannot be acted upon, mind in the passive sense is perishable), and without this nothing thinks.

NICOMACHEAN ETHICS

Book I (Chapters I-VII and XIII: Introduction to Ethics, The Good for Man, Happiness, Intellectual and Moral Virtues)

I. Every art and every investigation, and likewise every practical pursuit or undertaking, seems to aim at some good: hence it has been well said that the Good is That at which all things aim. (It is true that a certain variety is to be observed among the ends at which the arts and sciences aim: in some cases the activity of practising the art is itself the end, whereas in others the end is some product over and above the mere exercise of the art; and in the arts whose ends are certain things beside the practice of the arts themselves, these products are essentially superior in value to the activities.) But as there are numerous pursuits and arts and sciences, it follows that their ends are correspondingly numerous: for instance, the end of the science of medicine is health, that of the art

---

[8] *Sc.*, its previous activity.

of shipbuilding a vessel, that of strategy victory, that of domestic economy wealth. Now in cases where several such pursuits are subordinate to some single faculty—as bridle-making and the other trades concerned with horses' harness are subordinate to horsemanship, and this and every other military pursuit to the science of strategy, and similarly other arts to different arts again—in all these cases, I say, the ends of the master arts are things more to be desired than all those of the arts subordinate to them; since the latter ends are only pursued for the sake of the former. (And it makes no difference whether the ends of the pursuits are the activities themselves or some other thing beside these, as in the case of the sciences mentioned.)

II. If therefore among the ends at which our actions aim there be one which we wish for its own sake, while we wish the others only for the sake of this, and if we do not choose everything for the sake of something else (which would obviously result in a process *ad infinitum,* so that all desire would be futile and vain), it is clear that this one ultimate End must be the Good, and indeed the Supreme Good. Will not then a knowledge of this Supreme Good be also of great practical importance for the conduct of life? Will it not better enable us to attain what is fitting, like archers having a target to aim at? If this be so, we ought to make an attempt to determine at all events in outline what exactly this Supreme Good is, and of which of the theoretical or practical sciences it is the object.

Now it would be agreed that it must be the object of the most authoritative of the sciences—some science which is pre-eminently a master-craft. But such is manifestly the science of Politics; for it is this that ordains which of the sciences are to exist in states, and what branches of knowledge the different classes of the citizens are to learn, and up to what point; and we observe that even the most highly esteemed of the faculties, such as strategy, domestic economy, oratory, are subordinate to the political science. Inasmuch then as the rest of the sciences are employed by this one, and as it moreover lays down laws as to what people shall do and what things they shall refrain from doing, the end of this science must include the ends of all the others. Therefore, the Good of man must be the end of the science of Politics. For even though it be the case that the Good is the same for the individual and for the state, nevertheless, the good of the state is manifestly a greater and more perfect good, both to attain and to preserve. To secure the good of one person only is better than nothing; but to secure the good of a nation or a state is a nobler and more divine achievement.

This then being its aim, our investigation is in a sense the study of Politics.

III. Now our treatment of this science will be adequate, if it achieves that amount of precision which belongs to its subject matter. The same exactness must not be expected in all departments of philosophy alike, any more than in all the products of the arts and crafts. The subjects studied by political science are Moral Nobility and Justice; but these conceptions involve much difference of opinion and uncertainty, so that they are sometimes believed to be mere conventions and to have no real existence in the nature of things. And a similar uncertainty surrounds the conception of the Good, because it frequently occurs that good things have harmful consequences: people have before now been ruined by wealth, and in other cases courage has cost men their lives. We must therefore be content if, in dealing with subjects and starting from premises thus uncertain, we succeed in presenting a broad outline of the truth: when our subjects and our premises are merely generalities, it is enough if we arrive at generally valid conclusions. Accordingly we may ask the student also to accept the various views we put forward in the same spirit; for it is the mark of an educated mind to expect that amount of exactness in each kind which the nature of the particular subject admits. It is equally unreasonable to accept merely probable conclusions from a mathematician and to demand strict demonstration from an orator.

Again, each man judges correctly those matters with which he is acquainted; it is of these that he is a competent critic. To criticize a particular subject, therefore, a man must have been trained in that subject: to be a good critic generally, he must have had an all-round education. Hence the young are not fit to be students of Political Science. For they have no experience of life and conduct, and it is these that supply the premises and subject matter of this branch of philosophy. And moreover they are led by their feelings; so that they will study the subject to no purpose or advantage, since the end of this science is not knowledge but action. And it makes no difference whether they are young in years or immature in character: the defect is not a question of time, it is because their life and its various aims are guided by feeling; for to such persons their knowledge is of no use, any more than it is to persons of defective self-restraint. But Moral Science may be of great value to those who guide their desires and actions by principle.

Let so much suffice by way of introduction as to the student of the subject, the spirit in which our conclusions are to be received, and the object that we set before us.

IV. To resume, inasmuch as all studies and undertakings are directed to the attainment of some good, let us discuss what it is that we pronounce to be the aim of Politics, that is, what is the highest of all the goods that action can achieve. As far as the name goes, we may almost say that the great majority of mankind are agreed about this; for both the multitude and persons of refinement speak of it as Happiness, and conceive 'the good life' or 'doing well' to be the same thing as 'being happy.' But what constitutes happiness is a matter of dispute; and the popular account of it is not the same as that given by the philosophers. Ordinary people identify it with some obvious and visible good, such as pleasure or wealth or honour—some say one thing and some another, indeed very often the same man says different things at different times: when he falls sick he thinks health is happiness, when he is poor, wealth. At other times, feeling conscious of their own ignorance, men admire those who propound something grand and above their heads; and it has been held by some thinkers that beside the many good things we have mentioned, there exists another Good, that is good in itself, and stands to all those goods as the cause of their being good.

Now perhaps it would be a somewhat fruitless task to review all the different opinions that are held. It will suffice to examine those that are most widely prevalent, or that seem to have some argument in their favour.

And we must not overlook the distinction between arguments that start from first principles and those that lead to first principles. It was a good practice of Plato to raise this question, and to enquire whether the right procedure was to start from or to lead up to the first principles, as in a race-course one may run from the judges to the far end of the track or reversely. Now no doubt it is proper to start from the known. But 'the known' has two meanings—'what is known to us,' which is one thing, and 'what is knowable in itself,' which is another. Perhaps then for us at all events it is proper to start from what is known to us. This is why in order to be a competent student of the Right and Just, and in short of the topics of Politics in general, the pupil is bound to have been well trained in his habits. For the starting-point or first principle is the fact that a thing is so; if this be satisfactorily ascertained, there will be no need also to know the reason why it is so. And the man of good moral training knows first principles already, or can easily acquire them. As for the person who neither knows nor can learn, let him hear the words of Hesiod:

> Best is the man who can himself advise;
> He too is good who hearkens to the wise;
> But who, himself being witless, will not heed
> Another's wisdom, is worthless indeed.

V. But let us continue from the point where we digressed. To judge from men's lives, the more or less reasoned conceptions of the Good or Happiness that seem to prevail among them are the following. On the one hand the generality of men and the most vulgar identify the Good with pleasure, and accordingly are content with the Life of Enjoyment—for there are three specially prominent Lives, the one just mentioned, the Life of Politics, and thirdly, the Life of Contemplation. The generality of mankind then show themselves to be utterly slavish, by preferring what is only a life for cattle; but they get a hearing for their view as reasonable because many persons of high position share the feelings of Sardanapallus.

Men of refinement, on the other hand, and men of action think that the Good is honour—for this may be said to be the end of the Life of Politics. But honour after all seems too superficial to be the Good for which we are seeking; since it appears to depend on those who confer it more than on him upon whom it is conferred, whereas we instinctively feel that the Good must be something proper to its possessor and not easy to be taken away from him. Moreover men's motive in pursuing honour seems to be to assure themselves of their own merit; at least they seek to be honoured by men of judgement and by people who know them, that is, they desire to be honoured on the ground of virtue. It is clear therefore that in the opinion at all events of men of action, virtue is a greater good than honour; and one might perhaps accordingly suppose that virtue rather than honour is the end of the Political Life. But even virtue proves on examination to be too incomplete to be the End; since it appears possible to possess it while you are asleep, or without putting it into practice throughout the whole of your life; and also for the virtuous man to suffer the greatest misery and misfortune—though no one would pronounce a man living a life of misery to be happy, unless for the sake of maintaining a paradox. But we need not pursue this subject, since it has been sufficiently treated in the ordinary discussions.

The third type of life is the Life of Contemplation, which we shall consider in the sequel.

The Life of Money-making is a constrained kind of life, and clearly wealth is not the Good we are in search of, for it is only good as being useful, a means to something else. On this score indeed one might conceive the ends before mentioned to have a better claim, for they are approved for their own sakes. But even they do not really seem to be the Supreme Good; however, many arguments have been laid down in regard to them, so we may dismiss them.

VI. But perhaps it is desirable that we should examine the notion of a Universal Good, and review the difficulties that it involves, although such an enquiry goes against the grain because of our friendship for the authors of the Theory of Ideas. Still perhaps it would appear desirable, and indeed it would seem to be obligatory, especially for a philosopher, to sacrifice even one's closest personal ties in defence of the truth. Both are dear to us, yet 'tis our duty to prefer the truth.

The originators of this theory, then, used not to postulate Ideas of groups of things in which they posited an order of priority and posteriority (for which reason they did not construct an Idea of numbers in general). But Good is predicated alike in the Categories of Substance, of Quality, and of Relation; yet the Absolute, or Substance, is prior in nature to the Relative, which seems to be a sort of offshoot or 'accident' of Substance; so that there cannot be a common Idea corresponding to the absolutely good and the relatively good.

Again, the word 'good' is used in as many senses as the word 'is'; for we may predicate good in the Category of Substance, for instance of God or intelligence; in that of Quality—the excellences; in that of Quantity—moderate in amount; in that of Relation—useful; in that of Time—a favourable opportunity; in that of Place—a suitable 'habitat'; and so on. So clearly good cannot be a single and universal general notion; if it were, it would not be predicable in all the Categories, but only in one.

Again, things that come under a single Idea must be objects of a single science; hence there ought to be a single science dealing with all good things. But as a matter of fact there are a number of sciences even for the goods in one Category: for example, opportunity, for opportunity in war comes under the science of strategy, in disease under that of medicine; and the due amount in diet comes under medicine, in bodily exercise under gymnastics.

One might also raise the question what precisely they mean by their expression 'the Ideal so-and-so,' seeing that one and the same definition of man applies both to 'the Ideal man' and to 'man,' for in so far as both are man, there will be no difference between them; and if so, no more will there be any difference betwen 'the Ideal Good' and 'Good' in so far as both are good. Nor yet will the Ideal Good be any more good because it is eternal, seeing that a white thing that lasts a long time is no whiter than one that lasts only a day.

The Pythagoreans seem to give a more probable doctrine on the subject of the Good when they place Unity in their column of goods; and indeed Speusippus [1] appears to have followed them. But this subject must be left for another discussion.

We can descry an objection that may be raised against our arguments on the ground that the theory in question was not intended to apply to every sort of good, and that only things pursued and accepted for their own sake are pronounced good as belonging to a single species, while things productive or preservative of these in any way, or preventive of their opposites, are said to be good as a means to these, and in a different sense. Clearly then the term 'goods' would have two meanings, (1) things good in themselves and (2) things good as a means to these; let us then separate things good in themselves from things useful as means, and consider whether the former are called good because they fall under a single Idea. But what sort of things is one to class as good in themselves? Are they not those things which are sought after even without any accessory advantage, such as wisdom, sight, and certain pleasures and honours? for even if we also pursue these things as means to something else, still one would class them among things good in themselves. Or is there nothing else good in itself except the Idea? If so, the species will be of no use. If on the contrary the class of things good in themselves includes these objects, the same notion of good ought to be manifested in all of them, just as the same notion of white is manifested in snow and in white paint. But as a matter of fact the notions of honour and wisdom and pleasure, as being good, are different and distinct. Therefore, good is not a general term corresponding to a single Idea.

But in what sense then are different things called good? For they do not seem to be a case of things that bear the same name merely by chance. Possibly things are called good in virtue of being derived from one good; or because they all contribute to one good. Or perhaps it is rather by way of a proportion: that is, as sight is good in the body, so intelligence is good in the soul, and similarly another thing in something else.

Perhaps however this question must be dismissed for the present, since

---

[1] Speusippus was Plato's nephew, and succeeded him as head of the Academy.

a detailed investigation of it belongs more properly to another branch of philosophy. And likewise with the Idea of the Good; for even if the goodness predicated of various things in common really is a unity or something existing separately and absolute, it clearly will not be practicable or attainable by man; but the Good which we are now seeking is a good within human reach.

But possibly someone may think that to know the Ideal Good may be desirable as an aid to achieving those goods which are practicable and attainable: having the Ideal Good as a pattern we shall more easily know what things are good for us, and knowing them, obtain them. Now it is true that this argument has a certain plausibility; but it does not seem to square with the actual procedure of the sciences. For these all aim at some good, and seek to make up their deficiencies, but they do not trouble about a knowledge of the Ideal Good. Yet if it were so potent an aid, it is improbable that all the professors of the arts and sciences should not know it, nor even seek to discover it. Moreover, it is not easy to see *how* knowing that same Ideal Good will help a weaver or carpenter in the practice of his own craft, or how anybody will be a better physician or general for having contemplated the absolute Idea. In fact it does not appear that the physician studies even health in the abstract; he studies the health of the human being—or rather of some particular human being, for it is individuals that he has to cure.

Let us here conclude our discussion of this subject.

VII.   We may now return to the Good which is the object of our search, and try to find out what exactly it can be. For good appears to be one thing in one pursuit or art and another in another: it is different in medicine from what it is in strategy, and so on with the rest of the arts. What definition of the Good then will hold true in all the arts? Perhaps we may define it as that for the sake of which everything else is done. This applies to something different in each different art—to health in the case of medicine, to victory in that of strategy, to a house in architecture, and to something else in each of the other arts; but in every pursuit or undertaking it describes the end of that pursuit or undertaking, since in all of them it is for the sake of the end that everything else is done. Hence if there be something which is the end of all the things done by human action, this will be the practicable Good—or if there be several such ends, the sum of these will be the Good. Thus by changing its ground the argument has reached the same result as before. We must attempt however to render this still more precise.

Now there do appear to be several ends at which our actions aim; but as we choose some of them—for instance wealth, or flutes, and instruments generally—as a means to something else, it is clear that not all of them are final ends; whereas the Supreme Good seems to be something final. Consequently if there be some one thing which alone is a final end, this thing—or if there be several final ends, the one among them which is the most final—will be the Good which we are seeking. In speaking of degrees of finality, we mean that a thing pursued as an end in itself is more final than one pursued as a means to something else, and that a thing never chosen as a means to anything else is more final than things chosen both as ends in themselves and as means to that thing; and accordingly a thing chosen always as an end and never as a means we call absolutely final. Now happiness above all else appears to be absolutely final in this sense, since we always choose it for its own sake and never as a means to something else; whereas honour, pleasure, intelligence, and excellence in its various forms, we choose indeed for their own sakes (since we should be glad to have each of them although no extraneous advantage resulted from it), but we also choose them for the sake of happiness, in the belief that they will be a means to our securing it. But no one chooses happiness for the sake of honour, pleasure, etc., nor as a means to anything whatever other than itself.

The same conclusion also appears to follow from a consideration of the self-sufficiency of happiness—for it is felt that the final good must be a thing sufficient in itself. The term self-sufficient, however, we employ with reference not to oneself alone, living a life of isolation, but also to one's parents and children and wife, and one's friends and fellow citizens in general, since man is by nature a social being. On the other hand a limit has to be assumed in these relationships; for if the list be extended to one's ancestors and descendants and to the friends of one's friends, it will go on *ad infinitum*. But this is a point that must be considered later on; we take a self-sufficient thing to mean a thing which merely standing by itself alone renders life desirable and lacking in nothing, and such a thing we deem happiness to be. Moreover, we think happiness the most desirable of all good things without being itself reckoned as one among the rest; for if it were so reckoned, it is clear that we should consider it more desirable when even the smallest of other good things were combined with it, since this addition would result in a larger total of good, and of two goods the greater is always the more desirable.

Happiness, therefore, being found to be something final and self-sufficient, is the End at which all actions aim.

To say however that the Supreme Good is happiness will probably appear a truism; we still require a more explicit account of what constitutes happiness. Perhaps then we may arrive at this by ascertaining what is man's function. For the goodness or efficiency of a flute-player or sculptor or craftsman of any sort, and in general of anybody who has some function or business to perform, is thought to reside in that function; and similarly it may be held that the good of man resides in the function of man, if he has a function.

Are we then to suppose that, while the carpenter and the shoemaker have definite functions or businesses belonging to them, man as such has none, and is not designed by nature to fulfil any function? Must we not rather assume that, just as the eye, the hand, the foot and each of the various members of the body manifestly has a certain function of its own, so a human being also has a certain function over and above all the functions of his particular members? What then precisely can this function be? The mere act of living appears to be shared even by plants, whereas we are looking for the function peculiar to man; we must therefore set aside the vital activity of nutrition and growth. Next in the scale will come some form of sentient life; but this too appears to be shared by horses, oxen, and animals generally. There remains therefore what may be called the practical life of the rational part of man. (This part has two divisions, one rational as obedient to principle, the other as possessing principle and exercising intelligence). Rational life again has two meanings; let us assume that we are here concerned with the active exercise of the rational faculty, since this seems to be the more proper sense of the term. If then the function of man is the active exercise of the soul's faculties [2] in conformity with rational principle, or at all events not in dissociation from rational principle, and if we acknowledge the function of an individual and of a good individual of the same class (for instance, a harper and a good harper, and so generally with all classes) to be generically the same, the qualification of the latter's superiority in excellence being added to the function in his case (I mean that if the function of a harper is to play the harp, that of a good harper is to play the harp well): if this is so, and if we declare that the function of man is a certain form of life, and define that form of life as the exercise of the soul's faculties and activities in association with rational principle, and say that the function of a good man is to perform these activities well and rightly, and if a function is well performed when it is performed in accordance with its own proper excellence—from these premises it follows that the Good of man is the active exercise of his soul's faculties in conformity with excellence or virtue, or if there be several human excellences or virtues, in conformity with the best and most perfect among them. Moreover this activity must occupy a complete lifetime; for one swallow does not make spring, nor does one fine day; and similarly one day or a brief period of happiness does not make a man supremely blessed and happy.

Let this account then serve to describe the Good in outline—for no doubt the proper procedure is to begin by making a rough sketch, and to fill it in afterwards. If a work has been well laid down in outline, to carry it on and complete it in detail may be supposed to be within the capacity of anybody; and in this working out of details Time seems to be a good inventor or at all events coadjutor. This indeed is how advances in the arts have actually come about, since anyone can fill in the gaps. Also the warning given above must not be forgotten; we must not look for equal exactness in all departments of study, but only such as belongs to the subject matter of each, and in such a degree as is appropriate to the particular line of enquiry. A carpenter and a geometrician both seek after a right angle, but in different ways; the former is content with that approximation to it which satisfies the

---

[2] Literally 'activity of soul'; ψυχή however has a wider connotation than either 'soul' or 'mind,' and includes the whole of the vitality of any living creature.

purpose of his work; the latter, being a student of truth, looks for its essence or essential attributes. We should therefore proceed in the same manner in other subjects also, and not allow side issues to outweigh the main task in hand.

Nor again must we in all matters alike demand an explanation of the reason why things are what they are; in some cases it is enough if the fact that they are so is satisfactorily established. This is the case with first principles; and the fact is the primary thing—it *is* a first principle. And principles are studied—some by induction, others by perception, others by some form of habituation, and also others otherwise; so we must endeavour to arrive at the principles of each kind in their natural manner, and must also be careful to define them correctly, since they are of great importance for the subesquent course of the enquiry. The beginning is admittedly more than half of the whole, and throws light at once on many of the questions under investigation.

. . .

XIII. Inasmuch as happiness is a certain activity of soul in conformity with perfect goodness, it is necessary to examine the nature of goodness. For this will probably assist us in our investigation of the nature of happiness. Also, the true statesman seems to be one who has made a special study of goodness, since his aim is to make the citizens good and law-abiding men—witness the lawgivers of Crete and Sparta, and the other great legislators of history; but if the study of goodness falls within the province of Political Science, it is clear that in investigating goodness we shall be keeping to the plan which we adopted at the outset.

Now the goodness that we have to consider is clearly human goodness, since the good or happiness which we set out to seek was human good and human happiness. But human goodness means in our view excellence of soul, not excellence of body; also our definition of happiness is an activity of the soul. Now if this is so, clearly it behoves the statesman to have some acquaintance with psychology, just as the physician who is to heal the eye or the other parts of the body must know their anatomy. Indeed a foundation of science is even more requisite for the statesman, inasmuch as politics is a higher and more honourable art than medicine; but physicians of the better class devote much attention to the study of the human body. The student of politics therefore as well as the psychologist must study the nature of the soul, though he will do so as an aid to politics, and only so far as is requisite for the objects of enquiry that he has in view: to pursue the subject in further detail would doubtless be more laborious than is necessary for his purpose.

Now on the subject of psychology some of the teaching current in extraneous discourses is satisfactory, and may be adopted here: namely that the soul consists of two parts, one irrational and the other capable of reason. (Whether these two parts are really distinct in the sense that the parts of body or of any other divisible whole are distinct, or whether though distinguishable in thought as two they are inseparable in reality, like the convex and concave sides of a curve, is a question of no importance for the matter in hand.) Of the irrational part of the soul again one division appears to be common to all living things, and of a vegetative nature: I refer to the part that causes nutrition and growth; for we must assume that a vital faculty of this nature exists in all things that assimilate nourishment, including embryos—the same faculty being present also in the fully-developed organism (this is more reasonable than to assume a different nutritive faculty in the latter). The excellence of this faculty therefore appears to be common to all animate things and not peculiar to man; for it is believed that this faculty or part of the soul is most active during sleep, but when they are asleep you cannot tell a good man from a bad one (whence the saying that for half their lives there is no difference between the happy and the miserable). This is a natural result of the fact that sleep is a cessation of the soul from the activities on which its goodness or badness depends—except that in some small degree certain of the sense-impressions may reach the soul during sleep, and consequently the dreams of the good are better than those of ordinary men. We need not however pursue this subject further, but may omit from consideration the nutritive part of the soul, since it exhibits no specifically human excellence.

But there also appears to be another element in the soul, which, though irrational, yet in a manner participates in rational principle. In self-restrained and unrestrained people we approve their principle, or the rational part of their souls, because it urges them in the right way and exhorts them to the best course; but their nature seems also to contain another element beside that of rational principle, which combats and resists that principle. Exactly the same thing may take place in the soul as occurs with the body in a case of paralysis: when the patient wills to move his limbs to the right they swerve to the left; and similarly in unrestrained persons their impulses run counter to their principle. But whereas in the body we see the erratic member, in the case of the soul we do not see it; nevertheless it cannot be doubted that in the soul also there is an element beside that of principle, which opposes and runs counter to principle (though in what sense the two are distinct does not concern us here). But this second element also seems, as we said, to participate in rational principle; at least in the self-restrained man it obeys the behest of principle—and no doubt in the temperate and brave man it is still more amenable, for all parts of his nature are in harmony with principle.

Thus we see that the irrational part, as well as the soul as a whole, is double. One division of it, the vegetative, does not share in rational principle at all; the other, the seat of the appetites and of desire in general, does in a sense participate in principle, as being amenable and obedient to it (in the sense in fact in which we speak of 'paying heed' to one's father and friends, not in the sense of the term 'rational' in mathematics). And that principle can in a manner appeal to the irrational part, is indicated by our practice of admonishing delinquents, and by our employment of rebuke and exhortation generally.

If on the other hand it be more correct to speak of the appetitive part of the soul also as rational, in that case it is the rational part which, as well as the whole soul, is divided into two, the one division having rational principle in the proper sense and in itself, the other obedient to it as a child to its father.

Now virtue also is differentiated in correspondence with this division of the soul. Some forms of virtue are called intellectual virtues, others moral virtues: Wisdom or intelligence and Prudence are intellectual, Liberality and Temperance are moral virtues. When describing a man's moral character we do not say that he is wise or intelligent, but gentle or temperate; but a wise man also is praised for his disposition, and praiseworthy dispositions we term virtues.

Book II (*Chapters V-VII: Virtue and the Golden Mean*)

V. We have next to consider the formal definition of virtue.

A state of the soul is either (1) an emotion, (2) a capacity, or (3) a disposition; virtue therefore must be one of these three things. By the emotions, I mean desire, anger, fear, confidence, envy, joy, friendship, hatred, longing, jealousy, pity; and generally those states of consciousness which are accompanied by pleasure or pain. The capacities are the faculties in virtue of which we can be said to be liable to the emotions, for example, capable of feeling anger or pain or pity. The dispositions are the formed states of character in virtue of which we are well or ill disposed in respect of the emotions; for instance, we have a bad disposition in regard to anger if we are disposed to get angry too violently or not violently enough, a good disposition if we habitually feel a moderate amount of anger; and similarly in respect of the other emotions.

Now the virtues and vices are not emotions because we are not pronounced good or bad according to our emotions, but we are according to our virtues and vices; nor are we either praised or blamed for our emotions—a man is not praised for being frightened or angry, nor is he blamed for being angry merely, but for being angry in a certain way—but we are praised or blamed for our virtues and vices. Again, we are not angry or afraid from choice, but the virtues are certain modes of choice, or at all events involve choice. Moreover, we are said to be 'moved' by the emotions, whereas in respect of the virtues and vices we are not said to be 'moved' but to be 'disposed' in a certain way.

And the same considerations also prove that the virtues and vices are not capacities; since we are not pronounced good or bad, praised or blamed, merely by reason of our capacity for emotion. Again, we possess certain capacities by nature, but we are not born good or bad by nature: of this however we spoke before.

If then the virtues are neither emotions nor capacities, it remains that they are dispositions.

Thus we have stated what virtue is generically.

VI. But it is not enough merely to define virtue generically as a disposition; we must also say what species of disposition it is. It must then be premised that all excellence has a twofold effect on the thing to which it belongs: it not only renders the thing itself good, but it also causes it to perform its function well. For example, the effect of excellence in the eye is that the eye is good *and* functions well; since having good eyes means having good sight. Similarly excellence in a horse makes it a good horse, and also good at galloping, at carrying its rider, and at facing the enemy. If therefore this is true of all things, excellence or virtue in a man will be the disposition which renders him a good man and also which will cause him to perform his function well. We have already indicated what this means; but it will throw more light on the subject if we consider what constitutes the specific nature of virtue.

Now of everything that is continuous and divisible, it is possible to take the larger part, or the smaller part, or an equal part, and these parts may be larger, smaller, and equal either with respect to the thing itself or relatively to us; the equal part being a mean between excess and deficiency. By the mean of the thing I denote a point equally distant from either extreme, which is one and the same for everybody; by the mean relative to us, that amount which is neither too much nor too little, and this is not one and the same for everybody. For example, let 10 be many and 2 few; then one takes the mean with respect to the thing if one takes 6; $6 - 2 = 10 - 6$, and this is the mean according to arithmetical proportion. But we cannot arrive by this method at the mean relative to us. Suppose that 10 lb. of food is a large ration for anybody and 2 lb. a small one: it does not follow that a trainer will prescribe 6 lb., for perhaps even this will be a large ration, or a small one, for the particular athlete who is to receive it; it is a small ration for a Milo,[3] but a large one for a man just beginning to go in for athletics. And similarly with the amount of running or wrestling exercise to be taken. In the same way then an expert in any art avoids excess and deficiency, and seeks and adopts the mean—the mean, that is, not of the thing but relative to us. If therefore the way in which every art or science performs its work well is by looking to the mean and applying that as a standard to its productions (hence the common remark about a perfect work of art, that you could not take from it nor add to it—meaning that excess and deficiency destroy perfection, while adherence to the mean preserves it)—if then, as we say, good craftsmen look to the mean as they work, and if virtue, like nature, is more accurate and better than any form of art, it will follow that virtue has the quality of hitting the mean. I refer to moral virtue,[4] for this is concerned with emotions and actions,

---

3 A famous wrestler.
4 The formula of the mean does not apply to the intellectual virtues.

in which one can have excess or deficiency or a due mean. For example, one can be frightened or bold, feel desire or anger or pity, and experience pleasure and pain in general, either too much or too little, and in both cases wrongly; whereas to feel these feelings at the right time, on the right occasion, towards the right people, for the right purpose and in the right manner, is to feel the best amount of them, which is the mean amount—and the best amount is of course the mark of virtue. And similarly there can be excess, deficiency, and the due mean in actions. Now feelings and actions are the objects with which virtue is concerned; and in feelings and actions excess and deficiency are errors, while the mean amount is praised, and constitutes success; and to be praised and to be successful are both marks of virtue. Virtue, therefore, is a mean state in the sense that it is able to hit the mean. Again, error is multiform (for evil is a form of the unlimited, as in the old Pythagorean imagery, and good of the limited), whereas success is possible in one way only (which is why it is easy to fail and difficult to succeed —easy to miss the target and difficult to hit it); so this is another reason why excess and deficiency are a mark of vice, and observance of the mean a mark of virtue:

Goodness is simple, badness manifold.

Virtue then is a settled disposition of the mind determining the choice of actions and emotions, consisting essentially in the observance of the mean relative to us, this being determined by principle, that is, as the prudent man would determine it.

And it is a mean state between two vices, one of excess and one of defect. Furthermore, it is a mean state in that whereas the vices either fall short of or exceed what is right in feelings and in actions, virtue ascertains and adopts the mean. Hence while in respect of its substance and the definition that states what it really is in essence virtue is the observance of the mean, in point of excellence and rightness it is an extreme.

Not every action or emotion however admits of the observance of a due mean. Indeed the very names of some directly imply evil, for instance malice,[5] shamelessness, envy, and, of actions, adultery, theft, murder. All these and similar actions and feelings are blamed as being bad in themselves; it is not the excess or deficiency of them that we blame. It is impossible therefore ever to go right in regard to them—one must always be wrong; nor does right or wrong in their case depend on the circumstances, for instance, whether one commits adultery with the right woman, at the right time, and in the right manner: the mere commission of any of them is wrong. One might as well suppose there could be a due mean and excess and deficiency in acts of injustice or cowardice or profligacy, which would imply that one could have a medium amount of excess and of deficiency, an excessive amount of

---

[5] The word means 'delight at another's misfortune,' *Schadenfreude*.

excess and a deficient amount of deficiency. But just as there can be no excess or deficiency in temperance and justice, because the mean is in a sense an extreme, so there can be no observance of the mean nor excess nor deficiency in the corresponding vicious acts mentioned above, but however they are committed, they are wrong; since, to put it in general terms, there is no such thing as observing a mean in excess or deficiency, nor as exceeding or falling short in the observance of a mean.

VII. We must not however rest content with stating this general definition, but must show that it applies to the particular virues. In practical philosophy, although universal principles have a wider application, those covering a particular part of the field possess a higher degree of truth; because conduct deals with particular facts, and our theories are bound to accord with these.

Let us then take the particular virtues from the diagram. [*Here apparently the lecturer displayed a table of virtues, exhibiting each as a mean between two vices of excess and defect in respect of a certain class of action or feeling.*]

The observance of the mean in fear and confidence is Courage. The man that exceeds in fearlessness is not designated by any special name (and this is the case with many of the virtues and vices); he that exceeds in confidence is Rash; he that exceeds in fear and is deficient in confidence is Cowardly. In respect of pleasures and pains—not all of them, and to a less degree in respect of pains—the observance of the mean is Temperance, the excess Profligacy. Men deficient in the enjoyment of pleasures scarcely occur, and hence this character also has not been assigned a name, but we may call it Insensible. In regard to giving and getting money, the observance of the mean is Liberality; the excess and deficiency are Prodigality and Meanness, but the prodigal man and the mean man exceed and fall short in opposite ways to one another: the prodigal exceeds in giving and is deficient in getting, whereas the mean man exceeds in getting and is deficient in giving. For the present then we describe these qualities in outline and summarily, which is enough for the purpose in hand; but they will be more accurately defined later.

There are also other dispositions in relation to money, namely, the mode of observing the mean called Magnificence (the magnificent man being different from the liberal, as the former deals with large amounts and the latter with small ones), the excess called Tastelessness or Vulgarity, and the defect called Paltriness. These are not the same as Liberality and the vices corresponding to it; but the way in which they differ will be discussed later.

In respect of honour and dishonour, the observance of the mean is Greatness of Soul, the excess a sort of Vanity, as it may be called, and the deficiency, Smallness of Soul. And just as we said that Liberality is related to Magnificence, differing from it in being concerned with small amounts of money, so there is a certain quality related to Greatness of Soul, which is concerned with great honours, while this quality itself is concerned with small honours; for it is possible to aspire to minor honours in the right way, or more than is right, or less. He who exceeds in these aspirations is called ambitious, he who is deficient, unambitious; but the middle character has no name, and the dispositions of these persons are also unnamed, except that that of the ambitious man is called Ambitiousness. Consequently the extreme characters put in a claim to the middle position, and in fact we ourselves sometimes call the middle person ambitious and sometimes unambitious: we sometimes praise a man for being ambitious, sometimes for being unambitious. Why we do so shall be discussed later; for the present let us classify the remaining virtues and vices on the lines which we have laid down.

In respect of anger also we have excess, deficiency, and the observance of the mean. These states are virtually without names, but as we call a person of the middle character gentle, let us name the observance of the mean Gentleness, while of the extremes, he that exceeds may be styled irascible and his vice Irascibility, and he that is deficient, spiritless, and the deficiency Spiritlessness.

There are also three other modes of observing a mean which bear some resemblance to each other, and yet are different; all have to do with intercourse in conversation and action, but they differ in that one is concerned with truthfulness of speech and behaviour, and the other with pleasantness, in its two divisions of pleasantness in social amusement and pleasantness in the general affairs of life. We must then discuss these qualities also, in order the better to discern that in all things the observance of the mean is to be praised, while the extremes are neither right nor praiseworthy, but reprehensible. Most of these qualities also are unnamed, but in these as in the other cases we must attempt to coin names for them ourselves, for the sake of clearness and so that our meaning may be easily followed.

In respect of truth then, the middle character may be called truthful, and the observance of the mean Truthfulness; pretense in the form of exaggeration is Boastfulness, and its possessor a boaster; in the form of understatement, Self-depreciation, and its possessor the self-depreciator.

In respect of pleasantness in social amusement, the middle character is witty and the middle disposition Wittiness; the excess is Buffoonery and its possessor a buffoon; the deficient man may be called boorish, and his disposition Boorishness. In respect of general pleasantness in life, the man who is pleasant in the proper manner is friendly, and the observance of the mean is Friendliness; he that exceeds, if from no interested motive, is obsequious, if for his own advantage, a flatterer; he that is deficient, and unpleasant in all the affairs of life, may be called quarrelsome and surly.

There are also modes of observing a mean in the sphere of and in relation to the emotions. For in these also one man is spoken of as moderate and another as excessive—for example the bashful man whose modesty takes alarm at everything; while he that is deficient in shame, or abashed at nothing whatsoever, is shameless, and the man of middle character modest. For though Modesty is not a virtue, it is praised, and so is the modest man.

Again, Righteous Indignation is the observance of a mean between Envy and Malice, and these qualities are concerned with pain and pleasure felt at the fortunes of one's neighbours. The righteously indignant man is pained by undeserved good fortune; the jealous man exceeds him and is pained by all the good fortune of others; while the malicious man so far falls short of being pained that he actually feels pleasure.

These qualities however it will be time to discuss in another place. After them we will treat Justice, distinguishing its two kinds—for it has more than one sense—and showing in what way each is a mode of observing the mean.

Book III (*Chapters I-III and V: Responsibility*)

I. Virtue however is concerned with emotions and actions, and it is only voluntary actions for which praise and blame are given; those that are involuntary are condoned, and sometimes even pitied. Hence it seems to be necessary for the student of ethics to define the difference between the Voluntary and the Involuntary; and this will also be of service to the legislator in assigning rewards and punishments.

It is then generally held that actions are involuntary when done (*a*) under compulsion or (*b*) through ignorance; and that (*a*) an act is compulsory when its origin is from without, being of such a nature that the agent, who is really passive, contributes nothing to it: for example, when he is carried somewhere by stress of weather, or by people who have him in their power. But there is some doubt about actions done through fear of a worse alternative, or for some noble object—as for instance if a tryant having a man's parents and children in his power commands him to do something base, when if he complies their lives will be spared but if he refuses they will be put to death. It is open to question whether such actions are voluntary or involuntary. A somewhat similar case is when cargo is jettisoned in a storm; apart from circumstances, no one voluntarily throws away his property, but to save his own life and that of his shipmates any sane man would do so. Acts of this kind, then, are 'mixed' or composite; but they approximate rather to the voluntary class. For at the actual time when they are done they are chosen or willed; and the end or motive of an act varies with the occasion, so that the terms 'voluntary' and 'involuntary' should be used with reference to the time of action; now the actual deed in the cases in question is done voluntarily, for the origin of the movement of the parts of the body instrumental to the act lies in the agent; and when the origin of an action is in oneself, it is in one's own power to do it or not. Such acts therefore are voluntary, though perhaps involuntary apart from circumstances—for no one would choose to do any such action in and for itself.

Sometimes indeed men are actually praised for deeds of this 'mixed' class, namely when they submit to some disgrace or pain as the price of some great and noble object; though if they do so without any such motive they are blamed, since it is contemptible to submit to a great disgrace with no advantage or only a trifling one in view. In some cases again, such submission though not praised is condoned, when a man does something wrong through fear of penalties that impose too great a strain on human nature, and that no one could endure. Yet there seem to be some acts which a man cannot be compelled to do, and rather than do them he ought to submit to the most terrible death: for instance, we think it ridiculous that Alcmaeon in Euripides' play is compelled by certain threats to murder his mother! But it is sometimes difficult to decide how far we ought to go in choosing to do a given act rather than suffer a given penalty, or in enduring a given penalty rather than commit a given action; and it is still more difficult to abide by our decision when made, since in most of such dilemmas the penalty threatened is painful and the deed forced upon us dishonourable, which is why praise and blame are bestowed according as we do or do not yield to such compulsion.

What kind of actions then are to be called 'compulsory'? Used without qualification, perhaps this term applies to any case where the cause of the action lies in things outside the agent, and when the agent contributes nothing. But when actions intrinsically involuntary are yet in given circumstances deliberately chosen in preference to a given alternative, and when their origin lies in the agent, these actions are to be pronounced intrinsically involuntary but voluntary in the circumstances, and in preference to the alternative. They approximate however rather to the voluntary class, since conduct consists of particular things done, and the particular things done in the cases in question are voluntary. But it is not easy to lay down rules for deciding which of two alternatives is to be chosen, for particular cases differ widely.

To apply the term 'compulsory' to acts done for the sake of pleasure or for noble objects, on the plea that these exercise constraint on us from without, it to make every action compulsory. For (1) pleasure and nobility between them supply the motives of all actions whatsoever. Also (2) to act under compulsion and unwillingly is painful, but actions done for their pleasantness or nobility are done with pleasure. And (3) it is absurd to blame external things, instead of blaming ourselves for falling an easy prey to their attractions; or to take the credit of our noble deeds to ourselves, while putting the blame for our disgraceful ones upon the temptations of pleasure. It appears therefore that an act is compulsory when its origin is from outside, the person compelled contributing nothing to it.

(*b*) An act done through ignorance is in every case not voluntary, but it is involuntary only when it causes the agent pain and regret:

since a man who has acted through ignorance and feels no compunction
at all for what he has done, cannot indeed be said to have acted voluntarily, as he was not aware of his action, yet cannot be said to have acted
involuntarily, as he is not sorry for it. Acts done through ignorance
therefore fall into two classes: if the agent regrets the act, we think that
he has acted involuntarily; if he does not regret it, to mark the distinction we may call him a 'non-voluntary' agent—for as the case is
different it is better to give it a special name. Acting *through* ignorance
however seems to be different from acting *in* ignorance; for when a man
is drunk or in a rage, his actions are not thought to be done through
ignorance but owing to one or other of the conditions mentioned, though
he does act without knowing, and *in* ignorance. Now it is true that all
wicked men are ignorant of what they ought to do and refrain from
doing, and that this error is the cause of injustice and of vice in general.
But the term 'involuntary' does not really apply to an action when the
agent is ignorant of his true interests. The ignorance that makes an act
blameworthy is not ignorance displayed in moral choice (that sort of
ignorance constitutes vice)—that is to say, it is not general ignorance
(because that is held to be blameworthy), but particular ignorance,
ignorance of the circumstances of the act and of the things affected by it;
for in this case the act is pitied and forgiven, because he who acts in
ignorance of any of these circumstances is an involuntary agent.

Perhaps then it will be as well to specify the nature and number of
these circumstances. They are (1) the agent, (2) the act, (3) the thing
that is affected by or is the sphere of the act; and sometimes also (4)
the instrument, for instance, a tool with which the act is done, (5) the
effect, for instance, saving a man's life, and (6) the manner, for instance, gently or violently.

Now no one, unless mad, could be ignorant of all these circumstances
together; nor yet, obviously, of (1) the agent—for a man must know who
he is himself. But a man may be ignorant of (2) what he is doing, as
for instance when people say 'it slipped out while they were speaking,'
or 'they were not aware that the matter was a secret,' as Aeschylus said
of the Mysteries [6]; or that 'they let it off when they only meant to show
how it worked' as the prisoner pleaded in the catapult case. Again (3)
a person might mistake his son for an enemy, as Merope does [7]; or (4)
mistake a sharp spear for one with a button on it, or a heavy stone for
a pumice-stone; or (5) one might kill a man by giving him medicine
with the intention of saving his life; or (6) in loose wrestling [8] hit him
a blow when meaning only to grip his hand. Ignorance therefore being

---

[6] Aeschylus was accused before the Areopagus of having divulged the Mysteries
of Demeter in certain of his tragedies, but was acquitted. A phrase of his, 'It
came to my mouth,' became proverbial (Plato, *Rep.* 563 c, etc.), and he may
have used it on this occasion.

[7] In the lost *Cresphontes* of Euripides.

[8] A style of wrestling in which the adversaries only gripped each other's hands
without closing.

possible in respect of all these circumstances of the act, one who has acted in ignorance of any of them is held to have acted involuntarily, and especially so if ignorant of the most important of them; and the most important of the circumstances seem to be the nature of the act itself and the effect it will produce.

Such then is the nature of the ignorance that justifies our speaking of an act as involuntary, given the further condition that the agent feels sorrow and regret for having committed it.

An involuntary action being one done under compulsion or through ignorance, a voluntary act would seem to be an act of which the origin lies in the agent, who knows the particular circumstances in which he is acting. For it is probably a mistake to say that acts caused by anger or by desire are involuntary. In the first place, (1) this will debar us from speaking of any of the lower animals as acting voluntarily, or children either. Then (2) are none of our actions that are caused by desire or anger voluntary, or are the noble ones voluntary and the base involuntary? Surely this is an absurd distinction when one person is the author of both. Yet perhaps it is strange to speak of acts aiming at things which it is right to aim at as involuntary; and it is right to feel anger at some things, and also to feel desire for some things, for instance health, knowledge. Also (3) we think that involuntary actions are painful and actions that gratify desire pleasant. And again (4) what difference is there in respect of their involuntary character between wrong acts committed deliberately and wrong acts done in anger? Both are to be avoided; and also we think that the irrational feelings are just as much a part of human nature as the reason, so that the actions done from anger or desire also belong to the human being who does them. It is therefore strange to class these actions as involuntary.

II. Having defined voluntary and involuntary action, we next have to examine the nature of Choice. For this appears to be intimately connected with virtue, and to afford a surer test of character than do our actions.

Choice is manifestly a voluntary act. But the two terms are not synonymous, the latter being the wider. Children and the lower animals as well as men are capable of voluntary action, but not of choice. Also sudden acts may be termed voluntary, but they cannot be said to be done by choice.

Some identify Choice with (1) Desire, or (2) Passion, or (3) Wish, or (4) some form of Opinion. These views however appear to be mistaken.

(1) The irrational animals do not exercise choice, but they do feel desire, and also passion. Also a man of defective self-restraint acts from desire but not from choice; and on the contrary a self-restrained man acts from choice and not from desire. Again, desire can run counter to choice, but not desire to desire. And desire has regard to an object as pleasant or painful, choice has not.

(2) Still less is choice the same as passion. Acts done from passion seem very far from being done of deliberate choice.

(3) Again, choice is certainly not a wish, though they appear closely akin. Choice cannot have for its object impossibilities: if a man were to say he chose something impossible he would be thought a fool; but we can wish for things that are impossible, for instance immortality. Also we may wish for what cannot be secured by our own agency, for instance, that a particular actor or athlete may win; but no one chooses what does not rest with himself, but only what he thinks can be attained by his own act. Again, we wish rather for ends than for means, but choose the means to our end; for example, we wish to be healthy, but choose things to make us healthy; we wish to be happy, and that is the word we use in this connexion, but it would not be proper to say that we choose to be happy; since, speaking generally, choice seems to be concerned with things within our own control.

(4) Nor yet again can it be opinion. It seems that anything may be matter of opinion—we form opinions about what is eternal, or impossible, just as much as about what is within our power. Also we distinguish opinion by its truth or falsehood, not by its being good or bad, but choice is distinguished rather as being good or bad. Probably therefore nobody actually identifies choice with opinion in general. But neither is it the same as some particular opinion. For it is our choice of good or evil that determines our character, not our opinion about good or evil. And we choose to take or avoid some good or evil thing, but we opine what a thing is, or for whom it is advantageous, or how it is so: we do not exactly form an opinion to take or avoid a thing. Also we praise a choice rather for choosing the right thing, but an opinion for opining in the right way. And we choose only things that we absolutely know to be good, we opine things we do not quite certainly know to be true. Nor do the same persons appear to excel both at choosing and at forming opinions: some people seem to form opinions better, but yet to choose the wrong things from wickedness. That choice is preceded or accompanied by the formation of an opinion is immaterial, for that is not the point we are considering, but whether choice is the same thing as some form of opinion.

What then are the genus and differentia of Choice, inasmuch as it is not any of the things above mentioned? It manifestly belongs to the genus voluntary action; but not every voluntary act is chosen. Perhaps we may define it as voluntary action preceded by deliberation, since choice involves reasoning and some process of thought. Indeed previous deliberation seems to be implied by the very term *proaireton*, which denotes something *chosen before* other things.

III. As for Deliberation, do people deliberate about everything—are all things possible objects of deliberation—, or are there some things about which deliberation is impossible? The term 'object of deliberation' presumably must not be taken to include things about which a fool or a madman might deliberate, but to mean what a sensible person would deliberate about.

Well then, nobody deliberates about things eternal, such as the order of the universe, or the incommensurability of the diagonal and the side of a square. Nor yet about things that change but follow a regular process, whether from necessity or by nature or through some other cause: such phenomena for instance as the solstices and the sunrise. Nor about irregular occurrences, such as droughts and rains. Nor about the results of chance, such as finding a hidden treasure. The reason why we do not deliberate about these things is that none of them can be effected by our agency. We deliberate about things that are in our control and are attainable by action (which are in fact the only things that still remain to be considered; for Nature, Necessity, and Chance, with the addition of Intelligence and human agency generally, exhaust the generally accepted list of causes). But we do not deliberate about all human affairs without exception either: for example, no Lacedaemonian deliberates about the best form of government for Scythia; but any particular set of men deliberates about the things attainable by their own actions. Also there is no room for deliberation about matters fully ascertained and completely formulated as sciences; such for instance as orthography, for we have no uncertainty as to how a word ought to be spelt. We deliberate about things in which our agency operates but does not always produce the same results; for instance about questions of medicine and of business; and we deliberate about navigation more than about athletic training, because it has been less completely reduced to a science; and similarly with other pursuits also. And we deliberate more about the arts than about the sciences, because we are more uncertain about them.

Deliberation then is employed in matters which, though subject to rules that generally hold good, are uncertain in their issue; or where the issue is indeterminate, and where, when the matter is important, we take others into our deliberations, distrusting our own capacity to decide.

And we deliberate not about ends, but about means. A doctor does not deliberate whether he is to cure his patient, nor an orator whether he is to convince his audience, nor a statesman whether he is to secure good government, nor does anyone else debate about the end of his profession or calling; they take some end for granted, and consider how and by what means it can be achieved. If they find that there are several means of achieving it, they proceed to consider which of these will attain it most easily and best. If there is only one means by which it can be accomplished, they ask how it is to be accomplished by that means, and by what means that means can itself be achieved, until they reach the first link in the chain of causes, which is the last in the order of discovery. (For when deliberating one seems in the procedure described to be pursuing an investigation or analysis that resembles the analysis of a figure in geometry—indeed it appears that though not all investigation is deliberation, for example, mathematical investigation is not, yet all deliberation is investigation—and the last step in the analysis seems to be the first step in the execution of the design.) Then, if they have come up against an impossibility, they abandon the project—for instance, if it requires money and money cannot be procured; but if on the other hand it proves to be something possible, they begin to act. By possible, I mean able to be performed by our agency—things we do through the agency of our friends counting in a sense as done by ourselves, since the origin of their action is in us.

(In practising an art) the question is at one moment what tools to use, and at another how to use them; and similarly in other spheres, we have to consider sometimes what means to employ, and sometimes how exactly any given means are to be employed.

It appears therefore, as has been said, that a man is the origin of his actions, and that the province of deliberation is to discover actions within one's own power to perform; and all our actions aim at ends other than themselves. It follows that we do not deliberate about ends, but about means. Nor yet do we deliberate about particular facts, for instance, Is this object a loaf? or, Is this loaf properly baked? for these are matters of direct perception. Deliberation must stop at the particular fact, or it will embark on a process *ad infinitum*.

The object of deliberation and the object of choice are the same, except that when a thing is chosen it has already been determined, since it is the thing already selected as the result of our deliberation that is chosen. For a man stops enquiring how he shall act as soon as he has carried back the origin of action to himself, and to the dominant part of himself, for it is this part that chooses. This may be illustrated by the ancient constitutions represented in Homer: the kings used to proclaim to the people the measures they had chosen to adopt.

As then the object of choice is something within our power which after deliberation we desire, Choice will be a deliberate desire of things in our power; for we first deliberate, then select, and finally fix our desire according to the result of our deliberation.

Let this serve as a description in outline of Choice, and of the nature of its objects, and the fact that it deals with means to ends.

.   .   .

V. If then whereas we wish for our end, the means to our end are matters of deliberation and choice, it follows that actions dealing with these means are done by choice, and voluntary. But the activities in which the virtues are exercised deal with means. Therefore virtue also depends on ourselves. And so also does vice. For where we are free to act we are also free to refrain from acting, and where we are able to say No we are also able to say Yes; if therefore we are responsible for doing a thing when to do it is right, we are also responsible for not doing it when not to do it is wrong, and if we are responsible for rightly not doing a thing, we are also responsible for wrongly doing it. But if it is in our power to do and to refrain from doing right and wrong, and if, as we saw, being good or bad is doing right or wrong, it consequently depends on us whether we are virtuous or vicious. To say that

None would be vile, and none would not be blest

seems to be half false, though half true: it is true that no one is unwilling to be blessed, but not true that wickedness is involuntary; or else we must contradict what we just now asserted, and say that man is not the originator and begetter of his actions as he is of his children. But if it is manifest that a man is the author of his own actions, and if we are unable to trace our conduct back to any other origins than those within ourselves, then actions of which the origins are within us, themselves depend upon us, and are voluntary.

This conclusion seems to be attested both by men's behaviour in private life and by the practice of lawgivers; for they punish and exact redress from those who do evil (except when it is done under compulsion, or through ignorance for which the agent himself is not responsible), and honour those who do noble deeds, in order to encourage the one sort and to repress the other; but nobody tries to encourage us to do things that do not depend upon ourselves and are not voluntary, since it is no good our being persuaded not to feel heat or pain or hunger or the like, because we shall feel them all the same.

Indeed the fact that an offence was committed in ignorance is itself made a ground for punishment, in cases where the offender is held to be responsible for his ignorance; for instance, the penalty is doubled if the offender was drunk, because the origin of the offence was in the man himself, as he might have avoided getting drunk, which was the cause of his not knowing what he was doing. Also men are punished for offences committed through ignorance of some provision of the law which they ought to have known, and might have known without difficulty; and so in other cases where ignorance is held to be due to negligence, on the ground that the offender need not have been ignorant, as he could have taken the trouble to ascertain the facts.

It may be objected that perhaps he is not the sort of man to take the trouble. Well, but men are themselves responsible for having become careless through living carelessly, as they are for being unjust or profligate if they do wrong or pass their time in drinking and dissipation. They acquire a particular quality by constantly acting in a particular way. This is shown by the way in which men train themselves for some contest or pursuit: they practise continually. Therefore only an utterly senseless person can fail to know that our characters are the result of our conduct; but if a man knowingly acts in a way that will result in his becoming unjust, he must be said to be voluntarily unjust.

Again, though it is unreasonable to say that a man who acts unjustly or dissolutely does not wish to be unjust or dissolute, nevertheless this by no means implies that he can stop being unjust and become just merely by wishing to do so; any more than a sick man can get well by wishing, although it may be the case that his illness is voluntary, in the sense of being due to intemperate living and neglect of the doctors' advice. At the outset then, it is true, he might have avoided the illness, but once he has let himself go he can do so no longer. When you have thrown a stone, you cannot afterwards bring it back again, but nevertheless you are responsible for having taken up the stone and flung it, for the origin of the act was within you. Similarly the unjust and profligate might at the outset have avoided becoming so, and therefore they are so voluntarily, although when they have become unjust and profligate it is no longer open to them not to be so.

And not only are vices of the soul voluntary, but in some cases bodily defects are so as well, and we blame them accordingly. Though no one blames a man for being born ugly, we censure uncomeliness that is due to neglecting exercise and the care of the person. And so with infirmities and mutilations: though nobody would reproach, but rather pity, a person blind from birth, or owing to disease or accident, yet all would blame one who had lost his sight from tippling or debauchery. We see then that bodily defects for which we are ourselves responsible are blamed, while those for which we are not responsible are not. This being so, it follows that we are responsible for blameworthy moral defects also.

But suppose somebody says: "All men seek what seems to them good, but they are not responsible for its seeming good: each man's conception of his end is determined by his character, whatever that may be. Although therefore, on the hypothesis that each man is in a sense responsible for his moral disposition, he will in a sense be responsible for his conception of the good, if on the contrary this hypothesis be untrue, no man is responsible for his own wrongdoing. He does wrong through ignorance of the right end, thinking that wrongdoing will procure him his greatest Good; and his aim at his end is not of his own choosing. A man needs to be born with moral vision, so to speak, whereby to discern correctly and choose what is truly good. A man of good natural disposition is a man well endowed by nature in this respect; for if a thing is the greatest and noblest of gifts, and is something which cannot be acquired or learnt from another, but which a man will possess in such form as it has been bestowed on him at birth, a good and noble natural endowment in this respect will constitute a good disposition in the full and true meaning of the term."

Now if this theory be true, how will virtue be voluntary any more than vice? Both for the good man and the bad man alike, their view of their end is determined in the same manner, by nature or however it may be; and all their actions of whatever sort are guided by reference to their end as thus determined. Whether then a man's view of his end, whatever it may be, is not given by nature but is partly due to himself, or whether, although his end is determined by nature, yet virtue is voluntary because the good man's actions to gain his end are voluntary, in either case vice will be just as much voluntary as virtue; for the bad man equally with the good possesses spontaneity in his actions, even if not in his choice of an end. If then, as is said, our virtues are voluntary (and in fact we are in a sense ourselves partly the cause of our moral dispositions, and it is our having a certain character that makes us set up an end of a certain kind), it follows that our vices are voluntary also; they are voluntary in the same manner as our virtues.

We have then now discussed in outline the virtues in general, having indicated their genus [namely, that it is a mean, and a disposition], and having shown that they render us apt to do the same actions as those by which they are produced, and to do them in the way in which right reason may enjoin; and that they depend on ourselves and are voluntary.

But our dispositions are not voluntary in the same way as are our actions. Our actions we can control from beginning to end, and we are conscious of them at each stage. With our dispositions on the other hand, though we can control their beginnings, each separate addition to them is imperceptible, as is the case with the growth of a disease; though they are voluntary in that we were free to employ our capacities in the one way or the other.

But to resume, let us now discuss the virtues severally, defining the nature of each, the class of objects to which it is related, and the way in which it is related to them. In so doing we shall also make it clear how many virtues there are.

Book IV (*Chapter III: Greatness of Soul*)

III. Greatness of Soul,[9] as the word itself implies, seems to be related to great objects; let us first ascertain what sort of objects these are. It will make no difference whether we examine the quality itself or the person that displays the quality.

Now a person is thought to be great-souled if he claims much and deserves much; he who claims much without deserving it is foolish, but no one of moral excellence is foolish or senseless. The great-souled man is then as we have described. He who deserves little and claims little is modest or temperate, but not great-souled, since to be great-souled involves greatness just as handsomeness involves size: small people may be neat and well-made, but not handsome. He that claims much but does not deserve much is vain; though not everybody who claims more than he deserves is vain. He that claims less than he deserves is small-souled, whether his deserts be great or only moderate, or even though he deserves little, if he claims still less. The most small-souled of all would seem to be the man who claims less than he deserves when his deserts are great; for what would he have done had he not deserved so much?

Though therefore in regard to the greatness of his claim the great-souled man is an extreme, by reason of its rightness he stands at the mean point, for he claims what he deserves; while the vain and the small-souled err by excess and defect respectively.

If then the great-souled man claims and is worthy of great things and most of all the greatest things, Greatness of Soul must be concerned with

---

[9] μεγαλοψυχία, *magnanimitas*, means lofty pride and self-esteem rather than magnanimity or high-mindedness (in the modern sense of the word).

some one object especially. 'Worthy' is a term of relation: it denotes having a claim to goods external to oneself. Now the greatest external good we should assume to be the thing which we offer as a tribute to the gods, and which is most coveted by men of high station, and is the prize awarded for the noblest deeds; and such a thing is honour, for honour is clearly the greatest of external goods. Therefore the great-souled man is he who has the right disposition in relation to honours and disgraces. And even without argument it is evident that honour is the object with which the great-souled are concerned, since it is honour above all else which great men claim and deserve.

The small-souled man falls short both as judged by his own deserts and in comparison with the claim of the great-souled man; the vain man on the other hand exceeds as judged by his own standard, but does not however exceed the great-souled man.[10]

And inasmuch as the great-souled man deserves most, he must be the best of men; for the better a man is the more he deserves, and he that is best deserves most. Therefore the truly great-souled man must be a good man. Indeed greatness in each of the virtues would seem to go with greatness of soul. For instance, one cannot imagine the great-souled man running at full speed when retreating in battle,[11] nor acting dishonestly; since what motive for base conduct has a man to whom nothing is great? Considering all the virtues in turn, we shall feel it quite ridiculous to picture the great-souled man as other than a good man. Moreover, if he were bad, he would not be worthy of honour, since honour is the prize of virtue, and the tribute that we pay to the good. Greatness of Soul seems therefore to be as it were a crowning ornament of the virtues: it enhances their greatness, and it cannot exist without them. Hence it is hard to be truly great-souled, for greatness of soul is impossible without moral nobility.

Honour and dishonour then are the objects with which the great-souled man is especially concerned. Great honours accorded by persons of worth will afford him pleasure in a moderate degree: he will feel he is receiving only what belongs to him, or even less, for no honour can be adequate to the merits of perfect virtue, yet all the same he will deign to accept their honours, because they have no greater tribute to offer him. Honour rendered by common people and on trivial grounds he will utterly despise, for this is not what he merits. He will also despise dishonour, for no dishonour can justly attach to him. The great-souled man then, as has been said, is especially concerned with honour; but he will also observe due measure in respect to wealth, power, and good and bad fortune in general,

---

[10] That is, the small-souled man claims less than he deserves and less than the great-souled man deserves and claims; the vain man claims more than he deserves, but not more than the great-souled man deserves and claims.

[11] Literally 'fleeing swinging his arms at his side,' *i.e.* deficient in the virtue of Courage. If this be the meaning, the phrase recalls by contrast the leisurely retirement of Socrates from the stricken field of Delium (Plato, *Symposium,* 221 A).

as they may befall him; he will not rejoice overmuch in prosperity, nor grieve overmuch at adversity. For he does not care much even about honour, which is the greatest of external goods (since power and wealth are desirable only for the honour they bring, at least their possessors wish to be honoured for their sake); he therefore to whom even honour is a small thing will be indifferent to other things as well. Hence great-souled men are thought to be haughty.

But it is thought that the gifts of fortune also conduce to greatness of soul; for the high-born and those who are powerful or wealthy are esteemed worthy of honour, because they are superior to their fellows, and that which is superior in something good is always held in higher honour; so that even these gifts of fortune make men more great-souled, because their possessors are honoured by some people. But in reality only the good man ought to be honoured, although he that has both virtue and fortune is esteemed still more worthy of honour; whereas those who possess the goods of fortune without virtue are not justified in claiming high worth, and cannot correctly be styled great-souled, since true worth and greatness of soul cannot exist without complete virtue. It is true that even those who merely possess the goods of fortune may be haughty and insolent; because without virtue it is not easy to bear good fortune becomingly, and such men, being unable to carry their prosperity, and thinking themselves superior to the rest of mankind, despise other people, although their own conduct is no better than another's. The fact is that they try to imitate the great-souled man without being really like him, and only copy him in what they can, reproducing his contempt for others but not his virtuous conduct. For the great-souled man is justified in despising other people—his estimates are correct; but most proud men have no good ground for their pride.

The great-souled man does not run into danger for trifling reasons, and is not a lover of danger, because there are few things he values; but he will face danger in a great cause, and when so doing will be ready to sacrifice his life, since he holds that life is not worth having at every price.

He is fond of conferring benefits, but ashamed to receive them, because the former is a mark of superiority and the latter of inferiority. He returns a service done to him with interest, since this will put the original benefactor into his debt in turn, and make him the party benefited. The great-souled are thought to have a good memory for any benefit they have conferred, but a bad memory for those which they have received (since the recipient of a benefit is the inferior of his benefactor, whereas they desire to be superior); and to enjoy being reminded of the former but to dislike being reminded of the latter: this is why the poet makes Thetis not specify her services to Zeus; nor did the Spartans treating with the Athenians recall the occasions when Sparta had aided Athens, but those on which Athens had aided Sparta.

It is also characteristic of the great-souled man never to ask help from others, or only with reluctance, but to render aid willingly; and to be haughty towards men of position and fortune, but courteous towards those of moderate station, because it is difficult and distinguished to be superior to the great, but easy to outdo the lowly, and to adopt a high manner with the former is not ill-bred, but it is vulgar to lord it over humble people: it is like putting forth one's strength against the weak. He will not compete for the common objects of ambition, or go where other people take the first place; and he will be idle and slow to act, except when pursuing some high honour or achievement; and will not engage in many undertakings, but only in such as are important and distinguished. He must be open both in love and in hate, since concealment shows timidity; and care more for the truth than for what people will think; and speak and act openly, since as he despises other men he is outspoken and frank, except when speaking with ironical self-depreciation, as he does to common people. He will be incapable of living at the will of another, unless a friend, since to do so is slavish, and hence flatterers are always servile, and humble people flatterers. He is not prone to admiration, since nothing is great to him. He does not bear a grudge, for it is not a mark of greatness of soul to recall things against people, especially the wrongs they have done you, but rather to overlook them. He is no gossip, for he will not talk either about himself or about another, as he neither wants to receive compliments nor to hear other people run down (nor is he lavish of praise either); and so he is not given to speaking evil himself, even of his enemies, except when he deliberately intends to give offence. In troubles that cannot be avoided or trifling mishaps he will never cry out or ask for help, since to do so would imply that he took them to heart. He likes to own beautiful and useless things, rather than useful things that bring in a return, since the former show his independence more.

Other traits generally attributed to the great-souled man are a slow gait, a deep voice, and a deliberate utterance; to speak in shrill tones and walk fast denotes an excitable and nervous temperament, which does not belong to one who cares for few things and thinks nothing great.

Such then being the Great-souled man, the corresponding character on the side of deficiency is the Small-souled man, and on that of excess the Vain man. These also are not thought to be actually vicious, since they do no harm, but rather mistaken. The small-souled man deprives himself of the good things that he deserves; and his failure to claim good things makes it seem that he has something bad about him [and also that he does not know himself],[12] for (people argue), if he deserved any good, he would try to obtain it. Not that such persons are considered foolish, but rather too retiring; yet this estimate of them is thought to make them still worse, for men's ambitions show what they are worth, and if they hold aloof from noble enterprises and pursuits, and forgo the good things of life, presumably they think they are not worthy of them.

---

[12] These words seem to be interpolated. The small-souled man does not claim his deserts, but he may know what they are; he is not charged with ignorance of self, as is the vain man.

The vain on the other hand are foolish persons, who are deficient in self-knowledge and expose their defect: they undertake honourable responsibilities of which they are not worthy, and then are found out. They are ostentatious in dress, manner and so on. They want people to know how well off they are, and talk about it, imagining that this will make them respected.

Smallness of Soul is more opposed than Vanity to Greatness of Soul, being more prevalent and worse.

Greatness of Soul then, as we have said, is concerned with great honours.

Book VIII (*Chapter VIII: Giving and Receiving Love*)

VIII. Most men however, because they love honour, seem to be more desirous of receiving than of bestowing affection. Hence most men like flattery, for a flatterer is a friend who is your inferior, or pretends to be so, and to love you more than you love him; but to be loved is felt to be nearly the same as to be honoured, which most people covet. They do not however appear to value honour for its own sake, but for something incidental to it. Most people like receiving honour from men of high station, because they hope for something from them: they think that if they want something, the great man will be able to give it them; so they enjoy being honoured by him as a token of benefits to come. Those on the other hand who covet being honoured by good men, and by persons who know them, do so from a desire to confirm their own opinion of themselves; so these like honour because they are assured of their worth by their confidence in the judgment of those who assert it. Affection on the other hand men like for its own sake; from which we infer that it is more valuable than honour, and that friendship is desirable in itself.

But in its essence friendship seems to consist more in giving than in receiving affection: witness the pleasure that mothers take in loving their children. Some mothers put their infants out to nurse, and though knowing and loving them, do not ask to be loved by them in return, if it be impossible to have this as well, but are content if they see them prospering; they retain their own love for them even though the children, not knowing them, cannot render them any part of what is due to a mother. As then friendship consists more especially in bestowing affection, and as we praise men for loving their friends, affection seems to be the mark of a good friend. Hence it is friends that love each other as each deserves who continue friends and whose friendship is lasting.

Also it is by rendering affection in proportion to desert that friends who are not equals may approach most nearly to true friendship, since this will make them equal. Amity consists in equality and similarity, especially the similarity of those who are alike in virtue; for being true to themselves, these also remain true to one another, and neither request nor render services that are morally degrading. Indeed they may be said actually to restrain each other from evil: since good men neither err themselves nor permit their friends to err. Bad men on the other hand have no constancy in friendship, for they do not even remain true to their own characters; but they can be friends for a short time, while they take pleasure in each other's wickedness. The friendships of useful and pleasant people last longer, in fact as long as they give each other pleasure or benefit. It is friendship based on utility that seems most frequently to spring from opposites, for instance a friendship between a poor man and a rich one, or between an ignorant man and a learned; for a person desiring something which he happens to lack will give something else in return for it. One may bring under this class the friendship between a lover and the object of his affections, or between a plain person and a handsome one. This is why lovers sometimes appear ridiculous when they claim that their love should be equally reciprocated; no doubt if they are equally lovable this is a reasonable demand, but it is ridiculous if they have nothing attractive about them.

But perhaps there is no real attraction between opposites as such, but only accidentally, and what they actually desire is the mean between them (since this is the Good); the dry for instance striving not to become wet, but to reach an intermediate state, and so with the hot, and everything else. Let us however dismiss this question, as being indeed somewhat foreign to our subject.

Book IX (*Chapters IV and VIII: Self-Love*)

IV. The forms which friendly feeling for our neighbours take, and the marks by which the different forms of friendship are defined, seem to be derived from the feelings of regard which we entertain for ourselves. A friend is defined as (*a*) one who wishes, and promotes by action, the real or apparent good of another for that other's sake; or (*b*) one who wishes the existence and preservation of his friend for the friend's sake. (This is the feeling of mothers towards their children, and of former friends who have quarrelled.) Others say that a friend is (*c*) one who frequents another's society, and (*d*) who desires the same things as he does, or (*e*) one who shares his friend's joys and sorrows. (This too is very characteristic of mothers.) Friendship also is defined by one or other of these marks. But each of them is also found in a good man's feelings towards himself (and in those of all other men as well, in so far as they believe themselves to be good; but, as has been said, virtue and the virtuous man seem to be the standard in everything). For (*d*) the good man is of one mind with himself, and desires the same things with every part of his nature. Also (*a*) he wishes his own good, real as well as apparent, and seeks it by action (for it is a mark of a good man to exert himself actively for the good); and he does so for his own sake (for he does it on account of the intellectual part of himself, and this appears to be a man's real self). Also (*b*) he desires his own life and security, and especially that of his rational part. For existence is good for the virtuous man; and everyone wishes his own good: no one would choose to possess every good in the world on condition of becoming somebody else (for God possesses the good even as it is), but only while remaining himself, whatever he may be; and it would appear that the thinking part is the real self, or is so more than anything else. And (*c*) the good man desires his own company; for he enjoys being by himself, since he has agreeable memories of the past, and good hopes for the future, which are pleasant too; also his mind is stored with subjects for contemplation. And (*e*) he is keenly conscious of his own joys and sorrows; for the same things give him pleasure or pain at all times, and not different things at different times, since he is not apt to change his mind.

It is therefore because the good man has these various feelings towards himself, and because he feels towards his friend in the same way as towards himself (for a friend is another self), that friendship also is thought to consist in one or other of these feelings, and the possession of them is thought to be the test of a friend.

Whether a man can be said actually to feel friendship for himself is a question that may be dismissed for the present; though it may be held that he can do so in so far as he is a dual or composite being, and because very intense friendship resembles self-regard.

As a matter of fact, the feelings of self-regard described appear to be found in most people, even though they are of inferior moral worth. Perhaps men share them in so far as they have their own approval and believe in their own virtue; since the utterly worthless and criminal never possess them, or even have the appearance of doing so. Indeed it may almost be said that no morally inferior persons possess them. For (*d*) such persons are at variance with themselves, desiring one thing and wishing another: this is the mark of the unrestrained, who choose what is pleasant but harmful instead of what they themselves think to be good. (*a*) Others again, out of cowardice and idleness, neglect to do what they think best for their own interests. And (*b*) men who have committed a number of crimes, and are hated for their wickedness, actually flee from life and make away with themselves. Also (*c*) bad men constantly seek the society of others and shun their own company, because when they are by themselves they recall much that was unpleasant in the past and anticipate the same in the future, whereas with other people they can forget. Moreover they feel no affection for themselves, because they have no lovable qualities. Hence (*e*) such men do not enter into their own joys and sorrows, as there is civil war in their souls; one part of their nature, owing to depravity, is pained by abstinence from certain indulgences while another part is pleased by it; one part pulls them one way and another the other, as if dragging them asunder. Or if it be impossible to feel pain and pleasure at the same time, at all events after indulging in pleasure they regret it a little later, and wish they had never acquired a taste for such indulgences; since the bad are always changing their minds.

Thus a bad man appears to be devoid even of affection for himself, because he has nothing lovable in his nature. If then such a state of mind is utterly miserable, we should do our utmost to shun wickedness and try to be virtuous. That is the way both to be friends with ourselves and to win the friendship of others.

. . .

VIII.   The question is also raised whether one ought to love oneself or someone else most. We censure those who put themselves first, and 'lover of self' is used as a term of reproach. And it is thought that a bad man considers himself in all he does, and the more so the worse he is—so it is a complaint against him for instance that 'he never does a thing unless you make him'—whereas a good man acts from a sense of what is noble, and the better he is the more he so acts, and he considers his friend's interest, disregarding his own.

But the facts do not accord with these theories; nor is this surprising. For we admit that one should love one's best friend most; but the best friend is he that, when he wishes a person's good, wishes it for that person's own sake, even though nobody will ever know of it. Now this condition is most fully realized in a man's regard for himself, as indeed are all the other attributes that make up the definition of a friend; for it has been said already that all the feelings that constitute friendship for others are an extension of regard for self. Moreover, all the proverbs agree with this; for example, 'Friends have one soul between them,' 'Friends' goods are common property,' 'Amity is equality,' 'The knee is nearer than the shin.' All of these sayings will apply most fully to oneself; for a man is his own best friend. Therefore he ought to love himself most.

So it is naturally debated which of these two views we ought to adopt, since each of them has some plausibility.

Now where there is a conflict of opinion the proper course is doubtless to get the two views clearly distinguished, and to define how far and in what way each of them is true. So probably the matter may become clear if we ascertain what meaning each side attaches to the term 'self-love.'

Those then who make it a term of reproach call men lovers of self when they assign to themselves the larger share of money, honours, or bodily pleasures; since these are the things which most men desire and set their hearts on as being the greatest goods, and which accordingly they compete with each other to obtain. Now those who take more than their share of these things are men who indulge their appetites, and generally their passions and the irrational part of their souls. But most men are of this kind. Accordingly the use of the term 'lover of self' as a reproach has arisen from the fact that self-love of the ordinary kind is bad. Hence self-love is rightly censured in those who are lovers of self in this sense. And that it is those who take too large a share of things of this sort whom most people usually mean when they speak of lovers of self, is clear enough. For if a man were always bent on outdoing everybody else in acting justly or temperately or in displaying any other of the virtues, and in general were always trying to secure for himself moral nobility, no one will charge him with love of self nor find any fault with him. Yet as a matter of fact such a man might be held to be a lover of self in an exceptional degree. At all events he takes for himself the things that are noblest and most truly good. Also it is the most dominant part of himself that he indulges and obeys in everything. But (*a*) as in the state it is the sovereign that is held in the fullest sense to *be* the state, and in any other composite whole it is the dominant part that is deemed especially to be that whole, so it is with man. He therefore who loves and indulges the dominant part of himself is a lover of self in the fullest degree. Again (*b*), the terms 'self-restrained' and 'unrestrained' denote being restrained or not by one's intellect, and thus imply that the intellect is the man himself. Also (*c*) it is our reasoned acts that are felt to be in the fullest sense *our own* acts, *voluntary* acts. It is therefore clear that man is or is chiefly the dominant part of himself, and that a good man values this part of himself most. Hence the good man will be a lover of self in the fullest degree, though in another sense than the lover of self so-called by way of reproach, from whom he differs as much as living by principle differs from living by passion, and aiming at what is noble from aiming at what seems expedient. Persons therefore who are exceptionally zealous in noble actions are universally approved and commended; and if all men vied with each other in moral nobility and strove to perform the noblest deeds, the common welfare would be fully realized, while individuals also could enjoy the greatest of goods, inasmuch as virtue is the greatest good.

Therefore the good man ought to be a lover of self, since he will then both benefit himself by acting nobly and aid his fellows; but the bad man ought not to be a lover of self, since he will follow his base passions, and so injure both himself and his neighbours. With the bad man therefore, what he does is not in accord with what he ought to do, but the good man does what he ought, since intelligence always chooses for itself that which is best, and the good man obeys his intelligence.

But it is also true that the virtuous man's conduct is often guided by the interests of his friends and of his country, and that he will if necessary lay down his life in their behalf. For he will surrender wealth and power and all the goods that men struggle to win, if he can secure nobility for himself; since he would prefer an hour of rapture to a long period of mild enjoyment, a year of noble life to many years of ordinary existence, one great and glorious exploit to many small successes. And this is doubtless the case with those who give their lives for others; thus they choose great nobility for themselves. Also the virtuous man is ready to forgo money if by that means his friends may gain more money; for thus, though his friend gets money, he himself achieves nobility, and so he assigns the greater good to his own share. And he behaves in the same manner as regards honours and offices also: all these things he will relinquish to his friend, for this is noble and praiseworthy for himself. He is naturally therefore thought to be virtuous, as he chooses moral nobility in preference to all other things. It may even happen that he will surrender to his friend the performance of some achievement, and that it may be nobler for him to be the cause of his friend's performing it than to perform it himself.

Therefore in all spheres of praiseworthy conduct it is manifest that the good man takes the larger share of moral nobility for himself. In this sense then, as we said above, it is right to be a lover of self, though self-love of the ordinary sort is wrong.

Book X (*Chapters VI-VIII: The Highest Happiness*)

VI. Having now discussed the various kinds of Virtue of Friendship and of Pleasure, it remains for us to treat in outline of Happiness, inasmuch as we count this to be the End of human life. But it will shorten the discussion if we recapitulate what has been said already.

Now we stated that happiness is not a certain disposition of character; since if it were it might be possessed by a man who passed the whole of his life asleep, living the life of a vegetable, or by one who was plunged in the deepest misfortune. If then we reject this as unsatisfactory, and feel bound to class happiness rather as some form of activity, as has been said in the earlier part of this treatise, and if activities are of two kinds, some merely necessary means and desirable only for the sake of something else, others desirable in themselves, it is clear that happiness is to be classed among activities desirable in themselves, and not among those desirable as a means to something else; since happiness lacks nothing, and is self-sufficient.

But those activities are desirable in themselves which do not aim at any result beyond the mere exercise of the activity. Now this is felt to be the nature of actions in conformity with virtue; for to do noble and virtuous deeds is a thing desirable for its own sake.

But agreeable amusements also are desirable for their own sake; we do not pursue them as a means to something else, for as a matter of fact they are more often harmful than beneficial, causing men to neglect their health and their estates. Yet persons whom the world counts happy usually have recourse to such pastimes; and this is why adepts in such pastimes stand in high favour with princes, because they make themselves agreeable in supplying what their patrons desire, and what they want is amusement. So it is supposed that amusements are a component part of happiness, because princes and potentates devote their leisure to them.

But (i) perhaps princes and potentates are not good evidence. Virtue and intelligence, which are the sources of man's higher activities, do not depend on the possession of power; and if these persons, having no taste for pure and liberal pleasure, have recourse to the pleasures of the body, we must not on that account suppose that bodily pleasures are the more desirable. Children imagine that the things they themselves value are actually the best; it is not surprising therefore that, as children and grown men have different standards of value, so also should the worthless and the virtuous. Therefore, as has repeatedly been said, those things are actually valuable and pleasant which appear so to the good man; but each man thinks that activity most desirable which suits his particular disposition, and therefore the good man thinks virtuous activity most desirable. It follows therefore that happiness is not to be found in amusements.

(ii) Indeed it would be strange that amusement should be our End— that we should toil and moil all our life long in order that we may amuse ourselves. For virtually every object we adopt is pursued as a means to something else, excepting happiness, which is an end in itself; to make amusement the object of our serious pursuits and our work seems foolish and childish to excess: Anacharsis's motto, Play in order that you may work, is felt to be the right rule. For amusement is a form of rest; but we need rest because we are not able to go on working without a break, and therefore it is not an end, since we take it as a means to further activity.

(iii) And the life that conforms with virtue is thought to be a happy life; but virtuous life involves serious purpose, and does not consist in amusement.

(iv) Also we pronounce serious things to be superior to things that are funny and amusing; and the nobler a faculty or a person is, the more serious, we think, are their activities; therefore, the activity of the nobler faculty or person is itself superior, and therefore more productive of happiness.

(v) Also anybody can enjoy the pleasures of the body, a slave no less than the noblest of mankind; but no one allows a slave any measure of happiness, any more than a life of his own. Therefore happiness does not consist in pastimes and amusements, but in activities in accordance with virtue, as has been said already.

VII. But if happiness consists in activity in accordance with virtue, it is reasonable that it should be activity in accordance with the highest virtue; and this will be the virtue of the best part of us. Whether then this be the intellect, or whatever else it be that is thought to rule and lead us by nature, and to have cognizance of what is noble and divine, either as being itself also actually divine, or as being relatively the divinest part of us, it is the activity of this part of us in accordance with the virtue proper to it that will constitute perfect happiness; and it has been stated already that this activity is the activity of contemplation.

And that happiness consists in contemplation may be accepted as agreeing both with the results already reached and with the truth. For contemplation is at once the highest form of activity (since the intellect is the highest thing in us, and the objects with which the intellect deals are the highest things that can be known), and also it is the most continuous, for we can reflect more continuously than we can carry on any form of action. And again we suppose that happiness must contain an element of pleasure; now activity in accordance with wisdom is admittedly the most pleasant of the activities in accordance with virtue; at all events it is held that philosophy or the pursuit of wisdom contains pleasures of marvellous purity and permanence, and it is reasonable to suppose that the enjoyment of knowledge is a still pleasanter occupation than the pursuit of it. Also the activity of contemplation will be found to possess in the highest degree the quality that is termed self-sufficiency; for while it is true that the wise man equally with the just man and the rest requires the necessaries of life, yet, these being adequately supplied, whereas the just man needs other persons towards whom or with whose aid he may act justly, and so likewise do the temperate man and the brave man and the others, the wise man on the contrary can also contemplate by himself, and the more so the wiser he is; no doubt he will study better with the aid of fellow-workers, but still he is the most self-sufficient of men. Also the activity of contemplation may be held to be the only activity that is loved for its own sake: it produces no result beyond the actual act of contemplation, whereas from practical pursuits we look to secure some advantage, greater or smaller, beyond the action itself. Also happiness is thought to involve leisure for we do business in order that we may have leisure, and carry on war in order that we may have peace. Now the practical virtues are exercised in politics or in warfare; but the pursuits of politics and war seem to be unleisured—those of war indeed entirely so, for no one desires to be at war for the sake of being at war, nor deliberately takes steps to cause a war: a man would be thought an utterly bloodthirsty character if he declared war on a friendly state for the sake of causing battles and massacres. But the activity of the politician also is unleisured, and aims at securing something beyond the mere participation in politics—positions of authority and honour, or, if the happiness of the politician himself and of his fellow-citizens, this happiness conceived as something distinct from political activity (indeed we are clearly investigating it as so distinct).[13] If then among practical pursuits displaying the virtues, politics and war stand out pre-eminent in nobility and grandeur, and yet they are unleisured, and directed to some further end, not chosen for their own sakes: whereas the activity of the intellect is felt to excel in serious worth, consisting as it does in contemplation, and to aim at no end beyond itself, and also to contain a pleasure peculiar to itself, and therefore augmenting its activity: and if accordingly the attributes of this activity are found to be self-sufficiency, leisuredness, such freedom from fatigue as is possible for man, and all the other attributes of blessedness: it follows that it is the activity of the intellect that constitutes complete human happiness—provided it be granted a complete span of life, for nothing that belongs to happiness can be incomplete.

Such a life as this however will be higher than the human level: not in virtue of his humanity will a man achieve it, but in virtue of something within him that is divine; and by as much as this something is superior

---

[13] Probably the sentence should be curtailed to run 'or in fact the happiness of himself and his fellow-citizens; and happiness we are clearly investigating as something distinct from the art of politics [whose object it is].'

to his composite nature, by so much is its activity superior to the exercise of the other forms of virtue. If then the intellect is something divine in comparison with man, so is the life of the intellect divine in comparison with human life. Nor ought we to obey those who enjoin that a man should have man's thoughts and a mortal the thoughts of mortality, but we ought so far as possible to achieve immortality, and do all that man may to live in accordance with the highest thing in him; for though this be small in bulk, in power and value it far surpasses all the rest.

It may even be held that this is the true self of each, inasmuch as it is the dominant and better part; and therefore it would be a strange thing if a man should choose to live not his own life but the life of some other than himself.

Moreover what was said before will apply here also: that which is best and most pleasant for each creature is that which is proper to the nature of each; accordingly the life of the intellect is the best and the pleasantest life for man, inasmuch as the intellect more than anything else is man; therefore this life will be the happiest.

VIII. The life of moral virtue, on the other hand, is happy only in a secondary degree. For the moral activities are purely human: Justice, I mean, Courage and the other virtues we display in our intercourse with our fellows, when we observe what is due to each in contracts and services and in our various actions, and in our emotions also; and all of these things seem to be purely human affairs. And some moral actions are thought to be the outcome of the physical constitution, and moral virtue is thought to have a close affinity in many respects with the passions. Moreover, Prudence is intimately connected with Moral Virtue, and this with Prudence, inasmuch as the first principles which Prudence employs are determined by the Moral Virtues, and the right standard for the Moral Virtues is determined by Prudence. But these being also connected with the passions are related to our composite nature; now the virtues of our composite nature are purely human; so therefore also is the life that manifests these virtues, and the happiness that belongs to it. Whereas the happiness that belongs to the intellect is separate: so much may be said about it here, for a full discussion of the matter is beyond the scope of our present purpose. And such happiness would appear to need but little external equipment, or less than the happiness based on moral virtue. Both, it may be granted, require the mere necessaries of life, and that in an equal degree (though the politician does as a matter of fact take more trouble about bodily requirements and so forth than the philosopher); for in this respect there may be little difference between them. But for the purpose of their special activities their requirements will differ widely. The liberal man will need wealth in order to do liberal actions, and so indeed will the just man in order to discharge his obligations (since mere intentions are invisible, and even the unjust pretend to wish to act justly); and the brave man will need strength if he is to perform any action displaying his virtue; and the temperate man opportunity for indulgence: otherwise how can he, or the possessor of any other virtue, show that he is virtuous? It is disputed also whether purpose or performance is the more important factor in virtue, as it is alleged to depend on both; now the perfection of virtue will clearly consist in both; but the performance of virtuous actions requires much outward equipment, and the more so the greater and more noble the actions are. But the student, so far as the pursuit of his activity is concerned, needs no external apparatus: on the contrary, worldly goods may almost be said to be a hindrance to contemplation; though it is true that, being a man and living in the society of others, he chooses to engage in virtuous action, and so will need external goods to carry on his life as a human being.

The following considerations also will show that perfect happiness is some form of contemplative activity. The gods, as we conceive them, enjoy supreme felicity and happiness. But what sort of actions can we attribute to them? Just actions? but will it not seem ridiculous to think of them as making contracts, restoring deposits and the like? Then brave actions—enduring terrors and running risks for the nobility of so doing? Or liberal actions? but to whom will they give? Besides, it would be absurd to suppose that they actually have a coinage or currency of some sort! And temperate actions—what will these mean in their case? surely it would be derogatory to praise them for not having evil desires! If we go through the list we shall find that all forms of virtuous conduct seem trifling and unworthy of the gods. Yet nevertheless they have always been conceived as, at all events, living, and therefore living actively, for we cannot suppose they are always asleep like Endymion. But for a living being, if we eliminate action, and *a fortiori* creative action, what remains save contemplation? It follows that the activity of God, which is transcendent in blessedness, is the activity of contemplation; and therefore among human activities that which is most akin to the divine activity of contemplation will be the greatest source of happiness.

A further confirmation is that the lower animals cannot partake of happiness, because they are completely devoid of the contemplative activity. The whole of the life of the gods is blessed, and that of man is so in so far as it contains some likeness to the divine activity; but none of the other animals possess happiness, because they are entirely incapable of contemplation. Happiness therefore is co-extensive in its range with contemplation: the more a class of beings possesses the faculty of contemplation, the more it enjoys happiness, not as an accidental concomitant of contemplation but as inherent in it, since contemplation is valuable in itself. It follows that happiness is some form of contemplation.

But the philosopher being a man will also need external well-being, since man's nature is not self-sufficient for the activity of contemplation, but he must also have bodily health and a supply of food and other requirements. Yet if supreme blessedness is not possible without external goods, it must not be supposed that happiness will demand many or great possessions; for self-sufficiency does not depend on excessive abundance, nor does moral conduct, and it is possible to perform noble deeds even without being ruler of land and sea: one can do virtuous acts with quite moderate resources. This may be clearly observed in experience: private citizens do not seem to be less but more given to doing virtuous actions than princes and potentates. It is sufficient then if moderate resources are forthcoming; for a life of virtuous activity will be essentially a happy life.

Solon also doubtless gave a good description of happiness, when he said that in his opinion those men were happy who, being moderately equipped with external goods, had performed noble exploits and had lived temperately; for it is possible for a man of but moderate possessions to do what is right. Anaxagoras again does not seem to have conceived the happy man as rich or powerful, since he says that he would not be surprised if he were to appear a strange sort of person in the eyes of the many; for most men judge by externals, which are all that they can perceive. So our theories seem to be in agreement with the opinions of the wise.

Such arguments then carry some degree of conviction; but it is by the practical experience of life and conduct that the truth is really tested, since it is there that the final decision lies. We must therefore examine the conclusions we have advanced by bringing them to the test of the facts of life. If they are in harmony with the facts, we may accept them; if found to disagree, we must deem them mere theories.

And it seems likely that the man who pursues intellectual activity, and who cultivates his intellect and keeps that in the best condition, is also the man most beloved of the gods. For if, as is generally believed, the gods exercise some superintendence over human affairs, then it will be reasonable to suppose that they take pleasure in that part of man which is best and most akin to themselves, namely the intellect, and that they recompense with their favours those men who esteem and honour this most, because these care for the things dear to themselves, and act rightly and nobly. Now it is clear that all these attributes belong most of all to the wise man. He therefore is most beloved by the gods; and if so, he is naturally most happy. Here is another proof that the wise man is the happiest.

.   .   .

POETICS (*Chapters I-XV*)

I

I propose to treat of poetry in itself and of its several species, noting the essential quality of each; to inquire into the structure of the plot as requisite to a good poem; into the number and nature of the parts of which each species consists; and similarly into whatever else falls within the same inquiry. Following, then, the order of nature, let us begin with the principles which come first.

Epic poetry and Tragedy, Comedy also and dithyrambic poetry, and the greater part of the music of the flute and of the lyre are all in their general conception modes of imitation. They differ, however, from one another in three respects—the means, the objects, the manner of imitation being in each case distinct.

For as there are persons who, by conscious art or mere habit, imitate and represent various objects through the medium of color and form, or again by the voice; so in the arts above mentioned taken as a whole, the imitation is produced by rhythm, language, and 'harmony,' either singly or combined.

Thus in the music of the flute and the lyre 'harmony' and rhythm alone are employed; also in other arts such as that of the pipe, which are essentially similar to these; in dancing, rhythm alone is used without 'harmony'; for even dancing imitates character, emotion, and action, by rhythmical movement.

The art which imitates by means of language alone, and that either in prose or verse—which verse, again, may either combine different metres or consist of but one kind—has hitherto been without a name. For there is no common term we could apply to the mimes of Sophron and Xenarchus and to the Socratic dialogues; or, again, to poetic imitations in iambic, elegiac, or any similar metre. People do, indeed, commonly connect the idea of poetry or 'making' with that of verse, and speak of elegiac poets, or of epic (that is, hexameter) poets; implying that it is not imitation that makes them poets, but the metre that entitles them to the common name. Even if a treatise on medicine or natural philosophy be brought out in verse, the name of poet is by custom given to the author; and yet Homer and Empedocles have nothing in common except the metre: the former, therefore, is properly styled poet, the latter, physicist rather than poet.

So too if a writer should, in his poetic imitation, combine every variety of metre, like Chaeremon—whose *Centaur* is a rhapsody in which all metres are mingled—we must, according to usage, call him simply poet. So much then for these distinctions.

There are, again, certain kinds of poetry which employ all the means above mentioned—namely, rhythm, melody and metre. Such are dithyrambic and nomic poetry, and also Tragedy and Comedy; but between them the difference is, that in the first two cases these means are all employed at the same time, in the latter, separately.

Such, then, are the differences of the arts with respect to the means of imitation.

II

Since the objects of imitation are persons acting, and these persons must be either of a higher or a lower type (for moral character mainly answers to these divisions, goodness and badness being the distinguishing marks of moral differences), it follows that we must represent men either as better than in real life, or worse, or as they are. It is the same in painting. Polygnotus depicted men as nobler than they are, Pauson as less noble, Dionysius drew them true to life.

Now it is evident that each of the modes of imitation above mentioned will exhibit these differences, and become a distinct kind in imitating objects that are thus distinct. Such diversities may be found even in dancing, flute-playing, and lyre-playing. So again in prose compositions, and in verse unaccompanied by music. Homer, for example, makes men better than they are; Cleophon as they are; Hegemon the Thasian, the inventor of parodies, and Nicochares, the author of the *Deliad,* worse than they are. The same thing holds good of dithyrambs and nomes; here too one may portray lower types, as Timotheus and Philoxenus represented Cyclopes. The same distinction marks off Tragedy from Comedy; for Comedy aims at representing men as worse, Tragedy as better than in actual life.

III

There is still a third difference—the manner in which each of these objects may be imitated. For the means being the same, and the objects the same, the poet may imitate by narration—in which case he can either take another personality as Homer does, or speak in his own person, unchanged—or he may imitate by making all his actors live and move before us.

These, then, as we said at the beginning, are the three differences which distinguish artistic imitation—the means, the objects, and the manner. So that from one point of view, Sophocles is an imitator of the same kind as Homer—for both imitate higher types of character; from another point of view, of the same kind as Aristophanes—for both imitate persons acting and doing. Hence, some say, the name of 'drama' is given to such poems, as representing action. For the same reason the Dorians claim the invention both of Tragedy and Comedy. The claim to Comedy is put forward by the Megarians—not only by those of Greece proper, who allege that it originated under their democracy, but also by the Megarians of Sicily; the poet Epicharmus, who lived not long before Chionides and Magnes, being from their country. Tragedy too is claimed by certain Dorians of the Peloponnese. In each case they appeal to the evidence of language. Villages they say, are by them called χῶμαι, by the Athenians δῆμοι: and they assume that the name Comedians is derived not from χωμάζειν, 'to revel,' but from the performer wandering about the villages (χῶμαι), when still excluded from the city. They add also that the Dorian word for 'doing' is δρᾶν, and the Athenian, πράττειν.

This may suffice as to the number and nature of the various modes of imitation.

IV

Poetry in general seems to have sprung from two causes, each of them lying deep in our nature. First, the instinct of imitation is implanted in man from childhood, one difference between him and other animals being that he is the most imitative of creatures; and through imitation he acquires his earliest learning. And, indeed, every one feels a natural pleasure in things imitated. There is evidence of this in the effect produced by works of art. Objects which in themselves we view with pain, we delight to contemplate when reproduced with absolute fidelity: such as the forms of the most ignoble beasts and of dead bodies. The cause of this again is, that to learn is a lively pleasure, not only to philosophers but to men in general; whose capacity, however, of learning is more limited. Thus the reason why men enjoy seeing a likeness is, that in contemplating it they are engaged in learning—they reason and infer what each object is: 'this,' they say, 'is the man.' For if you happen not to have seen the original, the pleasure will be due not to the imitation as such, but to the execution, the colouring, or some such other cause.

Imitation, then, is one instinct of our nature. Next, there is the instinct for harmony and rhythm, metre being manifestly a species of rhythm. Persons, therefore, with this natural gift little by little improved upon their early efforts, till their rude improvisations gave birth to Poetry.

Poetry now branched off in two directions, according to the individual character of the writers. The more elevated poets imitated noble actions, and the actions of good men. The more trivial sort imitated the actions of meaner persons, at first composing satires, as the former did hymns to the gods and the praises of famous men. A poem of the satirical kind cannot indeed be put down to any author earlier than Homer; though many such writers probably there were. But from Homer onward, instances can be cited—his *Margites,* for example, and other similar compositions. The iambic metre was here introduced, as best fitted to the subject: hence the measure is still called the iambic or lampooning measure, being that in which the lampoons were written.

Thus the older poets were distinguished as writers either of heroic or of iambic verse. As, in the serious style, Homer is preeminent among poets, standing alone not only in the excellence, but also in the dramatic form of his imitations, so he too first sketched out the main lines of Comedy, by dramatising the ludicrous instead of writing personal satire. His *Margites* bears the same relation to Comedy that the *Iliad* and *Odyssey* do to Tragedy. But when Tragedy and Comedy had once appeared, writers applied themselves to one or other species of poetry, following their native bent. They composed Comedies in place of lampoons, and Tragedies in place of Epic poems, the newer forms of poetry being higher and more highly esteemed than the old.

Whether Tragedy has as yet perfected its proper types or not; and whether it is to be judged in itself, or in relation also to the stage—this raises another question. Be that as it may, Tragedy—as also Comedy—was at first mere improvisation. The one originated with the leaders of the dithyrambic, the other with those of the phallic songs, which are still in use in many of our cities. Tragedy advanced by slow degrees; each new element that showed itself was in turn developed. Having passed through many changes, it found its natural form, and there it stopped.

Aeschylus first introduced a second actor; he diminished the importance of the Chorus, and assigned the leading part to the dialogue. Sophocles raised the number of actors to three, and added scene-painting. It was not till late that the short plot was discarded for one of greater compass, and the grotesque diction of the earlier satyric form, for the stately manner of Tragedy. The iambic measure then replaced the trochaic tetrameter, which was originally employed when the poetry was of the satyric order, and had greater affinities with dancing. Once dialogue had come in, Nature herself discovered the appropriate measure. For the iambic is, of all measures, the most colloquial: we see it in the fact that conversational speech runs into iambic form more frequently than into any other kind of verse; rarely into hexameters, and only when we drop the colloquial intonation. The number of 'episodes' or acts was also increased, and the other embellishments added, of which tradition tells. These we need not here discuss; to enter into them in detail would, probably, be tedious.

V

Comedy is, as we have said, an imitation of characters of a lower type—not, however, in the full sense of the word bad; for the Ludicrous is merely a subdivision of the ugly. It may be defined as a defect or ugliness which is not painful or destructive. Thus, for example, the comic mask is ugly and distorted, but does not cause pain.

The successive changes through which Tragedy passed, and the authors of these changes are not unknown. It is otherwise with Comedy, which at first was not seriously treated. It was late before the Archon appointed a comic chorus; the performers were till then voluntary. From the time, however, when Comedy began to assume certain fixed forms, comic poets, distinctively so called, are recorded. Who introduced masks, or prologues, or increased the number of actors—these and other similar details remain unknown. As for the plot, it came originally from Sicily; but of Athenian writers Crates was the first who, abandoning the 'iambic' or lampooning form, generalised his themes and plots.

Epic poetry agrees with Tragedy in so far as it is an imitation in verse of characters of a higher type. They differ, in that Epic poetry admits but one kind of metre, and is narrative in form. They differ, again, in length: for Tragedy endeavours, as far as possible, to confine itself to a single revolution of the sun, or but slightly to exceed this limit; whereas the Epic action has no limits of time. This, then, is a second point of difference; though at first the same freedom was admitted in Tragedy as in Epic poetry.

Of their constituent parts some are common to both, some peculiar to Tragedy. Whoever, therefore, knows what is good or bad Tragedy, knows also about Epic poetry: for all the parts of an Epic poem are found in Tragedy, but what belongs to Tragedy is not all found in the Epic poem.

VI

Of the poetry which imitates in hexameter verse, and of Comedy, we will speak hereafter. Let us now discuss Tragedy, resuming its formal definition, as resulting from what has been already said.

Tragedy, then, is an imitation of an action that is serious, complete, and of a certain magnitude; in language embellished with each kind of artistic ornament, the several kinds being found in separate parts of the play; in the form of action, not of narrative; through pity and fear effecting the proper purgation of these emotions. By 'language embellished,' I mean language into which rhythm, 'harmony,' and song enter. By 'the several kinds in separate parts,' I mean, that some parts are rendered through the medium of verse alone, others again with the aid of song.

Now as tragic imitation implies persons acting, it necessarily follows, in the first place, that Scenic equipment will be a part of Tragedy. Next, Song and Diction, for these are the means of imitation. By 'Diction' I mean the mere metrical arrangement of the words: or for 'Song,' it is a term whose full sense is well understood.

Again, Tragedy is the imitation of an action; and an action implies personal agents, who necessarily possess certain qualities both of character and thought. It is these that determine the qualities of actions themselves; these—thought and character—are the two natural causes from which actions spring: on these causes, again, all success or failure depends. Hence, the Plot is the imitation of the action—for by plot I here mean the arrangement of the incidents. By Character I mean that in virtue of which we ascribe certain qualities to the agents. By Thought, that whereby a statement is proved, or a general truth expressed. Every Tragedy, therefore, must have six parts, which parts determine its quality—namely, Plot, Character, Diction, Thought, Scenery, Song. Two of the parts constitute the means of imitation, one the manner, and three the objects of imitation. And these complete the list. These elements have been employed, we may say, by almost all poets; in fact, every play contains Scenic accessories as well as Character, Plot, Diction, Song, and Thought.

But most important of all is the structure of the incidents. For Tragedy is an imitation, not of men, but of an action and of life—of happiness and misery; and happiness and misery consist in action, the end of human life being a mode of action, not a quality. Now the characters of men determine their qualities, but it is by their actions that they are happy or the reverse. Dramatic action, therefore, is not with a view to the representation of character: character comes in as subsidiary to the action. Hence the incidents and the plot are the end of a tragedy; and the end is the chief thing of all. Again, without action there cannot be a tragedy;

there may be without character. The tragedies of most of our modern poets fail in the rendering of character; and of poets in general this is often true. It is the same in painting; and here lies the difference between Zeuxis and Polygnotus. Polygnotus delineates character well: the style of Zeuxis is devoid of ethical quality. Again, if you string together a set of speeches expressive of character, and well finished in point of diction and thought, you will not produce the essential tragic effect nearly so well as with a play, which, however deficient in these respects yet has a plot and artistically constructed incident. Besides which, the most powerful elements of emotional interest in Tragedy—Reversals of Fortune, and Recognition scenes—are parts of the plot. A further proof is, that novices in the art are able to elaborate their diction and ethical portraiture, before they can frame the incidents. It is the same with almost all early poets.

The Plot, then, is the first principle, and, as it were, the soul of the tragedy: Character holds the second place. A similar fact is seen in painting. The most beautiful colours, laid on confusedly, will not give as much pleasure as the chalk outline of a portrait. Thus Tragedy is the imitation of an action, and of the agents, mainly with a view to the action.

Third in order is the Thought—that is, the faculty of saying what is possible and pertinent in given circumstances. In the case of the dramatic dialogue, this is the function of the political or the rhetorical art: for the older poets make their characters speak the language of civic life; the poets of our time, the language of the rhetoricians. Character is that which reveals moral purpose: it shows what kind of things, in cases of doubt, a man chooses or avoids. A dialogue, therefore, which in no way indicates what the speaker chooses or avoids, is not expressive of character. Thought, on the other hand, is that whereby we prove that something is or is not, or state a general maxim.

Fourth comes the Diction; by which I mean, as has been already said, the expression of our meaning in words; and its essence is the same both in verse and prose.

Of the remaining elements Song holds the chief place among the embellishments.

The Scenery has, indeed, an emotional attraction of its own, but, of all the parts, it is the least artistic, and connected least with poetic theory. For the power of Tragedy, we may be sure, is felt even apart from representation and actors. Besides, the production of scenic effects depends more on the art of the stage manager than on that of the poet.

VII

These principles being established, let us now discuss the proper structure of the Plot, since this is the first, and also the most important part of Tragedy.

Now, according to our definition, Tragedy is an imitation of an action, that is complete, and whole, and of a certain magnitude; for there may be a whole that is wanting in magnitude. A whole is that which has beginning, middle, and end. A beginning is that which does not itself follow anything by causal necessity, but after which something naturally is or comes to be. An end, on the contrary, is that which itself naturally follows some other thing, either by necessity, or in the regular course of events, but has nothing following it. A middle is that which follows something as some other thing follows it. A well constructed plot, therefore, must neither begin nor end at haphazard, but conform to the type here described.

Again, if an object be beautiful—either a living organism or a whole composed of parts—it must not only have its parts in orderly arrangement, it must also be of a certain magnitude. Hence no exceedingly small animal can be beautiful, for the view of it is confused, the object being seen in an almost imperceptible moment of time. Nor, again, can an animal of vast size be beautiful; for as the eye cannot take it all in at once, the unity and sense of the whole is lost for the spectator. So it would be with a creature a thousand miles long. As, therefore, in animate bodies and living organisms, a certain magnitude is necessary, and that such as may be easily embraced in one view; so in the plot, a certain length is necessary and that length one that may be easily embraced by the memory. The limit of length in relation to dramatic competition and sensuous presentment, is no part of artistic theory. For suppose a hundred tragedies had to be played against one another, the performance would be regulated by the hour-glass—a method, indeed, that is familiar enough otherwise. But the limit as fixed by the nature of the drama itself is this: —the greater the length, the more beautiful will the piece be in respect of such magnitude, provided that the whole be perspicuous. And as a general rule, the proper magnitude is comprised within such limits, that the sequence of events, according to the law of probability or necessity, will admit of a change from bad fortune to good, or from good fortune to bad.

VIII

Unity of plot does not, as some persons think, consist in the unity of the hero. For infinitely various are the incidents in one man's life, which cannot be reduced to unity; and so, too, there are many actions of one man out of which we cannot make one action. Hence the error, as it appears, of all poets who have composed a Heracleid, a Theseid, or other poems of the kind. They imagine that as Heracles was one man, the story of Heracles ought also to be a unity. But Homer, as in all else he is of surpassing merit, here too—whether from art or natural genius—seems to have happily discerned the truth. In composing the *Odyssey* he did not bring in all the adventures of Odysseus—such as his wound on Parnassus, or his feigned madness at the mustering of the host—incidents between which there was no necessary or probable connexion: but he made the *Odyssey*, and likewise the *Iliad,* to centre round an action, that in our sense of the word is one. As therefore in the other imitative arts, the imitation is one, when the object imitated is one, so the plot, being an imitation of an action, must imitate one action and that a whole, the structural union of the parts being such that, if any one of them is displaced or removed, the whole will be disjointed and disturbed. For that which may be present or absent without being perceived, is not an organic part of the whole.

IX

It is, moreover, evident from what has been said, that it is not the function of the poet to relate what has happened, but what may happen—what is possible according to the law of probability or necessity. The poet and the historian differ not by writing in verse or in prose. The work of Herodotus might be put into verse, and it would still be a species of history, with metre no less than without it. The true difference is that one relates what has happened, the other what may happen. Poetry, therefore, is a more philosophical and a higher thing than history: for poetry tends to express the universal, history the particular. The universal tells us how a person of given character will on occasion speak or act, according to the law of probability or necessity; and it is this universality at which Poetry aims in giving expressive names to the characters. The particular is—for example—what Alcibiades did or suffered. In Comedy this is now apparent: for here the poet first constructs the plot on the lines of probability, and then assumes any names he pleases—unlike the lampooners who write about a particular individual. But tragedians still keep to real names, the reason being that what is possible is credible: what has not happened we do not at once feel sure to be possible: but what has happened is manifestly possible; otherwise it would not have happened. Still there are some tragedies in which one or two names only are well known, the rest being fictitious. In others, none are well known—as in Agathon's *Flower*, where incidents and names alike are fictitious, and yet it pleases. We must not, therefore, at all costs keep to the received legends, which are the usual subjects of Tragedy. Indeed, it would be absurd to attempt it; for even familiar subjects are familiar only to a few, and yet give pleasure to all. It clearly follows that the poet or 'maker' should be the maker of plots rather than of verses; since he is a poet because he imitates, and what he imitates are actions. And if he chances to take an historical subject, he is none the less a poet; for there is no reason why some real events should not have that internal probability or possibility which entitles the author to the name of poet.

Of all plots and actions the episodic are the worst. I call a plot episodic in which the episodes or acts succeed one another without probable or necessary sequence. Bad poets compose such pieces by their own fault, good poets, to please the players; for, as they write for competing rivals, they draw out the plot beyond its capacity, and are often forced to break the natural continuity.

But again, Tragedy is an imitation not only of a complete action, but of events terrible and pitiful. Such an effect is best produced when the events come on us by surprise; and the effect is heightened when, at the same time, they follow from one another. The tragic wonder will then be greater than if they happened of themselves or by accident; for even accidents are most striking when they have an air of design. We may instance the statue of Mitys at Argos, which fell upon his murderer while he was looking at it, and killed him. Such events seem not to be due to mere chance. Plots, therefore, constructed on these principles are necessarily the best.

X

Plots are either simple or complicated; for such too, in their very nature, are the actions of which the plots are an imitation. An action which is one and continuous in the sense above defined, I call Simple, when the turning point is reached without Reversal of Fortune or Recognition: Complicated, when it is reached with Reversal of Fortune, or Recognition, or both. These last should arise from the internal structure of the plot, so that what follows should be the necessary or probable result of the preceding action. It makes all the difference whether one event is the consequence of another, or merely subsequent to it.

XI

A Reversal of Fortune is, as we have said, a change by which a train of action produces the opposite of the effect intended; and that, according to our rule of probability or necessity. Thus in the *Oedipus,* the messenger, hoping to cheer Oedipus, and to free him from his alarms about his mother, reveals his origin, and so produces the opposite effect. Again in the *Lynceus,* Lynceus is being led out to die, and Danaus goes with him, meaning to slay him; but the outcome of the action is, that Danaus is killed and Lynceus saved.

A Recognition, as the name indicates, is a change from ignorance to knowledge, producing love or hate between the persons destined by the poet for good or bad fortune. The best form of recognition is coincident with a reversal of fortune, as in the *Oedipus.* There are indeed other forms. Even inanimate things of the most trivial kind may sometimes be objects of recognition. Again, the discovery may be made whether a person has or has not done something. But the form which is most intimately connected with the plot and action is, as we have said, the recognition of persons. This, combined with a reversal of fortune, will produce either pity or fear; and actions producing these effects are those which, as we have assumed, Tragedy represents. Moreover, fortune or misfortune will depend upon such incidents. Recognition, then, being between persons, it may happen that one person only is recognised by the other—when the latter is already known—or the recognition may need to be on both sides. Thus Iphigenia is revealed to Orestes by the sending of the letter; but another means is required to make Orestes known to Iphigenia.

Two parts, then, of the Plot—Reversal of Fortune and Recognition—turn upon surprises. A third part is the Tragic Incident. The two former have been discussed. The Tragic Incident is a destructive or painful action, such as death on the stage, bodily torments, wounds and the like.

· XII

The parts of Tragedy, which must be treated as elements of the whole, have been already mentioned. We now come to the quantitative parts—the separate parts into which Tragedy is divided—namely, Prologos, Episode, Exodos, Choral element; this last being divided into Parados and Stasimon. These two are sung by the whole Chorus. The songs of the actors on the stage, and the Commoi, are sung by individuals.

The Prologos is that entire part of a tragedy which precedes the Parodos of the Chorus. The Episode is that entire part of a tragedy which is between whole choral songs. The Exodos is that entire part of a tragedy which has no choral song after it. Of the Choral part the Parodos is the first undivided utterance of the Chorus: the Stasimon is a choral ode without anapaests or trochees: the Commos is a joint lamentation of chorus and actors. The parts of Tragedy which must be treated as elements of the whole have been already mentioned. The quantitative parts—the separate parts into which it is divided—are here enumerated.

XIII

As the sequel to what has already been said, we must proceed to consider what the poet should aim at, and what he should avoid, in constructing his plots; and by what means Tragedy may best fulfil its function.

A perfect tragedy should, as we have seen, be arranged on the complicated not the simple plan. It should, moreover, imitate actions which excite pity and fear, this being the distinctive mark of tragic imitation. It follows plainly, in the first place, that the change of fortune presented must not be the spectacle of a perfectly good man brought from prosperity to adversity: for this moves neither pity nor fear; it simply shocks us. Nor, again, that of a bad man passing from adversity to prosperity: for nothing can be more alien to the spirit of Tragedy; it possesses no single tragic quality; it neither satisfies the moral sense, nor calls forth pity or fear. Nor, again, should the downfall of the utter villain be exhibited. A plot of this kind would, doubtless, satisfy the moral sense, but it would inspire neither pity nor fear; for pity is aroused by unmerited misfortune, fear by the misfortune of a man like ourselves. Such an event, therefore, will be neither pitiful nor terrible. There remains, then, the character between these two extremes—that of a man who is not eminently good and just, yet whose misfortune is brought about not by vice or depravity, but by some error or frailty. He must be one who is highly renowned and prosperous—a personage like Oedipus, Thyestes, or other illustrious men of such families.

A well constructed plot should, therefore, be single, rather than double as some maintain. The change of fortune should be not from bad to good, but, reversely, from good to bad. It should come about as the result not of vice, but of some great error or frailty, in a character either such as we have described, or better rather than worse. The practice of the stage bears out our view. At first the poets recounted any legends that came in their way. Now, tragedies are founded on the story of a few houses—on the fortunes of Alcmaeon, Oedipus, Orestes, Meleager, Thyestes, Telephus, and those others who have done or suffered something terrible. A tragedy, then, to be perfect according to the rules of art should be of this construction. Hence they are in error who censure Euripides just because he follows this principle in his plays, many of which end unhappily. It is, as we have said, the right ending. The best proof is that on the stage and in dramatic competition, such plays, if they are well represented, are most tragic in their effect; and Euripides, faulty as he is in the general management of his subject, yet is felt to be the most tragic of poets.

In the second rank comes the kind of tragedy which some place first. Like the *Odyssey*, it has a double thread of plot, and also an opposite catastrophe for the good and for the bad. It is generally thought to be the best owing to the weakness of the spectators; for the poet is guided in what he writes by the wishes of his audience. The pleasure, however, thence derived is not the true tragic pleasure. It is proper rather to Comedy, where those who, in the piece, are the deadliest enemies— like Orestes and Aegisthus—go forth reconciled at last, and no one slays or is slain.

XIV

Fear and pity may be aroused by the spectacle or scenic presentment; but they may also result from the inner structure of the piece, which is the better way, and indicates a superior poet. For the plot ought to be so constructed that, even without the aid of the eye, any one who is told the incidents will thrill with horror and pity at the turn of events. This is precisely the impression we should receive from listening to the story of the *Oedipus*. But to produce this effect by the mere spectacle is a less artistic method, and dependent on extraneous aids. Those who employ spectacular means to create a sense not of the terrible but of the monstrous, are strangers to the purpose of Tragedy; for we must not demand of Tragedy every kind of pleasure, but only that which is proper to it. And since the pleasure which the poet should afford is that which comes from pity and fear through imitation, it is evident that this quality must be stamped upon the incidents.

Let us then determine what are the circumstances which impress us as terrible or pitiful.

Actions capable of this effect must happen between persons who are either friends or enemies or indifferent to one another. If an enemy kills an enemy, there is nothing to excite pity either in the act or the intention—except so far as the suffering in itself is pitiful. So again with indifferent persons. But when the tragic incident occurs between those who are near or dear to one another—if, for example, a brother kills, or intends to kill, a brother, a son his father, a mother her son, a son his mother, or any other deed of the kind is done—here we have the situations which should be sought for by the poet. He may not indeed destroy the framework of the received legends—the fact, for instance, that Clytemnestra was slain by Orestes and Eriphyle by Alcmaeon—but he ought to show invention of his own, and skilfully adapt the traditional material. What is meant by skilfully, let us explain more clearly.

The action may be done willingly and with full knowledge on the part of the agents, in the manner of the older poets. It is thus, in fact, that Euripides makes Medea slay her children. Or, again, the deed of horror may be done, but done in ignorance, and the tie of kinship or friendship be discovered afterwards. The *Oedipus* of Sophocles is an example. Here, indeed, the incident is outside the drama proper; but cases occur where it falls within the action of the play: we may cite the *Alcmaeon* of Astydamas, or Telegonus in the *Wounded Odysseus*. Again, there is a third case, where some one is just about to do some irreparable deed through ignorance, and makes the discovery before it it done. These are the only possible ways. For the deed must either be done or not done—and that wittingly or unwittingly. But of all these ways, to be about to act knowing the consequences, and then not to act, is the worst. It is shocking without being tragic, for no disaster follows. It is, therefore, never, or very rarely, found in poetry. One instance, however, is in the *Antigone*, where Haemon intends to kill Creon. The next and better way is that the deed should be perpetrated. Still better, that it should be perpetrated in ignorance, and the discovery made afterwards. There is then nothing to shock us, while the discovery produces a startling effect. But the absolutely best way is the last mentioned. Thus in the *Cresphontes*, Merope is in the act of putting her son to death, but, recognising who he is, spares his life. So in the *Iphigenia*, the sister recognises the brother just in time. Again in the *Helle*, the son recognises the mother when on the point of giving her up. This, then, is why a few families only, as has been already observed, furnish the subjects of tragedy. It was not art, but happy chance, that led poets by tentative discovery to impress the tragic quality upon their plots. They are compelled, therefore, to have recourse to those houses in which tragic disasters have occurred.

Enough has now been said concerning the structure of the incidents, and the proper constitution of the plot.

XV

In respect of character there are four things to be aimed at. First, and most important, it must be good. Now any speech or action that manifests a certain moral purpose will be expressive of character: the character will be good if the purpose is good. This rule applies to persons of every class. Even a woman may be good, and also a slave; though the woman may be said to be an inferior being, and the slave is absolutely bad. The second thing to aim at is propriety. There is a type of manly valour; but for a woman to be valiant in this sense, or terrible, would be inappropriate. Thirdly, character must be true to life: for this is a distinct thing from goodness and propriety, as here described. The fourth point is consistency: for even though the original character, who suggested the type, be inconsistent, still he must be consistently inconsistent. As an example of character needlessly bad, we have Menelaus in the *Orestes:* of character incongruous and inappropriate, the lament of Odysseus in the *Scylla*, and the speech of Melanippe: of inconsistency, the *Iphigenia at Aulis*—for the suppliant Iphigenia in no way resembles her later self.

As in the structure of the plot, so too in the portraiture of character, the poet should always aim either at the necessary or the probable. Thus a person of a given character should speak or act in a given way, by the rule either of necessity or of probability; just as this event should follow that by necessary or probable sequence. It is therefore evident that the unravelling of the plot, no less than the complication, must be brought about by the plot itself, and not by Machinery—as in the *Medea*, or in the Return of the Greeks in the *Iliad*. Machinery should be employed only for events external to the drama—either such as are previous to it and outside the sphere of human knowledge, or subsequent to it and which need to be foretold and announced; for to the gods we ascribe the power of seeing all things. Within the action there must be nothing irrational. If the irrational cannot be excluded, it should be outside the scope of the tragedy. Such is the irrational element in the *Oedipus* of Sophocles.

Again, since Tragedy is an imitation of persons who are above the common level, the example of good portrait-painters should be followed. They, while reproducing the distinctive form of the original, make a likeness which is true to life and yet more beautiful. So too the poet, in representing men quick or slow to anger, or with other defects of character, should preserve the type and yet ennoble it. In this way Achilles is portrayed by Agathon and Homer.

These are rules the poet should observe. Nor should he neglect those appeals to the senses, which, though not among the essentials, are the concomitants of poetry: for here too there is much room for error. But of this we have said enough in our published treatises.

PART FOUR

HELLENISTIC
PHILOSOPHY

I

For many centuries, Plato and Aristotle were not followed by philosophers of comparable caliber. There was a decline of creative energy, in philosophy as well as in other fields. The great tragedians of the 5th Century had no successors either, nor did the Greeks produce another Homer or Thucydides.

Of Socrates' friends and disciples, at least two besides Plato are of some philosophic importance. Antisthenes, a rhetorician with an Athenian father and a Phrygian, non-Greek mother, had been a teacher in his own right before he met Socrates who made the profoundest impression on him. It seems to have been Socrates' character, his perfect self-control and self-sufficiency, his indifference to the cold of the winter (see the *Symposium*) and to the opinions of men (see the *Apology*), his serenely ironic superiority to every fate, that struck Antisthenes with the force of a revelation. What he learned from Socrates, was neither a metaphysic nor even a philosophic method but, as he, himself, put it, "to live with myself." He disposed of his possessions, keeping only a ragged old coat, whereupon Socrates is said to have taunted him: "I see your vanity through the holes of your coat." Antisthenes also taught the unity of God. He founded a school whose members received the nickname of Cynics, *kynikos* being Greek for doglike. They slept on the ground, neglected their clothes, let their beards grow to unusual lengths, and despised the run of men, insisting that virtue and happiness consist in self-control and independence. Of Antisthenes' disciples none was more famous than Diogenes, who went about during the day carrying a lantern and, asked what he was doing, would reply: "I am looking for an honest man." He made his home in a tub, and his eccentric behavior attracted the attention of Alexander the Great who went to visit him and, greatly impressed, asked whether there was anything at all that he could do to please the Cynic. Diogenes replied: "Yes, get out of my sunlight."

Another so-called Socratic school, that of the Cyrenaics, was founded by another of Socrates' associates and admirers, Aristippus of Cyrene, a city of Libya, in North Africa, about 10 miles from the Mediterranean coast. The Greeks had a colony there, and the city is also associated with one of the masterpieces of ancient sculpture, the Aphrodite of Cyrene, a Roman copy of a Greek statue. The Cyrenaics disparaged speculative philosophy and extolled pleasure, but, following Aristippus, they maintained that the purest pleasure attends self-mastery and the philosophic life. Only philosophy can protect men against passion, which spells suffering. While despising popular opinion, the Cyrenaics did consider custom, law, and altruism justifiable in terms of an appeal to long-range pleasures.

Before long, Cynicism became one of the tributaries of Stoicism, while the Cyrenaics were absorbed by the Epicureans; but it is worth noting to what extent the two dominant Hellenistic philosophies, which remained important and influential through the Roman era, received their inspiration, even if to some extent indirectly, from Socrates.

II

Epicurus was born on the island of Samos, like Pythagoras, approximately seven years after Plato's death, in 342/41 B.C. At 18, he went to Athens for a year, then joined his father in Colophon, the city where Xenophanes had been born. He studied the writings of Democritus before returning to Athens in 307, and there he bought a garden which became famous as the place where he taught his disciples. His emphasis on pleasure was distorted by his enemies, and "epicurean" became a synonym for "gourmet." In fact, he and the community that formed around him lived on water and barley bread, and an occasional drink of wine was considered something special. Unlike his critics, he found philosophy more pleasant than fine food.

His philosophy may be gleaned from the two works that follow, both being reprinted complete, without any omissions. His influence was very considerable and was felt for a long time after his death in 270 B.C. A Roman poet, Lucretius (98-55 B.C.), embraced the philosophy of Epicurus and expounded it in a celebrated poem, *De rerum natura* (Of the Nature of Things), which is still extant. Instead of excerpting necessarily inadequate prose translations that cannot hope to do justice to the poetry of the original, the present volume concentrates on Epicurus and Democritus, who were philosophers, not poets, and whose writings have so far been ever so much less accessible.

The last of the major Greek philosophers, like the first, Thales, was probably a Semite: Zeno of Citium, on the island of Cyprus, the founder of the Stoic school. The year of his birth is uncertain: some say 336 B.C., while others hold that he was 98 when he died in 264 B.C., there being agreement on the latter date. It is said that he discovered philosophy by reading Xenophon and that, Socrates being long dead, he attached himself for some time to the Cynics. He read very widely and was greatly respected for his learning and, if possible, even more for his character and the simplicity of his way of life. Like some of the pre-Socratics, he was a sage as well as a philosopher, and an immensely impressive personality besides being a great thinker.

The school received its name from the columned porch (Stoa, in Greek) where he taught. It survived him and proved to have special appeal to the Roman mind: not so much the ample speculative and theoretical contents of Stoicism, which owe much to Heraclitus and a variety of other sources, as the austere moral emphasis, the stress on self-control and superiority to pain. One might even say that in a recognizable sense the pillars of republican Rome all tended to be Stoics, even if they had never heard of Stoicism.

Zeno's first major disciple, Cleanthes, who is said to have starved himself to death at 90 (about 240 B.C.), is remembered chiefly for his "Hymn to Zeus," if for that, while the next major Stoic, Chrysippus, is known to few but specialists in Stoicism. Even Seneca, the tragic poet and philosopher who tutored the young Nero and later was forced by the emperor to commit suicide, in 65 A.D., is much more widely known than the earlier Greek Stoics. But most people associate Stoicism above all with Marcus Aurelius (121-180), who became Roman emperor in 161 and wrote a famous book of *Meditations*, and with Epictetus, an emancipated slave.

Epictetus' precise dates are not known, but he was born in Hierapolis in Phrygia, in Asia Minor, around 50 A.D., and lived most of his life in Rome. He died about 138 A.D. His *Manual* has been much admired as a concise and authentic summary of Stoicism.

The skepticism of Pyrrho, a philosopher from Elis on the Peloponnesus, who lived from about 360 to 270 B.C. but left no writings, is best presented in the *Outlines of Pyrrhonism,* written by Sextus Empiricus, a Greek physician and philosopher who lived in Alexandria and Athens during the first half of the 3rd Century A.D. Pyrrho suggested that we confront statements with their contradictories and develop an attitude of suspense of judgment (*epoché,* in Greek) and thus gradually attain to imperturbability (*ataraxia*).

Looking back on the development of Greek philosophy from the pre-Socratics to the Stoics, the Epicureans, and the Skeptics, one is struck by the overwhelming concern of the later schools with peace of mind. There is one quality which the pre-classical and classical Greeks possessed preeminently and which Skeptics, Stoics, and Epicureans lacked just as signally: enthusiasm. This may help to explain why, for all their intellectual and moral virtues, they could not compete with the growing appeal of Christianity.

The last great school of Greek philosophy was Neoplatonism, and its most famous representative was Plotinus, born in Lycopolis in Egypt of Roman parents in 204 A.D. He certainly did not lack enthusiasm but was, in spite of that, still more remote from classical Greek attitudes than the other Hellenistic philosophers. He extolled the spirit to the point of saying that he was ashamed to have a body, and his fervor was entirely directed toward mysticism and, to cite his famous words, "the flight of the Alone to the Alone." Thus he perfected the less classical tendencies of Plato's thought, merging them both with Neopythagoreanism and with such Oriental notions as the doctrine of progressive emanations from the One. The ultimate mystical union he sought, he is said to have attained four times before his death in 270 A.D. Porphyry, his pupil, edited his writings in the form of six groups of nine treatises, published as the so-called. *Enneads.*

Neoplatonism had a profound influence on Christian thought; for example, but by no means only, on Augustine. Indeed, if St. Thomas is considered an Aristotelian, St. Augustine may be called a Neoplatonist. Of the later non-Christian Neoplatonists, Proclus (410-485) was the most important. He influenced the German philosopher, Hegel; and Neoplatonism generally helped to mold the thought of such other German thinkers as Eckhart, Nicolas of Cusa, Jacob Boehme, and Schelling.

Proclus lived and taught in Athens, where the Academy Plato had founded survived. In 529, it was closed by the Christian emperor Justinian. That date may be said to mark the formal end of Greek philosophy.

III

The original texts of all the selections in Part Four, as in the first three Parts, were written in Greek, while the three men represented in Part Five wrote Latin.

Epicurus' *Letter to Herodotus* was incorporated by Diogenes Laertius in his *Lives of Eminent Philosophers*. The whole of the last book (Book X) of the *Lives* is devoted to Epicurus, and Diogenes Laertius concluded not only "this philosopher's life" but, as he himself emphasized, his "entire work" by also quoting in full Epicurus' *Principal Doctrines*. The whole of the *Lives* is available in The Loeb Classical Library, in two volumes, with the original text and an English translation by R. D. Hicks on facing pages. This is the translation offered here.

The translation of Cleanthes' *Hymn to Zeus* is that of James Adam.

The version of Epictetus' *Encheiridion*, or *Manual*, is that of W. A. Oldfather; the translation of Sextus Empiricus is by R. G. Bury. Both come from the bilingual Loeb editions, which also offer Epictetus' *Discourses*. The *Discourses* are longer than the *Manual* and consist of lectures recorded by Epictetus' pupil, Arrian.

Finally, Thomas Taylor's translation of *Select Works of Plotinus* has been used.

EPICURUS

A. LETTER TO HERODOTUS (*complete*)

"Epicurus to Herodotus, greeting.

"For those who are unable to study carefully all my physical writings or to go into the longer treatises at all, I have myself prepared an epitome [1] of the whole system, Herodotus, to preserve in the memory enough of the prinipal doctrines, to the end that on every occasion they may be able to aid themselves on the most important points, so far as they take up the study of Physics. Those who have made some advance in the survey of the entire system ought to fix in their minds under the principal headings an elementary outline of the whole treatment of the subject. For a comprehensive view is often required, the details but seldom.

---

[1] This, as the most authentic summary of Epicurean physics which we possess, serves as a groundwork in modern histories, *e.g.*, Zeller's.

"To the former, then—the main heads—we must continually return, and must memorize them so far as to get a valid conception of the facts, as well as the means of discovering all the details exactly when once the general outlines are rightly understood and remembered; since it is the privilege of the mature student to make a ready use of his conceptions by referring every one of them to elementary facts and simple terms. For it is impossible to gather up the results of continuous diligent study of the entirety of things, unless we can embrace in short formulas and hold in mind all that might have been accurately expressed even to the minutest detail.

"Hence, since such a course is of service to all who take up natural science, I, who devote to the subject my continuous energy and reap the calm enjoyment of a life like this, have prepared for you just such an epitome and manual of the doctrines as a whole.

"In the first place, Herodotus, you must understand what it is that words denote, in order that by reference to this we may be in a position to test opinions, inquiries, or problems, so that our proofs may not run on untested *ad infinitum*, nor the terms we use be empty of meaning. For the primary signification of every term employed must be clearly seen, and ought to need no proving; this being necessary, if we are to have something to which the point at issue or the problem or the opinion before us can be referred.

"Next, we must by all means stick to our sensations, that is, simply to the present impressions whether of the mind or of any criterion whatever, and similarly to our actual feelings, in order that we may have the means of determining that which needs confirmation and that which is obscure.

"When this is clearly understood, it is time to consider generally things which are obscure. To begin with, nothing comes into being out of what is non-existent. For in that case anything would have arisen out of anything, standing as it would in no need of its proper germs. And if that which disappears had been destroyed and become non-existent, everything would have perished, that into which the things were dissolved being non-existent. Moreover, the sum total of things was always such as it is now, and such it will ever remain. For there is nothing into which it can change. For outside the sum of things there is nothing which could enter into it and bring about the change.

"Further [*this he says also in the Larger Epitome near the beginning and in his First Book "On Nature"*], the whole of being consists of bodies and space. For the existence of bodies is everywhere attested by sense itself, and it is upon sensation that reason must rely when it attempts to infer the unknown from the known. And if there were no space (which we call also void and place and intangible nature), bodies would have nothing in which to be and through which to move, as they are plainly seen to move. Beyond bodies and space there is nothing which by mental apprehension or on its analogy we can conceive to exist. When we speak of bodies and space, both are regarded as wholes or separate things, not as the properties or accidents of separate things.

"Again [*he repeats this in the First Book and in Books XIV. and XV. of the work "On Nature" and in the Larger Epitome*], of bodies some are composite, others the elements of which these composite bodies are made. These elements are indivisible and unchangeable, and necessarily so, if things are not all to be destroyed and pass into non-existence, but are to be strong enough to endure when the composite bodies are broken up, because they possess a solid nature and are incapable of being anywhere or anyhow dissolved. It follows that the first beginnings must be indivisible, corporeal entities.

"Again, the sum of things is infinite. For what is finite has an extremity, and the extremity of anything is discerned only by comparison with something else. <Now the sum of things is not discerned by comparison with anything else:> hence, since it has no extremity, it has no limit; and, since it has no limit, it must be unlimited or infinite.

"Moreover, the sum of things is unlimited both by reason of the multitude of the atoms and the extent of the void. For if the void were infinite and bodies finite, the bodies would not have stayed anywhere but would have been dispersed in their course through the infinite void, not having any supports or counterchecks to send them back on their upward rebound. Again, if the void were finite, the infinity of bodies would not have anywhere to be.

"Furthermore, the atoms, which have no void in them—out of which composite bodies arise and into which they are dissolved—vary indefinitely in their shapes; for so many varieties of things as we see could never have arisen out of a recurrence of a definite number of the the same shapes. The like atoms of each shape are absolutely infinite; but the variety of shapes, though indefinitely large, is not absolutely infinite. [*For neither does the divisibility go on "ad infinitum," he says below; but he adds, since the qualities change, unless one is prepared to keep enlarging their magnitudes also simply "ad infinitum."*]

"The atoms are in continual motion through all eternity. [*Further, he says below, that the atoms move with equal speed, since the void makes way for the lightest and heaviest alike.*] Some of them rebound to a considerable distance from each other, while others merely oscillate in one place when they chance to have got entangled or to be enclosed by a mass of other atoms shaped for entangling.

"This is because each atom is separated from the rest by void, which is incapable of offering any resistance to the rebound; while it is the solidity of the atom which makes it rebound after a collision, however short the distance to which it rebounds, when it finds itself imprisoned in a mass of entangling atoms. Of all this there is no beginning, since both atoms and void exist from everlasting. [*He says below that atoms have no quality at all except shape, size, and weight. But that colour varies with the arrangement of the atoms he states in his "Twelve Rudi-*

ments"; further, that they are not of any and every size; at any rate
no atom has ever been seen by our sense.]

"The repetition at such length of all that we are now recalling to
mind furnishes an adequate outline for our conception of the nature
of things.

"Moreover, there is an infinite number of worlds, some like this world,
others unlike it. For the atoms being infinite in number, as has just been
proved, are borne ever further in their course. For the atoms out of
which a world might arise, or by which a world might be formed, have not
all been expended on one world or a finite number of worlds, whether like
or unlike this one. Hence there will be nothing to hinder an infinity of
worlds.

"Again, there are outlines or films, which are of the same shape as solid
bodies, but of a thinness far exceeding that of any object that we see.
For it is not impossible that there should be found in the surrounding
air combinations of this kind, materials adapted for expressing the hol-
lowness and thinness of surfaces, and effluxes preserving the same relative
position and motion which they had in the solid objects from which
they come. To these films we give the name of 'images' or 'idols.' Furthermore, so long as nothing comes in the way to offer resistance,
motion through the void accomplishes any imaginable distance in an
inconceivably short time. For resistance encountered is the equivalent
of slowness, its absence the equivalent of speed.

"Not that, if we consider the minute times perceptible by reason
alone, the moving body itself arrives at more than one place simultaneously (for this too is inconceivable), although in time perceptible
to sense it does arrive simultaneously, however different the point of
departure from that conceived by us. For if it changed its direction, that
would be equivalent to its meeting with resistance, even if up to that
point we allow nothing to impede the rate of its flight. This is an elementary fact which in itself is well worth bearing in mind. In the next
place the exceeding thinness of the images is contradicted by none
of the facts under our observation. Hence also their velocities are
enormous, since they always find a void passage to fit them. Besides, their
incessant effluence meets with no resistance, or very little, although
many atoms, not to say an unlimited number, do at once encounter
resistance.

"Besides this, remember that the production of the images is as quick
as thought. For particles are continually streaming off from the surface
of bodies, though no diminution of the bodies is observed, because other
particles take their place. And those given off for a long time retain the
position and arrangement which their atoms had when they formed
part of the solid bodies, although occasionally they are thrown into
confusion. Sometimes such films are formed very rapidly in the air,
because they need not have any solid content; and there are other
modes in which they may be formed. For there is nothing in all this
which is contradicted by sensation, if we in some sort look at the clear

evidence of sense, to which we should also refer the continuity of particles in the objects external to ourselves.

"We must also consider that it is by the entrance of something coming from external objects that we see their shapes and think of them. For external things would not stamp on us their own nature of colour and form through the medium of the air which is between them and us,[2] or by means of rays of light or currents of any sort going from us to them, so well as by the entrance into our eyes or minds, to whichever their size is suitable, of certain films coming from the things themselves, these films or outlines being of the same colour and shape as the external things themselves. They move with rapid motion; and this again explains why they present the appearance of the single continuous object, and retain the mutual interconnexion which they had in the object, when they impinge upon the sense, such impact being due to the oscillation of the atoms in the interior of the solid object from which they come. And whatever presentation we derive by direct contact, whether it be with the mind or with the sense-organs, be it shape that is presented or other properties, this shape as presented is the shape of the solid thing, and it is due either to a close coherence of the image as a whole or to a mere remnant of its parts. Falsehood and error always depend upon the intrusion of opinion <when a fact awaits> confirmation or the absence of contradiction, which fact is afterwards frequently not confirmed <or even contradicted> [*following a certain movement in ourselves connected with, but distinct from, the mental picture presented —which is the cause of error.*]

"For the presentations which, *e.g.*, are received in a picture or arise in dreams, or from any other form of apprehension by the mind or by the other criteria of truth, would never have resembled what we call the real and true things, had it not been for certain actual things of the kind with which we come in contact. Error would not have occurred, if we had not experienced some other movement in ourselves, conjoined with, but distinct from, the perception of what is presented. And from this movement, if it be not confirmed or be contradicted, falsehood results; while, if it be confirmed or not contradicted, truth results.

"And to this view we must closely adhere, if we are not to repudiate the criteria founded on the clear evidence of sense, nor again to throw all these things into confusion by maintaining falsehood as if it were truth.

"Again, hearing takes place when a current passes from the object, whether person or thing, which emits voice or sound or noise, or produces the sensation of hearing in any way whatever. This current is broken up into homogeneous particles, which at the same time preserve a certain mutual connexion and a distinctive unity extending to the object which emitted them, and thus, for the most part, cause the perception in that case or, if not, merely indicate the presence of the external object.

---

[2] This was the view of Democritus.

For without the transmission from the object of a certain interconnexion of the parts no such sensation could arise. Therefore we must not suppose that the air itself is moulded into shape by the voice emitted or something similar; for it is very far from being the case that the air is acted upon by it in this way. The blow which is struck in us when we utter a sound causes such a displacement of the particles as serves to produce a current resembling breath, and this displacement gives rise to the sensation of hearing.

"Again, we must believe that smelling, like hearing, would produce no sensation, were there not particles conveyed from the object which are of the proper sort for exciting the organ of smelling, some of one sort, some of another, some exciting it confusedly and strangely, others quietly and agreeably.

"Moreover, we must hold that the atoms in fact possess none of the qualities belonging to things which come under our observation, except shape, weight, and size, and the properties necessarily conjoined with shape. For every quality changes, but the atoms do not change, since, when the composite bodies are dissolved, there must needs be a permanent something, solid and indissoluble, left behind, which makes change possible: not changes into or from the non-existent, but often through differences of arrangement, and sometimes through additions and subtractions of the atoms. Hence these somethings capable of being diversely arranged must be indestructible, exempt from change, but possessed each of its own distinctive mass and configuration. This must remain.

"For in the case of changes of configuration within our experience the figure is supposed to be inherent when other qualities are stripped off, but the qualities are not supposed, like the shape which is left behind, to inhere in the subject of change, but to vanish altogether from the body. Thus, then, what is left behind is sufficient to account for the differences in composite bodies, since something at least must necessarily be left remaining and be immune from annihilation.

"Again, you should not suppose that the atoms have any and every size,[3] lest you be contradicted by facts; but differences of size must be admitted; for this addition renders the facts of feeling and sensation easier of explanation. But to attribute any and every magnitude to the atoms does not help to explain the differences of quality in things; moreover, in that case atoms large enough to be seen ought to have reached us, which is never observed to occur; nor can we conceive how its occurrence should be possible, *i.e.* that an atom should become visible.

"Besides, you must not suppose that there are parts unlimited in number, be they ever so small, in any finite body. Hence not only must we reject as impossible subdivision *ad infinitum* into smaller and smaller parts, lest we make all things too weak and, in our conceptions of the

---

[3] The opinion of Democritus.

aggregates, be driven to pulverize the things that exist, *i.e.* the atoms, and annihilate them; but in dealing with finite things we must also reject as impossible the progression *ad infinitum* by less and less increments.

"For when once we have said that an infinite number of particles, however small, are contained in anything, it is not possible to conceive how it could any longer be limited or finite in size. For clearly our infinite number of particles must have some size; and then, of whatever size they were, the aggregate they made would be infinite. And, in the next place, since what is finite has an extremity which is distinguishable, even if it is not by itself observable, it is not possible to avoid thinking of another such extremity next to this. Nor can we help thinking that in this way, by proceeding forward from one to the next in order, it is possible by such a progression to arrive in thought at infinity.

"We must consider the minimum perceptible by sense as not corresponding to that which is capable of being traversed, *i.e.* is extended, nor again as utterly unlike it, but as having something in common with the things capable of being traversed, though it is without distinction of parts. But when from the illusion created by this common property we think we shall distinguish something in the minimum, one part on one side and another part on the other side, it must be another minimum equal to the first which catches our eye. In fact, we see these minima one after another, beginning with the first, and not as occupying the same space; nor do we see them touch one another's parts with their parts, but we see that by virtue of their own peculiar character (*i.e.* as being unit indivisibles) they afford a means of measuring magnitudes: there are more of them, if the magnitude measured is greater; fewer of them, if the magnitude measured is less.

"We must recognize that this analogy also holds of the minimum in the atom; it is only in minuteness that it differs from that which is observed by sense, but it follows the same analogy. On the analogy of things within our experience we have declared that the atom has magnitude; and this, small as it is, we have merely reproduced on a larger scale. And further, the least and simplest things must be regarded as extremities of lengths, furnishing from themselves as units the means of measuring lengths, whether greater or less, the mental vision being employed, since direct observation is impossible. For the community which exists between them and the unchangeable parts (*i.e.* the minimal parts of area or surface) is sufficient to justify the conclusion so far as this goes. But it is not possible that these minima of the atom should group themselves together through the possession of motion.

"Further, we must not assert 'up' or 'down' of that which is unlimited, as if there were a zenith or nadir. As to the space overhead, however, if it be possible to draw a line to infinity from the point where we stand, we know that never will this space—or, for that matter, the space below the supposed standpoint if produced to infinity—appear to us to be at the same time 'up' and 'down' with reference to the same point; for this is inconceivable. Hence it is possible to assume one direction of motion, which we conceive as extending upwards *ad infinitum,* and another downwards, even if it should happen ten thousand times that what moves from us to the spaces above our heads reaches the feet of those above us, or that which moves downwards from us the heads of those below us. None the less is it true that the whole of the motion in the respective cases is conceived as extending in opposite directions *ad infinitum.*

"When they are travelling through the void and meet with no resistance, the atoms must move with equal speed. Neither will heavy atoms travel more quickly than small and light ones, so long as nothing meets them, nor will small atoms travel more quickly than large ones, provided they always find a passage suitable to their size, and provided also that they meet with no obstruction. Nor will their upward or their lateral motion, which is due to collisions, nor again their downward motion, due to weight, affect their velocity. As long as either motion obtains, it must continue, quick as the speed of thought, provided there is no obstruction, whether due to external collision or to the atoms' own weight counteracting the force of the blow.

"Moreover, when we come to deal with composite bodies, one of them will travel faster than another, although their atoms have equal speed. This is because the atoms in the aggregates are travelling in one direction during the shortest continuous time, albeit they move in different directions in times so short as to be appreciable only by the reason, but frequently collide until the continuity of their motion is appreciated by sense. For the assumption that beyond the range of direct observation even the minute times conceivable by reason will present continuity of motion is not true in the case before us. Our canon is that direct observation by sense and direct apprehension by the mind are alone invariably true.

"Next, keeping in view our perceptions and feelings (for so shall we have the surest grounds for belief), we must recognize generally that the soul is a corporeal thing, composed of fine particles, dispersed all over the frame, most nearly resembling wind with an admixture of heat, in some respects like wind, in others like heat. But, again, there is the third part which exceeds the other two in the fineness of its particles and thereby keeps in closer touch with the rest of the frame. And this is shown by the mental faculties and feelings, by the ease with which the mind moves, and by thoughts, and by all those things the loss of which causes death. Further, we must keep in mind that soul has the greatest share in causing sensation. Still, it would not have had sensation, had it not been somehow confined within the rest of the frame. But the rest of the frame, though it provides this indispensable condition for the soul, itself also has a share, derived from the soul, of the said quality; and yet does not possess all the qualities of soul. Hence on the departure of the soul it loses sentience. For it had not this power in itself; but something else, congenital with the body, supplied it to body: which other thing, through the potentiality actualized in it by means of motion, at once acquired for itself a quality of sentience, and, in virtue of the neighbourhood and interconnexion between them, imparted it (as I said) to the body also.

"Hence, so long as the soul is in the body, it never loses sentience through the removal of some other part. The containing sheath may be dislocated in whole or in part, and portions of the soul may thereby be lost; yet in spite of this the soul, if it manage to survive, will have sentience. But the rest of the frame, whether the whole of it survives or only a part, no longer has sensation, when once those atoms have departed, which, however few in number, are required to constitute the nature of soul. Moreover, when the whole frame is broken up, the soul is scattered and has no longer the same powers as before, nor the same motions; hence it does not possess sentience either.

"For we cannot think of it as sentient, except it be in this composite whole and moving with these movements; nor can we so think of it when the sheaths which enclose and surround it are not the same as those in which the soul is now located and in which it performs these movements. [*He says elsewhere that the soul is composed of the smoothest and roundest of atoms, far superior in both respects to those of fire; that part of it is irrational, this being scattered over the rest of the frame, while the rational part resides in the chest, as is manifest from our fears and our joy; that sleep occurs when the parts of the soul which have been scattered all over the composite organism are held fast in it or dispersed, and afterwards collide with one another by their impacts. The semen is derived from the whole of the body.*]

"There is the further point to be considered, what the incorporeal can be, if, I mean, according to current usage the term is applied to what can be conceived as self-existent. But it is impossible to conceive anything that is incorporeal as self-existent except empty space. And empty space cannot itself either act or be acted upon, but simply allows body to move through it. Hence those who call soul incorporeal speak foolishly. For if it were so, it could neither act nor be acted upon. But, as it is, both these properties, you see, plainly belong to soul.

"If, then, we bring all these arguments concerning soul to the criterion of our feelings and perceptions, and if we keep in mind the proposition stated at the outset, we shall see that the subject has been adequately comprehended in outline: which will enable us to determine the details with accuracy and confidence.

"Moreover, shapes and colours, magnitudes and weights, and in short all those qualities which are predicated of body, in so far as they are perpetual properties either of all bodies or of visible bodies, are knowable by sensation of these very properties: these, I say, must not be supposed to exist independently by themselves (for that is inconceivable), nor yet to be non-existent, nor to be some other and incorporeal entities cleaving to body, nor again to be parts of body. We must consider the whole body in a general way to derive its permanent nature from all of them, though it is not, as it were, formed by grouping them together in the same way as when from the particles themselves a larger aggregate is made up, whether these particles be primary or any magnitudes whatsoever less than the particular whole. All these qualities, I repeat, merely give the body its own permanent nature. They all have their own characteristic modes of being perceived and distinguished, but always along with the whole body in which they inhere and never in separation from it; and it is in virtue of this complete conception of the body as a whole that it is so designated.

"Again, qualities often attach to bodies without being permanent concomitants. They are not to be classed among invisible entities nor are they incorporeal. Hence, using the term 'accidents' in the commonest sense, we say plainly that 'accidents' have not the nature of the whole thing to which they belong, and to which, conceiving it as a whole, we give the name of body, nor that of the permanent properties without which body cannot be thought of. And in virtue of certain peculiar modes of apprehension into which the complete body always enters, each of them can be called an accident. But only as often as they are seen actually to belong to it, since such accidents are not perpetual concomitants. There is no need to banish from reality this clear evidence that the accident has not the nature of that whole—by us called body—to which it belongs, nor of the permanent properties which accompany the whole. Nor, on the other hand, must we suppose the accident to have independent existence (for this is just as inconceivable in the case of accidents as in that of the permanent properties); but, as is manifest, they should all be regarded as accidents, not as permanent concomitants, of bodies, nor yet as having the rank of independent existence. Rather they are seen to be exactly as and what sensation itself makes them individually claim to be.

"There is another thing which we must consider carefully. We must not investigate time as we do the other accidents which we investigate in a subject, namely, by referring them to the preconceptions envisaged in our minds; but we must take into account the plain fact itself, in virtue of which we speak of time as long or short, linking to it in intimate connexion this attribute of duration. We need not adopt any fresh terms as preferable, but should employ the usual expressions about it. Nor need we predicate anything else of time, as if this something else contained the same essence as is contained in the proper meaning of the word 'time' (for this also is done by some). We must chiefly reflect upon that to which we attach this peculiar character of time, and by which we measure it. No further proof is required: we have only to reflect that we attach the attribute of time to days and nights and their parts, and likewise to feelings of pleasure and pain and to neutral states, to states of movement and states of rest, conceiving a peculiar accident of these to be this very characteristic which we express by the word 'time.' [*He says this both in the second book "On Nature" and in the Larger Epitome.*]

"After the foregoing we have next to consider that the worlds and every finite aggregate which bears a strong resemblance to things we commonly see have arisen out of the infinite. For all these, whether small or great, have been separated off from special conglomerations of atoms; and all things are again dissolved, some faster, some slower, some through the action of one set of causes, others through the action of another. [*It is clear, then, that he also makes the worlds perishable, as their parts are subject to change. Elsewhere he says the earth is supported on the air.*]

"And further, we must not suppose that the worlds have necessarily one and the same shape. [*On the contrary, in the twelfth book "On Nature" he himself says that the shapes of the worlds differ, some being spherical, some oval, others again of shapes different from these. They do not, however, admit of every shape. Nor are they living beings which have been separated from the infinite.*] For nobody can prove that in one sort of world there might not be contained, whereas in another sort of world there could not possibly be, the seeds out of which animals and plants arise and all the rest of the things we see. [*And the same holds good for their nurture in a world after they have arisen. And so too we must think it happens upon the earth also.*]

"Again, we must suppose that nature too has been taught and forced to learn many various lessons by the facts themselves, that reason subsequently develops what it has thus received and makes fresh discoveries, among some tribes more quickly, among others more slowly, the progress thus made being at certain times and seasons greater, at others less.

"Hence even the names of things were not originally due to convention, but in the several tribes under the impulse of special feelings and special presentations of sense primitive man uttered special cries. The air thus emitted was moulded by their individual feelings or sense-presentations, and differently according to the difference of the regions which the tribes inhabited. Subsequently whole tribes adopted their own special names, in order that their communications might be less ambiguous to each other and more briefly expressed. And as for things not visible, so far as those who were conscious of them tried to introduce any such notion, they put in circulation certain names for them, either sounds which they were instinctively compelled to utter or which they selected by reason on analogy according to the most general cause there can be for expressing oneself in such a way.

"Nay more: we are bound to believe that in the sky revolutions, solstices, eclipses, risings and settings, and the like, take place without the ministration or command, either now or in the future, of any being who at the same time enjoys perfect bliss along with immortality. For troubles and anxieties and feelings of anger and partiality do not accord with bliss, but always imply weakness and fear and dependence upon one's neighbours. Nor, again, must we hold that things which are no more than globular masses of fire, being at the same time endowed with bliss, assume these motions at will. Nay, in every term we use we must hold fast to all the majesty which attaches to such notions as bliss and immortality, lest the terms should generate opinions inconsistent with this majesty. Otherwise such inconsistency will of itself suffice to produce the worst disturbance in our minds. Hence, where we find phenomena invariably recurring, the invariableness of the recurrence must be ascribed to the original interception and conglomeration of atoms whereby the world was formed.

"Further, we must hold that to arrive at accurate knowledge of the cause of things of most moment is the business of natural science, and that happiness depends on this (viz. on the knowledge of celestial and atmospheric phenomena), and upon knowing what the heavenly bodies really are, and any kindred facts contributing to exact knowledge in this respect.

"Further, we must recognize on such points as this no plurality of causes or contingency, but must hold that nothing suggestive of conflict or disquiet is compatible with an immortal and blessed nature. And the mind can grasp the absolute truth of this.

"But when we come to subjects for special inquiry, there is nothing in the knowledge of risings and settings and solstices and eclipses and all kindred subjects that contributes to our happiness; but those who are well-informed about such matters and yet are ignorant what the heavenly bodies really are, and what are the most important causes of phenomena, feel quite as much fear as those who have no such special information—nay, perhaps even greater fear, when the curiosity excited by this additional knowledge cannot find a solution or understand the subordination of these phenomena to the highest causes.

"Hence, if we discover more than one cause that may account for solstices, settings and risings, eclipses and the like, as we did also in particular matters of detail, we must not suppose that our treatment of these matters fails of accuracy, so far as it is needful to ensure our tranquillity and happiness. When, therefore, we investigate the causes of celestial and atmospheric phenomena, as of all that is unknown, we must take into account the variety of ways in which analogous occurrences happen within our experience; while as for those who do not recognize the difference between what is or comes about from a single cause and that which may be the effect of any one of several causes, overlooking the fact that the objects are only seen at a distance, and are moreover ignorant of the conditions that render, or do not render, peace of mind impossible—all such persons we must treat with contempt. If then we think that an event could happen in one or other particular way out of several, we shall be as tranquil when we recognize that it actually comes about in more ways than one as if we knew that it happens in this particular way.

"There is yet one more point to seize, namely, that the greatest anxiety of the human mind arises through the belief that the heavenly bodies are blessed and indestructible, and that at the same time they have volitions and actions and causality inconsistent with his belief; and through expecting or apprehending some everlasting evil, either because of the myths, or because we are in dread of the mere insensibility of death, as if it had to do with us; and through being reduced to this state not by conviction but by a certain irrational perversity, so that, if men do not set bounds to their terror, they endure as much or even more intense anxiety than the man whose views on these matters are quite vague. But mental tranquillity means being released from all these troubles and cherishing a continual remembrance of the highest and most important truths.

"Hence we must attend to present feelings and sense perceptions, whether those of mankind in general or those peculiar to the individual, and also attend to all the clear evidence available, as given by each of the standards of truth. For by studying them we shall rightly trace to its cause and banish the source of disturbance and dread, accounting for celestial phenomena and for all other things which from time to time befall us and cause the utmost alarm to the rest of mankind.

"Here then, Herodotus, you have the chief doctrines of Physics in the form of a summary. So that, if this statement be accurately retained and take effect, a man will, I make no doubt, be incomparably better equipped than his fellows, even if he should never go into all the exact details. For he will clear up for himself many of the points which I have worked out in detail in my complete exposition; and the summary itself, if borne in mind, will be of constant service to him.

"It is of such a sort that those who are already tolerably, or even perfectly, well acquainted with the details can, by analysis of what they know into such elementary perceptions as these, best prosecute their researches in physical science as a whole; while those, on the other hand, who are not altogether entitled to rank as mature students can in silent fashion and as quick as thought run over the doctrines most important for their peace of mind."

B. PRINCIPAL DOCTRINES (*complete*)

Come, then, let me set the seal, so to say, on my entire work as well as on this philosopher's life by citing his Sovran Maxims,[4] therewith bringing the whole work to a close and making the end of it to coincide with the beginning of happiness.

1. A blessed and eternal being has no trouble himself and brings no trouble upon any other being; hence he is exempt from movements of anger and partiality, for every such movement implies weakness. [*Elsewhere he says that the gods are discernible by reason alone, some being numerically distinct, while others result uniformly from the continuous influx of similar images directed to the same spot and in human form.*]

2. Death is nothing to us; for the body, when it has been resolved into its elements, has no feeling, and that which has no feeling is nothing to us.

3. The magnitude of pleasure reaches its limit in the removal of all pain. When pleasure is present, so long as it is uninterrupted, there is no pain either of body or of mind or of both together.

4. Continuous pain does not last long in the flesh; on the contrary, pain,

---

[4] This collection of forty of the most important articles of faith in the Epicurean creed was famous in antiquity. It consists of extracts from the voluminous writings of Epicurus, and may have been put together by a faithful disciple. On the other hand, Epicurus laid great stress on epitomes of his doctrine being committed to memory; so that his passion for personal direction and supervision of the studies of his pupils may have induced him to furnish them with such an indispensable catechism.

if extreme, is present a very short time, and even that degree of pain which barely outweighs pleasure in the flesh does not last for many days together. Illnesses of long duration even permit of an excess of pleasure over pain in the flesh.

5. It is impossible to live a pleasant life without living wisely and well and justly, and it is impossible to live wisely and well and justly without living pleasantly. Whenever any one of these is lacking, when, for instance, the man is not able to live wisely, though he lives well and justly, it is impossible for him to live a pleasant life.

6. In order to obtain security from other men any means whatsoever of procuring this was a natural good.

7. Some men have sought to become famous and renowned, thinking that thus they would make themselves secure against their fellow-men. If, then, the life of such persons really was secure, they attained natural good; if, however, it was insecure, they have not attained the end which by nature's own prompting they originally sought.

8. No pleasure is in itself evil, but the things which produce certain pleasures entail annoyances many times greater than the pleasures themselves.

9. If all pleasure had been capable of accumulation,—if this had gone on not only by recurrence in time, but all over the frame or, at any rate, over the principal parts of man's nature, there would never have been any difference between one pleasure and another, as in fact there is.

10. If the objects which are productive of pleasures to profligate persons really freed them from fears of the mind,—the fears, I mean, inspired by celestial and atmospheric phenomena, the fear of death, the fear of pain; if, further, they taught them to limit their desires, we should never have any fault to find with such persons, for they would then be filled with pleasures to overflowing on all sides and would be exempt from all pain, whether of body or mind, that is, from all evil.

11. If we had never been molested by alarms at celestial and atmospheric phenomena, nor by the misgiving that death somehow affects us, nor by neglect of the proper limits of pains and desires, we should have had no need to study natural science.

12. It would be impossible to banish fear on matters of the highest importance, if a man did not know the nature of the whole universe, but lived in dread of what the legends tell us. Hence without the study of nature there was no enjoyment of unmixed pleasures.

13. There would be no advantage in providing security against our fellow-men, so long as we were alarmed by occurrences over our heads or beneath the earth or in general by whatever happens in the boundless universe.

14. When tolerable security against our fellow-men is attained, then on a basis of power sufficient to afford support and of material prosperity arises in most genuine form the security of a quiet private life withdrawn from the multitude.

15. Nature's wealth at once has its bounds and is easy to procure; but the wealth of vain fancies recedes to an infinite distance.

16. Fortune but seldom interferes with the wise man; his greatest and highest interests have been, are, and will be, directed by reason throughout the course of his life.

17. The just man enjoys the greatest peace of mind, while the unjust is full of the utmost disquietude.

18. Pleasure in the flesh admits no increase when once the pain of want has been removed; after that it only admits of variation. The limit of pleasure in the mind, however, is reached when we reflect on the things themselves and their congeners which cause the mind the greatest alarms.

19. Unlimited time and limited time afford an equal amount of pleasure, if we measure the limits of that pleasure by reason.

20. The flesh receives as unlimited the limits of pleasure; and to provide it requires unlimited time. But the mind, grasping in thought what the end and limit of the flesh is, and banishing the terrors of futurity, procures a complete and perfect life, and has no longer any need of unlimited time. Nevertheless it does not shun pleasure, and even in the hour of death, when ushered out of existence by circumstances, the mind does not lack enjoyment of the best life.

21. He who understands the limits of life knows how easy it is to procure enough to remove the pain of want and make the whole of life complete and perfect. Hence he has no longer any need of things which are not to be won save by labour and conflict.

22. We must take into account as the end of all that really exists and all clear evidence of sense to which we refer our opinions; for otherwise everything will be full of uncertainty and confusion.

23. If you fight against all your sensations, you will have no standard to which to refer, and thus no means of judging even those judgements which you pronounce false.

24. If you reject absolutely any single sensation without stopping to discriminate with respect to that which awaits confirmation between matter of opinion and that which is already present, whether in sensation or in feelings or in any presentative perception of the mind, you will throw into confusion even the rest of your sensations by your groundless belief and so you will be rejecting the standard of truth altogether. If in your ideas based upon opinion you hastily affirm as true all that awaits confirmation as well as that which does not, you will not escape error, as you will be maintaining complete ambiguity whenever it is a case of judging between right and wrong opinion.

25. If you do not on every separate occasion refer each of your actions to the end prescribed by nature, but instead of this in the act of choice or avoidance swerve aside to some other end, your acts will not be consistent with your theories.

26. All such desires as lead to no pain when they remain ungratified are unnecessary, and the longing is easily got rid of, when the thing desired is difficult to procure or when the desires seem likely to produce harm.

27. Of all the means which are procured by wisdom to ensure happiness throughout the whole of life, by far the most important is the acquisition of friends.

28. The same conviction which inspires confidence that nothing we have to fear is eternal or even of long duration, also enables us to see that even in our limited conditions of life nothing enhances our security so much as friendship.

29. Of our desires some are natural and necessary; others are natural, but not necessary; others, again, are neither natural nor necessary, but are due to illusory opinion. [Epicurus regards as natural and necessary desires which bring relief from pain, as *e.g.* drink when we are thirsty; while by natural and not necessary he means those which merely diversify the pleasure without removing the pain, as *e.g.* costly viands; by the neither natural nor necessary he means desires for crowns and the erection of statues in one's honour.—Schol.]

30. Those natural desires which entail no pain when not gratified, though their objects are vehemently pursued, are also due to illusory opinion; and when they are not got rid of, it is not because of their own nature, but because of the man's illusory opinion.

31. Natural justice is a symbol or expression of expediency, to prevent one man from harming or being harmed by another.

32. Those animals which are incapable of making covenants with one another, to the end that they may neither inflict nor suffer harm, are without either justice or injustice. And those tribes which either could not or would not form mutual covenants to the same end are in like case.

33. There never was an absolute justice, but only an agreement made in reciprocal intercourse in whatever localities now and again from time to time, providing against the infliction or suffering of harm.

34. Injustice is not in itself an evil, but only in its consequence, viz. the terror which is excited by apprehension that those appointed to punish such offences will discover the injustice.

35. It is impossible for the man who secretly violates any article of the social compact to feel confident that he will remain undiscovered, even if he has already escaped ten thousand times; for right on to the end of his life he is never sure he will not be detected.

36. Taken generally, justice is the same for all, to wit, something found expedient in mutual intercourse; but in its application to particular cases of locality or conditions of whatever kind, it varies under different circumstances.

37. Among the things accounted just by conventional law, whatever in the needs of mutual intercourse is attested to be expedient, is thereby stamped as just, whether or not it be the same for all; and in case any law is made and does not prove suitable to the expediencies of mutual intercourse, then this is no longer just. And should the expediency which is expressed by the law vary and only for a time correspond with the prior conception, nevertheless for the time being it was just, so long as we do not trouble ourselves about empty words, but look simply at the facts.

38. Where without any change in circumstances the conventional laws, when judged by their consequences, were seen not to correspond with the notion of justice, such laws were not really just; but wherever the laws have ceased to be expedient in consequence of a change in circumstances, in that case the laws were for the time being just when they were expedient for the mutual intercourse of the citizens, and subsequently ceased to be just when they ceased to be expedient.

39. He who best knew how to meet fear of external foes made into one family all the creatures he could; and those he could not, he at any rate did not treat as aliens; and where he found even this impossible, he avoided all intercourse, and, so far as was expedient, kept them at a distance.

40. Those who were best able to provide themselves with the means of security against their neighbours, being thus in possession of the surest guarantee, passed the most agreeable life in each other's society; and their enjoyment of the fullest intimacy was such that, if one of them died before his time, the survivors did not lament his death as if it called for commiseration.

CLEANTHES' *HYMN TO ZEUS* (*complete*)*

    O God most glorious, called by many a name,
Nature's great King, through endless years the same;
Omnipotence, who by thy just decree
Controllest all, hail, Zeus, for unto thee
Behoves thy creatures in all lands to call.
We are thy children, we alone, of all
On earth's broad ways that wander to and fro,
Bearing thine image whereso'er we go.
Wherefore with songs of praise thy power I will forth show.
Lo! yonder Heaven, that round the earth is wheeled,
Follows thy guidance, still to thee doth yield
Glad homage; thine unconquerable hand
Such flaming minister, the levin brand,
Wieldeth, a sword two-edged, whose deathless might
Pulsates through all that Nature brings to light;
Vehicle of the universal Word, that flows
Through all, and in the light celestial glows
Of stars both great and small. A King of Kings
Through ceaseless ages, God, whose purpose brings
To birth, whate'er on land or in the sea
Is wrought, or in high heaven's immensity;

---

* See also Epictetus, section 53.

Save what the sinner works infatuate.
Nay, but thou knowest to make crooked straight:
Chaos to thee in order: in thine eyes
The unloved is lovely, who didst harmonize
Things evil with things good, that there should be
One Word through all things everlastingly.
One Word—whose voice alas! the wicked spurn;
Insatiate for the good their spirits yearn:
Yet seeing see not, neither hearing hear
God's universal law, which those revere,
By reason guided, happiness who win.
The rest, unreasoning, diverse shapes of sin
Self-prompted follow: for an idle name
Vainly they wrestle in the lists of fame:
Others inordinately riches woo,
Or dissolute, the joys of flesh pursue.
Now here, now there they wander, fruitless still,
For ever seeking good and finding ill.
Zeus the all-bountiful, whom darkness shrouds,
Whose lightning lightens in the thunder-clouds;
Thy children save from error's deadly sway:
Turn thou the darkness from their souls away:
Vouchsafe that unto knowledge they attain;
For thou by knowledge art made strong to reign
O'er all, and all things rulest righteously.
So by thee honoured, we will honour thee,
Praising thy works continually with songs,
As mortals should; nor higher meed belongs
E'en to the gods, than justly to adore
The universal law for evermore.

EPICTETUS' *ENCHEIRIDION* or *MANUAL* (*complete*)

1. Some things are under our control, while others are not under our control. Under our control are conception, choice, desire, aversion, and in a word, everything that is our own doing; not under our control are our body, our property, reputation, office and, in a word, everything that is not our own doing. Furthermore, the things under our control are by nature free, unhindered, and unimpeded; while the things not under our control are weak, servile, subject to hindrance, and not our own. Remember, therefore, that if what is naturally slavish you think to be free, and what is not your own to be your own, you will be hampered, will grieve, will be in turmoil, and will blame both gods and men; while if you think

only what is your own to be your own, and what is not your own to be, as it really is, not your own, then no one will ever be able to exert compulsion upon you, no one will hinder you, you will blame no one, will find fault with no one, will do absolutely nothing against your will, you will have no personal enemy, no one will harm you, for neither is there any harm that can touch you.

With such high aims, therefore, remember that you must bestir yourself with no slight effort to lay hold of them, but you will have to give up some things entirely, and defer others for the time being. But if you wish for these things also, and at the same time for both office and wealth, it may be that you will not get even these latter, because you aim also at the former, and certainly you will fail to get the former, which alone bring freedom and happiness.

Make it, therefore, your study at the very outset to say to every harsh external impression, "You are an external impression and not at all what you appear to be." After that examine it and test it by these rules which you have, the first and most important of which is this: Whether the impression has to do with the things which are under our control, or with those which are not under our control; and, if it has to do with some one of the things not under our control, have ready to hand the answer, "It is nothing to me."

2. Remember that the promise of desire is the attainment of what you desire, that of aversion is not to fall into what is avoided, and that he who fails in his desire is unfortunate, while he who falls into what he would avoid experiences misfortune. If, then, you avoid only what is unnatural among those things which are under your control, you will fall into none of the things which you avoid; but of you try to avoid disease, or death, or poverty, you will experience misfortune. Withdraw, therefore, your aversion from all the matters that are not under our control, and transfer it to what is unnatural among those which are under our control. But for the time being [1] remove utterly your desire; for if you desire some one of the things that are not under our control you are bound to be unfortunate; and, at the same time, not one of the things that are under our control, which it would be excellent for you to desire, is within your grasp. But employ only choice and refusal, and these too but lightly, and with reservations,[2] and without straining.

3. With everything which entertains you, is useful, or of which you are fond, remember to say to yourself, beginning with the very least things, "What is its nature?" If you are fond of a jug, say, "I am fond of a jug"; for when it is broken you will not be disturbed. If you kiss your own child or wife, say to yourself that you are kissing a human being; for when it dies you will not be disturbed.

[1] The remark, as many others of the admonitions, is addressed to a student or a beginner.
[2] See M. Aurelius, 1, 4, where Mr. Haines (in *L.C.L.*) suggests that the reference is to some such reservations as recommended in James iv. 15: "For that ye ought to say is, If the Lord will, we shall live, and do this, or that."

4. When you are on the point of putting your hand to some undertaking, remind yourself what the nature of that undertaking is. If you are going out of the house to bathe, put before your mind what happens at a public bath—those who splash you with water, those who jostle against you, those who vilify you and rob you. And thus you will set about your undertaking more securely if at the outset you say to yourself, "I want to take a bath, and, at the same time, to keep my moral purpose in harmony with nature." And so do in every undertaking. For thus, if anything happens to hinder you in your bathing, you will be ready to say, "Oh, well, this was not the only thing that I wanted, but I wanted also to keep your moral purpose in harmony with nature; and I shall not so keep it if I am vexed at what is going on."

5. It is not the things themselves that disturb men, but their judgements about these things. For example, death is nothing dreadful, or else Socrates too would have thought so, but the judgement that death is dreadful, *this* is the dreadful thing. When, therefore, we are hindered, or disturbed, or grieved, let us never blame anyone but ourselves, that means, our own judgements. It is the part of an uneducated person to blame others where he himself fares ill; to blame himself is the part of one whose education has begun; to blame neither another nor his own self is the part of one whose education is already complete.

6. Be not elated at any excellence which is not your own. If the horse in his elation were to say, "I am beautiful," it could be endured; but when you say in your elation, "I have a beautiful horse," rest assured that you are elated at something good which belongs to a horse. What, then, is your own? The use of external impressions. Therefore, when you are in harmony with nature in the use of external impressions, then be elated; for then it will be some good of your own at which you will be elated.

7. Just as on a voyage, when your ship has anchored, if you should go on shore to get fresh water, you may pick up a small shell-fish or little bulb [3] on the way, but you have to keep your attention fixed on the ship, and turn about frequently for fear lest the captain should call; and if he calls, you must give up all these things, if you would escape being thrown on board all tied up like the sheep. So it is also in life: If there be given you, instead of a little bulb and a small shell-fish, a little wife and child, there will be no objection to that; only, if the Captain calls, give up all these things and run to the ship, without even turning around to look back. And if you are an old man, never even get very far away from the ship, for fear that when He calls you may be missing.

8. Do not seek to have everything that happens happen as you wish, but wish for everything to happen as it actually does happen, and your life will be serene.

9. Disease is an impediment to the body, but not to the moral purpose, unless that consents. Lameness is an impediment to the leg, but not to

---

[3] The Greeks ate a good many different bulbous plants, and we use a variety of different plants for "greens."

the moral purpose. And say this to yourself at each thing that befalls you; for you will find the thing to be an impediment to something else, but not to yourself.

10. In the case of everything that befalls you, remember to turn to yourself and see what faculty you have to deal with it. If you see a handsome lad or woman, you will find continence the faculty to employ here; if hard labour is laid upon you, you will find endurance; if reviling, you will find patience to bear evil. And if you habituate yourself in this fashion, your external impressions will not run away with you.

11. Never say about anything, "I have lost it," but only "I have given it back." Is your child dead? It has been given back. Is your wife dead? She has been given back. "I have had my farm taken away." Very well, this too has been given back. "Yet it was a rascal who took it away." But what concern is it of yours by whose instrumentality the Giver called for its return? So long as He gives it to you, take care of it as of a thing that is not your own, as travellers treat their inn.

12. If you wish to make progress, dismiss all reasoning of this sort: "If I neglect my affairs, I shall have nothing to live on." "If I do not punish my slave-boy he will turn out bad." For it is better to die of hunger, but in a state of freedom from grief and fear, than to live in plenty, but troubled in mind. And it is better for your slave-boy to be bad than for you to be unhappy. Begin, therefore, with the little things. Your paltry oil gets spilled, your miserable wine stolen; say to yourself, "This is the price paid for a calm spirit, this the price for peace of mind." Nothing is got without a price. And when you call your slave-boy, bear in mind that it is possible he may not heed you, and again, that even if he does heed, he may not do what you want done. But he is not in so happy a condition that your peace of mind depends upon him.[4]

13. If you wish to make progress, then be content to appear senseless and foolish in externals, do not make it your wish to give the appearance of knowing anything; and if some people think you to be an important personage, distrust yourself. For be assured that it is no easy matter to keep your moral purpose in a state of conformity with nature, and, at the same time, to keep externals; but the man who devotes his attention to one of these two things must inevitably neglect the other.

14. If you make it your will that your children and your wife and your friends should live for ever, you are silly; for you are making it your will that things not under your control should be under your control, and that what is not your own should be your own. In the same way, too, if you make it your will that your slave-boy be free from faults, you are a fool; for you are making it your will that vice be not vice, but something else. If, however, it is your will not to fail in what you desire, this is in your power. Wherefore, exercise yourself in that which is in your power.

---

[4] That is, the slave-boy would be in a remarkable position of advantage if his master's peace of mind depended, not upon the master himself, but upon the actions of his slave-boy.

Each man's master is the person who has the authority over what the man wishes or does not wish, so as to secure it, or take it away. Whoever, therefore, wants to be free, let him neither wish for anything, nor avoid anything, that is under the control of others; or else he is necessarily a slave.

15. Remember that you ought to behave in life as you would at a banquet. As something is being passed around it comes to you; stretch out your hand and take a portion of it politely. It passes on; do not detain it. Or it has not come to you yet; do not project your desire to meet it, but wait until it comes in front of you. So act toward children, so toward a wife, so toward office, so toward wealth; and then some day you will be worthy of the banquets of the gods. But if you do not take these things even when they are set before you, but despise them, then you will not only share the banquet of the gods, but share also their rule. For it was by so doing that Diogenes and Heracleitus, and men like them, were deservedly divine and deservedly so called.

16. When you see someone weeping in sorrow, either because a child has gone on a journey, or because he has lost his property, beware that you be not carried away by the impression that the man is in the midst of external ills, but straightway keep before you this thought: "It is not what has happened that distresses this man (for it does not distress another), but his judgement about it." Do not, however, hesitate to sympathize with him so far as words go, and, if occasion offers, even to groan with him; but be careful not to groan also in the centre of your being.

17. Remember that you are an actor in a play, the character of which is determined by the Playwright: if He wishes the play to be short, it is short; if long, it is long; if He wishes you to play the part of a beggar, remember to act even this rôle adroitly; and so if your rôle be that of a cripple, an official, or a layman. For this is your business, to play admirably the rôle assigned you; but the selection of that rôle is Another's.[5]

18. When a raven croaks inauspiciously, let not the external impression carry you away, but straightway draw a distinction in your own mind, and say, "None of these portents are for me, but either for my paltry body, or my paltry estate, or my paltry opinion, or my children, or my wife. But for me every portent is favourable, if I so wish; for whatever be the outcome, it is within my power to derive benefit from it."

19. You can be invincible if you never enter a contest in which victory is not under your control. Beware lest, when you see some person preferred to you in honour, or possessing great power, or otherwise enjoying high repute, you are ever carried away by the external impression, and deem him happy. For if the true nature of the good is one of the things that are under our control, there is no place for either envy or jealousy; and you yourself will not wish to be a praetor, or a senator, or a consul, but a free man. Now there is but one way that leads to this, and that is to despise the things that are not under our control.

---

[5] A reverent designation for God.

20. Bear in mind that it is not the man who reviles or strikes you that insults you, but it is your judgement that these men are insulting you. Therefore, when someone irritates you, be assured that it is your own opinion which has irritated you. And so make it your first endeavour not to be carried away by the external impression; for if once you gain time and delay, you will more easily become master of yourself.

21. Keep before your eyes day by day death and exile, and everything that seems terrible, but most of all death; and then you will never have any abject thought, nor will you yearn for anything beyond measure.

22. If you yearn for philosophy, prepare at once to be met with ridicule, to have many people jeer at you, and say, "Here he is again, turned philosopher all of a sudden," and "Where do you suppose he got that high brow?" But do you not put on a high brow, and do you so hold fast to the things which to you seem best, as a man who has been assigned by God to this post; and remember that if you abide by the same principles, those who formerly used to laugh at you will later come to admire you, but if you are worsted by them, you will get the laugh on yourself twice.

23. If it should ever happen to you that you turn to externals with a view to pleasing someone, rest assured that you have lost your plan of life. Be content, therefore, in everything to *be* a philosopher, and if you wish also to be taken for one, show to yourself that you are one, and you will be able to accomplish it.

24. Let not these reflections oppress you: "I shall live without honour, and be nobody anywhere." For, if lack of honour is an evil, you cannot be in evil through the instrumentality of some other person, any more than you can be in shame.[6] It is not your business, is it, to get office, or to be invited to a dinner-party? Certainly not. How, then, can this be any longer a lack of honour? And how is it that you will be "nobody anywhere," when you ought to be somebody only in those things which are under your control, wherein you are privileged to be a man of the very greatest honour? But your friends will be without assistance? What do you mean by being "without assistance"? They will not have paltry coin from you, and you will not make them Roman citizens. Well, who told you that these are some of the matters under our control, and not rather things which others do? And who is able to give another what he does not himself have? "Get money, then," says some friend, "in order that we too may have it." If I can get money and at the same time keep myself self-respecting, and faithful, and high-minded, show me the way and I will get it. But if you require me to lose the good things that belong to me, in order that you may acquire the things that are not good, you can see for yourselves how unfair and inconsiderate you are. And which do you really prefer? Money, or a faithful and self-respecting friend?

---

[6] That is, every man is exclusively responsible for his own good or evil. But honour and the lack of it are things which are obviously not under a man's control, since they depend upon the action of other people. It follows, therefore, that lack of honour cannot be an evil, but must be something indifferent.

Help me, therefore, rather to this end, and do not require me to do those things which will make me lose these qualities.

"But my country," says he, "so far as lies in me, will be without assistance." Again I ask, what kind of assistance do you mean? It will not have loggias or baths of your providing. And what does that signify? For neither does it have shoes provided by the blacksmith, nor has it arms provided by the cobbler; but it is sufficient if each man fulfil his own proper function. And if you secured for it another faithful and self-respecting citizen, would you not be doing it any good? "Yes." Very well, and then you also would not be useless to it. "What place, then, shall I have in the State?" says he. Whatever place you *can* have, and at the same time maintain the man of fidelity and self-respect that is in you. But if, through your desire to help the State, you lose these qualities, of what good would you become to it, when in the end you turned out to be shameless and unfaithful?

25. Has someone been honoured above you at a dinner-party, or in salutation, or in being called in to give advice? Now if these matters are good, you ought to be happy that he got them; but if evil, be not distressed because you did not get them; and bear in mind that, if you do not act the same way that others do, with a view to getting things which are not under our control, you cannot be considered worthy to receive an equal share with others. Why, how is it possible for a person who does not haunt some man's door, to have equal shares with the man who does? For the man who does not do escort duty, with the man who does? For the man who does not praise, with the man who does? You will be unjust, therefore, and insatiable, if, while refusing to pay the price for which such things are bought, you want to obtain them for nothing. Well, what is the price for heads of lettuce? An obol, perhaps. If, then, somebody gives up his obol and gets his heads of lettuce, while you do not give your obol, and do not get them, do not imagine that you are worse off than the man who gets his lettuce. For as he has his heads of lettuce, so you have your obol which you have not given away.

Now it is the same way also in life. You have not been invited to somebody's dinner-party? Of course not; for you didn't give the host the price at which he sells his dinner. He sells it for praise; he sells it for personal attention. Give him the price, then, for which it is sold, if it is to your interest. But if you wish both not to give up the one and yet to get the other, you are insatiable and a simpleton. Have you, then, nothing in place of the dinner? Indeed you have; you have not had to praise the man you did not want to praise; you have not had to put up with the insolence of his doorkeepers.

26. What the will of nature is may be learned from a consideration of the points in which we do not differ from one another. For example, when some other person's slave-boy breaks his drinking-cup, you are instantly ready to say, "That's one of the things which happen." Rest assured, then, that when your own drinking-cup gets broken, you ought to behave in the same way that you do when the other man's cup is

broken. Apply now the same principle to the matters of greater importance. Some other person's child or wife has died; no one but would say, "Such is the fate of man." Yet when a man's own child dies, immediately the cry is, "Alas! Woe is me!" But we ought to remember how we feel when we hear of the same misfortune befalling others.

27. Just as a mark is not set up in order to be missed, so neither does the nature of evil arise in the universe.[7]

28. If someone handed over your body to any person who met you, you would be vexed; but that you hand over your mind to any person that comes along, so that, if he reviles you, it is disturbed and troubled— are you not ashamed of that?

29.[8] In each separate thing that you do, consider the matters which come first and those which follow after, and only then approach the thing itself. Otherwise, at the start you will come to it enthusiastically, because you have never reflected upon any of the subsequent steps, but later on, when some difficulties appear, you will give up disgracefully. Do you wish to win an Olympic victory? So do I, by the gods! for it is a fine thing. But consider the matters which come before that, and those which follow after, and only when you have done that, put your hand to the task. You have to submit to discipline, follow a strict diet, give up sweet cakes, train under compulsion, at a fixed hour, in heat or in cold; you must not drink cold water,[9] nor wine just whenever you feel like it; you must have turned yourself over to your trainer precisely as you would to a physician. Then when the contest comes on, you have to "dig in" beside your opponent, and sometimes dislocate your wrist, sprain your ankle, swallow quantities of sand, sometimes take a scourging, and along with all that get beaten. After you have considered all these points, go on into the games, if you still wish to do so; otherwise, you will be turning back like children. Sometimes they play wrestlers, again gladiators, again they blow trumpets, and then act a play. So you too are now an athlete, now a gladiator, then a rhetorician, then a philosopher, yet with your whole soul nothing; but like an ape you imitate whatever you see, and one thing after another strikes your fancy. For you have never gone out after anything with circumspection, nor after you had examined it all over, but you act at haphazard and half-heartedly.

In the same way, when some people have seen a philosopher and have heard someone speaking like Euphrates[10] (though, indeed, who can

---

[7] That is, it is inconceivable that the universe should exist in order that some things may go wrong; hence, nothing natural is evil, and nothing that is by nature evil can arise.—Thus in effect Simplicius, and correctly, it seems.

[8] This chapter is practically word for word identical with Arrian's *Discourses of Epictetus*, III. 15. Since it was omitted in Par., and not commented on by Simplicius, it may have been added in some second edition, whether by Arrian or not.

[9] That is, *cold* water not at all; while wine may be drunk, but only at certain times, *i.e.*, probably with one's meals. Such prohibitions are still common in Europe, particularly in popular therapeutics.

[10] An eminent Stoic lecturer.

speak like him?), they wish to be philosophers themselves. Man, consider first the nature of the business, and then learn your own natural ability, if you are able to bear it. Do you wish to be a contender in the pentathlon, or a wrestler? Look to your arms, your thighs, see what your loins are like. For one man has a natural talent for one thing, another for another. Do you suppose that you can eat in the same fashion, drink in the same fashion, give way to impulse and to irritation, just as you do now? You must keep vigils, work hard, abandon your own people, be despised by a paltry slave, be laughed to scorn by those who meet you, in everything get the worst of it, in honour, in office, in court, in every paltry affair. Look these drawbacks over carefully, if you are willing at the price of these things to secure tranquillity, freedom and calm. Otherwise, do not approach philosophy; don't act like a child—now a philosopher, later on a tax-gatherer, then a rhetorician, then a procurator of Caesar. These things do not go together. You must be one person, either good or bad; you must labour to improve either your own governing principle or externals; you must work hard either on the inner man, or on things outside; that is, play either the rôle of a philosopher or else that of a layman.

30. Our duties are in general measured by our social relationships. He is a father. One is called upon to take care of him, to give way to him in all things, to submit when he reviles or strikes you. "But he is a bad father." Did nature, then, bring you into relationship with a *good* father? No, but simply with a father. "My brother does me wrong." Very well, then, maintain the relation that you have toward him; and do not consider what he is doing, but what you will have to do, if your moral purpose is to be in harmony with nature. For no one will harm you without your consent; you will have been harmed only when you think you are harmed. In this way, therefore, you will discover what duty to expect of your neighbour, your citizen, your commanding officer, if you acquire the habit of looking at your social relations with them.

31. In piety towards the gods, I would have you know, the chief element is this, to have right opinions about them—as existing and as administering the universe well and justly—and to have set yourself to obey them and to submit to everything that happens, and to follow it voluntarily, in the belief that it is being fulfilled by the highest intelligence. For if you act in this way, you will never blame the gods, nor find fault with them for neglecting you. But this result cannot be secured in any other way than by withdrawing your idea of the good and the evil from the things which are not under our control, and placing it in those which are under our control, and in those alone. Because, if you think any of those former things to be good or evil, then, when you fail to get what you want and fall into what you do not want, it is altogether inevitable that you will blame and hate those who are responsible for these results. For this is the nature of every living creature, to flee from and to turn aside from the things that appear harmful, and all that produces them, and to pursue after and to admire the things that are helpful, and all that produces them. Therefore, it is impossible for a man who thinks

that he is being hurt to take pleasure in that which he thinks is hurting him, just as it is also impossible for him to take pleasure in the hurt itself. Hence it follows that even a father is reviled by a son when he does not give his child some share in the things that seem to be good; and this it was which made Polyneices and Eteocles enemies of one another, the thought that the royal power was a good thing. That is why the farmer reviles the gods, and so also the sailor, and the merchant, and those who have lost their wives and their children. For where a man's interest lies, there is also his piety. Wherefore, whoever is careful to exercise desire and aversion as he should, is at the same time careful also about piety. But it is always appropriate to make libations, and sacrifices, and to give of the firstfruits after the manner of our fathers, and to do all this with purity, and not in a slovenly or careless fashion, nor, indeed, in a niggardly way, nor yet beyond our means.

32.[11] When you have recourse to divination, remember that you do not know what the issue is going to be, but that you have come in order to find this out from the diviner; yet if you are indeed a philosopher, you know, when you arrive, what the nature of it is. For if it is one of the things which are not under our control, it is altogether necessary that what is going to take place is neither good nor evil. Do not, therefore, bring to the diviner desire or aversion, and do not approach him with trembling, but having first made up your mind that every issue is indifferent and nothing to you, but that, whatever it may be, it will be possible for you to turn it to good use, and that no one will prevent this. Go, then, with confidence to the gods as to counsellors; and after that, when some counsel has been given you, remember whom you have taken as counsellors, and whom you will be disregarding if you disobey. But go to divination as Socrates thought that men should go, that is, in cases where the whole inquiry has reference to the outcome, and where neither from reason nor from any other technical art are means vouchsafed for discovering the matter in question. Hence, when it is your duty to share the danger of a friend or of your country, do not ask of the diviner whether you ought to share that danger. For if the diviner forewarns you that the omens of sacrifice have been unfavourable, it is clear that death is portended, or the injury of some member of your body, or exile; yet reason requires that even at this risk you are to stand by your friend, and share the danger with your country. Wherefore, give heed to the greater diviner, the Pythian Apollo, who cast out of his temple the man who had not helped his friend when he was being murdered.[12]

---

[11] See *Discourses*, II. 7 where the principal points made here are illustrated at greater length.

[12] A few more unimportant details are given by Aelian, *Varia Historia*, 3, 44; and Simplicius in his commentary on this passage, p. 258 c ff. (Heinsius), or p. 411 (Schweighäuser). The point of the story is that a man does not need to go to a diviner in order to learn whether he should defend his country or his friends. That question was long ago settled by the greatest of diviners, Apollo at Delphi, who ordered to be cast out of his temple an inquirer that had once failed to defend his own friend.

33. Lay down for yourself, at the outset, a certain stamp and type of character for yourself, which you are to maintain whether you are by yourself or are meeting with people. And be silent for the most part, or else make only the most necessary remarks, and express these in few words. But rarely, and when occasion requires you to talk, talk, indeed, but about no ordinary topics. Do not talk about gladiators, or horse-races, or athletes, or things to eat or drink—topics that arise on all occasions; but above all, do not talk about people, either blaming, or praising, or comparing them. If, then, you can, by your own conversation bring over that of your companions to what is seemly. But if you happen to be left alone in the presence of aliens, keep silence.

Do not laugh much, nor at many things, nor boisterously.

Refuse, if you can, to take an oath at all, but if that is impossible, refuse as far as circumstances allow.

Avoid entertainments given by outsiders and by persons ignorant of philosophy; but if an appropriate occasion arises for you to attend, be on the alert to avoid lapsing into the behaviour of such laymen. For you may rest assured, that, if a man's companion be dirty, the person who keeps close company with him must of necessity get a share of his dirt, even though he himself happens to be clean.

In things that pertain to the body take only as much as your bare need requires, I mean such things as food, drink, clothing, shelter, and household slaves; but cut down everything which is for outward show or luxury.

In your sex-life preserve purity, as far as you can, before marriage, and, if you indulge, take only those privileges which are lawful. However, do not make yourself offensive, or censorious, to those who do indulge, and do not make frequent mention of the fact that you do not yourself indulge.

If someone brings you word that So-and-so is speaking ill of you, do not defend yourself against what has been said, but answer, "Yes, indeed, for he did not know the rest of the faults that attach to me; if he had, these would not have been the only ones he mentioned."

It is not necessary, for the most part, to go to the public shows. If, however, a suitable occasion ever arises, show that your principal concern is for none other than yourself, which means, wish only for that to happen which does happen, and for him only to win who does win; for so you will suffer no hindrance. But refrain utterly from shouting, or laughter at anyone, or great excitement. And after you have left, do not talk a great deal about what took place, except in so far as it contributes to your own improvement; for such behaviour indicates that the spectacle has aroused your admiration.

Do not go rashly or readily to people's public readings,[13] but when you do go, maintain your own dignity and gravity, and at the same time be careful not to make yourself disagreeable.

---

[13] A favourite way of introducing a new work of literature to the reading public, somewhat like our modern musical recitals, or artists' exhibitions. See also III. 23 for similar public lectures given by a philosopher.

When you are about to meet somebody, in particular when it is one of those men who are held in very high esteem, propose to yourself the question, "What would Socrates or Zeno have done under these circumstances?" and then you will not be at a loss to make proper use of the occasion. When you go to see one of those men who have great power, propose to yourself the thought, that you will not find him at home, that you will be shut out, that the door will be slammed in your face, that he will pay no attention to you. And if, despite all this, it is your duty to go, go and take what comes, and never say to yourself, "It was not worth all the trouble." For this is characteristic of the layman, that is, a man who is vexed at externals.

In your conversation avoid making mention at great length and excessively of your own deeds or dangers, because it is not as pleasant for others to hear about your adventures, as it is for you to call to mind your own dangers.

Avoid also raising a laugh, for this is a kind of behaviour that slips easily into vulgarity, and at the same time is calculated to lessen the respect which your neighbours have of you. It is dangerous also to lapse into foul language. When, therefore, anything of the sort occurs, if the occasion be suitable, go even so far as to reprove the person who has made such a lapse; if, however, the occasion does not arise, at all events show by keeping silence, and blushing, and frowning, that you are displeased by what has been said.

34. When you get an external impression of some pleasure, guard yourself, as with impressions in general, against being carried away by it; nay, let the matter wait upon *your* leisure, and give yourself a little delay. Next think of the two periods of time, first, that in which you will enjoy your pleasure, and second, that in which, after the enjoyment is over, you will later repent and revile your own self; and set over against these two periods of time how much joy and self-satisfaction you will get if you refrain. However, if you feel that a suitable occasion has arisen to do the deed, be careful not to allow its enticement, and sweetness, and attractiveness to overcome you; but set over against all this the thought, how much better is the consciousness of having won a victory over it.

35. When you do a thing which you have made up your mind ought to be done, never try not to be seen doing it, even though most people are likely to think unfavourably about it. If, however, what you are doing is not right, avoid the deed itself altogether; but if it is right, why fear those who are going to rebuke you wrongly?

36. Just as the propositions, "It is day," and "it is night," are full of meaning when separated, but meaningless if united; so also, granted that for you to take the larger share at a dinner is good for your body, still, it is bad for the maintenance of the proper kind of social feeling. When, therefore, you are eating with another person, remember to regard, not merely the value for your body of what lies before you, but also to maintain your respect for your host.

37. If you undertake a rôle which is beyond your powers, you both disgrace yourself in that one, and at the same time neglect the rôle which you might have filled with success.

38. Just as you are careful, in walking about, not to step on a nail or to sprain your ankle, so be careful also not to hurt your governing principle. And if we observe this rule in every action, we shall be more secure in setting about it.

39. Each man's body is a measure for his property,[14] just as the foot is a measure for his shoe. If, then, you abide by this principle, you will maintain the proper measure, but if you go beyond it, you cannot help but fall headlong over a precipice, as it were, in the end. So also in the case of your shoe; if once you go beyond the foot, you get first a gilded shoe, then a purple one, then an embroidered one. For once you go beyond the measure there is no limit.

40. Immediately after they are fourteen, women are called "ladies" by men. And so when they see that they have nothing else but only to be the bedfellows of men, they begin to beautify themselves, and put all their hopes in that. It is worth while for us to take pains, therefore, to make them understand that they are honoured for nothing else but only for appearing modest and self-respecting.

41. It is a mark of an ungifted man to spend a great deal of time in what concerns his body, as in much exercise, much eating, much drinking, much evacuating of the bowels, much copulating. But these things are to be done in passing; and let your whole attention be devoted to the mind.

42. When someone treats you ill or speaks ill of you, remember that he acts or speaks thus because he thinks it is incumbent upon him. That being the case, it is impossible for him to follow what appears good to you, but what appears good to himself; whence it follows that, if he gets a wrong view of things, the man that suffers is the man that has been deceived. For if a person thinks a true composite judgement to be false, the composite judgement does not suffer, but the person who has been deceived. If, therefore, you start from this point of view, you will be gentle with the man who reviles you. For you should say on each occasion, "He thought that way about it."

43. Everything has two handles, by one of which it ought to be carried and by the other not. If your brother wrongs you, do not lay hold of the matter by the handle of the wrong that he is doing, because this is the handle by which the matter ought not to be carried; but rather by the other handle—that he is your brother, that you were brought up together, and then you will be laying hold of the matter by the handle by which it ought to be carried.

---

[14] That is, property, which is of use only for the body, should be adjusted to a man's actual bodily needs, just as a shoe is (or at least should be) adjusted to the actual needs of a man's foot. The comparison seems to have been a commonplace; see Demophilus, *Similitudines,* 20 (Mullach); Horace, *Epist.* I. 7, 98 and 10, 42 f.

44. The following statements constitute a *non sequitur:* "I am richer than you are, therefore I am superior to you"; or, "I am more eloquent than you are, therefore I am superior to you." But the following conclusions are better: "I am richer than you are, therefore my property is superior to yours"; or, "I am more eloquent than you are, therefore my elocution is superior to yours." But *you* are neither property nor elocution.

45. Somebody is hasty about bathing; do not say that he bathes badly, but that he is hasty about bathing. Somebody drinks a good deal of wine; do not say that he drinks badly, but that he drinks a good deal. For until you have decided what judgement prompts him, how do you know that what he is doing is bad? And thus the final result will not be that you receive convincing sense-impressions of some things, but give your assent to others.

46. On no occasion call yourself a philosopher, and do not, for the most part, talk among laymen about your philosophic principles, but do what follows from your principles. For example, at a banquet do not say how people ought to eat, but eat as a man ought. For remember how Socrates had so completely eliminated the thought of ostentation, that people came to him when they wanted him to introduce them to philosophers, and he used to bring them along. So well did he submit to being overlooked. And if talk about some philosophic principle arises among laymen, keep silence for the most part, for there is great danger that you will spew up immediately what you have not digested. So when a man tells you that you know nothing, and you, like Socrates, are not hurt, then rest assured that you are making a beginning with the business you have undertaken. For sheep, too, do not bring their fodder to the shepherds and show how much they have eaten, but they digest their food within them, and on the outside produce wool and milk. And so do you, therefore, make no display to the laymen of your philosophical principles, but let them see the results which come from these principles when digested.

47. When you have become adjusted to simple living in regard to your bodily wants, do not preen yourself about the accomplishment; and so likewise, if you are a water-drinker, do not on every occasion say that you are a water-drinker. And if ever you want to train to develop physical endurance, do it by yourself and not for outsiders to behold; do not throw your arms around statues,[15] but on occasion, when you are very thirsty, take cold water into your mouth, and then spit it out, without telling anybody.

48. This is the position and character of a layman: He never looks for either help or harm from himself, but only from externals. This is the position and character of the philosopher: He looks for all his help or harm from himself.

---

[15] Diogenes the Cynic was said to have done that nude in cold weather, so as to harden himself. Diog. Laert. 6, 23.

Signs of one who is making progress are: He censures no one, praises no one, blames no one, finds fault with no one, says nothing about himself as though he were somebody or knew something. When he is hampered or prevented, he blames himself. And if anyone compliments him, he smiles to himself at the person complimenting; while if anyone censures him, he makes no defence. He goes about like an invalid, being careful not to disturb, before it has grown firm, any part which is getting well. He has put away from himself his every desire, and has transferred his aversion to those things only, of what is under our control, which are contrary to nature. He exercises no pronounced choice in regard to anything. If he gives the appearance of being foolish or ignorant he does not care. In a word, he keeps guard against himself as though he were his own enemy lying in wait.

49. When a person gives himself airs because he can understand and interpret the books of Chrysippus, say to yourself, "If Chrysippus had not written obscurely, this man would have nothing about which to give himself airs."

But what is it I want? To learn nature and to follow her. I seek, therefore, someone to interpret her; and having heard that Chrysippus does so, I go to him. But I do not understand what he has written; I seek, therefore, the person who interprets Chrysippus. And down to this point there is nothing to justify pride. But when I find the interpreter, what remains is to put his precepts into practice; this is the only thing to be proud about. If, however, I admire the mere act of interpretation, what have I done but turned into a grammarian instead of a philosopher? The only difference, indeed, is that I interpret Chrysippus instead of Homer. Far from being proud, therefore, when somebody says to me, "Read me Chrysippus," I blush the rather, when I am unable to show him such deeds as match and harmonize with his words.

50. Whatever principles are set before you, stand fast by these like laws, feeling that it would be impiety for you to transgress them. But pay no attention to what somebody says about you, for this is, at length, not under your control.

51. How long will you still wait to think yourself worthy of the best things, and in nothing to transgress against the distinctions set up by the reason? You have received the philosophical principles which you ought to accept, and you have accepted them. What sort of a teacher, then, do you still wait for, that you should put off reforming yourself until he arrives? You are no longer a lad, but already a full-grown man. If you are now neglectful and easy-going, and always making one delay after another, and fixing first one day and then another, after which you will pay attention to yourself, then without realizing it you will make no progress, but, living and dying, will continue to be a layman throughout. Make up your mind, therefore, before it is too late, that the fitting thing for you to do is to live as a mature man who is making progress, and let everything which seems to you to be best be for you a law that must not be transgressed. And if you meet anything that is

laborious, or sweet, or held in high repute, or in no repute, remember that *now* is the contest, and here before you are the Olympic games, and that it is impossible to delay any longer, and that it depends on a single day and a single action, whether progress is lost or saved. This is the way Socrates became what he was, by paying attention to nothing but his reason in everything that he encountered. And even if you are not yet a Socrates, still you ought to live as one who wishes to be a Socrates.

52. The first and most necessary division in philosophy is that which has to do with the application of the principles, as, for example, Do not lie. The second deals with the demonstrations, as, for example, How comes it that we ought not to lie? The third confirms and discriminates between these processes, as, for example, How does it come that this is a proof? For what is a proof, what is logical consequence, what contradiction, what truth, what falsehood? Therefore, the third division is necessary because of the second, and the second because of the first; while the most necessary of all, and the one in which we ought to rest, is the first. But we do the opposite; for we spend our time in the third division, and all our zeal is devoted to it, while we utterly neglect the first. Wherefore, we lie, indeed, but are ready with the arguments which prove that one ought not to lie.

53. Upon every occasion we ought to have the following thoughts at our command:

> Lead thou me on, O Zeus, and Destiny,
> To that goal long ago to me assigned.
> I'll follow and not falter; if my will
> Prove weak and craven, still I'll follow on.[16]

"Whoso has rightly with necessity complied,
We count him wise, and skilled in things divine." [17]

"Well, O Crito, if so it is pleasing to the gods, so let it be." [18]
"Anytus and Meletus can kill me, but they cannot hurt me." [19]

---

[16] From Cleanthes. Seneca, who translated these lines into Latin (*Epist.* 107. 11), has a fifth line: *Ducunt volentem fata, nolentem trahunt.* (The fates lead the willing and drag the unwilling.)

[17] Euripides, frag. 965 Nauck.

[18] Plato, *Crito,* 43 D (slightly modified).

[19] Plato, *Apology,* 30 C-4 (somewhat modified).

SEXTUS EMPIRICUS' *OUTLINES OF PYRRHONISM*

Book I

CHAPTER I—OF THE MAIN DIFFERENCE BETWEEN PHILOSOPHIC SYSTEMS

The natural result of any investigation is that the investigators either discover the object of search or deny that it is discoverable and confess it to be inapprehensible or persist in their search. So, too, with regard to the objects investigated by philosophy, this is probably why some have claimed to have discovered the truth, others have asserted that it cannot be apprehended, while others again go on inquiring. Those who believe they have discovered it are the "Dogmatists," specially so called —Aristotle, for example, and Epicurus and the Stoics and certain others; Cleitomachus and Carneades and other Academics treat it as inapprehensible: the Sceptics keep on searching. Hence it seems reasonable to hold that the main types of philosophy are three—the Dogmatic, the Academic, and the Sceptic. Of the other systems it will best become others to speak: our task at present is to describe in outline the Sceptic doctrine, first premising that of none of our future statements do we positively affirm that the fact is exactly as we state it, but we simply record each fact, like a chronicler, as it appears to us at the moment.

.   .   .

CHAPTER IV—WHAT SCEPTICISM IS

Scepticism is an ability, or mental attitude, which opposes appearances to judgements in any way whatsoever, with the result that, owing to the equipollence of the objects and reasons thus opposed, we are brought firstly to a state of mental suspense and next to a state of "unperturbedness" or quietude. Now we call it an "ability" not in any subtle sense, but simply in respect of its "being able." By "appearances" we now mean the objects of sense-perception, whence we contrast them with the objects of thought or "judgements." The phrase "in any way whatsoever" can be connected either with the word "ability," to make us take the word "ability," as we said, in its simple sense, or with the phrase "opposing appearances to judgements"; for inasmuch as we oppose these in a variety of ways—appearances to appearances, or judgements to judgements, or *alternando* appearances to judgements,—in order to ensure the inclusion of all these antitheses we employ the phrase "in any way whatsoever." Or, again, we join "in any way whatsoever" to "appearances and judgements" in order that we may not have to inquire how the appearances appear or how the thought-objects are judged, but may take these terms in the simple sense. The phrase "opposed judgements" we do not employ in the sense of negations and affirmations only but simply as equivalent to "conflicting judgements." "Equipollence" we use of equality in respect of probability and improbability, to indicate that no one of the conflicting judgements takes precedence of any other as being more probable. "Suspense" is a state of mental rest owing to which we neither deny nor affirm anything. "Quietude" is an untroubled and tranquil condition of soul. And how quietude enters the soul along with suspension of judgement we shall explain in our chapter (XII.) "Concerning the End."

. . .

CHAPTER VI—OF THE PRINCIPLES OF SCEPTICISM

The originating cause of Scepticism is, we say, the hope of attaining quietude. Men of talent, who were perturbed by the contradictions in things and in doubt as to which of the alternatives they ought to accept, were led on to inquire what is true in things and what false, hoping by the settlement of this question to attain quietude. The main basic principle of the Sceptic system is that of opposing to every proposition an equal proposition; for we believe that as a consequence of this we end by ceasing to dogmatize.

CHAPTER VII—DOES THE SCEPTIC DOGMATIZE?

When we say that the Sceptic refrains from dogmatizing we do not use the term "dogma," as some do, in the broader sense of "approval of a thing" (for the Sceptic gives assent to the feelings which are the necessary results of sense-impressions, and he would not, for example, say when feeling hot or cold "I believe that I am not hot or cold"); but we say that "he does not dogmatize" using "dogma" in the sense, which some give it, of "assent to one of the non-evident objects of scientific inquiry"; for the Pyrrhonean philosopher assents to nothing that is non-evident. Moreover, even in the act of enunciating the Sceptic formulae concerning things non-evident—such as the formula "No more (one thing than another)," or the formula "I determine nothing," or any of the others which we shall presently mention,—he does not dogmatize. For whereas the dogmatizer posits the things about which he is said to be dogmatizing as really existent, the Sceptic does not posit these formulae in any absolute sense; for he conceives that, just as the formula "All things are false" asserts the falsity of itself as well as of everything else, as does the formula "Nothing is true," so also the formula "No more" asserts that itself, like all the rest, is "No more (this than that," and thus cancels itself along with the rest. And of the other formulae we say the same. If then, while the dogmatizer posits the matter of his dogma as substantial truth, the Sceptic enunciates his formulae so that they are virtually cancelled by themselves, he should not be said to dogmatize in his enunciation of them. And, most important of all, in his enunciaton of these formulae he states what appears to himself and announces his own impression in an undogmatic way, without making any positive assertion regarding the external realities.

. . .

CHAPTER XII—WHAT IS THE END OF SCEPTICISM?

Our next subject will be the End of the Sceptic system. Now an "End" is "that for which all actions or reasonings are undertaken, while it exists for the sake of none"; or, otherwise, "the ultimate object of appetency." We assert still that the Sceptic's End is quietude in respect of matters of opinion and moderate feeling in respect of things unavoidable. For the Sceptic, having set out to philosophize with the object of passing judgement on the sense-impressions and ascertaining which of them are true and which false, so as to attain quietude thereby, found himself involved in contradictions of equal weight, and being unable to decide between them suspended judgement; and as he was thus in suspense there followed, as it happened, the state of quietude in respect of matters of opinion. For the man who opines that anything is by nature good or bad is for ever being disquieted: when he is without the things which he deems good he believes himself to be tormented by things naturally bad and he pursues after the things which are, as he thinks, good; which when he has obtained he keeps falling into still more perturbations because of his irrational and immoderate elation, and in his dread of a change of fortune he uses every endeavour to avoid losing the things which he deems good. On the other hand, the man who determines nothing as to what is naturally good or bad neither shuns nor pursues anything eagerly; and, in consequence, he is unperturbed.

The Sceptic, in fact, had the same experience which is said to have befallen the painter Apelles. Once, they say, when he was painting a horse and wished to represent in the painting the horse's foam, he was so unsuccessful that he gave up the attempt and flung at the picture the sponge on which he used to wipe the paints off his brush, and the mark of the sponge produced the effect of a horse's foam. So, too, the Sceptics were in hopes of gaining quietude by means of a decision regarding the disparity of the objects of sense and of thought, and being unable to effect this they suspended judgement; and they found that quietude, as if by chance, followed upon their suspense, even as a shadow follows its substance. We do not, however, suppose that the Sceptic is wholly untroubled; but we say that he is troubled by things unavoidable; for we grant that he is old at times and thirsty, and suffers various affections of that kind. But even in these cases, whereas ordinary people are afflicted by two circumstances,—namely, by the affections themselves and in no less a degree, by the belief that these conditions are evil by nature,—the Sceptic, by his rejection of the added belief in the natural badness of all these conditions, escapes here too with less discomfort. Hence we say that, while in regard to matters of opinion the Sceptic's End is quietude, in regard to things unavoidable it is "moderate affection." But some notable Sceptics have added the further definition "suspension of judgement in investigations."

CHAPTER XIII—OF THE GENERAL MODES LEADING TO SUSPENSION OF JUDGMENT

Now that we have been saying that tranquillity follows on suspension of judgement, it will be our next task to explain how we arrive at this suspension. Speaking generally, one may say that it is the result of setting things in opposition. We oppose either appearances to appearances or objects of thought to objects of thought or *alternando*. For instance, we oppose appearances to appearances when we say "The same tower appears round from a distance, but square from close at hand"; and thoughts to thoughts, when in answer to him who argues the existence of Providence from the order of the heavenly bodies we oppose the fact that often the good fare ill and the bad fare well, and draw from this the inference that Providence does not exist. And thoughts we oppose to appearances, as when Anaxagoras countered the notion that snow is white with the argument, "Snow is frozen water, and water is black; therefore snow also is black." With a different idea we oppose things present sometimes to things present, as in the foregoing examples, and sometimes to things past or future, as, for instance, when someone propounds to us a theory which we are unable to refute, we say to him in reply, "Just as, before the birth of the founder of the School to which you belong, the theory it holds was not as yet apparent as a sound theory, although it was really in existence, so likewise it is possible that the opposite theory to that which you now propound is already really existent, though not yet apparent to us, so that we ought not as yet to yield assent to this theory which at the moment seems to be valid."

But in order that we may have a more exact understanding of these antitheses I will describe the Modes by which suspension of judgement is brought about, but without making any positive assertion regarding either their number or their validity; for it is possible that they may be unsound or there may be more of them than I shall enumerate.

CHAPTER XIV—CONCERNING THE TEN MODES

The usual tradition amongst the older Sceptics is that the "modes" by which "suspension" is supposed to be brought about are ten in number; and they also give them the synonymous names of "arguments" and "positions." They are these: the first, based on the variety in animals; the second, on the differences in human beings; the third, on the different structures of the organs of sense; the fourth, on the circumstantial conditions; the fifth, on positions and intervals and locations; the sixth, on intermixtures; the seventh, on the quantities and formations of the underlying objects; the eighth, on the fact of relativity; the ninth, on the frequency or rarity of occurrence; the tenth, on the disciplines and customs and laws, the legendary beliefs and the dogmatic convictions. This order, however, we adopt without prejudice.

. . .

CHAPTER XV—OF THE FIVE MODES

The later Sceptics hand down Five Modes leading to suspension, namely these: the first based on discrepancy, the second on regress *ad infinitum*, the third on relativity, the fourth on hypothesis, the fifth on circular reasoning. That based on discrepancy leads us to find that with regard to the object presented there has arisen both amongst ordinary people and amongst the philosophers an interminable conflict because of which we are unable either to choose a thing or reject it, and so fall back on suspension. The Mode based upon regress *ad infinitum* is that whereby we assert that the thing adduced as a proof of the matter proposed needs a further proof, and this again another, and so on *ad infinitum*, so that the consequence is suspension, as we possess no starting-point for our argument. The Mode based upon relativity, as we have already said, is that whereby the object has such or such an appearance in relation to the subject judging and to the concomitant percepts, but as to its real nature we suspend judgement. We have the Mode based on hypothesis when the Dogmatists, being forced to recede *ad infinitum*, take as their starting-point something which they do not establish by argument but claim to assume as granted simply and without demonstration. The Mode of circular reasoning is the form used when the proof itself which ought to establish the matter of inquiry requires confirmation derived from that matter; in this case, being unable to assume either in order to establish the other, we suspend judgement about both.

That every matter of inquiry admits of being brought under these Modes we shall show briefly in this way. The matter proposed is either a sense-object or a thought-object, but whichever it is, it is an object of controversy; for some say that only sensibles are true, others only intelligibles, others that some sensible and some intelligible objects are true. Will they then assert that the controversy can or cannot be decided? If they say it cannot, we have it granted that we must suspend judgement; for concerning matters of dispute which admit of no decision it is impossible to make an assertion. But if they say that it can be decided, we ask by what is it to be decided. For example, in the case of the sense-object (for we shall base our argument on it first), is it to be decided by a sense-object or a thought-object? For if they say by a sense-object, since we are inquiring about sensibles that object itself also will require another to confirm it; and if that too is to be a sense-object, it likewise will require another for its confirmation, and so on *ad infinitum.* And if the sense-object shall have to be decided by a thought-object, then, since thought-objects also are controverted, this being an object of thought will need examination and confirmation. Whence then will it gain confirmation? If from an intelligible object, it will suffer a similar regress *ad infinitum;* and if from a sensible object, since an intelligible was adduced to establish the sensible and a sensible to establish the intelligible, the Mode of circular reasoning is brought in.

If, however, our disputant, by way of escape from this conclusion, should claim to assume as granted and without demonstration some postulate for the demonstration of the next steps of his argument, then the Mode of hypothesis will be brought in, which allows no escape. For if the author of the hypothesis is worthy of credence, we shall be no less worthy of credence every time that we make the opposite hypothesis. Moreover, if the author of the hypothesis assumes what is true he causes it to be suspected by assuming it by hypothesis rather than after proof; while if it is false, the foundation of his argument will be rotten. Further, if hypothesis conduces at all to proof, let the subject of inquiry itself be assumed and not some other thing which is merely a means to establish the actual subject of the argument; but if it is absurd to assume the subject of inquiry, it will also be absurd to assume that upon which it depends.

It is also plain that all sensibles are relative; for they are relative to those who have the sensations. Therefore it is apparent that whatever sensible object is presented can easily be referred to one of the Five Modes. And concerning the intelligible object we argue similarly. For if it should be said that it is a matter of unsettled controversy, the necessity of our suspending judgement will be granted. And if, on the other hand, the controversy admits of decision, then if the decision rests on an intelligible object we shall be driven to the regress *ad infinitum,* and to circular reasoning if it rests on a sensible; for since the sensible again is controverted and cannot be decided by means of itself because of the regress *ad infinitum,* it will require the intelligible object, just as also the intelligible will require the sensible. For these reasons, again, he who assumes anything by hypothesis will be acting illogically. Moreover, objects of thought, or intelligibles, are relative; for they are so named on account of their relation to the person thinking, and if they had really possessed the nature they are said to possess, there would have been no controversy about them. Thus the intelligible also is referred to the Five Modes, so that in all cases we are compelled to suspend judgement concerning the object presented.

Such then are the Five Modes handed down amongst the later
Sceptics; but they propound these not by way of superseding the Ten
Modes, but in order to expose the rashness of the Dogmatists with more
variety and completeness by means of the Five in conjunction with the
Ten.

. . .

PLOTINUS' *ENNEADS*

V. ii.

I. The one is all things, and yet no one of all. For the principle of
all is not all things; but *the one* is all, because all things run as it were
into it, or rather do not as yet exist, but will be. How, therefore, [does
multitude proceed] from *the one* which is simple, and in which no
variety, nor any duplicity present themselves to the view? Is it because
there was nothing in it, on this account all things are from it? Hence,
in order that being might exist, *the one* is not being, but being is the
progeny of it, and as it were its first-born. For *the one* being perfect, in
consequence of not seeking after, or possessing, or being in want of any
thing, it becomes as it were overflowing, and the superplenitude of it
produces something else. That, however, which is generated from it is
converted to it, and is filled, and was generated looking to it. But this
is intellect. And the permanency indeed of it about *the one*, produced
being; but its vision of *the one*, intellect. When, therefore, it is established
about *the one*, in order that it may see it, then it becomes at once intellect
and being. Hence, being in the same manner as *the one* produces things
similar to itself, through an effusion of abundant power. Its offspring also
has the form of it, in the same manner as prior to this it likewise flowed
forth from *the one*. And this energy from essence is soul, which was
generated from intellect permanently abiding. For intellect also was
generated, that which is prior to it abiding. Soul, however, does not
produce abiding, but being moved generates an image of itself. Soul,
therefore, looking thither whence it was generated, is filled. But proceeding into another and contrary motion, it generates an image of itself,
viz., sense, and the nature which is in plants. Nothing, however, is
separated or cut off from that which is prior to itself. Hence, also, the
soul of man is seen to proceed as far as to plants. For after *a certain*
manner it proceeds into them, because that which is in plants is derived
from it. Nevertheless, the whole of the human soul is not in plants, but
it is thus ingenerated in plants, because it so far proceeds into an inferior
nature, having made another hypostasis by its progression into and
propensity to that which is subordinate; since the soul which is prior
to this, being suspended from intellect, permits intellect to abide in itself.

VI. ix.

VI. How, therefore, can we speak of *the one*, and how can we adapt it to intellectual conception? Shall we say that this may be accomplished, by admitting that it is more transcendently one than the monad and a point? For in these, indeed, the soul taking away magnitude and the multitude of number, ends in that which is smallest, and fixes itself in a certain thing which is indeed impartible, but which was in a partible nature, and is in something different from itself. But *the one* is neither in another thing, nor in that which is partible. Nor is it impartible in the same way as that which is smallest. For it is the greatest of all things, not in magnitude, but in power. So that it is without magnitude in power. For the natures also which are [immediately] posterior to it, are impartible in powers, and not in bulk. The principle of all things likewise must be admitted to be infinite, not because he is magnitude or number which cannot be passed over, but because the power of him is incomprehensible. For when you conceive him to be intellect or God, he is more [excellent] than these. And again, when by the dianoetic power you equalize him with *the one*, or conceive him to be God, by recurring to that which is most united in your intellectual perception, he even transcends these appellations. For he is in himself, nor is any thing accidental to him. By that which is sufficient to itself also the unity of his nature may be demonstrated. For it is necessary that the principle of all things should be most sufficient both to other things, and to itself, and that it should also be most un-indigent. But every thing which is multitudinous and not one, is indigent; since consisting of many things it is not one. Hence the essence of it requires to be one. But *the one* is not in want of itself. For it is *the one*. Moreover, that which is many, is in want of as many things as it is. And each of the things that are in it, as it subsists in conjunction with others, and is not in itself, is indigent of other things; and thus a thing of this kind exhibits indigence, both according to parts and according to the whole. If, therefore, it is necessary there should be something which is most sufficient to itself, it is necessary there should be *the one*, which alone is a thing of such a kind, as neither to be indigent with reference to itself, nor with reference to another thing. For it does not seek after any thing in order that it may be, nor in order that it may be in an excellent condition, nor that it may be there established. For being the cause of existence to other things, and not deriving that which it is from others, nor its happiness, what addition can be made to it external to itself? Hence its happiness, or the excellency of its condition, is not accidental to it. For it is itself [all that is sufficient to itself]. There is not likewise any place for it. For it is not in want of a foundation, as if it were not able to sustain itself. For that which is established in another thing is inanimate, and a falling mass, if it is without a foundation. But other things are established on account of *the one*, through which also they at the same time subsist, and have the place in which they are arranged. That, however, which seeks after place is indigent. But the principle is not indigent of things posterior to itself. The principle, therefore, of all things is unindigent of all things. For that which is indigent, is indigent in consequence of aspiring after its principle. But if *the one* was indigent of any thing it would certainly seek not to be *the one;* so that it would be indigent of its destroyer. Every thing, however, which is said to be indigent, is indigent of a good condition, and of that which preserves it. Hence to *the one* nothing is good, and, therefore, neither is the wish for any thing good to it. But it is *super-good.* And it is not good to itself, but to other things, which are able to participate of it. Nor does *the one* possess intelligence, lest it should also possess difference; nor motion. For it is prior to motion, and prior to intelligence. For what is there which it will intellectually perceive? Shall we say itself? Prior to intellection, therefore, it will be ignorant, and will be in want of intelligence in order that it may know itself, though it is sufficient to itself. It does not follow, however, that because *the one* does not know itself, and does not intellectually perceive itself, there will be ignorance in it. For ignorance takes place where there is diversity, and when one thing is ignorant of another. That, however, which is *alone* neither knows any thing, nor has any thing of which it is ignorant. But being one, and associating with itself, it does not require the intellectual perception of itself; since neither is it necessary, in order that you may preserve *the one,* to adapt to it an association with itself. But it is requisite to take away intellectual perception, an association with itself, and the knowledge of itself, and of other things. For it is not proper to arrange it according to the act of perceiving intellectually, but rather according to intelligence. For intelligence does not perceive intellectually, but is the cause of intellectual perception to another thing. Cause, however, is not the same with the thing caused. But the cause of all things is not any one of them. Hence neither must it be denominated that good which it imparts to others; but it is after another manner *the good,* in a way transcending other goods.

· · ·

XI. This, therefore, is manifested by the mandate of the mysteries, which orders that they shall not be divulged to those who are uninitiated. For as that which is divine cannot be unfolded to the multitude, this mandate forbids the attempt to elucidate it to any one but him who is fortunately able to perceive it. Since, therefore, [in this conjunction with deity] there were not two things, but the perceiver was one with the thing perceived, as not being [properly speaking] vision but union; whoever becomes one by mingling with deity, and afterwards recollects this union, will have with himself an image of it. But he was also himself one, having with respect to himself no difference, nor with respect to other things. For then there was not any thing excited with him who had ascended thither; neither anger, nor the desire of any thing else nor reason, nor a certain intellectual perception, nor, in short, was even he himself moved, if it be requisite also to assert this; but being as it were in an ecstasy, or energizing enthusiastically, he became established in quiet and solitary union, not at all deviating from his own essence, nor revolving about himself, but being entirely stable, and becoming as it were stability itself. Neither was he then excited by any thing beautiful; but running above the beautiful, he passed beyond even the choir of the virtues. Just as if some one having entered into the interior of the adytum should leave behind all the statues in the temple which on his departure from the adytum will first present themselves to his view, after the inward spectacle, and the association that was there, which was not with a statue or an image, but with the thing itself [which the images represent], and which necessarily become the second objects of his perception. Perhaps, however, this was not a spectacle, but there was another mode of vision, viz. ecstasy, and an expansion and accession of himself, a desire of contact, rest, and a striving after conjunction, in order to behold what the adytum contains. But nothing will be present with him who beholds in any other way. The wise prophets, therefore, obscurely signified by these imitations how this [highest] God is seen. But the wise priest understanding the enigma, and having entered into the adytum, obtains a true vision of what is there. If, however, he has not entered, he will conceive this adytum to be a certain invisible thing, and will have a *knowledge* of the fountain and principle, as the principle of things. But when situated there, he will *see* the principle, and will be conjoined with it, by a union of like with like, neglecting nothing divine which the soul is able to possess. Prior to the vision also it requires that which remains from the vision. But that which remains to him who passes beyond all things, is that which is prior to all things. For the nature of the soul will never accede to that which is entirely non-being. But proceeding indeed downwards it will fall into evil; and thus into non-being, yet not into that which is perfect nonentity. Running, however, in a contrary direction, it will arrive not at another thing, but at itself. And thus not being in another thing, it is not on that account in nothing, but is in itself. *To be in itself alone, however, and not in being, is to be in God.* For God also is something which is not essence, but beyond essence. Hence the soul when in this condition, associates with him. He, therefore, who perceives himself to associate with God, will have himself the similitude of him. And if he passes from himself as an image to the archetype, he will then have the end of his progression. But when he falls from the vision of God, if he again excites the virtue which is in himself, and perceives himself to be perfectly adorned; he will again be elevated through virtue, proceeding to intellect and wisdom, and afterwards to the principle of all things. *This, therefore, is the life of the Gods, and of divine and happy men, a liberation from all terrene concerns, a life unaccompanied with human pleasures, and a flight of the alone to the alone.*

PART FIVE

THREE
CHRISTIAN
SAINTS

I

In their evaluations of medieval philosophy, interpreters are far apart, and religious attitudes become relevant. Many Catholic scholars and a minority of non-Catholics consider scholastic philosophy, and especially the system of Saint Thomas Aquinas, the culmination and fulfilment of Greek philosophy, while the great majority of non-Catholic philosophers take very little interest in medieval philosophy.

One striking discontinuity between ancient and medieval philosophy meets the eye: ancient philosophy was pagan, while the philosophies of Saint Augustine, Saint Anselm, and Saint Thomas Aquinas are Christian. To be sure, not all medieval philosophers were Christians: Moses Maimonides, for example, was a Jew. But he, too, like the Christians, appealed to God's revelation in Scripture.

References to God are encountered in Greek philosophy, too, though much more rarely than in medieval philosophy. But when Heraclitus, Plato, and Aristotle speak of God, they are not appealing to any Scripture, to any traditional revelation, or to any acknowledged authorities. They are not quoting earlier writers to establish

581

doctrines: on the contrary, when they refer to earlier thinkers, it is almost always to find fault.

The pre-Socratics broke with the exegetic mode of thought. Some openly derided Homer and the widely revered poems of the past, while others simply ignored previous writers. Each of these early Greek philosophers confronts us as a human being who insists on thinking for himself and who invites us to do likewise.

In the Middle Ages this is changed. The great Christian scholastics may be compared to the rabbis of the Talmud, as well as to Plato and Aristotle; unlike the Greeks, they are in the possession of sacred Scriptures and a great tradition which they accept with humility and pride. A large part of their elected task is to interpret this great heritage; but there is still ample room for acumen, originality, and ingenuity. After all, on the face of it, Scripture does not take up every problem; it treats many questions more than once, and it even seems to contain contradictions. Passages that to the lay mind are quite void of philosophical significance and possibly seem of no particular importance whatsoever are seen in a different light by the devout, who are quite certain that God's word is richly significant at every point. While some of the problems that confronted the religious thinkers of the Middle Ages were quite unlike any of the questions treated by the Greek philosophers—some of the problems about Christ, the Trinity, and angels, for example—most of the topics of ancient philosophy had to be reconsidered, too, in the light of revelation.

II

Saint Augustine (354-430) is as highly esteemed by many Protestants as he is by most Catholics. The story of his life is fairly well known and easily accessible because he himself recorded it in his celebrated *Confessions*. Originally written in Latin, like his many other works, the *Confessions* have been translated into all the major tongues. The book is of great interest for at least three reasons.

First, it may be considered the first great autobiography of world literature. The historical perspective of the Old Testament is here applied to an individual. The Jews, like the Greeks, had considered themselves different from all the other nations. But while the Greeks had believed that they were different by *nature* (according to Julius Jüthner's amply documented monograph on *Hellenen und Barbaren*, 1923, "the average Greek was convinced that he was even physically different form the barbarians," as different, in fact, as from the animals, and comparison of barbarians, i.e. non-Greeks, with animals was a "current commonplace"), the ancient Hebrews thought they were differentiated from other nations by their *history*. In large part, the Old Testament is the record of this history, but it also contains accounts of the growth of several individuals: Jacob and David are outstanding examples of this developmental approach to the human personality. Still lacking, however, was autobiography until Augustine, steeped in the Bible, founded this new genre.

Secondly, the *Confessions* is the autobiography of a particularly interesting person. His mother was a Christian, but he was brought up a pagan and relished a life that, as he grew older, seemed to him more and more a life of sin. Eventually, he became a Christian, after having first absorbed Manicheanism and Neoplatonism. The Manicheans were the heirs of Zoroaster's (or Zarathustra's) ancient Persian teaching that there are two great forces in the world, one good and one evil. (See the Preface to the selections from Heraclitus, above.)

Finally, there are some things of considerable philosophic interest in the *Confessions*, most notably the long discussion of time which is widely admired as the most striking sample of Augustine's philosophic acumen. This is reprinted here.

Of his many other works, *The City of God* is by far the most famous. During the 4th Century, Christianity had become the state religion of the Roman Empire; in 410 Rome fell to the Visigoths, and the eternal city was sacked for the first time. Naturally, there were many who considered the sack of Rome a punishment for the betrayal of the old Roman religion. Augustine wrote *The City of God* to answer this charge; but the book is no single-track tract. Rather, it is an encyclopedic work that purports to inform the reader not only about earthly matters but also about heaven and hell. One may thus compare it with Plato's *City* (known as *The Republic* in the English-speaking world). The two books differ, however, in that Plato's book is predominantly philosophical and contains only a little theology while Augustine's is for the most part theological and contains relatively little philosophy. In the following pages, only two short chapters from *The City of God* are offered: Book XI, Chapter 26, because it is one of several passages in Augustine's writings that more or less anticipate Descartes' celebrated *cogito ergo sum* (I think, therefore I am); and Book XXI, Chapter 12, which suggests at least a little of the over-all theological setting of Augustine's thought. While this final sample of Augustine's theology comes to little more than 1/30 of our total selections from his writings, it has probably been thirty times as influential as his philosophical reflections.

III

Saint Anselm of Canterbury (1033-1109) is chiefly remembered for an ingenious proof of God's existence that is usually called the ontological argument. Saint Thomas Aquinas did not accept this argument, but it was later taken up in various forms by Descartes, Spinoza, and Leibniz. Eventually, in 1781, Immanuel Kant tried to show in his *Critique of Pure Reason* that all arguments for God's existence are reducible to three, of which the ontological argument is one—and that the other two (to which he would reduce Saint Thomas' five) can be shown to fall back at a crucial point upon the ontological argument (which Thomas rejected). Kant's discussion is included in the companion volume, *Philosophic Classics: Bacon to Kant.*

In spite of Kant, a few later thinkers have returned to Anselm's argument. It has even been claimed that one's response to this proof shows whether one has any flair for metaphysics. Nor is appreciation of Anselm's argument confined to any one school. Philosophers of widely different outlooks have referred to it with great respect and have attempted to defend it.

IV

Saint Thomas Aquinas (1225-1274) has come to be generally considered the greatest of all the scholastics. An Italian, he studied with Albertus Magnus, an outstanding German theologian who outlived him. In those days, the philosophy of Aristotle had been newly rediscovered. For centuries, Aristotle had been known chiefly as a logician. Beginning a few years before Aquinas' birth, Aristotle's other works were translated into Latin, some from the original Greek, others from Arabic versions. There was an enormous excitement: a non-Christian world had come into view—an alternative to Christianity. Ten years before the saint's birth, Aristotle's works on metaphysics and on natural philosophy were banned at the University of Paris, where Thomas was to teach later. When Thomas was a little boy, in 1229, the faculty of the University of Toulouse announced lectures on Aristotle, hoping to attract students. In 1245, an attempt was made to extend the prohibition to Toulouse, but, as Father Frederick Copleston, S.J., puts it in his little book on *Aquinas,* "by that date it had become impossible to check the spread of Aristotelianism."

Thomas lived in an age of lively controversy, and though he enjoyed great prestige in his lifetime, he found, being a Dominican, that his arguments met with stubborn resistance among Franciscans, for example. And three years after his death, Robert Kilwardby, the archbishop of Canterbury, himself a Dominican, "followed the example of the bishop of Paris in censuring a number of propositions which included a few that had been held by Aquinas." In 1323, Aquinas was canonized, and then "the Parisian censures of 1277 were withdrawn, as far as they affected Aquinas" (Copleston).

In 1879, Pope Leo XII commended the study of Aquinas' philosophy in an encyclical, *Aeterni Patris*. This papal proclamation did not *launch* the revival of Thomism, as is often said, but it did lend an enormous impetus to the study of Thomas' writings. The encyclical praises the saint in the highest terms: "as far as man is concerned, reason can now hardly rise higher than she rose, borne up in the flight of Thomas; and Faith can hardly gain more helps from reason than those which Thomas gave her." Leo XIII also cited many previous popes who had spoken of Thomas in a similar vein. "Pius V acknowledges that heresies are confounded and exposed and scattered by his doctrine, and that by it the whole world is daily freed from pestilent errors. . . . The words of Blessed Urban V to the University of Toulouse seem to be most worthy of mention: 'It is our will, and by the authority of these letters we enjoin on you, that you follow the doctrine of Blessed Thomas as true and Catholic, and strive to unfold it with your whole strength.' This example of Urban was followed by Innocent XII . . . and by Benedict XIV . . ." Leo XIII cites, "as a crown, the testimony of Innocent VI: 'His doctrine above all other doctrine, with the one exception of the Holy Scriptures, has such a propriety of words, such a method of explanation, such a truth of opinions, that no one who holds it will ever be found to have strayed from the path of truth . . .' " Still, Leo XIII took care not to suggest that all of Thomas' teachings have to be accepted: "We, therefore, while We declare that everything wisely said should be received with willing and glad mind, . . . exhort all of you, Venerable Brothers, with the greatest earnestness to restore the golden wisdom of St. Thomas, and to spread it as far as you can . . . We say the wisdom of St. Thomas; for it is not by any means in our mind to set before this age, as a standard, those things which have been inquired into by Scholastic Doctors with too great subtlety; or anything taught by them with too little consideration, not agreeing with the investigations of a later age; or, lastly, anything that is not probable."

In much the same spirit, Etienne Gilson, as respected and renowned a Thomist as the 20th Century has produced, says in the Foreword to *The Christian Philosophy of St. Thomas Aquinas:* "Personally, I do not say of Thomas the he *was* right, but that he *is* right." Gilson does not mean that Thomas was right about every-thing. Although Thomas wrote detailed commentaries on the works of Aristotle, he read Aristotle in Latin translations, and Gilson ad-mits that, in his *Summa,* Thomas made "Aristotle say so many things he never said," and that he altogether metamorphosed Aristotle's doctrines by ascribing "a new meaning to Aristotle's principles." Gilson also concedes that Thomas used quotations from Augustine to buttress claims that are at variance with Augustine's real views. And it is a commonplace of modern scholarship that Dionysius, whom Aquinas very often cites to prove his point, was not a con-temporary of the Blessed Virgin and St. Paul, as Thomas thought, but a Neoplatonist of the 5th Century who wrote under the name of the first-Century Dionysius. In sum, even Aquinas' greatest devotees do not claim that he was infallible. And large numbers of Catholic philosophers, by no means all of them Franciscans, have no wish whatever to be identified as Thomists.

On the other hand, large numbers of non-Catholics would cheer-fully concede that Aquinas was one of the most remarkable thinkers of all time, and that he created a staggering synthesis of the Christian heritage he had received with the philosophy of Aristotle. Two more quotations from Gilson's great *History of Christian Philosophy in the Middle Ages* not only sum up the views of one outstanding historian, but may be safely accepted:

"The doctrine of Thomas Aquinas surprised his contemporaries. He was not a promoter of scientific learning like Albert the Great or Robert Grosseteste. To him the scientific knowledge of nature was in Aristotle, whose doctrine he had learned, commented upon and accepted, on the whole, in logic, physics, astronomy, biology, psy-chology, metaphysics and ethics" (p. 381). "Thomism was not the upshot of a better understanding of Aristotle. . . . Thomas uses the language of Aristotle everywhere to make the Philosopher say that there is only one God, the pure Act of Being, Creator of the World, infinite and omnipotent . . . Thomas changed the water of philosophy to the wine of theology. Thomas always considered himself a theo-logian. . . . In his own view, he was not only a theologian, but a monk who had no right to indulge in philosophical activities except in the spirit of his religious vocation" (p. 365).

His greatest work is, by common consent, the vast *Summa Theo-logica,* from which all of the following selections are taken. Among his many other writings, his *Summa Contra Gentiles* is probably best known. His complete works in Latin comprise 25 volumes; a superior edition, not completed yet, is expected to fill 34. Under these circum-stances it is difficult to give a clear idea of his thought in a few pages.

V

The *Summa Theologica* is divided into so-called Questions. Every question is broached in the same way: first it is posed; then an answer is offered which Thomas considers false; then this answer is buttressed with a few quotations that appear to support it; and next, we are confronted with a quotation that seems to contradict the stand defended so far. A dramatic tension is created, reminiscent of the disputatious climate of opinion in which Thomas wrote. It is resolved by the author's concise and straightforward *Respondeo,* or "I reply," which introduces his own view. He agrees with the immediately preceding quotation, gives his reasons, and then replies, one by one, to the objections raised before he stated his position. In this manner, every question is answered—no matter what its nature; for example, there are a vast number of questions about angels, including such fine points as whether an inferior angel can address a superior one, or, in the book on *Truth* which is generally regarded as exceptionally important, "Whether one angel can speak to another in such a way that others will not know what he is saying?" In the *Summa* itself, the proverbial question, how many angels can dance on the head of a needle, is asked in this form: "Whether several angels can be at the same time in the same place?" Other questions, treated in the same manner, may strike 20th Century readers as even stranger; for example, whether the semen in man is produced from surplus food?

Although it is well to keep in mind that comparable passages are found in Plato, there are also two differences. In Plato we find mostly philosophy, but also some material of this kind; in Thomas, the proportion is almost reversed, and one has to look for philosophic passages. Secondly, Plato generally offers matter of this sort in the form of frankly avowed myths, or says outright that the ideas presented are only probable; he neither cites nor claims authority, but offers, at most, his own view and often not even that. He writes dialogues, leaving the reader to decide what Plato's own conclusions might be. Plato is unsystematic and invites us to join a process of reflection and inquiry. In the *Summa* and the book on *Truth,* which is organized in the same way, the air is altogether different: the avowed purpose is to answer every question.

The following selections concentrate on matters of philosophic interest. From *Summa,* I, the second question, on "The Existence of God," is offered in its entirety. It contains the celebrated "five ways" of demonstrating God's existence. From Question 16, "On Truth," two Articles are offered. Concerning God and his relation to man, few questions are asked as frequently, and genuinely bother so many people as persistently, as the three from which selections are offered next: "Predestination," and quite especially "Whether God reprobates any man?" "The Power of God," and particularly "Whether God can do what he does not?" and "Whether God can do better than what he does?" "The Cause of Evil," and above all, "Whether the Supreme Good, God, is the cause of evil?"

From *Summa*, I-II, five Articles are offered from four Questions. The first concerns the old Socratic quandary "Whether ignorance causes involuntariness?" The second has a distinctly modern ring, as if it came from Oxford around the middle of the 20th Century: "Whether one can intend two things at the same time?" The third harks back to Aristotle and to Plato: "Whether there are four cardinal virtues?" And the last two deal with the natural law which is once again the focal point of much modern discussion.

Finally, from *Summa*, II-II, two articles from Question 11, "Of Heresy," are offered, which hark back to Plato's *Laws*. It may be fashionable to ignore this side of Thomas' thought, but that would be as misleading as to concentrate exclusively on the less pleasant aspects. These few pages, which contribute a great deal to our understanding of the climate of opinion in which Thomas thought, were easily as influential as his views on truth or virtue. A volume of selections should not suppress what the editor dislikes and offer a diffuse self-portrait. The present book includes the views of men tried for heresy, as well as the reasons men have given for condemning heretics to death. It is well to consider both.

AUGUSTINE

A. CONFESSIONS, *Book XI* (*The Discussion of Time*)

CHAPTER XII. WHAT GOD DID BEFORE THE CREATION OF THE WORLD

Behold, I answer to him who asks, "What was God doing before He made heaven and earth?" I answer not, as a certain person is reported to have done facetiously (avoiding the pressure of the question), "He was preparing hell," said he, "for those who pry into mysteries." It is one thing to perceive, another to laugh—these things I answer not. For more willingly would I have answered, "I know not what I know not," than that I should make him a laughing-stock who asks deep things, and gain praise as one who answers false things. But I say that Thou, our God, art the Creator of every creature; and if by the term "heaven and earth" every creature is understood. I boldly say that before God made heaven and earth, He made not anything. For if He did, what did He make unless the creature? And would that I knew whatever I desire to know to my advantage, as I know that no creature was made before any creature was made.

CHAPTER XIII. BEFORE THE TIMES CREATED BY GOD, TIMES WERE NOT

But if the roving thought of any one should wander through the images of bygone time, and wonder that Thou, the God Almighty, and All-creating, and All-sustaining, the Architect of heaven and earth, didst for innumerable ages refrain from so great a work before Thou wouldst make it, let him awake and consider that he wonders at false things. For whence could innumerable ages pass by which Thou didst not make, since Thou art the Author and Creator of all ages? Or what times should those be which were not made by Thee? Or how should they pass by if they had not been? Since, therefore, Thou art the Creator of all times, if any time was before Thou madest heaven and earth, why is it said Thou didst refrain from working? For that very time Thou madest, nor could times pass by before Thou madest times. But if before heaven and earth there was no time, why is it asked, What didst Thou then? For there was no "then" when time was not.

Nor dost Thou by time precede time; else wouldest not Thou precede all times. But in the excellency of an ever-present eternity, Thou precedest all times past, and survivest all future times, because they are future, and when they have come they will be past; but Thou art the same, and Thy years shall have no end. Thy years neither go nor come; but ours both go and come, that all may come. All Thy years stand at once since they do stand; nor were they when departing excluded by coming years, because they pass not away; but all these of ours shall be when all shall cease to be. Thy years are one day, and Thy day is not daily, but to-day; because Thy to-day yields not with to-morrow, for neither doth it follow yesterday. Thy to-day is eternity; therefore didst Thou beget the Co-eternal, to whom Thou saidst, "This day have I begotten Thee." Thou hast made all time; and before all times Thou art, nor in any time was there not time.

CHAPTER XIV. NEITHER TIME PAST NOR FUTURE, BUT THE PRESENT ONLY, REALLY IS

At no time, therefore, hadst Thou not made anything, because Thou hadst made time itself. And no times are co-eternal with Thee, because

Thou remainest for ever; but should these continue, they would not be times. For what is time? Who can easily and briefly explain it? Who even in thought can comprehend it, even to the pronouncing of a word concerning it? But what in speaking do we refer to more familiarly and knowingly than time? And certainly we understand when we speak of it; we understand also when we hear it spoken of by another. What, then, is time? If no one ask of me, I know; if I wish to explain to him who asks, I know not. Yet I say with confidence, that I know that if nothing passed away, there would not be past time; and if nothing were coming, there would not be future time; and if nothing were, there would not be present time. Those two times, therefore, past and future, how are they, when even the past now is not, and the future is not as yet? But should the present be always present, and should it not pass into time past, truly it could not be time, but eternity. If, then, time present—if it be time—only comes into existence because it passes into time past, how do we say that even this is, whose cause of being is that it shall not be—namely, so that we cannot truly say that time is, unless because it tends not to be?

CHAPTER XV. THERE IS ONLY A MOMENT OF PRESENT TIME

And yet we say that time is long and time is short; nor do we speak of this save of time past and future. A long time past, for example, we call a hundred years ago; in like manner a long time to come, a hundred years hence. But a short time past we call, say, ten days ago: and a short time to come, ten days hence. But in what sense is that long or short which is not? For the past is not now, and the future is not yet. Therefore let us not say, "It is long;" but let us say of the past, "It has been long," and of the future, "It will be long." O my Lord, my light, shall not even here Thy truth deride man? For that past time which was long, was it long when it was already past, or when it was as yet present? For then it might be long when there was that which could be long, but when past it no longer was; wherefore that could not be long which was not at all. Let us not, therefore, say, "Time past has been long;" for we shall not find what may have been long, seeing that since it was past it is not; but let us say that present time was long, because when it was present it was long. For it had not as yet passed away so as not to be, and therefore there was that which could be long. But after it passed, that ceased also to be long which ceased to be.

Let us therefore see, O human soul, whether present time can be long; for to thee is it given to perceive and to measure periods of time. What wilt thou reply to me? Is a hundred years when present a long time? See, first, whether a hundred years can be present. For if the first year of these is current, that is present, but the other ninety and nine are future, and therefore they are not as yet. But if the second year is current, one is already past, the other present, the rest future. And thus, if we fix on any middle year of this hundred as present, those before it are past, those after it are future; wherefore a hundred years cannot be present. See at least whether that year itself which is current can be present. For if its first month be current, the rest are future; if the second, the first has already passed, and the remainder are not yet. Therefore neither is the year which is current as a whole present; and if it is not present as a whole, then the year is not present. For twelve months make the year, of which each individual month which is current is itself present, but the rest are either past or future. Although neither is that month which is current present, but one day only: if the first, the rest being to come, if the last, the rest being past; if any of the middle, then between past and future.

Behold, the present time, which alone we found could be called long, is abridged to the space scarcely of one day. But let us discuss even that, for there is not one day present as a whole. For it is made up of four-and-twenty hours of night and day, of which the first has the rest future, the last has them past, but any one of the intervening has those before it past, those after it future. And that one hour passes away in fleeting particles. Whatever of it has flown away is past, whatever remains is future. If any portion of time be conceived which cannot now be divided into even the minutest particles of moments, this only is that which may be called present; which, however, flies so rapidly from future to past, that it cannot be extended by any delay. For if it be extended, it is divided into the past and future; but the present has no space. Where, therefore, is the time which we may call long? Is it future? Indeed we do not say, "It is long," because it is not yet, so as to be long; but we say, "It will be long." When, then, will it be? For if even then, since as yet it is future, it will not be long, because what may be long is not as yet; but it shall be long, when from the future, which as yet is not, it shall already have begun to be, and will have become present, so that there could be that which may be long; then does the present time cry out in the words above that it cannot be long.

CHAPTER XVI. TIME CAN ONLY BE PERCEIVED OR MEASURED WHILE IT IS PASSING

And yet, O Lord, we perceive intervals of times, and we compare them with themselves, and we say some are longer, others shorter. We even measure by how much shorter or longer this time may be than that; and we answer That this is double or treble, while that is but once, or only as much as that. But we measure times passing when we measure them by perceiving them; but past times, which now are not, or future times, which as yet are not, who can measure them? Unless, perchance, any one will dare to say, that that can be measured which is not. When, therefore, time is passing, it can be perceived and measured; but when it has passed, it cannot, since it is not.

CHAPTER XVII.   NEVERTHELESS THERE IS TIME PAST AND FUTURE

I ask, Father, I do not affirm. O my God, rule and guide me. Who is there who can say to me that there are not three times (as we learned when boys, and as we have taught boys), the past, present, and future, but only present, because these two are not? Or are they also; but when from future it becomes present, comes it forth from some secret place, and when from the present it becomes past, does it retire into anything secret? For where have they, who have foretold future things, seen these things, if as yet they are not? For that which is not cannot be seen. And they who relate things past could not relate them as true, did they not perceive them in their mind. Which things, if they were not, they could in no wise be discerned. There are therefore things both future and past.

CHAPTER XVIII.   PAST AND FUTURE TIMES CANNOT BE THOUGHT OF BUT AS PRESENT

Suffer me, O Lord, to seek further; O my Hope, let not my purpose be confounded. For if there are times past and future, I desire to know where they are. But if as yet I do not succeed, I still know, wherever they are, that they are not there as future or past, but as present. For if there also they be future, they are not as yet there; if even there they be past, they are no longer there. Wheresoever, therefore, they are, whatsoever they are, they are only so as present. Although past things are related as true, they are drawn out from the memory—not the things themselves, which have passed, but the words conceived from the images of the things which they have formed in the mind as footprints in their passage through the senses. My childhood, indeed, which no longer is, is in the time past, which now is not; but when I call to mind its image, and speak of it, I behold it in the present, because it is as yet in my memory. Whether there be a like cause of foretelling future things, that of things which as yet are not the images may be perceived as already existing, I confess, my God, I know not. This certainly I know, that we generally think before on our future actions, and that this premeditation is present; but that the action on which we premeditate is not yet, because it is future; which when we shall have entered upon, and have begun to do that which we were premeditating, then shall that action be, because then it is not future, but present.

In whatever manner, therefore, this secret preconception of future things may be, nothing can be seen, save what is. But what now is is not future, but present. When, therefore, they say that things future are seen, it is not themselves, which as yet are not (that is, which are future); but their causes or their signs perhaps are seen, which already are. Therefore, to those already beholding them, they are not future, but present, from which future things conceived in the mind are foretold. These conceptions again now are, and they who foretell those things behold these conceptions present before them. Let now so multitudinous a variety of things afford me some example. I behold daybreak; I foretell that the sun is about to rise. That which I behold is present; what I foretell is future—not that the sun is future, which already is; but his rising, which is not yet. Yet even its rising I could not predict unless I had an image of it in my mind, as now I have while I speak. But that dawn which I see in the sky is not the rising of the sun, although it may go before it, nor that imagination in my mind; which two are seen as present, that the other which is future may be foretold. Future things, therefore, are not as yet; and if they are not as yet, they are not. And if they are not, they cannot be seen at all; but they can be foretold from things present which now are, and are seen.

CHAPTER XIX. WE ARE IGNORANT IN WHAT MANNER GOD TEACHES FUTURE THINGS

Thou, therefore, Ruler of Thy creatures, what is the method by which Thou teachest souls those things which are future? For Thou hast taught Thy prophets. What is that way by which Thou, to whom nothing is future, dost teach future things; or rather of future things dost teach present? For what is not, of a certainty cannot be taught. Too far is this way from my view; it is too mighty for me, I cannot attain unto it; but by Thee I shall be enabled, when Thou shalt have granted it, sweet light of my hidden eyes.

CHAPTER XX. IN WHAT MANNER TIME MAY PROPERLY BE DESIGNATED

But what now is manifest and clear is, that neither are there future nor past things. Nor is it fitly said, "There are three times, past, present and future;" but perchance it might be fitly said, "There are three times; a present of things past, a present of things present, and a present of things future." For these three do somehow exist in the soul, and otherwise I see them not: present of things past, memory; present of things present, sight; present of things future, expectation. If of these things we are permitted to speak, I see three times, and I grant there are three. It may also be said, "There are three times, past, present and future," as usage falsely has it. See, I trouble not, nor gainsay, nor reprove; provided always that which is said may be understood, that neither the future, nor that which is past, now is. For there are but few things which we speak properly, many things improperly; but what we may wish to say is understood.

CHAPTER XXI.   HOW TIME MAY BE MEASURED

I have just now said, then, that we measure times as they pass, that we may be able to say that this time is twice as much as that one, or that this is only as much as that, and so of any other of the parts of time which we are able to tell by measuring. Wherefore, as I said, we measure times as they pass. And if any one should ask me, "Whence dost thou know?" I can answer, "I know, because we measure; nor can we measure things that are not; and things past and future are not." But how do we measure present time, since it has not space? It is measured while it passes; but when it shall have passed, it is not measured; for there will not be aught that can be measured. But whence, in what way, and whither does it pass while it is being measured? Whence, but from the future? Which way, save through the present? Whither, but into the past? From that, therefore, which as yet is not, though that which has no space, into that which now is not. But what do we measure, unless time in some space? For we say not single, and double, and triple, and equal, or in any other way in which we speak of time, unless with respect to the spaces of times. In what space, then, do we measure passing time? Is it in the future, whence it passes over? But what yet we measure not, is not. Or is it in the present, by which it passes? But no space we do not measure. Or in the past, whither it passes? But that which is not now, we measure not.

CHAPTER XXII.   HE PRAYS GOD THAT HE WOULD EXPLAIN THIS MOST ENTANGLED ENIGMA

My soul yearns to know this most entangled enigma. Forbear to shut up, O Lord my God, good Father—through Christ I beseech Thee—forbear to shut up these things, both usual and hidden, from my desire, that it may be hindered from penetrating them; but let them dawn through Thy enlightening mercy, O Lord. Of whom shall I inquire concerning these things? And to whom shall I with more advantage confess my ignorance than to Thee to whom these my studies, so vehemently kindled towards Thy Scriptures, are not troublesome? Give that which I love; for I do love, and this hast Thou given me. Give, Father, who truly knowest to give good gifts unto Thy children. Give, since I have undertaken to know, and trouble is before me until Thou dost open it. Through Christ, I beseech Thee, in His name, Holy of Holies, let no man interrupt me. For I believed, and therefore do I speak. This is my hope; for this do I live, that I may contemplate the delights of the Lord. Behold, Thou hast made my days old, and they pass away, and in what manner I know not. And we speak as to time and time, times and times—"How long is the time since he said this?" "How long the time since he did this?" and, "How long the time since I saw that?" and, "This syllable has double the time of that single short syllable." These words we speak, and these we hear; and we are understood, and we understand. They are most manifest and most usual, and the same things again lie hid too deeply, and the discovery of them is new.

CHAPTER XXIII. THAT TIME IS A CERTAIN EXTENSION

I have heard from a learned man that the motions of the sun, moon, and stars constituted time, and I assented not. For why should not rather the motions of all bodies be time? What if the lights of heaven should cease, and a potter's wheel run round, would there be no time by which we might measure those revolutions, and say either that it turned with equal pauses, or, if it were moved, at one time more slowly, at another more quickly, that some revolutions were longer, others less so? Or while we were saying this, should we not also be speaking in time? Or should there in our words be some syllables long, others short, but because those sounded in a longer time, these in a shorter? God grant to men to see in a small thing ideas common to things great and small. Both the stars and luminaries of heaven are for signs and for seasons, and for days and years. No doubt they are; but neither should I say that the circuit of that wooden wheel was a day, nor yet should he say that therefore there was no time.

I desire to know the power and nature of time, by which we measure the motions of bodies, and say (for example) that this motion is twice as long as that. For, I ask, since "day" declares not the stay only of the sun upon the earth, according to which day is one thing, night another, but also its entire circuit from east even to east—according to which we say, "So many days have passed" (the nights being included when we say "so many days," and their spaces not counted apart)—since, then, the day is finished by the motion of the sun, and by his circuit from east to east, I ask, whether the motion itself is the day, or the period in which that motion is completed, or both? For if the first be the day, then would there be a day although the sun should finish that course in so small a space of time as an hour. If the second, then that would not be a day if from one sunrise to another there were but so short a period as an hour, but the sun must go round four-and-twenty times to complete a day. If both, neither could that be called a day if the sun should run his entire round in the space of an hour; nor that, if, while the sun stood still, so much time should pass as the sun is accustomed to accomplish his whole course in from morning to morning. I shall not therefore now ask, what that is which is called day, but what time is, by which we, measuring the circuit of the sun, should say that it was accomplished in half the space of time it was wont, if it had been completed in so small a space as twelve hours; and comparing both times, we should call that single, this double time, although the sun should run his course from east to east sometimes in that single, sometimes in that double time. Let no man then tell me that the motions of the heavenly bodies are times, because, when at the prayer of one the sun stood still in order that he might achieve his victorious battle, the sun stood still, but time went on. For in such space of time as was sufficient was that battle fought and ended. I see that time, then, is a certain extension. But I do see it, or do I seem to see it? Thou, O Light and Truth, wilt show me.

CHAPTER XXIV. THAT TIME IS NOT A MOTION OF A BODY WHICH WE MEASURE BY TIME

Dost Thou command that I should assent, if any one should say that time is the motion of a body? Thou dost not command me. For I hear that no body is moved but in time. This Thou sayest; but that the very motion of a body is time, I hear not; Thou sayest it not. For when a body is moved, I by time measure how long it may be moving from the time in which it began to be moved till it left off. And if I saw not whence it began, and it continued to be moved, so that I see not when it leaves off, I cannot measure unless, perchance, from the time I began until I cease to see. But if I look long enough, I only proclaim that the time is long, but not how long it may be; because when we say, "How long," we speak by comparison, as, "This is as long as that," or, "This is double as long as that," or any other thing of the kind. But if we were able to note down the distances of places whence and whither comes the body which is moved, or its parts, if it moved as in a wheel, we can say in how much time the motion of the body or its part, from this place to that, was performed. Since, then, the motion of a body is one thing, that by which we measure how long it is another, who cannot see which of these is rather to be called time? For, although a body be sometimes moved, sometimes stand still, we measure not its motion only, but also its standing still, by time; and we say, "It stool still as much as it moved;" or, "It stood still twice or thrice as long as it moved;" and if any other space which our measuring has either determined or imagined, more or less, as we are accustomed to say. Time, therefore, is not the motion of a body.

CHAPTER XXV. HE CALLS ON GOD TO ENLIGHTEN HIS MIND

And I confess unto Thee, O Lord, that I am as yet ignorant as to what time is, and again I confess unto Thee, O Lord, that I know that I speak these things in time, and that I have already long spoken of time, and that very "long" is not long save by the stay of time. How, then, know I this, when I know not what time is? Or is it, perchance, that I know not in what wise I may express what I know? Alas for me, that I do not at least know the extent of my own ignorance! Behold, O my God, before Thee I lie not. As I speak, so is my heart. Thou shalt light my candle; Thou, O Lord my God, wilt enlighten my darkness.

CHAPTER XXVI. WE MEASURE LONGER EVENTS BY SHORTER IN TIME

Doth not my soul pour out unto Thee truly in confession that I do measure times? But do I thus measure, O my God, and know not what I measure? I measure the motion of a body by time; and the time itself do I not measure? But, in truth, could I measure the motion of a body, how long it is, and how long it is in coming from this place to that, unless I should measure the time in which it is moved? How, therefore, do I measure this very time itself? Or do we by a shorter time measure a longer, as by the space of a cubit the space of a crossbeam? For thus, indeed, we seem by the space of a short syllable to measure the space of a long syllable, and to say that this is double. Thus we measure the space of stanzas by the spaces of the verse, and the spaces of the verses by the spaces of the feet, and the spaces of the feet by the spaces of the syllables, and the spaces of long by the spaces of short syllables; not measuring by pages (for in that manner we measure spaces, not times), but when in uttering the words they pass by, and we say, "It is a long stanza because it is made up of so many verses; long verses, because they consist of so many feet; long feet, because they are prolonged by so many syllables; a long syllable, because double a short one." But neither thus is any certain measure of time obtained; since it is possible that a shorter verse, if it be pronounced more fully, may take up more time than a longer one, if pronounced more hurriedly. Thus for a stanza, thus for a foot, thus for a syllable. Whence it appeared to me that time is nothing else than extension; but of what I know not. It is wonderful to me, if it be not of the mind itself. For what do I measure, I beseech Thee, O my God, even when I say either indefinitely, "This time is longer than that;" or even definitely, "This is double that?" That I measure time, I know. But I measure not the future, for it is not yet; nor do I measure the present, because it is extended by no space; nor do I measure the past, because it no longer is. What, therefore, do I measure? Is it times passing, not past? For thus had I said.

CHAPTER XXVII. TIMES ARE MEASURED IN PROPORTION AS THEY PASS BY

Persevere, O my mind, and give earnest heed. God is our helper; He made us, and not we ourselves. Give heed, where truth dawns. Lo, suppose the voice of a body begins to sound, and does sound, and sounds on, and lo! it ceases—it is now silence, and that voice is past and is no longer a voice. It was future before it sounded, and could not be measured, because as yet it was not; and now it cannot, because it no longer is. Then, therefore, while it was sounding, it might, because there was then that which might be measured. But even then it did not stand still, for it was going and passing away. Could it, then, on that account be measured the more? For, while passing, it was being extended into some space of time, in which it might be measured, since the present has no space. If, therefore, then it might be measured, lo! suppose another voice has begun to sound, and still sounds, in a continued tenor without any interruption, we can measure it while it is sounding; for when it shall have ceased to sound, it will be already past, and there will not be that which can be measured. Let us measure it truly, and let us say how much it is. But as yet it sounds, nor can it be measured, save from that instant in which it began to sound, even to the end in which it left off. For the interval itself we measure from some beginning to some end. On which account, a voice which is not yet ended cannot be measured, so that it may be said how long or how short it may be; nor can it be said to be equal to another, or single or double in respect of it, or the like. But when it is ended, it no longer is. In what manner, therefore, may it be measured? And yet we measure times; still not those which as yet are not, nor those which no longer are, nor those which are protracted by some delay, nor those which have no limits. We, therefore, measure neither future times, nor past, nor present, nor those passing by; and yet we do measure times.

Deus Creator omnium; this verse of eight syllables alternates between short and long syllables. The four short, then, the first, third, fifth and seventh, are single in respect of the four long, the second, fourth, sixth, and eighth. Each of these has a double time to every one of those. I pronounce them, report on them, and thus it is, as is perceived by common sense. By common sense, then, I measure a long by a short syllable, and I find that it has twice as much. But when one sounds after another, if the former be short the latter long, how shall I hold the short one, and how measuring shall I apply it to the long, so that I may find out that this has twice as much, when indeed the long does not begin to sound unless the short leaves off sounding? That very long one I measure not as present, since I measure it not save when ended. But its ending is its passing away. What, then, is it that I can measure? Where is the short syllable by which I measure? Where is the long one which I measure? Both have sounded, have flown, have passed away, and are no longer; and still I measure, and I confidently answer (so far as is trusted to a practised sense), that as to space of time this syllable is single, that double. Nor could I do this, unless because they have past, and are ended. Therefore do I not measure themselves, which now are not, but something in my memory, which remains fixed.

In Thee, O my mind, I measure times. Do not overwhelm me with thy clamor. That is, do not overwhelm thyself with the multitude of thy impressions. In thee, I say, I measure times; the impression which things as they pass by make on Thee, and which, when they have passed by, remains, that I measure as time present, not those things which have passed by, that the impression should be made. This I measure when I measure times. Either, then, these are times, or I do not measure times. What when we measure silence, and say that this silence has lasted as long as that voice lasts? Do we not extend our thought to the measure of a voice, as if it sounded, so that we may be able to declare something concerning the intervals of silence in a given space of time? For when both the voice and tongue are still, we go over in thought poems and verses, and any discourse, or dimensions of motions; and declare concerning the spaces of times, how much this may be in respect of that, not otherwise than if uttering them we should pronounce them. Should any one wish to utter a lengthened sound, and had with forethought determined how long it should be, that man has in silence surely gone through a space of time, and, committing it to memory, he begins to utter that speech, which sounds until it be extended to the end proposed; truly it has sounded, and will sound. For what of it is already finished has surely sounded, but what remains will sound; and thus does it pass on, until the present intention carry over the future into the past; the past increasing by the diminution of the future, until, by the consumption of the future, all be past.

CHAPTER XXVIII. TIME IN THE HUMAN MIND, WHICH EXPECTS, CONSIDERS, AND REMEMBERS

But how is that future diminished or consumed which as yet is not? Or how does the past, which is no longer, increase, unless in the mind which enacts this there are three things done? For it both expects, and considers, and remembers, that that which it expects, through that which it considers may pass into that which it remembers. Who, therefore, denies that future things as yet are not? But yet there is already in the mind the expectation of things future. And who denies that past things are now no longer? But, however, there is still in the mind the memory of things past. And who denies that time present wants space, because it passes away in a moment? But yet our consideration endures, through which that which may be present may proceed to become absent. Future time, which is not, is not therefore long; but a "long future" is "a long expectation of the future." Nor is time past, which is now no longer, long; but a long past is "a long memory of the past."

I am about to repeat a psalm that I know. Before I begin, my attention is extended to the whole; but when I have begun, as much of it as becomes past by my saying it is extended in my memory; and the life of this action of mine is extended both ways between my memory, on account of what I have repeated, and my expectation, on account of what I am about to repeat; yet my consideration is present with me, through which that which was future may be carried over so that it may become past. The more this is done and repeated, by so much (expectation being shortened) the memory is enlarged, until the whole expectation be exhausted, when that whole action being ended shall have passed into memory. And what takes place in the entire psalm, takes place also in each individual part of it, and in each individual syllable: this holds in the longer action, of which that psalm is perchance a portion; the same holds in the whole life of man, of which all the actions of man are parts; the same holds in the whole age of the sons of men, of which all the lives of men are parts.

CHAPTER XXIX.   THAT HUMAN LIFE IS A DISTRACTION, BUT THAT THROUGH THE MERCY OF GOD HE WAS INTENT ON THE PRIZE OF HIS HEAVENLY CALLING

But because Thy loving-kindness is better than life, behold, my life is but a distraction, and Thy right hand upheld me in my Lord, the Son of man, the Mediator between Thee, The One, and us the many—in many distractions amid many things—that through Him I may apprehend in whom I have been apprehended, and may be re-collected from my old days, following The One, forgetting the things that are past; and not distracted, but drawn on, not to those things which shall be and shall pass away, but to those things which are before, not distractedly, but intently, I follow on for the prize of my heavenly calling, where I may hear the voice of Thy praise, and contemplate Thy delights, neither coming nor passing away. But now are my years spent in mourning. And Thou, O Lord, art my comfort, my Father everlasting. But I have been divided amid times, the order of which I know not; and my thoughts, even the inmost bowels of my soul, are mangled with tumultuous varieties, until I flow together unto Thee, purged and molten in the fire of Thy love.

CHAPTER XXX.   AGAIN HE REFUTES THE EMPTY QUESTION, "WHAT DID GOD BEFORE THE CREATION OF THE WORLD?"

And I will be immovable, and fixed in Thee, in my mould, Thy truth; nor will I endure the questions of men, who by a penal disease thirst for more than they can hold, and say, "What did God make before He made heaven and earth?" Or, "How came it into His mind to make anything when He never before made anything?" Grant to them, O Lord, to think well what they say, and to see that where there is no time, they cannot say "never." What, therefore, He is said "never to have made," what else is it but to say, that in no time was it made? Let them therefore see that there could be no time without a created being, and let them cease to speak that vanity. Let them also be extended unto those things which are before, and understand that thou, the eternal Creator of all times, art before all times, and that no times are co-eternal with Thee, nor any creature, even if there be any creature beyond all times.

CHAPTER XXXI.   HOW THE KNOWLEDGE OF GOD DIFFERS FROM THAT OF MAN

O Lord my God, what is that secret place of Thy mystery, and how far thence have the consequences of my transgressions cast me? Heal my eyes, that I may enjoy Thy light. Surely, if there be a mind, so greatly abounding in knowledge and foreknowledge, to which all things past and future are so known as one psalm is well known to me, that mind is exceedingly wonderful, and very astonishing; because whatever is so past, and whatever is to come of after ages, is no more concealed from Him than was it hidden from me when singing that psalm, what and how much of it had been sung from the beginning, what and how much remained unto the end. But far be it that Thou, the Creator of the universe, the Creator of souls and bodies—far be it that Thou shouldest know all things future and past. Far, far more wonderfully, and far more mysteriously, Thou knowest them. For it is not as the feelings of one singing known things, or hearing a known song, are—through expectation of future words, and in remembrance of those that are past—varied, and his senses divided, that anything happeneth unto Thee, unchangeably eternal, that is, the truly eternal Creator of minds. As, then, Thou in the Beginning knewest the heaven and the earth without any change of Thy knowledge, so in the Beginning didst Thou make heaven and earth without any distraction of Thy action. Let him who understandeth confess unto Thee; and let him who understandeth not, confess unto Thee. Oh, how exalted art Thou, and yet the humble in heart are Thy dwelling-place; for Thou raisest up those that are bowed down, and they whose exaltation Thou art fall not.

B. THE CITY OF GOD

Book XI

CHAPTER XXVI. OF THE IMAGE OF THE SUPREME TRINITY, WHICH WE FIND IN SOME SORT IN HUMAN NATURE EVEN IN ITS PRESENT STATE

And we indeed recognize in ourselves the image of God, that is, of the supreme Trinity, an image which, though it be not equal to God, or rather, though it be very far removed from Him—being neither co-eternal, nor, to say all in a word, consubstantial with Him—is yet nearer to Him in nature than any other of His works, and is destined to be yet restored, that it may bear a still closer resemblance. For we both are, and know that we are, and delight in our being, and our knowledge of it. Moreover, in these three things no true-seeming illusion disturbs us; for we do not come into contact with these by some bodily sense, as we perceive the things outside of us—colors, *e.g.*, by seeing, sounds by hearing, smells by smelling, tastes by tasting, hard and soft objects by touching—of all which sensible objects it is the images resembling them, but not themselves which we perceive in the mind and hold in the memory, and which excite us to desire the objects. But, without any delusive representation of images or phantasms, I am most certain that I am, and that I know and delight in this. In respect of these truths, I am not at all afraid of the arguments of the Academicians, who say, What if you are deceived? For if I am deceived, I am. For he who is not, cannot be deceived; and if I am deceived, by this same token I am. And since I am if I am deceived, how am I deceived in believing that I am? for it is certain that I am if I am deceived. Since, therefore, I, the person deceived, should be, even if I were deceived, certainly I am not deceived in this knowledge that I am. And, consequently, neither am I deceived in knowing that I know. For, as I know that I am, so I know this also, that I know. And when I love these two things, I add to them a certain third thing, namely, my love, which is of equal moment. For neither am I deceived in this, that I love, since in those things which I love I am not deceived; though even if these were false, it would still be true that I *loved* false things. For how could I justly be blamed and prohibited from loving false things, if it were false that I loved them? But, since they are true and real, who doubts that when they are loved, the love of them is itself true and real? Further, as there is no one who does not wish to be happy, so there is no one who does not wish to be. For how can he be happy, if he is nothing?

Book XXI

CHAPTER XII.   OF THE GREATNESS OF THE FIRST TRANSGRESSION, ON ACCOUNT OF WHICH ETERNAL PUNISHMENT IS DUE TO ALL WHO ARE NOT WITHIN THE PALE OF THE SAVIOUR'S GRACE

But eternal punishment seems hard and unjust to human perceptions, because in the weakness of our mortal condition there is wanting that highest and purest wisdom by which it can be perceived how great a wickedness was committed in that first transgression. The more enjoyment man found in God, the greater was his wickedness in abandoning Him; and he who destroyed in himself a good which might have been eternal, became worthy of eternal evil. Hence the whole mass of the human race is condemned; for he who at first gave entrance to sin has been punished with all his posterity who were in him as in a root, so that no one is exempt from this just and due punishment, unless delivered by mercy and undeserved grace; and the human race is so apportioned that in some is displayed the efficacy of merciful grace, in the rest the efficacy of just retribution. For both could not be displayed in all; for if all had remained under the punishment of just condemnation, there would have been seen in no one the mercy of redeeming grace. And, on the other hand, if all had been transferred from darkness to light, the severity of retribution would have been manifested in none. But many more are left under punishment than are delivered from it, in order that it may thus be shown what was due to all. And had it been inflicted on all, no one could justly have found fault with the justice of Him who taketh vengeance; whereas, in the deliverance of so many from that just award, there is cause to render the most cordial thanks to the gratuitous bounty of Him who delivers.

ANSELM'S *PROSLOGIUM*

CHAPTER II. TRULY THERE IS A GOD, ALTHOUGH THE FOOL HATH SAID IN HIS HEART, THERE IS NO GOD.

And so, Lord, do thou, who dost give understanding to faith, give me, so far as thou knowest it to be profitable, to understand that thou art as we believe; and that thou art that which we believe. And, indeed, we believe that thou art a being than which nothing greater can be conceived. Or is there no such nature, since the fool hath said in his heart, there is no God? (Psalms xiv. 1). But, at any rate, this very fool, when he hears of this being of which I speak—a being than which nothing greater can be conceived—understands what he hears, and what he understands is in his understanding; although he does not understand it to exist.

For, it is one thing for an object to be in the understanding, and another to understand that the object exists. When a painter first conceives of what he will afterwards perform, he has it in his understanding, but he does not yet understand it to be, because he has not yet performed it. But after he has made the painting, he both has it in his understanding, and he understands that it exists, because he has made it.

Hence, even the fool is convinced that something exists in the understanding, at least, than which nothing greater can be conceived. For, when he hears of this, he understands it. And whatever is understood, exists in the understanding. And assuredly that, than which nothing greater can be conceived, cannot exist in the understanding alone. For, suppose it exists in the understanding alone: then it can be conceived to exist in reality; which is greater.

Therefore, if that, than which nothing greater can be conceived, exists in the understanding alone, the very being, than which nothing greater can be conceived, is one, than which a greater can be conceived. But obviously this is impossible. Hence, there is no doubt that there exists a being, than which nothing greater can be conceived, and it exists both in the understanding and in reality.

CHAPTER III.   GOD CANNOT BE CONCEIVED NOT TO EXIST.—GOD IS
THAT, THAN WHICH NOTHING GREATER CAN BE CONCEIVED.—
THAT WHICH CAN BE CONCEIVED NOT TO EXIST IS NOT GOD.

And it assuredly exists so truly, that it cannot be conceived not to
exist. For, it is possible to conceive of a being which cannot be conceived
not to exist; and this is greater than one which can be conceived not to
exist. Hence, it that, than which nothing greater can be conceived, can
be conceived not to exist, it is not that, than which nothing greater can
be conceived. But this is an irreconcilable contradiction. There is, then,
so truly a being than which nothing greater can be conceived to exist,
that it cannot even be conceived not to exist; and this being thou art,
O Lord, our God.

So truly, therefore, dost thou exist, O Lord, my God, that thou canst
not be conceived not to exist; and rightly. For, if a mind could conceive
of a being better than thee, the creature would rise above the Creator;
and this is most absurd. And, indeed, whatever else there is, except thee
alone, can be conceived not to exist. To thee alone, therefore, it belongs
to exist more truly than all other beings, and hence in a higher degree
than all others. For, whatever else exists does not exist so truly, and hence
in a less degree it belongs to it to exist. Why, then, has the fool said
in his heart, there is no God (Psalms xiv. 1), since it is so evident, to
a rational mind, that thou dost exist in the highest degree of all? Why,
except that he is dull and a fool?

THOMAS AQUINAS—SUMMA THEOLOGICA

PART ONE

Question II—The existence of God (complete)

Because the chief aim of sacred doctrine is to teach the knowledge
of God not only as He is Himself, but also as He is the beginning of
things and their last end, and especially of rational creatures, as is clear
from what has been already said, therefore, in our endeavor to expound
this science, we shall treat: (1) of God; (2) of the rational creature's
movement towards God; (3) of Christ, Who as man is our way to God.

In treating of God there will be a threefold division:—

For we shall consider (1) whatever concerns the divine essence. (2)
Whatever concerns the distinctions of Persons. (3) Whatever concerns
the procession of creatures from Him.

Concerning the divine essence, we must consider:—

(1) Whether God exists? (2) The manner of His existence, or, rather, what is *not* the manner of His existence. (3) Whatever concerns His operations—namely, His knowledge, will, power.

Concerning the first, there are three points of inquiry:—

(1) Whether the proposition *God exists* is self-evident? (2) Whether it is demonstrable? (3) Whether God exists?

FIRST ARTICLE. WHETHER THE EXISTENCE OF GOD IS
SELF-EVIDENT?

We proceed thus to the First Article:—

Objection 1. It seems that the existence of God is self-evident. For those things are said to be self-evident to us the knowledge of which exists naturally in us, as we can see in regard to first principles. But as Damascene says, *the knowledge of God is naturally implanted in all*. Therefore the existence of God is self-evident.

Obj. 2. Further, those things are said to be self-evident which are known as soon as the terms are known, which the Philosopher says is true of the first principles of demonstration. Thus, when the nature of a whole and of a part is known, it is at once recognized that every whole is greater than its part. But as soon as the signification of the name *God* is understood, it is at once seen that God exists. For by this name is signified that thing than which nothing greater can be conceived. But that which exists actually and mentally is greater than that which exists only mentally. Therefore, since as soon as the name *God* is understood it exists mentally, it also follows that it exists actually. Therefore the proposition *God exists* is self-evident.

Obj. 3. Further, the existence of truth is self-evident. For whoever denies the existence of truth grants that truth does not exist: and, if truth does not exist, then the proposition *Truth does not exist* is true: and if there is anything true, there must be truth. But God is truth itself: *I am the way, the truth, and the life* (Jo. xiv. 6). Therefore *God exists* is self-evident.

On the contrary, No one can mentally admit the opposite of what is self-evident, as the Philosopher states concerning the first principles of demonstration. But the opposite of the proposition *God is* can be mentally admitted: *The fool said in his heart, There is no God* (Ps. lii. 1). Therefore, that God exists is not self-evident.

I answer that, A thing can be self-evident in either of two ways: on the one hand, self-evident in itself, though not to us; on the other, self-evident in itself, and to us. A proposition is self-evident because the predicate is included in the essence of the subject: *e.g., Man is an animal*, for animal is contained in the essence of man. If, therefore, the essence of the predicate and subject be known to all, the proposition will be self-evident to all; as is clear with regard to the first principles of demonstration, the terms of which are certain common notions that no one is ignorant of, such as being and non-being, whole and part, and the like. If, however, there are some to whom the essence of the predicate and subject is unknown, the proposition will be self-evident in itself, but not to those who do not know the meaning of the predicate and subject of the proposition. Therefore, it happens, as Boethius says, that there are some notions of the mind which are common and self-evident only to the learned, as that incorporeal substances are not in space. Therefore I say that this proposition, *God exists*, of itself is self-evident, for the predicate is the same as the subject, because God is His own existence as will be hereafter shown. Now because we do not know the essence of God, the proposition is not self-evident to us, but needs to be demonstrated by things that are more known to us, though less known in their nature—namely, by His effects.

Reply Obj. 1. To know that God exists in a general and confused way is implanted in us by nature, inasmuch as God is man's beatitude. For man naturally desires happiness, and what is naturally desired by man is naturally known by him. This, however, is not to know absolutely that God exists; just as to know that someone is approaching is not the same as to know that Peter is approaching, even though it is Peter who is approaching; for there are many who imagine that man's perfect good, which is happiness, consists in riches, and others in pleasures, and others in something else.

Reply Obj. 2. Perhaps not everyone who hears this name *God* understands it to signify something than which nothing greater can be thought, seeing that some have believed God to be a body. Yet, granted that everyone understands that by this name *God* is signified something than which nothing greater can be thought, nevertheless, it does not therefore follow that he understands that what the name signifies exists actually, but only that it exists mentally. Nor can it be argued that it actually exists, unless it be admitted that there actually exists something than which nothing greater can be thought; and this precisely is not admitted by those who hold that God does not exist.

Reply Obj. 3. The existence of truth in general is self-evident, but the existence of a Primal Truth is not self-evident to us.

SECOND ARTICLE. WHETHER IT CAN BE DEMONSTRATED THAT GOD EXISTS?

We proceed thus to the Second Article:—

Objection 1. It seems that the existence of God cannot be demonstrated. For it is an article of faith that God exists. But what is of faith cannot be demonstrated, because a demonstration produces scientific knowledge, whereas faith is of the unseen, as is clear from the Apostle (*Heb.* xi. 1). Therefore it cannot be demonstrated that God exists.

Obj. 2. Further, essence is the middle term of demonstration. But we cannot know in what God's essence consists, but solely in what it does not consist, as Damascene says. Therefore we cannot demonstrate that God exists.

Obj. 3. Further, if the existence of God were demonstrated, this could only be from His effects. But His effects are not proportioned to Him, since He is infinite and His effects are finite, and between the finite and infinite there is no proportion. Therefore, since a cause cannot be demonstrated by an effect not proportioned to it, it seems that the existence of God cannot be demonstrated.

On the contrary, The Apostle says: *The invisible things of Him are clearly seen, being understood by the things that are made* (*Rom.* i. 20). But this would not be unless the existence of God could be demonstrated through the things that are made; for the first thing we must know of anything is, whether it exists.

I answer that, Demonstration can be made in two ways: One is through the cause, and is called *propter quid*, and this is to argue from what is prior absolutely. The other is through the effect, and is called a demonstration *quia;* this is to argue from what is prior relatively only to us. When an effect is better known to us than its cause, from the effect we proceed to the knowledge of the cause. And from every effect the existence of its proper cause can be demonstrated, so long as its effects are better known to us; because, since every effect depends upon its cause, if the effect exists, the cause must pre-exist. Hence the existence of God, in so far as it is not self-evident to us, can be demonstrated from those of His effects which are known to us.

Reply Obj. 1. The existence of God and other like truths about God, which can be known by natural reason, are not articles of faith, but are preambles to the articles; for faith presupposes natural knowledge, even as grace presupposes nature and perfection the perfectible. Nevertheless, there is nothing to prevent a man, who cannot grasp a proof, from accepting, as a matter of faith, something which in itself is capable of being scientifically known and demonstrated.

Reply Obj. 2. When the existence of a cause is demonstrated from an effect, this effect takes the place of the definition of the cause in proving the cause's existence. This is especially the case in regard to God, because, in order to prove the existence of anything, it is necessary to accept as a middle term the meaning of the name, and not its essence, for the question of its essence follows on the question of its existence. Now the names given to God are derived from His effects, as will be later shown. Consequently, in demonstrating the existence of God from His effects, we may take for the middle term the meaning of the name *God*.

Reply Obj. 3. From effects not proportioned to the cause no perfect knowledge of that cause can be obtained. Yet from every effect the existence of the cause can be clearly demonstrated, and so we can demonstrate the existence of God from His effects; though from them we cannot know God perfectly as He is in His essence.

THIRD ARTICLE. WHETHER GOD EXISTS?

We proceed thus to the Third Article:—

Objection 1. It seems that God does not exist; because if one of two contraries be infinite, the other would be altogether destroyed. But the name *God* means that He is infinite goodness. If, therefore, God existed, there would be no evil discoverable; but there is evil in the world. Therefore God does not exist.

Obj. 2. Further, it is superfluous to suppose that what can be accounted for by a few principles has been produced by many. But it seems that everything we see in the world can be accounted for by other principles, supposing God did not exist. For all natural things can be reduced to one principle, which is nature; and all voluntary things can be reduced to one principle, which is human reason, or will. Therefore there is no need to suppose God's existence.

On the contrary, It is said in the person of God: *I am Who am* (*Exod.* iii. 14).

I answer that, The existence of God can be proved in five ways.

The first and more manifest way is the argument from motion. It is certain, and evident to our senses, that in the world some things are in motion. Now whatever is moved is moved by another, for nothing can be moved except it is in potentiality to that towards which it is moved; whereas a thing moves inasmuch as it is in act. For motion is nothing else than the reduction of something from potentiality to actuality. But nothing can be reduced from potentiality to actuality, except by something in a state of actuality. Thus that which is actually hot, as fire, makes wood, which is potentially hot, to be actually hot, and thereby moves and changes it. Now it is not possible that the same thing should be at once in actuality and potentiality in the same respect, but only in different respects. For what is actually hot cannot simultaneously be potentially hot; but it is simultaneously potentially cold. It is therefore impossible that in the same respect and in the same way a thing should be both mover and moved, *i.e.*, that it should move itself. Therefore, whatever is moved must be moved by another. If that by which it is moved be itself moved, then this also must needs be moved by another, and that by another again. But this cannot go on to infinity, because then there would be no first mover, and, consequently, no other mover, seeing that subsequent movers move only inasmuch as they are moved by the first mover; as the staff moves only because it is moved by the hand. Therefore it is necessary to arrive at a first mover, moved by no other; and this everyone understands to be God.

The second way is from the nature of efficient cause. In the world of sensible things we find there is an order of efficient causes. There is no case known (neither is it, indeed, possible) in which a thing is found to be the efficient cause of itself; for so it would be prior to itself, which is impossible. Now in efficient causes it is not possible to go on to infinity, because in all efficient causes following in order, the first is the cause of the intermediate cause, and the intermediate is the cause of the ultimate cause, whether the intermediate cause be several, or one only. Now to take away the cause is to take away the effect. Therefore, if there be no first cause among efficient causes, there will be no ultimate, nor any intermediate, cause. But if in efficient causes it is possible to go on to infinity, there will be no first efficient cause, neither will there be an ultimate effect, nor any intermediate efficient causes; all of which is plainly false. Therefore it is necessary to admit a first efficient cause, to which everyone gives the name of God.

The third way is taken from possibility and necessity, and runs thus. We find in nature things that are possible to be and not to be, since they are found to be generated, and to be corrupted, and consequently, it is possible for them to be and not to be. But it is impossible for these always to exist, for that which can not-be at some time is not. Therefore, if everything can not-be, then at one time there was nothing in existence. Now if this were true, even now there would be nothing in existence, because that which does not exist begins to exist only through something already existing. Therefore, if at one time nothing was in existence, it would have been impossible for anything to have begun to exist; and thus even now nothing would be in existence—which is absurd. Therefore, not all beings are merely possible, but there must exist something the existence of which is necessary. But every necessary thing either has its necessity caused by another, or not. Now it is impossible to go on to infinity in necessary things which have their necessity caused by another, as has been already proved in regard to efficient causes. Therefore we cannot but admit the existence of some being having of itself its own necessity, and not receiving it from another, but rather causing in others their necessity. This all men speak of as God.

The fourth way is taken from the gradation to be found in things. Among beings there are some more and some less good, true, noble, and the like. But *more* and *less* are predicated of different things according as they resemble in their different ways something which is the maximum, as a thing is said to be hotter according as it more nearly resembles that which is hottest; so that there is something which is truest, something best, something noblest, and, consequently, something which is most being, for those things that are greatest in truth are greatest in being, as it is written in *Metaph.* ii. Now the maximum in any genus is the cause of all in that genus, as fire, which is the maximum of heat, is the cause of all hot things, as is said in the same book. Therefore there must also be something which is to all beings the cause of their being, goodness, and every other perfection; and this we call God.

The fifth way is taken from the governance of the world. We see that things which lack knowledge, such as natural bodies, act for an end, and this is evident from their acting always, or nearly always, in the same way, so as to obtain the best result. Hence it is plain that they achieve their end, not fortuitously, but designedly. Now whatever lacks knowledge cannot move towards an end, unless it be directed by some being endowed with knowledge and intelligence; as the arrow is directed by the archer. Therefore some intelligent being exists by whom all natural things are directed to their end; and this being we call God.

Reply Obj. 1. As Augustine says: *Since God is the highest good, He would not allow any evil to exist in His works, unless His omnipotence and goodness were such as to bring good even out of evil.* This is part of the infinite goodness of God, that He should allow evil to exist, and out of it produce good.

Reply Obj. 2. Since nature works for a determinate end under the direction of a higher agent, whatever is done by nature must be traced back to God as to its first cause. So likewise whatever is done voluntarily must be traced back to some higher cause other than human reason and will, since these can change and fail; for all things that are changeable and capable of defect must be traced back to an immovable and self-necessary first principle, as has been shown.

Question XVI—On truth

FIRST ARTICLE.   WHETHER TRUTH RESIDES ONLY IN THE INTELLECT?

We proceed thus to the First Article:—

Objection 1. It seems that truth does not reside only in the intellect, but rather in things. For Augustine condemns this definition of truth, *That is true which is seen,* since it would follow that stones hidden in the bosom of the earth would not be true stones, as they are not seen. He also condemns the following, *That is true which is as it appears to the knower, who is willing and able to know;* for hence it would follow that nothing would be true, unless someone could know it. Therefore he defines truth thus: *The true is which is.* It seems, then, that truth resides in things, and not in the intellect.

Obj. 2. Further, whatever is true, is true by reason of truth. If, then, truth is only in the intellect, nothing will be true except in so far as it is understood. But this is the error of the ancient philosophers, who said that whatever seems to be true is so. Consequently contradictories can be true at the same time, since contradictories seem to be true as seen by different persons at the same time.

Obj. 3. Further, *that because of which a thing is so, is itself more so,* as is evident from the Philosopher. But *it is from the fact that a thing is or is not, that our thought or word is true or false,* as the Philosopher teaches. Therefore truth resides rather in things than in the intellect.

On the contrary, The Philosopher says, *The true and the false reside not in things, but in the intellect.*

I answer that, As *good* names that towards which the appetite tends, so *the true* names that towards which the intellect tends. Now there is this difference between the appetite and the intellect, or any knowledge whatsoever, that knowledge is according as the thing known is in the knower, while appetite is according as the desirer tends towards the thing desired. Thus the term of the appetite, namely good, is in the desirable thing, and the term of the intellect, namely the true, is in the intellect itself. Now as good exists in a thing so far as that thing is related to the appetite—and hence the aspect of goodness passes on from the desirable thing to the appetite, in so far as the appetite is called good if its object is good; so, since the true is in the intellect in so far as the intellect is conformed to the thing understood, the aspect of the true must needs pass from the intellect to the thing understood, so that also the thing understood is said to be true in so far as it has some relation to the intellect.

Now a thing understood may be in relation to an intellect either essentially or accidentally. It is related essentially to an intellect on which it depends as regards its being, but accidentally to an intellect by which it is knowable; even as we may say that a house is related essentially to the intellect of the architect, but accidentally to the intellect upon which it does not depend. Now we do not judge of a thing by what is in it accidentally, but by what is in it essentially. Hence, everything is said to be true absolutely, in so far as it is related to the intellect on which it depends; and thus it is that artificial things are said to be true as being related to our intellect. For a house is said to be true that fulfills the likeness of the form in the architect's mind; and words are said to be true so far as they are the signs of truth in the intellect. In the same way, natural things are said to be true in so far as they express the likeness of the species that are in the divine mind. For a stone is called true, which possesses the nature proper to a stone, according to the preconception in the divine intellect. Thus, then, truth resides primarily in the intellect, and secondarily in things according as they are related to the intellect as their source.

Consequently, there are various definitions of truth. Augustine says, *Truth is that whereby is made manifest that which is;* and Hilary says that *Truth makes being clear and evident:* and this pertains to truth according as it is in the intellect. As to the truth of things in so far as they are related to the intellect, we have Augustine's definition, *Truth is a supreme likeness, without any unlikeness, to its source;* also Anselm's definition, *Truth is rightness, perceptible by the mind alone;* for that is right which is in accordance with its source; also Avicenna's definition, *The truth of each thing is a property of the being which has been given to it.* The definition that *Truth is the equation of thought and thing* is applicable to it under either aspect.

Reply Obj. 1. Augustine is speaking about the truth of things, and from the notion of this truth excludes relation to our intellect; for what is accidental is excluded from every definition.

Reply Obj. 2. The ancient philosophers held that the species of natural things did not proceed from any intellect, but came about by chance. But as they saw that truth implies relation to intellect, they were compelled to base the truth of things on their relation to our intellect. From this fact there followed the various awkward consequences that the Philosopher attacks. Such consequences, however, do not follow, if we say that the truth of things consists in their relation to the divine intellect.

Reply Obj. 3. Although the truth of our intellect is caused by the thing, yet it is not necessary that the essence of truth should be there primarily, any more than that the essence of health should be primarily in medicine, rather than in the animal: for it is the power of medicine, and not its health, that is the cause of health, since the agent is no univocal. In the same way, the being of the thing, not its truth, is the cause of truth in the intellect. Hence the Philosopher says that an opinion or a statement is true *from the fact that a thing is, not from the fact that a thing is true.*

FIFTH ARTICLE. WHETHER GOD IS TRUTH?

We proceed thus to the Fifth Article:—

Objection 1. It seems that God is not truth. For truth consists in the intellect composing and dividing. But in God there is no composition and division. Therefore in God there is no truth.

Obj. 2. Further, truth, according to Augustine, is a *likeness to the source.* But in God there is no likeness to a source. Therefore in God there is no truth.

Obj. 3. Further, whatever is said of God, is said of Him as of the first cause of all things. Thus the being of God is the cause of all being, and His goodness the cause of all good. If therefore there is truth in God, all truth will be from Him. But it is true that someone sins. Therefore this will be from God; which is evidently false.

On the contrary, Our Lord says, *I am the Way, the Truth and the Life* (*Jo.* xiv. 6).

I answer that, As was said above, truth is found in the intellect according as it apprehends a thing as it is; and in things according as they have being conformable to an intellect. This is to the greatest degree found in God. For His being is not only conformed to His intellect, but it is the very act of His intellect; and His act of understanding is the measure and cause of every other being and of every other intellect; and He Himself is His own being and act of understanding. Whence it follows not only that truth is in Him, but that He is the highest and first truth itself.

Reply Obj. 1. Although in the divine intellect there is neither composition nor division, yet in His simple act of intelligence He judges of all things and knows all propositions; and thus there is truth in His intellect.

Reply Obj. 2. The truth of our intellect is according to its conformity with its source, that is to say, the things from which it receives knowledge. The truth also of things is according to their conformity with their source, namely, the divine intellect. Now this cannot be said, properly speaking, of divine truth; unless perhaps in so far as truth is appropriated to the Son, Who has a source. But if we speak of divine truth in its essence, we cannot understand what Augustine has said unless the affirmative proposition be resolved into the negative one, as when one says: *the Father is of Himself, because He is not from another.* Similarly, the divine truth can be called *a likeness of its source,* inasmuch as His being is not unlike His intellect.

Reply Obj. 3. Non-being and privation have no truth of themselves, but only in the apprehension of the intellect. Now all apprehension of the intellect is from God. Hence all the truth that exists in the statement,— *that this person commits fornication is true,* is entirely from God. But to argue, *Therefore that this person fornicates is from God,* is a fallacy of accident.

Question XXIII—Predestination

THIRD ARTICLE. WHETHER GOD REPROBATES ANY MAN?

We proceed thus to the Third Article:—

Objection 1. It seems that God reprobates no man. For nobody reprobates what he loves. But God loves every man, according to the words (*Wis.* xi. 25): *Thou lovest all things that are, and Thou hatest none of the things Thou hast made.* Therefore God reprobates no man.

Obj. 2. Further, if God reprobates any man, it would be necessary for reprobation to have the same relation to the reprobate as predestination has to the predestined. But predestination is the cause of the salvation of the predestined. Therefore reprobation will likewise be the cause of the loss of the reprobate. But this is false. For it is said (*Osee* xiii. 9): *Destruction is thy own, O Israel; Thy help is only in Me.* God does not, then, reprobate any man.

Obj. 3. Further, to no one ought anything to be imputed which he cannot avoid. But if God reprobates anyone, that one must perish. For it is said (*Eccles.* vii. 14): *Consider the works of God, that no man can correct whom He hath despised.* Therefore it could not be imputed to any man, were he to perish. But this is false. Therefore God does not reprobate anyone.

On the contrary, It is said (*Malach.* i. 2, 3): *I have loved Jacob, but have hated Esau.*

I answer that, God does reprobate some persons. For it was said above that predestination is a part of providence. To providence, however, it belongs to permit certain defects in those things which are subject to providence, as was said above. Thus, as men are ordained to eternal life through the providence of God, it likewise is part of that providence to permit some to fall away from that end; this is called *reprobation.* Thus,

as predestination is a part of providence, in regard to those divinely ordained to eternal salvation, so reprobation is a part of providence in
regard to those who turn aside from that end. Hence reprobation implies
not only foreknowledge, but also something more, as does providence, as
was said above. Therefore, as predestination includes the will to confer
grace and glory, so also reprobation includes the will to permit a person
to fall into sin, and to impose the punishment of damnation because of
that sin.

Reply Obj. 1. God loves all men and all creatures, inasmuch as He
wishes them all some good; but He does not wish every good to them all.
So far, therefore, as He does not wish for some this particular good—
namely, eternal life—He is said to hate or reprobate them.

Reply Obj. 2. Reprobation differs in its causality from predestination.
This latter is the cause both of what is expected in the future life by the
predestined—namely, glory—and of what is received in this life—namely,
grace. Reprobation, however, is not the cause of what is in the present—
namely, sin; but it is the cause of abandonment by God. It is the cause,
however, of what is assigned in the future—namely, eternal punishment.
But guilt proceeds from the free choice of the person who is reprobated
and deserted by grace. In this way the word of the prophet is true—
namely, *Destruction is thy own, O Israel.*

Reply Obj. 3. Reprobation by God does not take anything away from
the power of the person reprobated. Hence, when it is said that the reprobated cannot obtain grace, this must not be understood as implying absolute impossibility, but only conditional impossibility; just as it was said
above that the predestined must necessarily be saved, yet by a conditional
necessity, which does not do away with the liberty of choice. Whence,
although anyone reprobated by God cannot acquire grace, nevertheless,
that he falls into this or that particular sin comes from the use of his free
desire. Hence it is rightly imputed to him as guilt.

Question XXV—*The power of God*

FIFTH ARTICLE.　WHETHER GOD CAN DO WHAT HE DOES NOT?

We proceed thus to the Fifth Article:—

Objection 1. It seems that God can do only what He does. For God
cannot do what He has not foreknown and pre-ordained that He would
do. But He neither foreknew nor pre-ordained that He would do anything
except what He does. Therefore He can do only what He does.

Obj. 2. Further, God can do only what ought to be done and what is
just. But God is not bound to do what He does not; nor is it just that He
should do what He does not. Therefore He can do only what He does.

Obj. 3. Further, God cannot do anything that is not good and befitting creation. But it is not good for creatures nor befitting them to be otherwise than as they are. Therefore God can do only what He does.

On the contrary, It is said: *Thinkest thou that I cannot ask My Father, and He will give Me presently more than twelve legions of angels?* (*Matt.* xxvi. 53). But He neither asked for them, nor did His Father show them to refute the Jews. Therefore God can do what He does not.

I answer that, In this matter certain persons erred in two ways. Some laid it down that God acts from natural necessity in such way that, just as from the action of natural things nothing else can happen beyond what actually takes place—as, for instance, from the seed of man, a man must come, and from that of an olive, an olive; so from the divine operation there could not come forth other things, nor another order of things, than that which now is. But we showed above that God does not act from natural necessity, but that His will is the cause of all things; we showed also that the divine will is not naturally and from any necessity determined to these creatures. Whence in no way is the present scheme of things produced by God with such necessity that other things could not come to be.

Others, however, said that the divine power is restricted to this present scheme of things because of the order of the divine wisdom and justice, without which God does nothing. But since the power of God, which is His essence, is nothing else but His wisdom, it can indeed be fittingly said that there is nothing in the divine power which is not in the order conceived by the divine wisdom; for the divine wisdom comprehends the power of God in its entirety. However, the order established in creation by divine wisdom (in which the notion of His justice consists, as was said above), is not so equal to the divine wisdom that the divine wisdom should be restricted to it. For it is clear that the whole nature of the order which a wise man puts into the things made by him is taken from their end. So, when the end is proportionate to the things made for that end, the wisdom of the maker is restricted to a definite order. But the divine goodness is an end exceeding created things beyond all proportion. Therefore, the divine wisdom is not so restricted to any particular order that no other scheme of things could proceed from it. Hence we must say absolutely that God can do other things than those He has done.

Reply Obj. 1. In ourselves, in whom power and essence are distinct from will and intellect, and in whom intellect is distinct from wisdom, and will from justice, something can reside in our power which cannot reside in a just will or in a wise intellect. But in God, power, essence, will, intellect, wisdom and justice are one and the same. Whence, there can be found nothing in the divine power which cannot also be found in His just will or in His wise intellect. Now, because His will cannot be determined from necessity to this or that order of things, except upon supposition, as was said above; and because the wisdom and justice of God are likewise restricted not to this present order, as was shown above; for this reason, nothing prevents there being something in the divine power which He does not will, and which is not included in the order that He has established in things. Furthermore, because power is considered as *exe-*

cuting, will as *commanding*, and intellect and wisdom as *directing*, what is attributed to His power considered in itself God is said to be able to do in accordance with His *absolute power*. Of such a kind is everything which verifies the nature of being, as was said above. On the other hand, what is attributed to the divine power, according as it carries into execution the command of a just will, God is said to be able to do by His *ordained power*. In this manner, we must say that by His absolute power God can do other things than those He has foreknown and pre-ordained to do. But it could not happen that He should do anything which He has not foreknown and not pre-ordained that He would do. For His doing is subject to His foreknowledge and preordination, though His power, which is His nature, is not. For God does things because He so wills; yet He is able to do so, not because He so wills, but because He is such in His nature.

Reply Obj. 2. God is bound to nobody but Himself. Hence, when it is said that God can do only what He ought, nothing else is meant by this than that God can do nothing but what is for Him fitting and just. But these words *fitting* and *just* may be understood in two ways: one, in direct connection with the verb *is;* and thus they would be restricted to signifying the present order of things. They would therefore refer to His power under this restriction. In that case, what is said in the objection is false, for its meaning is that God can do nothing except what is now fitting and just. If, however, *fitting* and *just* are joined directly with the verb *can* (which has the effect of extending their application), and then secondly with *is*, the result will be a present signified in a confused and general way. The proposition would then be true, and its meaning would be: *God cannot do anything except that which, if He did it, would be suitable and just.*

Reply Obj. 3. Although the present order of things is restricted to what now exists, the divine power and wisdom are not thus restricted. Whence, although no other order would be suitable and good for the things which now exist, yet God can make other things and impose upon them another order.

SIXTH ARTICLE.   WHETHER GOD CAN DO BETTER THAN WHAT HE DOES?

We proceed thus to the Sixth Article:—

Objection 1. It seems that God cannot do better than He does. For whatever God does, He does in a most powerful and wise way. But a thing is so much the better done as it is more powerfully and wisely done. Therefore God cannot do anything better than He does.

Obj. 2. Further, Augustine argues thus: *If God could, but would not, beget a Son His equal, He would have been envious.* For the same reason, if God could have made better things than He has done, but was not willing so to do, He would have been envious. But envy is far removed from God. Therefore God has made everything perfect. He cannot therefore make anything better than He has done.

Obj. 3. Further, what is very good and the best of all cannot be bettered; because nothing is better than the best. But as Augustine says, *each thing that God has made is good, and, taken all together they are very good; because in them all consists the wondrous beauty of the universe.* Therefore the good in the universe could not be made better by God.

Obj. 4. Further, Christ as man is full of grace and truth, and possesses the Spirit without measure; and so He cannot be better. Again, created happiness is described as the highest good, and thus could not be better. And the Blessed Virgin Mary is raised above all the choirs of angels, and so cannot be better than she is. God cannot therefore make all things better than He has made them.

On the contrary, It is said (*Ephes.* iii. 20): *God is able to do all things more abundantly than we desire or understand.*

I answer that, The goodness of anything is twofold. One belongs to its essence:—thus, for instance, to be rational belongs to the essence of man. As regards this good, God cannot make a thing better than it is itself, although He can make another thing better than it. In the same way, He cannot make the number four greater than it is, because if it were greater it would no longer be four, but another number. For the addition of a substantial difference in definitions is after the manner of the addition of unity in numbers. Another kind of goodness is that which is over and above the essence; thus, the good of a man is to be virtuous or wise. As regards this kind of goodness, God can make better the things He has made. Absolutely speaking, however, God can make something else better than each thing made by Him.

Reply Obj. 1. When it is said that God can make better things than He does, if *better* is taken substantively, this proposition is true. For He can always make something else better than any individual thing: and He can make the same thing in one way better than it is, and in another way not; as was explained above. If, however, *better* is taken as an adverb, referring to the mode of God's activity, then God cannot make anything better than He makes it, because He cannot make it from greater wisdom and goodness. Finally, if it implies the mode of being in the things that God has made, then He can make something better; because He can give to things made by Him a better manner of being as regards accidents, although not as regards the substance.

Reply Obj. 2. It is of the nature of a son that he should be equal to his father, when he comes to maturity. But it is not of the nature of anything created that it should be better than it was made by God. Hence the comparison fails.

Reply Obj. 3. Given the things which actually exist, the universe cannot be better, for the order which God has established in things, and in which the good of the universe consists, most befits things. For if any one thing were bettered, the proportion of order would be destroyed; just as if one string were stretched more than it ought to be, the melody of the harp would be destroyed. Yet God could make other things, or add something to the present creation; and then there would be another and a better universe.

Reply Obj. 4. An infinite dignity, resulting from the infinite good which is God, is in a way possessed by the humanity of Christ because it is united to God; by created beatitude because it is the enjoyment of God; and by the Blessed Virgin because she is the mother of God. From this point of view, nothing better than these can be made; just as there cannot be anything better than God.

Question XLIX—*The cause of evil*

SECOND ARTICLE. WHETHER THE HIGHEST GOOD, GOD, IS THE CAUSE OF EVIL?

We proceed thus to the Second Article:—

Objection 1. It would seem that the highest good, God, is the cause of evil. For it is said (*Isa.* xlv. 5, 7): *I am the Lord, and there is no other God, forming the light, and creating darkness, making peace, and creating evil.* It is also said (*Amos* iii. 6), *Shall there be evil in a city, which the Lord hath not done?*

Obj. 2. Further, the effect of the secondary cause is reduced to the first cause. But good is the cause of evil, as was said above. Therefore, since God is the cause of every good, as was shown above, it follows that also every evil is from God.

Obj. 3. Further, as is said by the Philosopher, the cause of both *the safety and danger of the ship* is the same. But God is the cause of the safety of all things. Therefore He is the cause of all perdition and of all evil.

On the contrary, Augustine says that, *God is not the author of evil, because He is not the cause of tending to non-being.*

I answer that, As appears from what was said, the evil which consists in the defect of action is always caused by the defect of the agent. But in God there is no defect, but the highest perfection, as was shown above. Hence, the evil which consists in defect of action, or which is caused by defect of the agent, is not reduced to God as to its cause.

But the evil which consists in the corruption of some things is reduced to God as the cause. And this appears as regards both natural things and voluntary things. For it was said that some agent, inasmuch as it produces by its power a form which is followed by corruption and defect, causes by its power that corruption and defect. But it is manifest that the form which God chiefly intends in created things is the good of the order of the universe. Now, the order of the universe requires, as was said above, that there should be some things that can, and sometimes do, fail. And thus

God, by causing in things the good of the order of the universe, consequently and, as it were by accident, causes the corruptions of things, according to *I Kings* ii. 6: *The Lord killeth and maketh alive.* But when we read that *God hath not made death* (*Wis.* i. 13), the sense is that God does not will death for its own sake. Nevertheless, the order of justice belongs to the order of the universe; and this requires that penalty should be dealt out to sinners. And so God is the author of the evil which is penalty, but not of the evil which is fault, by reason of what is said above.

Reply Obj. 1. These passages refer to the evil of penalty, and not to the evil of fault.

Reply Obj. 2. The effect of the deficient secondary cause is reduced to the first non-deficient cause as regards what it has of being and perfection, but not as regards what it has of defect; just as whatever there is of motion in the act of limping is caused by the motive power, whereas what is unbalanced in it does not come from the motive power, but from the curvature of the leg. So, too, whatever there is of being and action in a bad action is reduced to God as the cause; whereas whatever defect is in it is not caused by God, but by the deficient secondary cause.

Reply Obj. 3. The sinking of a ship is attributed to the sailor as the cause, from the fact that he does not fulfill what the safety of the ship requires; but God does not fail in doing what is necessary for safety. Hence there is no parity.

FIRST PART OF THE SECOND PART

Question VI—On the voluntary and the involuntary

EIGHTH ARTICLE. WHETHER IGNORANCE CAUSES INVOLUNTARINESS?

We proceed thus to the Eighth Article:—

Objection 1. It would seem that ignorance does not cause involuntariness. For *the involuntary act deserves pardon,* as Damascene says. But sometimes that which is done through ignorance does not deserve pardon, according to *1 Cor.* xiv. 38: *If any man know not, he shall not be known.* Therefore ignorance does not cause involuntariness.

Obj. 2. Further, every sin implies ignorance, according to *Prov.* xiv. 22: *They err, that work evil.* If, therefore, ignorance causes involuntariness, it would follow that every sin is involuntary; which is opposed to the saying of Augustine, that *every sin is voluntary.*

Obj. 3. Further, *involuntariness is not without sadness,* as Damascene says. But some things are done out of ignorance, but without sadness. For instance, a man may kill a foe, whom he wishes to kill, thinking at the time that he is killing a stag. Therefore ignorance does not cause involuntariness.

On the contrary, Damascene and the Philosopher say that *what is done through ignorance is involuntary.*

I answer that, If ignorance cause involuntariness, it is in so far as it deprives one of knowledge, which is a necessary condition of voluntariness, as was declared above. But it is not every ignorance that deprives one of this knowledge. Accordingly, we must take note that ignorance has a threefold relationship to the act of the will: in one way, *concomitantly;* in another, *consequently;* in a third way, *antecedently. Concomitantly,* when there is ignorance of what is done, but so that even if it were known, it would be done. For then ignorance does not induce one to will this to be done, but it just happens that a thing is at the same time done and not known. Thus, in the example given, a man did indeed will to kill his foe, but killed him in ignorance, thinking to kill a stag. And ignorance of this kind, as the Philosopher states, does not cause involuntariness, since it is not the cause of anything that is repugnant to the will; but it causes *nonvoluntariness,* since that which is unknown cannot be actually willed.

Ignorance is *consequent* to the act of the will, in so far as ignorance itself is voluntary; and this happens in two ways in accordance with the two aforesaid modes of the voluntary. First, because the act of the will is brought to bear on the ignorance, as when a man wills not to know, that he may have an excuse for sin, or that he may not be withheld from sin, according to *Job* xxi. 14: *We desire not the knowledge of Thy ways.* And this is called *affected ignorance.*—Secondly, ignorance is said to be voluntary, when it regards that which one can and ought to know, for in this sense *not to act* and *not to will* are said to be voluntary, as was stated above. And ignorance of this kind happens either when one does not actually consider what one can and ought to consider (this is called *ignorance of evil choice,* and arises from some passion or habit), or when one does not take the trouble to acquire the knowledge which one ought to have; in which sense, ignorance of the general principles of law, which one ought to know, is voluntary, as being due to negligence.

Accordingly, if in either of these ways ignorance is voluntary, it cannot cause what is involuntary absolutely. Nevertheless it causes involuntariness in a certain respect, inasmuch as it precedes the movement of the will towards the act, which movement would not be, if there were knowledge.

Ignorance is *antecedent* to the act of the will when it is not voluntary, and yet is the cause of man's willing what he would not will otherwise. Thus a man may be ignorant of some circumstance of his act, which he was not bound to know, with the result that he does that which he would not do if he knew of that circumstance. For instance, a man, after taking proper precaution, may not know that someone is coming along the road, so that he shoots an arrow and slays a passer-by. Such ignorance causes what is involuntary absolutely.

From this may be gathered the solution of the objections. For the first objection deals with ignorance of what a man is bound to know. The second, with ignorance of choice, which is voluntary to a certain extent, as was stated above. The third, with that ignorance which is concomitant with the act of the will.

Question XII—On intention

THIRD ARTICLE. WHETHER ONE CAN INTEND TWO THINGS AT THE SAME TIME?

We proceed thus to the Third Article:—

Objection 1. It would seem that one cannot intend several things at the same time. For Augustine says that man's intention cannot be directed at the same time to God and to bodily benefits. Therefore, for the same reason, neither to any other two things.

Obj. 2. Further, intention designates a movement of the will towards a terminus. Now there cannot be several termini in the same direction of one movement. Therefore the will cannot intend several things at the same time.

Obj. 3. Further, intention presupposes an act of the reason or of the intellect. But *it is not possible to understand several things at the same time,* according to the Philosopher. Therefore, neither is it possible to intend several things at the same time.

On the contrary, Art imitates nature. Now nature intends two purposes by means of one instrument. Thus *the tongue* is *for the purpose of taste and speech.* Therefore, for the same reason, art or reason can at the same time direct one thing to two ends; so that one can intend several ends at the same time.

I answer that, Two things may be taken in two ways, namely, as related to one another, or as unrelated. And if they be related to one another, it is evident, from what has been said, that a man can intend several things at the same time. For intention is not only of the last end, as was stated above, but also of an intermediary end. Now a man intends, at the same time, both the proximate and the last end: *e.g.,* the mixing of a medicine and the giving of health.

But if we take two things that are not related to one another, thus also a man can intend several things at the same time. This is evident from the fact that a man prefers one thing to another because it is the better of the two. Now one of the reasons for which one thing is better than another is that it is available for more purposes; and so one thing can be chosen in preference to another because of the greater number of purposes for which it is available; so that evidently a man can intend several things at the same time.

Reply Obj. 1. Augustine means to say that man cannot at the same time direct his intention to God and to bodily benefits, as to two last ends; for, as was stated above, one man cannot have several last ends.

Reply Obj. 2. There can be several termini of the same movement and in the same direction, if one is related to the other; but there cannot be two unrelated termini of the same movement and in the same direction. At the same time, it must be observed that what is not one in reality may be taken as one by the reason. Now intention is a movement of the will to something already ordained by the reason, as was stated above. Therefore, where we have many things in reality, we may take them as one term of intention, in so far as the reason takes them as one; and this either because two things concur in the integrity of one whole, as a proper measure of heat and cold conduce to health, or because two things are included in one which may be intended. For instance, the acquiring of wine and clothing is included in wealth, as in something common to both; and so nothing hinders the man who intends to acquire wealth from intending both the others.

Reply Obj. 3. As was stated in the First Part, it is possible to understand several things at the same time in so far as, in some way, they are one.

Question LXI—*The cardinal virtues*

SECOND ARTICLE. WHETHER THERE ARE FOUR CARDINAL VIRTUES?

We proceed thus to the Second Article:—

Objection 1. It would seem that there are not four cardinal virtues. For prudence is the directing principle of the other moral virtues, as is clear from what has been said above. But that which directs others ranks before them. Therefore prudence alone is a principal virtue.

Obj. 2. Further, the principal virtues are, in a way, moral virtues. Now we are directed to moral works both by the practical reason and by a right appetite, as is stated in *Ethics* vi. Therefore there are only two cardinal virtues.

Obj. 3. Further, even among the other virtues one ranks higher than another. But in order that a virtue be principal, it need not rank above all the others, but above some. Therefore it seems that there are many more principal virtues.

On the contrary, Gregory says: *The entire structure of good works is built on four virtues.*

I answer that, Things may be numbered either in respect of their formal principles, or according to the subjects in which they are; and in either way we find that there are four cardinal virtues.

For the formal principle of the virtue of which we speak now is the good as defined by reason. This good can be considered in two ways. First, as existing in the consideration itself of reason, and thus we have one principal virtue called *prudence.*—Secondly, according as the reason puts its order into something else, and this either into operations, and then we have *justice,* or into passions, and then we need two virtues. For the need of putting the order of reason into the passions is due to their thwarting reason; and this occurs in two ways. First, when the passions incite to something against reason, and then they need a curb, which we thus call *temperance;* secondly, when the passions withdraw us from following the dictate of reason, *e.g.,* through fear of danger or toil, and then man needs to be strengthened for that which reason dictates, lest he turn back, and to this end there is *fortitude.*

In like manner, we find the same number if we consider the subjects of virtue. For there are four subjects of the virtue of which we now speak, viz., the power which is rational in its essence, and this is perfected by *prudence;* and that which is rational by participation, and is threefold, the will, subject of *justice,* the concupiscible power, subject of *temperance,* and the irascible power, subject of *fortitude.*

Reply Obj. 1. Prudence is absolutely the principal of all the virtues. The others are principal, each in its own genus.

Reply Obj. 2. That part of the soul which is rational by participation is threefold, as was stated above.

Reply Obj. 3. All the other virtues, among which one ranks before another, are reducible to the above four, both as to the subject and as to the formal principles.

Question XCIV—The natural law

FOURTH ARTICLE. WHETHER THE NATURAL LAW IS THE SAME IN ALL MEN?

We proceed thus to the Fourth Article:—

Objection 1. It would seem that the natural law is not the same in all. For it is stated in the *Decretals* that *the natural law is that which is contained in the Law and the Gospel.* But this is not common to all men, because, as it is written (*Rom.* x. 16), *all do not obey the gospel.* Therefore the natural law is not the same in all men.

Obj. 2. Further, *Things which are according to the law are said to be just,* as is stated in *Ethics* v. But it is stated in the same book that nothing is so just for all as not to be subject to change in regard to some men. Therefore even the natural law is not the same in all men.

Obj. 3. Further, as was stated above, to the natural law belongs everything to which a man is inclined according to his nature. Now different men are naturally inclined to different things,—some to the desire of pleasures, others to the desire of honors, and other men to other things. Therefore, there is not one natural law for all.

On the contrary, Isidore says: *The natural law is common to all nations.*

I answer that, As we have stated above, to the natural law belong those things to which a man is inclined naturally; and among these it is proper to man to be inclined to act according to reason. Now it belongs to the reason to proceed from what is common to what is proper, as is stated in *Physics* i. The speculative reason, however, is differently situated, in this matter, from the practical reason. For, since the speculative reason is concerned chiefly with necessary things, which cannot be otherwise than they are, its proper conclusions, like the universal principles, contain the truth without fail. The practical reason, on the other hand, is concerned with contingent matters, which is the domain of human actions; and, consequently, although there is necessity in the common principles, the more we descend towards the particular, the more frequently we encounter defects. Accordingly, then, in speculative matters truth is the same in all men, both as to principles and as to conclusions; although the truth is not known to all as regards the conclusions, but only as regards the principles which are called *common notions*. But in matters of action, truth or practical rectitude is not the same for all as to what is particular, but only as to the common principles; and where there is the same rectitude in relation to particulars, it is not equally known to all.

It is therefore evident that, as regards the common principles whether of speculative or of practical reason, truth or rectitude is the same for all, and is equally known by all. But as to the proper conclusions of the speculative reason, the truth is the same for all, but it is not equally known to all. Thus, it is true for all that the three angles of a triangle are together equal to two right angles, although it is not known to all. But as to the proper conclusions of the practical reason, neither is the truth or rectitude the same for all, nor, where it is the same, is it equally known by all. Thus, it is right and true for all to act according to reason, and from this principle it follows, as a proper conclusion, that goods entrusted to another should be restored to their owner. Now this is true for the majority of cases. But it may happen in a particular case that it would be injurious, and therefore unreasonable, to restore goods held in trust; for instance, if they are claimed for the purpose of fighting against one's country. And this principle will be found to fail the more, according as we descend further towards the particular, *e.g.*, if one were to say that goods held in trust should be restored with such and such a guarantee, or in such and such a way; because the greater the number of conditions added, the greater the number of ways in which the principle may fail, so that it be not right to restore or not to restore.

Consequently, we must say that the natural law, as to the first common principles, is the same for all, both as to rectitude and as to knowledge. But as to certain more particular aspects, which are conclusions, as it were, of those common principles, it is the same for all in the majority of cases, both as to rectitude and as to knowledge; and yet in some few cases it may fail, both as to rectitude, by reason of certain obstacles (just as natures subject to generation and corruption fail in some few cases because of some obstacle), and as to knowledge, since in some the reason is perverted by passion, or evil habit, or an evil disposition of nature. Thus at one time theft, although it is expressly contrary to the natural law, was not considered wrong among the Germans, as Julius Cæsar relates.

Reply Obj. 1. The meaning of the sentence quoted is not that whatever is contained in the Law and the Gospel belongs to the natural law, since they contain many things that are above nature; but that whatever belongs to the natural law is fully contained in them. Therefore Gratian, after saying that *the natural law is what is contained in the Law and the Gospel*, adds at once, by way of example, *by which everyone is commanded to do to others as he would be done by.*

Reply Obj. 2. The saying of the Philosopher is to be understood of things that are naturally just, not as common principles, but as conclusions drawn from them, having rectitude in the majority of cases, but failing in a few.

Reply Obj. 3. Just as in man reason rules and commands the other powers, so all the natural inclinations belonging to the other powers must needs be directed according to reason. Therefore it is universally right for all men that all their inclinations should be directed according to reason.

FIFTH ARTICLE. WHETHER THE NATURAL LAW CAN BE CHANGED?

We proceed thus to the Fifth Article:—
Objection 1. It would seem that the natural law can be changed. For on *Ecclus.* xvii. 9. (*He gave them instructions, and the law of life*) the *Gloss* says: *He wished the law of the letter to be written, in order to correct the law of nature.* But that which is corrected is changed. Therefore the natural law can be changed.

Obj. 2. Further, the slaying of the innocent, adultery and theft are against the natural law. But we find these things changed by God: as when God commanded Abraham to slay his innocent son (*Gen.* xxii. 2); and when He ordered the Jews to borrow and purloin the vessels of the Egyptians (*Exod.* xii. 35); and when He commanded Osee to take to himself *a wife of fornications* (*Osee* i. 2). Therefore the natural law can be changed.

Obj. 3. Further, Isidore says that *the possession of all things in common, and universal freedom, are matters of natural law.* But these things are seen to be changed by human laws. Therefore it seems that the natural law is subject to change.

On the contrary, It is said in the *Decretals: The natural law dates from the creation of the rational creature. It does not vary according to time, but remains unchangeable.*

I answer that, A change in the natural law may be understood in two ways. First, by way of addition. In this sense, nothing hinders the natural law from being changed, since many things for the benefit of human life have been added over and above the natural law, both by the divine law and by human laws.

Secondly, a change in the natural law may be understood by way of subtraction, so that what previously was according to the natural law, ceases to be so. In this sense, the natural law is altogether unchangeable in its first principles. But in its secondary principles, which, as we have said, are certain detailed proximate conclusions drawn from the first principles, the natural law is not changed so that what it prescribes be not right in most cases. But it may be changed in some particular cases of rare occurrence, through some specal causes hindering the observance of such precepts, as was stated above.

Reply Obj. 1. The written law is said to be given for the correction of the natural law, either because it supplies what was wanting to the natural law, or because the natural law was so perverted in the hearts of some men, as to certain matters, that they esteemed those things good which are naturally evil; which perversion stood in need of correction.

Reply Obj. 2. All men alike, both guilty and innocent, die the death of nature; which death of nature is inflicted by the power of God because of original sin, according to *1 Kings* ii. 6: *The Lord killeth and maketh alive.* Consequently, by the command of God, death can be inflicted on any man, guilty or innocent, without any injustice whatever.—In like manner, adultery is intercourse with another's wife; who is allotted to him by the law emanating from God. Consequently intercourse with any woman, by the command of God, is neither adultery nor fornication.—The same applies to theft, which is the taking of another's property. For whatever is taken by the command of God, to Whom all things belong, is not taken against the will of its owner, whereas it is in this that theft consists.—Nor is it only in human things that whatever is commanded by God is right; but also in natural things, whatever is done by God is, in some way, natural, as was stated in the First Part.

Reply Obj. 3. A thing is said to belong to the natural law in two ways. First, because nature inclines thereto: *e.g.*, that one should not do harm to another. Secondly, because nature did not bring with it the contrary. Thus, we might say that for man to be naked is of the natural law, because nature did not give him clothes, but art invented them. In this sense, *the possession of all things in common and universal freedom* are said to be of the natural law, because, namely, the distinction of possessions and slavery were not brought in by nature, but devised by human reason for the benefit of human life. Accordingly, the law of nature was not changed in this respect, except by addition.

SECOND PART OF THE SECOND PART

Question XI—Heresy

THIRD ARTICLE.   WHETHER HERETICS OUGHT TO BE TOLERATED?

We proceed thus to the Third Article:—

Objection 1. It seems that heretics ought to be tolerated. For the Apostle says (2 Tim. ii. 24, 25): *The servant of the Lord must not wrangle,*

... *with modesty admonishing them that resist the truth, if peradventure God may give them repentance to know the truth, and they may recover themselves from the snares of the devil.* Now if heretics are not tolerated but put to death, they lose the opportunity of repentance. Therefore it seems contrary to the Apostle's command.

Obj. 2. Further, Whatever is necessary in the Church should be tolerated. Now heresies are necessary in the Church, since the Apostle says (1 Cor. xi. 19): *There must be ... heresies, that they ..., who are reproved, may be manifest among you.* Therefore it seems that heretics should be tolerated.

Obj. 3. Further, The Master commanded his servants (Matth. xiii. 30) to suffer the cockle *to grow until the harvest,* i.e. the end of the world, as a gloss explains it. Now holy men explain that the cockle denotes heretics. Therefore heretics should be tolerated.

On the contrary, The Apostle says (Tit. iii. 10, 11): *A man that is a heretic, after the first and second admonition, avoid: knowing that he, that is such an one, is subverted.*

I answer that, With regard to heretics two points must be observed: one, on their own side, the other, on the side of the Church. On their own side there is the sin, whereby they deserve not only to be separated from the Church by excommunication, but also to be severed from the world by death. For it is a much graver matter to corrupt the faith which quickens the soul, than to forge money, which supports temporal life. Wherefore if forgers of money and other evil-doers are forthwith condemned to death by the secular authority, much more reason is there for heretics, as soon as they are convicted of heresy, to be not only excommunicated but even put to death.

On the part of the Church, however, there is mercy which looks to the conversion of the wanderer, wherefore she condemns not at once, but *after the first and second admonition,* as the Apostle directs: after that, if he is yet stubborn, the Church no longer hoping for his conversion, looks to the salvation of others, by excommunicating him and separating him from the Church, and furthermore delivers him to the secular tribunal to be exterminated thereby from the world by death. For Jerome commenting on Gal. v. 9, *A little leaven,* says: *Cut off the decayed flesh, expel the mangy sheep from the fold, lest the whole house, the whole paste, the whole body, the whole flock, burn, perish, rot, die. Arius was but one spark in Alexandria, but as that spark was not at once put out, the whole earth was laid waste by its flame.*

Reply Obj. 1. This very modesty demands that the heretic should be admonished a first and second time: and if he be unwilling to retract, he must be reckoned as already *subverted,* as we may gather from the words of the Apostle quoted above.

Reply Obj. 2. The profit that ensues from heresy is beside the intention of heretics, for it consists in the constancy of the faithful being put to the test, and *makes us shake off our sluggishness, and search the Scriptures more carefully,* as Augustine states (*De Gen. cont. Manich.* i.).

What they really intend is the corruption of the faith, which is to inflict very great harm indeed. Consequently we should consider what they directly intend, and expel them, rather than what is beside their intention, and so, tolerate them.

Reply Obj. 3. According to *Decret.* xxiv. (qu. iii., can. *Notandum*), *to be excommunicated is not to be uprooted.* A man is excommunicated, as the Apostle says (1 Cor. v. 5) that his *spirit may be saved in the day of Our Lord.* Yet if heretics be altogether uprooted by death, this is not contrary to Our Lord's command, which is to be understood as referring to the case when the cockle cannot be plucked up without plucking up the wheat, as we explained above (Q. X., A. 8, *ad* 1), when treating of unbelievers in general.

FOURTH ARTICLE. WHETHER THE CHURCH SHOULD RECEIVE THOSE WHO RETURN FROM HERESY?

We proceed thus to the Fourth Article:—

Objection 1. It seems that the Church ought in all cases to receive those who return from heresy. For it is written (Jerem. iii. 1) in the person of the Lord: *Thou hast prostituted thyself to many lovers; nevertheless return to Me saith the Lord.* Now the sentence of the Church is God's sentence, according to Deut. i. 17: *You shall hear the little as well as the great: neither shall you respect any man's person, because it is the judgment of God.* Therefore even those who are guilty of the prostitution of unbelief which is spiritual prostitution, should be received all the same.

Obj. 2. Further, Our Lord commanded Peter (Matth. xviii. 22) to forgive his offending brother *not* only *till seven times, but till seventy times seven times,* which Jerome expounds as meaning that *a man should be forgiven, as often as he has sinned.* Therefore he ought to be received by the Church as often as he has sinned by falling back into heresy.

Obj. 3. Further, Heresy is a kind of unbelief. Now other unbelievers who wish to be converted are received by the Church. Therefore heretics also should be received.

On the contrary, The Decretal about heretics (*Ad abolendam*) says that *those who are found to have relapsed into the error which they had already abjured, must be left to the secular tribunal.* Therefore they should not be received by the Church.

I answer that, In obedience to Our Lord's institution, the Church extends her charity to all, not only to friends, but also to foes who persecute her, according to Matth. v. 44: *Love your enemies; do good to them that hate you.* Now it is part of charity that we should both wish and work our neighbor's good. Again, good is twofold; one is spiritual, namely the health of the soul, which good is chiefly the object of charity, since it is this chiefly that we should wish for one another. Consequently, from this point of view, heretics who return after falling no matter how often, are admitted by the Church to Penance whereby the way of salvation is opened to them.

The other good is that which charity considers secondarily, viz. temporal good, such as the life of the body, worldly possessions, good repute, ecclesiastical or secular dignity, for we are not bound by charity to wish others this good, except in relation to the eternal salvation of them and of others. Hence if the presence of one of these goods in one individual might be an obstacle to eternal salvation in many, we are not bound out of charity to wish such a good to that person, rather should we desire him to be without it, both because eternal salvation takes precedence of temporal good, and because the good of the many is to be preferred to the good of one. Now if heretics were always received on their return, in order to save their lives and other temporal goods, this might be prejudicial to the salvation of others, both because they would infect others if they relapsed again, and because, if they escaped without punishment, others would feel more assured in lapsing into heresy. For it is written (Eccles. viii. 2): *For because sentence is not speedily pronounced against the evil, the children of men commit evils without any fear.*

For this reason the Church not only admits to Penance those who return from heresy for the first time, but also safeguards their lives, and sometimes by dispensation, restores them to the ecclesiastical dignities which they may have had before, should their conversion appear to be sincere: we read of this as having frequently been done for the good of peace. But when they fall again, after having been received, this seems to prove them to be inconstant in faith, wherefore when they return again, they are admitted to Penance, but are not delivered from the pain of death.

Reply Obj. 1. In God's tribunal, those who return are always received, because God is a searcher of hearts, and knows those who return in sincerity. But the Church cannot imitate God in this, for she presumes that those who relapse after being once received, are not sincere in their return; hence she does not debar them from the way of salvation, but neither does she protect them from the sentence of death.

Reply Obj. 2. Our Lord was speaking to Peter of sins committed against oneself, for one should always forgive such offences and spare our brother when he repents. These words are not to be applied to sins committed against one's neighbour or against God, for it is not left to our discretion to forgive such offences, as Jerome says on Matth. xviii. 15, *If thy brother shall offend against thee.* Yet even in this matter the law prescribes limits according as God's honour or our neighbour's good demands.

Reply Obj. 3. When other unbelievers, who have never received the faith are converted, they do not as yet show signs of inconstancy in faith, as relapsed heretics do; hence the comparison fails.

Acknowledgments

Acknowledgment is gratefully made, also, to the following:

Benziger Brothers, Inc., for Articles 3 and 4 of Question 11, Part II, of *The Summa Theologica of Saint Thomas Aquinas* translated by Fathers of the English Dominican Province. R. & T. Washbourne, Ltd., London, 1917.

Cambridge University Press, for selections from *The Pre-Socratic Philosophers: A Critical History with a Selection of Texts* by G. S. Kirk and J. E. Raven, 1957.

for selections from *Plato's Phaedo*. Translated with Introduction and Commentary by R. Hackforth, 1955.

for complete text of the dialogue in *Plato's Phaedrus*. Translated with Introduction and Commentary by R. Hackforth, 1952.

for "The Hymn of Cleanthes" from *The Vitality of Platonism* by James Adam, 1911.

Harvard University Press, for selections from *Ancilla to the Pre-Socratic Philosophers* by Kathleen Freeman, 1947.

The Loeb Classical Library:

for selections from Vol. I of *Sextus Empiricus: Outlines of Pyrrhonism* translated by The Rev. R. G. Bury, 1933, revised 1939.

for selections from *Plato's Seventh Letter* in Volume VII translated by The Rev. R. G. Bury, 1929, revised 1942.

for selections from both volumes of Aristotle's *Metaphysics* translated by Hugh Tredennick, 1933, 1935, the second volume revised 1936.

for selections from Aristotle's *The Nicomachean Ethics* translated by H. Rackham, 1926, revised 1934.

for selections from Aristotle's *On the Heavens* translated by W. K. C. Guthrie, 1939.

for selections from Aristotle's *On the Soul* translated by W. S. Hett, 1936, revised 1957.

for selections from Aristotle's "The Categories" and "An Interpretation" translated by Harold P. Cooke in *The Organon*, 1938.

for selections from both volumes of Aristotle's *Physics* translated by Philip H. Wicksteed and Francis M. Cornford, 1929, 1934, revised 1935, 1957.

for selections from Volume II of *Diogenes Laertius* translated by R. D. Hicks, 1925.

for selections from Volume II of *Epictetus* translated by W. A. Oldfather, 1928.

Oxford University Press, Inc., for selections from Aristotle's *Analytica Posteriora* translated by G. R. G. Mure in *The Works of Aristotle Translated into English* under the editorship of W. D. Ross.

Random House, Inc., for selections from Volumes I and II of *Basic Writings of Saint Thomas Aquinas* edited by Anton C. Pegis, 1945.

Routledge & Kegan Paul Ltd., for selections from *Plato's Theory of Knowledge*, 1935, *Plato's Cosmology*, 1937, and *Plato and Parmenides*, 1939, all translated by Professor F. M. Cornford.